American Society

American

CONSULTANTS

James H. Goetzinger
Chairman, Social Studies Department
Los Alamos High School
Los Alamos, New Mexico

Rudolph Gomez
Graduate Dean and Professor of Political Science
The University of Texas at El Paso
El Paso, Texas

Leroy E. Harris
Social Studies Specialist
San Diego City Schools
San Diego, California

Benita M. Jorkasky
Associate Professor, Department of Curriculum and Instruction
State University College at Brockport
Brockport, New York

Society

Jack Allen

AMERICAN BOOK SOCIAL STUDIES

American Book Company

JACK ALLEN, a past president of the National Council for the Social Studies, is Professor, Social Studies Faculty at George Peabody College for Teachers, Nashville, Tennessee. A former secondary school teacher, Dr. Allen has served as consultant to numerous school systems in the United States and in other countries. He is the author of a number of widely used textbooks, including HISTORY: USA, and of a variety of other teaching materials in government, civics, and history. Dr. Allen's activities in the area of citizenship education include a considerable range of professional publications and membership on a number of national committees and advisory boards.

Cover Design: Norman Gorbaty
    Cover Photos: Top Left—Mimi Forsyth from Monkmeyer; Top Center—Reaves from Alpha; Top Right—Nathan Benn from Black Star; Middle Left—Medford Taylor from Black Star; Middle—EPA Documerica; Middle Right—H. Burnstiner from FPG; Bottom Left—Jack Zehrt from Alpha; Bottom Center—Hallinan from FPG; Bottom Right—Bill Anderson from Monkmeyer

Book Design: Jack Lefkowitz

Charts and Maps: John Lind
    Chart Drawings: Ric Del Rossi

Text and photo acknowledgments are listed on pages 513 and 514.

AMERICAN BOOK COMPANY

New York   Cincinnati   Atlanta   Dallas   San Francisco

Copyright © 1978 by Litton Educational Publishing, Inc.

All rights reserved. Certain portions of this work copyright © 1973 by Litton Educational Publishing, Inc. No part of this work covered by the copyright hereon may be reproduced or used in any form or by any means—graphic, electronic, or mechanical, including photocopying, recording, taping, or information storage and retrieval systems—without written permission of the publisher. Manufactured in the United States of America.

ISBN: 0-278-46070-4

5 7 9 11 13 14 12 10 8 6

Contents

UNIT One — American Society: People and Values

Chapter 1 The People of a Proud Land — 2

U.S.A.: A Nation of Immigrants • Waves of Immigrants • Inquiry—Which Immigrant Groups Are Represented by the Students in Your Class? • Speaking Out—Jack Dennis and David Easton • Immigration Policies of the United States • Who Is an American Citizen? • Citizenship Laboratory

Chapter 2 Being a Part of American Society — 22

Membership in American Society • Inquiry—School Rules and Customs • The Values of American Culture • Speaking Out—Walter B. Wriston • Inquiry—Is There an "American Way of Life"? • Citizenship Laboratory

Chapter 3 A Heritage of Liberty — 42

Liberty and Citizenship • Toward Liberty and Self-Government • Liberty Through Constitutional Government • Inquiry—Who Shall Govern? • Speaking Out—Barbara Tuchman • 1976: A Year of Rededication • Citizenship Laboratory

UNIT Two — Government of All Americans

Chapter 4 Lawmaking in America — 66

The Constitution Establishes a National Congress • Inquiry—How Equal is Representation in the House? • Congress in Action • Congress and the People • Speaking Out—Vice Admiral H. G. Rickover • Lawmaking in the 50 States • Citizenship Laboratory

Chapter 5 Executive Leadership — 96

The Constitution Establishes the Office of President • The American President in Action • Inquiry—Who Has the Power to Make War? • The

Executive Branch • Speaking Out—George E. Reedy • Inquiry—How Well Do Presidential Nominating Conventions Serve the American People? • Inquiry—Is the Electoral College Outmoded? • The American Governor • Inquiry—How Powerful Is the Governor of Your State? • Citizenship Laboratory

Chapter 6 *The Role of the Courts* 128

An American System of Justice • Inquiry—Is Trial by Jury an Outmoded Practice? • The Constitution Establishes a Framework for a National System of Courts • State Court Systems • Speaking Out—The National Commission on the Causes and Prevention of Violence • American Judges • Inquiry—Can We Reestablish the Right to a Speedy Trial? • Citizenship Laboratory

UNIT Three Civic Rights and Responsibilities

Chapter 7 *Constitutional Rights of the American People* 150

Liberties Guaranteed in 1787 • Personal Liberties in the Bill of Rights • Speaking Out—William O. Douglas • Inquiry—Should the Rights Given in the 1st Amendment Apply to Students? • Legal Justice Guaranteed in the Bill of Rights • A General Statement of Liberty • Liberties for All Americans • Inquiry—Has the Struggle for Women's Rights Been Won? • Inquiry—How Would You Interpret the Words of the Constitution? • Citizenship Laboratory

Chapter 8 *Responsibilities of Free Citizens* 176

The Development of Responsible Opinions • The Media as Agents of Opinion Formation • Speaking Out—Edith Efron • Interest Groups as Agents of Opinion Formation • Inquiry—What Interest Groups Are Active in Your Community • Recognizing Propaganda • Inquiry—How Is Propaganda Used to Influence Our Opinions? • Practicing Responsible Citizenship • Inquiry—What Responsibilities Should Young People Have? • Citizenship Laboratory

Chapter 9 Responsible Government Through Political Parties   198

Political Parties • A Brief History of American Political Parties • Inquiry—Party Platforms—A Comparative Study • The Election Process • Speaking Out—Mrs. Jimmie Johnston • Inquiry—Who Votes in America? • Citizenship Laboratory

Chapter 10 The Costs of Democracy   222

American Society: Public and Private • Inquiry—What Are the Nation's Needs and How Shall We Pay for Them? • Government Spending • Speaking Out—James J. Kilpatrick • The Taxes We Pay • Inquiry—Can Tax Dollars Save American Federalism? • Citizenship Laboratory

UNIT Four   Life in American Communities

Chapter 11 Local Government: The American Way   246

Traditional Forms of Local Government • Inquiry—How Do Your Local Governments Affect You? • Local Government in Urban America • Speaking Out—Theodore J. Lowi • Inquiry—How Are the Cities in Your Area Governed? • The Government of the Great Metropolitan Areas • Citizenship Laboratory

Chapter 12 Local Issues: Housing and Education   268

Issues Affecting the American Family • Good Housing for All: A National Goal • The American Spirit in Education • Speaking Out—Susan Jacoby • Inquiry—Are Public Schools the Proper Agencies for Achieving Racial Integration? • Citizenship Laboratory

Chapter 13 The Urban Environment: Transportation, Pollution, and Crime   292

Transporting Urban People • Inquiry—Will Urban Mass Transit Meet the Cities' Needs? • Polluted Cities • Inquiry—What Can Individuals Do to

Fight Pollution? • Speaking Out—John C. Esposito • Safety on City Streets • Citizenship Laboratory

UNIT Five — Economic Life in Modern America

Chapter 14 Conserving Resources for All Americans — 316

America, Land of Plenty • Preserving Nature's Balance • Inquiry—How Many More People Can the Earth Support? • Conserving the Land • Using Mineral Resources Wisely • Conserving and Rebuilding Our Forests • Preserving the Natural Beauty of the Land • Protecting Our Nation's Wildlife • Conserving Water Resources • Speaking Out—Gus Tyler • Inquiry—How Serious Are Our Environmental Problems? • Citizenship Laboratory

Chapter 15 Developing National Systems of Transportation and Communication — 342

A National System of Highways • Speaking Out—David Hapgood • Railroads in the Nation's Economic Life • The Modern Age of Air Transport • Waterways as Avenues of Trade • Inquiry—Travel Data • Systems of Communication • Citizenship Laboratory

Chapter 16 The American Economy — 364

The Development of American Business • The American Economic System • Speaking Out—Alice Shabecoff • Government in the American Economy • Money and Credit in the American Economy • Poverty and Public Welfare in America • Inquiry—What Are the Goals of the American Economy? • Citizenship Laboratory

Chapter 17 Americans as Workers and Consumers — 390

A Machine Civilization • Organized Workers in a Capitalistic Society • Changing Work in a Changing Society • Inquiry—Choosing a Career • The Consumer in the American Economy • Speaking Out—Bess Myerson • Citizenship Laboratory

UNIT Six The United States in Today's World

Chapter 18 *The United States as a World Power* 414

United States' Rise to International Leadership • Inquiry—Foreign Policy Developments • Other Modern Centers of Power • The United States' Position in the World Economy • Speaking Out—Hans Morgenthau • Inquiry—What Should America's International Trade Policy Be? • Citizenship Laboratory

Chapter 19 *Democracy and Other Political Systems* 436

Political Systems and Ideas About Government • Democratic Political Systems • Inquiry—Democratic Traditions • Authoritarian Political Systems • Totalitarian Political Systems • Speaking Out—William Shirer and Barbara Tuchman • Citizenship Laboratory

Chapter 20 *The Search for a Peaceful World* 456

American Foreign Policy in the Making • Providing for National Security • Speaking Out—Sidney Lens • Inquiry—What Role Should the United States Play in World Politics? • Searching for a Peaceful World Through the United Nations • Citizenship Laboratory

Glossary 474

Constitution of the United States 483

Index 499

Acknowledgments 511

Charts

Immigration Policies of the United States	*15*
American Values	*31*
Principles That Safeguard American Liberties	*49*
Checks and Balances	*53*
Major Congressional Powers	*75*
Formal Organization of Congress	*82*
Standing Committees in Congress	*83*
How a Congressional Bill Becomes a Law	*85*
Major Presidential Powers	*101*
The Executive Branch of the Federal Government	*110*
Major Powers of the United States Supreme Court	*138*
The Federal Court System	*140*
The State Court System	*142*
Personal Liberties Guaranteed by the Bill of Rights	*157*
Legal Justice Guaranteed in the Bill of Rights	*162*
Agencies of Opinion Formation	*179*
Organization of the Democratic and Republican Parties	*201*
Forms of City Government	*256*
Landmarks in the Fight for Public Education in America	*277*
Street Patterns	*294*
Four Kinds of Economic Activity	*369*
Four Factors in the Economic Process	*369*
25 Top Growth Areas in the United States' Job Market	*398*
The United Nations	*469*

Graphs

Immigration to the United States	*8*
Political Parties of American Presidential Candidates	*205*
The Federal Budget Dollar	*229*
Rise in the National Debt	*230*
The National Debt as a Percent of the Gross National Product	*230*
State and Local Government Expenses	*231*
The Move to Cities and Towns	*253*
Automobiles in the United States	*296*
Common Noise Levels	*305*
Growth of Population in the United States	*323*
Air, Rail, and Bus Travel in the United States	*357*
The Rising Percentage of White-Collar Jobs in the United States	*397*
Changes in the Educational Level of the American Labor Force	*399*
Gross National Products of the World's Industrial Leaders	*425*
United States' Imports and Exports	*428*

Maps

Territory of the United States	*23*
Gerrymander of Massachusetts Congressional Districts (1811)	*78*
New York City Congressional Districts (1961)	*79*
State Sales and General Income Taxes	*235*
Counties in Three Modern States	*250*
National Parks	*332*
Railroad Routes Used by Amtrack	*349*
One Group's View of Political Systems in the World Today	*440*

Why Study AMERICAN SOCIETY?

We cannot know what the future will bring. There is too much about it that cannot be predicted. But each of you will have a chance to play some part in the future. You will have choices to make. As citizens of a free society, each of you can help shape the future. To make the best use of this opportunity, you need to be prepared. You need to gain knowledge, develop skills, and form beliefs so that you can do your part in building the kind of future you want.

AMERICAN SOCIETY was written to help you gain the knowledge, skills, and beliefs you need to be an active American citizen, now and in the future. Because none of us can be certain about the future, your book does not try to give you answers to every problem. Instead, it offers the tools you will need to come up with your own solutions.

Your book deals with definitions. What does it mean to be an American citizen? What things do we Americans have in common? How do we differ from each other? What kinds of governments have we set up to make the laws by which we are expected to live? What services can these governments provide? In what ways are we protected from unreasonable government interference? What opportunities do we have to take part in our government? What responsibilities do we have as American citizens?

Your book also deals with current issues. It examines American successes and problems in many fields. Among these are education, housing, transportation, ecology, communication, business, labor, and foreign affairs. What can be done to continue making the progress already being made? What can be done to solve the problems? What can be done to find solutions in the future? You will read about the solutions that other people have found. You will also read the opinions of people who disagree with these solutions. And, again, you will be asked to find your own solutions.

As you use your book, you will find a number of helpful features. Each chapter has a "Citizenship Laboratory." There you will find a list of the chapter's main ideas, a group of questions about the chapter topics, a vocabulary exercise, and a section devoted to the future. Within each chapter there are a number of other questions. Perhaps the most important are the "Getting the Facts" questions. They have been placed at the end of each section so you can quickly find out if you have gotten the essential details.

The book is filled with photographs, cartoons, charts, and graphs—all designed to make your study more enjoyable and more rewarding. You will also find a number of "Constitution Boxes." They will allow you to check the actual words of this important document as you read about the government it was written to form. The Constitution is not easy to read and understand. The language is difficult. For this reason, the entire Constitution has been placed at the end of the book along with explanations of each paragraph. Following the Constitution you will find a glossary and an index. With frequent use, both can serve you well.

There are two other features in your book that are likely to catch your attention immediately. These are the "Inquiry" and "Speaking Out" pages. The "Inquiry" pages present questions of current interest. Many of them deal with topics you will find in daily newspapers and nightly news reports. The "Speaking Out" pages present strongly held opinions of individuals or groups. The questions that are placed at the end of each "Speaking Out" page give you a chance to "speak back." That, after all, is part of your duty as an American citizen. To help create a better world, you must be able to form intelligent opinions, express them openly, and in the end act upon them.

ARCHIVES OF THE UNITED STATES OF AMERICA

Unit One

American Society: People and Values

1 The People of a Proud Land

America is people. It is people from many countries. It is people with different social backgrounds. It is people of various religions. Our nation—the United States of America—is truly a nation of nations. We, the people, are the product of every sort of racial and national background. In no other country is there so great a mixture.

Millions of us live closely together in huge cities. Other millions live in small cities, towns, and rural areas spread across the large land mass that makes up the United States. But whether we live in cities or on farms, we are the descendants of Europeans and Africans and Asians. We may be the descendants of immigrants who came within the last few hundred years. Or, we may be the descendants of the earliest Americans—Asians who crossed the Bering Strait thousands of years ago. We are all Americans.

From these varied places and pasts we have inherited differing customs, beliefs, and physical traits. Yet, with our many different backgrounds, we have been able to build and maintain a great and powerful country. We have created a republic based on the principles of freedom and self-government.

U.S.A.: A Nation of Immigrants

The United States of America is the result of the largest immigration of people in the history of the world. The immigrations probably began more than 20,000 years ago. At about that time, people from Asia began to cross the Bering Strait into what is now Alaska. From this corner of North America they spread over much of the Western Hemisphere. These people later came to be called Indians or Native Americans. It was thousands of years later—about 400 years ago—that people from Europe and Africa began to settle alongside the Indians here in America.

From those early times until now more than 40,000,000 people have immigrated to the United States from around the globe. What we have as a result is a country of well over 200,000,000 people. And thus it is that all of us Americans have either come from other lands or have forebears who came from other lands.

THE NATIVE AMERICANS

The Indians have lived in America for such a long time that they are called Native Americans. There are different opinions as to why their early ancestors left Asia. Whatever the reasons, they adapted well to their new land. They developed crops that grew well in American soil. They found ways to make use of American animals such as the buffalo and the beaver. They formed many different kinds of government suited to their needs.

Today Native Americans, like other Americans, may choose from among many different life styles. Some choose to follow the traditional ways of their own cultures. Others choose to follow less traditional ways.

THE PEOPLE OF A PROUD LAND

It is estimated that between 1,000,000 and 3,000,000 Indians were living in what is now the United States at the time Columbus arrived in the New World. In general, the coming of Europeans was not a happy occurrence for the Indians. As settlements were made the Indians were steadily pushed from their lands. In the process, many Indians died. Fewer Indians were born. In 1860, there were only 340,000 Indians in the United States. By 1910, there were only 220,000. In more recent times, however, there has been an end to this downward trend. The 1970 census showed that the Indian population had climbed to some 650,000. More important than just numbers is the fact that in recent decades Native Americans have had great success in their struggle to gain equal rights as American citizens. They have found new ways to achieve both individual and group goals.

WHY AMERICA?

The reasons why the Indians' ancestors came to the Western Hemisphere are still unclear to us. The same cannot be said of later immigrants. These people have had many different reasons for coming to America. The reasons have varied with different people and with changing times. However, most people were influenced by one of three important reasons. One was to escape economic troubles at home. Another was disagreement over the way government should be run. The third was lack of religious freedom. It is not at all difficult to understand why these three reasons were important. In today's world, people are still giving these same reasons for leaving their native lands.

Hope for better economic conditions was in the minds of many poor English immigrants in the 17th century. Some of these people worked as indentured servants to pay for their trips to the New World. Escape from poverty was also the major reason why almost 1,000,000 Irish left their native land during the potato famine of the 1840s. A better life was also in the minds of millions of Europeans and Asians who came in the late 19th and early 20th centuries. Large numbers came seeking work in the growing American factories. Others came to build America's canals and railroads.

Desire for political freedom has brought many people to America. Even before the United States became a nation, Americans had agreed to a Declaration of Independence that called for liberty for all people. A few years after the Constitution was written, a Bill of Rights was added. In it was a promise to respect the rights of the American people. Thus, when people have been subjected to tyranny in their own lands, those who valued human freedom have often looked with hope to the United States.

Desire for freedom has also arisen among people persecuted for religious beliefs. Unlike the United States, a number of countries have denied people the right to their own religious ideas and practices. Many immigrants have come to these shores in search of freedom of worship. They have brought with them many different kinds of religious beliefs. This very diversity has been a factor in keeping any one church or religion from having too great an influence in our country.

It is not unusual to find two churches or a church and a synagogue standing side by side in American communities. How many different religious buildings are there in your own community?

WHY THE AFRICANS CAME TO AMERICA

Freedom and opportunity brought large numbers of immigrants to America. However, the very opposite was true for one large group—blacks from Africa. Forced into slavery, these people were brought to the New World against their will.

Many Americans, from the time of the first slaves, did not like the idea of slavery. Even so, freedom for the slaves did not come easily or quickly. Most black Americans were still in bondage at the time the United States became a nation. The Declaration of Independence spoke of all people being created equal. Yet, when the Constitution was written in 1787, the people who disliked slavery gained only one small victory. Written into the Constitution was a provision that allowed Congress to end the importation of slaves in 1808.

Even after 1808 large numbers of slaves were brought to America illegally. Finally, in 1865, the 13th Amendment to the Constitution gave the slaves their freedom. However, it was another 100 years before this freedom was transformed into the beginnings of first-class citizenship for all black Americans.

AN END TO THE IMPORTATION OF SLAVES IN 1808: Article I, Section 9, Paragraph 1 of the Constitution

The migration or importation of such persons as any of the States now existing shall think proper to admit, shall not be prohibited by the Congress prior to the year one thousand eight hundred and eight, but a tax or duty may be imposed on such importation, not exceeding ten dollars for each person.

SLAVERY IS ABOLISHED IN 1865: The 13th Amendment to the Constitution, Section 1

Neither slavery nor involuntary servitude, except as a punishment for crime whereof the party shall have been duly convicted, shall exist within the United States, or any place subject to their jurisdiction.

Getting the Facts

1. Who were the first American "immigrants"?

2. Give three reasons why immigrants came to America.

3. Why did large numbers of Africans first come to America?

Examining the Issues

■ The United States has had more immigrants from more parts of the world than any other country. Think about your studies of world history and geography. What other options were open to people who wished to leave their homelands?

THE PEOPLE OF A PROUD LAND

Waves of Immigrants

The first United States census, in 1790, tells us something about immigration during colonial times. The census indicated that more than 60 percent of the white population were of English origin. Another 14 percent were Scotch or Scotch-Irish. The Scotch-Irish were people from Scotland who had moved first to Northern Ireland and then to America. There was also a large group of Germans, some 9 percent. About 10 percent of the white population were Irish, Dutch, French, or Swedish. The remaining 6 or 7 percent of the whites were people from a number of other lands.

The total United States population in 1790 was almost 4,000,000. This is only slightly more than the number of people living in Chicago today. Of this total, 757,000 were black Americans. Most of them were slaves. Only about 60,000 black people were free.

The 1790 census showed that the United States, even then, had people of more races and national origins than any other country in the world. The total number of people, however, was not large. The immigration to the New World in the colonial years was small in comparison to the waves of immigrants who reached American shores during the 19th and 20th centuries.

For some idea of the growing numbers of immigrants, consider these figures. During the 1820s, about 150,000 people came to the United States. During the 1840s, about 1,700,000 people came. During the 1880s, 5,200,000 newcomers arrived on American shores. Finally, during the first 10 years of the 20th century, the number of immigrants reached 8,800,000. More people came in that decade, between 1900 and 1909, than in any other decade in our history.

These figures, no matter how impressive, are at best only numbers. They tell nothing of the hopes and dreams that danced in the minds of the people who came. One immigrant expressed the feelings of thousands: "So at last I was going to America! Really, really going, at last! A million suns shone out for every star. The winds rushed in from outer space, roaring in my ears, 'America! America!' "

THE IRISH

The first great wave of immigrants to seek the promise of America were the Irish. Between 1830 and 1860, 2,000,000 of them left their native soil to seek a new life across the Atlantic. The most important cause for this large immigration was a plant disease that attacked the Irish potato during the 1840s. Through these terrible years almost one fourth of the Irish people died of hunger and disease.

But even after conditions improved in Ireland, the immigration continued. By 1920 well over 4,000,000 had come to the United States. Though most had been farmers in Ireland, they tended to settle in American cities along the Atlantic Coast. The reason was simple. Most were too poor to move farther west. In the cities, they often became involved in politics. Irish workers helped dig the Erie Canal and other early American waterways. And as railroads replaced the canals, Irish muscle figured heavily in their building.

This 1854 drawing shows a cartoonist's view of the promise America offered to the Irish. At left a poor young man is preparing to leave Ireland. Years later the same man, now well-to-do, thinks about returning to Ireland.

The arrival of large numbers of Irish, many of them poor and unskilled, caused resentment among many older groups of Americans. This often came from fear of competition for jobs. It was not uncommon in help-wanted ads of the day to see the words "No Irish need apply." To add to their problems, the Irish were the first Catholics to enter the United States in large numbers. The presence of so many new Catholics aroused the fears of many Protestants. In some cases, it even led to violence.

THE GERMANS

Between 1830 and 1930, 6,000,000 Germans came to the United States. Interestingly enough, there have been more immigrants from Germany than from any other country.

Unlike most of the Irish, most Germans came with some resources. Many of them had left their homeland, not because of poverty, but because they wanted more political freedom. As a consequence, many were able to move beyond the Atlantic Coast to cities and farms farther west. They helped populate such inland cities as Cincinnati, St. Louis, and Milwaukee. Many became well-to-do farmers. Some started their own businesses. Everywhere Germans were active in the development of public schools. They also helped further American music and art by supporting orchestras, choral groups, and museums.

THE PEOPLE OF A PROUD LAND

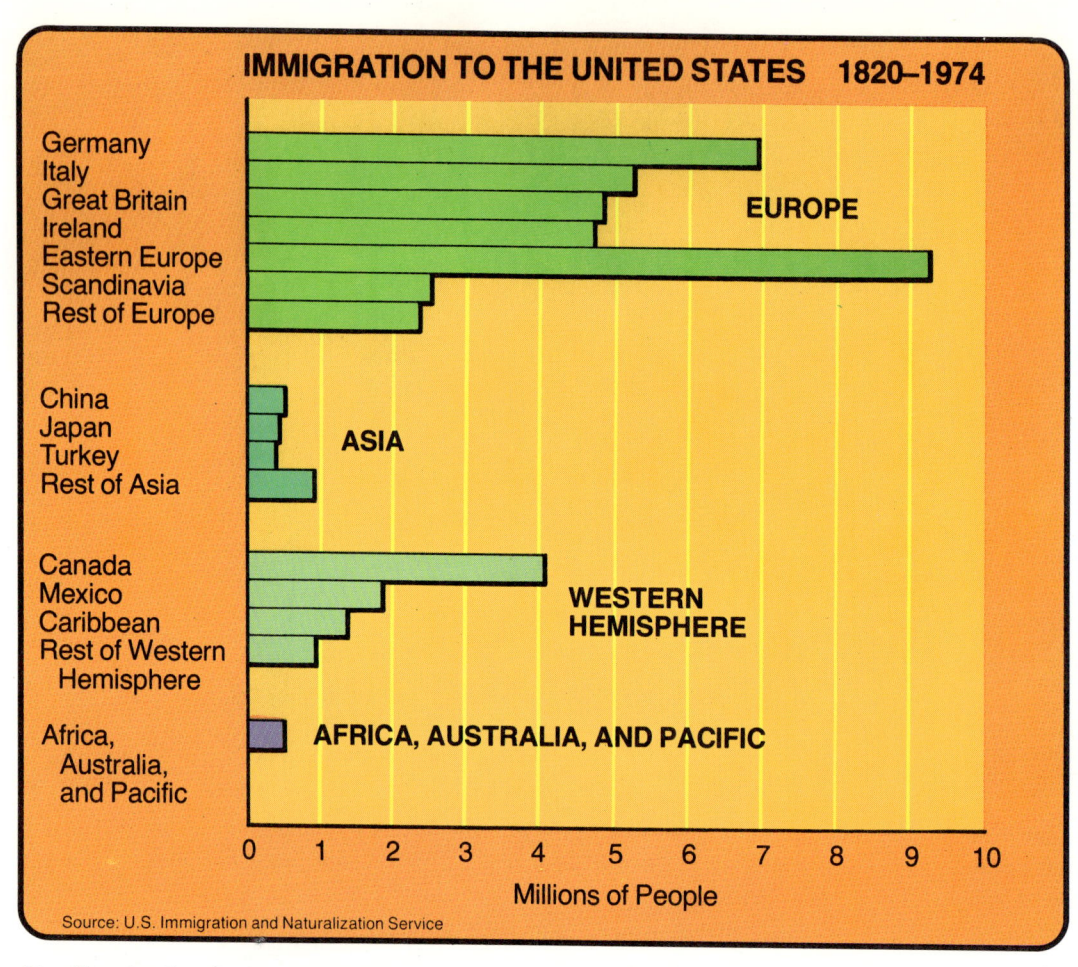

IMMIGRATION TO THE UNITED STATES 1820–1974

Europe
- Germany
- Italy
- Great Britain
- Ireland
- Eastern Europe
- Scandinavia
- Rest of Europe

Asia
- China
- Japan
- Turkey
- Rest of Asia

Western Hemisphere
- Canada
- Mexico
- Caribbean
- Rest of Western Hemisphere

Africa, Australia, and Pacific

Millions of People (0–10)

Source: U.S. Immigration and Naturalization Service

Reading the Graph: Over 9,000,000 immigrants came from eastern Europe between 1820 and 1974. About 500,000 came from China during the same period. About how many came from Great Britain?   Mexico?   Africa, Australia, and the Pacific?

THE SCANDINAVIANS

Viking sailors from Scandinavia may have been the first Europeans to explore the lands of the Western Hemisphere. Later Scandinavians, most of them Swedish, were among the early settlers in colonial America. It was not until the 1840s, however, that large numbers of Scandinavians began coming to the United States. Most came in search of good farmland and other economic opportunities.

Sweden has given us the largest group of Scandinavian immigrants—well over 1,000,000. Once on American soil, they tended to push westward along the Erie Canal and across the Great Lakes to the lands of the upper Middle West.

Other Scandinavians, from Norway, Denmark, and Finland, generally followed the same pattern. Like the Swedish people, these groups were inclined to settle in rural areas where they could become farmers or loggers. Norwegian immigration was somewhat smaller than the Swedish. Danish and Finnish immigration was smaller than either the Swedish or the Norwegian.

AMERICAN SOCIETY: PEOPLE AND VALUES

Of the many rich contributions of the Scandinavians to American culture, none has been greater than their support of education. They were especially active in the development of the colleges and universities of such states as Wisconsin, Minnesota, and Iowa.

THE ITALIANS

Italian immigrants began to arrive in America in large numbers in the 1880s. The number of Italians who have come to the United States is second only to the number of Germans. More than 5,000,000 have come.

The reasons for Italian immigration were mainly economic. People came to escape the poverty of their own land. Like many of the Irish of an earlier day, many Italians arrived in America with little more than a will to work and a desire to improve themselves and their families. Settling along the Atlantic Coast, they often found homes only in crowded tenements. Speaking a language unfamiliar to other Americans, they often had a hard time finding jobs. They generally had to take whatever was offered, usually at a low wage.

Many of these brave, uprooted people found comfort in strong family ties. Many looked to their local churches for a feeling of community. Clubs and other social groups were set up in the Italian neighborhoods. By learning English and some of the older American customs, more and more Italians made their way into the mainstream of American life. Some were able to set up their own businesses. Many, remembering the beautiful classical music of Italy, gave support to opera companies and symphony orchestras then being formed in America.

THE EASTERN EUROPEANS

At the time of the greatest Italian immigration, large numbers of people were also coming from eastern Europe. They came from Poland and Russia in northeastern Europe and from Greece in southeastern Europe. Others came from Czechoslovakia, Hungary, Austria, Rumania, and Bulgaria.

At the turn of the century, many immigrants moved into crowded tenement neighborhoods such as the one below. What are some of the many reasons why they chose such neighborhoods for their first homes in America?

The eastern Europeans came mainly in search of economic opportunity. They brought languages, religions, and beliefs about government that were different from those held by most earlier immigrants. With their customs and traditions, they added much to the richness of American life.

THE ASIANS

Asia, with so many more people than Europe, has nevertheless sent fewer immigrants to the United States. For one thing, the distance is far greater across the Pacific than across the Atlantic. And, for years, American immigration laws discriminated against Asians. Only about 2,000,000 people have come from all Asian countries. Of this total, the largest group has come from China.

Many West Coast cities such as Los Angeles still have flourishing Chinese-American neighborhoods. What ethnic neighborhoods can be found in the cities in your part of the country?

The first large group from China came to America in the 1840s. For a number of years they were welcomed on the West Coast where their labor was greatly needed. Chinese workers played an important part in the building of the western railroads.

Another Asian group, the Japanese, began to arrive in large numbers in the last years of the 19th century. Settling chiefly along the West Coast, most of them turned to farming.

Other countries of eastern and southern Asia have sent very few immigrants to the United States. Students have come from countries such as Korea and India to study in American colleges and universities. A few have come to make their homes in the United States. In the 1960s and 1970s, many Southeast Asians, especially from South Vietnam, came as a result of wars in their home countries.

Groups of immigrants from western Asia—the area we now call the Middle East—started to arrive in the United States early in the 19th century. People from Turkey came in small numbers as early as the 1820s. A large number of Syrians could be found among the many immigrants that came at the end of the 19th century. A large group of Armenians began to arrive during the present century.

THE CANADIANS

Often overlooked in the story of immigration to the United States are the Canadians. The movement between the two countries has been going on since colonial days. During the past 150 years, some 4,000,000 Canadians have come. The movement, however, has become much slower in the last few years. In fact, it is not uncommon today for citizens of the United States to turn the process around and emigrate to Canada.

THE MEXICANS

Another neighbor, Mexico, has also sent us a number of immigrants. Here the story is a long and interesting one. The Spanish began the colonization of Mexico long before there were any English colonies in North America. The Spanish colony was far larger than modern Mexico. It covered broad areas of what is now the southwestern part of the United States. The present border between the United States and Mexico was drawn up by a treaty in 1848, which ended a short war between the two countries, and by the Gadsden Purchase of 1853.

Because parts of our Southwest were once a part of Mexico, it is not easy to determine the true size of the Mexican immigration. It is likely that as many as 1,800,000 Mexicans have settled in the United States over the last 150 years. Today the influences of modern Mexican-Americans and of the old Spanish traditions can be clearly seen. Spanish words and Mexican arts and crafts are only a few of the things that add interest to American life wherever Mexican-Americans have settled.

PEOPLE FROM THE CARIBBEAN ISLANDS

Another group of people with Spanish traditions, the Puerto Ricans, have also made an impact on the American way of life. The island of Puerto Rico became a part of the United States in 1898 after the Spanish-American War. The people of Puerto Rico were made citizens of the United States in 1917. Thus, they can hardly be thought of as immigrants. Yet the movement of Puerto Ricans from the Caribbean to the mainland states has, in many ways, been like immigration from other countries. Many Puerto Ricans came to the mainland in the years following World War II. Most of them settled in New York and other large cities, mainly in the Northeast.

As American citizens, the people of Puerto Rico are not subject to immigration laws. They can come or leave as they please. In fact, improved economic conditions in Puerto Rico during the 1960s caused many to return to their homeland.

Large numbers of immigrants have been coming from the other Caribbean islands since the middle of the 19th century. Perhaps the most dramatic immigration was that of the Cuban refugees in the 1960s. They came because of their opposition to the government of Cuban leader Fidel Castro.

Getting the Facts

1. Immigrants from what three nationalities came in largest numbers after 1820?

2. Give two reasons why so few Asians have immigrated to the United States.

Examining the Issues

■ America is made up of people from many different national and cultural backgrounds. In what ways does the cultural background of American colonists still influence modern American culture? In what ways have the cultures of later groups influenced today's culture?

THE PEOPLE OF A PROUD LAND

Inquiry

Which Immigrant Groups Are Represented by the Students in Your Class?

While reading about the many different groups that have come together to make America, have you thought much about your own background? What about the backgrounds of the other students in your class? These might be interesting questions to explore at this point. Chances are that you will find more groups represented than you expected.

You may want to begin by asking members of your family, parents or others, about your own background. From here your investigations could lead you in a number of directions. How broadly and deeply you can explore will depend on the kinds of information available to you. If you can trace any of your ancestors back to the time that they came to America, try to answer the following questions.

- Where did they come from?
- When did they come?
- What were their reasons for coming?
- Where did they first settle? Why?
- Where have they and their descendants moved since they first came to America? Why did they make these moves?

There are a number of ways that you and others in the class can report the information gathered. Individual reports might be useful. So would a chart showing the different backgrounds of class members. Perhaps you can think of even better ways to present the findings.

AMERICAN SOCIETY: PEOPLE AND VALUES

Speaking Out

Jack Dennis and David Easton

Dennis and Easton are political scientists who are interested in American social development. Here they state their belief that the United States is *not* a "melting pot" society. They object to the theory that newcomers to America have accepted, or should accept, an "American" way of life. Instead they believe that there are, and should be, many separate ethnic groups in America, each with its own way of life.

"[It] does seem that the United States is and has been a multi-ethnic society, however unwilling it has been to conceptualize itself in these terms. For certain historical reasons, perhaps because the major minority racial group rose out of legal slavery and then has remained in social bondage for almost a century, American society has been able to deny the reality.

"The racial crisis of the 1960's has vividly revealed that even though the prevalent white and Anglo-Saxon ideology has been built around melting-pot aspirations and even though this has mitigated against alternative ways of conceptualizing the American social context, the United States has been unable to escape the strife and turbulence of many other multi-ethnic societies. American ideology has failed to constrain American reality. This may ultimately force the United States to alter its political self-image radically so that it may begin to reinterpret itself for what it really is, a society composed of several large and residentially concentrated ethnic groups—black, Puerto Rican, Mexican American, American Indian, and others—in tense juxtaposition to the dominant white, English-speaking population."

1. What are some arguments that could be used to support the "melting pot" theory—that newcomers to America have accepted, or should accept, the "American" way of life?

2. What are some arguments that could be used to support the belief of Dennis and Easton—that the United States is a multi-ethnic society of many different groups, each with different interests?

3. Which of the two beliefs—"melting pot" or multi-ethnic—do you think best describes the United States today? Explain.

THE PEOPLE OF A PROUD LAND   13

Immigration Policies of the United States

Standing majestically in the New York harbor is the Statue of Liberty. Written at the base of the statue are the words of Emma Lazarus: "Give me your tired, your poor, your huddled masses yearning to breathe free." From 1787 to 1921 these words were, with a few exceptions, an accurate expression of the immigration policy of the United States. There were, from time to time, expressions of fear and resentment of "foreigners." However, there was seldom anything serious enough to cause the passage of laws to restrict immigration. America was a growing country. Workers were needed in American factories and on American farms. In the early years of our country, people who came to help build America were more than welcome.

In the mid-19th century, railroads and factories often advertised in Europe, Asia, and the eastern part of the United States for workers and settlers to come and help build America.

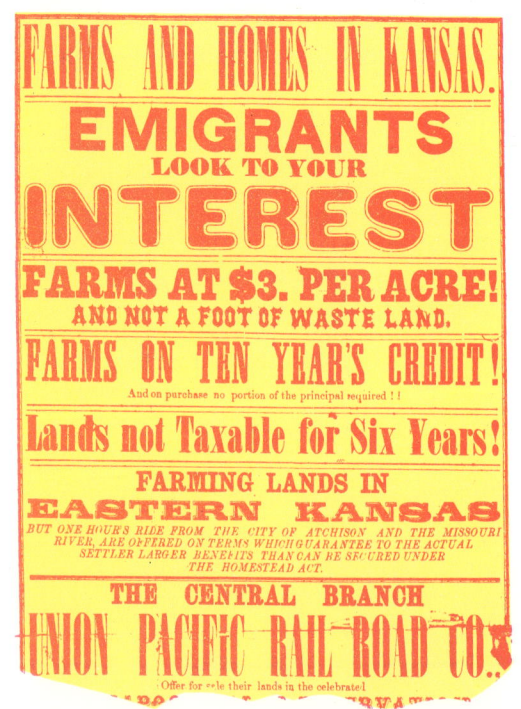

POLICIES BEFORE 1921

The first important change in policy came in 1882. In that year, Congress passed the Chinese Exclusion Act. This law put an end to the immigration of Chinese workers for a period of 10 years. The law also made it impossible for the Chinese to become citizens. The 10-year period was later extended and the law remained in force well into the 20th century. In the early 20th century, limits were also placed on the immigration of Japanese workers.

These laws were just one expression of the resentment many Americans felt against people with cultural backgrounds that were different from their own. These feelings grew quite strong at the end of the 19th century. Many of the immigrants at that time came from cultures that were very different from those of the earlier settlers.

These "new" immigrants came, for the most part, from eastern and southern Europe. Their customs, languages, and religions differed sharply from those of the so-called "old" immigrants. The old immigrants were chiefly from the British Isles and northwestern Europe. Large numbers of the new immigrants were unskilled workers. Many had been farmers in their own lands, but it was now much harder to find cheap land in America. Often they were illiterate. That is, they were unable to read and write their own languages.

The growing number of "new" immigrants led to another congressional

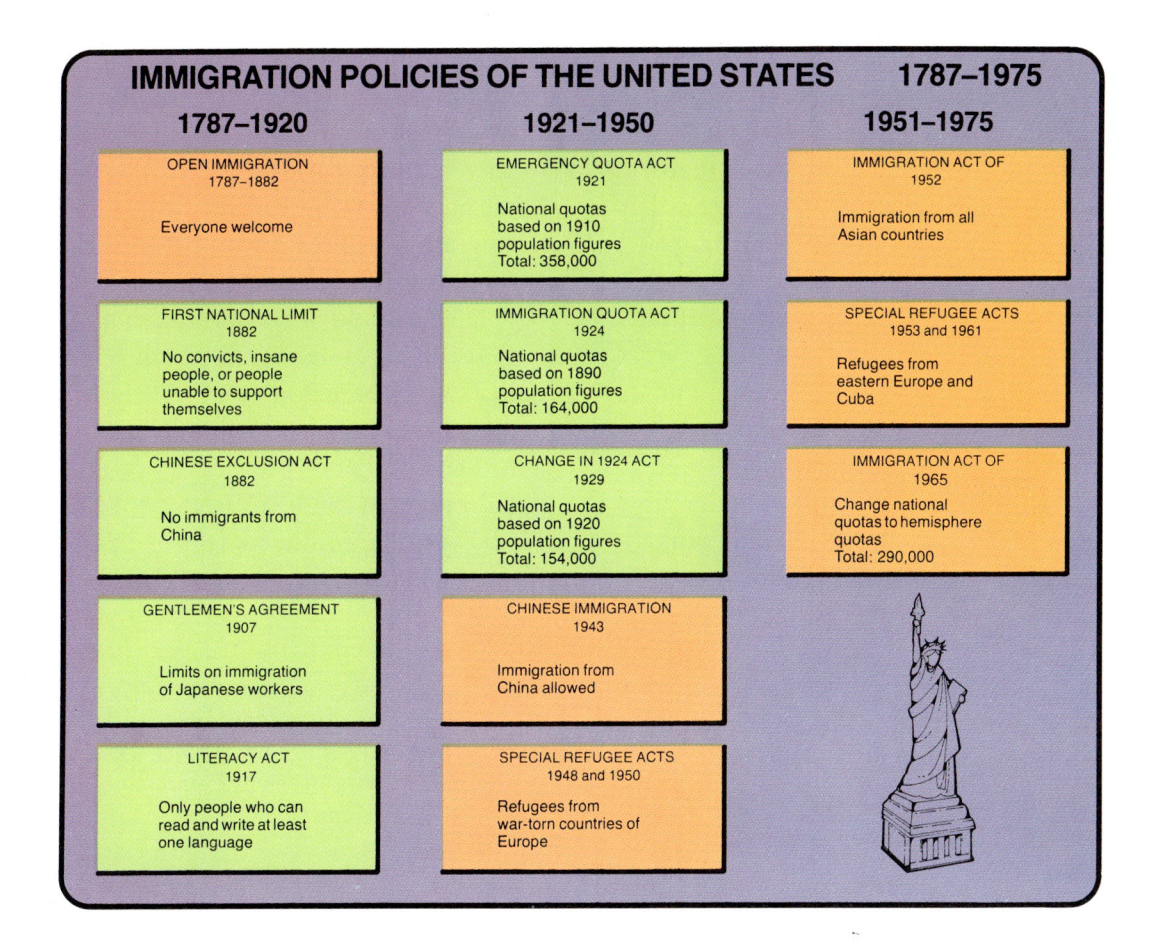

IMMIGRATION POLICIES OF THE UNITED STATES 1787–1975

1787–1920

OPEN IMMIGRATION
1787–1882
Everyone welcome

FIRST NATIONAL LIMIT
1882
No convicts, insane people, or people unable to support themselves

CHINESE EXCLUSION ACT
1882
No immigrants from China

GENTLEMEN'S AGREEMENT
1907
Limits on immigration of Japanese workers

LITERACY ACT
1917
Only people who can read and write at least one language

1921–1950

EMERGENCY QUOTA ACT
1921
National quotas based on 1910 population figures
Total: 358,000

IMMIGRATION QUOTA ACT
1924
National quotas based on 1890 population figures
Total: 164,000

CHANGE IN 1924 ACT
1929
National quotas based on 1920 population figures
Total: 154,000

CHINESE IMMIGRATION
1943
Immigration from China allowed

SPECIAL REFUGEE ACTS
1948 and 1950
Refugees from war-torn countries of Europe

1951–1975

IMMIGRATION ACT OF 1952
Immigration from all Asian countries

SPECIAL REFUGEE ACTS
1953 and 1961
Refugees from eastern Europe and Cuba

IMMIGRATION ACT OF 1965
Change national quotas to hemisphere quotas
Total: 290,000

---

effort to restrict immigration. A bill passed in 1897 stated that immigrants over 16 years of age must be able to read "not less than thirty . . . words in ordinary use." The bill was vetoed by President Cleveland. But, in 1917, a similar bill was passed over the veto of President Wilson.

POLICIES OF THE 1920s

The 1917 literacy law marked a turning point in American immigration policy. It was four years later, however, that the first truly major change took place. This was the Emergency Quota Act, passed by Congress in 1921. The total number of immigrants allowed to enter the United States in any one year was set at about 358,000. The law also restricted the number of immigrants in any one year to 3 percent of the number of foreign born of each nationality living in the United States in 1910. Clearly, this law was meant to favor the older immigrant groups. In 1910, there were more people from the British Isles and northwestern Europe than from southern and eastern Europe living in the United States.

But even this restrictive act was not enough to satisfy mounting anti-foreign feelings in the United States after World War I. Finally, in 1924, Congress passed a more permanent immigration law. By its terms the yearly quota of immigrants was lowered to about 164,000.

THE PEOPLE OF A PROUD LAND

The 1924 law also lowered the percentage of foreign-born people of each nationality to 2 percent. Moreover, the new limits were based on the United States population figures for 1890 rather than 1910. The use of the 1890 figures gave even greater advantage to groups from the British Isles and northwestern Europe.

In 1929, certain changes were made in the 1924 law. The great advantage enjoyed by older groups was lessened with the use of the 1920 population figures. At the same time, the total number of immigrants allowed to enter each year was again lowered, to about 154,000.

Clearly, the changes made in 1929 show that the restrictive acts were passed not just in prejudice against the "new" immigrants. There was also a feeling that the United States now had enough people.

CHANGES IN POLICY SINCE WORLD WAR II

For many years nothing more was done about immigration policy. But after World War II, many people began to take fresh looks at the old laws. In 1948 Congress passed a special act that made it possible for about 600,000 war refugees to enter the United States. There was another refugee act in 1953. It opened the door to some 200,000 people fleeing from the Communist countries of eastern Europe. A refugee act in 1961 allowed thousands of Cubans to enter the United States. In the mid-1970s, thousands of South Vietnamese war refugees came to the United States.

Along with these temporary acts, an important change was made in the overall immigration policy in 1952. The Immigration and Nationality Act of that year made it possible once again for Asians to become American citizens. Later, in 1965, Congress passed another Immigration and Nationality Act. This act continued to limit the number of people who could become American citizens. But it ended the use of the quota system based on national origins. Instead, it set up a worldwide quota system. The number of people who could enter remained small. The act allowed 120,000 immigrants to come each year from countries in the Western Hemi-

President Lyndon Johnson, in the middle of the cartoon below, strongly favored the 1965 Immigration and Naturalization Act. What is the cartoonist's view of the 1920s immigration laws and the 1965 law?

sphere. It allowed 170,000 people to come from countries outside the Western Hemisphere. In the years since 1965 there has been a drop in immigration from western Europe and an increase from southern Europe, Asia, and Latin America.

Getting the Facts

1. Give at least two reasons why America began to end its policy of open immigration in the late 19th and early 20th centuries.

2. How have immigration laws passed since World War II differed from those passed in the 1920s?

Forming an Opinion

■ American immigration policy is still based on a quota system but today the quotas are for hemispheres, not for nations. Do you think it is fair to distinguish between people in the Eastern and Western Hemispheres? Why, or why not?

Who Is an American Citizen?

American citizenship has been the goal of millions of immigrants. It was seldom easy for people to uproot themselves from their own lands. But many of them believed that in America they would find freedom and opportunity. They looked forward to becoming "Americans."

A basic definition of American citizenship is found in the 14th Amendment. "All persons born or naturalized in the United States, and subject to the jurisdiction thereof, are citizens of the United States and of the State wherein

> **AMERICAN CITIZENSHIP: The 14th Amendment to the Constitution, Section 1**
>
> All persons born or naturalized in the United States, and subject to the jurisdiction thereof, are citizens of the United States and of the State wherein they reside. No State shall make or enforce any law which shall abridge the privileges or immunities of citizens of the United States; nor shall any State deprive any person of life, liberty, or property, without due process of law; nor deny to any person within its jurisdiction the equal protection of the laws.

they reside." In other words, we become American citizens either by being born here or by being naturalized. But this is only the legal meaning of the words. Much more can be said about the true meaning of American citizenship.

CITIZENSHIP BY BIRTH

If you were born in the United States, you became a citizen at birth. This is true even if your parents were not American citizens. (In determining citizenship, "the United States" includes the 50 states, the District of Columbia, Puerto Rico, Guam, and the Virgin Islands of the United States. It also includes American embassies and legations around the world and American ships wherever they may be.)

If you were born outside the United States, and your parents were American citizens at the time of your birth, you may be an American citizen. You would likely be a citizen under one of two circumstances. Citizenship would be likely if either parent held American citizenship and had lived in the United States for at least 10 years, five of these after the age of 16. Citizenship would also be likely if you yourself live in the United States for at least five years between the ages of 13 and 21.

There are a number of other circumstances under which a person can hold citizenship by birth. Questions about special cases are answered by rulings of the United States Department of Justice.

CITIZENSHIP BY NATURALIZATION

It is also possible for a person to become a citizen through the process of naturalization. It is this process that has made it possible for immigrants to realize the dream of becoming full-fledged Americans.

Before they become citizens, people of foreign birth are known as aliens. The term "alien" means foreign or belonging to another country. In America, aliens enjoy most of the freedom and rights that our laws give to American citizens. They cannot, however, vote in elections.

To become a citizen by naturalization, an alien must be at least 18 years of age. A "petition for citizenship" can be filed after an alien has lived in the United States for five years. The person must be able to speak, read, and write the English language. The person must also show some understanding of the American system of government and American history. The alien must be of good moral character. A willingness to carry out the duties of American citizenship must be stated. Finally, an alien must give up citizenship in his or her native land and take an oath of allegiance to the United States. Some countries allow dual citizenship. In these countries, a person may hold citizenship in two countries. Citizens of the United States, however, can hold only one citizenship.

The naturalization process is handled by the courts. It is, in other words, a

The woman holding the baby is taking an oath of allegiance to become a citizen of the United States. The women with her are witnesses. Why is it very likely that her baby is already an American citizen?

legal procedure. After the process has been completed, the naturalized citizen has all the rights and duties of a native-born American, with one exception. Only native-born citizens may become President.

CITIZENSHIP AS ACTION

Citizenship, whether by birth or naturalization, gives us a number of legal rights. But there is more to being a citizen in a democracy such as ours. Citizenship is also action. It is action at all ages, not just after a person reaches voting age. American citizenship, for most people in the United States, begins the day they are born. Stated differently, the duties of citizenship belong to both children and adults. The important thing is that these duties are carried out in socially desirable ways.

What kinds of actions are socially desirable? This question will arise many times as you study this book. You are likely to form many different opinions about the answers to the question. However, there are three essentials. First, socially desirable actions must be based on knowledge. Second, citizens must think about the facts they have learned. Just gathering knowledge for the sake of having it is not enough. Finally, in order to act, citizens must form a sense of commitment. They must believe in something. Knowledge, thought, commitment, action—these are the basics of effective citizenship.

We all, to some degree, have our own ideas about what is desirable. Thinking about your own ideas, testing your own values and beliefs—these are some of the things you will be asked to do throughout your study of this book.

One way of turning our political knowledge, thoughts, and commitments into action is by taking part in political campaigns. What are some other actions that you would consider socially desirable?

One more thought. Nothing is so sure in our world today as change. You are used to it. You live with it daily. New facts and ideas pour forth year after year. How can you find the fresh information that you need? How can you use it to form new ideas? How can you turn your ideas into actions that will lead to a better America? These are basic questions for active American citizens. In the following chapters, many answers are suggested. In the end, of course, you must find your own answers.

Getting the Facts

1. Give at least two different ways in which a person can become an American citizen by birth.

2. What is an alien? Describe the process by which an alien can become a citizen of the United States.

Thinking About Citizenship

■ What are some of the ways in which you are fulfilling your duties of citizenship right now?

THE PEOPLE OF A PROUD LAND

Citizenship Laboratory

Review of Basic Ideas

1. The United States is a nation of nations. Modern America and modern Americans are the product of people from many races and national backgrounds. Immigrants have come to American shores for many different reasons. For the most part, people have come to fulfill a desire for economic, political, or religious freedom. One group offers an important exception. The African slaves were forced to come to America against their own wishes.

2. The United States has a greater mixture of people from different races and nations than any other country. In the colonial years and in the early 19th century, immigrants came mainly from northwestern Europe. By the end of the 19th century, immigrants were coming from all parts of the world. At different times in our nation's history, many of these immigrant groups have been resented by other immigrant groups that came at an earlier time.

3. For many years, America encouraged unlimited immigration. Many workers and farmers were needed to help build the new nation. Beginning in 1882 this policy changed. In the 1920s, quotas were set up to limit the number of immigrants from each country. In 1965, the law was changed to quotas for the Eastern and Western Hemispheres.

4. American citizenship may be acquired by birth or through naturalization. In both cases, desirable citizenship involves learning about government, thinking about political issues, and acting upon well informed beliefs.

Questions to Think About

1. What are some of the basic reasons why immigrants came to America in the 19th century? What are some examples of the ways these reasons still apply to people coming to the United States today?

2. Why do you suppose so many of the colonists and early immigrants were from northwestern Europe?

3. In terms of numbers, which have been the largest groups of American immigrants? Why do you think so many people have come from some countries and so few from others?

4. What are some arguments for and against the immigration laws that were passed in the 1920s?

5. Should the United States continue its policy of limited immigration? Why, or why not? If not, what changes would you favor?

6. Do you think American citizenship should be given automatically to people born in the United States? Why, or why not? Should the naturalization process be made more difficult? Should it be made easier? Explain your answers.

7. To what extent do you think people can be good citizens simply by minding their own business? How would you define good citizenship?

Citizenship Laboratory

Words and Relationships

Define each of the terms in the first column. Then show how each term is related to the item listed opposite it by using both items in a sentence or short paragraph.

1.	indentured servant	colonial labor force
2.	cultural difference	resentment
3.	"new" immigrants	religion
4.	"old" immigrants	political power
5.	literacy	public schools
6.	quota system	large population
7.	refugees	special laws
8.	citizenship	action
9.	naturalization	duties of citizens
10.	alien	American rights and freedom

Building a Future

Imagine that you are a member of a group that has been given the job of planning and developing a model American community. In doing so, you and your associates will have a chance to choose the kinds and classes of people who will be encouraged to settle in the new community. What kinds of people will you want for this community of the future? How many people would you want in your community? Prepare some good arguments for your choices in order to gain the support of your associates.

It is unlikely that many of us will ever be given the job of planning a model community. However, as American citizens and voters, we may be called upon to make decisions about America's future immigration policy. The world is moving rapidly toward a population of 4,000,000,000 people. Of these, more than 200,000,000 live in the United States—about 5 or 6 percent of the world's total. Because the United States is such a large country, there are still broad expanses of open land where there are few people. In addition, ours is a rich country where people live better than in most areas of the world. These factors make America an attractive place for people of lands that are poorer or more crowded. Should the United States open wide its gates to immigrants? If not, what restrictions should be placed on immigration? Should the limits be just in terms of numbers? Or should the limits involve things such as national background or educational background?

THE PEOPLE OF A PROUD LAND

2 Being a Part of American Society

Our country was built by the people of many different races and national backgrounds. For all kinds of reasons, people immigrated to these shores. With them they brought the customs and ways of their own lands. Living together in American communities, they began to develop new ways. New institutions—farms, businesses, schools, churches—were formed with a particularly American flavor. Over the years, the people developed a body of common customs and beliefs. All of these things helped to form our American way of life.

To understand a way of life, we must study the people themselves. We must think of the hopes, dreams, and ambitions of the people. The way people live and act as they follow their hopes and dreams becomes their way of life. To understand our American way of life, we must think about the customs and beliefs that we Americans hold in common. At the same time, we must always keep in mind the fact that ours is a country of great variety. Americans are alike in some ways and different in others. We should also remember that our American way of life is not something that suddenly came into being. It has been developing for hundreds of years. It will continue to change and develop as the American people search for a better tomorrow.

Membership in American Society

The people of any community in the United States are members of a larger group that we call American society. The word "society," when used this way, means the largest social body with which a group of people feel a strong relationship. We can expand this meaning by considering six points. To say that we belong to American society means that we have the following six things in common.

- We live in a country called the United States of America. It is a land that most Americans are willing to defend against invasion.
- We are governed by leaders chosen by the people.
- We have a commitment to continue our society by passing some or all of its customs and ways along to our children and grandchildren.
- We agree that we must maintain enough economic self-sufficiency to survive as a free country.
- We are governed by rules and laws that we generally accept.
- We share a common body of goals and values.

Let us now think about each of these six points.

DEFENSE OF NATIONAL TERRITORY

The United States of America includes 50 states and the District of Columbia. However, American territory includes much more than just the 50 states and the nation's capital. It includes the

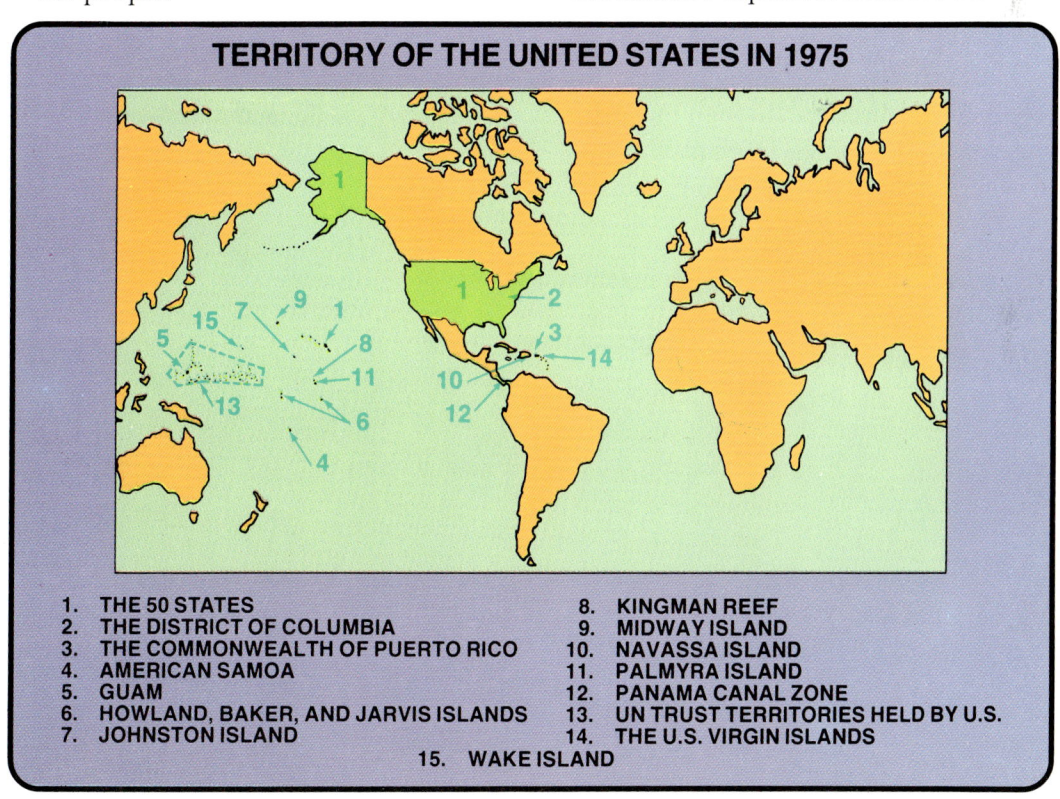

TERRITORY OF THE UNITED STATES IN 1975

1. THE 50 STATES
2. THE DISTRICT OF COLUMBIA
3. THE COMMONWEALTH OF PUERTO RICO
4. AMERICAN SAMOA
5. GUAM
6. HOWLAND, BAKER, AND JARVIS ISLANDS
7. JOHNSTON ISLAND
8. KINGMAN REEF
9. MIDWAY ISLAND
10. NAVASSA ISLAND
11. PALMYRA ISLAND
12. PANAMA CANAL ZONE
13. UN TRUST TERRITORIES HELD BY U.S.
14. THE U.S. VIRGIN ISLANDS
15. WAKE ISLAND

BEING A PART OF AMERICAN SOCIETY

island of Puerto Rico and the United States Virgin Islands in the Caribbean. It also includes a number of small islands in the Pacific Ocean, among them Guam and American Samoa. Finally, our territory includes water as well as land. It includes wide belts of ocean water around our coastal states and islands. And, it includes the rivers and lakes within our nation.

We, as citizens, are pledged to defend this broad territory.

LEADERSHIP THROUGH GOVERNMENT

We need leaders to help us organize American territory for defense. Leaders are also needed if we are to achieve the goals of our society. This leadership is provided by officers of our government.

We often call our government a democracy. The word "democracy" means rule by the people. Technically, the United States is a republic. The people rule indirectly—through their chosen representatives. In many ways, however, the people remain in control.

The leaders chosen by the people must remain responsible to the people. President Abraham Lincoln underscored this point in his Gettysburg Address. He described ours as a government "of the people, by the people, for the people."

THE CONTINUATION OF AMERICAN SOCIETY

We are members of a society brought into being by a revolt against British rule some 200 years ago. Today, we are still governed under the Constitution of 1787. This has been possible, in part, because the American people have been successful in passing along their inheritance to succeeding generations.

How has this been accomplished? For one thing, we have passed along membership in the society by giving people who are born here citizenship by birth. Equally important, we have made it possible for people of other countries to become full-fledged members of our society through the process of naturalization.

Our national government is run by the representatives we send to Washington, D.C. Yet, in the long-run, we the people remain in control. How?

Families and schools find many different ways to teach young children about their society. The group at the left is visiting Plymouth Rock. The group at the right is involved in a daily ceremony. What ideas are being stressed?

Membership in our society has also been passed along through social institutions. The family is one of the most important of these social institutions. It is within the family that young children first learn about people and their ways. Then there is the school. Here society's members learn about the ways of society. They learn how to live effectively in the society. Other social institutions continue the process.

NATIONAL SELF-SUFFICIENCY

Our society could not continue if we as a nation were not able to provide for our needs and wants. To supply the needs and wants of the American people organization and leadership in government and business are needed. The task of business and government has been made easier by the richness of the natural resources in our land. Over the years, the American people have made great use of these resources. The result is that the United States now has one of the strongest economic systems in the world. Members of American society enjoy an economic self-sufficiency unmatched by most other societies.

RULES AND LAWS

Even with all our freedom and self-sufficiency, there is a need for rules and laws. To be civilized is to be orderly. For a society to continue, its people must behave in an orderly fashion. Without these rules and laws our society, or any society for that matter, would fall apart.

BEING A PART OF AMERICAN SOCIETY

Along with rules and laws, there must be some means for enforcing them. If we ignore a rule or break a law, we can expect some form of punishment. The punishment may be no more than a scolding or a bit of ridicule. But it could be a long prison sentence or perhaps even death. In any case, punishment is society's way of keeping its members in some reasonable kind of order. It provides one means of persuading people to at least try to live in peace with one another.

In our American system we have legislative bodies that make the laws. We have executive leaders whose job it is to enforce the laws. And we have a judicial system of courts to interpret the laws so that every individual and group will be treated fairly.

GOALS AND VALUES

The rules and laws of our society express in large part our nation's goals and values. Our goals are the hopes and dreams we have for the American people as individuals and as groups. Our values are our beliefs about what thoughts and actions are desirable. They are things we believe to be right and good. They are things we believe our society should try to attain.

There is no better statement of American goals and values than that found in the Preamble to the Constitution of the United States. This document begins with the words "We, the people." The words are not "We, the delegates" or "We, the government." The people who wrote our Constitution chose to place emphasis on the people, all the people. In truth, it was a choice of a goal.

> **AMERICAN GOALS: The Preamble to the Constitution**
>
> We, the people of the United States, in order to form a more perfect union, establish justice, insure domestic tranquillity, provide for the common defense, promote the general welfare, and secure the blessings of liberty to ourselves and our posterity, do ordain and establish this Constitution for the United States of America.

Speaking in the name of the people, the Preamble lists a number of long-range goals for the people of the United States:

- To form a more perfect union
- To establish justice
- To insure domestic tranquility
- To provide for the common defense
- To promote the general welfare
- To secure the blessings of liberty to ourselves and our posterity.

These remain today among the goals of our society. They are still an important part of our nation's system of values.

Getting the Facts

1. Name at least four things that most or all Americans have in common.

2. What are some of the factors that have made it possible for the United States to develop a strong and relatively self-sufficient economy?

Forming an Opinion

■ What do you think are the greatest advantages of being a member of American society? What, if any, are the disadvantages?

School Rules and Customs

Your school is, of course, a part of American society. As an organized body it has certain rules. The things that are done in your school are also regulated to some extent by custom. Customs are practices and beliefs often handed down by word of mouth. They are less formal than rules and laws. But they can be just as effective in regulating what people do.

How well do you and your classmates understand the rules of your school? Do you know the reasons for each rule? How familiar are you with the nature and purposes of some of your school's more important customs? To increase your understanding of these matters, form one committee to study your school rules and a second to study school customs.

EXAMINING THE RULES: Do They Promote the School's Goals?

The first step for the committee on rules would be to get a copy of your school handbook or any other statement that lists your school rules. If a list exists, the committee should decide whether or not the list is complete. Any new or unlisted rules should be added. If there is no list, a list of rules can be prepared by interviewing administrators and teachers.

When the committee on school rules has completed its study, a report should be presented to the class. One way to analyze the rules would be to relate them to the goals of the school.

Listed below and at the top of the next page are a group of social goals.

- Guarantee of the rights of each individual
- Protection of property rights
- Protection of minority rights

Some school rules are very necessary. Learning traffic rules is stressed in most elementary schools. What other rules are generally stressed in elementary schools?

BEING A PART OF AMERICAN SOCIETY

Inquiry

- Protection of public health and safety
- Guarantee of freedom of movement
- Guarantee of freedom of assembly
- Respect for community standards
- Preservation of law and order

These are goals many people favor for American society in general. Each may also be a goal of your school. Are there any that are not? Do any of your school rules appear to conflict with certain of these goals? Do you think that some of the goals are possible for American society but not practical within a school?

EXAMINING CUSTOMS:
Are They Meaningful to Today's Students?

The committee on school customs may find some customs in the school handbook or in school yearbooks. Most likely, however, committee members will need to prepare a list of customs by talking to people around the school. Other people in the community may be able to give you information about the history of school customs. One thing this committee will need to keep in mind is that there may well be differing views about the reasons for school customs.

After the committee has completed its list of school customs, a report should be made to the class. Give each student a list of the customs. Have each person in the class place an "R" next to those customs she or he thinks are relevant today. Mark with an "O" those that are thought to be outmoded. Do class members agree? Discuss the reasons for any disagreements.

Does your school have a mascot? If so, what customs have been built up around the mascot?

Rules and Customs:
Questions to Consider

Now that you have studied the rules and customs of your school, consider the following questions.

Which of the rules are necessary to keep order in the school? Which of the rules help keep order, but seem more convenient than necessary?

Who makes the rules? What part do students play in making the rules? Do students play any part in enforcing the rules? Would you favor more or less student involvement in rule-making and rule-enforcing in your school?

Which, if any, of the school customs do you think should be changed? Why? Are there any students who still enjoy the customs that you think are out of date? What new customs, if any, would you like to see introduced in your school? What purposes would they serve?

The Values of American Culture

To live in American society is to be a part of American culture. Culture, broadly defined, is a society's way of life. Our American way of life is based, in part, on the government and laws that protect our rights and regulate our activities. The ways in which we provide ourselves with food, clothing, and shelter are part of our culture. Our social institutions and the way we relate to one another are also a part of our culture or way of life.

In many ways, our American values help shape and direct our way of life. Stated differently, our values help define our culture.

There is no ready-made list of American values. There is, however, general agreement among most people who study American society on a few specific values that must be included in any such list. Of course no list can be complete or final. Values are always being questioned. They are always subject to change.

This suggests another thought about our values. To label them "American" does not mean that all Americans think about them in exactly the same way. We disagree among ourselves about the meaning of certain values. Each of us has ideas about how they should be applied to our daily lives. The meanings given to these values may also differ from group to group. Finally, some values are viewed differently in different parts of our country.

There is one more thing to keep in mind. Identifying certain values as a

Which American values do you think would probably be shared by most of the people in a small town in Iowa and a large city in New Mexico? Which values might be viewed differently in the two places?

BEING A PART OF AMERICAN SOCIETY 29

part of American culture does not mean that they are found only in America. Certain values may also be a part of the cultures in other countries. Indeed, one of the great hopes for the future is that people and societies around the globe will be able to share many goals and values.

Keep these things in mind as you study the six basic values listed in this section. They have been chosen because they are values that most Americans hold in common.

IMPORTANCE AND WORTH OF THE INDIVIDUAL

There is nothing more basic to the American way of life than the belief that every human being has worth. In our families and schools, each child is treated as an individual. In our political system, citizens are urged to express their own opinions and to vote in elections. In our economic system, owners, managers, and workers all have certain rights.

In America we constantly dramatize the needs and achievements of the individual person. Advertisements on radio and TV and in newspapers and magazines offer products and services that are supposed to give the individual appeal, beauty, or success. Contests are held to pick the "teacher of the year," "homecoming queen," and so on. We make legendary figures out of brave individuals such as Daniel Boone, Harriet Tubman, and Amelia Earhart. We carry this emphasis to the highest levels of our government. Our President is generally considered not only the nation's representative, but its symbol.

Americans seem to be firmly committed to individualism. However, questions can be raised about how sincerely Americans believe in the importance and worth of *all*. Today and through our history, many examples can be found of our failure as Americans to support this value for all people and races.

INDIVIDUAL FREEDOM

As we Americans value the worth of every individual, so we respect the right of every person to be free. The meaning of this value can be expressed in many ways. When we are young, we want to be free to get an education. When we reach legal age, we want to be free to vote. We believe we should be free to express our own ideas about the ways that public affairs are run. We want to be free to move about. We want to be able to choose a vocation and to change jobs when we wish. We want to be free to marry the person of our choice. We believe we should be free to choose our own religious beliefs.

Our freedoms, however, are limited by the belief that we must show respect for the rights of others. Freedom without control can lead to total disorder. And so, we must have laws. There are laws that require attendance in school. Restrictions are placed on freedom of speech. Each state has laws that regulate marriage and divorce. A part of the money we earn must be returned to the government in the form of taxes. These, and other restrictions, have become a part of our way of life. They help advance one of the goals stated in the Preamble to the Constitution: to promote the general welfare.

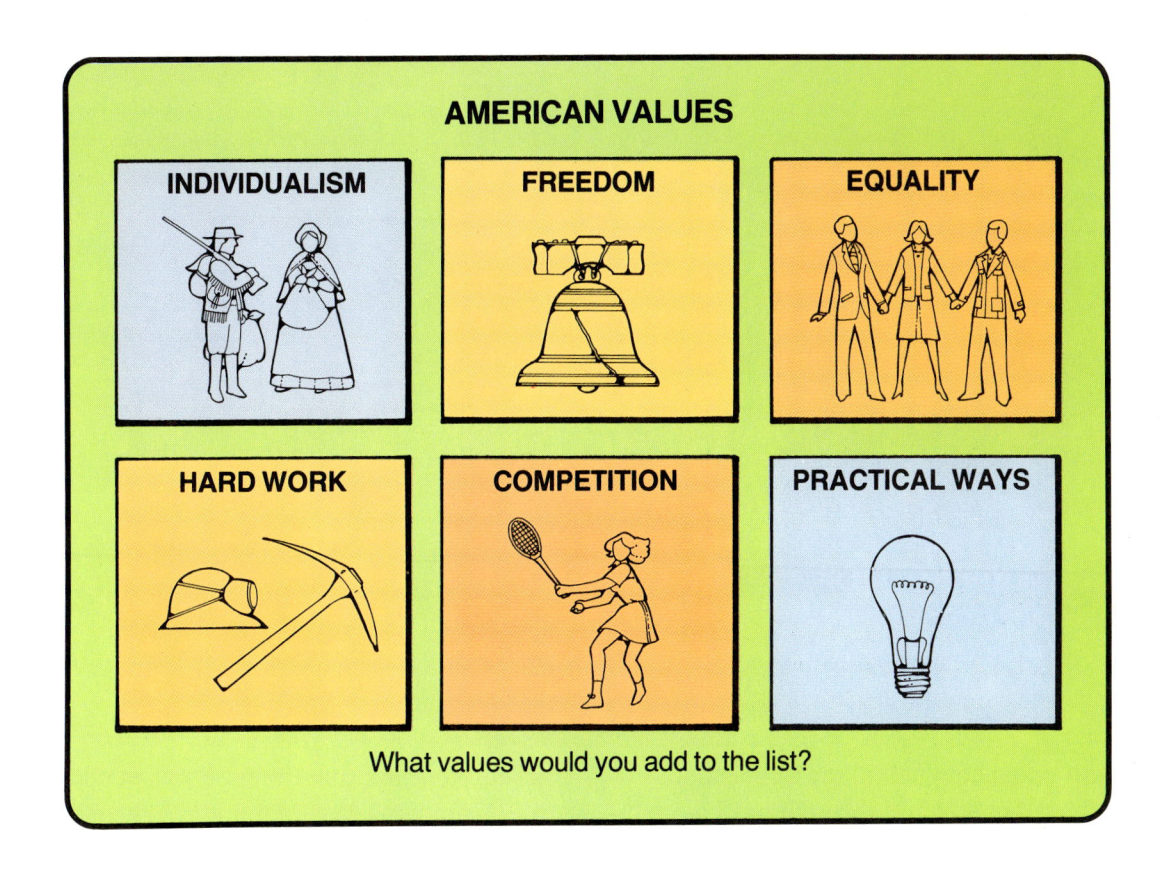

AMERICAN VALUES

- INDIVIDUALISM
- FREEDOM
- EQUALITY
- HARD WORK
- COMPETITION
- PRACTICAL WAYS

What values would you add to the list?

EQUALITY FOR ALL

Laws that restrict individual freedom in America are supposed to affect all people alike. Equality before the law is one of our most important ideals. This ideal of equality also applies to other aspects of our society. We value the ideal of social equality. We believe in equal opportunity in schools and in business.

The ideal of social equality includes the belief that each partner in a marriage should have equal rights. It also includes the belief that all children should be treated fairly by parents or guardians. It stresses the idea that all people should have a chance to improve their economic position. It stresses the need for equal access to the benefits of an education.

The ideal of equality was included in the Declaration of Independence. The American belief that all people are "created equal" has been expressed again and again through our history. Even so, we recognize that we do not always live up to this ideal. But generally when equal treatment and opportunity are denied, we find some Americans willing to speak out against the denial. Through our history, individuals and groups have struggled to gain equality for all. The value remains very much a part of American culture.

ACHIEVEMENT THROUGH WORK

Many Americans support the ideal of equal opportunity. At the same time, Americans have traditionally supported,

BEING A PART OF AMERICAN SOCIETY

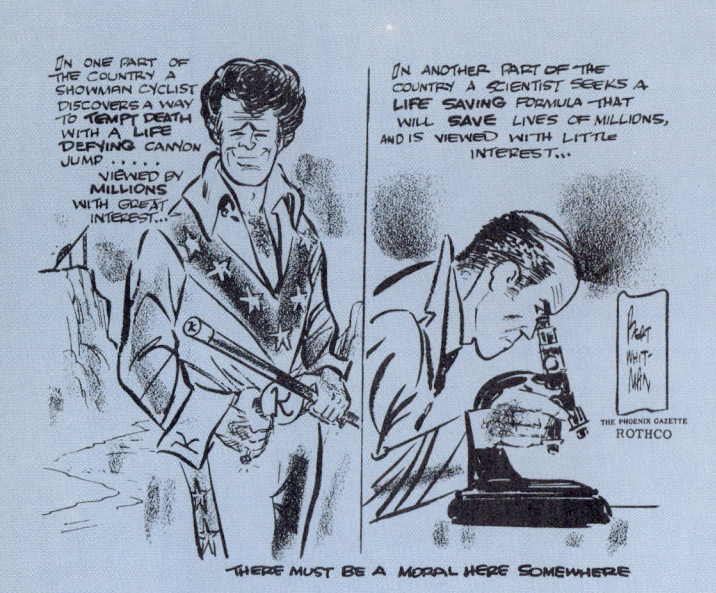

What are these two cartoonists saying about American values? How valid do you think their statements are?

"THERE MUST BE A MORAL HERE SOMEWHERE"

"Think of what this will mean to mankind, my boy! The easing of suffering, misery, and pain; the saving of untold numbers of lives, and a bright future and hope for healthy generations. It's a gold mine!"

with equal conviction, the belief that achievement comes through hard work. To get ahead in school one must "work at it." The same is true of success in business or a profession.

Americans tend to value individual achievement and success. In many quarters there is a tendency to measure a person's success by the amount of money made. We also tend to place value on the social distance a person is able to travel. A person who rises from a lowly background to achieve success is greatly admired.

Like so much else in American society, our values with regard to work may be changing. As technological changes reduce the hours of work, leisure time is increased. If work is good, so may leisure time be desirable. Both may be valued, each in its own way. Traditionally, leisure time was thought to be of value only if it made it possible for people to work more effectively. Today we tend to think that the time we spend away from work is valuable for its own sake.

COMPETITION

Along with the American belief in the value of individual achievement, there is a belief in the value of competition. Competition is stressed in the classroom and on the athletic field. We see it in contests for political office. Daily we are bombarded with competitive advertising as businesses try to convince us that we should buy a certain brand of soap or cola.

Underlying this stress on competition, there is a belief that the better person or product will win. And there is the feeling that the victory will be for the good of society.

Although our society places high value on competition, most Americans agree that competition should be regulated. Rules, laws, and public opinion seek to keep it under control. Winning is important, but it is equally important to win fairly. The referee or umpire is an important part of each contest. Competition need not lead to open conflict. When businesses compete to sell their goods or services, they are expected to do so peacefully and fairly. They are expected to follow the accepted laws and practices of our society.

PRACTICAL WAYS

Americans tend to value people and things that are practical. We like to see immediate results. We generally choose as heroes those women and men who are "doers" rather than "dreamers." An American philosopher once described this belief in practical things as a belief in the "cash value of an idea."

This belief in "cash value" strongly influences our way of life. Students are encouraged to stay in school for very practical reasons. They are told that a good education will lead to a good job, a high income, and a high social position. (In recent years, many people have learned that the process is not quite so simple.) American businesses are always in search of practical ways to be more efficient. Efficient ways of using time and money are also encouraged in schools, hospitals, and other institutions.

The belief is that practicality and efficiency will bring progress and better lives for the American people. Often progress and better lives are understood to mean the production of more goods and a rise in our standard of living. But the production of knowledge, especially scientific knowledge, is also seen as an important kind of progress. Americans believe that increased knowledge can lead to greater control over the forces of nature. Again, we are dealing with a practical matter. While greater control over nature may not lead to more goods and services, it can lead to better lives for Americans.

Getting the Facts

1. Name at least four values that most Americans hold in common.

2. What are some of the individual freedoms enjoyed by Americans? What are some of the ways in which individual freedom is limited in America?

Thinking About Your Own Values

■ Which of the values discussed in this chapter most closely resemble your own? With which of the values, if any, do you strongly disagree? Why?

In 1969, America placed the first person on the moon. What does this achievement say about American values?

Speaking Out

Walter B. Wriston

Wriston is the Chairman of Citibank, a large network of banks in New York City. Addressing a group of business students in 1976, he stated his belief that Americans must become more optimistic about the present and the future. We need to renew our traditional faith in progress and democracy.

"Birthday celebrations are always a time for looking back and looking forward. On the occasion of our 200th birthday, Americans have obeyed this natural tendency and look back in wonder at the distance we have come from scattered states in the wilderness to the world's premier democracy—the only stable democracy upon a continental scale in all human history. . . .

"Yet the accent today is not on the evidence of progress in a multitude of fields; the heaviest emphasis is upon failure. The media [TV, radio, newspapers, etc.] . . . would have us believe that things are not just going badly, they are growing progressively and rapidly worse. The dominant theme is the new American way of failure. No one wins; we always lose. . . . Let one scientist resign and say that nuclear power is a lethal accident waiting to happen and he is awarded the front page with pictures. He has unlimited interviews on television. The massive achievements of hundreds and hundreds of scientists and the comfort of millions of citizens who enjoy the products of nuclear power go for nothing. . . .

"It is this technique of incessantly accenting the negative that erodes optimism, one of the cornerstones of democracy. To function at all, a free society must be supported by the firm faith that man is capable of fashioning ways of life that time will prove better than his earlier efforts. . . .

"The fate of our Republic depends upon whether Americans can recover a profound belief in the democratic process. . . ."

---

1. Wriston states that the media stress the "negative" side of things. What examples of this negative stress do you find in TV news reports and local newspapers?

2. What examples do you find on TV and in newspapers of a positive view of American politics and society?

3. Are your own views about the future of the United States optimistic or pessimistic? Explain.

Is There an "American Way of Life"?

One way to study the American way of life and the many changes that are taking place is to look at a number of different communities in America. This was done a few years ago by a group of magazine writers. Each writer returned to his or her home town. Some had been away for many years. All reported their findings in their own ways. Portions of what they wrote about their home towns are quoted here. As you read about these five communities, think about the life style in your own community. Think about the ways in which all of the communities are alike and the ways in which they differ.

LIFE IN THE SOUTHWEST

Fort Worth floats like an ocean liner on the Texas plains. The city has always had a strong sense of its own identity. A returning native son finds much that he likes.

"There is an aura of gentleness that wraps my hometown, an aura constant as the Indian summer sun that burns from blue and unpolluted skies, an aura that once I interpreted as condemning, terminal dullness. Now I realize that the city I ran from a decade and a half ago has character of a deceiving sort: in the years that urban horror has assaulted the land, Fort Worth has met, matched, and if not totally bested the enemies at her gate, then she has achieved at least a tolerable standoff.

"Neither riot nor protest nor bombs nor yelling has molested her. She is prosperous, tranquil, ambitious and—above all—courteous. She seems, belatedly, to one prodigal, a wondrous place to live.

Her cinnamon brick boulevards . . . are clean. Her people nod and smile at one another on the sidewalks, and when a stranger seeks direction, if he cannot be told, then he will be guided. A helicopter prowls the lakes and rivers watching for pollutive discolorations, tracking them to the source: offenders are promptly ordered to cease and desist. All solid-waste industrial burning is prohibited. Her buildings and museums . . . are graceful, with room to breathe and look. Her downtown, which 10 years ago was dying . . . has been revitalized with a striking convention center that appears to be a giant flying saucer settled on the city. . . .

"Fort Worth is neither Southern nor Western but Southwestern, heir to a code of behavior that evolved a century ago when her North Side cattle yards were mecca for cowmen and for everything edible on four feet, a code that exalted physical strength, God, tolerance and honesty."

One writer's view of Fort Worth: "She is prosperous, tranquil, ambitious and—above all—courteous. She seems, belatedly, to one prodigal, a wondrous place to live."

Inquiry

BEING A PART OF AMERICAN SOCIETY

Inquiry

One writer's view of the Five Towns: "... the community has never had the coherence of a single town.... Like many other suburbs ... it has piled up on itself over the years and all run together ..."

LIFE IN THE NORTHEAST

From the Southwest we move to the Northeast to a cluster of five small towns or villages. Suburban neighborhoods on Long Island, they lie near our nation's largest city, New York.

"Actually the community has never had the coherence of a single town. It is rather a string of villages—Hewlett, Woodmere, Cedarhurst, Lawrence, Inwood—which runs in perhaps a five-mile strip along the south shore of Long Island and is known locally as the Five Towns. Like many other suburbs ... it has piled up on itself over the years and all run together with expansion. At the same time it seems now somehow wary and self-defensive, holding off, as it were, the ugly sprawl of the city of New York, whose outer limits are close by.

"It is not surprising that many of the more than 100,000 residents of the Five Towns would prefer to keep out the rest of the world. In many ways it is an excellent place to live, especially for the comfortably fixed. There are good golf courses and boating waters, and five ocean beaches are only a short drive away. Manhattan, where most of the men work, is an easy, 45-minute commute by train. Lovely old trees and superb planting set off the established residential areas, and some of the newer areas—especially Hewlett Harbor, which reportedly houses the wealthiest homeowners in the state—have the bleached wood-and-stone look and the hand-clipped manicuring of a place like Beverly Hills. At the end of many lawns here, yachts lie at docks. In startling contrast to this, the village of Inwood, at the other end of the Five Towns, has badly run-down sections, drab little pockets of ramshackle storefronts and housing, and a restless black population of 2,200 beset by all the grim and familiar pressures of urban poverty.

"One of the most obvious local problems of modern life in the Five Towns is noise pollution. Kennedy Airport is virtually next door, and at some air traffic times—the early evening hours, for example—tranquillity is utterly smashed by a parade of big, exhaust-spewing jets screaming low and often directly overhead on their ways up or down."

LIFE IN THE NORTHWEST

From the Atlantic we shift to Seattle on the shores of the Pacific.

"Dark and lowering north Pacific weather can leave Seattle gray, wet, horizonless and abject for weeks at a time; but when the sky turns blue it glows like few cities in the world. Its steep, populated hills stand against endless miles of glittering water, against distant vistas of black-green Douglas fir, and, beyond all, the icy mountains which rim it on every side. More than a million people now live in and around it along the shores of Puget Sound. It has built half the jet aircraft now flying in the Western world—planes which have long since ended its

One writer's view of Seattle: "In the back of its mind it still conceives itself to be a last, idyllic trading post . . . happily remote from life as it is lived 'back East.'"

own isolation from the rest of the continent. But in the back of its mind it still conceives itself to be a last, idyllic trading post, succored by wilderness and ocean and happily remote from life as it is lived 'back East.'

"These are not its only contradictions. It was settled by conservative New Englanders and dogged Scandinavians and grew up devoted to the public library, the Saturday night bath, high-grade sewer pipe, quality merchandise and concrete sidewalks. But it was also a seaport and sawmill town, and its police force was not above reducing drunken loggers, seamen and argonauts to the horizontal. . . . Left-wing politics bloomed in Seattle, and Dave Beck's Teamster goons battled Harry Bridges' longshoremen with boots and bicycle chains during the Great Depression. Time has altered the city and many of its aspirations but seems to have nurtured this duality."

LIFE IN THE MIDWEST

In midland America the capital city of Springfield, Illinois has its own special ways. Here the forces of tradition seem strong.

"That's how things were in Illinois when I was growing up. My generation was conceived in the Depression and brought up during World War II, but somehow those cataclysms scarcely registered on our bland and sheltered lives. . . . We wrote prompt thank-you notes, concealed most of our emotions, and rarely thought to question the authority of our teachers, our daddies, their daddies, or the occupants of any other seats of power.

"That's how things were and that, in a good many Illinois households, is how things still are. 'The biggest scandal on our block,' said the husband of one of my old friends, 'is that the neighbors down the street never know where their cat is. Our friends are so straight. . . .'

One writer's view of Springfield: "Tradition weighs heavy. Ancestors are revered; leaders are presumed to know what they're doing. Old is safe and good; new is suspect."

Inquiry

BEING A PART OF AMERICAN SOCIETY   37

Inquiry

"Illinois, as its car license plates perennially declare, is the land of Lincoln. Tradition weighs heavy. Ancestors are revered; leaders are presumed to know what they're doing. Old is safe and good; new is suspect. College kids may be brilliant, but they're inexperienced, and often more intolerant than their enemies. Street muggings and hijackings and campus bombings seem more threatening than (and unrelated to) the continuation of the war [in Vietnam]. A police state, even with National Guardsmen stationed every 10 feet, would be less awful than the anarchy recommended by Jerry Rubin and the Black Panthers. Coffee seems to cost a dime a pound more every time you go to Kroger's or the IGA. Thrift shops are doing better than department stores. There sure are a lot of houses on the market, but we shall overcome? Won't we? Haven't we always?"

LIFE ON THE WEST COAST

Although tradition seems to weigh heavily in Springfield, it has little influence in the California city of San Mateo. Much of the description is the writer's report of a conversation between two people who live in San Mateo. The last paragraph expresses the writer's own views.

" 'I've changed the way I think about how a fellow looks,' the salesman began. 'My daughter brings these guys home with hair down to their shoulders. I was upset at first, but I found out they're good students, they have ambition. I don't make an instant judgment anymore.'

" 'Don't you really?' the broker asked.

" 'Well, I think, "You've got two strikes on you, but I'll give you a third." '

" 'I grew a beard, you know,' the broker said, 'Just a silly little scraggy thing, and I had to see the president of my company. He says to me, very solemn, "We don't have people with beards." I want to keep my job so I shaved it off. . . .'

One writer's view of San Mateo: "When I was a boy . . . we could smell the bay three miles away. Now it's filled and occupied by a huge housing development. . . . Where do you find roots in a moving landscape?"

" 'What worries me most,' the salesman with the 19-year-old daughter said, 'is the breakdown of any respect for authority. There has to be a framework of laws or society won't work. But I also know we haven't left the greatest legacy in the world to these kids. We're worried about things now we never worried about before.'

" 'Right,' said the broker, father of a 20-year-old, 'and the kids brought it to our attention. My daughter thinks motherhood is almost a crime. She says she'll adopt, but she doesn't want to have children—because of over-population.'

" 'What scares me,' he went on, 'is that our economy is built on the use of goods—metals, fuel, etc. The kids think this is N.G. But where are they going to find jobs? Talk about creeping socialism, it's here, and it's going to creep more. I just don't know where the jobs are coming from.'

" 'I don't think we can deny socialism. . . . I enjoy the fringe benefits of capitalism, but I wonder—it seems we produce so many unnecessary things, big cars and all. The SST. The environmental effects are so bad I don't think we ought to have it.'

" 'Who needs that much speed?' asked the salesman. 'Somebody's going to have to say that's big enough, fast enough, don't grow any more.'

AMERICAN SOCIETY: PEOPLE AND VALUES

Inquiry

"The open land is gone. When I was a boy in San Mateo there was a large field across the street and plenty of room to hide. Now it's a row of high-rent 'town houses.' We could smell the bay three miles away. Now it's filled and occupied by a huge housing development called Foster City, 'Pop. 10,000 and growing beautifully,' the sign says. When I was going to high school in San Mateo in 1950, the population was around 42,000; now [1970] it is 80,000. If change is the norm, what do you measure change against? Where do you find roots in a moving landscape? One doesn't *come from* San Mateo; one rides it a while."

LIFE IN YOUR OWN COMMUNITY

Now that you have read about the five communities described by the magazine writers, think about how you would describe your own community. Perhaps you can describe it in the way each of the writers did. Or, you and your classmates may want to do a more complete job. If so, you will want to divide up the work. To help you with your study, topics are suggested in the following outline.

1. Geographic features
   a. Physical features—land, climate, natural resources, etc.
   b. Features made by people—size of population, amount of land within community borders, layout of streets, highways, location of homes and businesses, kinds of industry, etc.
2. Community history
   a. Kinds of people who first settled
   b. Reasons for settlement
   c. Later groups who came to area
   d. Reasons for growth or decline of the community
3. Local government
   a. Form of local government
   b. Services of local government
   c. Political activities
4. Social services
   a. Kinds of educational opportunities available
   b. Health services and recreation facilities
   c. Kinds of churches and religious groups
5. Community relationships with its surroundings
   a. Relationship of the community with other nearby communities
   b. Relationship of the community with the world both near and far

Comparing Six Communities

Having examined your own community and read about five others, think about these questions.

Which one of the five communities described by the writers is most like your own? What are the points of likeness? Which of the five is most different from your own? What are the points of difference?

To what extent do some of the communities seem tied to the past?

Do the six communities (including your own) have any common problems?

Can you name any American communities that are quite different from any of the six? In what ways are they different?

To what extent do the people in these communities seem to share the basic values of American culture discussed in this chapter? Should we speak of an "American *way* of life"? Or, would it make more sense to speak of "American *ways* of life"? Explain.

BEING A PART OF AMERICAN SOCIETY

Citizenship Laboratory

Review of Basic Ideas

1. American society is the largest social group with which we Americans, in general, feel a strong relationship. As members of American society we have a number of things in common. We live in a country called the United States of America. It is a land that most Americans would be willing to defend against invasion. We are governed by leaders chosen by the people. We have a commitment to continue our society by passing some or all of its customs and ways along to our children and grandchildren. We agree that we must maintain enough economic self-sufficiency to survive as a free country. We are governed by rules and laws that we generally accept. And, finally, we share a common body of goals and values.

2. American culture is the way of life in American society. The nature of this culture is determined, in large part, by the values that the American people hold in common. Certain of these values seem especially important. We believe in the worth of each individual. We believe in freedom for all. We accept the ideal of equality among all people. We believe that hard work and fair competition are necessary. And, we tend to favor those things and ways that seem to be most practical.

Questions to Think About

1. What are the territorial limits of the American society? Do you think any parts of this territory more worth defending than others? Explain.

2. In what specific ways do families, schools, and other social institutions help pass on the customs and ways of our society?

3. The Preamble to the Constitution lists a number of very general long-range goals for the American people. What more specific long-range goals would you favor for Americans? Why?

4. What are some examples that show the great value Americans place on individualism?

5. In what ways do American attitudes toward work seem to be changing? What changes, if any, do you see in American attitudes toward competition?

6. How would you define the word "practical" in terms of our American life style?

7. What features of American life are stressed in the descriptions you have read of five American communities? In which of these communities would you like to live? Why?

AMERICAN SOCIETY: PEOPLE AND VALUES

Citizenship Laboratory

Words and Relationships

Define each of the terms in the first column. Then show how each term is related to the item listed opposite it by using both items in a sentence or short paragraph.

1. institutions — American families, schools, and churches
2. community — American way of life
3. customs — rules and laws
4. self-sufficiency — natural resources
5. values — actions
6. culture — social relationships
7. individualism — pioneers
8. competition — American business
9. technology — scientific achievements
10. practicality — progress

Building a Future

In the "Building a Future" section at the end of Chapter 1, you were asked to think about the way you would plan a model community. In that exercise, emphasis was placed on what people and how many of them you would want in your community. As you might easily guess, there is much more to planning a model community.

    Imagine that you have again been chosen to serve on the planning board for a model community. The community must be located somewhere within our American territory. Where would you locate your community? What kind of climate and physical features would be important in the choice of location? How would such matters as daily living, work, and leisure influence the arrangement of homes, businesses, and recreational areas? What steps would be taken to bring about a feeling of community spirit and a sense of tradition? Are there some "instant traditions" that could be created? Do you think such things as community spirit and tradition are necessary? What purposes might they serve? What long-range goals would you choose for the members of your community? What values would you hope to find among the people in the community? To what extent would you want the way of life in your community to resemble the American way of life?

BEING A PART OF AMERICAN SOCIETY

3 A Heritage of Liberty

The word "liberty" has a good sound to American ears. It is perhaps the most important of all American values. Probably more than any other word, it defines the beliefs and hopes of the people of the United States. References to liberty fill the pages of our history. In the years before the American Revolution, groups called the Sons of Liberty were formed to protest British taxes. When American colonists proclaimed their independence in 1776, the Liberty Bell in Philadelphia rang out the news. A hundred years later, in New York harbor, the Statue of Liberty was set up, a gift from the people of France. When America entered World War I, Liberty Bonds were sold to help pay for what President Wilson called a war to "make the world safe for democracy."

What is the meaning of liberty? Actually, the word has many meanings. But when all is said, chances are that its meaning will come down to one idea—the idea of freedom. Liberty and freedom, the words go hand in hand. When we sing "My country, 'tis of thee," we call it "Sweet land of liberty." And from this land, we say, "Let freedom ring." For Americans, liberty and freedom are two ways of saying the same thing.

Liberty and Citizenship

As members of the American society, we enjoy a number of different kinds of liberty. Citizenship in the United States provides at least three different kinds of liberty: personal liberty, civil liberty, and political liberty.

Personal liberty involves our right as citizens to come and go as we please. It gives us the freedom to choose our own religions. It offers us a chance to express our own ideas. It allows us to feel that any property that we own is reasonably safe.

Civil liberty protects us from unreasonable government interference. It means that the power of the government of the United States is limited. Our 50 state governments and our national government are all limited by written constitutions. Each of the constitutions tells what the government may do and what it may not do.

Political liberty gives us the right to be active in our government. It gives us the right to vote in free elections. It offers a chance to disagree with actions taken by our political leaders.

THE NEED FOR LAW

American liberty does not give us the right to do anything we want. The American definition of liberty takes account of the fact that people are not perfect. It is because people are not perfect that governments are set up. It is through these governments that laws are made to limit the freedom of the people. Even in a government based upon the idea of liberty, laws that limit freedom are needed. Imagine, for example, the

The reasons behind some of the rules and laws in our society are quite easy to understand. How many cars do you think the parking lot above would hold if people parked as they pleased?

problems there would be if there were no traffic laws.

In order to enjoy the benefits of liberty, it is necessary to adjust the desires and actions of individual people to the welfare of the group. This idea was stated by the English political thinker John Locke almost 300 years ago:

"The end of the law is not to abolish or restrain, but to preserve and enlarge freedom.... Where there is no law there is no freedom. For liberty is to be free from restraint and violence from others, which cannot be where there is no law."

A HERITAGE OF LIBERTY

The meaning of John Locke's statement is clear. If we wish to enjoy liberty, we must have both liberty and law. Thus, liberty and law are close allies. Even so, one thing is clear. In our democratic society, law is only the means to an end. The end or the goal of American society is liberty.

HOW MUCH LIBERTY AND HOW MUCH LAW?

Governments in some form or another have been in existence for thousands of years. In simplest terms, government means the making of rules to guide the behavior of the people. It also involves setting up some kind of power to make sure that the people follow the rules.

Through the ages, governments have taken many forms. This continues to be true today. It is possible, however, to group modern governments into three different types: totalitarian, authoritarian, and democratic. Examples of each are given in Chapter 19. For our purposes here, each will be described briefly.

In a totalitarian form of government, the rules are made by one person or by a small number of people. The government tries to control all aspects of the people's lives. In other words, the ruler and the government seek to have *total* control over the lives of the people.

In an authoritarian form of government, the people have more freedom than the people in a totalitarian form of government have. As in totalitarian governments, one or a few people make the rules. And the rules are enforced by a strong leader or by a powerful group. The difference lies in the fact that the people are allowed some freedom in the conduct of their daily lives. An authoritarian form of government does not try to control all aspects of daily life.

In a democratic form of government, the people make the rules. In a pure democracy, they make the rules directly. In a representative democracy such as ours, the people choose representatives to make the rules for them. The rules are enforced by leaders chosen by the people.

As you can see, a basic difference found in the three types of governments is the amount of liberty and the amount of law that each government finds necessary. At one extreme, in a totalitarian form of government, great emphasis is placed on the law and little concern is shown for liberty. At the other extreme, in a democratic form of government, the people have a great amount of liberty. They even have the liberty to change the laws when they choose.

Getting the Facts

1. What purpose can laws serve in a free country?

2. What are the three main types of government in the world today? How do they differ?

Examining the Issues

■ The government of the United States is a representative democracy. However, this does not mean that democratic ways are followed everywhere in America. Our state and federal prisons are definitely not run on a democratic basis. What are other examples of non-democratic rule in the United States? To what extent do you think the lack of democracy is necessary in each case?

Toward Liberty and Self-Government

The idea that people should govern themselves is not new. It is true, however, that most people in earlier times had little to say about the choice of rulers. Although people might dislike the actions of their rulers, there was little they could do to change the actions.

EARLY GROWTH OF SELF-GOVERNMENT

An important step forward for the ideas of democracy and self-government came in the ancient Greek city-state of Athens. Here, during one period, almost one third of the people were given the right to vote. Democratic ideas also made some headway in ancient Rome. During the days of the Roman Republic, it is estimated that more than a third of the people were given the right to vote.

Following the decline of Rome and the breakup of its empire, there developed in Europe an economic and social system called feudalism. In the feudal societies of the Middle Ages, most of the people were peasants who worked on the land. They had no say in government. Only the ruler, members of the nobility, and certain important religious leaders had any voice in the government. And only these ruling groups had any right to own land.

In time, the feudal rulers began to lose their great political power. One important change came in the year 1215. A group of nobles in England forced King John to sign the Magna Charta—the Great Charter.

The people who wrote our Constitution greatly admired the early governments of Greece and Rome. It is no accident that the interior design of our Senate chamber today resembles the Roman Senate in the drawing below.

The drawing above shows a 13th century English Parliament. Note that, as in the Roman Senate, all the members are men. Although England had a number of powerful woman rulers, it was not until 1919 that a woman became a member of Parliament. Our own Congress seated its first woman in 1917.

The Magna Charta was not in itself an important victory for liberty and self-government. It simply promised the English nobles that the king or queen would respect their special rights. Even so, the Magna Charta was written in general terms. As time passed, the rights granted by the charter came to be applied to more and more people. One section of the charter, for example, contained these words: "No free man shall be taken or imprisoned or dispossessed or outlawed or banished, or in any way destroyed . . . except by . . . the law of the land." Here we have one of the great statements in the progress toward human liberty.

Within 50 years after the Magna Charta, the English Parliament, or law-making body, began to increase its power at the expense of the ruler. A number of especially powerful rulers, among them Henry VIII and Elizabeth I, caused temporary setbacks. Nevertheless, the idea of representative government began to gain ground. In the 1600s, the struggle for power in England between the ruler and the Parliament led to a bitter civil war. In this struggle, Parliament finally gained the upper hand. The ruler was forced to give up some of the royal power and obey "the will of the people." It was during this century of struggle that permanent English colonies were first set up in the New World.

GROWTH OF LIBERTY IN THE NEW WORLD

The English ideas about liberty were transplanted in the English colonies in the New World. Part of the "baggage" that early colonists brought with them was a belief in their basic rights as English subjects to govern themselves. Typical of the attitude was the language of the Fundamental Orders of Connecticut, written in 1639. This document, often considered to be the first written constitution in America, contains these words:

". . . we the inhabitants and residents of Windsor, Hartford and Wethersfield . . . dwelling in and upon the River of Connecticut and the land thereunto adjoining; And well knowing . . . that to maintain the peace and union of such a people there should be an orderly and decent government established according to God . . . do therefore associate and conjoine ourselves to the one Public State or Commonwealth."

Thus, in the Connecticut wilderness, far removed from their Old World leaders, we find a group of people experimenting with their own ideas of self-government.

Experiments with different forms of self-government were carried on throughout the English colonies. Many of these experiments were made possible by the vast distances that separated the colonies from the government in England. In addition, England often neglected its colonies in America because of important matters in England, in Europe, and in other parts of the world.

In New England, the town meeting was developed. Here, in open meeting, a large number of people had the right to take part in the government of their local areas. In contrast to the New England town governments, southern colonies set up local governments organized on the basis of counties. In the other colonies such as Pennsylvania and New York, experiments were carried on with combinations of county and town government.

Representative government was also developed on a colony-wide basis. The first representative assembly in the New World, the House of Burgesses, was set up in the colony of Virginia as early as 1619. Similar lawmaking bodies were set up later in other colonies.

The idea of liberty was advancing in other directions as well. Through the efforts of such people as Anne Hutchinson and Roger Williams, the idea of freedom of religion gradually became accepted. More and more people began to agree that all people should be permitted to choose their own religious beliefs. Victories were also won for such important rights as freedom of speech and freedom of the press.

An important victory for freedom of the press was won in the court case of John Peter Zenger. Zenger was a newspaper publisher in New York City. His newspaper, the *New York Weekly Journal,* printed stories that attacked the policies of the British colonial governor and administration. Upset by the charges, the British leaders publicly burned copies of Zenger's paper. Zenger was arrested and brought to trial in 1735. The jury decided that the stories Zenger had printed were true. They voted him not guilty.

Great progress toward freedom and self-government was made in colonial America. However, some people did not gain as much freedom as others. In most colonies, it was necessary to own a certain amount of property in order to vote

Which of the American colonists in the scene below were likely to have had the right to vote?

A HERITAGE OF LIBERTY

and hold office. In the 1600s, in some colonies, the vote was given only to church members. Throughout the colonial period, and for many years after, the right to vote was generally not given to women, blacks, and Indians. A lack of equality was also seen in the way representatives were chosen to attend the colonial assemblies. The people who arrived first in a colony usually were able to gain control of the assembly. As the colony grew larger, those in control often refused to give up their power. In many cases, they refused to give equal rights of representation to the people who settled in the newer frontier areas.

LIBERTY IN A NEW NATION

The spirit of liberty among American colonists was one of the factors that led to the break with Great Britain. The reasons for the break were listed in the Declaration of Independence. The War for Independence produced a new nation—the United States of America.

Thirteen states made up the young republic. During the war, each state set up its own government with its own constitution. While the war was still in progress, a national government was also formed. It was organized under a set of rules called the Articles of Confederation.

It soon became clear that the government set up by the Articles of Confederation was very weak. Each of the 13 states kept its independence and power as a separate government. The Congress of the new nation did not even have the power to tax the people directly. Many people doubted that the new nation could survive if changes were not made to strengthen the national government.

To make changes in the Articles of Confederation, delegates from 12 of the 13 states met at Independence Hall in Philadelphia in May of 1787. Among these delegates were some of the most respected leaders in America.

The delegates soon decided that instead of making a few changes in the Articles of Confederation they wanted to form a new government. Through the hot summer of 1787 they worked to write our Constitution.

Our Constitution remains today a short but complex document. No one is ever certain exactly what it means. Scholars have spent their lives trying to understand even small parts of it. Justices of the United States Supreme Court disagree over short passages. Is this because the people who wrote the Constitution were such poor constitution makers? Quite the opposite. The evidence is that these farsighted people knew what they were doing. They had reasons for preparing a complex, rather than a simple, instrument. It was a constitution written for a government and a country that would always be willing to make changes to meet new conditions.

For all their wisdom, the delegates failed to deal directly and specifically with an important aspect of liberty. They failed to give guarantees of all the rights the people felt they should possess. For this reason, one of the first things the new government did was to add 10 amendments—the Bill of Rights—to the new Constitution. These amendments, added in 1791, were specifically written for a republican, or representative, form of government. The people who wrote the Bill of Rights knew that the danger to liberty in the new United

States would not be from a queen or king. Instead, there was always the chance that the majority of the citizens would prevent the minority from enjoying their rights. The Bill of Rights was, and is today, a means of protecting Americans from control by other Americans. These amendments, together with certain other parts of the Constitution, are guarantees that ours is a government of laws rather than a government of powerful people.

Getting the Facts

1. Trace the progress of liberty and self-government in Europe and colonial America in the years before 1776.

2. What were the Articles of Confederation? What was the basic weakness of the Articles?

3. Why was the Bill of Rights added to the Constitution?

Forming an Opinion

■ In a democracy, the desires of the majority are generally followed. But what about the people in the minority? To what extent do you think it necessary to protect the rights of people who do not agree with most Americans? What rights do you think all Americans should enjoy, whether they hold popular or unpopular views?

PRINCIPLES THAT SAFEGUARD AMERICAN LIBERTIES

- FEDERALISM — National Government / 50 State Governments
- DIVISION OF NATIONAL POWERS — President, Congress, Supreme Court
- LIMITED GOVERNMENT
- JUDICIAL REVIEW — The Supreme Court
- AMENDING PROCESS

Liberty Through Constitutional Government

Three important principles of government were written into the Constitution. A fourth principle was developed through interpretation of the Constitution in the early 19th century. The four principles are (1) federalism, (2) division of national powers, (3) limited government, and (4) judicial review. Each has helped give us a stable government that is able to change when change is needed. Together, the four principles have helped to protect the liberties that Americans value so highly.

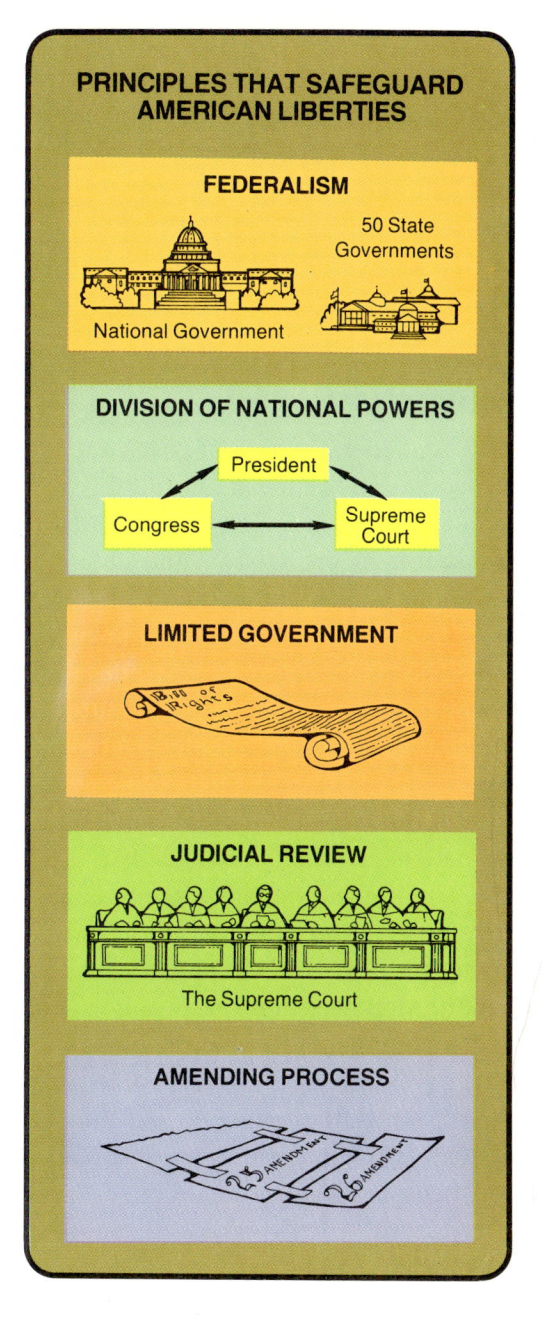

A HERITAGE OF LIBERTY

To further protect American liberties and to allow the American government to change and grow with the times, the constitution makers set up a method of amending the Constitution. The people of the new nation soon found a need for amendments. In 1791, the first 10 amendments were added, giving us our Bill of Rights.

FEDERALISM

Ours is a federal system of government. By federalism, we mean a form of government in which the power is divided and shared by the national and state governments. (Note that the word "federal" has two slightly different meanings. The "federal system" includes the national and state governments. But the "federal government" means just one of these governments—the national government. Likewise, the "federal courts" are the national courts.)

The Constitution gives the national government powers to deal with those matters that are of concern to the whole nation. All powers not specifically given to the national government belong to the state governments, or to the people. The ways in which these state powers may be used are given in the state constitutions.

Because of the nature of our federal system, most Americans are citizens of both a nation and of a state. (Exceptions to this rule are people living in the District of Columbia, Puerto Rico, Guam or other outlying areas. But all of us are citizens of a nation and some other smaller government.) We look to the government in Washington to deal with problems that affect us as a nation. We look to our state governments to handle many other kinds of problems. Generally, state governments deal with matters that seem closer to our daily lives. It is quite likely that the school you are in now is part of your state's system of education. You may have seen a patrol car of the state police on your way to school. You may have paid a state sales tax the last time you bought something. The government of your state is very much a part of your daily life.

When we think about all the different governments—state and national—that make up our federal system of government, a basic question comes to mind. Why was such a complex system set up?

The people who wrote the Constitution were thinking in terms of a large republic. They wanted to set up a government that would represent the people of 13 states and of the territory in the West. It is interesting to note that they were acting against the beliefs of many important political thinkers of the time. These thinkers believed that it was not possible to have a republic that covered a large land area or a large number of people. When a republic became too large, they reasoned, the central government would need more and more power in order to control the nation. In their belief, the central government of an extended republic would eventually destroy the rights of the people. Self-government would not last.

To deal with the problem of a central government with too much power, Americans turned to a political idea known as federalism. They set up a system of many governments within one government. They found ways in which power could be divided and shared by different levels of government.

In addition to this wish to limit the power of a strong central government, there was another, perhaps more practical, reason for adopting a federal system of government. During the American Revolution, the colonies began to function as independent states with their own governments and constitutions. These many independent states were not eager to give up their newly won power. As a result, the first national government, set up under the Articles of Confederation, was very weak. The states wished to keep as much power as possible.

One of the most important laws passed by the Congress of the Articles of Confederation government was one that made it possible for more governments to be added to the American federal system. The Northwest Ordinance of 1787 provided that new states set up within the Northwest Territory could enter the Union on an equal basis with the older states. (In 1787, the "Northwest" was the region north of the Ohio River and east of the Mississippi River.) When a stronger national government was set up under the Constitution a short time later, this idea was extended to include any new state. In 1791, Vermont became

In 1787, the problem of industrial pollution was practically nonexistent. Why does it make sense today to have national or at least regional government involvement in the control of pollution?

the 14th state. Finally, in 1959, the number was rounded out to 50 with the admission of Hawaii.

Like other aspects of our government, federalism allows us to make changes that are needed. A good example of the need for change may be seen in the revolution in transportation that has taken place since the Constitution was written. Originally, roads and other travel networks were a responsibility of state governments. The coming of the railroad, then the automobile, and finally the airplane, brought great changes in travel. To have tried to maintain state control of these kinds of transportation would have been to keep a form of "horse-and-buggy" federalism. Today, major travel systems are the responsibility of the national government. State governments are still responsible for state highway systems.

> **NEW STATES: Article IV, Section 3, Paragraph 1 of the Constitution**
>
> New States may be admitted by the Congress into this Union; but no new State shall be formed or erected within the jurisdiction of any other State; nor any State be formed by the junction of two or more States, or parts of States, without the consent of the legislatures of the States concerned as well as of the Congress.

A HERITAGE OF LIBERTY

DIVISION OF NATIONAL POWER: Checks and Balances

The Constitution divided the national government into three branches: legislative, executive, and judicial. Each branch was given certain duties and powers. Here we have a good example of how the Constitution was made complex rather than simple. For while power is divided among the three branches of government, it is also shared by each branch. Because powers are shared by the three branches, it is very difficult for any one branch to become all-powerful.

This system of shared powers is often referred to as the system of checks and balances. The chart at the right shows the many different ways in which power is divided and shared by the three branches of the national government. Let us take a closer look at one example: national lawmaking power. Article I of the Constitution states that "All legislative powers herein granted shall be vested in a Congress of the United States." Yet, despite this clear language, the President, the head of the executive branch, also has legislative powers. The

---

THREE BRANCHES OF GOVERNMENT: Established by Articles I, II, and III of the Constitution

A Legislative Branch Is Formed: Article I, Section I

All legislative powers herein granted shall be vested in a Congress of the United States, which shall consist of a Senate and House of Representatives.

An Executive Branch Is Formed: Article II, Section 1, Paragraph 1

The executive power shall be vested in a President of the United States of America. He shall hold his office during the term of four years, and, together with the Vice President, chosen for the same term, be elected as follows.

A Judicial Branch Is Formed: Article III, Section 1

The judicial power of the United States shall be vested in one Supreme Court, and in such inferior courts as the Congress may from time to time ordain and establish. The judges, both of the Supreme and inferior courts, shall hold their offices during good behavior, and shall, at stated times, receive for their services, a compensation which shall not be diminished during their continuance in office.

THE PRESIDENT'S LEGISLATIVE POWERS: Listed in Articles I and II of the Constitution

Vetoing Laws: Article I, Section 7, Paragraph 2

Every bill which shall have passed the House of Representatives and the Senate, shall, before it becomes a law, be presented to the President of the United States; if he approve he shall sign it, but if not he shall return it, with his objections to that House in which it shall have originated, who shall enter the objections at large on their journal, and proceed to reconsider it. If after such reconsideration two thirds of that House shall agree to pass the bill, it shall be sent, together with the objections, to the other House, by which it shall likewise be reconsidered, and if approved by two thirds of that House, it shall become a law. . . .

Carrying Out Laws: Article II, Section 3

. . . he [the President] shall take care that the laws be faithfully executed . . .

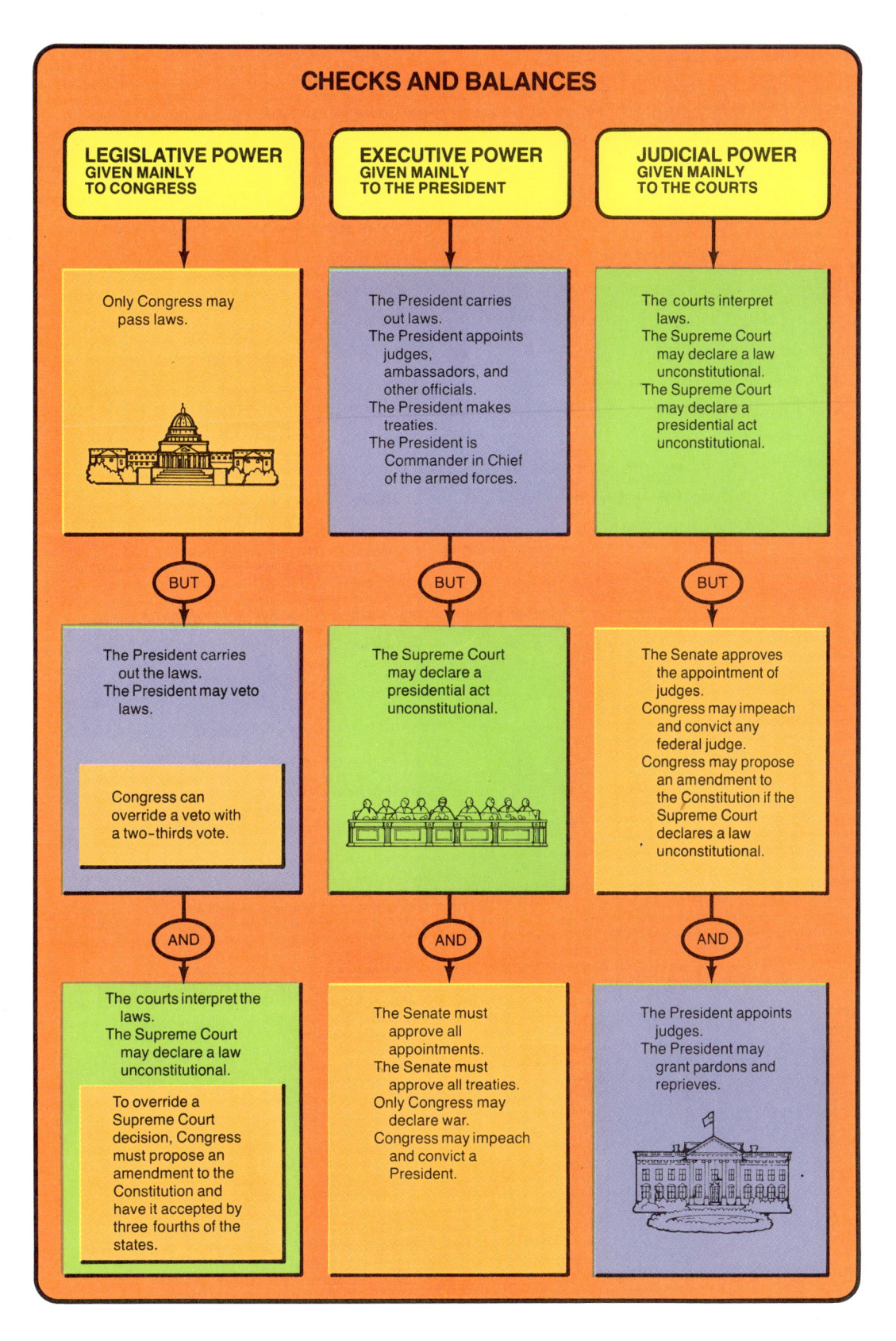

CHECKS AND BALANCES

LEGISLATIVE POWER
GIVEN MAINLY TO CONGRESS

Only Congress may pass laws.

BUT

The President carries out the laws.
The President may veto laws.

Congress can override a veto with a two-thirds vote.

AND

The courts interpret the laws.
The Supreme Court may declare a law unconstitutional.

To override a Supreme Court decision, Congress must propose an amendment to the Constitution and have it accepted by three fourths of the states.

EXECUTIVE POWER
GIVEN MAINLY TO THE PRESIDENT

The President carries out laws.
The President appoints judges, ambassadors, and other officials.
The President makes treaties.
The President is Commander in Chief of the armed forces.

BUT

The Supreme Court may declare a presidential act unconstitutional.

AND

The Senate must approve all appointments.
The Senate must approve all treaties.
Only Congress may declare war.
Congress may impeach and convict a President.

JUDICIAL POWER
GIVEN MAINLY TO THE COURTS

The courts interpret laws.
The Supreme Court may declare a law unconstitutional.
The Supreme Court may declare a presidential act unconstitutional.

BUT

The Senate approves the appointment of judges.
Congress may impeach and convict any federal judge.
Congress may propose an amendment to the Constitution if the Supreme Court declares a law unconstitutional.

AND

The President appoints judges.
The President may grant pardons and reprieves.

A HERITAGE OF LIBERTY

President has the right to veto laws. In other words, the head of the executive branch of the national government may refuse to approve acts of the legislative branch of the government. Congress can override vetoed laws, but with a two-thirds majority vote rather than a simple majority vote. The President and other members of the executive branch can also exercise a kind of legislative power by enforcing or carrying out laws in certain ways. In the judicial branch, the United States Supreme Court also has certain legislative powers. It can interpret congressional laws. That is, the Court may be called upon to say what a law really means.

Recently, a number of Americans have begun to wonder whether our system of checks and balances works as well as the constitution makers thought it would. In Chapter 5, we will consider the question of whether or not one branch of government—the executive branch—has become stronger than the other two.

Some people feel that the system may still work but that it is often too slow. When Congress considered the impeachment of a President in the early 1970s, it took months and months of preparation time. However, few people disagree with the idea of a system of checks and balances. Most critics would simply like to strengthen the system.

Most state constitutions divide state powers between the different branches of government in much the same way that the national Constitution does. All 50 state constitutions call for three branches of government: legislative, executive, and judicial. To some extent, the state constitutions also provide systems of checks and balances. Almost all governors, for example, have the power to veto laws. But in some states this veto can be overridden by a simple majority in both houses of the state legislature.

LIMITED GOVERNMENT

The people who wrote our Constitution were familiar with humanity's long struggle for liberty. They themselves had been colonial subjects. For these rea-

What is the cartoonist's view of the way the checks and balances system is working today? To what extent do you agree or disagree with this view?

sons, they decided to place limits on the power of government. To do this they balanced power. They set up a federal system in which some power was given to the national government, some to the states, and some to the people. In like manner, they set up a system of checks and balances for the three branches of the national government.

To further limit government, they wrote into the Constitution certain rights that the government could not take away. As we have seen, however, these rights were not enough to suit the people's wishes. To make sure that the new Constitution would be accepted by the American people, it was necessary to add the Bill of Rights. These 10 amendments are still another limitation on the power of government. Today, all 50 of the state constitutions also have bills of rights to protect the liberties of the people.

JUDICIAL REVIEW

The principle of judicial review refers to the power of the Supreme Court of the United States to declare acts of Congress unconstitutional. The Court, in other words, has the power to rule that an act of Congress is contrary to the meaning of the Constitution. If the Court rules against an act of Congress, the act can no longer be considered a law.

The Constitution does not specifically give judicial review to the Supreme Court. It is, nevertheless, a power that became clearly accepted early in the history of our country. This principle covers laws passed by all governments in the United States—national, state, and local.

AMENDING THE CONSTITUTION

In the years between 1791 and 1971, Americans added 26 amendments to the Constitution. A number of these have greatly increased our freedom as American citizens. They have guaranteed our personal and legal rights. They have given us the right to vote directly for members of the national Senate. They have given the vote to black Americans and to women.

Only one of the amendments added to the Constitution has been repealed. In 1919, Americans decided that the sale of

What is this cartoonist saying about the American system of checks and balances? How can judicial review help protect the rights of individual Americans?

"Can You See Me Now?"

A HERITAGE OF LIBERTY

intoxicating liquors should be prohibited. The 18th Amendment made the production, sale, and transportation of most forms of alcoholic drink illegal. In 1933, with the 21st Amendment, Americans changed their minds. Liquor again became legal except in states where laws prohibited it.

One of the reasons why almost all of the amendments have lasted so long is that the process set up in the Constitution makes it hard to add amendments. The box at the right lists the steps that must be followed. The process takes a great deal of time. In some cases, Americans have had years to consider possible new amendments. Finally, each amendment must be accepted by a large majority of the states. This process has assured that each new amendment will be carefully studied and thought out before it becomes a part of our Constitution.

AN AMENDMENT IS REPEALED:
The 18th Amendment to the Constitution Is Repealed by the 21st Amendment

Prohibition: The 18th Amendment, Section 1

After one year from the ratification of this article the manufacture, sale, or transportation of intoxicating liquors within, the importation thereof into, or the exportation thereof from the United States and all territory subject to the jurisdiction thereof for beverage purposes is hereby prohibited.

Repeal of Prohibition: The 21st Amendment, Section 1

The eighteenth article of amendment to the Constitution of the United States is hereby repealed.

AMENDING THE CONSTITUTION:
Article V of the Constitution

The Congress, whenever two thirds of both Houses shall deem it necessary, shall propose amendments to this Constitution, or on the application of the legislatures of two thirds of the several States, shall call a convention for proposing amendments, which, in either case, shall be valid to all intents and purposes, as part of this Constitution, when ratified by the legislatures of three fourths of the several States, or by conventions in three fourths thereof, as the one or the other mode of ratification may be proposed by the Congress; provided that no amendment which may be made prior to the year one thousand eight hundred and eight shall in any manner affect the first and fourth clauses in the ninth section of the first article; and that no State, without its consent, shall be deprived of its equal suffrage in the Senate.

Getting the Facts

1. What is a federal system of government?

2. How is power divided between the different branches of the national government? Give at least five examples of the way the system of checks and balances works.

3. How does the principle of judicial review work?

Examining the Issues

■ For many reasons it seemed to make sense to set up a federal system of government in 1787. Do you think the federal system still works well today? Why, or why not? Would you favor a plan that would change the 50 states into about a dozen regional areas with common interests? Why, or why not?

Who Shall Govern?

The search for liberty has had a long history. In terms of political power, the search involved the question of who shall govern. Should government be left in the hands of an all-powerful ruler? Should power be given to a chosen few? Or should all people have political rights and duties? From the distant past to our own time, there have always been people who believed that most people are not able to govern themselves. These people have maintained that political power should rest with one or a few people who, for some reason, are qualified to govern. Yet, there have always been others who believed that political power would be more wisely used if held by a much larger group. And, of course, there are many people, especially today, who believe that political power should be held by all people.

In the ancient world, it was common for one person or a small group of people to rule. Most people seemed to think this was natural. In Egypt, for example, the men and women who ruled as pharaohs were generally thought of as being godlike. Who could question the right of a godlike person to rule?

However, as early as the 5th century B.C., there were people who did not agree with this common view. Pericles, an important political leader in Athens, believed that the people of Athens could rule themselves. In the following words, he described how the government of Athens worked:

"It is true that we are called a democracy, for the administration is in the hands of the many and not the few. But while the law secures equal justice to all alike in their private disputes, the claim of excellence is also recognized; and when a citizen is in any way distinguished, he is preferred to the public service, not as a matter of privilege, but as a reward of merit. Neither is poverty a bar, but a man may benefit his country whatever be the obscurity of his condition. There is no exclusiveness in our public life, and in our private intercourse we are not suspicious of one another, nor angry with our neighbor if he does what he likes. . . . We alone regard a man who takes no interest in public affairs, not as a harmless, but as a useless character; and if few of us are originators, we are all sound judges of policy."

It is easy to be misled by Pericles' words. His statements about the government in Athens refer to men only. The women in Athens could become citizens, but they could not vote or hold office. If so many of the males in Athens were given the right to govern themselves, why were the females not given the same right?

Some women, as members of ruling families, did hold positions of great power in the ancient world. However, the opinion was widespread that women in general could not be trusted with political power. The words of a high ranking official in ancient Rome show the strength of this feeling. In arguing that Rome should keep certain laws restricting female dress, movement, and possession of money, the official shows a general mistrust of women:

"Our ancestors would have no woman transact even private business except through her guardian; they placed them under the tutelage of parents or brothers or husbands. We suffer them now to dabble in politics and mix themselves up with the business of the Forum

Inquiry

A HERITAGE OF LIBERTY

Inquiry

and public debates and election contests. What are they doing now in the public roads and at street corners but recommending to the plebs [common people] the proposal of their tribunes and voting for the repeal of the law? . . . This is the smallest of those restrictions which have been imposed upon women by ancestral custom or by laws, and which they submit to with such impatience. What they really want is unrestricted freedom . . .and if they win on this occasion what is there that they will not attempt?"

Arguments such as this have been used through the years by people seeking to keep women and other groups of people from sharing political power. Nevertheless, it is clear that in parts of the ancient world the idea of liberty for at least some of the people was accepted.

Hundreds of years later the question of who should have political power was still very much alive. In Europe, we find a number of rulers claiming power for themselves alone. Such power, they said, was a gift from God. One of these rulers was King James I of England. In 1609, he stated his beliefs in the following manner:

"Kings are justly called Gods, for that they exercise a manner of resemblance of Divine power upon earth. For if you will consider the attributes of God, you shall see how they agree in the person of a King. God hath power to create, or destroy, make or unmake at His pleasure, to give life, or send to death, to judge all, and to be judged nor accountable to none, to raise low things, and to make high things low at His pleasure, and to God are both soul and body due. And the like power have Kings. They make and unmake their subjects, they have power of raising, and casting down, of life, and of death, judges over all their subjects, and in all causes, and yet accountable to none but God only. . . ."

Rulers such as James I of England believed that God had granted them the power to rule over subjects who were unable to rule themselves.

Other people, in England and in other countries, held a view different from that of James I. One was the political thinker John Locke. Writing in 1690, Locke stated his belief that governments are created by the people. As such the governments are subject to the laws of the people rather than the will of a ruler.

"Men being . . . by nature all free, equal, and independent, no one can be put out of this estate, and subjected to the political power of another without his consent. The only way by which anyone divests himself of his natural liberty and puts on the bonds of civil society is by agreeing with other men to join and unite into a community for their comfortable, safe, and peaceable living one amongst another, in a secure enjoyment of their properties, and a greater security against any that are not of it."

John Locke's ideas were not forgotten in America. Almost 100 years later, in 1776, they appeared in the Declaration of Independence. Included in this famous statement of American liberties are these words:

"We hold these truths to be self-evident, that all men are created equal, that they are endowed by their Creator with certain unalienable rights, that among these are life, liberty and the pursuit of happiness. That to secure these rights, governments are instituted among men, deriving their just powers from the consent of the governed, that whenever any form of government becomes destructive of these ends, it is the right of the people to alter or abolish it, and to institute new government, laying its foundation on such principles, and organizing its powers in such form, as to them shall seem most likely to effect their safety and happiness."

Americans won their independence. The United States was set up as a republic based on government by the people. These actions, however, did not end the age-old arguments about human freedom and who should govern, even in our own country. During the 1850s, the arguments reached fever pitch in the controversy over slavery. One of the Americans who argued in defense of slavery was George Fitzhugh, a Virginia lawyer. Fitzhugh could not agree with the words of the Declaration of Independence. He believed that people are basically unequal.

"Men are not 'born entitled to equal rights'! It would be far nearer the truth to say that 'some were born with saddles on their backs, and others booted and spurred to ride them'—and the riding does them good. They need the reins, the bit, and the spur. No two men by nature are exactly equal or exactly alike. No institutions can prevent the few from acquiring rule and ascendancy over the many. Liberty and free competition invite and encourage the attempt of the strong to master the weak and insure their success."

So strong were the disagreements among Americans over the rights of people and the rights of the national and state governments to limit or expand human freedom that a bloody war was fought. The Civil War freed all black Americans from the bonds of slavery. It did not, however, settle all questions about human rights.

The freed slaves were given the right to vote soon after the Civil War. However, state and local restrictions often prevented them from actually voting. In most places, women were also denied the right to vote. Arguments for and against an end to these restrictions continued well into the 20th century. Under the leadership of such people as Carrie Chapman Catt and Martin Luther King, Jr., these groups have gained a greater role in government.

Examining Questions of Liberty and Power

You have read a number of statements covering some 2,500 years of history. All are concerned with liberty and the right of people to govern themselves. With these statements in mind, think about these questions:

In what ways does the democracy in Pericles' Athens seem to be like our American democracy? In what ways does it seem different?

What arguments would you offer to support or oppose the arguments of the Roman official?

What is the basic disagreement found in the statements of Locke and Fitzhugh? To what extent can Fitzhugh's argument be used to deny equal rights to all people? What counter arguments could you use to support the idea of equal rights for all people?

A HERITAGE OF LIBERTY

Speaking Out

Barbara Tuchman

Historian Barbara Tuchman has twice won the Pulitzer Prize. Looking back over the last 200 years of our country's history, she sees both successes and failures in the American struggle for democracy and liberty. In spite of the failures, however, she feels that America is still the country in which these goals are most likely to be reached.

"The United States is a nation consciously conceived, not one that evolved slowly out of an ancient past. It was a planned idea of democracy, of liberty of conscience and pursuit of happiness. It was the promise of equality of opportunity and individual freedom within a just social order, as opposed to the restrictions and repressions of the Old World...

"... The founding idea of the United States remained, on the whole, dominant through the first 100 years. With reservations, it was believed in by Americans, by visitors who came to aid our Revolution or later to observe our progress, by immigrants who came by the hundreds of thousands to escape an intolerable situation in their native lands.

"... But slowly in the struggle the idea lost ground, and at a turning point around 1900 ... it lost dominance....

"In the United States [today] we have a society pervaded from top to bottom by contempt for the law. Government—including the agencies of law enforcement—business, labor, students, the military, the poor no less than the rich, outdo each other in breaking the rules and violating the ethics that society has established for its protection....

"Yet the idea does not die. Americans are not passive under their faults. We expose them and combat them. Somewhere every day some group is fighting a public abuse.... The U.S. has slid a long way from the original idea. Nevertheless ... it still offers a greater opportunity for social happiness, that is to say, for well-being combined with individual freedom and initiative, than is likely elsewhere. The ideal society for which mankind has been striving through the ages will remain forever beyond our grasp. But if the great question, whether it is still possible to reconcile democracy with social order and individual liberty, is to find a positive answer, it will be here."

1. What particular fault does the author find widespread in American society today? Considering your own experiences as an American, how widespread do you believe this fault is? Give examples to support your answer.

2. What reason does the author give for her belief that the United States "still offers a greater opportunity for social happiness ... than is likely elsewhere"? To what extent do you agree with her belief? Why?

1976: A Year of Rededication

There was a rededication to our heritage of liberty during the year 1976. Across this land of ours, we Americans celebrated the 200th anniversary of our Declaration of Independence. In hundreds of ways, during this Bicentennial Celebration, we recalled the contributions of earlier Americans to the cause of freedom. With pride, we remembered the many Americans who have contributed to the greatness of the United States.

Thoughts of past achievements, nevertheless, were coupled with an awareness of future challenges. Do all Americans now have equal opportunities? In our complex modern world, will we still be able to govern ourselves? Questions such as these continue to concern us as citizens. New answers to them must repeatedly be found if our democracy is to live and grow.

Getting the Facts

■ What anniversary did Americans celebrate in 1976?

Thinking About the Future

■ What do you think are the greatest challenges Americans will face in the next 100 years? How do you think these challenges should be met?

Americans celebrated the Bicentennial in many different ways—some of them serious, others simply fun. How did the people in your community celebrate our country's 200th anniversary?

A HERITAGE OF LIBERTY

Citizenship Laboratory

Review of Basic Ideas

1. The American people have a number of different kinds of liberty. Among these are personal freedom, protection from unreasonable government interference, and the right to take an active part in the government. Even in a government based on the idea of liberty, some laws that limit personal freedom are needed. To some extent, it is necessary to limit the actions of individual people to promote the welfare of all people. The amount of liberty and the number of restricting laws vary from government to government. In very general terms, there are three different types of modern government: totalitarian, authoritarian, and democratic. In totalitarian governments, an effort is made to control all aspects of the people's lives. Authoritarian governments allow people some freedom in the conduct of their daily lives. The goal of democracy is to give people as much freedom as possible.

2. The people who settled the English colonies in North America brought with them a heritage of liberty and a number of ideas about self-government. In the colonies and in the new nation, they continued to experiment with new forms of self-government.

3. The American government is based on four constitutional principles of government: federalism, division of national powers, limited government, and judicial review. Each helps protect the liberties of the American people. In our federal system of government, powers are divided and shared between the national and state governments. The powers of the national government are divided and shared by the legislative, executive, and judicial branches. The power of each branch is limited by a system of checks and balances. Government is also limited by a number of guarantees of freedom written into the Constitution and the Bill of Rights. The principle of judicial review gives the United States Supreme Court the power to say that acts of Congress are unconstitutional. American liberties have also been furthered by the fact that amendments can be added to the Constitution to bring about needed changes.

4. The American Bicentennial Celebration of 1976 gave the American people a chance to review past achievements and think about future challenges.

Questions to Think About

1. What forms of liberty, if any, do you think Americans should have but do not yet have? How could these liberties be gained?

2. To what extent do you agree that a society must have laws if its people are to enjoy liberty? What are some examples of necessary laws in America today?

3. It is very likely that many of the problems nations face today are more complex and more difficult to solve than the problems nations faced 100 years ago. Which of the three types of modern government do you think is best able to deal with such things as energy shortages, threats of nuclear war, and overpopulation? Explain.

4. In what ways did the ideas of liberty and self-government flourish in colonial America? What factors made experiments with these ideas possible?

5. Our Constitution is so complex that no one is ever certain exactly what it means. To what extent do you think this complexity has been useful?

6. In what ways are the powers of the national government limited? Could the government work more efficiently if some of these limitations were removed? Or would it be better if even more limitations were placed on the power of the national government? Explain your answer.

Words and Relationships

Define each of the words in the first column. Then show how each term is related to the item listed opposite it by using both items in a sentence or short paragraph.

1.	liberty	the right to vote
2.	law	freedom of religion
3.	totalitarian	freedom of the press
4.	authoritarian	political power
5.	democracy	change
6.	inequality	colonial America
7.	Bill of Rights	protection of minority rights
8.	federalism	states' rights
9.	checks and balances	legislative power
10.	judicial review	limited government

Building a Future

The idea of liberty has had a long history. It has developed in different ways in different parts of the world. Think about the idea as it works today. Think about how it may change in the years to come.

To what extent are we Americans a free people? Do we need more liberty if we are to have a truly free society? Think about other countries and people. Which of them seem to have the largest amount of freedom? In which countries is liberty very restricted?

If more liberty is a desirable goal, how can it be gained? Could it best be gained in our own country through the orderly process of passing laws? Or are protests and rebellion needed to gain more liberty? Should the process be different in the United States than in certain other countries? Are there some countries where liberty is not likely to be gained? Will it be possible for these nations to live peaceably alongside nations whose people have more freedom?

Finally, there is another kind of question. As we look into the increasingly complex world of the future, is more liberty really a desirable goal? Is it possible that, in a world of advanced technology and larger populations, it will prove necessary to place more restrictions on people's actions? Stated differently, can this new kind of world afford more freedom? Does this suggest new ways of thinking about the old relationships between liberty and law?

A HERITAGE OF LIBERTY

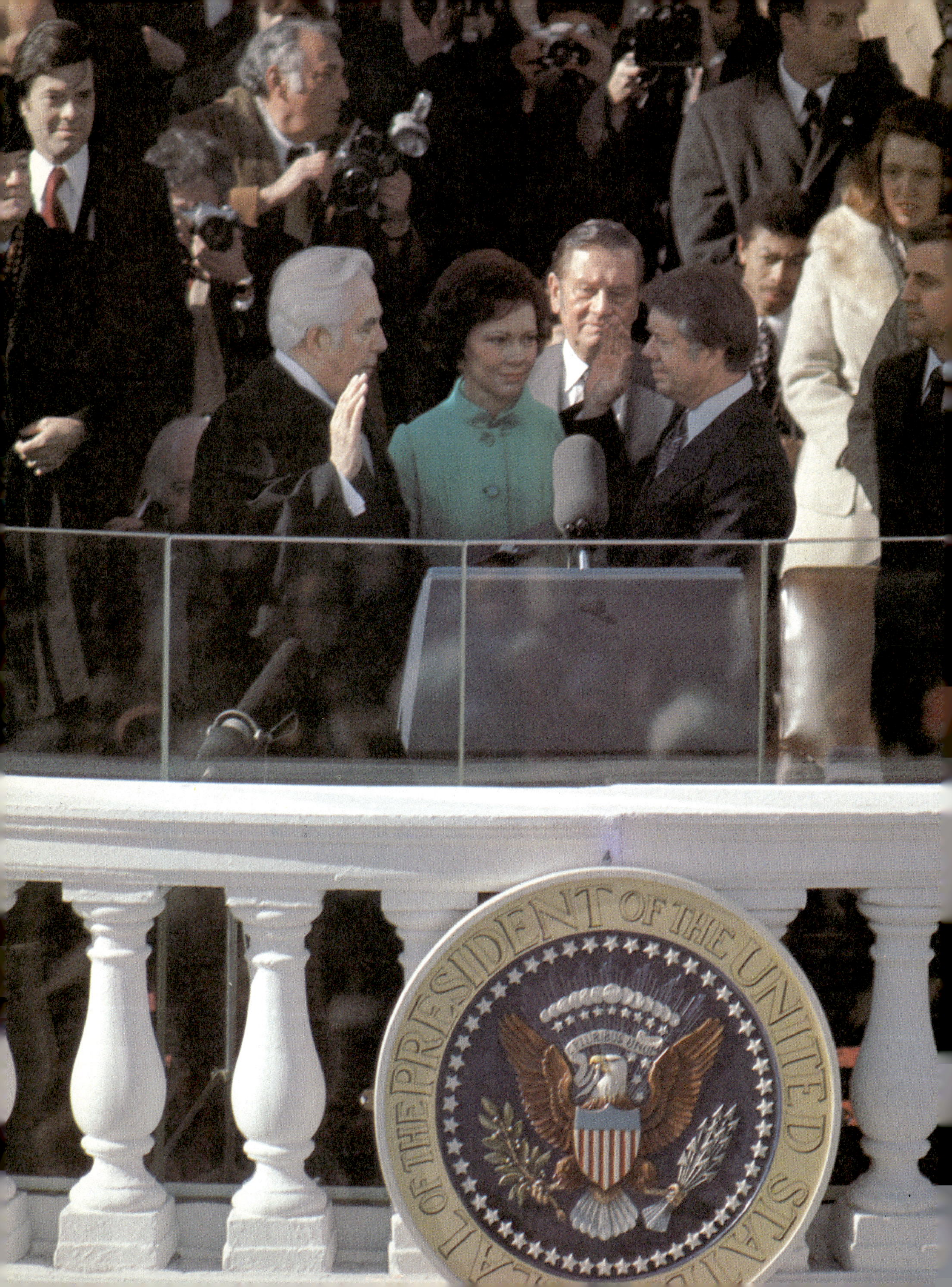
SEAL OF THE PRESIDENT OF THE UNITED STATES
E PLURIBUS UNUM

Unit Two
Government of All Americans

4 Lawmaking in America

We citizens of the United States live in an independent nation that is governed by the people. It is a nation with a special way of life that we call "American." Created in the late 18th century through revolution and constitution making, it is a nation based on the principle of self-government.

The people who established our government did more than just set up a new government. They set up a very special form of government: a federal republic. By "republic" these early Americans meant a form of government in which people would be ruled by laws passed by their representatives. Views differed as to whether the right to vote should be given to all or to only a few. But there was general agreement that the government must be based on representative principles. There was a strong feeling that provisions must be made for some expression of the people's desires.

Most closely representing the people of the new United States were the members of Congress. To assure that the wishes of the people would be heard, the constitution makers made this national lawmaking body a very powerful part of the new government.

State Capitol in Montpelier, Vermont
National Capitol in Washington, D.C.
State Capitol in Austin, Texas

GOVERNMENT OF ALL AMERICANS

The Constitution Establishes a National Congress

The Constitution calls for three branches of government. National power is divided and shared by the legislative branch, the executive branch, and the judicial branch. The legislative, or lawmaking, branch is the Congress.

A STRONG CONGRESS

The makers of the Constitution placed great emphasis on the legislative branch of the new government. The first article of the Constitution begins with these words: "All legislative powers herein granted shall be vested in a Congress of the United States . . ." Not only is this lawmaking article the first article in the Constitution, it is also by far the longest article in the Constitution. Its location, its length, and its wording were not matters of chance. Clearly, the people who wrote the Constitution wished to stress the importance of the national lawmaking body.

Although they set up a government with an executive branch, the constitution makers feared a strong executive. They had seen the people's liberties endangered by kings and queens and by royal governors. For this reason, they wanted to make sure that Congress had at least as much power as the other two branches of government. Some felt that Congress should have even more power than the other two branches. They believed that Congress would be the branch most likely to protect the liberties of the American people.

In England and in the colonies, the lawmaking body had always been the branch of government that best represented the people's wishes. In the election process set up by the Constitution, this tradition was continued. The states were given the power to set voter qualifications but the Constitution offered certain guidelines. In the box on page 68 you can see the guidelines set up for choosing officers of the three branches of the federal government. Members of the lower house of Congress, the House of Representatives, were the only officers to be elected directly by the people. Members of the upper house of Congress, the Senate, were to be chosen by the people's representatives in the state legislatures. (This was changed to direct election with the 17th Amendment to the Constitution in 1913.) In contrast, the President was to be chosen by electors who would be chosen in some manner by the state legislatures. Even today, the Electoral College is directly responsible for the election of the American President. These electors still have the power to choose a President who has lost the popular election. They did this twice in the 19th century. Today it is highly unlikely but still possible. When the Constitution was written, however, the Electoral College was expected to make an independent decision. The people were not to be consulted except through

> **A LEGISLATIVE BRANCH IS FORMED: Article I, Section 1 of the Constitution**
>
> All legislative powers herein granted shall be vested in a Congress of the United States, which shall consist of a Senate and House of Representatives.

LAWMAKING IN AMERICA

METHODS OF CHOOSING FEDERAL OFFICERS: Given in Articles I and II of the Constitution

Members of the House of Representatives: Article I, Section 2, Paragraph 1
The House of Representatives shall be composed of members chosen every second year by the people of the several States, and the electors in each State shall have the qualifications requisite for electors of the most numerous branch of the State legislature.

Members of the Senate: Article I, Section 3, Paragraph 1
The Senate of the United States shall be composed of two senators from each State, chosen by the legislature thereof for six years; and each senator shall have one vote.

The President: Article II, Section 1, Paragraph 2
Each state shall appoint, in such manner as the legislature thereof may direct, a number of electors, equal to the whole number of senators and representatives to which the State may be entitled in the Congress: but no senator or representative, or person holding an office of trust or profit under the United States, shall be appointed an elector.

Justices of the United States Supreme Court: Article II, Section 2, Paragraph 2
He [the President] shall have power, by and with the advice and consent of the Senate, to make treaties, provided two thirds of the senators present concur; and he shall nominate, and by and with the advice and consent of the Senate, shall appoint ambassadors, other public ministers and consuls, judges of the Supreme Court, and all other officers of the United States, whose appointments are not herein otherwise provided for, and which shall be established by law: but the Congress may by law vest the appointment of such inferior officers, as they think proper, in the President alone, in the courts of law, or in the heads of departments.

DIRECT ELECTION OF SENATORS BEGINNING IN 1913: **The 17th Amendment to the Constitution, Section 1**

The Senate of the United States shall be composed of two senators from each State, elected by the people thereof, for six years; and each senator shall have one vote. The electors in each State shall have the qualifications requisite for electors of the most numerous branch of the State legislatures.

their representatives in the state legislatures. Finally, the officers of the third branch of government, the justices of the United States Supreme Court, were to be appointed by the President with the advice and consent of Senate. Clearly, the Congress set up by the constitution makers in 1787 was by far the most representative of the three branches of government.

A CONGRESS OF TWO HOUSES

Following the pattern of the English Parliament and most colonial legislatures, Article I of the Constitution calls for a Congress of two houses: a Senate and a House of Representatives. This bicameral, or two-house, pattern was followed for at least two reasons. Many believed that two houses were needed so that one could serve as a check on the other. But there was another, perhaps more practical reason. With two houses, it was possible to please both the small and the large states. Each state was given two members in the Senate. Without this equal representation of states in the Senate it is likely that some of the states with smaller populations would

All 535 members of the two houses of Congress meet together at least once a year to hear the President's annual State of the Union message.

not have accepted the Constitution. Representation in the House of Representatives was based on population. This, of course, pleased the states with larger populations. This compromise was just one of many that have been needed over the years to make our democratic political system work.

With two senators from each state, we now have a Senate of 100 members. All are elected on a state-wide basis. Through the years, the fact that we have just two senators from each state has offered certain benefits. Senators represent more than just the people of relatively small districts. At the very least, a senator is the representative of an entire state. Quite often senators are more. They often respond to the social, economic, and political interests of the people of entire regions of the country.

The House of Representatives, with its membership based on population, is much larger than the Senate. Each state, no matter how small its population, has at least one representative. On the other hand, some states have many representatives. After the 1970 census, the state with the most people was California. California was given 43 representatives. New York was second with 39.

REPRESENTATION IN THE TWO HOUSES OF CONGRESS: **Given in Article I of the Constitution**

Two Members from Each State in the Senate: Article I, Section 3, Paragraph 1
The Senate of the United States shall be composed of two senators from each State, chosen by the legislature thereof for six years; and each senator shall have one vote.

Representation Based on Population in the House of Representatives: Article I, Section 2, Paragraph 3
Representatives and direct taxes shall be apportioned among the several States which may be included within this Union, according to their respective numbers, which shall be determined by adding to the whole number of free persons, including those bound to service for a term of years, and excluding Indians not taxed, three fifths of all other persons. The actual enumeration shall be made within three years after the first meeting of the Congress of the United States, and within every subsequent term of ten years, in such manner as they shall by law direct. The number of representatives shall not exceed one for every thirty thousand, but each State shall have at least one representative; and until such enumeration shall be made, the State of New Hampshire shall be entitled to choose three, Massachusetts eight, Rhode Island and Providence Plantations one, Connecticut five, New York six, New Jersey four, Pennsylvania eight, Delaware one, Maryland six, Virginia ten, North Carolina five, South Carolina five, and Georgia three.

LAWMAKING IN AMERICA

coming up for election every two years. Members of the House are elected for two-year terms. Senators must be at least 30 years old. Members of the House must be 25 or older. Senators must have held United States citizenship for at least nine years before they can be elected. Members of the House have to have been citizens for only seven years.

The constitution makers apparently believed that if they set longer terms and slightly higher qualifications for senators, members of the Senate would have greater strength and dignity and a higher level of ability than members of the House. Following the same line of reasoning, the House of Representatives is often called the "lower house" of Congress. The Senate is called the "upper house." These terms, however, can be

In some ways the job of a senator is more difficult than the job of a member of the House. A senator from Pennsylvania must consider the interests of all areas of the state, including the two very different areas shown above.

The total membership of the House was fixed at 435 by a congressional act in 1929. Because of this fixed number, the growth and movement of the nation's population causes some states to gain and others to lose representatives from time to time. Changes are made after each 10-year census.

Senators are elected for six-year terms, with one third of the senators

QUALIFICATIONS FOR MEMBERS OF CONGRESS: Given in Article I of the Constitution

Qualifications for Senators: Article I, Section 3, Paragraph 3

No person shall be a senator who shall not have attained to the age of thirty years, and been nine years a citizen of the United States, and who shall not, when elected, be an inhabitant of that State for which he shall be chosen.

Qualifications for Members of the House of Representatives: Article I, Section 2, Paragraph 2

No person shall be a representative who shall not have attained to the age of twenty-five years, and been seven years a citizen of the United States, and who shall not, when elected, be an inhabitant of that State in which he shall be chosen.

GOVERNMENT OF ALL AMERICANS

> **MONEY BILLS BEGIN IN THE HOUSE OF REPRESENTATIVES:**
> **Article I, Section 7, Paragraph 1 of the Constitution**
>
> All bills for raising revenue shall originate in the House of Representatives; but the Senate may propose or concur with amendments as on other bills.

misleading. As far as lawmaking power is concerned, the two houses are equal. Spending and money bills, for example, must begin in the House. The Senate, on the other hand, is the only body that can ratify a treaty. It is also the Senate that confirms the President's appointments of government officials.

CONSTITUTIONAL POWERS GIVEN TO CONGRESS

The most important power given to Congress was, of course, the power to make laws. But what kinds of laws could Congress make? To answer this question, the constitution makers listed a number of specific powers in Section 8 of Article I.

More than half of these powers deal with money and the armed forces. As you can see in the chart on the next page, Congress was given the power (1) to collect taxes and (2) to borrow money. (The numbers in parentheses refer to the paragraphs in Section 8.) In order to set up a national currency, Congress was given the power (5) to coin money. To protect this currency, Congress was also given the power (6) to punish counterfeiters. Congressional war powers included the right (11) to declare war, (12) to raise an army, (13) to provide a navy, and (15) to call forth the state militias. To carry out these war powers, Congress was also given the right to pass laws (14) to regulate land and naval forces and (16) to regulate the state militias.

A number of the powers given to Congress were of great interest to the growing businesses of the new nation. Under the earlier Articles of Confederation government, the states had the power to regulate trade. It was not uncommon for one state to place taxes on the products of another state. This created endless problems for businesses that wished to expand their markets. Under the Constitution, Congress was given the power (3) to regulate trade among the states and with foreign countries. Congress was also allowed (4) to pass uniform bankruptcy laws and (5) to set up a uniform system of weights and measures. Finally, Congress was allowed (8) to grant patents and copyrights to protect inventors and authors.

As the national lawmaking body, Congress was given the power (4) to set up rules for naturalization so that people from other countries could become citizens. To draw the country closer together, Congress was directed (7) to set up post offices and post roads. Article III of the Constitution set up the United States Supreme Court, but Congress was directed (9) to set up a system of federal courts to work under the Supreme Court. Because piracy was still a major problem at the end of the 18th century, Congress was given the power (10) to punish acts of piracy.

The last of the powers specifically listed in Section 8 gave Congress the right (17) to set up and govern certain national lands. The constitution makers

> **POWERS GIVEN TO CONGRESS:**
> **Listed in Article I of the Constitution**
>
> **To Collect Taxes:** Article I, Section 8, Paragraph 1
>
> The Congress shall have power to lay and collect taxes, duties, imposts and excises, to pay the debts and provide for the common defense and general welfare of the United States; but all duties, imposts and excises shall be uniform throughout the United States;
>
> **To Borrow Money:** Article I, Section 8, Paragraph 2
>
> To borrow money on the credit of the United States;
>
> **To Regulate Trade:** Article I, Section 8, Paragraph 3
>
> To regulate commerce with foreign nations, and among the several States, and with the Indian tribes;
>
> **To Pass Naturalization and Bankruptcy Laws:** Article I, Section 8, Paragraph 4
>
> To establish an uniform rule of naturalization, and uniform laws on the subject of bankruptcies throughout the United States;
>
> **To Coin Money and Set Up a Standard System of Weights and Measures:** Article I, Section 8, Paragraph 5
>
> To coin money, regulate the value thereof, and of foreign coin, and fix the standard of weights and measures;
>
> **To Punish Counterfeiters:** Article I, Section 8, Paragraph 6
>
> To provide for the punishment of counterfeiting the securities and current coin of the United States;
>
> **To Set Up Post Offices and Post Roads:** Article I, Section 8, Paragraph 7
>
> To establish post offices and post roads;
>
> **To Pass Patent and Copyright Laws:** Article I, Section 8, Paragraph 8
>
> To promote the progress of science and useful arts by securing for limited times to authors and inventors the exclusive right to their respective writings and discoveries;
>
> **To Create a System of Federal Courts:** Article I, Section 8, Paragraph 9
>
> To constitute tribunals inferior to the Supreme Court;

were looking forward to the time when the federal government would be relocated on land not governed by any state. (The federal government moved to Washington, D.C. in 1800. Before that the government had been based first in New York and later in Philadelphia.)

The 18th power listed in Section 8 of Article I is quite different from the first 17. It says that Congress shall have power to make all laws "necessary and proper for carrying into execution the foregoing powers." This is the well-known "elastic clause." It is called "elastic" because its meaning can be stretched to include a huge number of different kinds of congressional powers. It can be used to give Congress many powers that are not listed in the Constitution. These additional powers given by the elastic clause are often called the "implied powers."

To Punish Piracy: Article I, Section 8, Paragraph 10

To define and punish piracies and felonies committed on the high seas, and offenses against the law of nations;

To Declare War: Article I, Section 8, Paragraph 11

To declare war, grant letters of marque and reprisal, and make rules concerning captures on land and water;

To Raise an Army: Article I, Section 8, Paragraph 12

To raise and support armies, but no appropriation of money to that use shall be for a longer term than two years;

To Maintain a Navy: Article I, Section 8, Paragraph 13

To provide and maintain a navy;

To Regulate the Armed Forces: Article I, Section 8, Paragraph 14

To make rules for the government and regulation of the land and naval forces;

To Call Forth the State Militias: Article I, Section 8, Paragraph 15

To provide for calling forth the militia to execute the laws of the Union, suppress insurrections and repel invasions;

To Regulate the State Militias: Article I, Section 8, Paragraph 16

To provide for organizing, arming, and disciplining the militia, and for governing such part of them as may be employed in the service of the United States, reserving to the States respectively the appointment of the officers, and the authority of training the militia according to the discipline prescribed by Congress;

To Govern Federal Lands: Article I, Section 8, Paragraph 17

To exercise exclusive legislation in all cases whatsoever, over such district (not exceeding ten miles square) as may, by cession of particular States and the acceptance of Congress, become the seat of the government of the United States, and to exercise like authority over all places purchased by the consent of the legislature of the State in which the same shall be, for the erection of forts, magazines, arsenals, dockyards, and other needful buildings; and

To Pass Laws Needed to Carry Out the Powers Given to Congress in the Constitution: Article I, Section 8, Paragraph 18

To make all laws which shall be necessary and proper for carrying into execution the foregoing powers, and all other powers vested by this Constitution in the government of the United States, or in any department or officer thereof.

Looking back over the 17 specific powers, you will no doubt be able to think of examples of the way the elastic clause has been used. Think, for example, of the power to regulate trade. Railroads and modern interstate highways are not mentioned. They did not exist in 1787. But the power to regulate trade has been stretched to include the regulation of railroads and the building of highways. Think also of the powers dealing with the armed forces. It would have been impossible to mention an air force in the Constitution. Again the powers have been stretched so that today's Congress can maintain not only an army and navy but also an air force.

A complete list of congressional powers must include two important powers that do not appear in Section 8 of Article I. Article II, Section 2 gives the Senate the power to approve all

LAWMAKING IN AMERICA

treaties and presidential appointments. If two thirds of the members of the Senate do not approve a treaty it must be renegotiated or rejected. In like manner, when a majority of the senators refuse to approve a presidential appointment, the President must make a new appointment, again subject to approval by the Senate. Article I, Sections 2 and 3 give the Congress powers of impeachment. The House of Representatives has the power to impeach—accuse of wrongdoing—any officer of the federal government. The Senate has the power to conduct trials of impeached officers. If two thirds of the senators vote for conviction, the impeached officer will be removed from office.

LIMITS ON THE POWER OF CONGRESS

While stressing the importance of Congress, the people who wrote the Constitution did place a number of limitations on the power of Congress. This was done in two ways. First, the Constitution lists certain kinds of laws that Congress may not pass. Second, the Constitution gives the President certain ways of rejecting bills passed by Congress. This was done as part of the system of checks and balances set up to limit the power of all three branches of the national government.

Congress was specifically forbidden to pass six kinds of laws in Article I, Section 9 of the Constitution. The chart at the right gives the complete list. To protect the interests of slaveholders, Congress was forbidden to pass any law limiting the slave trade in the years before 1808. To protect the rights of all Americans, limits were placed on the

---

THE SENATE IS GIVEN THE POWER TO APPROVE TREATIES AND PRESIDENTIAL APPOINTMENTS: Article II, Section 2, Paragraph 2 of the Constitution

He [the President] shall have power, by and with the advice and consent of the Senate, to make treaties, provided two thirds of the senators present concur; and he shall nominate, and by and with the advice and consent of the Senate, shall appoint ambassadors, other public ministers and consuls, judges of the Supreme Court, and all other officers of the United States, whose appointments are not herein otherwise provided for, and which shall be established by law: but the Congress may by law vest the appointment of such inferior officers, as they think proper, in the President alone, in the courts of law, or in the heads of departments.

CONGRESSIONAL POWERS OF IMPEACHMENT: Found in Article I of the Constitution

The House of Representatives May Impeach Federal Officers: Article I, Section 2, Paragraph 5

The House of Representatives shall choose their speaker and other officers, and shall have the sole power of impeachment.

The Senate May Try Cases of Impeachment: Article I, Section 3, Paragraph 6

The Senate shall have the sole power to try all impeachments. When sitting for that purpose, they shall be on oath or affirmation. When the President of the United States is tried, the chief justice shall preside: and no person shall be convicted without the concurrence of two thirds of the members present.

POWERS DENIED CONGRESS:
Listed in Article I of the Constitution

No Laws Against Slave Trade Until 1808: Article I, Section 9, Paragraph 1

The migration or importation of such persons as any of the States now existing shall think proper to admit, shall not be prohibited by the Congress prior to the year one thousand eight hundred and eight, but a tax or duty may be imposed on such importation, not exceeding ten dollars for each person.

Limited Suspension of the Writ of *Habeas Corpus:* Article I, Section 9, Paragraph 2

The privilege of the writ of *habeas corpus* shall not be suspended, unless when in cases of rebellion or invasion the public safety may require it.

No Bills of Attainder and *Ex Post Facto* Laws: Article I, Section 9, Paragraph 3

No bill of attainder or *ex post facto* law shall be passed.

Limited Power to Levy Direct Taxes: Article I, Section 9, Paragraph 4

No capitation, or other direct, tax shall be laid, unless in proportion to the census or enumeration herein before directed to be taken.

No Taxes on Trade Between States: Article I, Section 9, Paragraph 5

No tax or duty shall be laid on articles exported from any State.

No Preference to Be Given to the Trade of Any State: Article I, Section 9, Paragraph 6

No preference shall be given by any regulation of commerce or revenue to the ports of one State over those of another: nor shall vessels bound to, or from, one State be obliged to enter, clear, or pay duties in another.

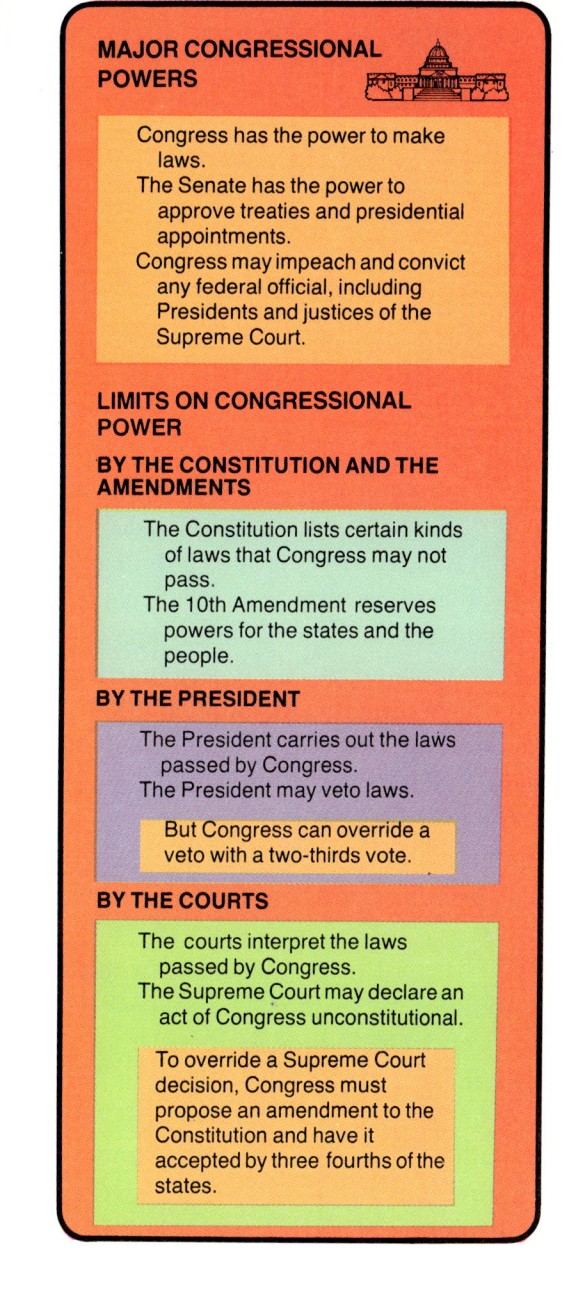

MAJOR CONGRESSIONAL POWERS

- Congress has the power to make laws.
- The Senate has the power to approve treaties and presidential appointments.
- Congress may impeach and convict any federal official, including Presidents and justices of the Supreme Court.

LIMITS ON CONGRESSIONAL POWER

BY THE CONSTITUTION AND THE AMENDMENTS

- The Constitution lists certain kinds of laws that Congress may not pass.
- The 10th Amendment reserves powers for the states and the people.

BY THE PRESIDENT

- The President carries out the laws passed by Congress.
- The President may veto laws.
  - But Congress can override a veto with a two-thirds vote.

BY THE COURTS

- The courts interpret the laws passed by Congress.
- The Supreme Court may declare an act of Congress unconstitutional.
  - To override a Supreme Court decision, Congress must propose an amendment to the Constitution and have it accepted by three fourths of the states.

kinds of situations in which the writ of *habeas corpus* could be suspended. In most cases, this made it impossible to hold people in jail without allowing them to ask for and receive a prompt hearing before a judge. Congress was also forbidden to pass bills of attainder and *ex post facto* laws. A bill of attainder

LAWMAKING IN AMERICA

> **CONGRESS IS GIVEN THE POWER TO COLLECT INCOME TAXES BEGINNING IN 1913: The 16th Amendment to the Constitution**
>
> The Congress shall have power to lay and collect taxes on incomes, from whatever source derived, without apportionment among the several States, and without regard to any census or enumeration.

is a law that singles out a person or group and punishes them without a trial by jury. An *ex post facto* law punishes a person for an action that was not illegal at the time the action occurred. Section 9 also places limits on Congress's power to levy direct taxes. This was changed in 1913 when the 16th Amendment gave Congress the power to levy income taxes. Finally, Congress was not allowed to tax goods shipped from one state to another or to favor the trade of one state over the trade of any of the other states.

The constitution makers knew that it would be impossible to list all laws that were to be forbidden. In order to limit the chance that Congress would pass unlisted but highly undesirable laws, the Constitution gave the President the power to veto acts of Congress. After both houses of Congress pass a bill by a majority vote, the bill is sent to the President. If the President signs the bill it becomes a law. The bill also becomes a law if the President holds the bill without signing for 10 days while the Congress is in session. However, the President may choose to veto a bill by sending it back to Congress within 10 days without signing it. In that case, the bill becomes a law only if two thirds of the members of each house vote in favor of the bill. The President may also use what is called a "pocket veto." Toward the end of a congressional session, the President may choose to veto a bill by holding it. If the congressional session ends within the 10-day period, the bill can not become a law. In order to pass such a bill, Congress must vote again at the beginning of the next session. The people who wrote the Constitution set up this complicated veto procedure to make sure that a great

> **PRESIDENTIAL POWER TO VETO LAWS: Article I, Section 7, Paragraph 2 of the Constitution**
>
> Every bill which shall have passed the House of Representatives and the Senate, shall, before it becomes a law, be presented to the President of the United States; if he approve he shall sign it, but if not he shall return it, with his objections to that House in which it shall have originated, who shall enter the objections at large on their journal, and proceed to reconsider it. If after such reconsideration two thirds of that House shall agree to pass the bill, it shall be sent, together with the objections, to the other House, by which it shall likewise be considered, and if approved by two thirds of that House, it shall become a law. But in all such cases the votes of both Houses shall be determined by yeas and nays, and the names of the persons voting for and against the bill shall be entered on the journal of each House respectively. If any bill shall not be returned by the President within ten days (Sundays excepted) after it shall have been presented to him, the same shall be a law, in like manner as if he had signed it, unless the Congress by their adjournment prevent its return, in which case it shall not be a law.

deal of thought would be given to congressional bills before they became the law of the land.

In the years that followed the writing of the Constitution, a number of other limitations were placed on the power of the Congress. Among the most important are those found in the first 10 amendments to the Constitution. These amendments—our Bill of Rights—are discussed in detail in Chapter 7. The first nine of these amendments were written to guarantee certain rights to the American people. Indirectly these amendments place limits on Congress. Because the 1st Amendment guarantees freedom of religion, Congress cannot pass laws that would seriously jeopardize religious freedom. In like manner, Congress cannot pass laws that would jeopardize the rights of an accused person given in the 6th Amendment. All nine of these amendments place indirect limits on the power of Congress. The 10th Amendment is different. It deals directly with power. It reserves all powers not given to the national government to the states and the people. As we have noted, the Constitution does not give Congress the power to set voter qualifications. This power was reserved for the states. The Constitution does not mention schools or welfare services.

Again, these powers were left to the states.

In the early years of the new nation, another important limitation was placed on the power of Congress. The Constitution says nothing about the United States Supreme Court's right of judicial review. However, this right was recognized early in the history of our country. It has become an important part of the constitutional system of checks and balances. The right of judicial review allows the Supreme Court to review laws of Congress when they arise in court cases and to decide whether these laws should stand. If the Supreme Court decides that a congressional law is contrary to the meaning of the Constitution, it can declare the law unconstitutional. The law is rejected. At that point, only an amendment to the Constitution can bring the law back to life.

Getting the Facts

1. Why did the constitution makers wish to make Congress a strong branch of government?

2. How do the two houses of Congress differ in size and membership?

3. Name at least eight powers given to Congress in the Constitution.

4. Name at least three ways in which the power of Congress is checked.

Forming an Opinion

■ The constitution makers allowed direct election of only one group of federal officials—the members of the House of Representatives. What are some arguments for and against direct election of senators? of American Presidents? of federal judges?

POWERS RESERVED FOR THE STATES: **The 10th Amendment to the Constitution**

The powers not delegated to the United States by the Constitution, nor prohibited by it to the States, are reserved to the States respectively, or to the people.

Inquiry

How Equal Is Representation in the House?

The United States Constitution has very little to say about the way in which the states are to choose members of the House of Representatives. It simply states that members shall be chosen "by the people of the several States." For many years the states chose their representatives in any way they wished. Some states set up congressional districts. Others elected representatives from the state at large. Finally, in 1842, Congress passed a law that set up one system for all states. Under this law, each state legislature was required to divide the state into congressional districts, one for each representative.

The 1842 law has been changed in minor ways from time to time. But the district plan is still followed for the most part. The plan seems fair and reasonable. However, in practice, it is often not fair at all. It is the job of the state legislature to set up districts. In the legislature, the majority political party is in a position to set up districts in such a way as to help the party. A Republican-controlled legislature, for example, might divide an area where the Democratic Party is strong into several small parts. These parts could then be placed in districts where they could be absorbed by a safe Republican majority. Or the same legislature might simply put a number of Democratic areas together. In this way they could keep the number of Democratic districts to a minimum.

The shaping of congressional districts for political advantage is called "gerrymandering." It is an old practice that gets its name from a Massachusetts politician, Elbridge Gerry. In 1811, Gerry was involved in setting up the districts in his state. A political opponent exclaimed that one of the districts was shaped so oddly that it looked like a salamander. "No," said a bystander, "better say a Gerrymander."

A picture of the original gerrymander is shown below. Note how the areas were strung out to form the shape. An artist has added the beak, claws, and wing to make it look even more like an animal.

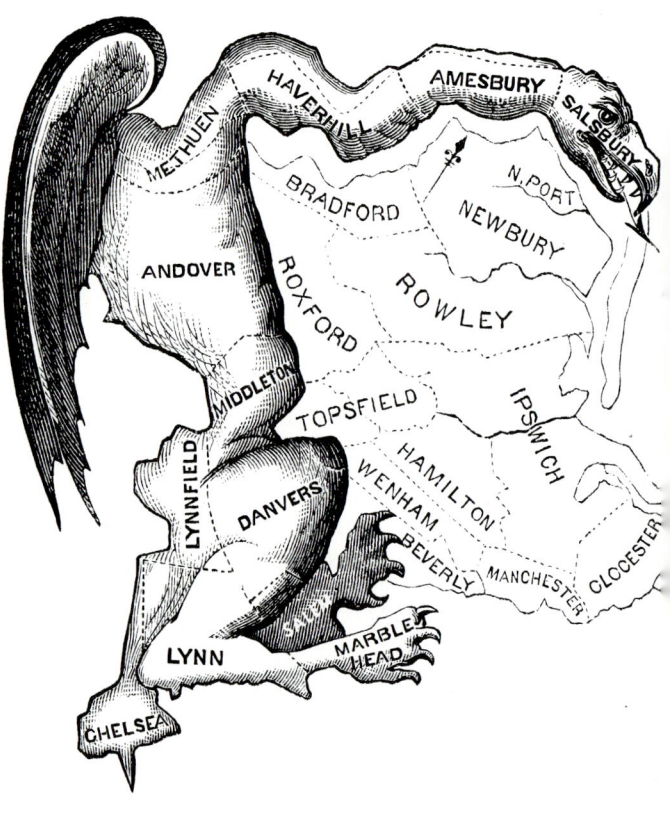

The map at the right shows a situation in New York City in 1961, 150 years after the original gerrymander. In it is shown a series of congressional districts. As you can see, many of the districts have very odd shapes. So intriguing were their shapes, that critics took

GOVERNMENT OF ALL AMERICANS

delight in trying to name them in good gerrymander fashion. Here are some of the names they came up with: the Upside-Down Crocodile, the Cow That Jumped over the Moon, and the Jaws of the Wrench. Perhaps you can think of other names to describe some of these districts. Is it possible that districts could be set up in this way and still be fair to both political parties? Is it likely?

An interesting follow-up to this discussion would be a study of congressional districting in your own state. Did your state gain or lose representatives after the last census? If there was a change in the number of representatives, what kinds of issues arose in the state legislature? Your local newspaper would be a good source for this kind of information. What is the present plan of congressional districts in your state? A useful exercise would be to prepare a large state map showing the pattern of congressional districts. With the help of a few people who know about your state's politics, you can get a good idea of whether or not any gerrymandering has taken place.

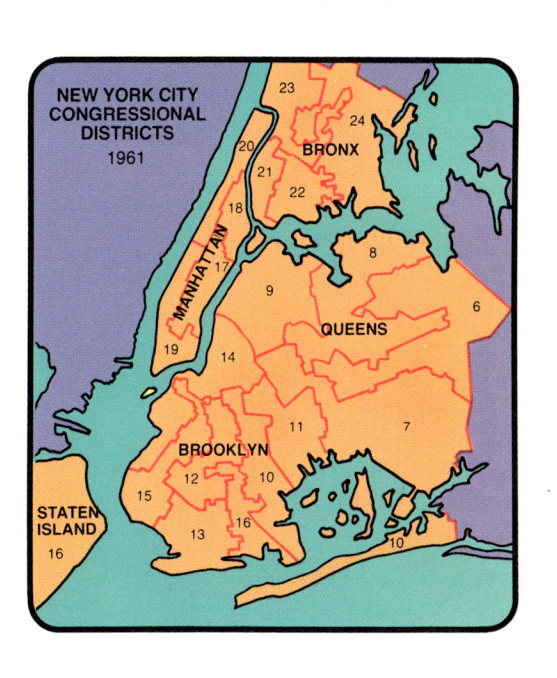

Gerrymandering is still a problem today. However, important steps have been taken to solve other problems and make members of the House more representative of all Americans. One of these was a decision of the United States Supreme Court in 1964. In the case of *Wesberry v. Sanders*, the Court ruled that congressional districts within each state must be relatively equal in population. The decision was specifically directed at a number of state legislatures that had repeatedly failed to redraw congressional districts to follow changes in population. Studies showed that certain districts in some states had four or five times as many people as other districts in the same state.

After the *Wesberry* decision almost all states made changes in their district plans. However, the real shift of power is likely to take place over a long period of time. The decision promotes redistricting after each 10-year census. In the future, power will follow population or be challenged in the courts.

Equal Representation: Analyzing the Problem

If state legislatures continue to draw up district plans, it is likely that some gerrymandering will always be seen. To what other group or groups might the job of forming districts be given?

In what way has our system of checks and balances been involved in the fight to gain equal representation in Congress? Do you think the system of checks and balances has worked well in this case? Why, or why not?

LAWMAKING IN AMERICA

Congress in Action

Congress as a body, and members of Congress as individuals, are constantly in the public eye. Reporters from the news media are ever alert to congressional actions. Members of Congress are seen on TV when running for office or considering important issues. In this section we will take a look at the less dramatic, day-to-day activities of our national representatives.

CONGRESSIONAL PRIVILEGES

Members of Congress have some rights and privileges that are not granted to other Americans. These rights are given so that members may be free to attend sessions and to speak and vote without interference. When speaking in Congress, they may say whatever they choose without fear of being sued for slander. (Slander means to make false and unfair statements that could hurt a person's reputation.) While attending sessions of Congress, they are free from arrest for minor offenses. This freedom, however, does not cover major criminal offenses.

Members of Congress are also given franking privileges and travel allowances. The franking privilege gives members of Congress the right to mail personal letters, printed speeches, and other materials without paying postage charges. A travel allowance is given to pay for the trips to and from Washington, D.C. at the beginning and end of each session of Congress. Members may also make other free trips when they need to gain information that will be useful in their work. Critics, however, believe that some of these trips are really just pleasure trips, or "junkets," taken at the public expense.

CONGRESSIONAL SESSIONS

The Constitution states that "Congress shall assemble at least once in every year." The Constitution also gives the President the power to call either or both houses of Congress into special session. In recent years, the regular sessions of Congress have become longer. A session may last through most of the year. This does not mean that a member of Congress is always in Washington. When Congress is in session most members find it necessary or desirable to spend part of the time in their home states or districts. Some who live close to Washington are even said to belong to a so-called "Tuesday to Thursday Club." These members often spend only three days a week in Washington. Since members are often away from Washington, absenteeism can be a problem. There may not be enough members present to have a vote, or enough committee members present to hold a hearing.

PRIVILEGES GIVEN TO MEMBERS OF CONGRESS: Article I, Section 6, Paragraph 1 of the Constitution

The senators and representatives shall receive a compensation for their services, to be ascertained by law, and paid out of the Treasury of the United States. They shall in all cases, except treason, felony and breach of the peace, be privileged from arrest during their attendance at the session of their respective Houses, and in going to and returning from the same; and for any speech or debate in either House, they shall not be questioned in any other place.

> **CONGRESSIONAL SESSIONS:** Given in Articles I and II of the Constitution
>
> **One Required Meeting Each Year:** Article I, Section 4, Paragraph 2
>
> The Congress shall assemble at least once in every year, and such meeting shall be on the first Monday in December, unless they shall by law appoint a different day.
>
> **The President May Call Special Meetings of Congress:** Article II, Section 3
>
> He [the President] shall from time to time give to the Congress information of the state of the Union, and recommend to their consideration such measures as he shall judge necessary and expedient; he may, on extraordinary occasions, convene both Houses, or either of them, and in case of disagreement between them with respect to the time of adjournment, he may adjourn them to such time as he shall think proper; he shall receive ambassadors and other public ministers; he shall take care that the laws be faithfully executed, and shall commission all the officers of the United States.

THE LEADERSHIP

The Constitution provides presiding officers for both houses of Congress. In Article I, Section 2 the members of the House of Representatives are directed to choose a Speaker. In Article I, Section 3 the Vice President of the United States is made President of the Senate. Because the Vice President may not always be available to act as presiding officer of the Senate, the members of the Senate are directed to choose a President *pro tempore* to preside in the absence of the Vice President.

The Speaker of the House is elected at the opening of each new Congress. The candidate of the political party that holds the majority of the seats in the House generally wins with no difficulty. The role of Speaker is very powerful. The role has been well described by political scientist Stephen K. Bailey:

"The Speaker occupies the most powerful single office in Congress. He combines majority party leadership with the traditional parliamentary responsibility of impartial umpire. . . . He also . . . is expected to provide the majority party membership with a party line on important issues. In this role he becomes an important broker between the President of the United States and the majority party membership in the House of Representatives. He is never totally the President's man; he is never totally the instrument of the majority party; he is never totally the impartial umpire of the

> **PRESIDING OFFICERS OF CONGRESS:** Listed in Article I of the Constitution
>
> **Officers of the House of Representatives:** Article I, Section 2, Paragraph 5
>
> The House of Representatives shall choose their speaker and other officers, and shall have the sole power of impeachment.
>
> **Officers of the Senate:** Article I, Section 3, Paragraphs 4 and 5
>
> The Vice President of the United States shall be President of the Senate, but shall have no vote, unless they be equally divided.
>
> The Senate shall choose their other officers, and also a president *pro tempore*, in the absence of the Vice President, or when he shall exercise the office of President of the United States.

LAWMAKING IN AMERICA   81

FORMAL ORGANIZATION OF CONGRESS

	HOUSE OF REPRESENTATIVES	SENATE
OFFICERS:	The Speaker of the House	President of the Senate (Vice President of the United States); President *pro tempore*
COMMITTEES:	Standing Committees; Subcommittees of the Standing Committees; Special Committees; Select Committees	Standing Committees; Subcommittees of the Standing Committees; Special Committees; Select Committees
	Joint Committees	

POLITICAL ORGANIZATION OF CONGRESS

	HOUSE OF REPRESENTATIVES	SENATE
OFFICERS:	Majority and Minority Party Floor Leaders; Majority and Minority Party Whips	Majority and Minority Party Floor Leaders; Majority and Minority Party Whips
COMMITTEES:	Majority and Minority Party Caucuses; Majority and Minority Party Steering Committees	Majority and Minority Party Caucuses; Majority and Minority Party Policy Committees

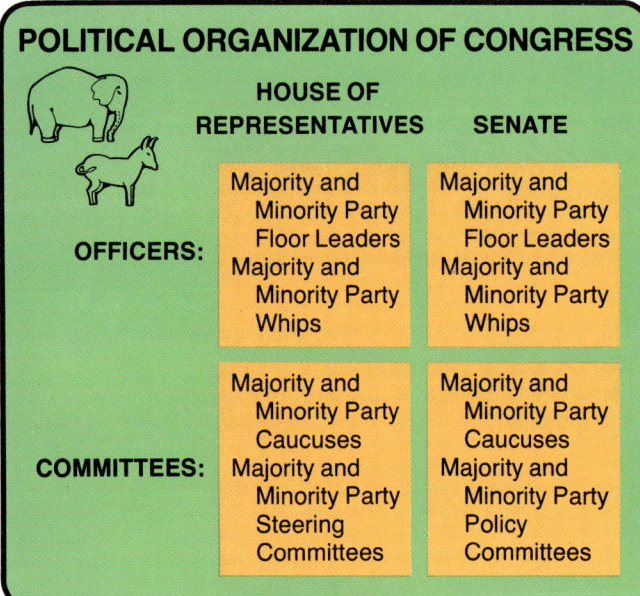

whole House. And yet to a degree he is all of these things. His success as a Speaker is related to his capacity to play these diverse and sometimes divergent roles with integrity and skill, and to negotiate honorably and flexibly with the minority party leadership on matters affecting 'both sides of the aisle.'"

The roles of the two presiding officers in the Senate are much less powerful than the role of the Speaker of the House. The Vice President is not even allowed to vote on Senate bills unless an extra vote is needed to break a tie.

In the Senate, the person whose power and influence comes closest to that of the Speaker of the House is the Senate majority leader. This leader is part of a leadership system not mentioned in the Constitution. As you can see in the chart at the left, a system of political party leadership has been developed over the years in both houses of Congress.

Most of the members of Congress belong to one of the two major parties in the United States: the Democratic Party and the Republican Party. The party with the majority of the members in a house of Congress has come to be called the "majority party." In like manner, the party with fewer members is called the "minority party."

At the beginning of each session of Congress, party caucuses in each house choose leaders and party whips. The "whips" act as assistants to the party leaders. They generally have more direct contacts with the rest of the party members. Both the party leaders and the party whips must be able to guide and lead other members of their parties. Generally this ability to lead depends more on personal qualities than on any formal powers. Each party in each house also sets up a policy or steering committee to help the leaders and to make decisions about bills that arise in the course of the congressional session.

GOVERNMENT OF ALL AMERICANS

THE COMMITTEE SYSTEM

To carry on the work of the Congress, a system of committees has been set up. Such a system seems to be needed. Clearly, the thousands of bills introduced during any regular session of Congress and the many other kinds of business that come before the members could not be handled by the bodies as a whole.

Proposals that come before the Congress are sent to committees. As you can see in the chart at the right, each committee has a special area of interest. A proposal dealing with farmlands would be sent to the House Agriculture Committee or the Senate Agriculture and Forestry Committee. In a committee, a measure is considered and recommendations are made. The committee then decides whether or not

The Senate committee in the photograph is holding a public hearing on a proposed bill. What other functions do congressional committees serve?

STANDING COMMITTEES OF CONGRESS

HOUSE OF REPRESENTATIVES	SENATE
Agriculture	Aeronautical and Space Sciences
Appropriations	Agriculture and Forestry
Armed Services	Appropriations
Banking, Currency and Housing	Armed Services
Budget	Banking, Housing and Urban Affairs
District of Columbia	Budget
Education and Labor	Commerce
Government Operations	District of Columbia
House Administration	Finance
Interior and Insular Affairs	Foreign Relations
International Relations	Government Operations
Interstate and Foreign Commerce	Interior and Insular Affairs
Judiciary	Judiciary
Merchant Marine and Fisheries	Labor and Public Welfare
Post Office and Civil Service	Post Office and Civil Service
Public Works and Transportation	Public Works
Rules	Rules and Administration
Science and Technology	Veterans' Affairs
Small Business	
Standards of Official Conduct	
Veterans' Affairs	
Ways and Means	

the proposal should be sent to the entire membership of the House or the Senate for a vote.

Because so much business comes before the Congress, it is hard to keep the number of committees from growing out of bounds. In 1975, there were 22 standing committees in the House of

LAWMAKING IN AMERICA

Representatives and 18 in the Senate. All of these committees were further divided into subcommittees. In addition, special committees and select committees are set up from time to time to deal with special problems. There are also a number of joint committees in which members of both houses meet together.

Members of the House generally belong to only one major committee. This allows them to learn a great deal about a subject over a period of years. The committee work load in the Senate is heavier. Each senator belongs to a number of committees.

Congress does most of its real work in the committees. That is why a visit to the House or Senate during a congressional session can be disappointing. Chances are that, at any given time, the proceedings will seem very dull. There will likely be few members in their seats. Those that are present may be reading newspapers and paying little attention to the person who is making a speech or carrying on some other business. The high drama of the lawmaking process can be seen only when a key vote comes before all the members.

MAKING LAWS

The chart on the next page describes in detail all the steps that must be followed before a congressional bill can become a law. Notice that a bill may be killed at a number of points. A committee may decide to "pigeonhole" a bill by holding it indefinitely. A committee may also decide to amend, rewrite, or simply drop a bill. A bill can be killed if the majority of the members of the house where it was introduced vote against it. A bill can also be killed if it fails to receive a majority vote when it is sent to the second house. A bill that is passed by one house and changed by the other house is generally reconsidered in a joint conference committee. It is then sent back to both houses for a vote. It cannot become a law unless it receives a majority vote in both houses. Finally, the President can veto a bill. A vetoed bill can become a law only if it is approved by two thirds of the members of each house.

MEMBERS OF THE CLUB

Congress has been described by one observer as "a headless, leaderless body composed of 535 independent and individualistic spirits who are accountable, in the final analysis, not to the Congress of the United States but to their constituencies in their home states." This same observer goes on to comment that "the very vagueness and ambiguities of its rules can often be turned to individual advantage . . . [members] are protected in the maintenance of their influence in many instances by this imprecise, easygoing system. 'Let well enough alone' is their axiom, and it finds wide acceptance among the membership at large." Yet this same observer calls Congress "a pretty wonderful institution" that has met "most of its great challenges and responsibilities."

Just what kind of organization is this institution that some have called "the world's greatest deliberative body"? Hundreds of books have been written about Congress. The halls of Congress are filled with stories of its membership.

There is, for instance, the story of a nervous new senator from Missouri

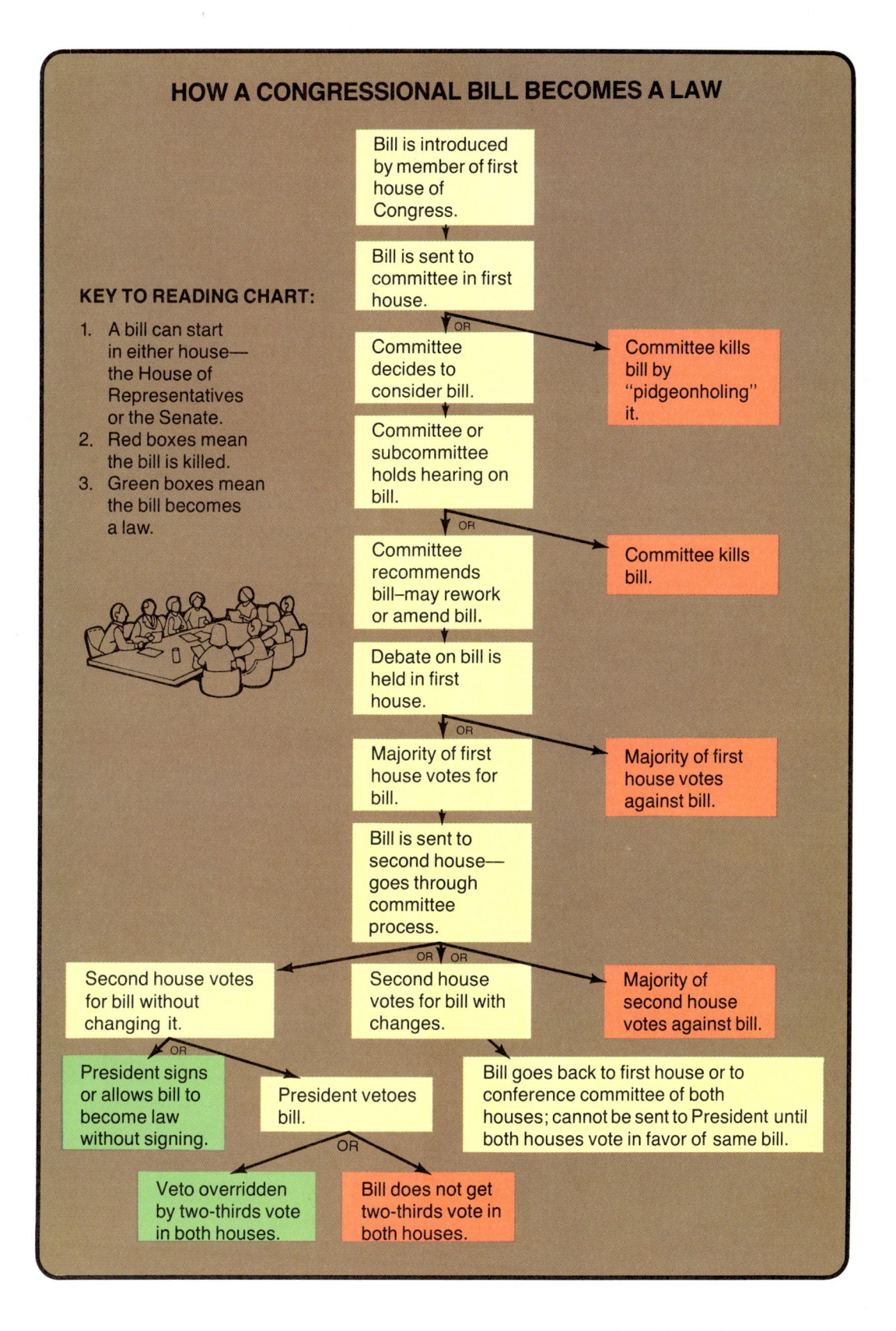

HOW A CONGRESSIONAL BILL BECOMES A LAW

KEY TO READING CHART:

1. A bill can start in either house—the House of Representatives or the Senate.
2. Red boxes mean the bill is killed.
3. Green boxes mean the bill becomes a law.

- Bill is introduced by member of first house of Congress.
- Bill is sent to committee in first house.
  - OR → Committee kills bill by "pidgeonholing" it.
- Committee decides to consider bill.
- Committee or subcommittee holds hearing on bill.
  - OR → Committee kills bill.
- Committee recommends bill–may rework or amend bill.
- Debate on bill is held in first house.
- Majority of first house votes for bill.
  - OR → Majority of first house votes against bill.
- Bill is sent to second house—goes through committee process.
  - Second house votes for bill without changing it.
  - OR Second house votes for bill with changes. → Bill goes back to first house or to conference committee of both houses; cannot be sent to President until both houses vote in favor of same bill.
  - OR → Majority of second house votes against bill.
- President signs or allows bill to become law without signing.
- OR President vetoes bill.
  - Veto overridden by two-thirds vote in both houses.
  - OR Bill does not get two-thirds vote in both houses.

LAWMAKING IN AMERICA

named Harry S Truman. Sitting uneasily on the edge of his back-row seat in the Senate on his first day in office, he was surprised when a distinguished-looking gentleman in a cutaway coat and bristling red beard approached him. It was the veteran senator from Illinois, James Hamilton Lewis. Placing his hand on Truman's shoulder, Senator Lewis smiled and said, "I know how you feel, young man, but don't let it worry you. You will spend your first six months wondering how in the world you got here, and the rest of your life wondering how all these others got in."

Getting the Facts

1. Who is the most powerful leader in the House of Representatives? in the Senate?

2. Why does Congress have a system of committees?

3. Describe the steps by which a congressional bill becomes a law.

Forming an Opinion

■ What privileges do members of Congress have that are not granted to other American citizens? Which of the privileges do you think are justifiable? Which do you think are not justifiable? Explain.

Congress and the People

Not too many years ago the contacts between the average American and the government in Washington were few and far between. There was the federal employee who delivered the mail. There was a report each year to the income tax collector. There was little else. How different it is today. The same government seems to touch the lives of almost all of us every day. People in business may have government contracts. Doctors may fill out reports under Medicare. Grandparents may collect social security checks. Many people who have been in the military attend college with their veteran benefits.

Young or old, rich or poor, there are government laws and programs that directly affect the lives of every American. A number of problems and concerns arise out of these many laws and programs. Who are the people best able to help Americans with these matters? Many people turn to the members of the House from their districts or to the senators from their states.

CONGRESSIONAL CHORES

The people about whom a member of Congress is most directly concerned are the member's constituents. The constituents of a House member are the people who live in the member's district. The constituents of a senator are the people who live in the senator's state.

Members of Congress spend a great deal of time running errands for their constituents. Some have estimated that 50 to 90 percent of their time is given to such chores. The number and variety are endless. The following are examples of requests that may come to the office of a member of Congress on any given day.

- A local Chamber of Commerce hears a rumor that a nearby military base may be shut down. Is there any truth to it? If there is, can the member of Congress stop it?
- Two important citizens write that their children are graduating from college

and would like to work in a Washington government bureau. What can be done to help them find good jobs?
- A college has asked for a government grant to build a dormitory. Can the member of Congress help them to get an answer quickly?
- Members of a civics class write their representative asking for a list of the kinds of chores constituents ask the representative to do.

Requests such as these flow into the congressional offices in a steady stream. Mail to a member of the House can easily run to several hundred letters a week. A senator from a large state would likely receive two or three times this amount. Some of the letters deal with important matters. Others are about trivial matters. However, the office staff must answer all letters quickly and politely. It is all part of the way in which members of Congress keep their fences built back home.

KEEPING IN TOUCH

Mail is one important way in which members of Congress keep in touch with their constituents. It is by no means the only way. It is very important that members of Congress be available in their states or districts for all important occasions. They may be asked to cut the ribbon at the opening of a new hospital. They may be asked to make a high school graduation address. They may be asked to launch a fund-raising drive. Often they are asked to hear problems and complaints of constituents. The list of occasions goes on and on. Here is how one member described these activities:

"I read 48 weekly newspapers and clip every one of them myself. Whenever there is a particularly interesting item

The office of a United States senator is a busy place. Much of the work involves answering requests from constituents. What are the advantages and disadvantages of spending so much time filling these requests?

about anyone, that person gets a note from me. We also keep a complete list of the change of officers in every organization in our district. Then when I am going into a town I know exactly who I should like to have at the meeting. I learned early that you had to make your way with Democrats as well as Republicans. And you cannot let the matter of elections go until the last minute. I budget 17 trips home each session and somehow I have never managed to go less than 21 times."

Getting the Facts

■ What are some of the things that members of Congress are called upon to do for their constituents?

Examining the Issues

■ One of the reasons why members of Congress spend so much time taking care of constituent requests is that they must stand for reelection every two or six years. Would you favor terms longer than two years for members of the House? What about increasing the six-year terms of senators? What factors other than time spent on constituent requests should be considered?

LAWMAKING IN AMERICA

Speaking Out

Vice Admiral H. G. Rickover

Admiral Rickover was one of the pioneers of nuclear submarine research. He has also been a long-standing critic of American education. Here he speaks about what he believes is another national problem of great importance. He feels that Congress is losing too much of its power.

"As a realist, I must say that about the only real power Congress has left is the negative power of denying funds. Surely this was never the intention of the framers of the Constitution, nor has it come about by the proper procedure of constitutional amendment. Take the bill to limit the ability of the executive to carry on indefinitely an undeclared war. I thoroughly approve the intent of the bill. But ought it to be necessary? Does not the Constitution vest in Congress and in Congress alone the power 'to declare war'? . . .

"When Congress does not exercise the power vested exclusively in it to make the laws that govern the United States, its power to do so atrophies. Indeed, I submit that Congress has already lost much of its power by not using it.

"Congress may change the Administration's budget by 1 or 2 per cent, but to all intents and purposes Congress no longer has control over the budget. Like any other parliamentary body in a free society, it does, however, have the power of legislative oversight as well as the right to refuse to vote appropriations if it judges that in the past they have not been used in accordance with the laws it has enacted. . . .

"Since Congress itself can no longer control in detail how appropriated moneys are spent, its constitutional control of the purse strings now depends more than ever on the judicious exercise of its investigatory function, and on the negative power to refuse funds."

1. What is meant by "the negative power of denying funds"?

2. In what ways can Congress use "legislative oversight" and its "investigatory function" to place limits on the power of the President?

3. To what extent do you agree with Rickover's statement that "Congress has already lost much of its power"? What steps could be taken by Congress to gain more power?

Lawmaking in the 50 States

The states and the national government share the power to make our laws. This sharing of the lawmaking power is a basic part of our federal system of government.

The Constitution deals mainly with the lawmaking powers of the national government. However, as noted earlier in this chapter, the 10th Amendment to the Constitution gives a broad but indefinite grant of powers to the states and the people. Powers not given to the national government are reserved for the states and the people.

CHANGES IN STATE POWER

A belief in the rights of the states was very strong in the early years of our history. For this reason, the 10th Amendment was added to the Constitution. State leaders kept careful watch to make sure that the national government did not overstep the powers it had been given in the Constitution. A number of times in the early 19th century, states threatened to pull out of the Union because they did not like the actions of the national government. Generally, it was argued that the national government was taking away the rights of the states.

A number of states finally did leave the Union in 1861. Their withdrawal led to the Civil War. As a result of this bloody war, many people began to agree that the authority of the national government must be strengthened. The feeling was strong enough to bring about the adoption of the 14th Amendment to the Constitution. The amendment stressed the fact that the people of all states were American citizens and must be treated equally by the states as well as by the national government. The amendment also gave Congress the power to enforce the provisions of the amendment.

The 20th century has brought other important changes in the way power is divided between the states and the national government. These changes have taken place because of changes in our way of life. Consider a few examples. At one time state governments could, if they wished, control the way in which horses and buggies moved along country roads. But can a single state control the movement of jets whizzing overhead at hundreds of kilometers per hour? A local government in an earlier time might have regulated the activities of a small iron foundry. But can even a state government regulate the activities of a major steel company?

> **THE AUTHORITY OF THE NATIONAL GOVERNMENT IS STRENGTHENED IN 1868:** **The 14th Amendment to the Constitution, Sections 1 and 5**
>
> All persons born or naturalized in the United States, and subject to the jurisdiction thereof, are citizens of the United States and of the State wherein they reside. No State shall make or enforce any law which shall abridge the privileges or immunities of citizens of the United States; nor shall any State deprive any person of life, liberty, or property, without due process of law; nor deny to any person within its jurisdiction the equal protection of the laws.
>
> The Congress shall have power to enforce, by appropriate legislation, the provisions of this article.

Even though state governments have lost some powers they still have a number of important powers today. While far from complete, the following list gives some of the important powers that each state has today.

- States set up and provide most of the money for systems of public schools, including state colleges and state universities.
- States build most of the highways within their state borders.
- States manage and provide most of the money for networks of hospitals and prisons.
- States manage and provide money for programs of public welfare, either on a state-wide basis or on a local basis.
- States grant charters to corporations.
- States control the terms of business contracts.
- States license professional people, including doctors, teachers, and lawyers.
- States regulate public utilities, including gas and electric companies.
- States pass laws concerning marriage, divorce, and child adoption.
- States pass laws to prevent pollution.

As you can see, states still have a number of important powers. Even so,

Which of the signs shown below are state highway signs? (If you're from the Southeast you probably noticed that the two signs for Route 21 are in the shape of the state of Alabama. They're the only state highway signs in the group. The rest are federal highway signs.)

Both the state and the federal governments operate prisons.

in many cases, they seek the help and cooperation of the national government when they use these powers.

The modern movement toward an increase in the power of the national government and a decrease in the power of state governments has been very strong. Today, some efforts are being made to end this movement. Early in the 1970s, President Nixon made proposals for what he termed a "new federalism." One of the important features was a plan known as "revenue sharing." Under this plan, taxes collected by the national government could be shared with state and local governments. In 1972, Congress passed a revenue-sharing bill. To some extent, this has helped state and local governments use their powers more effectively.

STATE LEGISLATURES

Like the national Constitution, the constitutions of our 50 states all call for three branches of government. Each state has a legislative branch, an executive branch, and a judicial branch. In general, however, most of the responsibility for carrying out the powers of the states rests with the state legislatures. One of the most striking differences between the state and national governments is the difference in the amount of power given the executive leaders. The governors of most of our states have far less power than the President.

In structure, most of the state lawmaking bodies are much like Congress. All but one of the state legislatures are bicameral, or two-house, bodies. (Nebraska has a unicameral, or one-house,

Our state legislatures resemble the national Congress in many ways, including a generally small number of women representatives. What social factors help explain this situation?

legislature.) The "lower house" is generally called the House of Representatives. It usually has two to three times more members than the "upper house"—the Senate.

A number of students of government believe that most of the state legislatures are too large. A recent count showed that about four fifths of the state legislatures have more than 100 members. A few have more than 200 members. There was also a wide variation in representation. At one extreme, New Hampshire had one legislator in its lower house for every 1,500 people in the state. At the other extreme, California had one representative for every 200,000 people.

One of the major problems of state legislatures today involves another aspect of representation. Most states entered the Union at a time when their populations were mostly rural. Their constitutions often remained the same even after many people moved to towns and cities. Because the state constitutions did not change, rural voters often ended up having a greater representation than urban voters. Some of the constitutions, however, were written by people who anticipated the possibility that the population would shift and grow. These constitutions called for changes to be made in representation from time to time to take account of population changes. Even so, legislators were often reluctant to make such changes. Some chose to ignore their state constitutions so as not to lose power.

During the 19th century and into the 20th century, more and more people moved to towns and cities. Many urban voters began to complain that they were being underrepresented in the state legislature. Many agreed with the words of a Michigan citizen in the early 1950s: "As a city dweller, I'm becoming rather piqued at my rural neighbor's stolid conviction that I'm not fit to be trusted with a full vote in matters of state government."

The feeling expressed by the city dweller in Michigan was also present in other states. One was Tennessee. That state had failed again and again to change its representation in the legisla-

"DEALER WINS AND WINNER DEALS."

What is the cartoonist saying about representation in American lawmaking bodies? What steps have been taken to improve the situation?

ture even though the constitution clearly called for a change. The Tennessee constitution stated that the legislature must reapportion itself every 10 years to follow population changes shown in the federal census. For 60 years the legislature failed to act. The search for a change was finally brought to a federal court by a group of Tennessee citizens. They stated that failure of the legislature to reapportion denied them their rights of equal protection under the law. Such rights, they said, were guaranteed by the 14th Amendment.

In a landmark decision, *Baker v. Carr* (1962), a majority of the United States Supreme Court upheld the claim of the group from Tennessee. The Court noted that 37 percent of the voters of Tennessee were electing 61 percent of the state senators. It also observed that 40 percent of the voters were electing 64 percent of the members of the state House of Representatives. Given the failure of the legislature to make any changes, a majority of the Court felt that action must be taken by the national government. A minority of the Court disagreed, however. One justice who disagreed argued that those who have the responsibility for setting up a system of representation should be allowed to consider factors other than population. The justice pointed to the United States Senate as an example. The majority opinion, nevertheless, led to a number of important changes. Within two years, some changes in the apportionment of legislative seats were made, not just in Tennessee, but in a total of 42 states.

Getting the Facts

1. Name at least four powers of state governments.

2. How has the balance of power between the national and state governments changed in the years since the Constitution was written?

3. How did the United States Supreme Court decision in *Baker v. Carr* affect the state legislatures?

Examining the Issues

■ In *Baker v. Carr* one Supreme Court justice stated the minority opinion that representation need not be based on population. The United States Senate was offered as an example. Do you agree or disagree with this minority opinion? Why? If you agree, explain how you would organize representation in the state legislatures.

LAWMAKING IN AMERICA

Citizenship Laboratory

Review of Basic Ideas

1. The Constitution calls for three branches of government: legislative, executive, and judicial. Legislative, or lawmaking, powers at the national level are given mainly to Congress. Congress is a bicameral, or two-house, body. Membership in the House of Representatives is based on population. In the Senate, each state has two representatives. The Constitution gives the Congress a number of powers. The power of Congress is limited by a constitutional list of powers forbidden to Congress, the 10th Amendment, the President's veto power, and the United States Supreme Court's right of judicial review.

2. The Constitution calls for the selection of a Speaker to preside over meetings of the House of Representatives. To preside over meetings of the Senate, the Constitution appoints the Vice President of the United States and calls for the selection of a President *pro tempore* to preside in the absence of the Vice President. In both houses, a system of political leadership has developed in the years since the Constitution was written. The role of the Speaker of the House remains powerful. However, in the Senate the most powerful leader is the majority leader. Most congressional work, including work on laws, is carried out in committees.

3. Members of Congress spend a great amount of time handling requests from the people of their states or districts.

4. The Constitution deals mainly with the lawmaking powers of the national government, but the 10th Amendment reserves all powers not given to the national government for the states and the people. Over the years, the national government has gained power at the expense of the states. Today the states still have a number of important powers. These include setting up and maintaining systems of public schools, systems of state highways, and public welfare programs. State lawmaking powers are given mainly to the state legislatures. Modern state legislatures have been criticized for not being truly representative. Decisions of the United States Supreme Court have helped to make both the state legislatures and the national House of Representatives more representative of the American people.

Questions to Think About

1. What are some arguments in favor of having a bicameral, or two-house, legislature? What are arguments in favor of a unicameral, or one-house, legislature?

2. In what ways can the executive and judicial branches of the national government limit the power of Congress? In what ways can Congress limit the power of the executive and judicial branches?

3. What changes, if any, would you make in the lawmaking process and the procedure used to veto a law? Explain.

4. Do you agree that it is important for members of Congress to be readily available to the people of their states or districts at all times? Or would you favor rules that greatly limited the amount of time members could spend away from Washington during congressional sessions? Explain.

5. In what ways does the Constitution provide for the dividing and sharing of powers by the national and state governments? In what ways does the Constitution allow for changes in the way powers are divided and shared by these governments?

6. Do state governments have enough duties to perform? What additional duties and powers do you think should be given to the states? What duties and powers should be taken away from the states? Why?

Words and Relationships

Define each of the terms in the first column. Then show how each term is related to the item listed opposite it by using both items in a sentence or short paragraph.

1.	republic	self-government
2.	Senate	regional interests
3.	"elastic clause"	"implied powers"
4.	veto	checks and balances
5.	gerrymander	inequality
6.	House of Representatives	Speaker of the House
7.	slander	congressional privileges
8.	constituents	representative government
9.	revenue sharing	state power
10.	bicameral	state legislatures

Building a Future

Early in the 1970s President Richard Nixon proposed what he called a "new federalism." The proposal was based on the belief that too much power was being concentrated at the national level. The President's plan was to reverse the flow of power by placing more responsibility and more money in the hands of state and local governments. To a limited extent, this plan is being followed today.

Think about the future of our federal system. Would you favor an increase in national power, an increase in state power, or an increase in local power? Consider two specific examples:

- Our public schools and colleges are controlled and largely supported by state and local governments. Should the state systems be made stronger with more money from federal tax dollars? Or would it be better to have one national system of education?

- Today a number of social service programs are controlled by state and local governments. Other programs such as the social security system are centered in Washington. Would it be better to have just one program in Washington? Or can the state and local governments better meet the needs of their people?

What other state powers, if any, would you like to see turned over to the national government? What national powers, if any, would you like to see given to the state and local governments? Why?

5 Executive Leadership

During the late 1950s, a group of Connecticut students, grades four through eight, were asked certain questions about American political leaders. Among the fourth graders, 96 percent could name the President. Fewer of them—90 percent—knew the mayor of their city. All of the eighth graders could name the President. Almost all of the eighth graders—97 percent—knew their mayor.

The students' knowledge of what these two leaders did was another matter. Only 23 percent of the fourth graders could name any of the President's duties. Only 25 percent could name any of the mayor's duties. The older students knew a great deal more about these duties. Among the eighth graders, 66 percent could name some of the presidential duties and 67 percent could name some of the duties of the mayor.

Interestingly enough, these Connecticut students seemed to know much less about their state government. Only 8 percent of the fourth graders could name any of the governor's duties. Only 5 percent knew anything about the role of the state legislature. Even among eighth graders, only 43 percent knew any of the governor's duties. Only 37 percent knew anything about the role of the state legislature.

Most of the students tended to view their political leaders in friendly ways.

They saw them all as leaders who were working for the good of the people.

Less favorable views were found a few years later among children in a county in eastern Kentucky. In this area, the young people questioned were not so kindly disposed toward their political leaders.

There may be a number of reasons for this difference in attitude. It could have been a result of the change in the times. One study was done in the 1950s. One was done in the 1960s. The different areas in which the students lived could have made a difference.

Whatever the differences, one result was similar in both studies. All students were aware that some form of political authority or executive leadership did exist. Also clear, in both studies, was the fact that the students were much more aware of the leader as a person than they were of the nature of the leader's office.

Is this last finding true of older students and adults today? Most of us know a good many things about our President or our governor. But what do we know of the presidency, or the governorship? This brings us to our purpose here. In this chapter, we will examine the way in which executive leadership functions in our federal system of government.

The Constitution Establishes the Office of President

Our first national government, under the Articles of Confederation, had no executive branch. In that government, the legislative branch was supreme. The national government set up later under the Constitution did, of course, have an executive branch. However, even in the Constitution, great emphasis was placed on the legislative branch. By placing legislative powers in Article I the people who wrote the Constitution seemed to have had in mind a "congressional government." Congress, in other words, was placed before the President.

Nevertheless, in Article II of the Constitution, the American President is given a number of important powers. Some of these were given to check the power of Congress. Others were given so that the new nation might have a chief representative—a person who could deal with the heads of other countries. Still others were given so that the United States would have a leader able to carry out the daily affairs of the national government.

CONSTITUTIONAL POWERS OF THE AMERICAN PRESIDENT

The opening sentence of Article II states that "the executive power shall be vested in a President of the United States . . ." As used by the constitution makers, the term "executive power" meant the power needed to execute—or carry out—the daily affairs of government. More specifically, it meant the

---

AN EXECUTIVE BRANCH IS FORMED: Article II, Section 1, Paragraph 1 of the Constitution

The executive power shall be vested in a President of the United States of America. He shall hold his office during the term of four years, and, together with the Vice President, chosen for the same term, be elected as follows.

power needed to execute—or carry out—the laws passed by Congress.

Powers given to the President are listed in Sections 2 and 3 of Article II. In contrast to the list of powers given to the Congress, this list appears quite short. Like much of our Constitution, however, these few words say a great deal. They give the President five broad kinds of constitutional power.

1. Commander in Chief. It is not by chance that the very first grant of power names the President Commander in Chief. The people who wrote our Constitution wanted to be certain that the country's military leaders would be con-

---

POWERS GIVEN TO THE PRESIDENT: Listed in Article II of the Constitution

To Command the Army and the Navy, Ask Opinions of the Officers of the Executive Departments, and Grant Reprieves and Pardons: Article II, Section 2, Paragraph 1

The President shall be commander in chief of the army and navy of the United States, and of the militia of the several States, when called into the actual service of the United States; he may require the opinion, in writing, of the principal officer in each of the executive departments, upon any subject relating to the duties of their respective offices, and he shall have power to grant reprieves and pardons for offenses against the United States, except in cases of impeachment.

To Make Treaties and Appoint Diplomats, Judges, and Other Federal Officers with the Approval of the Senate: Article II, Section 2, Paragraph 2

He shall have power, by and with the advice and consent of the Senate, to make treaties, provided two thirds of the senators present concur; and he shall nominate, and by and with the advice and consent of the Senate, shall appoint ambassadors, other public ministers and consuls, judges of the Supreme Court, and all other officers of the United States, whose appointments are not herein otherwise provided for, and which shall be established by law: but the Congress may by law vest the appointment of such inferior officers, as they think proper, in the President alone, in the courts of law, or in the heads of departments.

To Make Temporary Appointments When the Senate Is Not in Session: Article II, Section 2, Paragraph 3

The President shall have power to fill up all vacancies that may happen during the recess of the Senate, by granting commissions which shall expire at the end of their next session.

To Make Recommendations to Congress, Call Special Meetings of Congress, Receive Ambassadors, Carry Out Laws, and Commission Military Officers: Article II, Section 3

He shall from time to time give to the Congress information of the state of the Union, and recommend to their consideration such measures as he shall judge necessary and expedient; he may, on extraordinary occasions, convene both Houses, or either of them, and in case of disagreement between them with respect to the time of adjournment, he may adjourn them to such time as he shall think proper; he shall receive ambassadors and other public ministers; he shall take care that the laws be faithfully executed, and shall commission all the officers of the United States.

trolled by a nonmilitary leader. They knew that military leaders had, through history, used their armies to gain control of governments.

The constitution makers also gave the President the power to commission all military officers. This further strengthened the President's power over the military.

2. Chief Administrator. The opening sentence of Article II makes the President the executive, or administrative, head of the national government. Additional grants of this kind of power are found in Sections 2 and 3. The President must gather information about national affairs and, from time to time, address the Congress, giving members the information gathered. The President is given power to appoint a number of government officials. The President may, in certain cases, call the Congress into session and, again in certain cases, adjourn congressional sessions. By far the most important of the President's administrative powers and duties, however, is found near the end of Section 3. There it is stated that the President "shall take care that the laws be faithfully executed."

Even in 1787 it would have been difficult for one person to carry out all these administrative powers and duties. The Constitution does not specifically direct the President to form a Cabinet. However, the Constitution does state that the President "may require the opinion, in writing, of the principal officer in each of the executive departments." Using the permission granted by these words, President Washington set up a four-member Cabinet. Presidents in later years increased the size of the Cabinet. They also used their powers of appointment to hire other officials to help carry out the work of the executive branch. Today the executive branch has almost 3,000,000 nonmilitary employees. Most of them are now chosen, not by appointment, but by examinations.

3. Chief Diplomat. In Sections 2 and 3, you will also find clauses that give the President power to represent our country in dealing with the rest of the world. These clauses also deal with the President's treaty-making power and the President's power to appoint and receive ambassadors.

Like most other 20th century Presidents, Nixon found it necessary to meet directly with the heads of other nations. What purposes might these meetings serve?

EXECUTIVE LEADERSHIP 99

4. Judicial Authority. As a part of our government's system of checks and balances, the Constitution gives the President the power to grant reprieves and pardons to people who have been convicted of federal offenses in the federal courts. A more important part of the system of checks and balances is the President's power to appoint judges to the United States Supreme Court and to lesser federal courts.

5. Legislative Responsibility. The Constitution clearly gives major legislative powers to Congress. However, the President has a strong influence in the field of lawmaking. First, the President is directed to give Congress information about national affairs and to recommend certain measures or laws that the President believes are needed. Carrying out this duty, our Presidents now present a legislative program to Congress each January in a State of the Union address. This message, together with other messages the President may send to Congress from time to time, becomes to an important extent the agenda that Congress follows in setting up a program of legislation.

As has been noted, the President is also given the power to call Congress into session and to adjourn sessions of Congress in certain cases. Finally, the President must see that congressional laws are "faithfully executed."

The President may also veto laws of Congress. This power is found, not in Article II, but in Article I. A discussion of the ways this veto power may be used is found in Chapter 4. This presidential power continues to be a vital part of the constitutional system of checks and balances.

LIMITS ON THE POWER OF THE PRESIDENT

A number of important limits on the power of the President are included along with the presidential powers in Article II. In Section 2, the President's diplomatic powers are greatly limited. Although the President is given the power to carry out treaty negotiations with other countries, no treaty can be accepted without the consent of two thirds of the members of the Senate. A similar limit is placed on the President's power to appoint ambassadors, Supreme Court judges, and other government officials. A simple majority of the members of the Senate can force the President to withdraw an appointment. If the Senate rejects an appointment, the President must appoint someone else and again ask for the Senate approval.

President Ford, shown signing one bill, used his presidential power to veto a large number of other bills. This often happens when the President's party is not in control of the Congress.

MAJOR PRESIDENTIAL POWERS

- The President is Commander in Chief of the armed forces.
- The President appoints judges, ambassadors, and other officials.
- The President carries out the laws.
- The President makes treaties.
- The President may grant pardons and reprieves.
- The President may veto laws.

LIMITS ON PRESIDENTIAL POWER

BY THE CONGRESS

- The Senate must approve all treaties and appointments.
- Congress may impeach and convict a President.
- Congress may override a presidential veto with a two-thirds vote.

BY THE COURTS

- The Supreme Court may declare a presidential act unconstitutional.

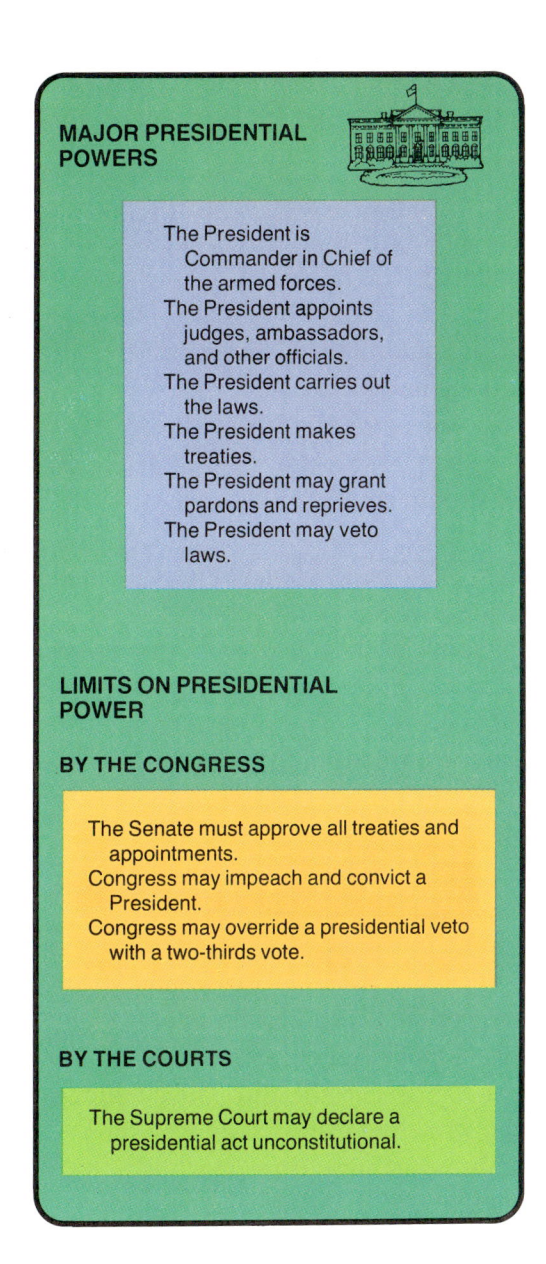

The last section of Article II deals with congressional powers of impeachment and conviction. Using these powers, Congress may remove a President, a Vice President, or any other nonmilitary officer of the national government. The method by which the President and others may be removed is given in Article I. (See page 74.) No President has ever been removed from office as a direct result of the impeachment process. In the 1860s, President Andrew Johnson was impeached but not convicted. In the 1970s, President Richard Nixon resigned from office in the midst of impeachment proceedings.

Another important limit on the power of the President is found in Article I. Although the President may veto laws of Congress, Congress is allowed to override the President's veto with a two-thirds vote. In this way, Congress can pass laws without the consent of the President.

Although it is not mentioned in the Constitution, the United States Supreme Court also has a means of checking the power of an American President. If the Court believes an action of the President is contrary to the meaning of the Constitution, it may declare the action unconstitutional. According to the law of the land, the President must then reverse the action or cease doing whatever it is that the Court has declared unconstitutional.

The power of the American President is also limited by the fact that the President must stand for reelection every four years. If American voters do not approve of the actions of the President

IMPEACHING A PRESIDENT:
Article II, Section 4 of the Constitution

The President, Vice President, and all civil officers of the United States, shall be removed from office on impeachment for, and conviction of, treason, bribery, or other high crimes and misdemeanors.

EXECUTIVE LEADERSHIP   **101**

> **PRESIDENTS ARE LIMITED TO TWO TERMS BEGINNING IN 1951: The 22nd Amendment to the Constitution, Section 1, Paragraph 1**
>
> No person shall be elected to the office of the President more than twice, and no person who has held the office of President, or acted as President, for more than two years of a term to which some other person was elected President shall be elected to the office of the President more than once.

they can vote the President out of office. Today there is yet another limit on the President's power. The 22nd Amendment, added in 1951, limits each President to just two terms in office.

Getting the Facts

1. Why, in the early years of our country, was there fear of executive power?

2. Name at least five powers given to the President by the Constitution.

3. Name at least three ways in which the Constitution limits the power of the President.

Examining the Issues

■ Only one President has ever been impeached. No President has ever been convicted. Bearing in mind the fact that other federal officials have been impeached and convicted, what do you think the lack of presidential convictions implies about (a) the quality of American Presidents and (b) the constitutional system of impeachment. What other factors might help explain the fact that no Presidents have ever been removed from office through the process of impeachment?

The American President In Action

The job of the President of the United States has been described as the toughest in the world. Long ago Thomas Jefferson said of the office, "It brings nothing but unceasing drudgery and daily loss of friends." A modern Vice President, Hubert Humphrey, spoke of the presidency as "an office that demands perhaps more judgment, wisdom, and maturity than any single man possesses." Still, a modern state governor spoke of the office as one "no political leader in our national life should dread or shun." The governor added that the burdens of the presidency "do not awe me, only its honor."

THE EXPANSION OF EXECUTIVE AUTHORITY

The power of the executive branch of the national government has increased through the years. Our Presidents today have a great deal more power than most of their predecessors did. The people who wrote the Constitution would no doubt be greatly surprised at the power and scope of the American presidency today. The office of the President has expanded to include many high level presidential associates and almost 3,000,000 civil servants. These civil servants staff a number of different departments and offices.

The growth in the power and size of the executive branch has been tremendous. Much of the executive power has been gained at the expense of the power of the legislative branch. Although the constitution makers seem to have had a

GOVERNMENT OF ALL AMERICANS

"congressional government" in mind, today it would seem more accurate to say that the United States has a "presidential government."

DUTIES AND POWERS BEYOND THE CONSTITUTION

If a person follows the activities of the President for a few days, chances are the person will see the use of many powers not given in the Constitution. Many of these extra-constitutional duties and powers involve matters the constitution makers did not foresee.

1. Party Leader. The Constitution makes no mention of political parties. For this reason one of the presidential duties that was not mentioned is leadership of the President's political party. Indeed, President Washington was strongly opposed to the idea of parties. By the time of Thomas Jefferson, however, American Presidents came to realize that party leadership was very important. One reason was that political leadership and political power made it easier for them to lead the entire country. It made it easier for them to get the bills they favored passed. It helped strengthen their national position.

Presidents lead their parties in a number of ways. They work to gain the support of party members in Congress and of party leaders in the states. They campaign for party candidates, most often in congressional elections. They can use their power of appointment as a means of keeping control. They often work with party groups in states and cities to gain support for their programs. In these and other ways, Presidents play the role of politician. They do this in an effort to lead people in the direction that they believe is best for the nation.

2. Ceremonial Head. During the President's normal day many things occur that can only be described as ceremonial. A war hero may appear on the White House steps to receive a medal. A Christmas message may be delivered as the White House Christmas tree is lighted. A state dinner may be held for a visiting chief of state.

When carrying out these duties, the President is acting much like a king or queen. Indeed, because Presidents have been given these ceremonial duties along with their broad constitutional powers, they have sometimes been called "rulers of the Americans." In some ways the President's family does seem like a royal family.

To what extent does the position of an American President such as President Ford resemble the position of a royal head of state such as Queen Elizabeth of Great Britain?

EXECUTIVE LEADERSHIP **103**

Before the comparison with royalty is carried too far, however, one should remember that the President is the chief executive only until the next election.

3. Molder of Public Opinion. To lead, the President must influence public opinion. In a free country such as ours, an informed public opinion is very necessary. Every President has been aware of this. Each has tried to influence opinions. Each has tried to educate the public in certain ways.

Modern communications media—especially radio and TV—have made us very aware of the President as a molder of public opinion. President Franklin Roosevelt made good use of folksy "fireside chats" on radio. The coming of TV has given the President an even more powerful educational tool. We see Presidents use it in a number of ways. They may hold large press conferences, give interviews, or make reports to the people.

You are likely to have seen presidential press conferences, speeches, or debates on TV. Have they affected your opinions about public issues? If so, in what ways?

THE GLORY AND POWER OF THE OFFICE

The honor of the presidency and its almost royal trappings are among its more redeeming features. Presidents do seem to enjoy the stately White House and all that it stands for. There is the ever-present TV camera. There is the corps of White House correspondents to carry messages from the President to the people. During the course of a presidential day, there is everything from a steady stream of important officials and visitors to the glitter of a state dinner. On the White House lawn, a helicopter waits, ready to take the President and family, friends, or associates to a jet that can carry them to any part of the world.

Most of all, there is a profound sense of power. A sentence from the President's lips can send waves through the society. The President is Commander in Chief of one of the strongest military forces in the world. The President's decisions can affect the lives of millions.

Getting the Facts

1. In what ways has the power of the executive branch of the national government changed since 1787?

2. What are some of the President's extra-constitutional duties and powers?

Forming an Opinion

■ You are likely to have lived under the administrations of at least four American Presidents. Which of them do you think used their constitutional and extra-constitutional powers most effectively to increase the power of the executive branch? Which used these powers to bring the greatest benefits to the American people?

Who Has the Power to Make War?

In Article I, Section 8 of the Constitution are these words: "The Congress shall have power . . . to declare war . . . to raise and support armies . . . to provide and maintain a navy. . . ." In Article II, Section 2 is this statement: "The President shall be commander in chief of the army and navy of the United States . . . when called into the actual service of the United States. . . ." The words seem clear enough. The Constitution gives Congress the power to *declare* war. To the President, the Constitution gives the power to *conduct* war. Like many other constitutional matters, however, the issue is not so simple. It is clouded by one overriding question. How much power should the President have to take the country into war?

In an age of nuclear weapons and intercontinental missiles, the people of the world have come to recognize the fact that a major war could begin in a matter of minutes. If such a war were to take place, it would be difficult for the United States to follow the words of the Constitution and wait for a congressional declaration of war. To many it has made sense to give the President the power to act immediately. However, if the President is given the power to take our country into a nuclear war how can the President be prevented from using this same power to take the United States into a more limited war? The question leads to another, perhaps more important, question. Should the President ever be prevented from using presidential power to take us into a war the President believes necessary? In other words, should the Constitution be changed so that the President, and not the Congress, would have the constitutional power to declare war?

Through the years of the War in Vietnam, Americans tried to find answers to these questions. The first attempts at answers came in the summer of 1964 as the result of President Johnson's report of an attack on United States destroyers in the Gulf of Tonkin. According to the President's report the destroyers had been attacked by North Vietnamese PT boats after a South Vietnamese raid on the coast of North Vietnam. At the time, the United States had thousands of military personnel in South Vietnam. However, the United States had not yet been involved in any attack on North Vietnamese territory. In retaliation for the reported attack the President ordered a massive air attack on North Vietnam. He followed these orders with a TV address to the American people. The following words are a part of that message:

"My fellow Americans:
"As President and Commander-in-Chief, it is my duty to the American people to report that renewed hostile actions against United States ships on the high seas in the Gulf of Tonkin have today required me to order the military forces of the United States to take action in reply. . . .
"Aggression by terror against the peaceful villages of South Vietnam has now been joined by open aggression on the high seas against the United States of America. The determination of all Americans to carry out our full commitment to the people and to the government of South Vietnam will be redoubled by this outrage. . . .

Inquiry

EXECUTIVE LEADERSHIP

Inquiry

"We Americans know—although others appear to forget—the risk of spreading conflict. We still seek no wider war. . . .

"I have today met with the leaders of both parties in the Congress of the United States, and I have informed them that I shall immediately request the Congress to pass a resolution making it clear that our Government is united in its determination to take all necessary measures in support of freedom and in defense of peace in Southeast Asia. . . ."

Support for the President came from many people in all parts of the country. In less than a week the Congress overwhelmingly approved the "Gulf of Tonkin" resolution. It authorized the President to "take all necessary measures to repel any armed attack against the forces of the United States and to prevent further aggression."

In the years following 1964, America's role in the War in Vietnam expanded greatly. The war dragged on through the 1960s and into the 1970s. As time passed, more and more Americans began to question the President's use of executive war-making powers.

In 1966, in an article in the magazine *Foreign Affairs*, political journalist James Reston described what he considered the basic problem: the long-term growth of the President's power.

"I believe the power of the Presidency has been increasing steadily since the Second World War, particularly since the introduction of nuclear weapons, and that the power of the press and even of the Congress to restrain him has declined proportionately during this same period.

"The Presidential power in the foreign field is in direct proportion to the size of the issue. The press can still embarrass him by premature disclosure of his plans, and the Congress can still oppose and even defy him on peripheral issues, but on the great acts of foreign policy, especially those involving the risk or even the act of war, he is more powerful in this age than in any other, freer to follow his own bent than any other single political leader in the world—and the larger and more fateful the issue, the greater is his authority to follow his own will.

"As the leader of a world-wide coalition of nations engaged in constant contention with hostile forces in scores of different theaters of action or manoeuvre, he is virtually assured of support once he proclaims his intentions. The Congress, of course, retains its power to deny him the funds to carry out his plans, but it cannot do so without repudiating him in the face of the enemy and assuming responsibility for the crisis that would surely follow. . . .

"The gravity of the issues since the advent of the cold war and atomic weapons has clearly enhanced the power of the President. In fact, I cannot think of a single major foreign-policy move any President wanted to make since the Second World War that he was unable to carry through because of the opposition of the press or of Congress."

The reason generally given for this growth of presidential power was that the President had to be able to respond quickly to threats to the nation's security. Senator Gale McGee of Wyoming, a supporter of strong presidential power, stated it this way: "The decision-making process may be reduced by events to a single day, or even hours. For more than one occasion the time allotted by crisis incidents to those who must make the decisions has been less than the time it would take to assemble a quorum of the Congress."

This view has been disputed by witnesses appearing before the Senate Foreign Relations Committee. Among those who disagreed was an American historian, Henry Steele Commager. In his remarks to the committee, Professor Commager stated, "If we turn to the many examples of Presidential war-making in the past twenty years we are, I submit, impressed by the fact that in almost every instance the Congress was actually in session and available for consultation: [However, Congressional approval was not sought in] the Korean intervention, the landing of troops in Lebanon, the Bay of Pigs, the occupation of the Dominican Republic by President Johnson and the successive series of forays into Viet Nam, Cambodia, and Laos."

By the late 1960s, most Americans had formed strong opinions about the Vietnamese War and the President's use of war-making powers. Some agreed with Senator McGee. Others agreed with Professor Commager. As the war dragged into the 1970s and as other Southeast Asian countries became more involved, more and more people began to question American involvement in the war.

What strong opinions about the Vietnamese War are shown in these two photographs? Looking back upon the war, what is your opinion?

EXECUTIVE LEADERSHIP

Inquiry

Congressional disapproval of American actions in Cambodia and Laos was very strong. In 1970, both houses approved a measure banning the use of American troops in either of these countries. In addition, the Senate voted to repeal the "Gulf of Tonkin" resolution. Later in 1973, Congress passed, over President Nixon's veto, the War Powers Act. It stated that the President must report to the Congress within 48 hours after sending American troops into foreign combat. It called for the same kind of report if the President decided to increase "substantially" the number of troops fighting in a foreign country. The act also stated that the President must end any hostilities within 60 days unless Congress specifically authorizes the use of American troops.

In the early years of the Vietnamese War, few Americans spoke out against American involvement. What are some of the factors that may have led many people to oppose the war in later years?

As would be expected, many people saw this act as a dangerous interference with presidential power. Others hoped the act would greatly limit the President's war-making powers.

In 1975, shortly after the end of the War in Vietnam, the United States merchant ship *Mayaquez* was captured by Cambodian forces. We were not officially at war with Cambodia but President Ford ordered an air attack and sent United States Marines into the area. The ship and its crew were quickly returned and the crisis ended. According to the War Powers Act of 1973, a President can take this kind of action provided that a report is made to Congress within 48 hours. Thus, to a large extent, American Presidents still have major war-making powers. The extent to which Congress will, in future years, share these powers remains an open question.

Examining a Question of Power

Do you think President Johnson acted wisely in ordering a massive air attack as a result of the reported events in the Gulf of Tonkin? Why, or why not? What other actions could he have taken?

Do you think Congress should have approved the "Gulf of Tonkin" resolution? What might have happened if Congress had not approved? What other actions might Congress have taken?

To what extent do you agree with the argument that nuclear power has made it necessary to destroy the old balance between the war-making powers of Congress and the President? Would you favor a reestablishment of the balance? Why, or why not? Do you think the War Powers Act of 1973 is strong enough to restore the balance? Why, or why not?

The Executive Branch

The duties of the executive branch in today's government are far too many for one person. So, while the President is one person, the presidency involves many people. These people help the President carry out the executive duties.

Some idea of the growth of the American presidency may be seen in figures covering a brief 40 years. In 1932, there were fewer than 100 presidential assistants. By 1972, there were more than 2,000. Added to this group are millions of civilian and military employees in the departments and agencies of the executive branch of the government.

PERSONAL ADVISERS

The President's office is located in one wing of the White House. The White House is a family residence. But it also contains the offices of many presidential assistants, secretaries, and other employees. The building is, in fact, a giant communications center. It is a place into which messages and mail constantly flow. Here the information is recorded, filed, and prepared for the President and others who must make decisions. Next door to the White House is the former State Department Building. This building now houses most of the remaining presidential staff.

In addition to the help of the White House staff, the President receives assistance from three agencies. These are the Office of Management and Budget, the Council of Economic Advisers, and the National Security Council.

The Office of Management and Budget helps the President prepare the annual budget for the national government. Each year this agency prepares a detailed financial statement. It is so detailed that it is generally the size of a large city telephone book. The statement spells out ways the President believes money should be spent to run the national government in the coming year. This presidential budget must be approved by Congress. The President must be ready to make compromises. Congress tends to make changes in the budget to suit its own ideas about how the government's money should be spent.

The Council of Economic Advisers helps the President deal with the country's financial affairs. It was set up in 1946. The major job of the council is keeping track of the country's economic health. To do this, the council collects information about production, employment, and other economic matters. When economic problems arise, recommendations are made to the President about ways to restore the nation's economic strength.

The National Security Council advises the President on relations with other countries. Set up in 1947, the council includes the President, the Vice President, the Secretary of State, and the Secretary of Defense. Also included are others from the executive branch whose advice the President feels might be needed. The council's task is to keep alert to anything that may affect our security as a nation.

In addition to these three agencies, certain others are set up from time to time, often on a temporary basis. They may deal with such subjects as energy, environment, drug abuse, and price controls.

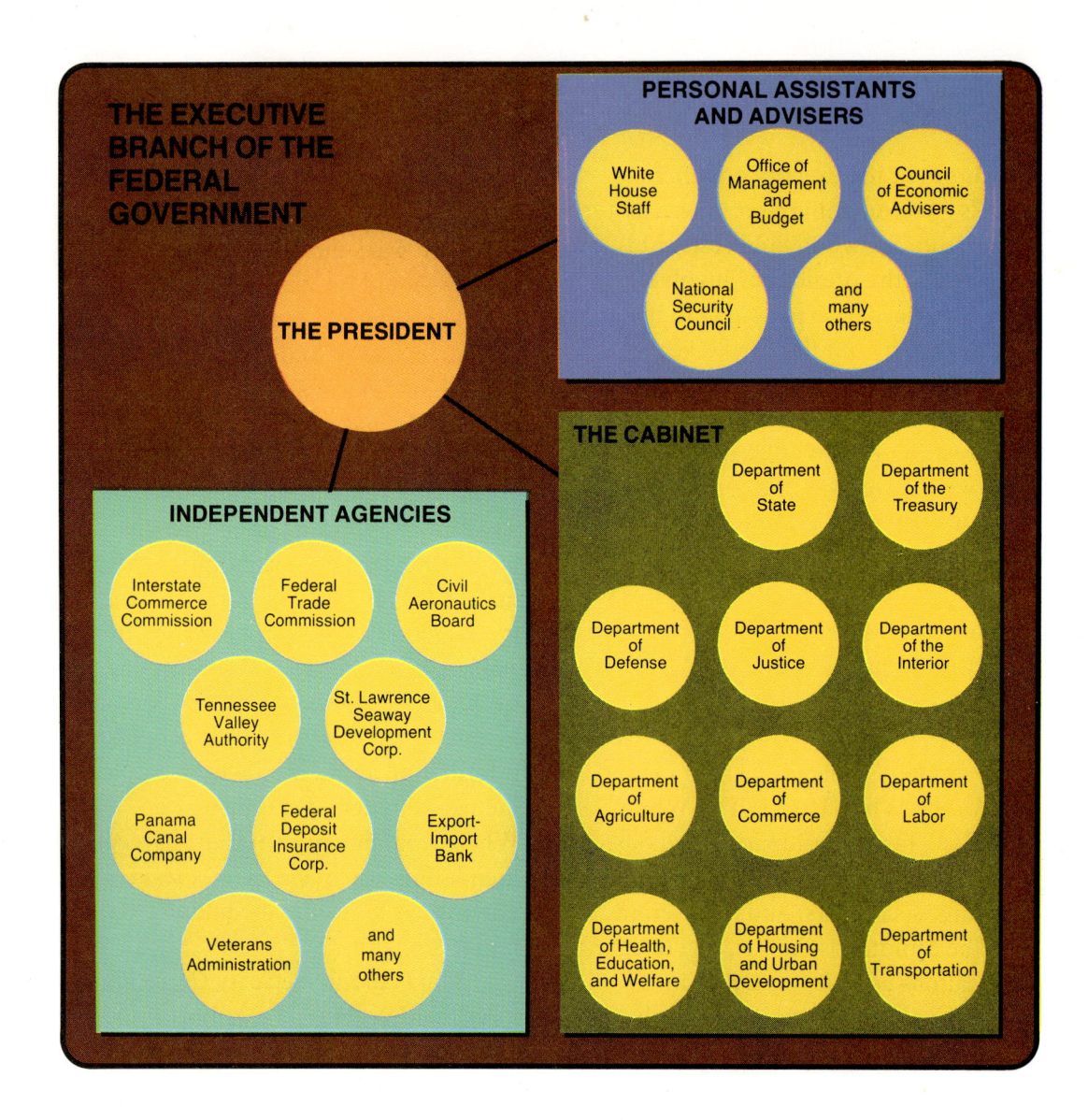

THE EXECUTIVE BRANCH OF THE FEDERAL GOVERNMENT

THE PRESIDENT

PERSONAL ASSISTANTS AND ADVISERS
- White House Staff
- Office of Management and Budget
- Council of Economic Advisers
- National Security Council
- and many others

INDEPENDENT AGENCIES
- Interstate Commerce Commission
- Federal Trade Commission
- Civil Aeronautics Board
- Tennessee Valley Authority
- St. Lawrence Seaway Development Corp.
- Panama Canal Company
- Federal Deposit Insurance Corp.
- Export-Import Bank
- Veterans Administration
- and many others

THE CABINET
- Department of State
- Department of the Treasury
- Department of Defense
- Department of Justice
- Department of the Interior
- Department of Agriculture
- Department of Commerce
- Department of Labor
- Department of Health, Education, and Welfare
- Department of Housing and Urban Development
- Department of Transportation

THE PRESIDENT'S CABINET

Equally important to the President is the advice of the members of the President's Cabinet. Each Cabinet member is the head of a giant department in the executive branch of government. Each is appointed by the President. They must then be approved by the Senate.

As has been noted, the Constitution makes no mention of a Cabinet. There is, however, a clause stating that the President "may require the opinion, in writing, of the principal officer in each of the executive departments." This strongly suggests that the constitution makers were thinking of a group similar to the Cabinet.

George Washington was aware of the need both for advice and for people to serve as department heads. When he became President, he set up four Cabinet posts. He chose a Secretary of State, a Secretary of the Treasury, a Secretary of War, and an Attorney General. In later years other Presidents added new Cabinet posts and executive departments. In 1966 the number of posts and departments rose to 11.

Since the days of President Washington, the departments have grown not only in number, but also in size. The many duties of each department cannot be described in a few pages. We can, however, look at some of the major duties of each department.

The Department of State is in charge of the overall direction of our foreign policy. Its head, the Secretary of State, is the President's chief foreign policy adviser. From its main office in Washington, D.C., the department directs the work of officials around the world. These people look after the interests of the United States in foreign countries and cities. We have an ambassador in almost every country in the world. In most large foreign cities we have a consul. The consul's office looks after the interests of American business. It also stands ready to help Americans who are working or traveling in the country. We Americans travel a great deal. Thus, it is well to be reminded of another important duty of the Department of State. It issues passports. These documents allow us to enter and leave different countries.

The Department of the Treasury is in charge of the country's monetary matters. Its head, the Secretary of the Treasury, is the President's chief adviser on financial and tax matters. This is the department that collects our taxes. It prints our money. And it watches over our government's public debt. Interestingly enough, it also has some law enforcement duties. The Secret Service, which protects the President and our monetary system, is a part of the department.

The Department of Defense is in charge of our country's armed military forces. Its head, the Secretary of Defense, is the President's major adviser on matters of national security. To carry out such duties, the Secretary, who is a civilian (nonmilitary) official, works directly with a group of military advisers. This group is called the Joint Chiefs of Staff. The head of the Joint Chiefs is also the head of all the country's armed forces. Other members of the group are the Chiefs of the Army, Air Force, and Navy. The Marine Corps is a part of the Navy. For this reason, the Commandant of Marines also meets with the Joint Chiefs of Staff. The main office of the Department of Defense is in a huge building called the Pentagon. From the Pentagon, orders go out to our military forces in countries around the world. In its offices, a number of other activities are carried out. These include general supervision of officer-training schools at Annapolis, Maryland (Navy), West Point, New York (Army), Colorado

---

THE CONSTITUTIONAL BASIS FOR A CABINET: Article II, Section 2, Paragraph 1 of the Constitution

The President shall be commander in chief of the army and navy of the United States, and of the militia of the several States, when called into the actual service of the United States; he may require the opinion, in writing, of the principal officer in each of the executive departments, upon any subject relating to the duties of their respective offices, and he shall have power to grant reprieves and pardons for offenses against the United States, except in cases of impeachment.

Which one of these Defense Department officials is the Secretary of Defense? How can you tell?

Springs, Colorado (Air Force), and New London, Connecticut (Coast Guard). The department's duties also include carrying on research programs and engineering projects.

The Department of Justice is concerned with the enforcement of federal laws. Its head, the Attorney General, is the nation's chief law officer. The department gives legal advice to government officials. It represents the government in the federal courts. To carry out these duties, the department has a number of offices, boards, divisions, and bureaus. One of the best known is the Federal Bureau of Investigation—the FBI. Newspaper headlines often mention three other important divisions of the Justice Department. The first of these—the Anti-Trust Division—works to prevent unfair business combinations that threaten to seriously limit free competition. The second division—the Civil Rights Division—helps protect the legal rights of all Americans. The third division—the Immigration and Naturalization Service—assists people from other countries who wish to become American citizens.

The Department of the Interior was set up in 1849. It was the first department created after the four set up by President Washington. Its head, the Secretary of the Interior, can be thought of as the "caretaker" of our country's natural resources. This responsibility is carried out with the help of three assistant secretaries. One works with matters concerning fish, wildlife, and parks. Another takes care of matters involving energy and minerals. The third is concerned with land and water resources. Another important official is the Commissioner of Indian Affairs. As head of the Bureau of Indian Affairs, the official is concerned with the welfare of American Indians.

Today only about 30 percent of the Native Americans in the United States live on the reservations run by the Bureau of Indian Affairs.

112 GOVERNMENT OF ALL AMERICANS

The Department of Agriculture, set up in 1862, looks after the interests of America's farmers. Its head, the Secretary of Agriculture, advises the President on all matters related to the raising and marketing of farm products. The Secretary is interested in what is best for American farmers in markets at home and in other countries. This department offers a number of farm services. These include loans, rural electrification, soil conservation, research, and educational activities.

The Department of Commerce was set up in 1913. Its most important duty is to serve the interests of American industry and business. Its head, the Secretary of Commerce, advises the President on all matters that affect American business, industry, and technology. The department serves American business both at home and in other countries. The department includes a number of smaller agencies that offer other services. The United States Travel Service encourages tourism. The Census Bureau counts the American people every 10 years. The National Bureau of Standards maintains the American system of weights and measures. The Office of Minority Business Enterprise works in the interests of businesses owned by members of American minority groups.

The Department of Labor was set up at the same time the Department of Commerce was in 1913. It watches over the interests of the country's workers. Its head, the Secretary of Labor, advises the President on matters related to working conditions and job opportunities. The Secretary has the help of agencies that collect information about such matters as wages and jobs. From its Washington office, the department works closely with offices across the country. Special agencies have been set up to help young workers, older workers, war veterans, women, and other groups.

The Department of Health, Education, and Welfare was set up in 1953. To form this huge new department, Congress put together a number of older agencies and bureaus. Among them were the Public Health Service, Office of Education, Food and Drug Administration, and Children's Bureau. Today, the Secretary of Health, Education, and Welfare directs a department of nine major agencies. The department is responsible, in one way or another, for the general welfare of all Americans.

The Department of Housing and Urban Development, set up in 1965, is a reflection of a growing interest in the well-being of American cities and towns. Its head, the Secretary of Housing and Urban Development, recommends to the President policies related to housing and community development. To help in the work of the department, regional offices have been set up in 10 cities in different parts of the country.

The Department of Transportation was set up in 1966. It was formed to take charge of our national highway programs, develop automobile safety programs, and deal with problems of mass transit. Its head, the Secretary of Transportation, is responsible for these matters and many others associated with transportation. One of the Secretary's other duties is supervision of the United States Coast Guard. The Coast Guard protects American shipping. It also keeps people and goods from entering our country illegally.

EXECUTIVE LEADERSHIP

Besides running the departments of the executive branch and giving the President needed advice, the members of the Cabinet also serve another function. By act of Congress they are among the government officials listed as possible successors to the President. If a President dies or becomes disabled, the Vice President takes over. If the Vice President dies or for any reason cannot fill the office, the Speaker of the House becomes President. Next in line is the President *pro tempore* of the Senate followed by the Cabinet heads.

INDEPENDENT AGENCIES

In addition to the President's personal advisers and the Cabinet, the executive branch includes a number of independent agencies. There are almost 50 in all. Each was set up by Congress. All report directly to the President. The independent agencies were set up to allow small groups—commissions or boards—to apply the knowledge of experts to certain government problems.

The most important agencies are those that serve as regulatory commissions. Their job is to regulate or watch over certain aspects of the country's economic life. The first regulatory agency was the Interstate Commerce Commission. It was set up in 1887. This body watches over the activities of surface carriers—railroads, trucks, buses—engaged in business that crosses state lines. Another such agency that has been in existence for many years is the Federal Trade Commission. Set up in 1915, this agency watches over the activities of American business. Its job is to protect our system of free competition. A newer agency, set up in 1938, is the Civil Aeronautics Board. This agency watches over air traffic in our country.

Another kind of independent executive agency is the government corporation. These have been set up to carry out certain business-related functions of the national government. They were very popular during the 1930s. At one time, there were almost 100 of them. Now there are not quite a dozen. Three government corporations are in charge of the development and use of important waterways. These are the Tennessee Valley Authority, the St. Lawrence Seaway Development Corporation, and the Panama Canal Company. Two important corporations—the Federal Deposit Insurance Corporation and the Export-Import Bank of the United States—are concerned with banking.

Getting the Facts

1. Name at least three different agencies that have been set up to give the President advice or assistance.

2. Name at least eight services performed by the departments of the President's Cabinet.

3. What is the purpose of the regulatory commissions?   the government corporations?

Examining the Issues

■ One way to analyze the reasons for the growth of the executive department of the national government is to consider the way in which the President's Cabinet has grown. What four Cabinet departments did President Washington set up? Why do you think these departments seemed necessary in the late 18th century? Why do you think the other Cabinet departments were created when they were?

Speaking Out

George E. Reedy

Reedy is a student of American government and a former presidential press secretary. Here he argues that Presidents tend to lose contact with the outside world.

"From the president's standpoint, the greatest staff problem is that of maintaining his contact with the world's reality that lies outside the White House walls. Very few have succeeded in doing so. They start their administrations fresh from the political wars, which have a tendency to keep men closely tied to the facts of life, but it is only a matter of time until the White House assistants close in like a pretorian guard. Since they are the only people a president sees on a day-to-day basis, they become to him the voice of the people. They represent the closest approximation that he has of outside contacts, and it is inevitable that he comes to regard them as humanity itself....

"A 'strong' president, if strength is defined as determination to have one's own way, paradoxically is more liable to suffer from the operations of the White House staff system than one who is 'weak.' The strong man has a propensity to create an environment to his liking and to weed out ruthlessly those assistants who might persist in presenting him with irritating thoughts. It is no accident that White House staffs under the regime of a forceful president tend to become more and more colorless and more and more nondescript as time goes on. Palace-guard survivors learn early to camouflage themselves with a coating of battleship gray."

---

1. What problems are likely to arise if a President loses contact with the outside world?

2. What actions might a President take to keep from being walled off from the outside world?

3. Why does Reedy believe that a strong President is more apt to be removed from the views of the outside world than a weak President?

EXECUTIVE LEADERSHIP

Inquiry

How Well Do Presidential Nominating Conventions Serve the American People?

Every four years, during certain weeks in the summer, the American people see on TV two unlikely, but very American, spectacles. These are the presidential nominating conventions of the Republican and Democratic parties. They have been a part of our political tradition for about a century and a half.

Delegates to these conventions are chosen in a number of different ways. Each state chooses its own method. In some states, delegates are chosen directly by the state Democratic and Republican party organizations. In about 30 states, presidential preference primaries are held by each party. Voters registered in a party may vote for a delegate or, in some states, directly for a candidate who will then be represented by a delegate chosen by the party organization. However, in many of the states that hold presidential preference primaries, the delegates are not committed to vote for specific candidates. In these states, voters have very limited control over the choice of candidate.

Over the years, a number of people have criticized the way in which presidential candidates are chosen. Many object to the way in which delegates are chosen. There are criticisms about the way in which the national nominating conventions are run. Even the need for holding any conventions at all is questioned.

These criticisms are not new. Consider for example these comments made at the beginning of this century.

"At last, after a session of several days, the end is reached; the convention adjourns. . . . All is over. As you step out of the building you inhale with relief the gentle breeze which tempers the scorching heat of July; you come to yourself; you recover your sensibility, which has been blunted by the incessant uproar, and your faculty of judgment, which has been held in abeyance amid the pandemonium in which day after day has been passed. You collect your impressions, and you realize what a colossal travesty of popular institutions you have just been witnessing. A greedy crowd of office-holders, or of office-seekers, disguised as delegates of the people, on the pretense of holding the grand council of the party, indulged in, or were the victims of, intrigues and manoeuvres, the object of which was the chief magistracy of the greatest Republic of two hemispheres,—the succession to the Washingtons and the Jeffersons."

After voicing these highly critical thoughts, however, the same observer went on to face a central problem. For some reason, the system seems to work.

"Yet when you carry your thoughts back from the scene which you have just witnessed and review the line of Presidents, you find that if they have not all been great men—far from it—they were all honourable men; and you cannot help repeating the American saying: 'God takes care of drunkards, of little children, and of the United States!'"

Many people today believe that a better way of choosing presidential candidates would be to hold a national primary. The political parties involved in the primary would be committed to follow the choice of the voters. The idea is quite appealing. Most of our other political candidates are chosen by primaries. Yet the national primary idea, like the nominating conventions, has its critics.

Inquiry

In 1966 former President Dwight D. Eisenhower spoke out against the way in which conventions are run. Yet he stated that he would rather have conventions than national primary elections.

"First, I want to make it clear that I am not among those who wish to abolish the nominating conventions in favor of a national primary. Over the years, the conventions have done a reasonably good job of choosing men of ability and honor. There are, moreover, compelling arguments against a national primary. . . . If we nominated by primary, only wealthy men could normally run for the Presidency. Any campaign which attempts to cover this big country is enormously expensive. . . . Therefore I feel that the nominating conventions must be retained. . . .

"There is, however, no reason under heaven why these conventions must be exercises in chaos and tumult—unmannerly, undignified, ridiculous. Here we have men and women meeting to perform a vital task. The same atmosphere of dignity should prevail that we find in Con-

Tradition was followed at the 1976 Republican Convention. What arguments does Eisenhower offer against following this particular tradition? What arguments can be offered in favor of the tradition?

Because of new rules drawn up by the Democratic Party for its 1976 convention, Chairman Robert Strauss's job of calling the delegates to order was relatively easy.

gress or in any other major deliberative body. Yet our conventions now resemble a rioting mob of juvenile delinquents.

"The floor often becomes a scene of milling humanity, and the din is such that the delegates frequently cannot hear what is said on the podium. The thumping of the chairman's gavel, as he futilely tries to restore order, is an endless refrain to television viewers, many of whom turn off their sets in frustration. . . .

"The ultimate in mob scenes occurs, of course, after each candidate is placed in nomination. The band plays the candidate's theme song, *ad infinitum,* and the parade of demonstrators begins. The theory seems to be that the man who gets a 20-minute ovation would make twice as good a candidate as the 10-minute man."

A number of people have defended the conventions because they seem to work. A student of American government, A. B. Wildavsky, offers another reason for keeping the conventions. Wildavsky believes conventions are needed to build party unity.

"No one will deny that presidential nominating conventions are peculiar. After all, they perform a peculiar function. The task of the convention is to unite a party which is not inherently united, behind a popular candidate who

EXECUTIVE LEADERSHIP   **117**

Inquiry

After months of campaigning for a number of different candidates, convention delegates nominate one person to carry the party's banner to the November election.

is unpopular with many delegates, in order to speak for all the people after battling half of them in an election. It would be surprising if a political institution which must accomplish these goals did not reflect some of the contradictions it is designed to embody."

Another student of government, Philip Green, offers a compromise solution. He favors the convention. However, he thinks a national primary should be held in all states before the conventions.

"Without conventions . . . factions would lose the major forum they presently have in which to exert some influence on the winning candidate even while themselves losing. They would have to find some substitute. Their obvious temptation . . . would be to split off and form new, essentially special-interest, parties. . . .

"For these reasons . . . the *pre-convention national primary* ought to be considered as a more feasible alternative to the present system. The idea behind this proposal is to do away, not with the national conventions, but with the pre-convention *state* conventions that precede it, and with all the opportunities they offer for gross misrepresentation of popular desires.

"Under the proposed system, the major parties would hold primary elections in *all* the states. . . . The primaries would be open to any entrant. There would be no 'official' party candidate. . . .

"Thus the drama of the convention would be retained and so would the opportunity for bargaining and compromise that the convention offers. That bargaining and compromise, however, would take place among delegates whose power would be based almost solely on the number of voters they represented (and on their bargaining skill, of course)."

Analyzing a Political Institution

Most of us have watched national nominating conventions on TV. Think about your own reactions to the conventions. To what extent do you agree with the criticisms of the way in which the conventions are run? What changes, if any, do you think should be made?

How are delegates to the national conventions chosen in your state? How well do you think the delegates represent the wishes of the people in your state?

As early as 1913 an American President suggested that we stop having national nominating conventions. President Wilson suggested that we have primary elections instead. As you can see, a number of others have agreed with him through the years. Which of the criticisms of the conventions do you think are strongest? Which of the arguments in favor of conventions do you think are strongest? How do you think presidential candidates should be chosen? Why?

Is the Electoral College Outmoded?

Just as people question the method used to nominate presidential candidates, people question the method used to elect a President. The Constitution deals with the matter in Article II, Section 1. It calls for a group of electors that together form what is known as the Electoral College. These electors were to be chosen as each state legislature directed.

The method originally provided for the selection of a Vice President did not work well. By the original method, the person with the second largest number of presidential electoral votes became Vice President. The method was changed in 1804 by the 12th Amendment. (See box on page 120.) Electors now vote in two separate elections: one for the President and the other for the Vice President.

The Electoral College, however, has continued through the years. Like the nominating convention, it has often come under attack. Many people have argued that Americans should be able to vote directly for a President. They point to the fact that in the 19th century two presidential candidates lost the popular election but won the majority of the votes in the Electoral College. They both became President.

From time to time, constitutional amendments have been proposed to

---

THE ELECTORAL COLLEGE IS FORMED: Article II, Section 1, Paragraphs 2 and 3 of the Constitution

Each State shall appoint, in such manner as the legislature thereof may direct, a number of electors, equal to the whole number of senators and representatives to which the State may be entitled in the Congress: but no senator or representative, or person holding an office of trust or profit under the United States, shall be appointed an elector.

The electors shall meet in their respective States, and vote by ballot for two persons, of whom one at least shall not be an inhabitant of the same State with themselves. And they shall make a list of all the persons voted for, and of the number of votes for each; which list they shall sign and certify, and transmit sealed to the seat of the government of the United States, directed to the president of the Senate. The president of the Senate shall, in the presence of the Senate and House of Representatives, open all the certificates, and the votes shall then be counted. The person having the greatest number of votes shall be the President, if such number be a majority of the whole number of electors appointed; and if there be more than one who have such majority, and have an equal number of votes, then the House of Representatives shall immediately choose by ballot one of them for President; and if no person have a majority, then from the five highest on the list the said house shall in like manner choose the President. But in choosing the President, the votes shall be taken by States, the representation from each State having one vote; a quorum for this purpose shall consist of a member or members from two thirds of the States, and a majority of all the States shall be necessary to a choice. In every case, after the choice of the President, the person having the greatest number of votes of the electors shall be the Vice President. But if there should remain two or more who have equal votes, the Senate shall choose from them by ballot the Vice President.

EXECUTIVE LEADERSHIP

Inquiry

THE METHOD OF CHOOSING A PRESIDENT AND A VICE PRESIDENT IS CHANGED IN 1804: The 12th Amendment to the Constitution

The electors shall meet in their respective States, and vote by ballot for President and Vice President, one of whom, at least, shall not be an inhabitant of the same State with themselves; they shall name in their ballots the person voted for as President, and in distinct ballots the person voted for as Vice President, and they shall make distinct lists of all persons voted for as President and of all persons voted for as Vice President, and of the number of votes for each, which lists they shall sign and certify, and transmit sealed to the seat of government of the United States, directed to the president of the Senate;—The president of the Senate shall, in the presence of the Senate and House of Representatives, open all the certificates and the votes shall then be counted;—The person having the greatest number of votes for President shall be the President, if such number be a majority of the whole number of electors appointed; and if no person have such majority, then from the persons having the highest numbers not exceeding three on the list of those voted for as President, the House of Representatives shall choose immediately, by ballot, the President. But in choosing the President, the votes shall be taken by States, the representation from each State having one vote; a quorum for this purpose shall consist of a member or members from two thirds of the States, and a majority of all the States shall be necessary to a choice. And if the House of Representatives shall not choose a President whenever the right of choice shall devolve upon them, before the fourth day of March next following, then the Vice President shall act as President, as in the case of the death or other constitutional disability of the President. The person having the greatest number of votes as Vice President shall be the Vice President, if such number be a majority of the whole number of electors appointed, and if no person have a majority, then from the two highest numbers on the list, the Senate shall choose the Vice President; a quorum for the purpose shall consist of two thirds of the whole number of senators, and a majority of the whole number shall be necessary to a choice. But no person constitutionally ineligible to the office of President shall be eligible to that of Vice President of the United States.

change the system. Typical of the arguments in favor of an amendment are these comments made by political columnist Clayton Fritchey in the late 1960s:

"It might as well be admitted that we have the Electoral College because the Founding Fathers (advanced as they were) could not quite bring themselves to rely altogether on direct democracy in choosing the President. Instead of a national election, they invented a system by which each state (depending on its population) would vote for a certain number of so-called electors. Naturally, it was assumed all the electors would be wise and lofty citizens who would know best how to select a President. No oligarchy in any country has even demonstrated that, in the long run, it could do better than the common people, and the American electoral oligarchy proved to be no exception. . . .

"Originally, it had been assumed that the electors, in their infinite wisdom, would exercise individual judgment in voting for the various candidates, but with the quick emergence of political parties, the electors in each state were pledged to vote as a group for their candidate if he carried the state."

GOVERNMENT OF ALL AMERICANS

The Electoral College, however, has continued to have a number of supporters. One is Richard N. Goodwin, a man who served as adviser to Presidents Kennedy and Johnson. About an amendment proposed in the late 1960s, he stated:

"There is good reason to believe that direct popular election of the President may end the two-party system that has helped make the United States one of the most stable and long-lasting democracies in the history of the world. Coming, as it does, at a time of deepening national division and ideological strife, that result is even more likely.

"Yet this immense possibility—a likelihood in my judgment—has been barely mentioned in the curiously muted debate over a proposal to change a constitutional system which has worked well for two centuries. . . .

"The Electoral College has not only faithfully reflected the popular will, it has usually strengthened it by giving a candidate with a narrow popular margin a far larger electoral mandate. Against this historical experience is now set the argument that the electoral system offends the theoretical democratic principle of 'one man, one vote.'

"This is certainly so, at least in abstract possibility. We must remember, however, that this is not the uniform principle of our Government. The Supreme Court, with its power to overrule President and Congress, is responsible to no electorate, and its insulation from popular will has helped strengthen it to protect popular liberties."

What is this cartoonist saying about the presidential election system? How valid do you think the statement is?

"WHEW! CAN'T WE FIND SOME OTHER ROUTE?"

The Electoral College: Source of Strength or Weakness?

Each state has the same number of members in the Electoral College that it has in Congress. Thus, the choice of the members of the College is only partially based on population. Why do you think the system was set up this way? Do you think a system based only on population would be better? Why, or why not?

Is the fact that the Electoral College has served our country as well as it has over the last 200 years a good reason for keeping the system? Why, or why not?

What do you think is the strongest reason for keeping the Electoral College system? What do you think is the strongest argument for giving it up?

The American Governor

Just as the President is the chief executive in the national government, the governor is the chief executive in each state. The governor's role as head of the executive department of state government involves a number of important duties. Governors generally play a major part in setting up goals for their states. They work with the many agencies of state government to develop specific proposals and programs that will lead the states toward their goals. And they work with the state legislatures to pass the kind of laws that will allow the states to move forward.

Virginia's colonial executive lived in the Governor's Palace. What does the name of the residence imply about the power of the executive? What is the name given to the residences of most governors today?

HISTORICAL LIMITS TO POWER

Governors in most states have a very limited amount of power. Some of this lack of power can be traced back to the first state constitutions. Remembering the strong, autocratic rule of many colonial governors, the constitution makers in all but three of the original states decided that the governor should be chosen by the state legislature. The powers given to each governor were quite limited. In most states, the governor's term of office was for one year only.

During the first half of the 19th century the power of governors was in some ways strengthened and in other ways weakened. Generally their terms in office grew longer. Instead of one-year terms, many were given two-year terms and even four-year terms. The four-year term remains the most common today. In addition, the choice of governor in most states was taken away from the state legislatures and given to the people. This made it possible for governors to act more independently. However, in many states governors lost much of the control they had earlier held over the executive branch of the state government. Along with the belief that governors should be elected directly by the people came the belief that other officers of the executive branch should be elected. In most states today, the heads of executive departments are still elected by popular vote. This greatly limits the power of the governors in these states. They lack the important power the President and a few governors have to appoint the heads of executive departments and agencies.

Only in the 20th century has there been a real movement toward strong

122 GOVERNMENT OF ALL AMERICANS

One of the most powerful of all 20th century governors was Huey Long of Louisiana. Yet Governor Long chose to exchange his powerful state office for a seat in the United States Senate.

governors. In part, this increase in power can be traced to a number of strong leaders who have been elected governor in the 20th century. The growth of the power of the state executive has been apparent most recently in the administration of Nelson Rockefeller, four-term governor of New York. Still, the power given to the executive branch in most states today remains limited. In general, the historical growth in the power of governors has not been in any way so great as the growth of the power of the President.

Despite these historical limitations, there have been a number of governors who have held a great deal of power. Many have used the governor's office as a stepping-stone to the presidency. Among these are Woodrow Wilson, Calvin Coolidge, and Franklin D. Roosevelt. Other governors have moved on to powerful positions in Congress.

THE GOVERNOR AS LEGISLATIVE LEADER

Governors are generally elected in November. They then take office the following January. Immediately after taking office the governors in most states are expected to present plans for the coming year or years to the legislature. This is a heavy duty for governors to be given so quickly. To overcome this problem, a few states delay the meeting time of their legislatures until late winter or spring. This gives an incoming governor time to prepare a legislative program.

While the legislature is in session, the governor can be thought of as a partner in the lawmaking process. Governors recommend programs. They try to use their power as party leaders to get certain kinds of laws passed. In all states but one, North Carolina, they have the power to veto acts of the legislature. In a few states the governor's veto can be overridden by a simple majority of the members in each house. In most states, however, a two-thirds or three-fifths majority is required to override the governor's veto.

THE GOVERNOR AS ADMINISTRATIVE HEAD

As the chief executives of state governments, governors are the administrative heads of a number of departments, boards, and commissions. There are well over 2,000,000 people working in state agencies across the country.

Governors often find it difficult to maintain effective control over the many different agencies in their states. In a number of cases, state constitutions and laws do not give the governors enough power over the departments and agencies of state government. Here again the power of most governors is much more limited than the power of the President. Only in a few states can the governor be said to have effective authority over the administration of state government. Often the heads of state agencies have closer ties with similar agencies in the national government than they do with the governor's office in their own state.

OTHER POWERS AND DUTIES

As the state's chief executive, the governor is responsible for carrying out the state's laws. This makes the governor the head of the state's police force. Governors also have control of the National Guard, which they may use in state emergencies. The National Guard, however, is responsible to both a state and the national government. For this reason, National Guard units may be called into service by the national government in time of war or national emergency.

Governors also have certain kinds of judicial powers. These include, in every state, the power to grant pardons and reprieves to people who have been convicted of crimes in the state courts. Using their power to pardon, they can free a person from paying a legal penalty. By granting a reprieve, they can order a delay in the execution of a court action. Most states have pardon and parole boards that report to the governor. Using their power to parole, governors may release a prisoner before the person has served a full sentence.

Getting the Facts

1. Why were the powers of most governors greatly limited by the early state constitutions?

2. Which of the powers given to the President are also given to most state governors? Which presidential powers are not given to most state governors?

Forming an Opinion

■ Your textbook points out a number of ways in which the constitutional powers given to most state governors are weaker than the constitutional powers given to the President. Think about the responsibilities, both national and international, of the American President. Do governors need as much power as Presidents? Why, or why not?

How Powerful Is the Governor of Your State?

The role of governor can be described in as many ways as there are states. The purpose of this inquiry is to learn more about your own state's chief executive. Most important is an understanding of the duties and powers of your governor. Basic information about the governor can be found in a manual of your state government. The manual is generally published by the office of the Secretary of State in your state capital. Use the manual and a copy of your state constitution to gather basic information:

- term of office and limits on number of terms;
- minimum age and state residence requirement;
- annual salary, official residence, expense allowance;
- constitutional powers.

It is much harder to obtain information about the real powers available to the governor in each state. This kind of information is sometimes found in books and articles about state government. It can also be gained by speaking to government workers, political leaders, and newspaper writers. You may also gain information from others who, for a number of reasons, have become interested in the way state government works. Using such sources what can you learn about the actual power available to your governor? Has the power made the executive branch weak or strong in your state?

Authority and leadership are used more by some than by others. What of your present governor? Do people see your governor as a strong or weak executive? Does the governor work well with the legislature? How much authority does the governor have over administrative departments? What political background does the governor bring to the office? Finally, what personal attributes does the governor bring to the office—age, education, family, former career, interests, and so on? Do any parts of the governor's personal background have an influence on the amount of power the governor has? If so, in what way?

Three governors and a member of the national Senate are shown below at a meeting of the National Conference of State Governors in 1977. Can you name them? (Hint: the senator is from Tennessee and the governors are from Alabama, Georgia, and Connecticut.)

Inquiry

EXECUTIVE LEADERSHIP

Citizenship Laboratory

Review of Basic Ideas

1. The Constitution gives the President power to carry out a number of duties. These include the President's duties as Commander in Chief of the armed forces and as administrative head of the federal government. The President is also responsible for representing American interests in other countries, appointing federal judges, and presenting a legislative program to Congress. The President's power is limited by our government's system of checks and balances. The Senate must approve presidential appointments and treaties. The President may veto laws but this veto can be overriden by a two-thirds vote in both houses of Congress. Finally, the President can be removed from office if impeached and convicted by Congress.

2. The growth in the power of the executive branch leads to the conclusion that the United States now has a "presidential government" rather than a "congressional government." Among the President's many extra-constitutional duties are those of party leader, ceremonial head of state, and molder of public opinion.

3. The executive branch of the national government includes a large number of assistants and advisers. Personal assistants help the President prepare the national budget, watch over matters of national security, and set up programs needed to solve national problems. The President's Cabinet is made up of the heads of a number of large executive departments. In addition, the President receives advice from a number of independent executive agencies.

4. The governor is the chief executive in each of our state governments. Like the President, governors have a number of powers and duties. In general, however, the power of the state governors is much more limited than the power of the President. One reason is that many members of the state executive branches are elected rather than appointed by the chief executive.

Questions to Think About

1. One study shows that young students in Connecticut knew more about national and local leaders than about their state governor. Do you think this is true of most young Americans? Explain.

2. The constitution makers emphasized the importance of the legislative branch. In many ways, they set up a "congressional government." To what extent do you agree that we now have a "presidential government"? What factors helped bring about changes in the balance of power?

3. Which of the President's constitutional powers do you think have been most important in bringing about the growth of presidential power? In what ways can Presidents use their extra-constitutional powers and duties to help increase their authority?

4. The executive branch of the national government has been growing larger and larger for years. In what ways could the many agencies and departments be regrouped to create a smaller, perhaps more efficient, executive branch? Do you think such a regrouping would be wise? Why, or why not?

5. Candidates for congressional seats are generally chosen in direct primaries. General elections are then held and people can cast their votes directly for the candidate of their choice. Why is this system not used for selecting Presidents?

6. Why do governors in most states have less power than they need? What powers would you add to make them more effective?

Words and Relationships

Define each of the terms in the first column. Then show how each term is related to the item listed opposite it by using both items in a sentence or short paragraph.

1.	treaty making	Senate
2.	pardon	judicial authority
3.	veto	legislative power
4.	presidential government	checks and balances
5.	party leader	power of appointment
6.	National Security Council	advice
7.	Cabinet	Constitution
8.	Joint Chiefs of Staff	civilian control
9.	nominating conventions	party unity
10.	Electoral College	democratic elections

Building a Future

American political leaders who would like to be President must first give thought to their "availability." They may have decided they are available to try for office, but whether or not they possess availability is another matter. Availability is a rather loosely defined principle that involves certain practical matters that must be considered by any serious presidential candidate. A number of things can make a candidate "unavailable." The person may live in a state with few electoral votes. The person may be a member of a particular racial or ethnic minority. The person may be female or may have extreme views on certain sensitive issues.

Availability factors change from time to time. A good illustration is membership in the Catholic church. For years it made candidates unavailable. The Democrats tried unsuccessfully to change this in 1928 by running Alfred E. Smith for President. Later, in 1960, they succeeded by electing John F. Kennedy. He was our first Catholic President.

Looking to the future, consider some other bars to availability. Think of American women. When, if ever, do you think it will be possible for a woman to become President? What of black leaders? From a religious viewpoint, should the presidency be "available" to atheists or non-believers? In sum, should such things as sex, race, or religious beliefs be availability principles? What requirements would you put in your own list?

EXECUTIVE LEADERSHIP

6 The Role of the Courts

A system of courts is basic to our American way of government. The court system forms the third of the three branches of government—the judicial branch. Like the legislative and executive branches of government, the judicial branch has a special job to perform. It is the job of the courts, and the judges of the courts, to hear disputes concerning the law and to reach decisions about the disputes. In this manner, courts interpret the laws by which we Americans are governed.

The fact that legal disputes arise is clear evidence that laws can have different meanings to different people. It is not enough simply to say, "It is the law." Judges must give meaning to laws by applying them to specific cases. Although for the most part judges must apply the laws passed by lawmaking bodies or turn to decisions made by earlier judges, they do have some freedom. The meanings of the laws and past judgments are seldom so clear and absolute that judges cannot in some way mold the meanings to fit the specific cases they are judging. Cases may also arise in which there are no specific laws to apply. In these cases, the judges must decide, on the basis of facts, what is right and fair. It is through this system of courts and judges that we try to reach the democratic ideal of justice for all.

An American System of Justice

EQUAL JUSTICE UNDER LAW—these words are written above the entrance of a gleaming white building in Washington, D.C. The building houses the United States Supreme Court. The words have been placed there to emphasize the goal of American courts.

Let's examine the words more closely. Like any ideal, "equal justice" can be hard to attain. But in a democratic country it is a goal worth striving for. Then there are the words "under law." In the United States, government is based on laws, not on the desires of a few powerful leaders. Our tradition is to seek justice through the law. And it is to our courts that we generally turn to seek such justice.

This American tradition has been stressed by many leaders, among them President Abraham Lincoln. Warning that if the laws are disregarded, and American rights are not protected, the people will lose faith in their government, he said:

"Let every American, every lover of liberty, every well-wisher to his posterity swear by the blood of the Revolution never to violate in the least particular the laws of the country and never to tolerate their violation by others....

"Let every man remember that to violate the law is to trample on the blood of his father and to tear the charter of his own and his children's liberty. Let reverence for the law be breathed by every American mother to the lisping babe that prattles on her lap. Let it be taught in schools, in seminaries and in colleges....

"Let it be preached from the pulpit, proclaimed in legislative halls and enforced in courts of justice. And, in short, let it become the *political religion* of the nation...."

To promote the ideal of "equal justice under law" a number of court systems have been set up in America. We have state courts to deal with state and local matters. We have federal courts to deal with national matters. And finally we have the United States Supreme Court—a court that has been given the power to review the actions of all the other courts in the United States.

Before we turn to a discussion of the many court systems in America, let us look at some of the important features of the American legal system.

DIFFERENT KINDS OF LAWS

Until now we have studied only one kind of law—the kind of law made by legislative bodies. These laws are called statutory laws. Judges in American courts deal not only with statutory laws but also with common law and with laws, or rules, of equity.

America inherited common law from England. Beginning almost 1,000 years ago, English judges decided cases according to the customs of their day. Slowly these decisions were built into a vast body of law. Judges were able to turn to this body of law for help in making new decisions. Gradually the process of turning back to the decisions made by earlier judges became an accepted practice in English courts. This English system was brought to America early in the colonial period. Today common law is still widely used, especially in state courts.

Judges sometimes hear cases in which a direct application of common law or statutory law would lead to great injustice. This is especially likely to happen when a contract or a will has been badly written. In such cases judges may turn to a set of laws or rules called equity. These rules give judges freedom to depart from the strict meaning of common law and statutory law. Within broad limits, judges are able to make decisions that they think will best promote justice.

DIFFERENT KINDS OF COURT CASES

In general, American courts handle two different kinds of cases. These are civil cases and criminal cases.

Civil cases involve disputes between private individuals. The cases may involve any of a number of our private rights. They may deal with our right to own property. They may involve an attack against a person's character and good name. Civil cases may deal with the rights of marriage partners or of members of a family. They often involve the rights of people who have signed contracts. These are only a few of the many private matters that may be involved in civil cases.

Criminal cases involve acts that are considered major offenses against individuals or against society. Each state has statutory laws that define the kinds of acts that are considered crimes in the state.

More serious crimes are called felonies. Felonies include such crimes as murder, robbery, perjury, arson, and counterfeiting. Lesser crimes are called misdemeanors. Included in this category are such crimes as assault and battery, bribery, disturbing the peace, and violating public health laws.

Generally speaking, we are much more aware of criminal cases than we

Placing a person behind bars is a serious matter. Do you agree with the often stated belief that it is better to let a few guilty people go than run the risk of imprisoning an innocent person? Why, or why not?

are of civil cases. Criminal cases are more likely to be reported in the newspaper and on TV. The fact is, however, most court cases are civil cases.

THE RIGHTS OF THE ACCUSED

Deeply rooted in the American system of legal justice is the belief that a person is innocent until proven guilty. A person may be brought before a court and accused of an unlawful act. It is then the job of the person's accusers to prove beyond doubt that the person is guilty. This is the very opposite of what happens in many countries. In many European countries, for example, accused people are believed to be guilty until they can prove their own innocence.

Four amendments to the Constitution provide further protection of the rights of people accused of crimes. These amendments—the 5th, 6th, 7th, and 8th—are examined in detail in the next chapter. Together they help to assure that any American accused of a crime will be treated fairly in American courts. Note that all four are a part of the Bill of Rights. They were all among the first 10 amendments added to the Constitution in 1791. Americans have long supported the goal of equal justice.

TRIAL BY JURY

One of the most important of the many rights we Americans enjoy is our right in most criminal cases and in many civil cases to a trial by jury. Trial by jury is called for in Article III, Section 2 of the Constitution. It is also mentioned in the 6th and 7th Amendments to the Constitution. And finally, trial by jury is called for in state constitutions.

TRIAL BY JURY: Mentioned in Article III and the 6th and 7th Amendments to the Constitution

Trial by Jury Guaranteed in Federal Criminal Cases: Article III, Section 2, Paragraph 3

The trial of all crimes, except in cases of impeachment, shall be by jury; and such trial shall be held in the State where the said crimes shall have been committed; but when not committed within any State, the trial shall be at such place or places as the Congress may by law have directed.

Right to a "Speedy and Public" Trial by Jury in Federal Criminal Cases: The 6th Amendment

In all criminal prosecutions, the accused shall enjoy the right to a speedy and public trial, by an impartial jury of the State and district wherein the crime shall have been committed, which district shall have been previously ascertained by law, and to be informed of the nature and cause of the accusation; to be confronted with the witnesses against him; to have compulsory process for obtaining witnesses in his favor, and to have the assistance of counsel for his defense.

Trial by Jury Guaranteed in Certain Federal Common Law Cases: The 7th Amendment

In suits at common law, where the value in controversy shall exceed twenty dollars, the right of trial by jury shall be preserved, and no fact tried by a jury shall be otherwise reexamined in any court of the United States, than according to the rules of the common law.

Like much of our legal tradition, trial by jury can be traced back to England. We are all likely to be reasonably familiar with the system. We see juries on popular TV programs and in movies.

What are some of the functions of judges in American courts? To what extent may they exercise their own judgment?

We read about the actions of juries in our newspapers. And each year more than 1,000,000 Americans spend some time serving on juries.

Juries are of two kinds: grand and petit. A grand jury may have anywhere from 12 to 23 members. Its job is to hear charges against a person who is suspected of a crime. If the evidence presented seems good and sufficient, the grand jury hands down an indictment.

An indictment is a formal accusation. Once an indictment has been issued, a petit jury is selected to hear the case. The petit jury is the "trial jury." It generally has 12 members.

In civil cases there are no grand juries. There may, or may not, be petit juries. There are grand juries in many criminal cases and petit juries in most criminal cases. In both civil and criminal cases the job of petit juries is to decide questions of fact. It is the job of the trial judge to instruct members of the jury about the law that should apply in each case.

In criminal cases, the jury decides whether or not the accused person is guilty. If the verdict is guilty, it becomes the responsibility of the judge to decide what the punishment shall be. In civil cases, the petit juries may not only reach verdicts, but may also award specific damages.

Getting the Facts

1. What kinds of law are described by the terms "statutory," "common law," and "equity"?

2. What is the basic difference between civil cases and criminal cases?

3. What is the basic job of a grand jury? of a petit jury?

Forming an Opinion

■ In the Inquiry section that follows you will read arguments for and against the use of juries in American courts. Before you read this section, consider your own views about trial by jury. What are its greatest strengths and weaknesses? Which do you think are stronger, the strengths or the weaknesses? Explain.

132 GOVERNMENT OF ALL AMERICANS

Is Trial by Jury an Outmoded Practice?

According to our democratic tradition, a trial by jury offers a reasonably fair judgment based on the common sense of the people. Juries are assumed to be made up of men and women from every social class and from all races and religions. But it is often hard to put together a group that truly represents the community. There is also an important question that must be asked. Should a group of people, untrained in the law, have responsibility for the kinds of legal matters that come before the courts?

For these and other reasons, our jury system has often come under sharp attack. Yet it continues to have many strong defenders. Among critics and defenders we find many people who are well qualified to speak about legal matters. This is shown in the two selections that follow. The first selection, "Something's Wrong With Our Jury System," is from an article by United States Circuit Court Judge Jerome Frank. The second selection, "In Defense of Our Jury System," is from an article by Federal District Court Judge Louis E. Goodman.

In his article Judge Frank offers strong criticism of the jury system. He believes the system is the "weakest spot in our judicial system."

"If a surgeon were to call in 12 men untrained in surgery, give them an hour's talk on the instruments used in appendectomies, and then let them remove a patient's appendix, we would be appalled. Yet similar operations on men's legal rights are performed every day by juries, amateurs entrusted with the use of legal rules which lawyers and judges understand only after long special training.

"No sensible business outfit would decide on the competence and honesty of a prospective executive by seeking the judgment of 12 men and women, taken from a group selected almost at random —and from which all those had been weeded out who might have special qualifications for deciding the question. Yet juries chosen in this way are given the job of ascertaining facts on which depend a man's property, his reputation, his very life. . . .

"At the beginning of a trial every juror takes an oath, as a public official, that he will 'well and truly try the matters in issue and a true verdict render according to the law and the evidence.' After the evidence and the lawyers' arguments have been heard, the judge addresses— or 'charges'—the jurors. He describes the 'law'—the legal rules—which, he says, must govern their verdict. He instructs them that it is their sworn duty to apply those legal rules, whether or not they like them, to the facts they 'find'; that their 'finding' of the facts must be based entirely on the evidence they have heard during the trial, and not on any personal knowledge; and that they must dismiss from their minds all bias for or against either party to the suit, and act fairly and impartially.

"The jurors then retire to the jury room for secret deliberations. If they agree on the result, they come back to the courtroom and report their verdict. They are not required to, nor do they, give any explanation whatever of this verdict. What went on in their secret session, whether they acted in accordance with their oaths and with the judge's instructions—this the judge very seldom learns.

"But it is known, through later interviews with jurors, that juries frequently pay no heed to what the judge tells them to do. In many a civil trial the jurors decided for one side or another on the

Inquiry

THE ROLE OF THE COURTS

Inquiry

flip of a coin. In one instance the jurors agreed to draw a number between 1 and 100, the decision to be that of the juror whose age came closest to the number he drew. Then, too, there are cases in which one of the jurors who disagreed with the others surrendered his honest judgment because he mistakenly thought he had to go along with the majority, or because the other jurors threatened him, or because he was anxious to go home.

"Of course not all juries behave this way. But there is reason to believe that if full reports were made on all jury deliberations, public confidence in jury trials would be badly shaken....

"Although trial by jury can be improved, in my opinion it will remain the weakest spot in our judicial system—reform it as we may."

If you were the defendant in a criminal trial, what qualities would you wish to find in the jury chosen to judge your guilt or innocence?

Replying to Judge Frank, Judge Goodman offers a number of reasons for keeping the jury system.

"A new plague is upon us here in America. The 'efficiency expert' wants experts to take the place of juries in our administration of justice. He wants motorists to decide accident cases, physicians to decide malpractice cases, accountants to decide tax cases, engineers to decide engineering cases, chemists to decide chemical cases, real-estate experts to decide lease cases, and so on....

"Critics of our jury system ... cite or write books or scenarios about cases of mistake or misfeasances committed by jurors, and then conclude that juries are not competent and should be done away with. It is true that some highly placed judges have or have had this view. But I have not heard of a competent trial judge of experience who has expressed such a belief....

"Practically, what does a lawyer or trial judge learn about juries? A trial judge sits in most courtrooms within 10 feet of the jury. The lawyers sit almost as close. What happens in a courtroom in the selection and functioning of a jury?

"The judge questions those who are not excused from serving, as do the lawyers in many courts, concerning their qualifications to serve in a particular case. Day in and day out, year in and year out, the trial judge hears the views jurors may have on social or economic problems, what they think about law-enforcement officers or taxes or insurance companies, and even judges and lawyers. And so as time passes, the judge begins to get a firsthand knowledge and understanding of the people who make up the jury panels, their likes, their dislikes, their weaknesses, their strong points, their capacity to be fair.

"The judge observes the impact, upon the 12 people who sit as jurors, of the testimony of witnesses, of the attitudes and habits of lawyers...."

GOVERNMENT OF ALL AMERICANS

"Even after the case has been submitted to the jury and they have retired to deliberate, the judge's contact with the jury does not end. The jurors frequently call on the judge during their deliberations. They want to know about the exhibits. They want clarification of some instruction. They want advice on the materiality of evidence or documents or exhibits. . . .

"The fact that a layman cannot perform a surgical operation does not mean he cannot decide a question of fact, that he cannot use his common sense and decide who is telling the truth.

"Judge Frank makes the bald statement that in 'many' civil trials the jury decides for one side or the other on the flip of a coin. I am curious as to how and where such evidence was obtained. In 36 years, no such case has come to my attention. Judges and lawyers to whom I have talked have had no such knowledge. . . .

"All this sort of argument, and the citing of picturesque instances, proves is that human beings make mistakes. In equally important issues of life and death and in civil and property-right matters, judges make mistakes. If the trial judge makes a mistake [the case can be appealed—sent to a higher court—and] the appellate judges can correct the mistake and reverse the judgment. Sometimes, if the question is important enough, the Supreme Court may intercede and make its own decision.

"It must not be overlooked that the verdict of the jury is not final. It may be reviewed by the trial judge; it can be set aside by him. In like manner it can be reviewed and set aside by the higher court. This is part and parcel of the system of checks and balances which is inherent in our constitutional form of government. It applies to jurors just as much as it applies to the executive, administrative or legislative departments. No judge of integrity or conscience will let an unjust verdict stand. . . .

"It is true that many improvements are needed in the administration of the jury system. Better techniques in selecting jury panels are necessary. We need better methods of training jurors and in the procedure of instructing jurors. More careful screening of potential jurors to eliminate the unfit is undoubtedly needed. Progress is being made in these directions. We aim to have much more. But reformations are also needed in other phases of our administration of justice. Before us always is the warning that to make justice work, eternal vigilance and constant and intelligent effort are essential.

"I say: Hold fast to the jury system. It is of the essence of democracy. It is a symbol of freedom. To abolish it is to step toward totalitarianism."

Two Judges—Two Opinions

Now that you have read and studied Judge Frank's criticisms and Judge Goodman's defense of the jury system, consider these questions.

To what extent do you agree with Judge Frank's suggestion that people chosen for jury duty should have special qualifications that relate to the case?

How well do you think Judge Goodman answers Judge Frank's criticism of the manner in which juries reach their verdicts?

In neither selection is anything said about age of jurors. Now that 18-year-olds have the right to vote should they also be allowed to serve on juries? Why, or why not?

Do you think that the jury system should be replaced entirely? If so, with what should it be replaced? If not, why not?

What are possible ways of reforming the jury system to get verdicts that are fairer?

The Constitution Establishes a Framework for a National System of Courts

Having set up the legislative branch of the national government in Article I of the Constitution and the executive branch in Article II, the constitution makers went on to set up the third branch of government in Article III. This third article, dealing with the judicial branch of government, is by far the shortest of the three articles. It sets up only the barest framework for a national system of courts. Only one court, the United States Supreme Court, is mentioned specifically in the Constitution. Congress is directed to set up other federal courts as needed.

Yet in a few words, Article III accomplishes a great deal. The powers of the national courts are limited by a specific list of the kinds of cases that are to be tried in federal courts. The Supreme Court is given special powers over the other courts. The right to trial by jury in all federal criminal cases except cases of impeachment is guaranteed. And finally, a limited definition of treason is given.

In many ways, Article III can be seen as a set of limits. The powers given to the judicial branch seem much weaker than those given the legislative and executive branches. Indeed in the early years of our nation a number of prominent people turned down appointments to the Supreme Court. However, by expanding the powers given in the Constitution, the United States Supreme Court gradually became a very powerful part of the national government.

A JUDICIAL BRANCH IS FORMED: Article III, Section 1 of the Constitution

The judicial power of the United States shall be vested in one Supreme Court, and in such inferior courts as the Congress may from time to time ordain and establish. The judges, both of the Supreme and inferior courts, shall hold their offices during good behavior, and shall, at stated times, receive for their services, a compensation which shall not be diminished during their continuance in office.

POWERS OF THE UNITED STATES SUPREME COURT

At the beginning of Article III it is stated that "the judicial power of the United States shall be vested in one Supreme Court, and in such inferior courts as the Congress may from time to time ordain and establish." In a later part of the article, the Supreme Court is given "original jurisdiction" over only two kinds of cases. The only kinds of cases that can begin in the Supreme Court are cases involving members of the diplomatic corps and cases involving one or more of the states. However, the Supreme Court is also given "appellate jurisdiction" over all federal cases. This means that if people are not satisfied with the decision made by a lower federal court they may appeal the case to the Supreme Court. The Supreme Court can overrule the decision of any of the other federal courts. Although it is not mentioned in the Constitution, this right of "appellate jurisdiction" soon came to cover decisions made by the state courts in cases involving the national Constitution or national laws.

> **POWERS GIVEN TO THE JUDICIAL BRANCH:** Listed in Article III of the Constitution
>
> **Cases to Be Tried in Federal Courts:** Article III, Section 2, Paragraph 1
>
> The judicial power shall extend to all cases, in law and equity, arising under this Constitution, the laws of the United States, and treaties made, or which shall be made, under their authority;—to all cases affecting ambassadors, other public ministers and consuls;—to all cases of admiralty and maritime jurisdiction;—to controversies to which the United States shall be a party;—to controversies between two or more States;—between a State and citizens of another State;—between citizens of different States,—between citizens of the same State claiming lands under grants of different States, and between a State, or the citizens thereof, and foreign States, citizens or subjects.
>
> **Special Powers of the Supreme Court:** Article III, Section 2, Paragraph 2
>
> In all cases affecting ambassadors, other public ministers and consuls, and those in which a State shall be a party, the Supreme Court shall have original jurisdiction. In all the other cases before mentioned, the Supreme Court shall have appellate jurisdiction, both as to law and fact, with such exceptions, and under such regulations as the Congress shall make.

The Constitution also fails to mention another important power of the Supreme Court. This power, known as judicial review, is now a major part of our system of checks and balances. It became recognized in the early years of our nation. Stated in simplest terms, judicial review allows the Court to decide whether a law passed by a lawmaking body is in accord with the meaning and intent of the Constitution. If the Court finds the law opposed to the meaning of the Constitution, it can declare the law unconstitutional. The law then loses its effect as a law. Like the right of "appellate jurisdiction," the right of judicial review is not limited to the national government. The United States Supreme Court may declare state and local laws unconstitutional if, when brought before the Court in test cases, they are found to be opposed to the meaning of the Constitution.

LIMITS ON THE POWER OF THE SUPREME COURT

The Constitution calls for a Supreme Court. It mentions that inferior courts may be established. Power to translate these words into action, however, is given to Congress and to the President. In Section 2 of Article II, the President is given the power to appoint judges of the Supreme Court. The Senate is given the power to approve these presidential appointments. In this way the constitution makers made certain that the people serving on the Court would be acceptable to the other two branches of government, at least at the time of their appointment. Judges, or justices, of the Supreme Court may hold their offices "during good behavior." Thus it is possible that years will go by with no justice resigning or dying. At other times, Presidents and senators have been able to make a number of new appointments. In all cases, however, the original choice of justices is made by the other two branches of government.

Congress is given a number of other ways of limiting the power of the Court.

Congress is responsible for setting up all other federal courts. While Congress cannot abolish the Supreme Court, it does have the power to fix its size. As first set up in 1789, the Supreme Court consisted of one Chief Justice and five associate justices. From time to time the number of justices has been changed. In 1869 the size of the Court was fixed at nine members. It has remained this size ever since.

Congress also has the power to impeach justices of the Court. The process of impeaching and convicting justices is the same as the process of impeaching and convicting Presidents.

Finally, Congress may take steps to see that a law declared unconstitutional by the Supreme Court is reestablished as an effective law. To do this Congress must propose an amendment to the Constitution. If such an amendment is accepted by three fourths of the states it becomes a part of the Constitution. The law can no longer be considered "unconstitutional."

THE SUPREME COURT IN ACTION

Most of the cases that come before the United States Supreme Court have been appealed from the lower federal courts or from the highest courts of the states. Cases that reach this highest court in the land are generally concerned with questions about the meaning of the Constitution or with other matters of great importance to the nation. Most of these cases are test cases. They are brought to the Supreme Court to "test" certain issues. Generally the people who bring these cases to the Supreme Court hope that the Court will decide against some state or national law. If the decision is against a state law it will hold against all other similar state laws.

Examples of test cases are found in the many civil rights cases brought before the Supreme Court in the years since 1950. One of the most famous of these was the case of *Brown v. Board of Education of Topeka* (1954). The case in-

---

MAJOR POWERS OF THE UNITED STATES SUPREME COURT

- The Supreme Court interprets laws.
- The Supreme Court can hear appeals from any federal court cases.
- The Supreme Court can hear appeals from state court cases that involve the Constitution or national laws.
- The Supreme Court may declare a law unconstitutional.
- The Supreme Court may declare a presidential act unconstitutional.

LIMITS ON THE POWER OF THE SUPREME COURT

BY THE PRESIDENT

- The President appoints judges.
- The President may grant paroles and reprieves.

BY THE CONGRESS

- The Senate approves the appointments of judges.
- Congress has the power to set up federal courts under the Supreme Court.
- Congress may impeach and convict any federal judge.
- Congress may propose an amendment to the Constitution if the Supreme Court declares a law unconstitutional.

The nine justices on the United States Supreme Court can make decisions that will affect the lives of all Americans. What steps can be taken—by the people, the states, and Congress—to counteract a Court decision?

volved a segregated school system in Topeka, Kansas. When the Supreme Court ruled against segregation of black and white students in the Topeka schools, it was, in effect, ruling against segregation based on racial differences in all public schools.

In decisions of the Supreme Court the opinions of all nine justices have equal weight. The Chief Justice of the Court does have a number of special duties. Among them are the duty of administering the oath of office to an incoming President and the duty of presiding at trials of Presidents who have been impeached. However, the Chief Justice has no special power over the legal decisions that are made by the Court.

After studying a case, the justices meet to discuss their views. The Court's final decision is that of the majority of the justices who cast votes. Justices can abstain from voting in cases in which they have or have had a personal or professional interest.

Once a majority has agreed on a decision, one of the justices who voted with the majority is asked to write the opinion of the Court. Any member who differs with the majority view may write a dissenting opinion. Such an opinion states the reasons why the judge disagrees. Some of the dissenting opinions that have been written by Supreme Court justices are as well known and respected as the majority actions of the Court.

THE ROLE OF THE COURTS **139**

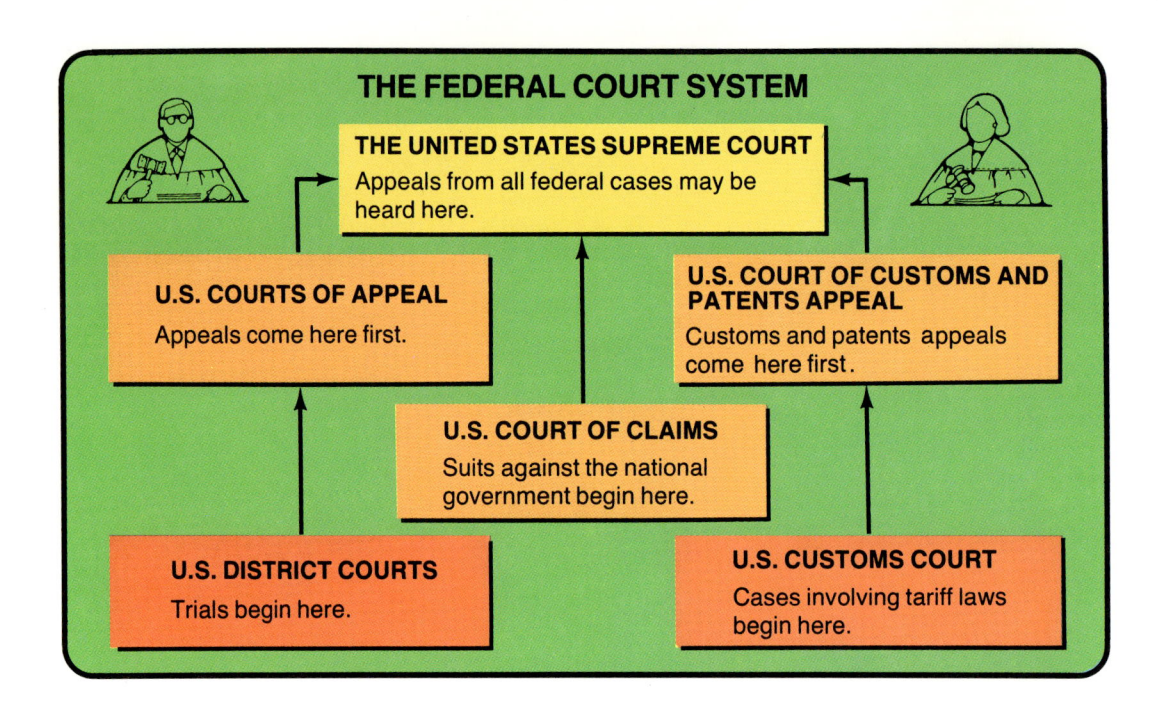

THE FEDERAL COURT SYSTEM

THE UNITED STATES SUPREME COURT
Appeals from all federal cases may be heard here.

U.S. COURTS OF APPEAL
Appeals come here first.

U.S. COURT OF CUSTOMS AND PATENTS APPEAL
Customs and patents appeals come here first.

U.S. COURT OF CLAIMS
Suits against the national government begin here.

U.S. DISTRICT COURTS
Trials begin here.

U.S. CUSTOMS COURT
Cases involving tariff laws begin here.

LESSER FEDERAL COURTS

Among the most important of the federal courts created by Congress are the United States District Courts and the United States Courts of Appeal.

There are nearly 100 District Courts. By acts of Congress, the United States has been divided into districts with one District Court in each. A District Court may have one judge or many. The number depends upon the amount of work. The District Courts are the lowest courts in the federal system. Known as courts of "original jurisdiction," these are the courts where cases begin. It is here that trials are held. Most of the cases involve crimes against the Constitution, the laws of Congress, or treaties.

Cases may be appealed from the District Courts to the United States Courts of Appeal. There are 11 Courts of Appeal in the United States. There are at least three judges presiding over each of these courts. If the work load of a court is large, there may be many more. No cases begin in these "appellate courts." The main job of the courts is to decide whether the judge in the trial court—the District Court—has made any mistakes in applying the law. The decisions of the Courts of Appeal may also be appealed—to the Supreme Court.

Congress has also set up certain special courts to serve particular purposes. The oldest of these is the Court of Claims. Set up in 1855, the Court holds its sessions in Washington, D.C. It hears cases in which claims are made against the national government. It is the only court in which the national government may be sued for damages. If the Court upholds a claim, Congress provides the money to pay it.

Two other special courts are the United States Customs Court and the United States Court of Customs and Patent Appeals. The nine judges of the Customs court hear cases that involve our tariff laws. Tariffs are charges on goods entering the country. The Court of Customs and Patent Appeals is a body of five judges. It hears cases that are appealed from the Customs Court and from the United States Patent Office. The Patent Office is a government agency that gives people and groups exclusive rights to such things as inventions.

Closely associated with the federal court system is the Department of Justice. This department is a unit within the executive branch of government. It is headed by a member of the President's Cabinet, the Attorney General. The Justice Department provides legal advice and represents the government in the federal courts. Working with the office of the Attorney General are a number of United States District Attorneys. There is one District Attorney for each District Court. The District Attorney's job is to prepare for trial any government case that arises in the district.

Getting the Facts

1. What special powers does the United States Supreme Court have as the "highest court in the land"?

2. What powers do Congress and the President have that limit the power of the Supreme Court?

3. Describe the various "inferior" courts in the federal court system.

Examining the Issues

■ What evidence is there that the constitution makers wished to make the judicial branch the weakest branch of the federal government? For what reasons might they have made such a decision?

State Court Systems

In keeping with our federal system, each state has set up its own system of courts. As one would guess, there are some differences from state to state. The different state systems do tend, however, to follow a general pattern.

THE HIGHEST STATE COURTS

The highest court in each state is the state supreme court. These courts are known by other names in some states but each state has a highest court. The work of these courts is almost exclusively that of hearing appeals from the lower state courts.

To cut down the work load of the state supreme courts, a few states have set up intermediate courts. Appeals heard by these courts are generally those thought to be of lesser importance.

State cases involving the national Constitution and national laws can, of course, be appealed from the highest state courts to the United States Supreme Court.

MAJOR STATE TRIAL COURTS

In every state there are general trial courts in which major civil and criminal cases involving state law begin. These courts are often called circuit courts. In some states the courts are called district courts, superior courts, county courts, or courts of common pleas. The states also have special trial courts called probate courts. These bodies hear cases involving wills, the inheritance of property, and other similar matters.

MINOR STATE TRIAL COURTS

In addition to the major state trial courts, there are minor courts that hear cases involving local matters. Many cities have municipal courts. These courts are concerned with such things as the violations of city ordinances. Ordinances are the laws passed by city councils. These courts try a wide range of cases dealing with such things as traffic violations and disorderly conduct.

In many small towns and rural areas there are justice of the peace courts. Like municipal courts, these courts hear cases involving small sums of money or minor offenses.

In many cities, a number of courts have been set up to handle special kinds of problems. Juvenile courts deal with cases in which young people are accused of wrongdoing. Domestic relations courts try to settle disagreements within families. Small claims courts hear cases involving small sums of money. Traffic courts handle traffic violations. Through these special courts an attempt is made to provide justice at the lowest level of government.

Getting the Facts

1. What different kinds of courts are found in the state court systems? What are the functions of the different kinds of courts?

2. What kinds of cases can be appealed from the state courts to the United States Supreme Court?

Forming an Opinion

■ In the United States a number of courts have been set up to hear appeals, both at the national and at the state level. What are the advantages of having so many appellate courts? What are the disadvantages?

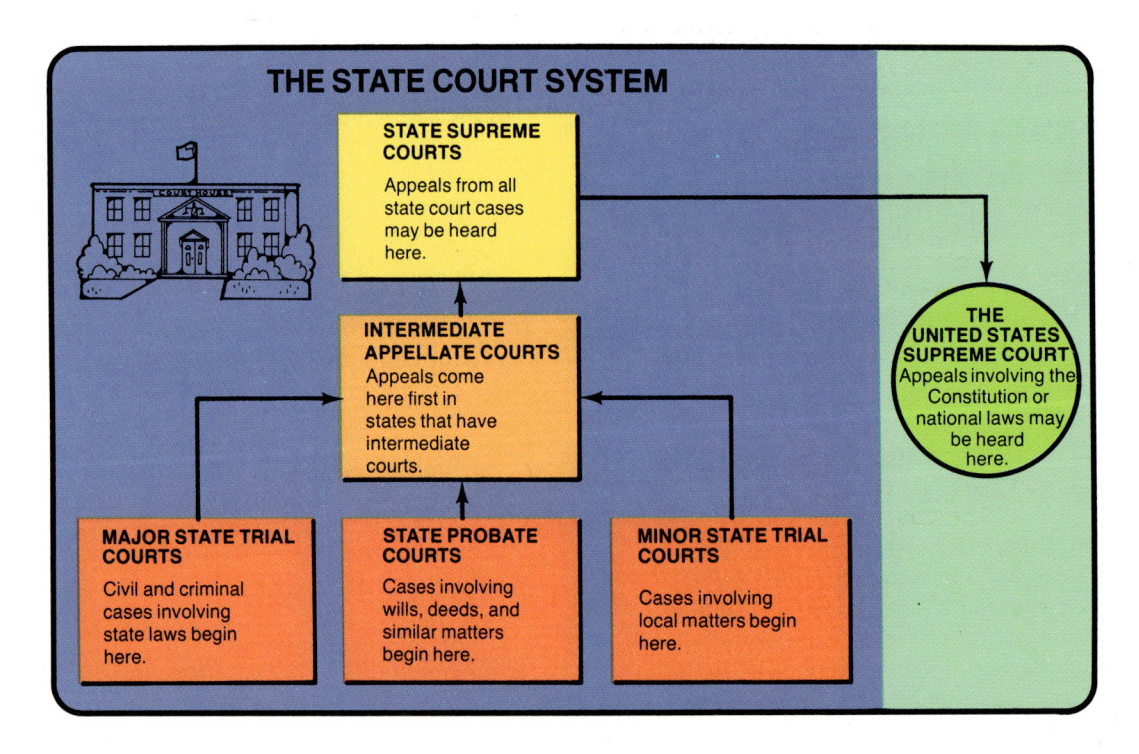

THE STATE COURT SYSTEM

STATE SUPREME COURTS
Appeals from all state court cases may be heard here.

INTERMEDIATE APPELLATE COURTS
Appeals come here first in states that have intermediate courts.

MAJOR STATE TRIAL COURTS
Civil and criminal cases involving state laws begin here.

STATE PROBATE COURTS
Cases involving wills, deeds, and similar matters begin here.

MINOR STATE TRIAL COURTS
Cases involving local matters begin here.

THE UNITED STATES SUPREME COURT
Appeals involving the Constitution or national laws may be heard here.

GOVERNMENT OF ALL AMERICANS

Speaking Out

The National Commission on the Causes and Prevention of Violence

The National Commission on the Causes and Prevention of Violence was set up in the wake of the riots of the mid-1960s. In the following statement, a commission task force asserts that poor people in America receive a kind of justice different from that enjoyed by the rest of the American people. The commission finds this to be especially true in the special state courts set up to handle urban problems.

"The last resort of the poor as well as the rich is in the courts. They are there to do justice, whatever the cost. They must stand between the individual citizen and the carnivorous merchant, the profiteering landlord, the arbitrary administrator. If he cannot find justice there, the poor man is lost.

"The courts of the poor are the courts of 'inferior' jurisdiction, the 'people's courts.' The judges in these lower courts tend to be younger, less experienced, from less prestigious law schools. The caseloads of these courts tend to be the greatest. . . . Cases of enormous importance to the participants are handled in assembly-line fashion, with less than five minutes to a case.

"Specialized 'social' courts—family courts, drunk courts, juvenile courts—or specialized 'legal' courts—landlord-tenant courts, small claims courts—handle the bulk of cases involving the urban poor. In the 'social courts' the judges rely, too heavily if at all, on reports of probation officers, intake officers, social workers, and referees to dispose of the parties' complaints. The reports are often not available to the parties, they contain inadmissible and hearsay evidence, and their drafters cannot be cross-examined. In the 'legal courts,' no account at all is taken of the equities: the tenant owes rent, the debtor owes money; that is that.

"In these courts, parties are most often not represented by counsel; the proceedings are not recorded; appeals are infrequent. Dispositions are commonly arrived at in such courts without a full adversary hearing. Without a formal challenge to the other party's facts in open court, the poor person is usually at a disadvantage."

1. According to the task force report, what are the weaknesses of the courts of inferior jurisdiction? Why would these weaknesses affect poor people more than middle class and wealthy people?

2. In criminal cases, all people may have lawyers whether or not they can pay the lawyers' fees. Do you think lawyers should be provided for everyone in civil cases? Why, or why not?

3. What changes would make the courts of inferior jurisdiction more effective?

THE ROLE OF THE COURTS

American Judges

Justice in our court system depends a great deal on the quality of the judges. Because of this, it is worthwhile to examine the different ways in which our judges are chosen and the different terms of office they are given.

APPOINTMENT OR ELECTION?

In the federal court system, all judges are appointed by the President with the approval of the Senate. In a few states, governors appoint judges. However, most of the judges in the state courts are not appointed. In 41 states some or all of the judges are elected.

The election of state court judges began in the early 19th century. Part of the general belief of those times was that one person was as qualified to hold public office as another. Such a belief, as it relates to the choice of judges, has changed only very slowly. Many people today still favor the election of judges because it seems more democratic. But most students of government favor appointment. They see the appointment method as a better means for obtaining judges who are highly qualified. It is also seen as a way of removing the choice of judges, to some extent, from political influences.

The election of judges presents one special problem. People tend to cast their ballots for judges in a rather blind fashion. This can be seen in the results of a survey made in New York City. In a 1966 election, half of the New Yorkers who voted in the election stated that they did not vote for any of the judges. What's more, very few who voted even remembered the names of any of the candidates for judge a week or so after the election.

SHORT OR LONG TERMS?

Once in office, how long should a judge's term be? At present many of the terms are short. Often they are for only four years. Students of government, however, tend to favor long terms in office. They believe this is one way to protect judges from political influence. A 1967 presidential commission, for example, recommended that the terms of all major trial court judges be for 10 years or more. Other authorities recommend that judges be appointed for life. Generally, they also recommend that judges be required to retire if they live to a certain age.

Judges in the federal courts are appointed for life. Life tenure in some form is also used in at least two states, Massachusetts and Rhode Island. But the most common term of office for judges in major state trial courts is four to six years. The term is often somewhat longer for judges in the highest state courts.

Getting the Facts

1. What methods are used to select the judges in the federal and state courts?

2. How do the lengths of term given to judges vary in the different courts?

Forming an Opinion

■ What length of term would you favor for judges in American courts? Why? Do you think the length of term should vary with the level of the court? Why, or why not?

Inquiry

Can We Reestablish the Right to a Speedy Trial?

The two cartoons on this page direct attention to a problem well known to those familiar with American courts. The problem is the clogging up of the machinery of justice. The courts are clogged by unreasonable delays in both civil and criminal cases. To make matters worse, the backlog of cases waiting trial continues to grow. The 6th Amendment guarantees "a speedy and public trial." What can be done to unclog American courts?

The 8th Amendment to the Constitution forbids "cruel and unusual punishments." Do you agree with this cartoonist's use of the word "cruel"? Why, or why not?

What are some of the things this cartoonist identifies as causing problems in American courts? What can be done to solve these problems?

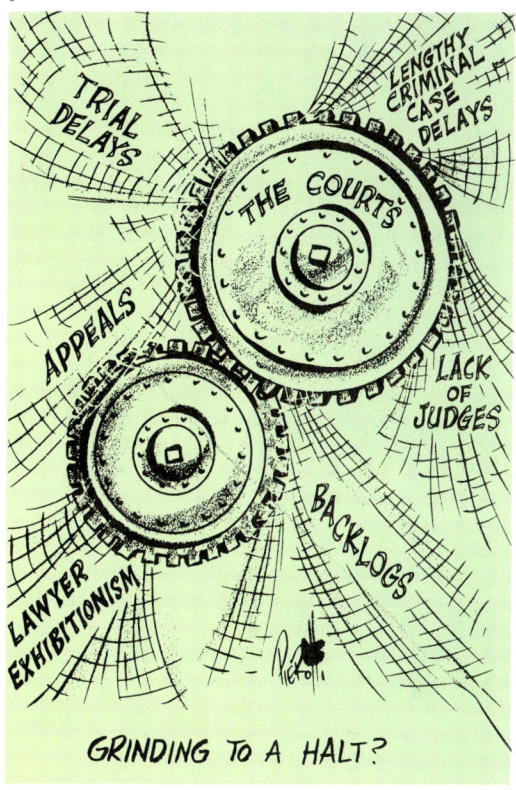

With this problem in mind, investigate the work load of courts in your own community. Your best sources of information will likely be judges and other court officials, reporters who cover court cases, and lawyers. Using these sources, ask about the problem of clogged courts. Many people believe that speedier trials give us one of the best means of fighting crime. There is also the feeling that speedier trials offer better justice for the accused. Do the people interviewed agree with these beliefs? Having made an investigation, do you think there are any major difficulties in obtaining justice in your local courts? What changes might improve the local courts?

THE ROLE OF THE COURTS

Citizenship Laboratory

Review of Basic Ideas

1. The United States has a government based on law, not on the desires of a few strong leaders. These laws are upheld and at times interpreted by judges in American courts. Although most American law is statutory—passed by legislative bodies—American courts also use common law and equity. Most court cases are civil cases. However, criminal cases generally receive more public attention. Among the many rights Americans have in our court system is the right to a trial by jury in most criminal cases and in many civil cases. Civil cases may be decided by petit juries or by judges. Criminal cases are generally heard first by grand juries and then by petit juries.

2. The United States Supreme Court, the highest court in the land, is the only court mentioned specifically in the Constitution. Cases involving the Constitution and other matters of national importance can be appealed to the Supreme Court from federal and state courts. The right of judicial review allows the Supreme Court to declare acts of Congress unconstitutional. The power of the Supreme Court is checked by the presidential power of appointment and by a number of congressional powers. Congress may set the size of the Supreme Court, impeach officers of the Court, and propose amendments to the Constitution. Over the years, Congress has set up a number of lesser federal courts. Today there are almost 100 United States District Courts, each with a United States District Attorney. Federal cases can be appealed from the District Courts to the 11 United States Courts of Appeal and then, if necessary, to the Supreme Court. The federal court system also includes special courts such as the Court of Claims and the Customs Court.

3. Each state also has a supreme court, although the name of this court varies from state to state. States also have a number of major state trial courts and even more minor state trial courts. In many cities, there are courts set up to hear special kinds of cases. Among these are juvenile courts, small claims courts, and traffic courts.

4. All judges in the federal courts are appointed by the President with the approval of the Senate. These federal judges have lifetime terms. By contrast, most of the judges in the state courts are elected. Generally, they are given relatively short terms.

Questions to Think About

1. How would you interpret the phrase "equal justice under law"? To what extent do you think equal justice is available to all Americans today?

2. Should a judge, in deciding a case, depend more on legal tradition, statutory law, or the nature of present-day conditions? Explain your answer.

3. How does equity differ from common law and statutory law? In what kinds of cases might equity be used?

4. What is the difference between civil cases and criminal cases? Why do you think there is more likely to be a jury trial in criminal cases? Would you favor jury trials for most civil cases? Why, or why not?

5. In what ways can judicial review be used to protect the liberties of all Americans?

6. Many cities have set up juvenile courts to deal with cases involving young people. Do you favor or oppose the idea of special courts for young people? Why?

7. Do you think the judges in the state courts should be appointed? Why, or why not?

Words and Relationships

Define each of the terms in the first column. Then show how each term is related to the item listed opposite it by using both items in a sentence or short paragraph.

1.	common law	English tradition
2.	equity	equal justice
3.	statutory law	legislative branch
4.	civil case	private rights
5.	criminal case	social rights
6.	felony	safety on the streets
7.	misdemeanor	personal protection
8.	grand jury	indictment
9.	petit jury	legal training
10.	appeal	United States Supreme Court

Building a Future

In the summer of 1967, the Senate, by an overwhelming majority, approved President Johnson's appointment of Thurgood Marshall to the Supreme Court. Marshall was the son of a Pullman porter and great-grandson of a slave. In 1967, he became the first black justice in the country's history. His appointment drew attention to a basic feature of our judicial system—the judges who preside over the courts.

As America continues to pursue the goal of equal rights, one important movement is toward equal access to the judiciary, whether through appointment or election. More and more people agree that judgeships must be open to all qualified Americans. Evidence of the strength of the movement is seen in the appointment and election of black judges. It is also seen in the appointment and election of women judges.

Examine the makeup of the courts in your state. Who are the judges in your state court system? Is there evidence of judges with few qualifications? Would it appear desirable to have more younger judges? Are there many women judges? Is there any evidence that black lawyers or lawyers from other ethnic minorities do not have an equal opportunity to become judges? If there is evidence of a lack of equal opportunity, what can be done to improve the situation?

Citizenship Laboratory

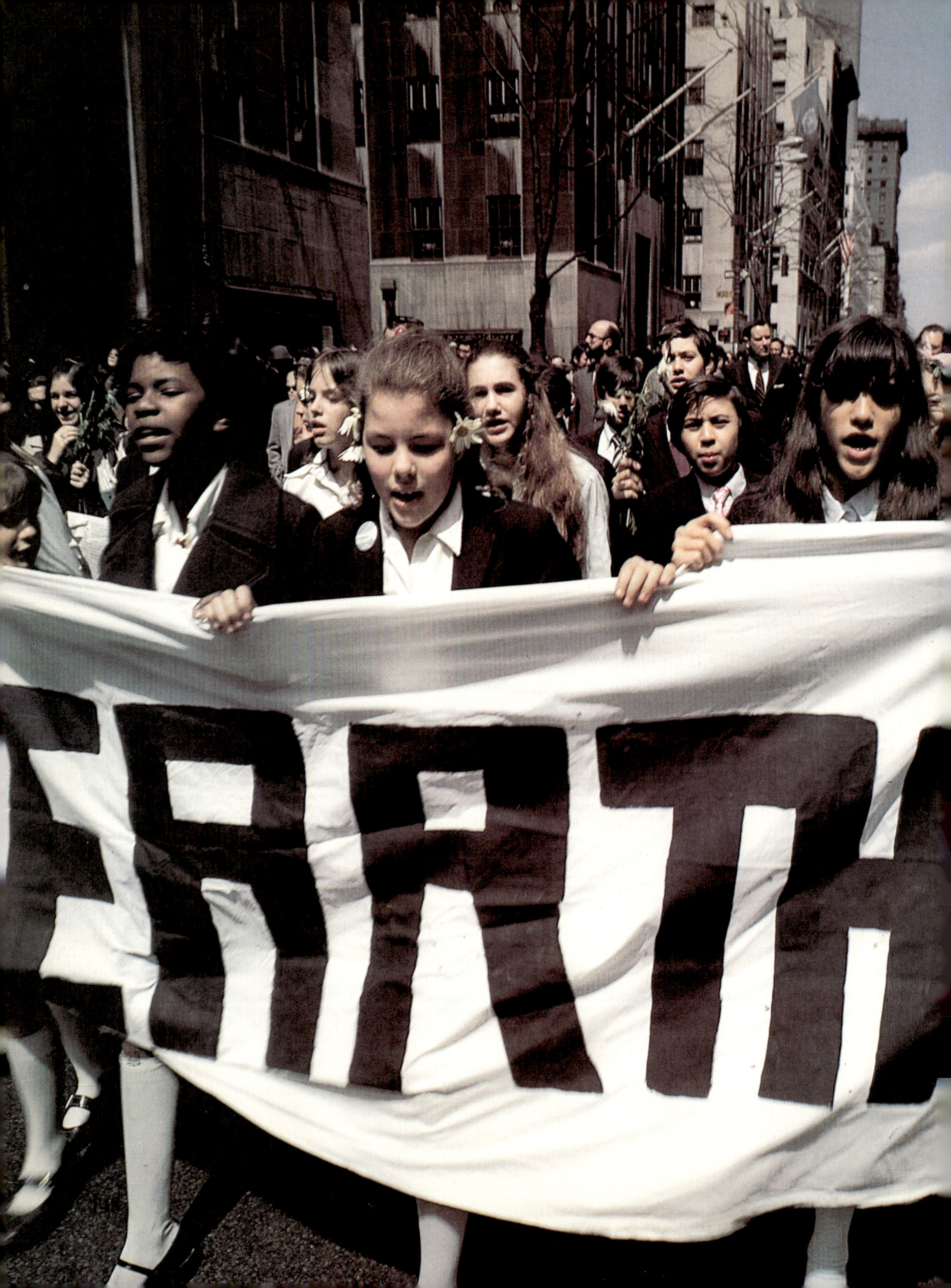

Unit Three
Civic Rights and Responsibilities

7 Constitutional Rights of the American People

One of the most important guarantees of American liberties and freedom is the United States Constitution. That is why it is a part of your textbook. You will find the complete Constitution at the end of the book.

Certain parts of the Constitution are especially important to us as guarantees of our liberty. Mention has already been made of the first 10 amendments. These amendments are generally called the Bill of Rights. However, the idea of an American bill of rights can easily be expanded to include the 13th, 14th, and 15th Amendments. These were added after the Civil War, mainly to protect the rights of newly freed black Americans. The 19th Amendment could also be added. It gave women the right to vote. And the 26th Amendment, which lowered the voting age to 18, might also be considered a part of our bill of rights. There are also a number of clauses in the original Constitution that are directly concerned with our rights.

In this chapter we will study these clauses and amendments. We will try to understand how each relates to our liberties as Americans. But the Constitution is a complex document. Even judges disagree about its exact meaning. So be prepared for less than exact answers.

Liberties Guaranteed in 1787

The Constitution, as written in 1787, contains certain basic guarantees of liberty. These guarantees protect us from arbitrary or unreasonable actions by the government. Each is the result of certain experiences people have had in the long struggle for human freedom.

HABEAS CORPUS
Article I, Section 9

Section 9 of Article I of the Constitution lists a number of powers denied to Congress. In the box below you can see the clause concerning *habeas corpus.* The clause forbids Congress to suspend the writ of *habeas corpus* except under special conditions. A writ of *habeas corpus* is a written court order concerning a person who has been arrested. It requires that an arrested person be brought before a judge. The judge must decide whether or not the person should be kept in jail before being tried. The purpose of such a writ is to prevent unreasonable imprisonment. By forbidding the suspension of the writ, the people who wrote our Constitution sought to protect this important right of the American people.

So important is *habeas corpus* that a leading authority has called it "the most important human rights provision in the Constitution." The reason for making the writ of *habeas corpus* a part of our Constitution goes very deep into English history, back to the Magna Charta. Without the protection of *habeas corpus*, it was common for rulers to throw people who did not agree with them into prison. No reasons had to be given for throwing these people into prison. The people were given no chance to have a hearing before a judge.

One thing to note are those words in the clause that allow our government to ignore the writ of *habeas corpus* in certain cases. The writ may be suspended "when in cases of rebellion or invasion the public safety may require it." Here we have one of many constitutional complexities. How, for instance, might people differ about the meaning of the word "rebellion"? Who is to decide when the public safety might require suspension of the writ?

Does public safety call for the suspension of the writ of habeas corpus *in situations such as the one shown below? How would you define "public safety"?*

> **LIMITED SUSPENSION OF THE WRIT OF *HABEAS CORPUS*:**
> **Article I, Section 9, Paragraph 2 of the Constitution**
>
> The privilege of the writ of *habeas corpus* shall not be suspended, unless when in cases of rebellion or invasion the public safety may require it.

CONSTITUTIONAL RIGHTS OF THE AMERICAN PEOPLE

The writ has been suspended only once in American history. This was in 1861, at the beginning of the Civil War. President Lincoln issued a general proclamation aimed at people who were charged with being disloyal to the Union. Thousands of people were arrested and brought before military courts. They were thus denied trial by jury. The President agreed that, because of his action, these people were not allowed to enjoy a basic right. He defended his action, however, on the grounds that it would keep people from being influenced to commit acts of treason.

Lincoln's act was challenged as unconstitutional by the United States Supreme Court. The Court argued that the power to suspend the writ rested with Congress. Lincoln ignored the Court. Finally in 1863 Congress passed an act giving the President power to suspend the writ when, in the President's judgment, the action was needed to protect the country. The weight of legal opinion since that time is that President Lincoln did act unconstitutionally, but that he had good reasons for doing so.

PROTECTION FROM BILLS OF ATTAINDER AND *EX POST FACTO* LAWS   Article I, Sections 9 and 10

Two other important rights are also guaranteed in Section 9 of Article I. In the box at the top of the next column you will see two terms: bill of attainder and *ex post facto*. These terms are names for two forms of law that are not allowed in the United States.

A bill of attainder is a law that singles out one person or one group of people and punishes them without a trial by jury. A few years ago, the United

> **CONGRESS MAY NOT PASS BILLS OF ATTAINDER AND *EX POST FACTO* LAWS: Article I, Section 9, Paragraph 3 of the Constitution**
>
> No bill of attainder or *ex post facto* law shall be passed.

States Supreme Court decided that a law passed by Congress included a bill of attainder. One part of the law made it a crime for a member of the Communist Party to serve as an officer or employee of a labor union. In other words, the law singled out members of the Communist Party for punishment without trial by jury. The Supreme Court decided that this part of the law was unconstitutional.

An *ex post facto* law is a law that punishes a person for doing something that was not illegal when the person did it. Right now in the United States, people can legally buy and sell gold. At some time in the future, Congress may pass a law that makes it illegal to buy and sell gold. But Congress may not pass a law that would lead to the arrest of those who had bought and sold gold only before the new law was passed.

Section 9 of Article I deals only with laws passed by Congress. As you can see in the box below, Section 10 of Article I places the same limits on laws passed by state legislatures.

> **STATES MAY NOT PASS BILLS OF ATTAINDER AND *EX POST FACTO* LAWS: Article I, Section 10, Paragraph 1 of the Constitution**
>
> No State shall . . . pass any bill of attainder, *ex post facto* law, or law impairing the obligation of contracts . . .

LIMITED DEFINITION OF TREASON   Article III, Section 3

Section 3 of Article III (shown in the box at the right) deals with American ideas about treason. The first paragraph is of special interest. It gives a definition of treason against the United States. Treason is the only crime defined in the Constitution.

Why did the constitution makers define treason? They knew from their own experiences and from their study of history how often simple criticism of the government had been called treason. For this reason, they believed it necessary to define treason in very specific terms.

The second paragraph of Section 3 is also of interest. In it the constitution makers showed that they were against a certain practice still common at the time in Europe. In Europe, the entire family of a person convicted of treason was often forced to give up all its property. Sometimes all members of the family were forced to leave the country. The words in the second paragraph of Section 3 keep this from happening in the United States.

During two relatively recent periods of American history, there were those who thought that large numbers of Americans were committing treason. Following World War I, people in the United States Department of Justice accused thousands of people of having radical ideas. One result of the so-called "Red Scare" was that a large number of aliens were forced to leave the United States. Following World War II, during what has been called the McCarthy Era, many Americans were accused of being influenced by the Communist Party.

> **LIMITED DEFINITION OF TREASON:**
> **Article III, Section 3,**
> **Paragraphs 1 and 2 of the Constitution**
>
> Treason against the United States shall consist only in levying war against them, or in adhering to their enemies, giving them aid and comfort. No person shall be convicted of treason unless on the testimony of two witnesses to the same overt act, or on confession in open court.
>
> The Congress shall have power to declare the punishment of treason, but no attainder of treason shall work corruption of blood, or forfeiture except during the life of the person attainted.

Among those accused, often with no proof at all, were a number of government officials. Today many people feel that, during these two periods, the definition of treason was expanded far beyond its constitutional meaning.

Getting the Facts

1. In what way is each of the following a protection of individual liberty: (a) a limited suspension of the writ of *habeas corpus*; (b) a ban on bills of attainder; (c) a ban on *ex post facto* laws?

2. How does the Constitution define treason? Why is treason defined?

Thinking About Liberty

■ In the next few sections you will read about the additional liberties guaranteed in the amendments to the Constitution. Before you read these sections make your own list of important liberties that are missing from the Constitution as it was written in 1787. Save the list and review it after you complete this chapter.

CONSTITUTIONAL RIGHTS OF THE AMERICAN PEOPLE

Personal Liberties in the Bill of Rights

The first four amendments to the Constitution concern, in one way or another, matters of personal liberty. They protect our rights to think our own thoughts, to act the way we choose, and to enjoy privacy in our own homes.

FREEDOM OF RELIGION, EXPRESSION, AND ASSOCIATION
The 1st Amendment

As you can see in the box at the right, the language of the 1st Amendment is short and simple. Don't let this simplicity fool you. The amendment says a great deal in a few words. A justice of the United States Supreme Court has called the 1st Amendment "the heart of our government." The kind of protection it gives from government interference had never before been given to any people in any country.

The 1st Amendment speaks of three kinds of freedom. These are freedom of religion, freedom of expression, and freedom of association.

The first of the rights given in the 1st Amendment is the right to choose our own religions. In Europe, and in many of the English colonies, the people had been forced to follow the religion of the government.

The 1st Amendment also gives the American people the right to express their own ideas, both orally and in writing. The right to "petition the government" gives the American people yet another way to express their ideas.

Finally, the American people are given the right to meet together. They

> **FREEDOM OF RELIGION, EXPRESSION, AND ASSOCIATION:** The 1st Amendment to the Constitution
>
> Congress shall make no law respecting an establishment of religion, or prohibiting the free exercise thereof; or abridging the freedom of speech, or of the press; or the right of the people peaceably to assemble, and to petition the government for a redress of grievances.

have the right to form associations, or groups, of like-minded people. Today the right to form whatever groups we please seems natural. However, at one time, governments felt that it was necessary to control such groups. They were afraid that groups might be formed for the purpose of overthrowing the government.

Which two of the rights guaranteed in the 1st Amendment are these people making use of?

CIVIC RIGHTS AND RESPONSIBILITIES

As written, the 1st Amendment covered only laws of Congress. This was changed in 1868 when the 14th Amendment was added to the Constitution. Through later decisions by the United States Supreme Court, the 14th Amendment made the 1st Amendment binding on all governments in our country—national, state, and local.

THE RIGHT TO BEAR ARMS AND THE RIGHT *NOT* TO QUARTER TROOPS
The 2nd and 3rd Amendments

As you read the 2nd and 3rd Amendments, you may decide that they are the products of another day and age. The 3rd Amendment may bring to mind certain events in American history. You may remember how the British forced colonists to let soldiers live in their homes during the period just before the American Revolution. It was because of this kind of action that the 3rd Amendment was written. You are probably right if you think that this amendment is not of great importance to us today. No one has tried to quarter troops in American homes for the last 200 years.

The wording of the 2nd Amendment is also old-fashioned but the ideas are still important today. We seldom use the word militia now. However, states still have their own militias. Oddly enough, these state militias are now called the National Guard. Much of the money used to support the National Guard comes from the national government. But the National Guard units are still under state control. The units are generally called into action during natural disasters such as floods. They may also be called into action during civil disturbances when local police forces seem to need help.

The right to bear arms is also a live issue today. In today's terms, this part of

> **THE RIGHT TO BEAR ARMS:** The 2nd Amendment to the Constitution
>
> A well regulated militia, being necessary to the security of a free State, the right of the people to keep and bear arms, shall not be infringed.

> **THE RIGHT *NOT* TO QUARTER TROOPS:** The 3rd Amendment to the Constitution
>
> No soldier shall, in time of peace, be quartered in any house, without the consent of the owner, nor in time of war, but in a manner to be prescribed by law.

What is this cartoonist saying about guns in America today? Do you agree or disagree? Why?

"HEY, POP, YOU THINK CIGARETTES ARE REALLY DANGEROUS?"

CONSTITUTIONAL RIGHTS OF THE AMERICAN PEOPLE

What purposes did firearms serve in the early years of our country? What purposes do they serve today? Do you think this change in the use of firearms should make any difference in the way the 2nd Amendment is interpreted today? Why, or why not?

the 2nd Amendment involves our right to own and use guns, rifles, and other such weapons. Recently, many people have begun to question this right. Some have argued that it should be greatly limited. Pressures to limit the right to bear arms became very strong after the assassinations of President John F. Kennedy, presidential candidate Robert F. Kennedy, and black leader Martin Luther King, Jr. More recently, Americans have seen attempts on the lives of former Alabama Governor George Wallace and President Gerald Ford. However, others argue that we should keep what they feel is an important American right. Many of these people enjoy the sport of hunting. Others feel they need guns to protect themselves, their families, and their property. What attitudes do you find in your own community toward gun control laws?

THE RIGHT OF PRIVACY
The 4th Amendment

Under the terms of the 4th Amendment, a law-enforcement officer may not search a person or a person's home without first getting a warrant from a judge. A warrant is also needed before a person's property can be taken. Warrants are legal documents. A warrant must give the name of the person or a descrip-

> **THE RIGHT OF PRIVACY: The 4th Amendment to the Constitution**
>
> The right of the people to be secure in their persons, houses, papers, and effects, against unreasonable searches and seizures, shall not be violated, and no warrants shall issue, but upon probable cause, supported by oath or affirmation, and particularly describing the place to be searched, and the persons or things to be seized.

156 CIVIC RIGHTS AND RESPONSIBILITIES

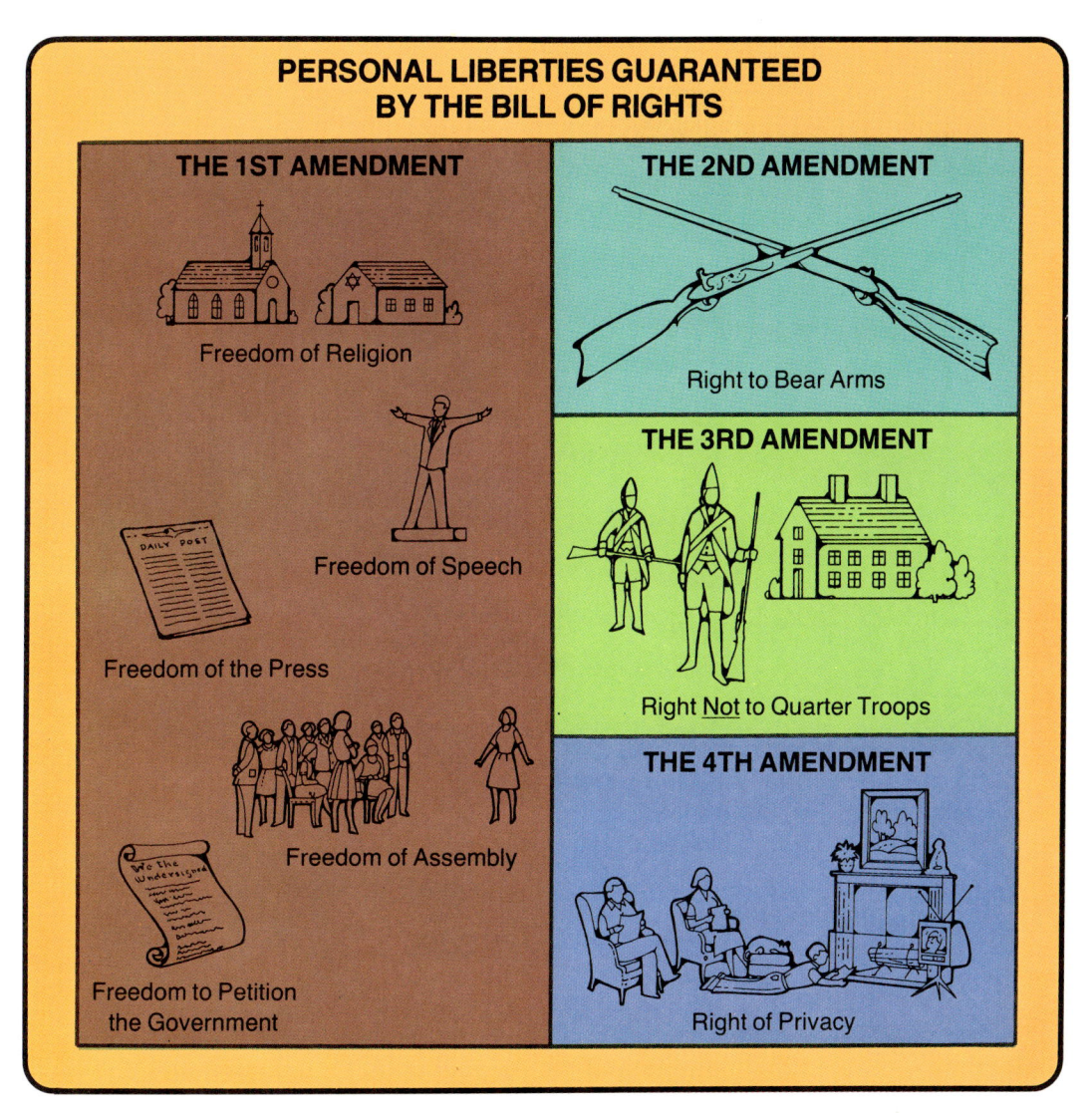

PERSONAL LIBERTIES GUARANTEED BY THE BILL OF RIGHTS

THE 1ST AMENDMENT
- Freedom of Religion
- Freedom of Speech
- Freedom of the Press
- Freedom of Assembly
- Freedom to Petition the Government

THE 2ND AMENDMENT
- Right to Bear Arms

THE 3RD AMENDMENT
- Right Not to Quarter Troops

THE 4TH AMENDMENT
- Right of Privacy

---

tion of the place to be searched. Any property to be taken must also be listed.

Judges may not give warrants unless there is a good reason. Usually, the reason involves the prevention of a crime. In most cases, a general warrant—that is, one that lists no specific person, place, or thing—is not legal.

For obvious reasons, the 4th Amendment has generally come to be known as the "right of privacy" amendment. Imagine what it would be like to live in a country where there is no such right.

Getting the Facts
■ Give at least one personal liberty that is guaranteed by each of the first four amendments to the Constitution.

Examining the Issues
■ It has been argued that the need to obtain warrants from judges greatly limits the efficiency of law-enforcement officers. Which do you think more important: (a) possibly capturing more law-breakers by removing the need for warrants, or (b) continuing to protect the privacy of all Americans by keeping the need for warrants? Explain.

CONSTITUTIONAL RIGHTS OF THE AMERICAN PEOPLE

Speaking Out

William O. Douglas

William O. Douglas served for many years as an associate justice of the United States Supreme Court. He often spoke in favor of civil liberty for all Americans. Here he states his belief that legal dissent has often been treated as unlawful conduct in this country. He believes that certain people and groups who do not agree with the opinion of the majority have not been given a fair chance to voice their opinions publicly.

"Although television and radio time as well as newspaper space is available to the affluent members of this society to disseminate their views, most people cannot afford that space. Hence, the means of protest, and the customary manner of dissent in America, from the days of the American Revolution, has been pamphleteering.

"Other methods of expression, however, are also protected by the First Amendment—from picketing, to marching on the city streets, to walking to the State Capital or to Congress, to assembling in parks and the like.

"It was historically the practice of state police to use such labels as 'breach of the peace' or 'disorderly conduct' to break up groups of minorities who were protesting in these unorthodox ways. The real crime of the dissenters was that they were out of favor with the Establishment, and breach of the peace or disorderly conduct was used merely as a cloak to conceal the true motive of the prosecution."

---

1. If you were a member of a group with a great amount of money, what ways would you choose to voice your opinions? What ways would you choose if you were a member of a group without much money?

2. Justice Douglas argues that protest groups are often not allowed to voice their opinions. What recent examples can you find to support or oppose his argument?

3. To what extent do you agree with Justice Douglas's argument that an equal right of expression should be guaranteed to all groups in America?

Should the Rights Given in the 1st Amendment Apply to Students?

The Bill of Rights gives a number of important freedoms to the American people. Possibly the most important of these are the freedoms of expression and association. These are given in the 1st Amendment. The wording is quite direct. "Congress shall make no law . . . abridging the freedom of speech, or of the press; or the right of the people peaceably to assemble, and to petition the government for a redress of grievances." Without these freedoms, our democracy could not exist. With them, we can discuss, criticize, and even disagree with our government.

More than simply personal rights, these freedoms provide a kind of self-correcting mechanism for our democracy. Because we as citizens can discuss and criticize our government, problems can be identified quickly. Public pressure can be used to help correct the problems. This is one reason why democracy works. In totalitarian and authoritarian governments, the people are not free to criticize the government. Government leaders may not even know that certain problems exist. This lack of knowledge may lead to the downfall of their governments.

However, even in a democracy there are limitations on freedom. Freedom of speech, as one justice of the United States Supreme Court put it, does not give a person the right to cry "fire!" in a crowded theater—when there is no fire. Freedom of speech and freedom of the press are limited by libel and slander laws. Libel is a written statement that unfairly dishonors the character of a person. Slander is a spoken statement that does the same thing. Both are illegal. However, court decisions are generally needed to decide whether or not some statement is truly a matter of libel or slander.

Do most young people in America have as much freedom as adults do? Do they enjoy the same rights of expression and association? If not, should they enjoy these rights?

A number of reasons can be given for not giving young students in school the same freedoms that adults enjoy. Many argue that before students can begin to fully enjoy the rights of citizenship they must learn about the responsibilities of citizenship. Students must also learn about the limits of American freedom—about laws such as those covering libel and slander. They must learn about the consequences of overstepping the limits placed on our freedom. Another argument against giving young students full rights involves the question of legal responsibility. Although laws vary from state to state, it is generally true that young people under the age of 18 do not have the same legal responsibility for their actions that adults do. If students print libelous statements in a school newspaper, the school might well be called upon to bear the costs of a legal suit. For reasons such as these, many parents and schools continue to place limits on what young people may say and write.

A somewhat different point of view is seen in a resolution on "Rights and Responsibilities for Senior High School Students." It was adopted by the New

Inquiry

These young people are protesting the building of a nuclear power plant in their community. Do you think they should be allowed to carry this protest action into the public schools? Why, or why not?

York City Board of Education in 1969. The following is a part of the resolution:

"Students may exercise their constitutionally protected rights of free speech and assembly so long as they do not interfere with the operation of the regular school program. (a) Students have a right to wear political buttons, arm bands and other badges of symbolic expression. (b) Students may distribute political leaflets, newspapers, and other literature, without prior authorization, at locations adjacent to the school. (c) Students shall be allowed to distribute leaflets, newspapers, and other literature with prior authorization at specified locations and times designated within the school for that purpose . . . it is clearly the intention of the Board of Education to promote the dissemination of diverse viewpoints and to foster discussion of all political and social issues. Decisions under this section restricting the distribution of literature within the school for the reasons stated above shall be made by the Principal, or with his agreement by some other body which shall consist of students and faculty. Such decisions may be reviewed by the supervising assistant superintendent and later by the Chancellor and the central board. (d) Students may form political and social organizations, including those that champion unpopular causes, providing they are open to all students and governed by the regulations pertaining to student government regarding extracurricular activities."

Freedom for Students?

Do you think the statement by the New York City Board of Education gives students too much liberty, too little liberty, or just about the right amount of liberty?

What arguments could be used to defend the idea that students should stick to their books and not bother school boards with issues that may have nothing to do with school? What arguments could be used to oppose this idea?

Does your school system have any statement of student rights? If not, would you favor or oppose a statement such as the one you have just read. Explain.

Legal Justice Guaranteed in the Bill of Rights

Justice in courts of law is a matter of great importance to the people of a free country. It is a matter that is dealt with in a number of ways in the Bill of Rights. The 5th, 6th, 7th, and 8th Amendments all deal with our rights to legal justice.

THE GRAND JURY, DOUBLE JEOPARDY, SELF-INCRIMINATION, AND DUE PROCESS OF LAW
The 5th Amendment

The 5th Amendment is one of the most important amendments to the Constitution. It is also one of the most controversial. Many people have argued strongly for and against the rights given by this amendment.

> **RIGHT TO GRAND JURY HEARING, PROTECTION FROM DOUBLE JEOPARDY AND SELF-INCRIMINATION, RIGHT TO DUE PROCESS OF LAW:**
> **The 5th Amendment to the Constitution**
>
> No person shall be held to answer for a capital, or otherwise infamous crime, unless on a presentment or indictment of a grand jury, except in cases arising in the land or naval forces, or in the militia, when in actual service in time of war or public danger; nor shall any person be subject for the same offense to be twice put in jeopardy of life or limb; nor shall be compelled in any criminal case to be a witness against himself, nor be deprived of life, liberty, or property, without due process of law; nor shall private property be taken for public use without just compensation.

In one short paragraph, it gives a whole series of protections. It helps protect our very basic right to life, liberty, and property. Four basic rights are listed in the 5th Amendment. These involve the grand jury, the ideas of double jeopardy and self-incrimination, and our right to due process of law.

First let us look at that part of the amendment that deals with the grand jury. The amendment states that people cannot be brought to trial for a crime without the decision of a grand jury. A grand jury is a group of citizens appointed by a court to hear charges against an accused person. The grand jury decides if the charges are important enough to bring the person to trial. As the amendment states, the only exception to this rule is in the case of a person serving in the armed forces in time of war or other national emergency.

Next, let us consider the idea of double jeopardy. The 5th Amendment states that no person shall "be subject for the same offense to be twice put in jeopardy of life or limb." In today's terms this means that, after a person has been acquitted or cleared by a court, the person may not be brought to trial again for the same crime. With this right, people found innocent of crimes are free to resume their normal lives. Without the right, these people might be tried again and again. They might be forced to live the rest of their lives in fear of being, at some point, found guilty. The idea of protecting people from double jeopardy has been around for a long time. It was written into the Body of Liberties of Massachusetts in 1641. It was also a part of many early state constitutions. Today, all but five states

LEGAL JUSTICE GUARANTEED IN THE BILL OF RIGHTS

THE 5TH AMENDMENT

Right to grand jury hearing in criminal cases

Protection from double jeopardy: People cannot be tried twice for the same crime.

Protection from self-incrimination: People do not have to testify against themselves in criminal cases.

Right to due process of law: Legal procedures protect people from unreasonable government interference.

THE 6TH AMENDMENT

Right to a fair and speedy trial by jury in criminal cases

THE 7TH AMENDMENT

Right to trial by jury in certain civil cases

THE 8TH AMENDMENT

Right to fair bail, fair fines, and fair punishment

---

have double-jeopardy clauses in their constitutions.

The idea of double jeopardy seems simple enough. However, it is often difficult for the courts to interpret. An interesting example of this difficulty can be seen in a court case in Louisiana. A person was sentenced to death but remained alive because the electric chair did not work. The condemned person appealed to the United States Supreme Court, arguing that a second death warrant issued by the state was an example of double jeopardy. The Supreme Court denied the appeal. The Court upheld the state's right to execute the prisoner. The Court's decision, however, was 5 to 4. That is, four of the Supreme Court justices believed that the second warrant did, indeed, place the prisoner in double jeopardy.

The 5th Amendment also protects people from self-incrimination. The amendment states that people cannot be forced to testify against themselves in criminal cases. When people follow this part of the 5th Amendment and refuse to testify against themselves, they are often said to be "taking the 5th." In general, they are simply refusing to say that they are guilty of any crimes.

In recent years, many Americans have begun to question our right to protect ourselves from self-incrimination. They are aware of the fact that known criminals have refused to testify against themselves hundreds of times during congressional investigations. Many people today believe that known lawbreakers should not be given the right to "take the 5th."

The people who wrote the Bill of Rights, on the other hand, had strong feelings about this part of the 5th Amendment. They remembered the way that torture and other cruel measures had been used to force innocent people to give false testimony against themselves. In our own time, a justice of the United States Supreme Court has called our protection from self-incrimination "one of the greatest heritages we have."

Finally, let us turn to our right to due process of law. The 5th Amendment states that no person shall "be deprived of life, liberty, or property, without due process of law." The idea of due process of law has deep roots in our heritage of liberty. The words are found in English laws as early as the 14th century. Yet, even today, the words are hard to define. In one sense, due process of law protects us from unreasonable actions taken by the government against our lives, liberty, or property. In a broader sense, it means a guarantee that all our liberties will be protected.

One example of the way the due process of law idea works is seen in a case brought before the United States Supreme Court in 1966. Twelve years earlier, in Cleveland, Ohio, a doctor had been convicted of murder. In an 8 to 1 decision, the Supreme Court ruled that the doctor had not been given a fair trial. The correct legal process had not been followed. The Court ordered that the doctor be freed from prison or retried. In its decision, the Court stated that the original trial had been conducted in a "carnival atmosphere." Much of the blame was placed on the trial judge. While the trial was going on, many newspaper and radio reports had expressed the opinion that the doctor was guilty. The Supreme Court said that the judge should have taken steps to make sure that the jury did not see or hear these reports. Speaking about criminal trials in general, the Court stated, "We note that unfair and prejudicial news comment on pending trials has become increasingly prevalent . . . given the pervasiveness of modern communications, and the difficulty of effacing prejudicial publicity from the minds of the jurors, the trial courts must take strong measures to insure that the balance is never weighed against the accused."

The Supreme Court has also shown concern that young people receive due process of law. Most states have set up special courts to try young people accused of crimes. In general, this is because the punishments for young people are not as severe as those for adults. However, the Supreme Court has taken steps to make sure that the rights of these young people are protected in the same way the rights of an adult are protected. In a case in 1967, involving a

"COME NOW—THERE IS NO SUCH THING AS A BAD BOY..."

What is the cartoonist saying about recent Court interpretations of the Bill of Rights? What changes, if any, do you think should be made in the way people accused of crimes are treated in American courts?

young boy, the Court spoke of the rights of young people:

"A boy is charged with misconduct. The boy is committed to an institution where he may be restrained of liberty for years. It is of no constitutional consequence . . . that the institution to which he is committed is called an industrial school. . . .

"In view of this, it would be extraordinary if our Constitution did not require the procedural regularity and the exercise implied in the phrase 'due process.' Under our Constitution, the condition of being a boy does not justify a kangaroo court. . . .

"In respect of proceedings to determine delinquency which may result in commitment to an institution in which the juvenile's freedom is curtailed, the child and his parent must be notified of the child's right to be represented by counsel retained by them, or if they are unable to afford counsel, the counsel will be appointed to represent the child. . . ."

FAIR TRIALS IN CRIMINAL CASES The 6th Amendment

The 6th Amendment guarantees a fair trial to all people accused of crimes. As with most legal questions, opinions differ about the exact meaning of some of the words in the 6th Amendment. For example, how much time does a "speedy" trial take? Does it take a few days? Or can it take weeks or months? Actually, the time may vary from case to case. In some cases, lawyers may need a long period of time to prepare for trial. Key witnesses may be difficult to locate. The accused person may become sick.

164 CIVIC RIGHTS AND RESPONSIBILITIES

The United States Supreme Court has clearly defined one part of the 6th Amendment. The right of counsel is the right to have legal aid whether or not an accused person can pay for it. In *Gideon v. Wainwright* (1963), the Court ruled that states must supply free lawyers to poor people accused of crimes. The decision included these words:

". . . any person haled into court, who is too poor to hire a lawyer, cannot be assured a fair trial unless counsel is provided for him. . . . Governments, both state and federal, quite properly spend vast sums of money to establish machinery to try defendants accused of crime. Lawyers to prosecute are everywhere deemed essential to protect the public's interest in an orderly society. Similarly, there are few defendants charged with crime, few indeed, who fail to hire the best lawyers they can get to prepare and present their defense. That government hires lawyers to prosecute and defendants who have the money hire lawyers to defend are the strongest indications of the widespread belief that lawyers in criminal courts are necessities and not luxuries. . . ."

What is this cartoonist's view of justice in America? To what extent do you agree or disagree?

TRIAL BY JURY IN CIVIL CASES
The 7th Amendment

As we saw in Chapter 6, Article III, Section 2 of the Constitution guarantees trial by jury in all federal criminal cases except in cases of impeachment. The 6th Amendment offers guarantees that such trials be as fair as possible. The importance of the 7th Amendment lies in its

---

RIGHT TO A FAIR TRIAL IN FEDERAL CRIMINAL CASES:
The 6th Amendment to the Constitution

In all criminal prosecutions, the accused shall enjoy the right to a speedy and public trial, by an impartial jury of the State and district wherein the crime shall have been committed, which district shall have been previously ascertained by law, and to be informed of the nature and cause of the accusation; to be confronted with the witnesses against him; to have compulsory process for obtaining witnesses in his favor, and to have the assistance of counsel for his defense.

RIGHT TO TRIAL BY JURY IN FEDERAL CIVIL CASES: **The 7th Amendment to the Constitution**

In suits at common law, where the value in controversy shall exceed twenty dollars, the right of trial by jury shall be preserved, and no fact tried by a jury shall be otherwise reexamined in any court of the United States, than according to the rules of the common law.

guarantee, under certain conditions, of the right to trial by jury in federal civil cases. The conditions are that the case must involve a sum of more than $20 and be tried according to common law.

Today, with a few exceptions, the right to trial by jury is generally guaranteed in state criminal cases. A number of states also guarantee jury trials, under certain conditions, in civil cases.

Interestingly enough, the Constitution never defines the term trial by jury. At the time the Constitution was written, most juries were made up of 12 people. The United States Supreme Court has generally ruled that a jury of 12 people is needed for federal court trials. State courts, on the other hand, have experimented with juries of different sizes.

FAIR BAIL, FAIR FINES, AND FAIR PUNISHMENT
The 8th Amendment

The 8th Amendment is very short, but it does need some explanation. One part of the amendment involves the idea of bail. When a person is arrested, the court may allow the person to pay a certain amount of money, known as bail. After paying bail, the person is set free until the time for the trial. The bail acts as a guarantee that the person will return for trial. The money is given back when the person returns. However, if the person does not return, the court keeps the bail. The 8th Amendment prevents the courts from asking for unfair amounts of bail.

The 8th Amendment also prevents the courts from setting fines that are too high or prison sentences that are too long. Cruel forms of punishment such as torture are forbidden.

> **RIGHT TO FAIR BAIL, FAIR FINES, AND FAIR PUNISHMENT:**
> **The 8th Amendment to the Constitution**
>
> Excessive bail shall not be required, nor excessive fines imposed, nor cruel and unusual punishments inflicted.

The problem presented by the words of the 8th Amendment is obvious. What is the meaning of the words "excessive," "cruel," and "unusual"? As you might guess, courts differ widely in the ways they define these words. Even so, the words act as a reminder that all Americans should be treated fairly by the American courts. Furthermore, if a person feels that a court has not followed the words of the 8th Amendment, it may be possible to have the case appealed to a higher court.

Getting the Facts

1. List at least six ways in which the Bill of Rights seeks to guarantee fair trials to all Americans.

2. Why is the 5th Amendment so controversial?

3. What decision did the United States Supreme Court make in *Gideon v. Wainwright*?

Examining the Issues

■ The 5th Amendment contains so many details that one of the guarantees—the right to a grand jury hearing—is often overlooked. In what ways does such a guarantee protect the rights of individual citizens? In what way does it serve the government and society?

A General Statement of Liberty

The people who wrote the Bill of Rights knew that it would be impossible to include every human right in the Constitution. They included the ones they thought were most important. They also knew that it would be impossible to list all powers that the state governments should have. For these reasons, the 9th and 10th Amendments were added to the Constitution.

RIGHTS FOR THE PEOPLE
The 9th Amendment

The language used in the 9th Amendment is much more general than the language used in the first eight amendments. The 9th Amendment simply points out that the Constitution does not name every right that the people have. The fact that a right is not named does not mean that the people do not have that right.

> **RIGHTS RETAINED BY THE PEOPLE: The 9th Amendment to the Constitution**
>
> The enumeration in the Constitution of certain rights shall not be construed to deny or disparage others retained by the people.

POWERS RESERVED FOR THE STATES AND THE PEOPLE
The 10th Amendment

The language of the 10th Amendment is also very general. The amendment notes that the national government has been given certain powers by the Constitution. The Constitution also lists certain powers that the national and state governments do not have. However, there are many powers that are not mentioned at all in the Constitution. Following the terms of the 10th Amendment, all powers not mentioned belong to the states or to the American people. The amendment serves two purposes. First, it offers further protection of the rights of the people. Second, it acts to strengthen the idea of a federal system of government.

> **POWERS RESERVED FOR THE STATES AND THE PEOPLE: The 10th Amendment to the Constitution**
>
> The powers not delegated to the United States by the Constitution, nor prohibited by it to the States, are reserved to the States respectively, or to the people.

Getting the Facts

1. What general statement about rights and liberties is contained in the 9th Amendment to the Constitution?

2. What general statement about power is contained in the 10th Amendment to the Constitution?

Forming an Opinion

■ You have now read about all 10 of the amendments in the Bill of Rights. If you had to limit the Bill of Rights to only five amendments which five would you choose? In other words, which five do you think offer the greatest protection of American liberties? Explain the reasons for your choices.

Liberties for All Americans

As noted earlier, the idea of an American bill of rights can easily be expanded to include more than just the first 10 amendments. In fact, if we wish to speak of a bill of rights for all Americans, it is essential to include more than just these 10. When they were written, the first 10 amendments, in many cases, applied only to adult white males. A number of later amendments, added since the Civil War, have helped to guarantee rights to all Americans.

RIGHTS FOR BLACK AMERICANS
The 13th, 14th, and 15th Amendments

The 13th, 14th, and 15th Amendments are sometimes called the emancipation amendments. Emancipation is the act of setting people free. In this case emancipation refers to the end of slavery in America.

As you can see, the 13th Amendment is short. It was added late in 1865, the year the Civil War came to an end. The basic purpose of the amendment was to free slaves in all states and territories of the United States.

The 14th Amendment, in contrast to the 13th, is quite long. It was added in 1868, partly to protect the rights of black Americans. However, it gives important rights to all Americans. For our purposes here, Section 1 and part of Section 2 are most important. Section 1 states, in clear language, the meaning of American citizenship. In like manner, it sets limits on the power of the states to interfere with the rights of Americans.

SLAVERY IS ABOLISHED IN 1865: The 13th Amendment to the Constitution, Section 1

Neither slavery nor involuntary servitude, except as a punishment for crime whereof the party shall have been duly convicted, shall exist within the United States, or any place subject to their jurisdiction.

THE AUTHORITY OF THE NATIONAL GOVERNMENT IS STRENGTHENED IN 1868: The 14th Amendment to the Constitution, Sections 1 and 2

All persons born or naturalized in the United States, and subject to the jurisdiction thereof, are citizens of the United States and of the State wherein they reside. No State shall make or enforce any law which shall abridge the privileges or immunities of citizens of the United States; nor shall any State deprive any person of life, liberty, or property, without due process of law; nor deny to any person within its jurisdiction the equal protection of the laws.

Representatives shall be apportioned among the several States according to their respective numbers, counting the whole number of persons in each State, excluding Indians not taxed. But when the right to vote at any election for the choice of electors for President and Vice President of the United States, representatives in Congress, the executive and judicial officers of a State, or the members of the legislature thereof, is denied to any of the male inhabitants of such State, being twenty-one years of age, and citizens of the United States, or in any way abridged, except for participation in rebellion, or other crime, the basis of representation therein shall be reduced in the proportion which the number of such male citizens shall bear to the whole number of male citizens twenty-one years of age in such State.

Citizens of the United States, the 14th Amendment says, are citizens both of the nation and of the state in which they may live. Each of us, it says, has a right to "equal protection of the laws." That is, our laws may not favor one person over another. Finally, the amendment states that due process of law must be followed by state governments as well as by the national government. The 5th Amendment had guaranteed due process of law only in cases involving the national government.

Section 2 of the 14th Amendment is rather wordy. What it does, among other things, is set up a form of punishment for states that prevent adult male citizens from voting in state or national elections. If a state prevents a person from voting, the state's representation in Congress will be reduced. The real purpose of this was to force states to let black citizens vote. However, in the years since the 14th Amendment was added, no state has ever been punished in this way. In 1965, Congress felt it was necessary to pass a Voting Rights Act. This act led to the registration of thousands of new black voters.

Guaranteeing the right to vote was also the purpose of the 15th Amendment. Added in 1870, the 15th Amendment states that no citizen shall be denied the right to vote because of race or because the person was once a slave.

**RIGHTS FOR AMERICAN WOMEN
The 19th Amendment**

Another amendment having to do with voting rights was added in 1920. The 19th Amendment gave the right to vote to women. Before 1920, women had gained full voting rights in a few states.

> **RIGHT TO VOTE CANNOT BE DENIED BECAUSE OF RACE BEGINNING IN 1870:** The 15th Amendment to the Constitution, Section 1
>
> The right of citizens of the United States to vote shall not be denied or abridged by the United States or by any State on account of race, color, or previous condition of servitude.

> **RIGHT TO VOTE IS GIVEN TO WOMEN IN 1920:** The 19th Amendment to the Constitution, Section 1
>
> The right of citizens of the United States to vote shall not be denied or abridged by the United States or by any State on account of sex.

In other states, women were allowed to take part only in certain types of elections. Often, this involved only the right to vote in school board elections. In many states, women had no voting rights at all. The 19th Amendment gave all American women the right to vote in all elections.

Many Americans thought that giving the vote to women would bring major changes in the kind of candidates elected. How would you explain the fact that no major changes seem to have occurred?

CONSTITUTIONAL RIGHTS OF THE AMERICAN PEOPLE

> **RIGHT TO VOTE IS GIVEN TO 18-YEAR-OLDS IN 1971: The 26th Amendment to the Constitution, Section 1**
>
> The right of citizens of the United States who are eighteen years of age or older to vote shall not be denied or abridged by the United States or by any State on account of age.

RIGHTS FOR YOUNG AMERICANS
The 26th Amendment

Voting rights were extended in another way when the 26th Amendment was added in 1971. This addition to the Constitution gave the right to vote to all citizens who were 18 years of age or older. One effect of the amendment was the addition of more than 11,000,000 young people to the voting roles. Another effect was seen in the fact that many states gave those over age 17 complete rights as adults. Laws that had previously given 21 as a minimum age were changed in many states.

Getting the Facts

1. Why are the 13th, 14th, and 15th Amendments often referred to as the emancipation amendments?

2. In what ways have voting rights been extended by the amendments to the Constitution?

Forming an Opinion

■ The 14th Amendment strengthened the power of the national government. It specifically limited the states' power to run state courts and set voter qualifications. However, as you have seen, it was many years before the states were forced to follow all these limitations. Do you favor or oppose these limitations on state power? Explain.

These young Americans are registering to vote for the first time. At what age do you think American citizens should be given the right to vote? Why?

170   CIVIC RIGHTS AND RESPONSIBILITIES

Has the Struggle for Women's Rights Been Won?

The 19th Amendment was the result of a long struggle for equal rights for American women. It was not as if the contributions of American women had been ignored before 1920. As long ago as the 1830s, the French writer de Tocqueville commented, "If I were asked . . . to what the singular prosperity and growing strength of that people [Americans] ought mainly to be attributed, I should reply: to the superiority of their women."

Be that as it may, many American women in the 1830s keenly felt their lack of certain basic rights. In 1848, a group of women led by Lucretia Mott and Elizabeth Cady Stanton held a convention in Seneca Falls, New York. At this meeting, they adopted the Declaration of Seneca Falls. Written in the style of the Declaration of Independence, it stated, in part:

"We hold these truths to be self evident: that all men and women are created equal; that they are endowed by their Creator with certain inalienable rights; that among these are life, liberty and the pursuit of happiness. . . .

"The history of mankind is a history of repeated injuries and usurpations on the part of man toward woman, having in direct object the establishment of an absolute tyranny over her. To prove this, let the facts be submitted to a candid world.

- He has never permitted her to exercise her inalienable right to the elective franchise [vote].
- He has compelled her to submit to laws in the formation of which she had no voice.
- He has withheld from her rights which are given to the most ignorant and degraded men, both natives and foreigners.
- Having deprived her of this first right of a citizen, the elective franchise, thereby leaving her without representation in the halls of legislation, he has oppressed her on all sides. . . .

"Now, in view of this entire disfranchisement of one-half of the people of this country, their social and religious degradation, in view of the unjust laws above mentioned, and because women do feel themselves aggrieved, oppressed, and fraudulently deprived of their most sacred rights, we insist that they have immediate admission to all rights and privileges which belong to them as citizens of the United States. . . ."

Note that there was an interval of 72 years between the Seneca Falls declaration and the adoption of the 19th Amendment. But even this amendment was not enough to end the struggle for women's rights. In 1972, a new struggle began. Its purpose was to add a second women's rights amendment to the Constitution. This amendment would give more than voting rights. It was hoped that it would include words such as these: "Equal rights under the law shall not be denied or abridged by the United States or by any state on account of sex."

Whether or not another women's rights amendment is really needed has been a matter of debate for years. Those who favor a new amendment point to such things as discrimination against women in certain kinds of jobs. They point out that in many cases women have received lower pay than men who have the same kinds of jobs. Those who are against the new amendment have pointed to the conclusion reached by the presidential Commission on the Status of Women in 1963. Chaired by Eleanor

Inquiry

Very few women are employed in the American construction industry. To what extent does this fact support the argument that women do not enjoy equal rights in the United States?

Some American women, including Governor Grasso of Connecticut, have been elected to high office. To what extent does this fact support the argument that American women enjoy equal opportunities?

Roosevelt, the commission report stated that "since the commission is convinced that the U.S. Constitution now embodies equality of rights for men and women, we conclude that a constitutional amendment need not now be sought in order to establish this principle."

The conclusion reached by the Roosevelt Commission has recently been strongly opposed by Congresswoman Shirley Chisholm of New York. Chisholm argued not only against the claim that women already have equal rights but also against the idea that women need special protection.

"Existing laws are not adequate to secure equal rights for women. Sufficient proof of this is the concentration of women in lower paying, menial, unrewarding jobs and their incredible scarcity in the upper level jobs. If women are already equal, why is it such an event whenever one happens to be elected to Congress?

"It is obvious that discrimination exists. Women do not have the opportunities that men do. And women that do not conform to the system, who try to break with the accepted patterns, are stigmatized as 'odd' and 'unfeminine.'

The fact is that a woman who aspires to be chairman of the board . . . does so for exactly the same reasons as any man. . . .

"Regarding special protection for working women, I cannot understand why it should be needed. Women need no protection that men do not need. What we need are laws to protect working people, to guarantee them fair pay, safe working conditions, protection against sickness and layoffs, and provisions for dignified, comfortable retirement. Men and women need these things equally. That one sex needs protection more than the other is a male supremacist myth as ridiculous and unworthy of respect as the white supremacist myths that society is trying to cure itself of at this time."

Forming an Opinion

In what ways have the injustices listed in the Seneca Falls declaration of 1848 been corrected?

You have studied the rights guaranteed by the Constitution. To what extent do you agree with the conclusion of the Commission on the Status of Women?

With which of Chisholm's arguments do you agree or disagree? Why?

How Would You Interpret the Words of the Constitution?

As noted before, the Constitution is a complex document. People often do not agree about the meaning of the words in the Constitution and the amendments.

In 1960, a poll was taken to find out how a number of high school students would interpret the words of the Constitution. The students were given a number of statements and asked to say whether or not they thought the ideas expressed in the statements were in accord with the meaning of the Constitution and the amendments. Five of the statements are listed here. Some of them involve the meaning of the first 10 amendments—that is, the meaning of the Bill of Rights. Others involve the meaning of later amendments and some involve the meaning of more than one amendment. Included with each statement are four or five different possible answers. Also included are the percentages of students who gave each answer.

As you read each statement, relate it to one or more of the amendments. Next, give your own response to each statement. Conduct a class survey to find out how many of your classmates choose each of the answers. You now have two sets of data: the 1960 percentages, and the percentages in your own class. Using these two sets of information, conduct an analysis of the results. How do opinions of the students in your class differ from those of students in 1960? If there are major differences, try to find possible reasons for them. In the same way, examine the differences of opinion found within your own class.

1. Newspapers and magazines should be allowed to print anything they want except military secrets.
Agree	29%
Disagree	51%
Undecided	19%
No response	1%

2. The government should prohibit some people from making public speeches.
Agree	25%
Disagree	51%
Uncertain	22%
No response	2%

3. In some cases, the police should be allowed to search a person or his home, even though they do not have a warrant.
Agree	33%
Disagree	57%
Uncertain	8%
No response	2%

4. Pupils of all races and nationalities should attend school together everywhere in this country.
Agree	49%
Undecided; probably agree	18%
Undecided; probably disagree	8%
Disagree	24%
No response	1%

5. People who have wild ideas and don't use good sense should not have the right to vote.
Agree	28%
Undecided; probably agree	13%
Undecided; probably disagree	15%
Disagree	43%
No response	1%

Inquiry

CONSTITUTIONAL RIGHTS OF THE AMERICAN PEOPLE

Citizenship Laboratory

Review of Basic Ideas

1. The Constitution, as written in 1787, contains guarantees of a number of basic liberties. Included here are the rights protected by writs of *habeas corpus*, protection from bills of attainder and *ex post facto* laws, and a limited definition of treason.

2. A number of personal liberties are guaranteed in the first four amendments to the Constitution. The 1st Amendment guarantees freedom of religion, expression, and association. The 2nd Amendment concerns state militias and our right to bear arms. The 3rd Amendment, perhaps the least important of the amendments today, protects us from having to shelter troops in our homes. The 4th Amendment involves our right of privacy.

3. A number of amendments help to guarantee equal justice in American courts. The 5th Amendment gives us the right to a grand jury hearing and protects us from double jeopardy. It also protects us from self-incrimination. Some believe that this right not to testify against ourselves is too often misused by known law-breakers. Others regard it as a basic American liberty. The 5th Amendment also requires federal courts to follow due process of law. The 14th Amendment later extended our right to due process of law to cases in state courts. In many ways, our right to due process of law helps to protect all of our American liberties. The 6th Amendment gives people involved in criminal cases the right to counsel, even if they are too poor to pay a lawyer. The 7th Amendment involves our right to trial by jury in civil cases. The 8th Amendment forbids unfair bail, fines, and punishment.

4. The 9th Amendment was written to protect freedoms that were not specifically mentioned in the Constitution. The 10th Amendment gives all powers that are not mentioned in the Constitution to the states or to the people.

5. In many ways, the first 10 amendments—the Bill of Rights—guaranteed full rights only to adult white males. A number of later amendments helped to guarantee liberties for all Americans. The 13th, 14th, and 15th Amendments were added to protect the rights of black Americans. In addition, the 14th Amendment places certain limits on the power of the state governments. The 19th Amendment was passed to give women the right to vote in all elections. The 26th Amendment has given voting rights to all citizens who are 18 years of age or older.

Questions to Think About

1. What important guarantee of human rights is provided by the *habeas corpus* clause of the Constitution? Under what conditions do you think this right should be suspended?

2. What limits, if any, do you think should be placed on the rights guaranteed in the 1st Amendment? Explain.

3. Which of the legal rights guaranteed in the 5th, 6th, 7th, and 8th Amendments do you think are most important to the majority of the American people? Why?

4. In some places, a person who is well known in a community can be released

from jail without paying any bail. This is called "release on recognizance." Do you think this is a fair procedure? What are some arguments for and against this practice?

5. In what ways does the 10th Amendment help to preserve our federal system of government?

6. Why might it be argued that the 14th Amendment gives American citizens more freedoms than are given by any other amendment?

Words and Relationships

Define each of the terms in the first column. Then show how each term is related to the item listed opposite it by using both items in a sentence or short paragraph.

1.	*habeas corpus*	limited government
2.	bill of attainder	trial by jury
3.	*ex post facto* law	United States Supreme Court
4.	petition	totalitarian governments
5.	grand jury	rights of the accused
6.	double jeopardy	legal justice
7.	self-incrimination	known law-breakers
8.	due process of law	unfair trial
9.	right to counsel	poverty
10.	14th Amendment	federalism

Building a Future

The United States Constitution has been amended a number of times. Many of these amendments have had as their purpose the protection of American liberties. Yet, despite these amendments, many people believe that rights are not equally distributed among the American people. Some groups seem to enjoy more privileges than others. In many cases, the laws seem to operate unfairly.

What can interested citizens do to help assure an equal sharing of rights among all Americans? A useful way to start is with valid information. Using the information in this chapter, prepare a list of constitutional rights. For each right, form an opinion about which groups of citizens may not be receiving full benefits. Gather as many facts as you can to support your opinions. Compare your judgments with those of your classmates.

From the information and ideas gathered, consider actions that might be taken to help bring about greater equality in America. Is it possible, for example, that even in your own school there are some students who have more rights than others? If enough of you feel that this condition exists, think of steps that might be taken to improve the condition. What about your community? Can you find situations here that need correction? Finally, are any situations of inequality so widespread that they require action by congressional legislation or even constitutional amendment?

CONSTITUTIONAL RIGHTS OF THE AMERICAN PEOPLE

8 Responsibilities of Free Citizens

Just as there are two sides to a coin, there are two sides to citizenship in a democracy. One side is liberty. The other is responsibility. Liberty is a great and wonderful gift. But it is a gift that can be given only if people agree to use it in responsible ways.

What are the responsibilities of free citizens? For one thing, responsible citizens should have opinions and ideas that are well thought out. Each of us, in other words, should try to become a member of what early American leaders called an "informed citizenry."

Civic responsibility is not something "for adults only." Most Americans are citizens from the day they are born. For young Americans, one of the most important civic responsibilities is to get an education. Indeed, the strongest argument for setting up our system of free education was the need for every citizen to learn about our society and our government.

In addition to gaining knowledge, civic responsibility involves action. A person may be a well informed citizen but, because of inactivity, a useless one. We can carry out our civic responsibilities in many ways. We can work with others in groups that have been set up for any number of purposes. We can also work for political parties. Certainly, when we reach voting age, we can vote in elections.

The Development of Responsible Opinions

One of the most important responsibilities of young people in a democracy is the development of informed opinions. Nothing is more central to the democratic idea than the idea that government is an expression of the will of the people. It follows that the effectiveness of democracy is measured to an important degree by the extent to which people express intelligent opinions on public issues.

In some ways, it is becoming more and more difficult to form intelligent opinions about public issues. In the early years of our country, voters often had few political decisions to make. Sometimes all they had to do was to choose between the personalities of two people seeking office. In national elections today, by contrast, political parties have long platforms. They state positions on many different public issues.

It is to the credit of the American people that they have tried to keep up with the great changes that are taking place in today's world. Almost a century ago a noted English jurist, James Bryce, came to the United States to see how American government worked. He decided that public opinion in the United States is "on the whole more alert, more vigilant, and more generally active through every class and section of the nation than in any other great state." He went on to say that "nowhere does there exist so large a percentage who have an opinion, and can say why they have an opinion, regarding the merits of a question or of a politician."

THE NATURE OF PUBLIC OPINION

A group of individual opinions makes up something we call "public opinion." In a democracy, the term "public opinion" is also used when we speak of the opinion held by a majority of the people on any question or issue.

One way to better understand the idea of public opinion is to look at the way in which the American political system works. At the base are the opinions of individual Americans. Each of these opinions is the product of many influences. Some come from inside the person. Others come from the world in which the person lives.

The next stage in opinion formation takes place when people with similar views come together. They may do this to protect their interests or to promote certain ideas. To achieve these goals, many different kinds of groups are formed. Some can be quite informal. A group of neighbors may meet in a living room to talk about a problem that concerns them all. Other groups can be very formal and, sometimes, very large. Business associations, labor unions, and farmers' organizations may have hundreds or thousands of members. Any of these groups may use their influence to try to cause government to follow their wishes.

Groups often try to influence government by working through political parties. Each party is interested, of course, in getting its own candidates into office. So each party tries to get as much support as possible from interested people and groups. Almost always, in the process, conflicts arise between different opinions. Parties and candidates generally decide to make compromises,

Candidates for political office often seek out individual opinions so that they can better predict "public opinion."

since they want to get the support of as many people and groups as possible. The party that wins an election can then try to put into practice the opinions of the people who voted for the party.

As you can see, public opinion starts with individual people. Groups are formed. Political parties listen to the opinions of the people and the groups. In this way, the "will of the people" has a great influence on government. To a great extent, the actions of our government are based on the opinions of the American people.

AGENCIES OF OPINION FORMATION

Our opinions are the products of information and influences that come from many sources. In the earliest years of childhood, the socialization process within the family is very important. Throughout childhood and adolescence, school plays a major part in the ideas and points of view that we form. During these years and into adulthood, churches, clubs, and friends may all play important roles. All these people and groups may influence our opinions.

There are many other ways in which information is directed to us. These include printed matter such as newspapers, magazines, and books. We are also influenced by TV, radio, and the movies.

Getting the Facts

1. What are two meanings of the term "public opinion"?

2. List at least six different factors that have a major influence on opinion formation.

Forming an Opinion

■ What are some specific examples of the way in which public opinion has influenced political parties and government in America? What are some examples of the way parties and government have ignored public opinion? To what extent do you think "the will of the people" is being followed today?

AGENCIES OF OPINION FORMATION

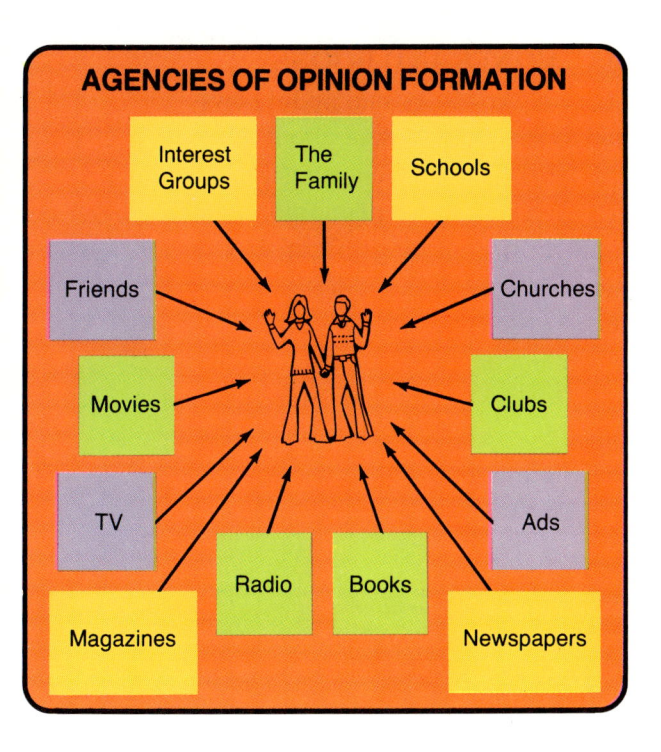

(Interest Groups, The Family, Schools, Friends, Churches, Movies, Clubs, TV, Ads, Magazines, Radio, Books, Newspapers)

The Media as Agents of Opinion Formation

We live in a media age. The word "media" is heard more and more in today's world. "Media" is a useful term. It includes most of the different forms of communication that influence us—newspapers, magazines, books, TV, radio, and many others.

Daily we are bombarded with words and images from these media. TV marches the affairs of the world before our eyes. The voice of radio is with us wherever we go. Movies bring us the real and the unreal. The printed word is seen in a number of forms.

In the United States, citizens have no problem obtaining information from the media. Our problem is instead one of finding out how to make the best use of the wealth of information with which we are daily presented.

We must decide which of the many different channels of information can give us the specific kinds of information we need. We must also decide which of the channels are likely to give us the fairest interpretation of current issues. Only by making such decisions can we make good use of information in fulfilling our civic responsibilities.

NEWSPAPERS

Newspapers have long been seen as a strong influence in forming public opinion. One writer has called the newspaper "the bible of democracy." Their wide circulation and their power to persuade causes newspapers to be criticized by many people. Those who do not agree with the views printed in newspapers sometimes fear that newspapers have too much power to influence.

Newspapers in the United States are privately owned. They do not serve as the voice of an all-powerful government, as in totalitarian countries. The price that people pay for American newspapers is generally not enough to pay for their publication. Two thirds or more of the cost is usually paid for by advertising. For this reason, newspapers are sometimes said to distort or suppress the news in the interests of their advertisers. On the other hand, there is reason to believe that this may be an exaggeration. Newspapers with large circulations generally have many different advertisers. This fact may allow them to present very independent views.

Another criticism of American newspapers is that, in order to increase their circulations, they have helped lower public tastes. They are accused of printing news stories that play up conflict. They are said to fill their pages with stories about crime and items of poor taste. There is some truth to these charges. However, we must remember that newspapers are private businesses. To remain in business, papers must be sold. If newspapers seem to carry too many stories about conflict, crime, and the like, it may be because many people want such news.

MAGAZINES AND BOOKS

Many of the things said about newspapers may also be said about magazines. Like newspapers, magazines with large circulations depend upon advertisers for the cost of publication. But they, too, have many different advertisers. For this reason, they can show a great deal of independence.

Books also influence our opinions. Some books may be seen mainly as storehouses of information. In many ways, your school books fit this descrip-

What magazines do you read? Do they tend to voice the same opinions or do they offer a wide range of opinions? Are there other magazines you know of that offer opinions greatly different from the ones you read?

tion. Certainly this is true of encyclopedias and other reference books. Then, there are books written mainly to present a point of view and influence the reader to think a certain way. Other books, such as novels and books of poetry, may be written mainly to entertain people.

Some books have a greater influence on the formation of opinion than others. At the same time, all books present information. This information provides grist for our opinion mills. When we read books, we collect information in our minds. You are doing this now as you read this book. When the need arises, we can fit this information together for our own special purposes.

RADIO, TV, AND MOVIES

Many other media also provide us with information and ideas that shape our opinions. Among these are two powerful agencies of "mass communication," radio and TV. Both can be found in almost every American home.

Radio has been a part of American life since the 1920s. Its influence on opinion formation over the years has been noted in many ways. One historical example is often used. President Franklin Roosevelt's "fireside chats" were very important in helping to build support for his New Deal program. With the rise of TV in the late 1940s, many people predicted the decline of the radio. But this has not been the case. It might be added that perhaps no group has been as important in keeping radio alive and growing as American teenagers.

At the same time, the development of TV can only be described as phenomenal. Much more than pure entertainment, it has become a powerful medium of opinion formation.

One area where the importance of TV has been noted is in the socialization process of young children. Most young children in the United States spend a great amount of time in front of a TV set. It is hard to determine exactly what children learn from these early experiences. Those who study such matters, however, agree that quite a lot is learned. They think TV plays an important part in the development of concepts and the formation of values.

The coming of TV led to predictions not only of a decline in radio, but also of a decline in the importance of movies. For a time, it appeared that the movies might lose their grip on the interest of the American people. This has not happened. The interest in movies is seen in the number of people who go to theaters. Interest is also seen in the fact that many movies are shown on TV. More than just entertainment, movies, like radio and TV, can be influential in shaping our opinions.

Getting the Facts

1. What are the six major forms of media in the United States?

2. What kinds of information are offered by each form of media you listed in Question 1?

Examining the Issues

■ Government regulations require TV stations to present a wide range of different viewpoints. How successful do you think these regulations have been? How would you describe the points of view presented by the TV stations in your area?

Speaking Out

Edith Efron

Efron is a journalist who specializes in studies of the political impact of TV on our society. Here she argues against government regulation of the TV networks. She believes that such regulation violates the 1st Amendment and makes it impossible for TV and radio to offer a free exchange of ideas.

"In broadcasting, from the ground up, the system has been totally destroyed; the First Amendment has been violated at every crucial stage of the marketing process. . . .

"Thus, unlike publishers, who may own and use their own printing presses at will, the broadcasters may not own and use their broadcasting facilities at will. The airwaves are declared to be "publicly owned," which boils down, simply, to ownership by the State [the federal government]. The State then chooses the individuals who will have access to the airwaves, by a licensing system. . . . The government—in the person of the FCC, the Congress, the Executive and the Courts, etc.—sets a variety of standards for content and standards for hiring, firing, selling, etc.—that influence content. Centralized, nationwide standards, if you please, with which all broadcasters must comply.

"And right away, as if by magic, we have the most extraordinary development in the history of American communications: huge monopoly production centers, churning out an absolutely identical product from coast to coast. . . .

". . . A relatively small group of men are able to create a uniform political orientation in a mass communications system, to the unending distress of those whose political views clash with theirs. Thus does government intervention work in the broadcasting industry. . . .

"And what is the excuse for this catastrophic violation of the First Amendment in our major communications system? *Consumerism*, of course. Originally called "the public interest." The rationalization for every step of the intervention process, from licensing to the setting of program types and standards, to ownership and sales arrangements, to Congressional investigations of the content of plays and of news . . . all of this is allegedly in the name of the public which must be protected from . . . from what? From private property and private ownership of the means of production. . . . Translation: from a free market of ideas."

1. What specific reasons does Efron give for opposing government regulation of TV and radio? To what extent do you agree with her arguments?

2. What are some arguments in favor of government regulation of TV and radio?

Interest Groups as Agents of Opinion Formation

A TV commercial may be made to influence us to eat more eggs or to develop a more favorable attitude toward America's railroads. In either case, the message presented comes from some interest group.

An interest group is a group of people with a common interest. It can be a powerful, well organized body with members in all parts of the nation. Or it can be a small group of people organized for a short period of time to gain a single goal. In any case, in a free society such as ours, there will always be a number of interest groups.

James Madison, often called the "father of the Constitution," saw this clearly. At the time the Constitution was being written, he wrote, "the landed interest, a manufacturing interest, a mercantile interest, a monied interest, and many lesser interests, grow out of necessity in civilized nations, and divide them into different classes, actuated by different sentiments and views." Shortly after Madison wrote these words, the 1st Amendment was added to the Constitution. It serves as a guarantee that interest groups may be formed.

> **FREEDOM OF ASSOCIATION:**
> **The 1st Amendment to the Constitution**
>
> Congress shall make no law respecting an establishment of religion, or prohibiting the free exercise thereof; or abridging the freedom of speech, or of the press; or the right of the people peaceably to assemble, and to petition the government for a redress of grievances.

There are a great number of different interest groups in our country. We often misunderstand and mistrust the roles they play. It is well to remember that interest groups are nothing more or less than groups of American people trying to influence government and society for their own purposes. They are really no better or worse than each of us as individuals.

In dealing with interest groups, we should try to find out what each group is seeking to gain. We should do this whether or not we agree with the group's activities or stated goals.

Interest groups must also be a concern of government. As James Madison wrote, "The interest of these various and interfering interests forms the principal task of modern legislation. It involves the spirit of party and faction in the necessary operation of government." This means that our government must constantly be aware of the activities of interest groups. More than that, the government must control any actions that may be a threat to the welfare of others.

The government controls interest groups in many ways. Limits are placed on the amount of money an interest group can give to a person running for public office. The government controls the way in which certain products such as cigarettes are advertised. There are laws regulating the quality of food and medicine.

There are so many interest groups in our country that it is impossible to think of them in more than general terms. The best we can do is to consider a few types. In some cases, we have given historical as well as modern examples. This is done to stress the fact that interest groups have always been a part of American life.

GROUPS INTERESTED IN POLITICAL AND SOCIAL REFORM

The pages of American history are filled with accounts of interest groups seeking reforms in government and society. Some of these have disbanded as their goals were reached. One was the American Anti-Slavery Society, set up in 1833 from a number of local groups that date back to the time of the American Revolution. Another important group was the National Civil Service Reform League, set up in 1881. Its aim was to reduce political favoritism and to get better qualified people into government. A third group was the National American Woman Suffrage Association. Set up in 1890, its goal was to gain the right to vote for women. In 1895, a group called the Anti-Saloon League was formed to limit the sale of alcohol. During the same period, a desire to improve local politics in the large cities led to the establishment of a number of voters' leagues. The first was the Municipal Voters' League of Chicago, set up in 1896.

Important among groups working today in the interest of good government is the League of Women Voters of the United States. Another national group is concerned with the protection of our constitutional rights. This group is called the American Civil Liberties Union. Other groups, among them the Foreign Policy Association and the American Association for the United Nations, are interested in our relations with other countries.

INTEREST GROUPS IN BUSINESS

Among some of the most powerful and best organized interest groups in America are those that represent industry and business. Three of the largest and best known are the National Association of Manufacturers, the Chamber of Commerce of the United States, and the American Retail Federation.

The National Association of Manufacturers was set up in 1895. It represents more than 20,000 of the country's largest industries. It carries on a widespread public relations program. It also conducts lobbying activities in state capitals and in Washington, D.C. The term "lobbying" is used to describe the work that interest groups do to influence laws and other forms of government action.

The Chamber of Commerce of the United States represents thousands of state and local chambers of commerce. Through the many local and state chambers, great influence is brought to bear on state and local governments.

The American Retail Federation is an organization that represents about 70 state and national retail groups. Like other business groups, it is interested in government policies that have impact on the economic life of the country.

These business groups spend a great amount of time trying to influence the government. They may, for example, try to influence government to pass tax laws that favor business interests. They may also work with other groups in their own communities. They often support Junior Achievement programs and scout groups. In this way, they benefit the communities and help to build a favorable image for business in the minds of the people.

What two opposing interest groups are shown here? With which group do you identify more strongly? Why?

LABOR ORGANIZATIONS

Comparable in power and influence to the national business groups is the organization known as the AFL-CIO. The full name of the AFL-CIO is the American Federation of Labor–Congress of Industrial Organizations. This giant interest group is the parent body for a number of large national trade and industrial unions. Among these are the large unions of steel workers, electricians, and retail clerks. Under its spreading umbrella can be found much of the nation's organized labor. One part of the organization, the AFL, was first set up in its present form in 1886. The CIO came into being in 1938, as a result of a split with the AFL. From then until 1955, the AFL and CIO operated as two separate labor groups. During this period they often disagreed strongly with each other. But on matters of interest to workers, they generally agreed.

In 1955, the two groups settled their differences and formed the present body. Today, more than 16,000,000 American workers belong to the AFL-CIO.

Outside the AFL-CIO are a number of other unions. Some of these are also large national groups. They, too, are often able to have a great influence on government and public opinion.

The influence of these groups is used in different ways. Labor groups are always ready to back political candidates who favor their cause. Community support for a strike may be sought through newspaper advertising. Good will may be gained by contributions to local charities.

FARM GROUPS

American farmers have formed three large national groups. The National Grange is the oldest of these. It was set up in 1867. It has about 600,000 members today.

The most powerful of the farm groups is the American Farm Bureau Federation. First set up in New York in 1917, the Farm Bureau became a national body in 1919. Today it represents more than 1,500,000 farm families in the United States. Its members generally have large mechanized farms. Their farms are the ones that produce most of the country's food.

The third group, the National Farmers' Union, represents mainly farmers

RESPONSIBILITIES OF FREE CITIZENS **185**

Which of the many different farm groups do you think is best able to promote the interests of these seasonal workers? Why?

with small farms, farm workers, and tenant farmers. The group was set up in 1902. On many public issues the interests of the Farmers' Union are closer to those of labor than to those of the farmers in the Farm Bureau. In recent years, some farm workers have even formed labor unions. The United Farm Workers of America is one of the strongest. Many of its members are seasonal workers who work on large farms harvesting such products as grapes and lettuce. Under the leadership of Cesar Chavez and others, these workers are seeking union contracts and better working conditions.

PROFESSIONAL GROUPS

Almost all of the professions in the United States have set up organizations to care for their special interests. The American Medical Association represents a large number of American doctors. The American Bar Association works for the interests of American lawyers. The largest group of American teachers is the National Education Association. All of these groups, and many others like them, are parent bodies with related groups at state and local levels.

OTHER SPECIAL INTEREST GROUPS

Religious and ethnic groups have also formed a number of special interest groups. Two of the largest religious groups are the Federal Council of Churches of America and the National Catholic Welfare Conference. Among well-known ethnic interest groups are the National Association for the Advancement of Colored People and the Anti-Defamation League of B'nai B'rith.

A list of important special interest groups in America could go on and on. All add vitality and interest to our democracy. They are able to form and act because ours is a free country. They are kept in bounds, often by other groups that oppose them. If this kind of opposition is not enough, there remains the power of government to regulate them in the interest of all the people.

Getting the Facts

1. Name at least six specific American interest groups.

2. In what ways is the power of interest groups controlled?

Thinking About Citizenship

■ Which, if any, of the interest groups discussed in this section do you think you may someday belong to? What policies would you want the group or groups you join to follow? What individual and general benefits would you expect to gain from membership?

Inquiry

What Interest Groups Are Active in Your Community?

Your community, like others, has many kinds of interest groups. The purpose of this inquiry is to study the goals and activities of some of these groups. Using the discussion in this chapter as a guide, prepare a list of interest groups in your community. From the list, choose a number of groups for study. Try to include groups that have opposing views on certain subjects. For example, a business group and a labor group might have different views about local taxes.

All class members may help prepare the list of interest groups. However, a committee might be better able to conduct the investigation. Committee members should collect any useful printed materials prepared by the groups. These materials may help to explain the views of the groups. You may also be able to set up interviews with members of the interest groups. Ask them about group views, group activities, and the ways in which the group tries to persuade others to agree with their views. Newspaper stories and other people in your community may also help explain how these groups use their influence.

The materials and information collected should be examined carefully. Do the printed materials deal with the facts? Or are they statements of group opinions? Is the wording fair or slanted? In what other ways do the groups try to influence public opinion?

When the committee has ended its study, the findings should be reported to the class. The report should include a display of any printed materials collected. It should also include comments on any interviews held with leaders of interest groups.

What is this cartoonist saying about the strength of interest groups at the national level? Do you agree or disagree? How powerful do you find the interest groups in your own community?

Comparing Local Interest Groups

After the committee has made its report, all members of the class should consider the following questions.

Which of the groups seem to be best organized and best financed? Do these groups have more influence on public opinion than groups with less organized methods and less money?

Do the methods used by some of the groups seem to be more fair than the methods used by other groups? What methods do you consider unfair?

With which groups' arguments and views do you agree? Why?

RESPONSIBILITIES OF FREE CITIZENS

Recognizing Propaganda

Whenever you form opinions about political candidates or products you are likely to encounter different forms of persuasion. TV commercials, newspaper ads, or leaflets may be used to try to influence your opinion. "Persuasion," as one person has noted, "has become a conscious art and a regular organ of popular government." The techniques used to influence our thinking and persuade us to act in certain ways can be thought of in a general sense as "propaganda."

There is, of course, nothing wrong with the use of persuasion. Nor is propaganda itself bad. It is just that we have become very sensitive about the use of propaganda in this age of mass communication. And we often have reason to be concerned about the misuse of these techniques. During World War I, the American people first became acutely aware of the misuse of propaganda. Certain of the warring governments sent out war reports that were very misleading. Many Americans came to believe that all propaganda was bad.

To help Americans understand and interpret different kinds of propaganda, the Institute for Propaganda Analysis was set up in 1937. A nonprofit organization, the Institute has made studies of the ways that information is used to influence us. To help us decide which forms of propaganda are fair and which are not, the Institute has identified a number of different propaganda techniques. The techniques may or may not be harmful. However, it is important to be aware of them. We must face the fact that all of us meet them in our daily lives. As thoughtful individuals, we must be able to recognize the fact that propaganda is being used. We must also recognize that propaganda is telling only one side of the story. The following are common forms of propaganda identified by the Institute for Propaganda Analysis.

1. Name Calling. This device is used to give "good" or "bad" names to people or groups. The names act as a substitute for a true description of the people or groups. A "good" political candidate may be called a "champion of the people" or a person who believes in an "honest" dollar. A "bad" candidate may be called a "radical" or a "coward." In neither case does the propagandist give any information to back up the names that are used.

What is this cartoonist saying about "name calling"? Do you agree or disagree? Why?

"You Disloyal American! You Communist!"

2. Glittering Generalities. We are all familiar with such noble words as freedom, equality, and honor. All of us approve of the ideas behind such words. For this reason, such words are often used to influence our opinions. We should recognize that, in many cases, they are merely glittering generalities. They are used to make broad and meaningless statements with which anyone can agree. Another kind of generality, often used by advertisers, is the word "new." We Americans tend to react favorably to something we think is new. Thus, we often find the word "new" attached to an old product. Or some small change in a product may be called a "revolutionary development."

3. Transfer. Transfer involves making a connection between something most people like or dislike and something else about which most people have no strong feeling. Propagandists who use the transfer device generally start with a respected symbol. The American flag is often used. By flying the flag at a meeting, the organizers may hope to fix in the mind of the audience the feeling that the group is very patriotic. The flag may also be used by an advertiser with a product to sell. By using the flag, or maybe just the colors red, white, and blue, the advertiser may hope that the public will make some connection between the product and America. The transfer device may also be used in a negative way. In a TV commercial, the competitor's product may be favored by a very rude person.

4. Testimonial. The testimonial, or endorsement, is often used by politicians and advertisers. Many political candidates have appeared on stage or before TV cameras in the company of well-known entertainers. A common form of advertising is to have a well-known sports figure endorse a product. No one claims that these people have any special knowledge or qualifications for the tasks. It is not likely, in fact, that most entertainers are also specialists in politics. It is also not likely that most tennis stars have expert knowledge about gasoline. However, politicians and advertisers hope that people will be influenced by the choices made by these entertainers and sports figures.

Advertisers have been using propaganda techniques for a long time. What techniques do you find in this 1930s photograph?

RESPONSIBILITIES OF FREE CITIZENS

This label stands for:
- **The creativity of American design.**
- **The skill of American workmanship.**
- **The importance of American jobs.**

Look for our label when you shop.

As seen in newspapers throughout the country March 21, 1972.

Would it be fair to say that a propaganda technique is being used in this ad? Why, or why not? If you think one is being used, which one?

5. Plain Folks. The plain folks appeal is very much a part of our democratic tradition. It places emphasis on the average person and the American way of life. A person running for office may make this appeal by visiting city ghettos or shaking hands at a factory gate. Political speeches may emphasize the American dream by calling attention to the fact that the candidate came from a poor family. Advertisers also use the plain folks appeal in many ways. We often hear about the taste of "home baked" bread and the smell of "country" sausages.

6. Card Stacking. This is a device that presents true statements in a very misleading way. A newspaper may do this by using headlines and front page space to report the activities of the party or candidate it supports. Reports about the other party may be placed on the inside pages. The same technique may be used by an advertiser in reporting the results of tests involving competing products. The results favoring the advertiser's product are listed first or they are printed in larger type.

7. Bandwagon. The bandwagon device tries to persuade us to "join the crowd." It is a technique based on the idea that if something is said often enough and loud enough most people will believe it. It is also based on the fact that many people want to support a winner. If people are told that a product is "number one," they may not want to settle for second best. If people can be convinced that a candidate is going to win they may decide not to waste a vote on the opponent.

Getting the Facts

1. What is the basic purpose of propaganda?

2. Name at least five propaganda techniques and give an example of each.

Examining the Issues

■ If you were taking part in an election campaign which, if any, of the propaganda techniques would you use? If you were trying to sell some product to raise money for your school which, if any, of the techniques would you use? Why would you use the ones you chose? If you chose none, why not?

Inquiry

How Is Propaganda Used to Influence Our Opinions?

You have just studied seven different propaganda techniques. They are name calling, glittering generalities, transfer, testimonial, plain folks, card stacking, and bandwagon. However, just knowing the names and definitions is not enough. All of us should be able to recognize these techniques when they are used to persuade us.

Organize an investigation to be carried on by members of your class. Each student should prepare a file of clippings from newspapers and magazines. Include advertisements and political stories that show the use of different techniques. Each student should also prepare a file for TV and radio. Include examples from commercials and from political news reports.

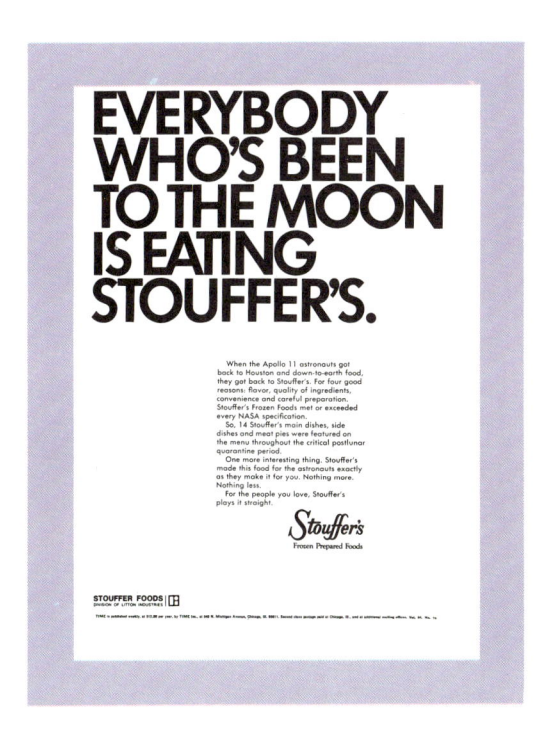

Bring your files to class and compare your findings with those of your classmates. Some of the material may be used to make a bulletin board display showing uses of each technique.

As a final stage, try to place the materials collected into two different groups. In one group place items that represent a fair and honest effort to persuade. In the second group, place items that the class feels have deliberately tried to mislead people. In some cases, members of the class may not agree about whether an ad or political story involves honest persuasion or deliberate deception. Analyze these items with greater care.

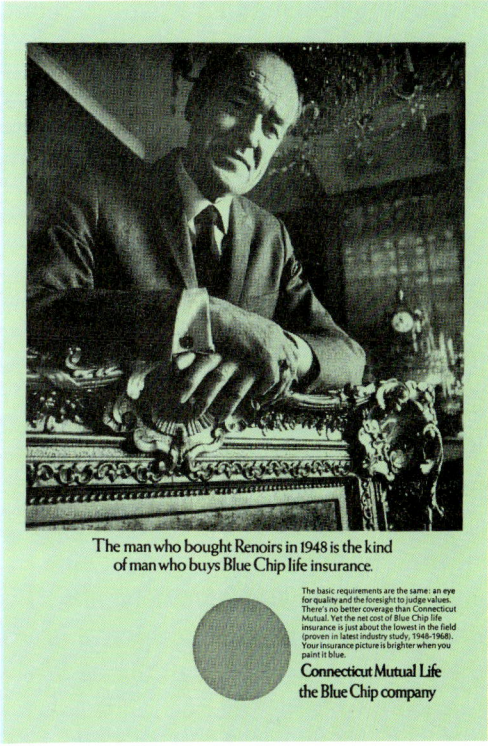

Propaganda techniques are often used, not to mislead, but simply to persuade. What persuasive techniques are being used in these two ads?

RESPONSIBILITIES OF FREE CITIZENS

Practicing Responsible Citizenship

Being a responsible citizen in a democracy places a number of demands on each of us. One demand is that we gain enough knowledge to be able to develop informed opinions about civic affairs. We have seen how information is provided by the media and interest groups. Information also comes from our families, schools, and other agencies of society. A second demand is that we develop skill in using our knowledge to help solve social problems. An important task of American schools is helping students develop such skill. Finally, there is the demand that we think about our values. Families, churches, schools, friends, interest groups—all bring their influence to bear on our feelings. All try to influence our thoughts and actions in ways they think are right. We must recognize that we are being influenced by others. We must decide for ourselves what we think is right.

CITIZENSHIP AS ACTION

Knowledge, skills, and well considered values are very important. But responsible citizenship is much more. Good citizens must be willing to act for the good of society. Unfortunately, not all Americans are willing to be active in their government. Many of the best informed people in America fail to take an active part in the government of their communities.

One reason that well informed people may fail to act is because they lack practice. The practice of civic action can begin at an early age. It can be done by each of us, as individuals, and as members of groups. Through practice, perhaps by working on local projects, we can improve our skills. Added skill can, in turn, increase our confidence in our ability to get things done. The hope, finally, is that more people will become action-oriented. In this way, all of us can contribute our share to the betterment of society.

YOUTH IN ACTION

In recent years, the young people in America have shown civic responsibility in many ways. Across the country, one can find ways that young people have turned information and values into socially desirable activities. Let us look at a few examples.

- A group of teenagers in Lawrence, Massachusetts found some answers to teenage complaints about nothing to do and no place to go. They set up a Teen Betterment Committee. The group took as one project the task of cleaning up a city park. It involved a week's work by 100 young people. Another project was to set up a Jobs for Teens program. With help from the state's employment agency, jobs were found for more than 300 teenagers during a single summer. So effective were the actions of these young people that grateful adults helped them start a new teen center. During the first year of the teenagers' activities there was a large drop in teenage vandalism in Lawrence. City officials and parents were convinced that the drop was the direct result of the group's efforts.

All of these young citizens have chosen to direct their actions toward improving the environment. What are some of the many other ways in which young people can turn citizenship into action?

RESPONSIBILITIES OF FREE CITIZENS 193

- Stopping vandalism of school buses was the goal of students in a New York City high school. Leaders in student government, members of athletic teams, and other interested students launched an educational campaign within the school. The result was a major reduction in vandalism. Losses caused by vandalism were cut from $180,000 a year to almost nothing.

- The city council in Seattle, Washington decided to build a garbage disposal plant near a high school. The students in the school disliked the council's decision. They decided to take action. Student leaders prepared a report on the situation. Their report helped persuade the city council to change its decision. The garbage disposal plant was not built near the high school.

- "Spectacular" is a good word for the results achieved by students in a Detroit, Michigan high school. Aware of the need for better facilities in a city hospital, they conducted a number of interviews and collected a great deal of information. An action group was formed, composed of several hundred students. With the help of other students in the city, the group carried a petition supporting the hospital's request for funds to the Detroit Common Council. When the council held its budget hearing, more than 500 students were present. The students also gained access to the news media of the city. The result was that the council gave even more money to the city hospital than the hospital had originally asked for.

- In a Philadelphia school, a group of students became interested in political action after attending a local political party meeting. One of their projects was the collection of money to help in a voter registration drive. Money raising activities included a school dance and the sale of cakes. As a result, the students were able to collect more than $1000 for the voter registration drive.

- In Kansas City, Missouri, students from different schools worked together to set up a youth court. The court had a municipal judge and a 12-member jury of students. The court heard certain kinds of cases involving young people. Cases of traffic violations by young people were a major part of the court's work. In each case it was up to the student jury to reach a decision.

- A major event each year in a junior high school in Wheaton, Illinois is a carefully planned model congress. Students play the roles of senators and representatives. They introduce bills and those that are passed are sent to the school principal to be signed or vetoed.

Getting the Facts

■ What are some of the demands of responsible citizenship in America?

Thinking About Citizenship

■ How would you define responsible citizenship? To what extent do you think good citizens must be action-oriented?

Inquiry

What Responsibilities Should Young People Have?

When is an American old enough or mature enough to take on civic responsibilities? Part of the answer is determined by a person's physical growth and development. Another part of the answer is determined by the kind of culture in which a person grows up. Stated another way, growing up is regulated to some extent by what a society expects of its young people.

In America, there have been important changes in what society expects from its young people. The roles played by young people in the 18th and 19th centuries were in many ways different from the roles played by young people today.

The two columns at the right show the changes in American beliefs about the role of young people. In the first column, certain beliefs and practices that were common in earlier times are listed. In the second, beliefs and practices that are common today are listed. As you read the two lists, think of your own role as a young person. In other words, think about each item as it relates to you personally.

Earlier Times	Today
Short period between childhood and adulthood.	Long period to prepare for adult responsibilities.
Early marriages and large families generally thought desirable.	Great variations in marriage age and in family size.
Parents often involved in choice of marriage partner.	Individual freedom in choice of marriage partner.
Boys generally expected to follow occupation of father or enter the military, politics, or the ministry.	Almost unlimited choice of future occupation.
Most girls given training only as homemakers.	Equal education for both sexes.
High school education only for a few.	High school education for all.
Little regard for special interests and needs of children and young people.	Much interest in and study of special interests and needs of young people.
General feeling that young people should not question the decisions of parents and other older people.	Emphasis on individual freedom and the formation of individual ideas, even at very young ages.

The Responsibilities of Youth: Yesterday, Today, and Tomorrow

How do you see yourself in relation to each set of items given in the chart? Is there any place where you might fit more nearly in the "Earlier Times" column than in the "Today" column?

If you were to add a third column headed "Tomorrow," which of the "Today" items would you change? What, in other words, might you want for American youth that may be denied them today?

Does the list of "Today" items suggest that youth can assume all of the kinds of responsibilities described in this chapter? Or should most young people wait until they are mature before undertaking these responsibilities?

RESPONSIBILITIES OF FREE CITIZENS

Citizenship Laboratory

Review of Basic Ideas

1. A basic responsibility of citizens in a democracy is the development of informed and responsible opinions about public issues. Public opinion, a collection of the individual opinions of citizens, has an important influence on democratic government. The formation of opinions is influenced by families, friends, schools, the media, interest groups, and the government.

2. The media have an important influence on opinion formation. We may see newspapers, magazines, books, radio, TV, and movies primarily as entertainment or as sources of information. However, each presents a number of ideas and opinions to the American people.

3. Interest groups play an essential role in democratic society. Their right to form and act is guaranteed by the 1st Amendment. Some interest groups are formed to seek reforms in government and society. Others act to protect the interests of various business, labor, farm, professional, and special interest groups.

4. Interest groups, advertisers, and politicians often use propaganda to persuade people to think or act in certain ways. We should recognize the different forms of propaganda and realize that propaganda often involves half-truths.

5. Liberty can exist only in a society whose people exercise civic responsibility. Civic responsibility demands both knowledge and action. Civic duty is not for the few but for citizens of all ages.

Questions to Think About

1. Given the complexities of modern society, to what extent is it possible to form opinions on all public issues? For which public issues do you think it most important that Americans form intelligent opinions?

2. For what reasons is it possible that what we call public opinion is often just the expression of a few loud voices? What can be done to make sure that public opinion includes the voices of all Americans?

3. Which of the media do you think have the most influence on the formation of opinions? Which have the least influence? Why?

4. In what ways does the government control interest groups? Would you favor more or less control by government? Why?

5. The power of one interest group is often balanced by the power of another interest group with opposing views. What are some examples of this balance among the interest groups you have just studied?

6. Which of the seven propaganda techniques do you think are the most dangerous? Why? Which, if any, of the techniques have become so common and overused that they no longer persuade people?

7. Some of the social actions by young people described in this chapter were of great value to the communities. In what ways were these actions also of great value to the young people involved?

Citizenship Laboratory

Words and Relationships

Define each of the terms in the first column. Then show how each term is related to the item listed opposite it by using both items in a sentence or short paragraph.

1.	public opinion	the will of the people
2.	media	political speeches
3.	lobbying	interest groups
4.	propaganda	advertising
5.	glittering generalities	progress
6.	transfer	communism
7.	testimonial	expert knowledge
8.	plain folks	country living
9.	card stacking	fair coverage
10.	bandwagon	be right

Building a Future

The future of American democracy depends, in part, on intelligent and informed public opinion. But forming intelligent opinions becomes harder as society grows more complex and as the amount of information increases. Another problem today involves the sources of information. In many cases, a few powerful groups have a great amount of control over the information we receive. In part, this is because large organizations have the money to gather information more efficiently. Consider the following facts.

- Radio and TV: Most shows and news programs are produced by a few giant networks.
- Newspapers: In recent years, many large city newspapers have gone out of business. With fewer newspapers, fewer views are presented. Most national and international news comes from two major wire services.
- Mass circulation magazines: Only a few are left today.
- Interest groups: The well financed public relations departments of a number of large interest groups use a variety of persuasion techniques to gain public support.

These examples illustrate the problem of obtaining accurate information. Do we need more sources of information? If so, what actions might be taken by government or private groups to give us more sources of information? Given our present sources of information, how can we use our knowledge about the sources to gain a better idea of the truth?

RESPONSIBILITIES OF FREE CITIZENS

9 Responsible Government Through Political Parties

The United States Constitution guarantees freedom of expression to all Americans. It gives interest groups the right to form and act in their own behalf. Both guarantees are vital elements of our government. Without them, it is likely that our democracy would not work. A third element of our government is equally important. Political parties and free elections have become an essential part of our American democracy.

Political parties are the best means that Americans have found to achieve their goals through government. As important as parties are, however, it is interesting to note that the Constitution does not mention them. In fact, political parties as we know them are relatively new. Here in the United States two major political groups began to form as early as the administration of President George Washington. But Washington himself spoke out against the idea of political parties. He feared that parties would divide Americans and make it very hard for them to work together for the good of the country. Nevertheless, parties were formed. Both in our country and in other democratic countries, the creation of a party system can now be seen as a great political achievement.

Political Parties

In all large socieites there are two groups of people. There are the rulers or leaders. And there are those who are ruled or governed. How are the leaders chosen? How can the leaders be made to serve the best interests of the people they govern? These are two questions a society must answer.

In earlier times, a society ruled by a queen or a king had simple answers to these questions. The ruling power was passed on from parent to child. There were few if any constitutional limitations on a ruler's power. The ruler needed to pay attention only to those people or groups with military or economic power.

Modern totalitarian governments are somewhat similar. Here, a major problem may arise when a leader dies. Many of these countries have no generally accepted way of replacing a leader. For this reason, a great struggle for power often takes place. The person or group that wins the struggle may then force the opposition into private life or exile. Some of these people may even be put to death.

In democratic countries such as ours, political parties and free elections are the means by which the people who are to be governed choose their leaders. If the leaders fail to serve the best interests of the people, they can be replaced. The process is carried on in a peaceful manner. It follows accepted laws and procedures. In many cases, elected officials may serve only limited terms in office. In some of our states, for example, a governor may not serve for two terms in a row. The President of the United States is limited to two terms by the 22nd Amendment. In this way, the people in office are prevented from using the power of the office to gain permanent control of the government.

> **PRESIDENTS ARE LIMITED TO TWO TERMS BEGINNING IN 1951:** The 22nd Amendment to the Constitution, Section 1, Paragraph 1
>
> No person shall be elected to the office of the President more than twice, and no person who has held the office of President, or acted as President, for more than two years of a term to which some other person was elected President shall be elected to the office of the President more than once.

THE VALUE OF PARTIES

In accepting the important responsibility of peaceful transfer of power, political parties serve us in a number of ways. For one thing they help cut down the number of people who run for each office. Take, for example, the election of a President. The campaign generally narrows down to two people, the candidates of the two major parties.

Parties also help the voters focus on important issues. Before an election, the parties decide which issues they think are the most important to the country. During the campaign, the issues are discussed by the candidates. In this way, voters can get some idea of what a candidate or party plans to do if elected.

As we have noted, parties help assure a peaceful transfer of political power. They also help us settle other political questions in a peaceful way. The people in totalitarian countries often find it hard to understand the peaceful

In 1976 Ronald Reagan made an unsuccessful bid for the Republican presidential nomination. He is shown here thanking his supporters for their efforts. Why do you think political defeat is accepted so calmly in the United States?

results of our elections. During elections, parties carry on heated battles of words. Interest groups of all kinds join in. But in the end, the voters choose one of the candidates. The people vote "yes" or "no" on certain issues. The losing candidates and the people who voted for the losing candidates and issues accept the results. Even the battle of words dies down.

A final value of parties is the fact that they offer Americans from all walks of life a chance to take part in government. Our history books remind us that many Americans have moved from the log cabin and other poor homes to the White House. We have read about the ways in which Irish immigrants were able to gain political offices even though "native" American groups were formed in prejudice against them. Today, when we read of a Chicano representative to Congress, or a woman governor, or a black mayor we see evidence that our party system is still helping Americans to fulfill the American dream.

THE TWO-PARTY SYSTEM

In general terms, the American political system can be called a two-party system. Third parties do spring up frequently. But they generally do not last very long. They generally do not become very powerful.

Why does America seem to favor a two-party system? Other democratic countries such as France have a number of major political parties. No one really knows why America has settled into a two-party system. However, a number of possible reasons have been suggested.

Some feel that our two-party system is largely a matter of custom. Another possible reason is that many Americans like to vote for a winner. Often a vote for a third-party candidate is seen as a wasted vote. Our British political heritage offers another possible reason. For most of their history, the British have had two major parties. We may have adopted the British system almost without thought. It is also important to remember that our two major parties are generally open to new ideas. When third parties come up with new ideas that interest large number of voters, the same ideas generally appear later in the program of one of the major parties.

PARTY ORGANIZATION

Unless they take part in party activities, most Americans know little about the organization of our major political parties. All of us hear about party activities when local elections are held. And every four years we watch Democrats and Republicans choose their candidates for President. But few Americans know much about what happens between local elections and national conventions.

It is not hard to describe the general organization of the two major parties. It is the same for both parties. Both have local committees in each ward or precinct. These committees are given the job of keeping in touch with the voters. They also work to "get out the vote" on election day.

Each party also has city and county committees. These groups coordinate the activities of the ward and precinct groups under them. The leaders of the city and county groups are often powerful members of the party. This is especially true in large cities.

The activities of the city and county groups are coordinated by a state central committee. The ways of choosing the members of the state group are decided by the party in each state. In some states, members are chosen by state party conventions. In others, they are chosen by district elections. The work of the state committee becomes most important when elections are held for state or national offices. At these times the committee raises money for the campaign. Political rallies are held and party literature is printed. In some states, the committee sets requirements for voting in party primaries. If the winner of a party primary dies or withdraws before the general election, the state committee has the power to choose a new candidate.

At the top of the party organization is the national committee. This body includes one man and one woman from each state. One man and one woman are also chosen from the District of Columbia and certain American territories. Its most important job is to try to get the party's presidential candidate elected. At other times the national committee is less important.

Getting the Facts

1. Name at least three general services of political parties in a democracy.

2. Describe the organization of the two major political parties.

Examining the Issues

■ What do you consider the advantages of having only two major parties? What are the disadvantages? Which do you think are stronger, the advantages or the disadvantages? Why?

ORGANIZATION OF THE DEMOCRATIC AND REPUBLICAN PARTIES

NATIONAL COMMITTEE

STATE CENTRAL COMMITTEES

COUNTY AND CITY COMMITTEES

PRECINCT OR WARD COMMITTEES

VOTERS REGISTERED IN THE PARTY

RESPONSIBLE GOVERNMENT THROUGH POLITICAL PARTIES

A Brief History of American Political Parties

The spirit that leads people to form political parties was present in colonial America. People who lived in the colonies tended to divide themselves into two groups. In one group were many of the wealthy landowners, professionals, and business leaders. For the most part, these people supported the British colonial government. The second group was made up of shopkeepers, wage earners, and people with small farms. In many cases, these were the people who helped stir up the revolt against the British government.

Of course, these are generalizations. Not all of the wealthier people favored the British rule. Nor did all of the poorer people have common interests. In fact, in the 1770s, people from all walks of life joined to make a revolution. Nevertheless, as you can see, even in the colonial period, America had two major groups with different political views.

FEDERALISTS AND DEMOCRATIC-REPUBLICANS

Some of the colonial ideas about political groups carried over into the new government set up under the Constitution. Washington did not favor the formation of political groups. In his Farewell Address, he spoke out against the "spirit of party." He called this spirit the "worst enemy" of popular government. Yet many people trace the beginnings of our two-party system to the political differences between Thomas Jefferson, who was Washington's Secretary of State, and Alexander Hamilton, who was Washington's Secretary of the Treasury.

People who favored Hamilton's policies formed the core of a party that took the name Federalists. They believed in a strong central government. They also had an interest in the development of business and industry. This gave the party strong support from most business groups in America. In 1796, when Washington finished his second term as President, the Federalists had enough power to elect John Adams.

By the election of 1800, however, those opposing the Federalists were able to elect Thomas Jefferson as President. The group supporting Jefferson was known as the Democratic-Republican Party. (The party's name, "Democratic-Republican," may be confusing to modern Americans. Many of today's Democrats feel that their party can trace its roots back to Jefferson's Democratic-Republicans. Today's Republican Party traces its roots to a party formed later—just before the Civil War.) In contrast to the Federalists, the Democratic-Republicans wanted to give power to state governments. They were also more interested in helping farmers and workers than in helping business groups.

Between 1800 and 1824, the Democratic-Republicans had complete control of the national government. Like the Federalists before them, they greatly disliked having any real political opposition. In the early days of our country, political opposition was often seen as unpatriotic and even unconstitutional. Thus, in many ways, the government of the United States had a kind of one-party structure during its early years.

DEMOCRATS AND WHIGS

The success of Jefferson's Democratic-Republicans caused the Federalists to die out as a national party after the election of 1816. By the election of 1824, the Democratic-Republicans were also in deep trouble. So many different factions had developed within the party that four candidates were named for the presidency. By the 1830s, America had two new parties. These were the Democrats and the Whigs. Both became major political parties.

The leader of the new Democratic Party was Andrew Jackson. The Jacksonian Democrats drew many of their followers from the old Democratic-Republican Party. Included were workers in the Northeast, farmers in the West and South, and a number of other interest groups.

The strongest support for the newly formed Whig Party came from business and industrial leaders in the Northeast, some political leaders in the West, and wealthy planters in the South. During the 1830s, the party was united on only one issue. This was opposition to Andrew Jackson. Opposition was strong enough to elect Whigs to the presidency in 1840 and 1848. The Whigs, however, could not agree on any well defined political program. The party died in the 1850s in the heat of the slavery controversy.

The Democratic Party continued to follow a program along the lines favored by Jackson. During the 1850s, however, control of the party moved largely into the hands of its southern leaders.

DEMOCRATS AND REPUBLICANS

With the Whigs divided over the issue of slavery, and the Democrats controlled mainly by Southerners, many Americans found nowhere to turn. The result was the formation of the Republican Party in 1854.

In the presidential campaign of 1840 Whig Party leaders spent more time talking about their candidate's military record and poor childhood than they did about issues such as slavery. Log cabins and hard cider were the symbols of the campaign.

American parties still use symbols such as the Republican elephant and the Democratic donkey. What symbols do you find in the photographs above? What purposes do these symbols serve?

Born in a tiny schoolhouse in Ripon, Wisconsin, the Republican Party began as a party opposed to the further extension of slavery. However, the party soon attracted support from people with other interests. Many northern Whigs and farmers who had been northern Democrats joined the party. In 1860 it was able to elect the first Republican President, Abraham Lincoln.

From 1860 to 1932, the Republican Party dominated American government. The only Democratic Presidents during these years were Grover Cleveland and Woodrow Wilson. In Congress, Republican control was even more complete. It was a time when the nation's two-party system was divided on the basis of geography. The Republican Party was most powerful in the North and West. The Democratic Party held power in the South.

Two important events in American history brought an end to Republican control. First, a huge number of immigrants settled in the northern cities during the early years of the 20th century. Because Democratic Party leaders in the big cities were often willing to help the immigrants adjust to life in America, many of the immigrants became Democrats. The second event was the Great Depression of the 1930s. A number of people blamed the Republicans for the depression. Others simply felt it was time for a change. During most of the 1930s, all of the 1940s, and most of the 1960s, America had Democratic Presidents. Through all these years, and even during the Eisenhower presidency of the 1950s, the Democrats controlled the Congress.

In these years, the old geographic centers of party power began to disappear. Democrats gained power in the North and West. The Republican Party grew stronger in the South. Each party had to face many issues that were national rather than regional. Both had to answer questions about the amount of

204 CIVIC RIGHTS AND RESPONSIBILITIES

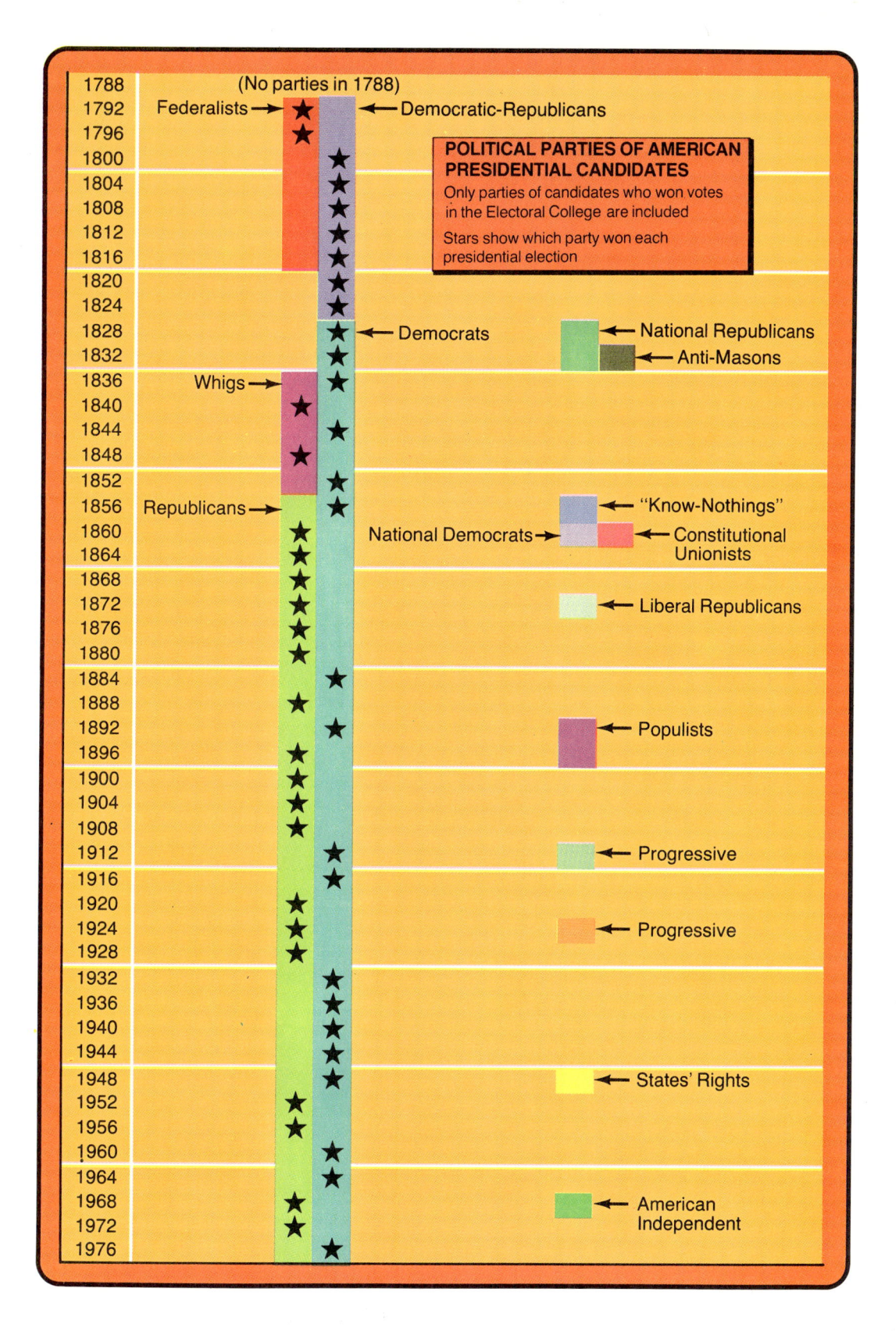

POLITICAL PARTIES OF AMERICAN PRESIDENTIAL CANDIDATES

Only parties of candidates who won votes in the Electoral College are included

Stars show which party won each presidential election

1788	(No parties in 1788)
1792	Federalists ★ / Democratic-Republicans
1796	★
1800	★
1804	★
1808	★
1812	★
1816	★
1820	★
1824	★
1828	★ Democrats / National Republicans / Anti-Masons
1832	★
1836	Whigs ★
1840	★
1844	★
1848	★
1852	★
1856	Republicans ★ / "Know-Nothings" / National Democrats / Constitutional Unionists
1860	★
1864	★
1868	★
1872	★ / Liberal Republicans
1876	★
1880	★
1884	★
1888	★
1892	★ Populists
1896	★
1900	★
1904	★
1908	★
1912	★ Progressive
1916	★
1920	★
1924	★ Progressive
1928	★
1932	★
1936	★
1940	★
1944	★
1948	★ States' Rights
1952	★
1956	★
1960	★
1964	★
1968	★ American Independent
1972	★
1976	★

RESPONSIBLE GOVERNMENT THROUGH POLITICAL PARTIES

government involvement needed to solve all the economic and social problems of America. Both had to answer questions about the extent to which the United States should become involved in the political, economic, and military affairs of the rest of the world. Differences between Democrats and Republicans on these important issues were largely matters of how far and how much.

THIRD-PARTY MOVEMENTS

Whatever the policies of the two major parties, there are often issues that many people feel the major parties are ignoring or not handling well. This situation has often led to the rise of third-party movements. Some of these have been weak, with little influence. Others have played important parts in American history.

1. Anti-Masonic Party. The first important third party was the Anti-Masonic Party. The party was set up in the early 1830s in opposition to the secret meetings of Masonic groups. The Anti-Masons also opposed Democratic President Jackson, a member of the Masons. Anti-Masons won a number of congressional seats and state offices in 1832. Believing they were strong enough to win the presidency, party leaders called a national presidential nominating convention. The device had never before been used in America. Up until this time, presidential candidates had been chosen by party members in Congress. The senators and representatives from each party had held meetings known as caucuses. The Anti-Masonic Party lost the presidential election. But their idea of national nominating conventions was soon adopted by all major parties.

2. Know-Nothing Party. Another early third-party movement led to the American or "Know-Nothing" Party. (The name "Know-Nothing" came from the answer party members gave when they were questioned about the party's organization.) The "Know-Nothing" Party rose to importance in the mid-1850s. Set up mainly to work for restrictions on immigration, the party had some success. It gained control of a number of state legislatures and, at one time, had 70 members in Congress. It declined when the party split over the issue of slavery.

3. Prohibition Party. In the years following the Civil War, a number of third-party movements were started. In 1869, the Prohibition Party was formed. The party's goal was to limit the sale of alcohol in America. The success of its efforts can be seen in the adoption of the 18th Amendment.

THE PROHIBITION PARTY WINS A SHORT-LIVED VICTORY

Prohibition in 1919: The 18th Amendment to the Constitution, Section 1

After one year from the ratification of this article the manufacture, sale, or transportation of intoxicating liquors within, the importation thereof into, or the exportation thereof from the United States and all territory subject to the jurisdiction thereof for beverage purposes is hereby prohibited.

Repeal of Prohibition in 1933: The 21st Amendment to the Constitution, Section 1

The eighteenth article of amendment to the Constitution of the United States is hereby repealed.

4. Populist Party. The best known of the late 19th century third-party movements was the People's or Populist Party. It became a national party in 1892. However, most of its members were farmers in the Middle West and South. Fighting for such things as inflated currency and government ownership of the railroads, the party had great influence for a number of years. It became inactive after the election of 1908.

5. Progressive Parties. At least three third-party movements in the 20th century have taken the name "Progressive." The first was formed in 1912 because of a split in the Republican Party. The major goal of this Progressive Party was the election of Theodore Roosevelt as President. With Roosevelt's defeat the party ended.

Another Progressive Party was formed in 1924. Its members believed that government and industry in the United States were being controlled by giant business corporations. Its goal was to end this control. In 1924, the party's presidential candidate was Senator Robert M. La Follette of Wisconsin. La Follette's defeat ended the party.

A third Progressive Party was formed in 1948. Like the parties of 1912 and 1924, it was formed mainly to support a presidential candidate. In this case, the candidate was former Democratic Vice President Henry Wallace. Again, a defeat brought an end to the party.

6. States' Rights Democratic Party. Most of the Wallace Progressives of 1948 were left-wing Democrats who were unhappy with the policies of the Democratic Party. They felt that the Democrats were not doing enough to improve government and society. At the other extreme, in 1948, was a group of Democrats who thought the Democrats had too many reform ideas. They particularly disliked President Truman's civil rights proposals. The group set up the States' Rights Democratic Party. It was often called the "Dixiecrat" Party because many members were from the South. The party came to an end after its candidate, Strom Thurmond, was defeated in the 1948 presidential election.

7. American Independent Party. The presidential election of 1968 produced a new third-party movement—the American Independent Party. Its platform stressed the need for law and order in the United States. Its presidential nominee, former Governor George C. Wallace of Alabama, made a strong showing. He won 45 electoral votes. This was the largest number for a third-party candidate in more than 100 years. Still, the party died after the election.

Getting the Facts

1. Who were the Federalists? the Democratic-Republicans? How did their programs differ?

2. Trace the history of today's Democratic and Republican parties.

3. Name at least four of the more important third-party movements. Why was each party formed?

Thinking About Politics

■ Use your knowledge of American history and politics to decide which party you would have supported in 1796, 1840, 1860, 1896, 1912, and 1948. What are your reasons for each choice?

Inquiry

Party Platforms—A Comparative Study

Every four years the two major political parties hold nominating conventions. Here they name their candidates for President and Vice President. Before the nominations are made, a committee in each party sets up a party platform. The platforms are statements of party principles. To a large extent, presidential candidates are expected to base their campaigns on these platforms.

The platform committee in each party hopes that its platform will attract a majority of the voters. For this reason, party platforms tend to avoid extremes. They are inclined to be worded in very middle-of-the-road terms.

Although both parties are likely to avoid extremes, the platforms can and often do differ in important ways. Some examples of differences can be found in the Democratic and Republican platforms of 1976. Both are much too long to reprint in full. Instead, party views on a number of issues are given here. As you read the following paragraphs, note the subjects upon which the parties appear to disagree. Note also the subjects upon which the parties appear to be in agreement.

Why do the party platforms of our two major political parties often seem to be offering "something for everyone"?

DEMOCRATIC PLATFORM 1976

Busing: Democrats believe that busing to achieve racial integration of public schools should be used only as a "judicial tool of last resort."

Crime: Democrats favor banning small handguns called "Saturday-night specials." They call for the national government to work with the states to place tighter contols on other kinds of handguns. They favor mandatory sentences for people who commit crimes using guns.

Defense: Democrats favor large cuts in the military budget unless there is a "major change in the international situation." At the same time they believe that the United States should have military strength at least equal to that of the Soviet Union.

Energy: Democrats are in favor of continuing price controls on oil and natural gas. They believe we should seek alternative sources of energy. They favor placing limits on the activities of big oil companies when there is evidence of inadequate competition. They would like to hold the country's dependence on nuclear power to a minimum.

Foreign Affairs: Democrats favor pursuing better relations with the Soviet Union through "hard bargaining," while strengthening ties with our traditional allies and with the nations of the "third world." They favor continued support of Israel. They oppose settlement of the conflicts in the Middle East by formulas brought in from outside.

Government: Democrats call for a review of government programs to end overlapping and duplication of services.

REPUBLICAN PLATFORM 1976

Busing: Republicans oppose "forced busing to achieve racial balance" in public schools.

Crime: Republicans oppose federal registration of firearms. They call for the national government to continue helping state and local law-enforcement agencies. They favor compulsory minimum sentences for people who commit federal crimes using dangerous weapons.

Defense: Republicans are in favor of continuing the military's "major modernization program," adding new army divisions, and developing new weapons. They believe that the United States must maintain "a superior national defense."

Energy: Republicans would like to end price controls on oil and natural gas. They favor providing government incentives to encourage the exploration and development of our country's energy resources. They are against any moves to break up big oil companies. They would like to sharply reduce our country's dependence on other nations for energy.

Foreign Affairs: Republicans believe that we should explore new ways of reducing tensions with the Soviet Union. They favor maintaining "friendly relations" with Mainland China and, at the same time, continuing to support the independence of Nationalist China on Taiwan. They would like to continue "decisive support" of Israel while seeking a "negotiated peace" among countries in the Middle East.

Government: Republicans call for reducing federal regulation and bureaucratic interference in the lives of the

Inquiry

RESPONSIBLE GOVERNMENT THROUGH POLITICAL PARTIES

Inquiry

DEMOCRATIC PLATFORM 1976

They also favor having Congress review all federal programs from time to time so that any programs that no longer seem useful can be rejected.

Health: Democrats favor a national compulsory health insurance program for all Americans. The program would be paid for with federal tax money and payroll taxes.

Housing: Democrats would like to see greater efforts made to make sure that women and members of minority groups have an equal chance to obtain mortgage credit. They also favor building more low-income and middle-income housing.

Inflation: Democrats believe rising prices can be slowed down by an increase in business production. They favor the use of wage and price controls if necessary, but do not believe they are necessary at the present time.

REPUBLICAN PLATFORM 1976

American people. They would favor a requirement that federal programs "meet strict tests of their usefulness and effectiveness."

Health: Republicans oppose Democrats' health insurance program because it "could require a personal income-tax increase of approximately 20 per cent." They support greater protection from "catastrophic illness" for all Americans who cannot otherwise obtain protection.

Housing: Republicans favor "expanding housing opportunities," while "reducing the degree of direct federal involvement in housing." They also favor "continued incentives to support the development of low and moderate-income housing."

Inflation: Republicans favor ending the federal government's policy of deficit spending—spending more money than is taken in. They oppose wage and price controls.

After writing their 1976 party platforms, the parties chose Ford and Carter to represent them in the November election. Would it make more sense to write the platforms after choosing the candidates? Why, or why not?

CIVIC RIGHTS AND RESPONSIBILITIES

DEMOCRATIC PLATFORM 1976

Taxes: Democrats believe that the federal tax system should be overhauled. They would like to eliminate unfair tax benefits, particularly for wealthy tax payers. They favor continuing the policy of cutting taxes to prevent recession.

Transportation: Democrats support more flexible use of federal transportation money. They also support the use of a larger part of highway money for mass transport.

Unemployment: Democrats call for lowering the unemployment rate to 3 percent within four years. They believe this should be done by stimulating the economy and, if necessary, by setting up a program to provide "useful public jobs."

Welfare: Democrats favor an income-maintenance program that would provide a minimum income for the working poor and for people who are not able to work. They believe that benefits should be taken away from people who refuse to work. They favor a policy that would gradually lower the share of welfare costs now paid by state and local governments.

Women: Democrats support ratification of the Equal Rights Amendment. They oppose any constitutional amendment that would make abortions illegal.

REPUBLICAN PLATFORM 1976

Taxes: Republicans favor reforming and simplifying tax laws. They call for a reduction in tax rates along with a balance in the federal budget. They favor tax policies that encourage the economy to expand.

Transportation: Republicans favor giving local officials more flexibility so that they can set up a system best suited to local needs. They also favor a system that would allow state and local governments to use highway money for more important local needs such as mass transport.

Unemployment: Republicans favor a policy that would help businesses expand so that businesses would be able to provide more jobs. They oppose a "massive, federally-funded public-employment program."

Welfare: Republicans believe that the "truly needy" should be provided with an adequate income. They would like to end welfare fraud and set up stricter work requirements. They oppose giving the national government the major responsibility for welfare programs.

Women: Republicans support ratification of the Equal Rights Amendment. They also favor a constitutional amendment that would "restore protection of the right to life for unborn children."

Comparing Party Platforms

Having studied the various provisions of the two platforms, think about these questions.

On which subjects do the two platforms seem to disagree most sharply?

Where do the disagreements seem to be very minor?

At what points do the two parties seem in general agreement?

Which platform do you find more appealing? Why?

RESPONSIBLE GOVERNMENT THROUGH POLITICAL PARTIES

The Election Process

We Americans seem always to be electing someone or something. Even young children in their first years of school vote for class officers or group leaders. In the adult world it is the same story. Elections can be very informal. Nominations may come from the floor. Elections may be by a show of hands. On the other hand, the election process can be very complex. It can call for long, noisy campaigns. Elaborate voting procedures can be used. It is this second kind of election process that brings political parties so much into play. But, simple or complex, elections are very American. It is the way we make democracy work.

Although the primaries are the first step in elections the first step for each voter is registration.

The process used for political elections in America involves two stages. First there are the primary elections usually held in the spring or summer. These are followed by general elections in November. This is not always the case, however. In some places, local elections are held in the spring. This is done so that local issues will not become confused with state and national issues.

PRIMARY ELECTIONS

During the early years of our country, candidates for office were usually nominated by party leaders. Even in state and local elections, the majority of the people had little to say about who would be nominated. Opposition to this procedure gradually developed. People became aware that party caucuses and conventions could be controlled by a few important party leaders. In most states, party conventions have now been replaced with direct primaries.

The direct primary gives voters a chance to choose party nominees from among two or more candidates. One of two different methods is generally followed. The most common is the "closed primary." In a closed primary, each ballot lists the names of the candidates of only one party. Voters are usually asked to indicate in some manner the party to which they belong. They are then given the ballot of that party.

A few states follow a different method. This second method is called the "open primary." In an open primary, the names of all candidates of all parties are printed on one ballot. Voters can choose the candidate of any party. Although open primaries do give voters a greater choice, many people oppose their use. One argument against open primaries is that they allow voters in one party to vote for a weak candidate in the other party. By doing this they hope that their party's candidate will be able to run against a candidate who is easy to beat.

Whether closed or open, the reformers who fought for the direct primary felt that it would weaken the control of political machines. ("Machines" are powerful party organizations set up to control politics and, to a large extent, the government of a local area or a state. Often the leaders of the machines have never been elected to any government position. They may, however, have a great deal of influence over party members who have been elected to official positions.) In general, the reformers were right, but not in all cases. The problem is that many voters feel that the primary is less important than the general election. The result is that in primary elections only a small number of people vote. With a low vote, a political machine often finds it very easy to nominate its own candidates. Machine leaders make sure that people who will vote for their candidates get to the polls. This can be prevented only if large numbers of independent people show enough interest to vote.

The presidential preference primary is a special kind of primary. These primaries are held in about 30 states every four years just before a presidential election. They have become better known to Americans in the last few years because of heavy coverage by TV and newspapers. Unlike direct primaries, the preferential primaries do not nominate candidates. They just show how the voters of a state feel about certain candidates. In many states, however, winning candidates do gain delegates who are pledged to support them at the national party convention.

GENERAL ELECTIONS

All party candidates nominated in the direct primary are listed on the same ballot in the general election. Voters may mark their ballots as they choose, regardless of their party affiliations. Usually, the general election is of greater interest to voters than the primary. In most cases, more people vote. An exception to this rule is sometimes seen in states or localities where one of the major parties has almost complete control. However, this is becoming less and less common. As we have noted, our political parties are becoming less geographical in support and makeup. They are becoming more concerned with national issues. For these reasons, there are no longer as many "one-party" areas in the United States.

CONDUCTING ELECTIONS

Both primary and general elections are generally conducted by a city or county board of elections. These boards are usually bipartisan (two-party) bodies made up of an equal number of Democrats and Republicans. In some places, there are no election boards. In these places, the elections are run by the city council or county officials.

A major responsibility of these boards is to divide their areas into election districts or precincts. In each precinct, the board sets up a polling place where people can vote. Voting places are often set up in public buildings such as schools, fire stations, or town halls. However, private buildings are sometimes rented for the purpose.

The people who work in the precincts are appointed by the election board. The number of election officials and the roles they play vary from state to state. In many states, each precinct has three judges and two clerks. Only two of the three judges may belong to the same party. The two clerks must belong to different parties. Generally, the same precinct officials run both primary and general elections.

A qualified voter who for some reason is unable to vote at the local polling place may cast an "absentee ballot." The ballot is marked by the voter and mailed to the election board before election day.

Both at the polls and with absentee ballots, election officials must make sure that only eligible voters are allowed to vote. Voters are often asked to sign their names in front of the election officials. Their signatures may then be compared with the name they signed when they registered to vote. Officials may "challenge" voters if they think the voters are not eligible. When people are challenged, they may be asked, under oath, to answer a number of questions about their right to vote.

Voters may also be challenged by people known as "watchers." These people are placed at the polls by parties that have candidates in the election. The candidates may also be allowed to have watchers. Watchers have the right to check the records. They are present to see that the elections are run in an honest way.

IMPROVING THE ELECTION PROCESS

The most important thing in a polling place may well be the voting machine. Voting machines were first used in New York in 1892. Today, the voting machine has replaced the traditional paper ballot and the ballot box in most places. The machines are easy to operate. They make vote counting quicker and easier. More important, they increase the accuracy of counting and reduce the chances for dishonesty.

The widespread use of voting machines has greatly improved the election process. Another improvement came even earlier than the voting machine. The secret ballot was first used in the United States in 1888. Before this time, voting was done either by word of mouth or on paper ballots that were handed to election officials. Voting was anything but secret. Because the votes were given publicly, there was a great deal of dishonesty. A voter could easily be bribed or threatened.

Another change in election procedure has been taking place slowly over the years. In many places, the "long ballot" has been replaced by the "short ballot." A long ballot is so named because it contains long lists of candidates for many different offices. Most voters will know only a few of the candidates. The situation may be even worse if the terms of office are short. By the time voters become familiar with most of the names that have appeared on the long ballots in the past, new candidates will appear. In primary elections, long ballots tend to work in favor of political machines. In general elections, voters with long ballots often vote "straight tickets." That is,

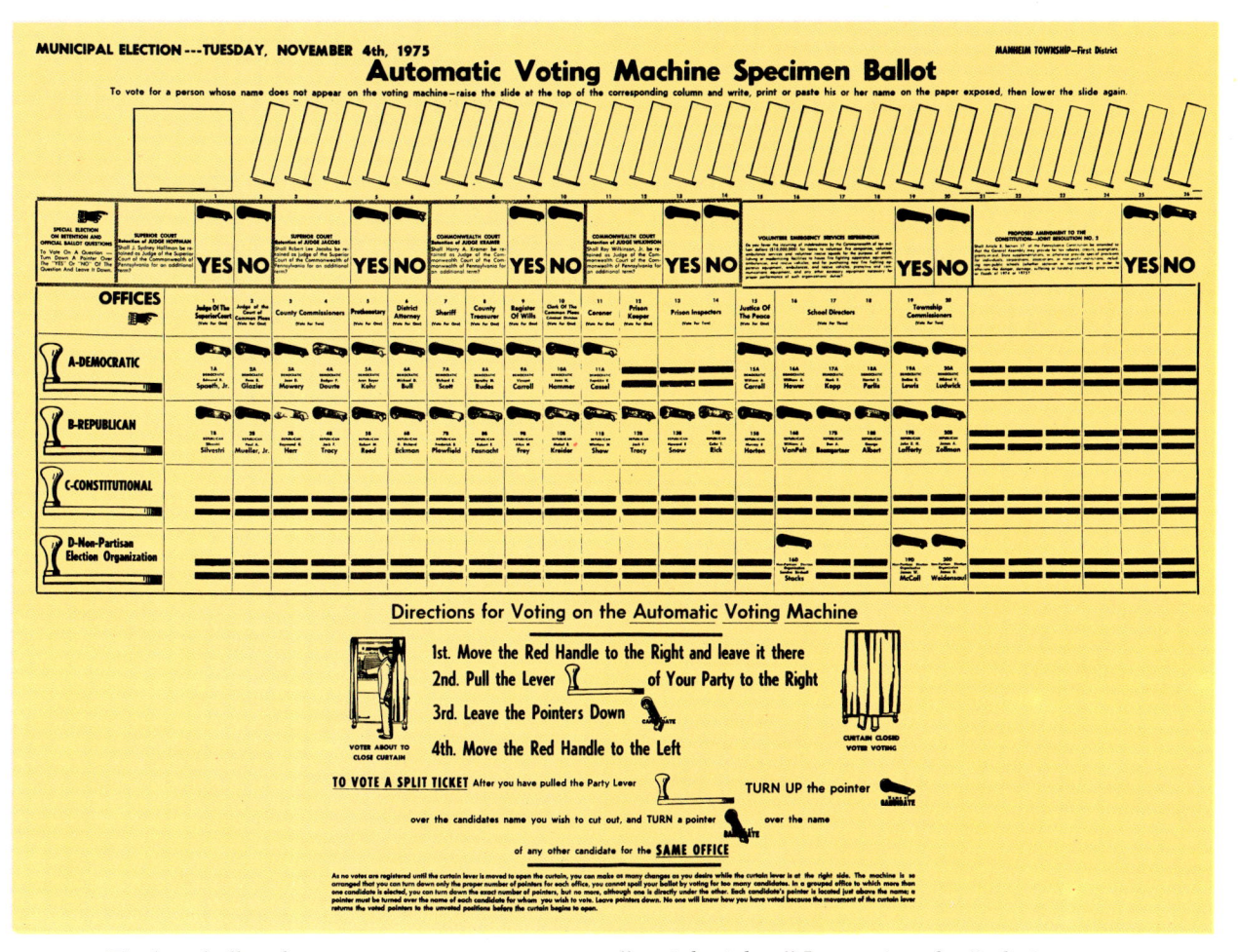

The long ballot above encourages voters to vote a "straight ticket." Instructions for "splitting a ticket"—voting for people in different parties—are given only at the bottom in small print.

instead of choosing a candidate for each office, voters make one mark to show that they are voting for all the candidates in one party.

With the short ballot, some elective offices become appointive. In other words, many of the offices once filled by elected officials are filled by officials chosen by other officials. Governors or mayors may be given the right to appoint members of their cabinets. Those who favor the use of a short, rather than a long, ballot have at least two strong arguments. They believe that with fewer names voters will become better acquainted with the people for whom they are voting. They also believe that the officials who appoint other officials can be made clearly responsible for their actions. The voter, in other words, will know who deserves praise or blame.

Another change in the election process may be coming soon. On election day, polling places generally open early in the morning and close early in the evening. This gives people 12 to 15 hours to vote. But, while this may seem to be a lot of time, there is a growing

RESPONSIBLE GOVERNMENT THROUGH POLITICAL PARTIES

feeling that it is not enough. The National Conference of State Governors, for example, has proposed that voters be given a full 24 hours to vote. There is also a question concerning the day of the week. Generally, elections are held in the middle of the week. Some people think that election day should be made a national holiday and fall on Mondays.

Many people have suggested another possible change in our election process. They believe that all of the polls across the country should close at the same time. Because voting machines are so widely used, we get the results of elections very quickly. Because of the difference in time zones, voters in California often hear the results in Massachusetts before they vote. It is possible that many of the West Coast voters are influenced by the news from the East Coast. If all of the polls closed at the same time, this problem would not exist.

Getting the Facts

1. Why did reformers want the direct primary? What is the difference between an "open primary" and a "closed primary"?

2. What are the responsibilities of a board of elections?

3. Describe at least two changes that have been made to improve the election process.

Examining the Issues

■ Many believe that one of the major problems of our election process is the fact that so many people do not vote. Do you agree that this is a major problem? Why, or why not? If you agree, what, if anything, do you think should be done to increase the number of voters?

What statement is 19th century cartoonist Thomas Nast making about the power of political machines run by bosses such as Tweed? What changes in the election process have helped weaken the power of such machines?

"THAT'S WHAT'S THE MATTER."
BOSS TWEED. "As long as I count the Votes, what are you going to do about it? say?"

216 CIVIC RIGHTS AND RESPONSIBILITIES

Speaking Out

Mrs. Jimmie Johnston

Mrs. Johnston lives in a rural community in Kansas. She wrote the following letter to the *Farm Journal* to express her firm belief that Americans should learn about political issues and vote.

"We had a special election last summer, here in Labette County, Kan. Most farmers were so busy they didn't bother to find out what the issue was all about.

"We only knew it pertained to a watershed [a water drainage area]. We did not know if we were for or against the bill; we had read nothing in our local newspaper other than when and where to vote. Less than 10% of the eligible voters voted. We were among the other 90%.

"But all 100% sat up and took notice when they received their personal and real estate tax notices. Lo and behold, we were being taxed two mills [.2¢] for Watershed District No. 96.

"A neighbor picked up my husband to go and find out what was happening. After several phone calls and visits, they ended up at the local ASCS office, where they were shown a map of the proposed watershed which extends into other counties.

"Apparently, those of us who live upland will hold back the water from heavy rains so that farmers in the bottoms will not be flooded out. Does it not matter if we in the upland have our crops and pastures stand under water a few days so the lowland farmers can keep theirs dry?

"They also stopped at the county courthouse. Personnel there knew nothing about the bill, but suggested they visit the county attorney. He was unavailable, so they saw his assistant, who explained.

"The notice of this special election had to be printed only once in one of the county newspapers. (Not all farmers take all county newspapers.) No petition could be circulated to kill the bill if it was not done within 90 days of the special election.

"The two-mill watershed levy cost us nearly $50 this year. How many more years will we be paying on something we knew nothing about?

"From now on, if we don't know what the issue is, we'll find out and let our voice be heard. Don't sit back and let George do it! He won't. Or, he might vote for the other side."

---

1. What reasons does Mrs. Johnston give for the small voter turn-out in her community?

2. In many places, voter turn-out is larger for presidential elections than for local elections. Why do you think this is so often true?

3. What, if anything, do you think should be done to increase voter turn-out in all elections?

RESPONSIBLE GOVERNMENT THROUGH POLITICAL PARTIES

Inquiry

Who Votes in America?

There was a time when the only American voters were white males, 21 years of age or older. In some states, a voter even had to own a certain amount of property. The property requirements, where they existed, were not long-lived. However, all other limitations lasted until the 15th Amendment was passed in 1870. This constitutional change was written to add black males to the voter lists. However, for years it was a right that existed mainly on paper. Another Amendment, the 19th, was added in 1920. It gave voting rights to women. Soon after that all restrictions on the voting rights of American Indians were removed.

The vote was limited to people 21 years of age or over until 1970. In that year, Congress gave American citizens who were 18 years of age and older the right to vote in national elections. The 26th Amendment was adopted soon after. It gave those 18 years old or over the right to vote in all elections, local and state as well as national.

This brief history is useful background information. It tells something about who has the right to vote today. But it says nothing about what American voters are like today. It tells nothing about their political preferences. For this, political analyses are needed.

One way of learning about the political character of Americans is through a study of voter preferences. The chart below shows the results of Gallup Polls taken in 1965, 1970, and 1975. In each year, a representative sample of voters were asked, "In politics, as of today, do you consider yourself a Republican, Democrat, or Independent?"

	1965	1970	1975
Republican	27%	29%	22%
Democrat	50%	45%	45%
Independent	23%	26%	33%

How would you explain the increase in the number of Independents? With so many voters calling themselves Democrats in 1965 and 1970, how would you explain the fact that a Republican President was elected in 1968 and again in 1972? How do these percentages compare with the political preferences of members of your class?

ADDITIONS TO THE RANKS OF AMERICAN VOTERS: Given in the 15th, 19th, and 26th Amendments to the Constitution

Vote Given to Men of All Races in 1870: The 15th Amendment, Section 1

The right of citizens of the United States to vote shall not be denied or abridged by the United States or by any State on account of race, color, or previous condition of servitude.

Vote Given to Women in 1920: The 19th Amendment, Section 1

The right of citizens of the United States to vote shall not be denied or abridged by the United States or by any State on account of sex.

Vote Given to 18-Year-Olds in 1971: The 26th Amendment, Section 1

The right of citizens of the United States who are eighteen years of age or older to vote shall not be denied or abridged by the United States or by any State on account of age.

Another way to study the American voter is to look at statistics dealing with all Americans. This is what political analyst Richard M. Scammon has done. Writing about the American voter in 1970, Scammon came to these conclusions:

"(1) . . . the American electorate is increasingly metropolitan. That doesn't mean urban—the big cities are going down just as the farms are going down. Perhaps the two biggest social movements in America in the last twenty-five years have been the flight from the land and the flight from the cities [to the suburbs].

"(2) . . . it is an electorate that has more women than men. There have been more women than men in the adult population for some years now, but they haven't voted as frequently as men. Beginning about 1964 or 1966, there have been more women voters than men.

"(3) . . . the electorate in America today is middle-aged. Despite all you may read, the 1970's are not going to be the years of the politics of the diaper but rather the politics of the man who has been voting for 20 years. The average of the voters in 1968 was 47. And with the enfranchisement of 18-year-olds, the average will still be well over 40."

With these three points in mind, place yourself in the shoes of a politician. To gain the support of the voting groups identified by Scammon, what kinds of policies might you favor? How accurate could you be about this? Could you, for instance, know with any real certainty that a public policy or law would have more appeal to women than men? Could you know that it would have more appeal to middle-aged voters than to young or old voters?

Having placed a majority of the voters in three broad groups, Scammon makes a general observation.

". . . while the American voter is not an intellectual when it comes to politics, neither is he a jerk. He is not an uninformed slob who simply goes out and votes his emotions or his ethnic background or whatever it might be. He is a moderately well-intentioned, moderately well-informed moderate, who, by and large, will do the best he can with the political decisions which he is asked to make."

How well do you think this statement describes the average American voter? With which parts of Scammon's description do you agree or disagree?

What are these cartoonists saying about American voters? Which do you think offers the fairer view?

RESPONSIBLE GOVERNMENT THROUGH POLITICAL PARTIES   219

Citizenship Laboratory

Review of Basic Ideas

1. Though the United States Constitution makes no mention of political parties, a party system has developed. It is a means by which Americans achieve their goals through government. The party system helps limit the number of candidates for political office and helps voters focus on important issues. The party system also helps us to resolve conflicts peacefully and offers a way in which all Americans can become political leaders. The American party system consists of two major parties. Minor, or third, parties arise from time to time. Both major parties are organized from the national level down to the local ward.

2. The two-party system began to appear during the presidency of George Washington. Until the 1830s, however, one party generally held most of the power. The modern-day Republican Party was first set up in 1854. From 1860 to 1932, the Republican Party generally controlled the national government. During this period, the Democrats generally controlled the state governments in the South. Today, both parties share power in almost all parts of the country. Although there were third-party movements as early as the 1830s, the best known third parties appeared during the late 19th and early 20th centuries.

3. The election process is the means by which political parties achieve results. It consists of two stages, a primary and a general election. Both are conducted by local boards. The election process has been improved by the use of voting machines and by short ballots.

Questions to Think About

1. In what ways have our political parties helped to reduce conflict in our society?

2. Why do third-party movements in America often have very short lives?

3. How are the major parties organized at the national, state, and local level? Which aspects of the organization seem most democratic? Do any aspects of party organization seem undemocratic?

4. Although we have a two-party tradition in America, in some places and during some periods we have actually had a one-party system. Why do you think this has happened in a democracy with a two-party tradition?

5. When did the modern Democratic and Republican parties come into being? What interest groups were involved in the formation of these parties? To what extent do the parties still draw support from these interest groups?

6. To what extent, through their histories, have the Democratic and Republican parties been regional parties? For what reasons have they lost much of their regional power today?

7. In what ways have primary elections brought more democracy into the election process?

8. The use of the short ballot means that there will be more appointive than elective offices. What are some arguments for and against the use of a short ballot in a democracy?

Words and Relationships

Define each of the terms in the first column. Then show how each term is related to the item listed opposite it by using both items in a sentence or short paragraph.

1.	totalitarian	transfer of power
2.	precinct	party organization
3.	third party	political reform
4.	party platform	voter appeal
5.	primary elections	nominating process
6.	closed primary	independent voter
7.	presidential preference primary	committed delegates
8.	bipartisan	fair elections
9.	absentee ballot	qualified voter
10.	long ballot	straight ticket

Building a Future

The addition of the 26th Amendment to the Constitution meant young citizens could begin voting at 18 rather than 21 years of age. This has given the high school years a new kind of political importance.

How can young citizens approach this new responsibility? Though this is a broad question, here are two suggestions.

- Think about your political values. Do you like things pretty much as they are? Do you think change should be approached slowly and carefully? Or, are you dissatisfied with much that you see in society? Do you want to see some big changes in many of our traditional institutions? Perhaps you would really like to turn our American way of life around and return to what you regard as the good old days.
- As you think about your values, consider ways in which you might become politically involved in helping to further your beliefs. Think about the politics of your community, state, and nation. Do you prefer the Republican or Democratic Party? Perhaps you think of yourself as an Independent? Or is there a third-party movement that attracts your interest? Whatever the political party of your choice, give some thought to working in it now. Volunteers are often needed at local headquarters, particularly near election time. Many political candidates began as party volunteers.

Citizenship Laboratory

RESPONSIBLE GOVERNMENT THROUGH POLITICAL PARTIES

10 The Costs of Democracy

"Taxes," an American judge once said, "are the price we pay for civilization." A statement with an unusual twist, it still leaves much unsaid. What kind of "civilization" do we Americans want? How much of it do we want to "buy" with our taxes? These are the sorts of questions that the judge's statement leaves unanswered. Implied in the statement are, however, four important ideas.

- Government is essential to civilized society.
- Government costs money.
- People have to pay for government.
- The way to pay for government is through taxes.

These are some of the ideas that we will examine in this chapter.

Another important question involves the allocation of funds. Where should our tax dollars go? Should money from taxes be allocated mainly through the federal government? Should state and local governments have a far greater role in allocating tax dollars?

Museums and concert halls in the United States depend heavily on support from the private sector. What are the advantages and disadvantages of this reliance on private wealth?

American Society: Public and Private

Because we live in a democratic country, we Americans are repeatedly called upon to make decisions as to whether our money will be used for public or private purposes. As individuals, we use some of our money to supply our private needs and wants. As citizens, we elect representatives to vote for taxes to satisfy our public needs and wants.

PUBLIC AND PRIVATE SECTORS

One way to examine civilization in the United States is to look at the public and private aspects of our society. Those aspects that we set up and support through government are called the "public sector." Those that we maintain through the use of private wealth are called the "private sector."

To understand the distinction between the public and private sectors, let us consider something as familiar as the collection of garbage. A local government may decide that garbage collection will be one of the services it will provide. In this case, the service will be paid for with tax dollars. Garbage collection will become part of the public sector. Another local government, however, may decide that all property owners will pay for their own garbage collection. They may either pay a privately owned company to do it, or they may do it themselves. The activity then becomes a part of the private sector. In the same manner, public schools come within the public sector. Independent and parochial schools are part of the private sector.

THE COSTS OF DEMOCRACY   **223**

There are many examples that could be given to show the differences between the two sectors. However, it should be noted that many activities in our country are carried on with money from both the public and private sectors. A privately owned university may receive grants of money from the government so that it can carry on activities deemed important for the public good. A private company may receive government money to design new aircraft for the Department of Defense. What other examples can you suggest of public money being used by private groups?

What all this means is that many of the decisions we must make about the use of our national wealth cannot be categorized as completely private or public. Even so, there remains an important question for people in our country. How shall we use our resources and our money? Shall we do what we think needs to be done by turning to government—the public sector? Or shall we turn to the private sector and do things as private people and groups with our private wealth?

BIG GOVERNMENT: GROWTH OF THE PUBLIC SECTOR

The growing public sector raises a fear, among many Americans, of a government that will threaten our liberty. This is not a new fear. An expression of it can be found in the Declaration of Independence. Among the grievances listed in the Declaration of Independence was the assertion that the British government had "erected a multitude of new offices, and sent . . . swarms of officers to harrass our people and eat out their substance."

Some two centuries later an American President had comparable words on the subject. "The rapid and largely unplanned expansion of the federal government," the President asserted, "has resulted in a structure so complicated, so confused, so contradictory, that it can neither serve the people well, nor respond reliably to the direction of the people's elected representatives."

There is no question about growth of government in the United States. It has grown both in size and in scope. In 1800 the federal government had fewer than 3,000 civilian employees. In 1970 there were almost 3,000,000 civilian workers. Military personnel in 1970 also numbered almost 3,000,000. In 1800 there were only about 5,000.

Perhaps even more important are certain growth figures for the 10 years between 1960 and 1970. During this decade the American population increased 13 percent. The number of civilian workers in the government, however, grew 51 percent. Stated another way, one out of every eight civilian workers in the United States in 1960 worked for the government—federal, state, and local. By 1970 the number of civilian government workers had risen to one out of every six.

But, before we become too concerned about these increases, let us look at certain other kinds of information. Let us look at the country's ability to support a growing government. Let us also look at the ways in which the government is spending its growing funds. The years after 1940 saw a huge increase in the production of goods and services in the United States. The total of all goods and services produced in the

United States is called the "gross national product," or the GNP. With the growth in the GNP after 1940, came a great increase in government spending for national defense. When we look at the non-defense expenditures of government between 1940 and 1970, the picture is quite different. Over these 30 years the percentage of the GNP used by government for non-defense expenditures decreased. In other words, the American government was spending less of its wealth for non-defense purposes in 1970 than it was in 1940. Viewed in these terms, it is hardly surprising that outcries were heard for government to begin spending more for cleaner air and water, better schools, and so on. Apparently these voices were heard. In the mid-1970s there was some decrease in the percentage of the GNP used for national defense. By 1974, spending by the Department of Health, Education, and Welfare had, for the first time, become greater than spending by the Department of Defense.

WHY THE GROWTH OF GOVERNMENT?

Regardless of how we look at government spending, the fact remains that there has been a steady growth of government in America. It is growth that has been very great in recent times. Why has this been so? Such a question is one about which entire books have been written. A simple answer is that government has grown because of changes that have taken place in American society.

Since society is people, consider, as part of an answer, two important changes in our population. When the United States was founded, there were fewer than 4,000,000 people in the entire country. In the next two centuries, the number grew to more than 200,000,000. In the early years most Americans lived on farms. Today most Americans live in large towns or cities.

To carry on our search for answers, we need to think of two other important changes. The first is the revolution in American technology. The second is the emergence of the United States as a world power.

Technology has revolutionized our lives. It has given us a world of science and machines. Think of communications. In 1790 it took about six months for a message to go back and forth between the United States and Europe.

Almost all of our modern transportation systems receive some government support. Public money is spent to build highways, run mass transit systems, and subsidize the operation of railroads and airlines.

Today we can talk directly to people in Europe by telephone. Rapid communication has become an important part of our lives. The telephone and telegraph services that make this kind of communication possible have become essential. Think of business. At the beginning of our nation's history, goods were produced and sold in small shops. Today economic life is dominated by large factories and businesses. These technological changes have placed many demands on government. A number of government agencies have been set up to regulate today's huge communication networks and businesses. The agencies help protect the interests of all Americans by controlling the power of huge enterprises.

The second major change, America's rise to world power, also helps answer questions about the growth of government. The demands of World War II led to great increases in government spending. The number of people needed to run the government increased as well. It is easy to understand why government would grow larger during a war. But why do our military forces and expenditures now remain high in times of peace? Why does peace itself seem different today than, say, 100 years ago? For one thing, the technology that has brought the people of the world closer together has also given us the atomic bomb. The threat of total destruction is always present. Many countries, including the United States, now feel that they must support large military forces even in times of peace.

Perhaps the most important reason for the growth of government lies in the fact that, over the years, the American people have come to expect more from American governments. Demands on governments at all levels have risen greatly. Today our governments are expected to provide many social services that were once provided only by private charities. Today government supported public schools are taken for granted. Americans have learned to turn to government for answers to major problems. Our governments are expected to find ways to control pollution and cure cancer. They may be called upon to find jobs for the unemployed.

When we think about all of the changes that have taken place in America in the last two centuries—changes in population, technology, and expectations—it is hardly surprising that government has grown. And with this growth, of course, has come a rise in the amount of money Americans must pay to support the government.

Getting the Facts

1. Give examples to show the difference between the public sector and the private sector in the United States today.

2. What is the meaning of the term "GNP"?

3. What are some of the reasons why public expenditures have grown so large?

Examining the Issues

■ Make a list of the many government services you benefit from. How do you think your life would change if these services were no longer provided by the government? Do you think the private sector would do a better job or a worse job of providing these same services?

Inquiry

What Are the Nation's Needs and How Shall We Pay for Them?

In 1971, the Economic Policy Committee of the AFL-CIO, our country's largest labor organization, issued a report about the future needs of America. The report was entitled Public Investment to Meet America's Needs. It stressed the need for government spending, calling public investment "America's new frontier." The following is part of the report.

"In the 1970's, America needs a long-range, national effort to greatly expand and improve public investments in facilities and services. Planned public programs will be needed throughout the remainder of the 20th century to revitalize the nation's urban areas as centers of American civilization and to improve the quality of life of the American people. Such effort is essential to strengthen the basic foundation of American society by meeting the requirements of a growing and increasingly urban population, in the midst of rapid and radical changes in technology, urban growth and race relations.

"For 40 years, the country has been undergoing vast social changes, with rapidly multiplying needs for every kind of public investment from sewer systems and waste treatment facilities to urban mass transit, education, health care, public safety, libraries, roads and airports. Despite efforts to meet these growing needs in the past 25 years—and particularly during the latter 1960's—large backlogs of unmet needs have remained and some have expanded to monumental size...."

Clearly, those who wrote this report believed that the kinds of needs identified should be paid for by the government. The investments should be made in the public sector, with tax dollars. Not all Americans would agree, however. Some of these investments, many feel, should be made by private people and groups—the private sector. Many people also disagree about priorities. There is only so much money to invest. What are

Who should pay for day-care centers and mass transit systems? Why?

Inquiry

the most important needs? Which kinds of investments should receive priority?

You have your own ideas about these matters. To make decisions about your own values, look at the following list of national needs. Opposite each need are two sets of choices. The first choice involves the importance you would assign each need. The second choice involves the method of paying for the need. Which choices most nearly match your own beliefs? (List your choices on a separate sheet of paper.)

Having made your choices, compare them with those of your classmates. Think about your own value judgments. Do the reasons that support your judgments seem as sound as differing ones used by classmates? Is one person's judgment as good as another's on matters such as these? On what bases should value judgments be made?

National Needs	Important Need	Lesser Need	Public Money	Private Money
1. Housing for low-income families	___	___	___	___
2. Jobs for the unemployed	___	___	___	___
3. Day-care centers for young children	___	___	___	___
4. A national health insurance program	___	___	___	___
5. Health care facilities	___	___	___	___
6. Elementary and secondary education	___	___	___	___
7. College education	___	___	___	___
8. Parks and other recreation areas	___	___	___	___
9. Control of air and water pollution	___	___	___	___
10. Waste treatment plants	___	___	___	___
11. Police and fire protection	___	___	___	___
12. Mass transportation	___	___	___	___
13. New airports	___	___	___	___
14. New sources of energy	___	___	___	___

Government Spending

Each year federal, state, and local governments must make decisions about the ways they will spend their money in the coming year. Generally, this decision making process begins in the executive branch.

At the national level the President, each January, sends an annual budget message to Congress. The purpose of this message is two-fold. First, it sets forth the kinds and amounts of spending the President thinks the federal government should plan for the year. Then, it sets forth the kinds and amounts of taxes the President believes should be levied to bring in the money the government will need. Much the same procedure is followed by governors and mayors.

The President's budget is studied by Congress. Changes are often made by Congress. The same thing takes place in state legislatures and city councils.

But, even after final decisions are made, changes in spending and taxing plans may be made for a number of reasons. As individuals and families with their own budget plans well know, unforeseen events can arise. In the case of the federal government, there can be something as unexpected as a war or a business recession. A war can bring about a sudden increase in spending for national defense. A recession can bring a decrease in the amount the government hoped to receive from taxes.

THE FEDERAL BUDGET

The budget of the national government is the product of months of work by the President and the Office of Management and Budget. When Congress receives the budget more work is done.

A federal budget runs to hundreds of pages. It weighs a number of kilograms. For a general idea of what the budget contains, look at the chart on this page.

The chart shows two kinds of estimates for fiscal year 1976. As used by the federal government, "fiscal year 1976" means the 12-month period that began on July 1, 1975 and ended on June 30, 1976.

The left bar in the chart shows where the national government expected to get its money for the year. Note that, for fiscal year 1976, individual income taxes were expected to furnish the

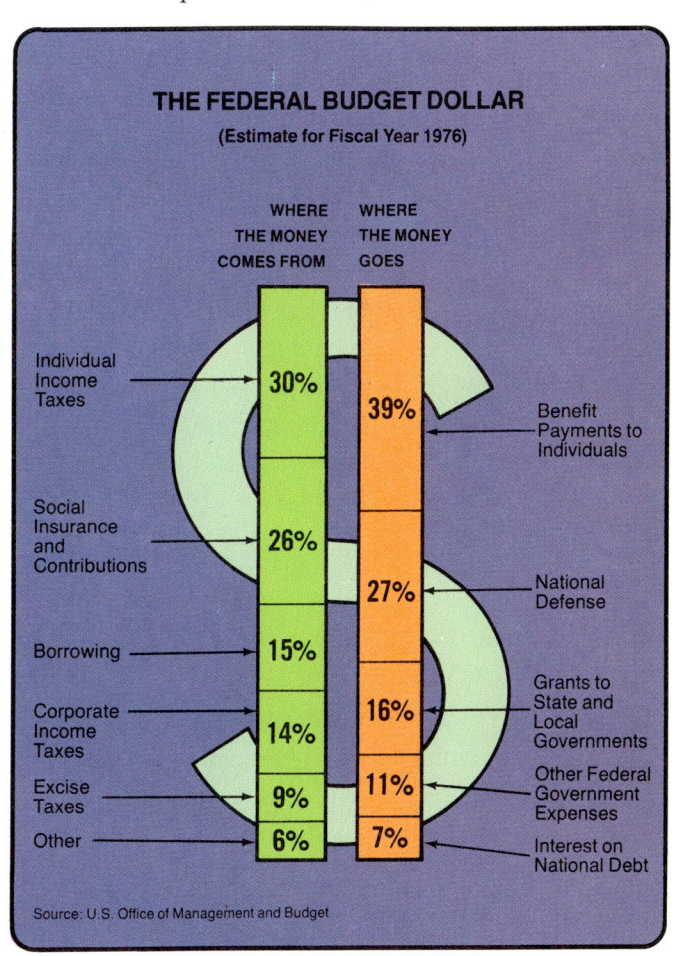

THE FEDERAL BUDGET DOLLAR
(Estimate for Fiscal Year 1976)

WHERE THE MONEY COMES FROM	WHERE THE MONEY GOES
Individual Income Taxes — 30%	39% — Benefit Payments to Individuals
Social Insurance and Contributions — 26%	27% — National Defense
Borrowing — 15%	16% — Grants to State and Local Governments
Corporate Income Taxes — 14%	11% — Other Federal Government Expenses
Excise Taxes — 9%	7% — Interest on National Debt
Other — 6%	

Source: U.S. Office of Management and Budget

THE COSTS OF DEMOCRACY

largest single source of money needed to run the government.

The right bar in the chart describes the ways the President wanted the national government to spend its money. The largest planned expenditures for fiscal year 1976 were benefit payments to individuals. Social security and veterans' benefits were expected to make up a large part of this portion of the budget. These payments and many of the grants to state and local governments were meant to promote the health and welfare of millions of Americans. Also included in the planned expenses for 1976 were large amounts of money for education and housing. Another sizable item among the expected expenses was for national defense. Included here is the money that the President thought would be needed to support the country's armed forces and programs of military aid to other countries.

The last item among the expected expenses is the money that was needed to pay interest on the national debt. The national debt is the money the federal government has borrowed. The government borrows money by issuing bonds and other securities. These are bought by private people and by banks and other institutions. This is the government's way of getting the money it needs beyond what it gets through taxes.

SPENDING BY STATE AND LOCAL GOVERNMENTS

The budgets of state and local governments are quite different from the budget of the federal government. To better understand this difference, compare the chart on the next page with the one on page 229. The chart on the next page shows major state and local expenses. The chart on page 229 shows estimated national expenses. What are the most important differences in the two charts?

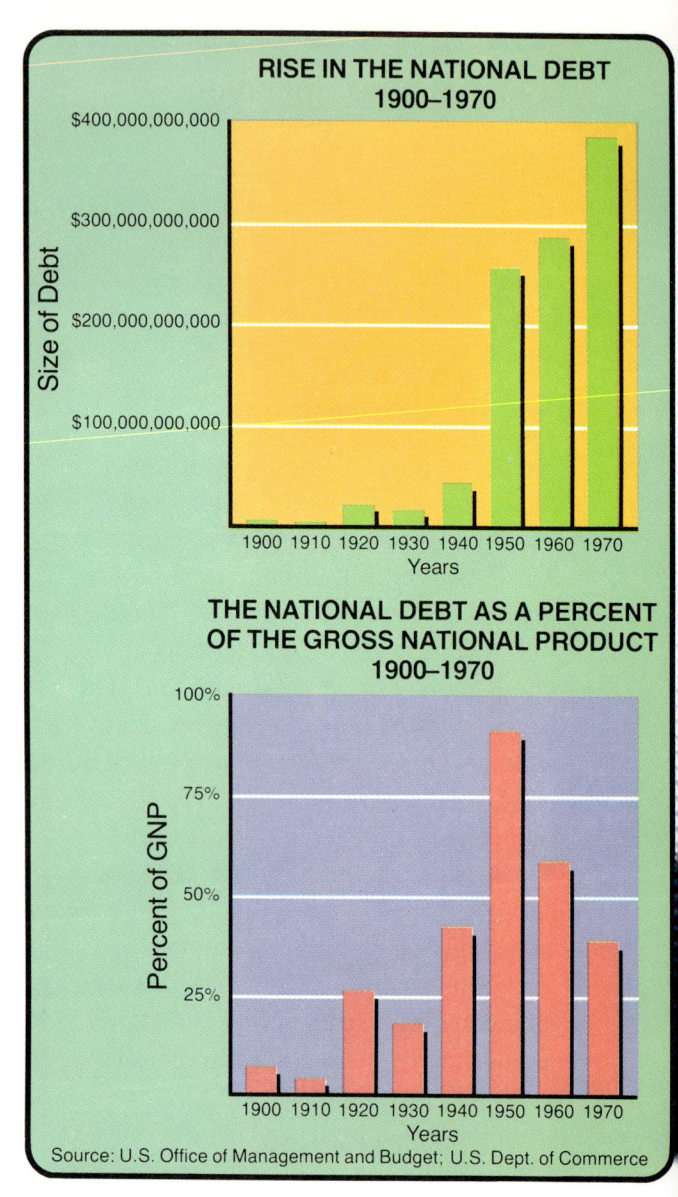

Reading the Graphs: *The first graph shows that the national debt was about $40,000,000,000 in 1940. How high had the debt grown by 1970? The second graph shows that the national debt was about 90% of the GNP in 1950. What percent was it in 1970?*

To make this comparison possible, it has been necessary to lump together and average the spending of the many different state and local governments in the United States. There are so many governments that it would be out of the question to try to look at each of them. We can, by combining them, at least get a general view of the important ways the states and local governments spent their money during one year.

You have probably already noted that the largest amount of spending by state and local governments was for education. This is understandable when we recall that education in the United States has traditionally been a major responsibility of state and local governments. Most of this money was spent for elementary and secondary education. Less than a fourth of the money was spent for higher education, that is, for public colleges and universities. Another large item was public welfare. Two other sizable items were expenditures for highways and health. Still another large expenditure was for police and fire protection.

As we look at the ways state and local governments spend their money, there is one important thing to keep in mind. Governments, like people, change their habits and ways. What seems important at one time may not seem so at another. Things that the governments used their money for in 1973 may not seem as important today. There may also be differences from city to city and from state to state.

Getting the Facts

1. What are the roles of the President and Congress in the preparation of the federal budget?

2. What are the major expenses of the federal government?   of state and local governments?

Forming an Opinion

■ Study the chart of federal income and expenses. What items do you think should be changed? Would you change any of the ways in which the government gets its money? What changes, if any, would you make in the ways the money is spent?

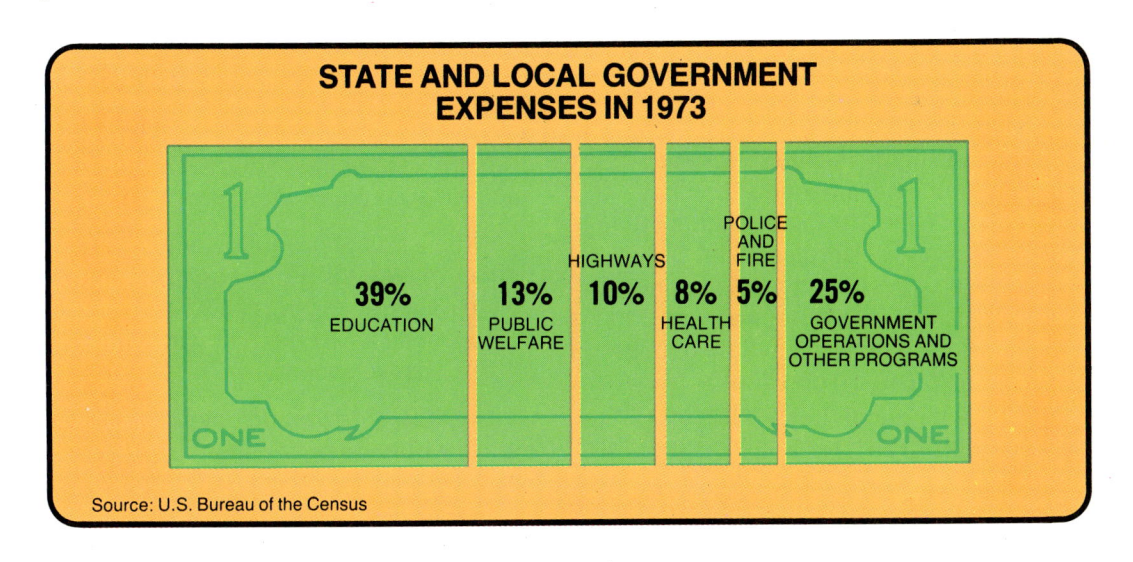

STATE AND LOCAL GOVERNMENT EXPENSES IN 1973

| 39% EDUCATION | 13% PUBLIC WELFARE | 10% HIGHWAYS | 8% HEALTH CARE | 5% POLICE AND FIRE | 25% GOVERNMENT OPERATIONS AND OTHER PROGRAMS |

Source: U.S. Bureau of the Census

Speaking Out

James J. Kilpatrick

Kilpatrick is a widely read newspaper columnist. Here he shows his concern about the growth of spending by the federal government.

". . . Federal spending, let us face it, is out of hand. With the best will in the world, neither Congress nor the White House can bring these monstrous outlays under control. The figures are literally beyond comprehension: the mind of man is incapable of comprehending the expenditure of more than a billion dollars a day. Recurring deficits [debts]—staggering deficits—have become an inflationary way of life. The fiscal [financial] cancer cries out for surgical relief.

"And the governmental crisis is not merely a fiscal crisis. In the broadest sense, we face a political and philosophical crisis also. The old constitutional system, relying upon federalism and the separation of powers, is gasping for survival. Today the federal hand is everywhere; the constraints, the regimentation, the endless rules and regulations of executive agencies spread across the whole of society. We are smothering in benevolence.

". . . Let us systematically seek to restore those precepts of state and local responsibility that were among the foundation stones of our Republic. Let us undertake to confine the national government to those functions that are plainly national in scope; as for the rest, let us keep government close to the people governed."

---

1. If the federal government spends about $1,000,000,000 a day, how much does it spend in a minute? If each of the approximately 200,000,000 Americans paid an equal share of the federal government's expenses, how much would each American pay each day?

2. What kinds of programs and expenses do you think must be managed by the national government? What kinds could just as easily be run by the state and local governments?

3. Do you agree that much of our tax money would be better spent if it were kept "close to the people governed"? Why, or why not?

The Taxes We Pay

We pay the cost of government through taxes. Taxes provide the money for public education, national defense, and all the other public services we enjoy. Since taxes touch the pocketbooks of all of us, they cause a great deal of controversy. Americans often disagree about the kind and amount of taxes government should levy.

PURPOSES OF TAXES

The main purpose of taxes is to raise money for running government programs. However, taxes are also levied for other reasons. In general, the other reasons involve the government's power to promote certain ideas and to regulate the activities of powerful groups.

The government's use of this power can be seen in taxes levied on personal incomes. These taxes are "progressive." That is, the rate of taxation becomes greater as the size of a person's income increases. A person with a relatively small income may pay only 15 percent of the income in taxes. A person with a higher income may pay 50 percent or more of it in taxes. Progressive taxes are based on ability-to-pay. The belief is that wealthier people should pay a much larger share of income in taxes. Suppose, on the other hand, that people with larger incomes did not have to spend a large part of their money for taxes. They could invest the money in business or spend it on luxury goods. Instead, our government uses its power to regulate the flow of this money. Because of the progressive income tax, the flow is directed into the public sector.

Another kind of government regulation can be found in the high taxes that are generally placed on such things as alcohol and tobacco. One reason for these heavy taxes may be to reduce the use of such products.

The government's desire to promote certain ideas and activities through taxes can also be easily seen. As a general rule, privately owned hospitals, churches, schools, and colleges are not taxed. This is because it is recognized that they contribute to people's welfare. However, there are exceptions. These offer another illustration of the government's power to regulate. Businesses owned by churches or colleges may, in a number of cases, be subject to taxation.

Through our country's history, the government has used taxes to promote and regulate American trade with other countries. This is done mainly through

The Marble House in Newport, Rhode Island is one of many splendid mansions built in the years before federal income taxes were collected.

the use of tariffs. Tariffs are taxes on goods brought in from foreign countries or sent out to foreign countries. In the United States there are tariffs only on goods coming into the country. A high tariff may be placed on a foreign product to keep it from competing with an American product. On the other hand, tariffs may be lowered to promote certain kinds of international trade.

DIFFERENT FORMS OF TAXES

From these few illustrations you can see that taxes can serve a number of purposes. It would be hard, however, to find one tax that could fill every purpose or raise all the money needed. For these reasons, today's governments collect several different forms of taxes.

1. Personal Income Taxes. Personal income taxes are levied on the earnings of individual people. This form of tax is now so important that it brings in about half of all the tax money received by the federal government. It was not until the 16th Amendment was added to the Constitution in 1913, however, that it became legal.

Most states and a number of cities also levy personal income taxes. However, these taxes are generally less important as a source of money to states and cities than they are to the federal government.

As we have noted, federal income taxes are progressive taxes. To a great extent, they are based on ability-to-pay. The same is true, but to a lesser degree, of the income taxes levied by states. In 1975, for example, federal income tax rates ranged from 14 percent on the first $1,000 of taxable income to 70 percent on income above $200,000. In New York, the state income tax rates ranged from 2 percent on the first $1,000 of taxable income to 15 percent on all taxable income over $25,000. In California, the rates ranged from 1 percent on the first $1,000 to 11 percent over $15,500. By contrast, Indiana's tax was 2 percent regardless of the size of income. City income taxes in 1975 ranged from 1 percent to as much as 3½ percent. Generally, the rate of city taxes remained the same regardless of the size of income. In other words, these city taxes were not based on ability-to-pay.

2. Corporate Income Taxes. A corporation is a form of business organization. To carry on its business, a corporation receives a charter, generally from a state government. The income earned by corporations is taxed by the federal government somewhat in the same way that personal income is taxed.

In contrast to personal income taxes, however, corporation income taxes are not progressive. The percent of tax charged is a flat, or fixed, rate. The exception is a lower rate paid by very small businesses.

Corporation income taxes are the second largest source of income for the national government. Many states also levy corporate taxes.

> **CONGRESS IS GIVEN THE POWER TO COLLECT INCOME TAXES BEGINNING IN 1913:** **The 16th Amendment to the Constitution**
>
> The Congress shall have power to lay and collect taxes on incomes, from whatever source derived, without apportionment among the several States, and without regard to any census or enumeration.

STATE SALES AND GENERAL INCOME TAXES

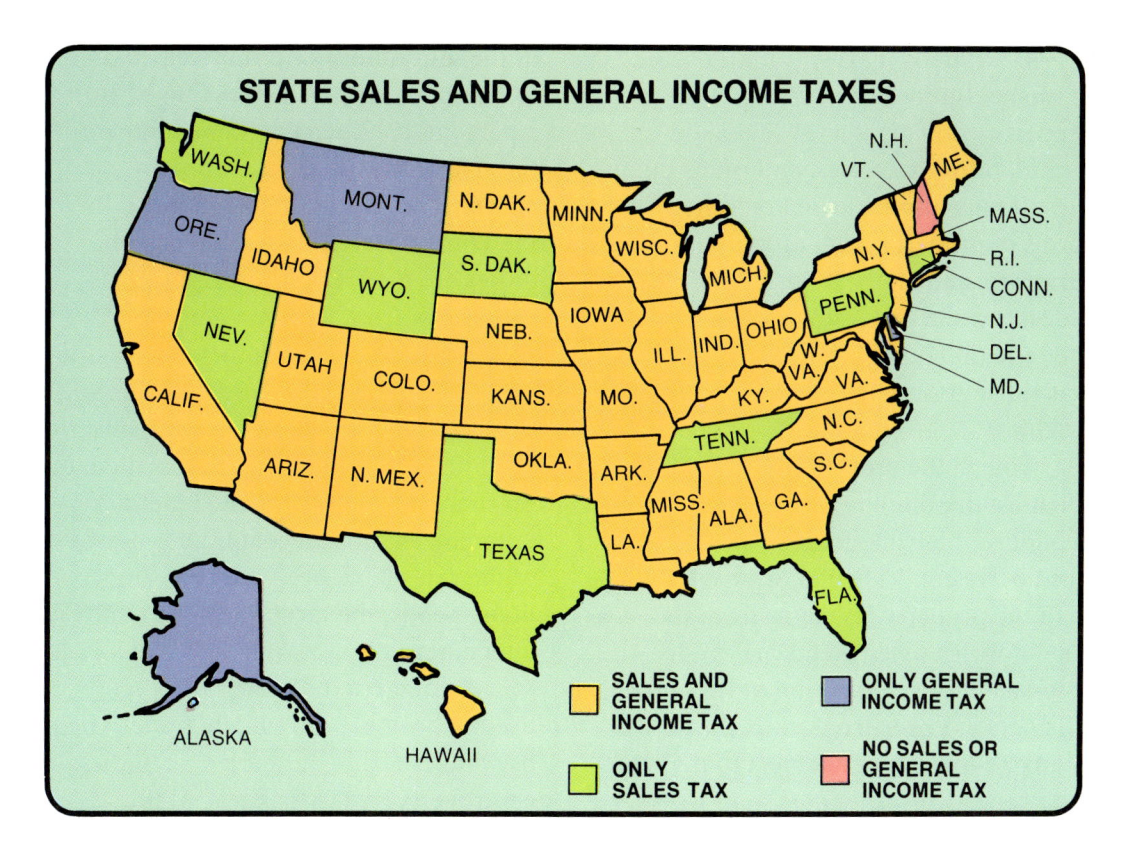

Legend:
- Sales and general income tax
- Only sales tax
- Only general income tax
- No sales or general income tax

3. Sales and Excise Taxes. Among the major sources of money for state and local governments are sales and excise taxes. These are taxes levied on the sale of goods and services.

Some form of general sales tax can be found in almost every state. A sales tax is a certain percent charged on retail sales. The rate is generally 3, 4, or 5 percent. It is collected directly by merchants from buyers. The idea of a general sales tax also appeals to many city governments. Many cities today feel the need for additional money. A sales tax offers an important source of funds.

A general sales tax has the virtue of being easy to collect. Many people also find it a relatively painless way to pay taxes. Critics, however, point to the fact that it is a "regressive" tax. As such, it differs greatly from the progressive personal income tax. The regressive sales tax levies the same rate on rich and poor alike. Many people feel that it is especially unfair to place a regressive tax on such goods as food and medicine. These are necessities that every family must buy. Yet these are the kinds of goods on which sales taxes are often levied.

These objections are not raised as strongly against excise taxes. A special kind of sales tax, excise taxes are levied on such goods as jewelry, cigarettes, and cosmetics. You will recognize that many of these are so-called "luxury" items. They are not things that everyone needs. One excise tax, however, that many Americans are concerned about is that charged on gasoline by the state and federal governments. You can see this excise tax posted on the tanks in any filling station.

THE COSTS OF DEMOCRACY

4. Property Taxes. A major source of money for local governments is the property tax. This is a tax levied on homes, farms, factories, and office buildings. It may also be levied on other forms of property, such as automobiles, furniture, and clothes. It is one of the oldest taxes in our history. It dates from the time that land, rather than income, was the most important source of wealth.

Today, the property tax may well be the most unpopular tax in America. One economist has called it the "sick giant of our tax system." The major problem with the property tax stems from the way in which assessments are made. An assessment is a calculation of the value of a person's property for tax purposes. Many people strongly object to the way the property assessment system works. One critic has described it as "nothing short of scandalous." In many places, assessments are seldom updated. Owners of newer homes often pay much higher taxes because their homes were assessed after long periods of inflation. Many local officials have been forced to search for ways to reform their assessment procedures or to find new sources of money for their hard-pressed governments.

5. Estate and Gift Taxes. A very small part of the federal and state government money comes from estate and gift taxes. Estate taxes are levied on money or property left by someone who dies. Gift taxes are taxes on gifts of money or property, over a certain value. The taxes are generally paid by the person giving the gift.

Both are progressive taxes. Like the rates on income taxes, the rates on estate and gift taxes become larger as the value of the inheritance or gift increases. In 1975, the federal estate tax ranged from 3 percent to 77 percent, depending on the size of the estate.

6. Tariffs and Custom Duties. In the United States, tariffs and custom duties are often charged on goods brought in from foreign countries. Tariff rates vary, depending on the kinds of goods imported. Before the 16th Amendment gave Congress the power to levy income taxes, the tariff was the largest source of money for the federal government. In more recent times, many of the rates have been lowered. For many goods, the tariff has been removed altogether.

As suggested earlier, tariffs can be used to promote or regulate trade. Their use makes tariffs the subject of endless controversy. A tariff affects all the people in America. It increases the cost of a foreign product wherever it is sold in our country. Often, however, it helps only the businesses in certain areas. It may, for example, protect the makers of American wines or the growers of American sugar cane, while raising the price of foreign wine or sugar that other Americans wish to buy. Equally important, tariffs can slow down international trade. A tariff on another country's cars may make it much harder for that country to sell cars in the United States. In turn, with smaller profits from American car sales, that country may not be able to buy as many American-made goods. The writing of tariff laws becomes, in other words, a never-ending process of trying to balance out different sets of interests.

Less controversial than tariffs are customs duties. Customs duties are taxes charged on products that travellers bring with them when they enter the United States. They affect only a relatively small number of people. "Going through customs" is often a memorable experience for people returning to the United States from abroad. However, it is possible to bring a certain amount into the country without paying any duties. For this reason, many tourists pay no custom duties at all.

7. **Licenses and Fees.** A final source of government money can be found under the general heading of licenses and fees. These are an important source of money for state and local governments. This kind of tax is perhaps most often seen in the form of automobile license tags. Less apparent are licenses that businesses must buy from local governments. These give businesses permission to operate. Then, there are licenses for fishing, hunting, and the like.

State governments receive large amounts of money from truck and bus license charges. This income is often earmarked for construction and maintenance of highways. There are also many kinds of fees charged by local officials to carry out certain services for citizens. These include charges to record deeds to property and other legal documents.

Getting the Facts

1. What purposes other than raising money do taxes serve?

2. Name at least five different forms of taxes collected in the United States.

3. What is a progressive tax? a regressive tax?

Forming an Opinion

■ Many of our state and local governments are in need of more money. One source may be the federal government. What other methods do you think state and local governments should use to raise money? If more money must be raised through taxes, which forms of taxes should be raised? Why?

What purposes does this tax serve?

Inquiry

Can Tax Dollars Save American Federalism?

American federalism, a unique system of government created in 1787, is in trouble. (You will find a discussion of the way federalism works on pages 50–51.) Much of the difficulty stems from money—or the lack of it. One insight into the money problem can be found in the map on page 235. Note the large number of states that have both sales and income taxes. Not too many years ago such a map would have shown neither kind of tax. At one time, the general property tax was the major source of money for state and local governments. In the years before 1913, the federal government also had no income tax. It collected money from a number of sources, including the tariff. The result was a kind of balance between the different levels of government in our federal system, at least as far as taxes were concerned.

This balance in American federalism was challenged greatly by the development of huge businesses and industries. It was also challenged by the growth of great cities. Giant oil refineries set up pipe lines stretching hundreds of kilometers. Large chain stores began to market their products from coast to coast. These businesses could not be contained within state boundaries. For this reason, they could not be controlled by state laws. Huge cities generally developed interests very different from those of the rest of the state in which they happened to be located. Many of the cities objected to various forms of state control.

One response to these changing conditions came in 1913. The 16th Amendment was added to the Constitution. This amendment gave the federal government power to impose a tax on personal incomes. Within half a century the income tax was bringing in some $100,000,000,000 a year.

Huge amounts of money began to flow into the federal treasury. It was inevitable that the American people and their state and local governments would turn to Washington for money to help them solve their problems. It was a trend that had its beginning during the depression years of the 1930s. Even then there were many who saw in the trend a weakening of American federalism. One was British political scientist Harold J. Laski who expressed the following views in 1939:

"My plea . . . is for the recognition that the federal form of state is unsuitable to the stage of economic and social development that America has reached.

"I infer from this . . . two conclusions: first, that the present division of powers . . . is inadequate to the needs America confronts; and, second, that any revision of these powers is one which must take place in Washington, and Washington only. . . .

"I infer, in a word, that the epoch of federalism is over, and that only a centralized system can effectively confront the problems of a new time. . . .

"Whether we take the conditions of labor, the level of taxation, the standards of education, public health, or the supply of amenities like housing and recreation, it has become clear that the true source of decision is no longer at the circumference, but at the center. . . ."

Because a number of people held views similar to those of Professor Laski, Congress appointed a Commission on Inter-Governmental Relations. The commission was asked to make a study of our federal system. In a 1955 report the commission saw much hope for federalism.

"The continuing vitality of state and local government affords the most solid evidence that our federal system is still an asset and not a liability.

"To be sure, it is not a neat system, and not an easy one to operate. It makes large demands on our sense of responsibility, our patience, our self-restraint. It requires toleration of diversity with respect to taxes, roads, schools, law enforcement, and many other important matters. Those who have a passion for streamlining can easily point to awkward features.

"Nevertheless, the federal principle, along with the principle of checks and balances, remains one of the great institutional embodiments of our traditional distrust of too much concentrated authority in government. . . ."

Some comfort could be found in the commission's words. However, the drift toward centralized government did not stop. Washington grew in power. It became an even greater source of money. During the last five years of the 1960s, for example, some 250 programs giving money to state and local governments were set up by Congress. These programs involved the use of federal money for such things as schools, transportation, and economic development. Viewing this continued trend with alarm, President Richard Nixon addressed the problem in his 1971 State of the Union message. He called for a "new American Revolution."

"As we approach our 200th anniversary in 1976, we remember that this nation launched itself as a loose confederation of separate states, without a workable central government. At the time, the mark of its leaders' vision was that they quickly saw the need to balance the separate powers of the states with a government of central powers.

"And so they gave us a Constitution of balanced powers . . . and so clear was their vision that it survives today as the oldest written constitution still in force in the world.

"Almost two centuries since—and dramatically in the 1930's—at those great turning points when the question has been between the states and the federal government, that question has been resolved in favor of a stronger central government. . . .

"The time has now come in America to reverse the flow of power and resources from the states and communities to Washington and start power and resources flowing back from Washington to

What is this cartoonist saying about modern changes in the federal system? Do you agree or disagree? Why?

THE COSTS OF DEMOCRACY 239

Inquiry

the states and communities and, more important, to the people, all across America."

To reverse this flow of power and money, the President suggested a "revenue-sharing" plan. The plan would give state and local governments a larger amount of the federal tax money. There hardly seemed any question about the need for money. State after state reported having to spend more than it could collect in state taxes. Cities were forced to end important public services because of rising costs and too little tax money.

The most important question involved control of the federal tax money. Should the federal government continue its rather tight control over the money given to state and local governments? Or should control of the federal purse strings be loosened to allow states and cities greater freedom in the use of federal money? One view was expressed by Democratic Senator Hubert H. Humphrey of Minnesota.

"I think that close and continual scrutiny of the pros and cons of revenue sharing is fine. We must explore this concept thoroughly before deciding the specifics of a sharing program. However, I warn against just talking about helping the states and localities. They are in grave financial condition. What they need is not an elaborate diagnosis of their ills. They don't need to be told who is to blame for their fiscal mess. What they need, and need now, is cash. . . .

"When we see city after city sinking into a state of administrative paralysis—when fire houses are closed for lack of funds—when adequate police protection is lacking—when these basic housekeeping functions of local government are beginning to be eroded and disappear, then we in Washington must act and act soon. . . .

FIRST ALLOWANCE

A NEW-BORN FREEDOM

What two opposing views of revenue sharing are shown in the cartoons on this page? What is your view of the program?

240 CIVIC RIGHTS AND RESPONSIBILITIES

"I realize that some critics of revenue sharing say it makes no sense to give state and local governments any more money. They say that states and localities cannot manage what they have now and increased Federal funding will only continue propping up out-dated and inefficient government systems. . . .

"We must not permit ourselves to get bogged down in detail. . . . There must be a flexibility here. A flexibility that will permit us to join together in securing these vitally needed funds to save our local governments from dying on the vine."

A similar view was expressed by Republican Senator Barry M. Goldwater of Arizona.

"When you get down to the crux of this fight, you run into the bureaucratic claim that states and local communities cannot be trusted to spend their tax money wisely.

"Time and again, in congressional committees and in government agencies, the claim is made that if a portion of the federal revenue is returned to the states and local communities, it may not be used for the purposes that the all-wise Washington experts think it should. . . .

"It never seems to sink in on the professional Washington bureaucrat that some of the nation's intelligence and brains reside beyond the boundaries of the District of Columbia. It never seems to occur to them that people living in Phoenix, Arizona, for example, know best what money should be spent for what in that community. . . .

"I have long rejected . . . the idea that government in Washington is more wise, more honest and more efficient than government at local or state levels. Judging from my own experience, I would venture to say that more wisdom, honesty and efficiency can be found at the lower levels of government than in the Nation's Capital. Certainly, more information exists at the local level about needs at that level."

The Future of Federalism: Analyzing Conflicting Views

The material you have just read presents a number of different points of view about our federal system. What you have read fits into two broad categories. First, there is the question of how tax money should be distributed. Second, there is the question of how political power should be shared. As an American voter, you will have to make many decisions about these matters. Think of this responsibility as you consider the following questions.

Professor Laski stated his belief that federalism was an outdated system even in the 1930s. The Commission on Inter-Governmental Relations took an opposite view, speaking of the system's "continuing vitality." Which of these points of view seems more nearly correct today? Explain.

Today we have a limited revenue-sharing program. Would you favor a greatly expanded program? To what extent do you think the federal government should control the use of federal money given to the states and cities? Do you think an expanded revenue-sharing program can solve the problems of American cities? Explain your answers.

Speaking against revenue sharing, one member of Congress said, "I sincerely believe that with the pleasure of spending funds should also be the odium of collecting them." Following this opinion, do you agree that a state or city will be more careful about the way it spends its own tax money than about the way it spends tax money collected by the federal government? Why, or why not?

To what extent do you agree with Senator Goldwater's statement that "more wisdom, honesty and efficiency can be found at the lower levels of government than in the Nation's Capital"?

Inquiry

Citizenship Laboratory

Review of Basic Ideas

1. Americans are often called upon to make decisions about the use of their incomes. They must decide whether money should be channeled into the public or private sector of the economy. Recent years have brought a great expansion of the public sector. This growth has been the result of two important developments. First, there has been a revolution in technology. Second, the United States has become a world power.

2. Government budget recommendations begin in the executive branch. As finally adopted, a budget is the result of agreements between the executive and legislative branches. The two largest items in the federal budget are for human needs—health, welfare, education, and housing—and for national defense. The largest expenditures of state and local governments are for education. Other major state and local expenditures are for roads, health, public safety, and welfare.

3. The main purpose of taxes is to raise money for running the government. Governments also use taxes to promote or regulate certain ideas and certain actions of citizens and businesses. Income taxes provide the largest source of money for the federal government. Among the largest sources of money for state and local governments are sales and excise taxes. Another major source of money for local governments is the property tax.

Questions to Think About

1. The public sector of the American economy has grown a great deal over the past 100 years. What kinds of services were once provided mainly by the private sector but are now provided mainly by the public sector? Do you favor a continued growth of the public sector? Why, or why not?

2. Why has the federal government grown so rapidly in recent times? What changes might slow or stop the growth of the federal government?

3. Describe the process by which government budgets are drawn up. In what ways are decisions about budgets related to beliefs about the directions that government should take?

4. What are some arguments for and against the idea of progressive taxes? To what extent can you justify the use of regressive sales taxes by cities and states? For what reasons do you think the policy of not taxing churches, hospitals, and private schools is fair or unfair? What are some arguments for and against the use of tariffs to regulate foreign trade?

5. Why is the property tax referred to as the "sick giant of our tax system"? If it became necessary to replace property taxes as the major source of money for local governments, what kind of tax would you favor as a replacement? Why?

Words and Relationships

Define each of the terms in the first column. Then show how each term is related to the item listed opposite it by using both items in a sentence or short paragraph.

1.	gross national product	American economy
2.	technology	changes in life styles
3.	budget	purposes of government
4.	income tax	ability-to-pay
5.	sales tax	painless-to-collect
6.	excise tax	"luxury" items
7.	assessment	property taxes
8.	estate and gift taxes	progressive tax
9.	tariff	international trade
10.	customs duties	overseas travel

Building a Future

The only way a government can spend the money it receives from taxes wisely is by making budgets. These plans for spending tax money are closely related to the government's general plans for carrying out certain policies and programs. Planning a budget is a useful process for anyone to follow. Just as the government relates income to policy plans, we can make decisions about our own activities based on our own incomes.

    At this stage, making your own budget need not be a big and complicated process. Here is one way to approach the matter with very little bother. Buy a small notebook that can be carried easily. For a month or two record in it everything you spend—for movies, snacks, parties, and everything else that is supposed to be covered by your allowance or income. At the end of this trial period, total your spending and balance it against your income. Do your income and spending balance?

    Whatever the result, analyze your spending carefully. Think of each expenditure in terms of what you really want and need. If you have come out ahead, would it make sense to place the extra money in a savings account and make plans for something you want in the future? If you spent more than your income, where can you cut back? Or, what can you do to increase your income? These are important questions. They are questions that will become more important as you grow older. They are the kinds of questions government and business must ask as they plan.

Citizenship Laboratory

THE COSTS OF DEMOCRACY

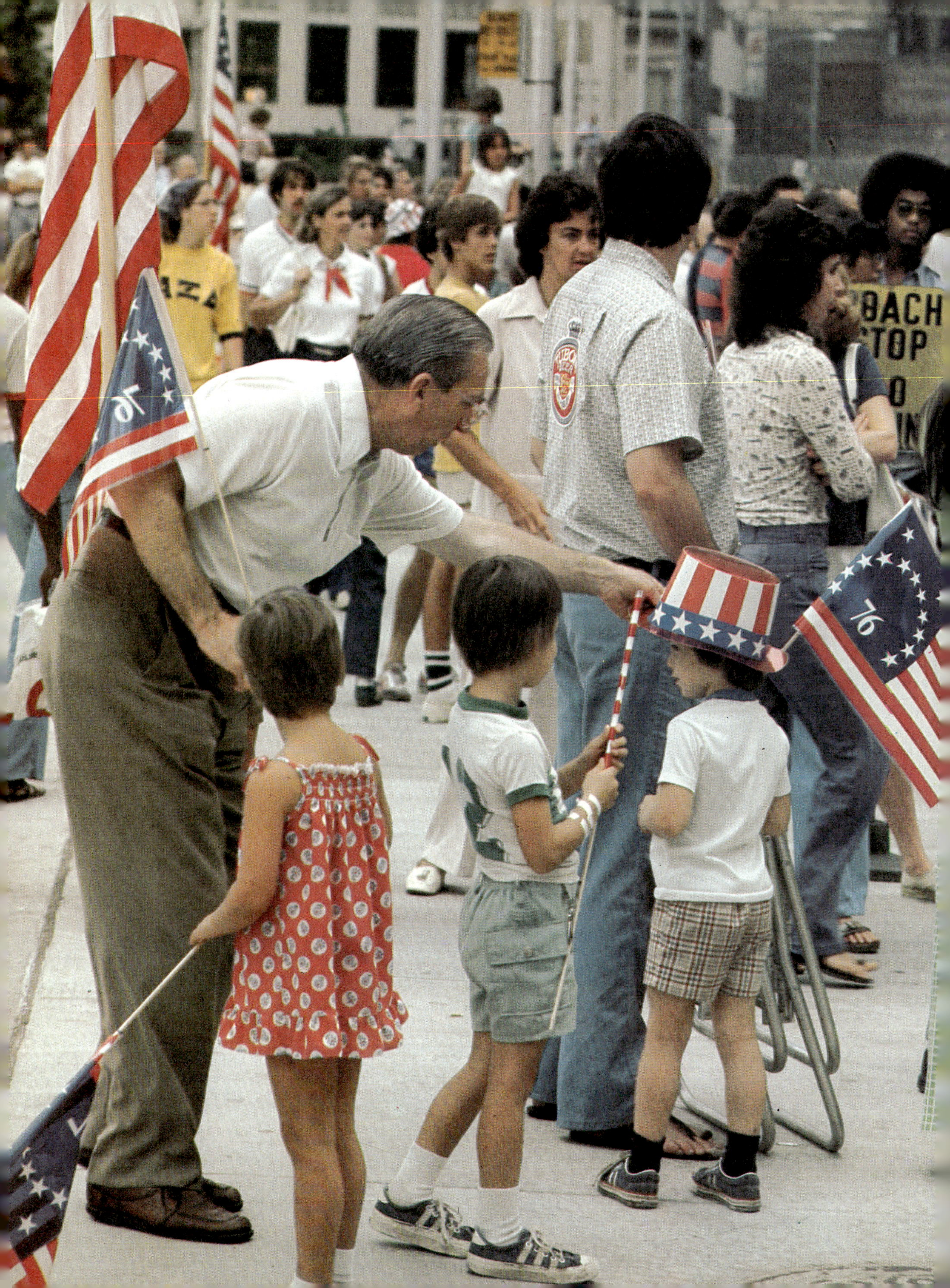

Unit Four

Life in American Communities

11 Local Government: The American Way

Los Angeles is one of the great cities of the world. When we think of Los Angeles, we generally see visions of endless freeways filled with ant-like files of automobiles. We think of busy airports with jets arriving from and departing for all parts of the world. From sandy beaches along the Pacific to towering inland mountains, Los Angeles sprawls across southern California. It almost seems a city without end.

Yet, for all its size, Los Angeles is in many ways like other American cities. It is a place with clearly defined boundaries. It has its own local government and its own elected officials. It has a city school system, police and fire departments, and so on. Spread out around the boundaries of Los Angeles are a number of other communities. They have their own governments, their own schools, their own police and fire departments.

The city of Los Angeles is a modern metropolis. The word "metropolis" is Greek. First used to describe ancient Greek city-states such as Sparta and Athens, it means "mother city." Today, in the United States, there are many metropolises. Each is a city with smaller communities clustered about it. We call these clusters "metropolitan areas."

Local government in the United States, however, is more than just the governments of the great metropolitan areas. It is government in smaller urban communities as well. ("Urban" is the word used by the United States Bureau of the Census for all communities with populations of 2,500 or more.) It is also government in rural areas. ("Rural" is the Census Bureau's term for communities with fewer than 2,500 people.)

Strong local government, whether rural or urban, is very much a part of the American tradition. At first, most of our local governments were rural since most people lived on farms or in villages. Over the years, however, there has been a steady movement of Americans toward urban centers. In the young United States of 1790 about 95 percent of the people lived in rural areas. By contrast, the 1970 census found more than 70 percent of Americans living in urban areas. Stated differently, about three out of four Americans are now urban residents. One of our major needs today is to adapt our local governments to these changing circumstances.

Traditional Forms of Local Government

Most local governments in the United States are an inheritance from earlier times. They take many forms. Generally, these governments have kept some rural features. This is because they were set up when most Americans lived in small villages or on farms.

Small scattered settlements were the means by which our country was colonized. They were also the means by which the early settlers learned the ways of self-government. The people of Jamestown acted under the authority of their home government in England. In similar manner, those in early Santa Fe were subjects of the government in Spain. However, both settlements were separated from their governments by the great distance across the broad Atlantic Ocean. In general, settlers had to find their own ways of protecting themselves, providing food, and forming an orderly society. They could not forever be running to their home governments for help.

In early Jamestown, the leaders were forced to take stern measures to save the people from starvation. A council was formed to force the settlers to work and to obtain corn from the Indians.

As settlers spread from Jamestown into other parts of eastern Virginia, they developed more ideas about local government. By 1619, only 12 years after the first settlement, the Virginia colony had grown so large that it was divided into 11 boroughs. In July of that year representatives from each borough met in Jamestown to form the House of Burgesses. It was the first representative legislative body ever to meet in America.

Ideas about local self-government were carried by pioneers into the American frontier. There the spirit of local government continued to flourish. These people, like those in the early colonies, were far removed from the power of a central government.

In the course of our country's history, ideas about local government have led to the more than 100,000 units of local government that we now have in the United States. These units are of different forms. They serve a number of different functions.

THE COUNTY

All states but two are divided into political units called counties. Louisiana has similar units, but they are called parishes. Alaska is divided into organized and unorganized boroughs.

As a unit of government, the county has a long history. English in origin, the county idea was brought to the New World by the early settlers. It proved a useful form of government for Americans who lived on farms and in small, scattered settlements. These rural people needed a center of government such as the county seat where deeds, contracts, and other legal documents could be recorded. People needed these documents to protect the land they owned. They needed a government that would acquire tax money to build local market roads, set up public schools, and provide some health services. They needed a system of courts and a means of law enforcement.

Most counties were set up before the development of modern highway systems and other means of rapid transportation and communication. For this reason, counties are generally quite small. In drawing the boundaries of a county, the idea was to make them small enough that a person could leave home, travel to the county seat by horse or carriage, transact business, and return home—all in the same day. The result is that we find today an average of more than 60 counties in each state. Delaware, with three counties, has the fewest. Texas, with 254, has the most.

The sign above lists some of the many services provided by a county in New Jersey. The Extension Service deals with agricultural matters such as the local 4-H Club.

Clearly, this inheritance from a horse-and-buggy era leaves much to be desired as a means of governing heavily populated urban areas of our country. But, for much of rural America, county government still works well. It provides many needed services.

One characteristic of most county governments is a large number of elected officials. Most of them run their own departments in the manner they think appropriate. There is generally no chief executive to coordinate government activities. Often county officials are not required or even expected to have any special qualifications for the offices they hold.

The officer most like a chief executive in many county governments is the county judge. This officer presides over a court that hears certain kinds of law suits. The judge's most important job, however, is to preside at meetings of the county board. The board is made up of officials elected from districts in the county. These officials, called magistrates in some counties, act as general managers of the county government. The business records of the county are kept in the office of the county clerk. The county's legal business may be handled by a county attorney. Law enforcement is in the hands of a sheriff and a group of appointed deputies. Counties generally have a number of other officials. Many of these are appointed rather than elected. They may include a superintendent of schools, a county health officer, and a county agricultural agent.

Important as such officials have been, the fact is that many are finding less and less to do in all but very rural counties. If the trend toward urban life continues, county governments may find even fewer functions to carry out.

THE NEW ENGLAND TOWN

The county idea found its greatest acceptance in the southern colonies. The New England colonies developed a different form of local government—the town. A town would often begin in a fort or small village. From there it would spread to take in the surrounding farm families. The area would generally range in size from about 64 to 100 square kilometers. Today these town governments continue to provide many kinds of local administration in all six of the New England states. These states also have counties, but the county governments have little power.

Perhaps the most interesting feature of town government is the town meeting.

Which of the traditional American values you studied in Chapter 2 are reflected by the New England town meeting?

Generally held in March of each year, a town meeting is traditionally open to all qualified voters in the town. However, in the more heavily populated towns today, a group of citizens are often chosen to represent the rest of the people in the town meeting. Even so, the number of representatives is large. Those who attend the town meeting elect a presiding officer. The discussions may touch on any matters of local concern—election of town officials, taxes, schools, public works, local ordinances or laws. Any question brought to a vote is decided by a majority of the people present.

Town meetings are generally held only a day or two each year. For this reason, each town must have a group of officials to carry on the daily work of government. The chief governing body is usually called the "Board of Selectmen." The group generally has from

LOCAL GOVERNMENT: THE AMERICAN WAY

COUNTIES IN THREE MODERN STATES

In the New England State of Massachusetts

Town governments have always been more important than county governments in New England.

In the Southern State of South Carolina

County governments have always been important in the South.

In the Mid-Western State of Michigan

Township and county governments are important in the Mid-West. Note how the counties follow the township squares.

THE TOWNSHIP

Not quite so old a form of local government as the New England town, but in some ways like it, is the township. Today townships make up a part of local government in more than a dozen states.

The township idea began in the colonies of New York, Pennsylvania, and New Jersey. Townships later became an important form of local government in the area north of the Ohio River and west of the Appalachian Mountains. In opening this Northwest Territory for settlement, the Congress of the Articles of Confederation government passed the Land Ordinance of 1785. The Ordinance stated that the territory should be surveyed and the land laid out in squares. Each square, an area of 36 square miles

In many parts of the Old Northwest roads and fields still follow the squares plotted at the end of the 18th century.

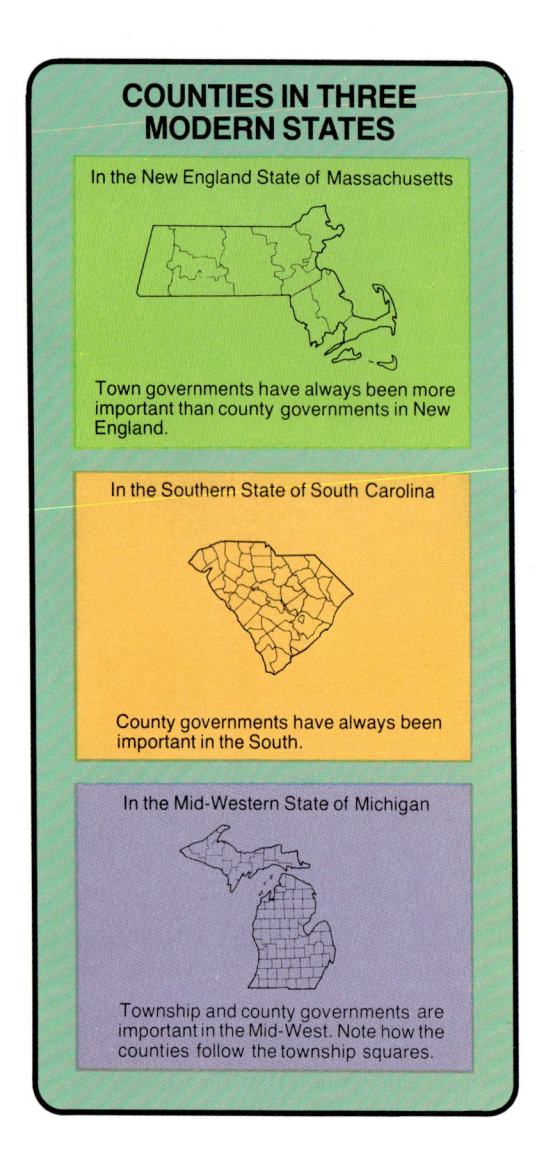

three to nine members. These people handle many town matters, including the spending of tax money and the control of town property. Towns may also have other governing bodies such as school boards.

The democratic flavor of the town meeting and the important part it allows all citizens to play in local government are valued features of our American heritage. However, we may question the appropriateness of the town government for modern urban areas.

250   LIFE IN AMERICAN COMMUNITIES

(about 94 square kilometers), became a township.

The Land Ordinance was not passed to form units of local government. It was meant to provide a means of filling these public lands quickly. Settlers and land companies could buy the land they wanted and receive deeds listing the boundaries of the land. However, many, but not all, townships soon became units of local government. Those that serve as governments are called "civil townships." Those that have remained no more than surveyed land units are called "congressional townships."

Most civil townships are units of rural governments with responsibility for such things as country roads and schools. Generally, they do not have as many responsibilities as a county or a New England town.

THE INCORPORATED VILLAGE

Driving through the American countryside, a person is likely to encounter many small communities that seem to be "just wide places in the road." Often a highway sign will give the name of the village followed by the word "unincorporated." This means that the village has no government of its own.

Many small villages, however, are "incorporated." This means that the residents have formed a local government by securing a charter from their state government. A charter of incorporation gives the village certain powers and rights. The chief governing body is generally an elected board. There may also be other officials such as law enforcement officers and school board members.

Regulations concerning incorporation vary widely from state to state. Often a village is required to have at least 500 or 600 people. State regulations may also deal with the amount of land an incorporated village can cover and the kinds of government services it may provide.

THE SPECIAL DISTRICT

Without question, the form of local government found most often in the United States is the special district. There are more than 90,000 special districts in our country. Normally, a special district is formed to provide a single government service.

School districts are a common form of special district in rural areas. Other rural districts may be concerned with such matters as soil conservation, irrigation, and land reclamation. In urban areas, special districts may be set up to provide such services as water, heat, light, and sewage disposal.

Getting the Facts

1. Name at least four forms of local government.

2. What are the basic responsibilities of each of the forms of local government you named in Question 1?

Examining the Issues

■ Which of the many services provided by local governments do you think must be provided by some form of local government? Which, if any, do you think could be provided just as well by state governments, the national government, or private groups? Explain.

Inquiry

How Do Your Local Governments Affect You?

There are units of local government all around us. They often touch our lives in ways that we neither know nor even suspect. In this inquiry, you are asked to examine your own local government or governments. An investigation might begin with these general questions:

- How aware are you of the county in which you live?
- If you live in New England, how much do you know about your town government?
- Is your home located in or near a civil township?
- If you do not live in a small incorporated village, are there any nearby?
- What special districts are there in your area?

To deal with these questions, and others that flow naturally from them, set up as many committees as needed. There should be one committee for each of the local governments in your area.

Often answers to questions about government organization or structure can be found in printed materials prepared by the local government.

Beyond matters of structure, there are more important questions of government function. In the course of your studies, you will need to deal with questions such as these:

- If you live in a city or suburb, are there any features of your county government that seem more appropriate for a rural area than for your own urban area?
- If you have a town government, do you think your town meeting is truly representative of local views? Or is your town so large and urbanized that the town meeting is controlled by a few individuals?
- Do you believe that the police in a small incorporated village should have the right to set up a radar system, in part to control traffic, but also to serve as a means of collecting money in the form of fines for running the local government?
- If your area has any special districts, what services do they perform? Are there other, larger governments in the area that offer the same services? Would it make sense to combine the services under the larger government?
- To what extent do you agree or disagree with the view that certain local government units exist largely to provide jobs for local government officials and workers?
- If your community or county were absorbed into a larger government unit, what benefits would you expect to gain or lose?

Committee reports about government structure could be presented in the form of charts and maps. Questions about government functions and appropriateness, however, might best be presented for class discussion. Much of the discussion will involve values. You may, for example, be able to offer good arguments as to why it would be more efficient for a small government to be absorbed by a larger one. You may, on the other hand, be more concerned with preserving traditions of local self-government.

Local Government in Urban America

Nothing is more characteristic of American society than the steady movement of people to the city. It is a process known as urbanization. The rapid growth of cities in the United States is shown in the graph on this page.

Every American city is, by law, a municipality. A municipality is a city or district that has a charter giving it powers of local self-government. Each municipal government functions according to the provisions of a charter granted by the state in which the city is located. The charter is in some ways like a constitution. It is a statement of the rights and powers granted to the city. Today, in the United States, there are more than 1,800 municipal governments.

DEVELOPMENT OF CITY GOVERNMENT

The earliest American cities were governed by elected bodies or councils. During the 1820s, in imitation of the state and national governments, cities began to set up separate legislative and executive branches. The council became the legislative body. The executive role

Reading the Graph: In 1870 almost 75% of the people in the United States lived in rural areas. Only a little over 25% of the people lived in urban areas. What percentage of the people lived in urban areas in 1920? in 1970?

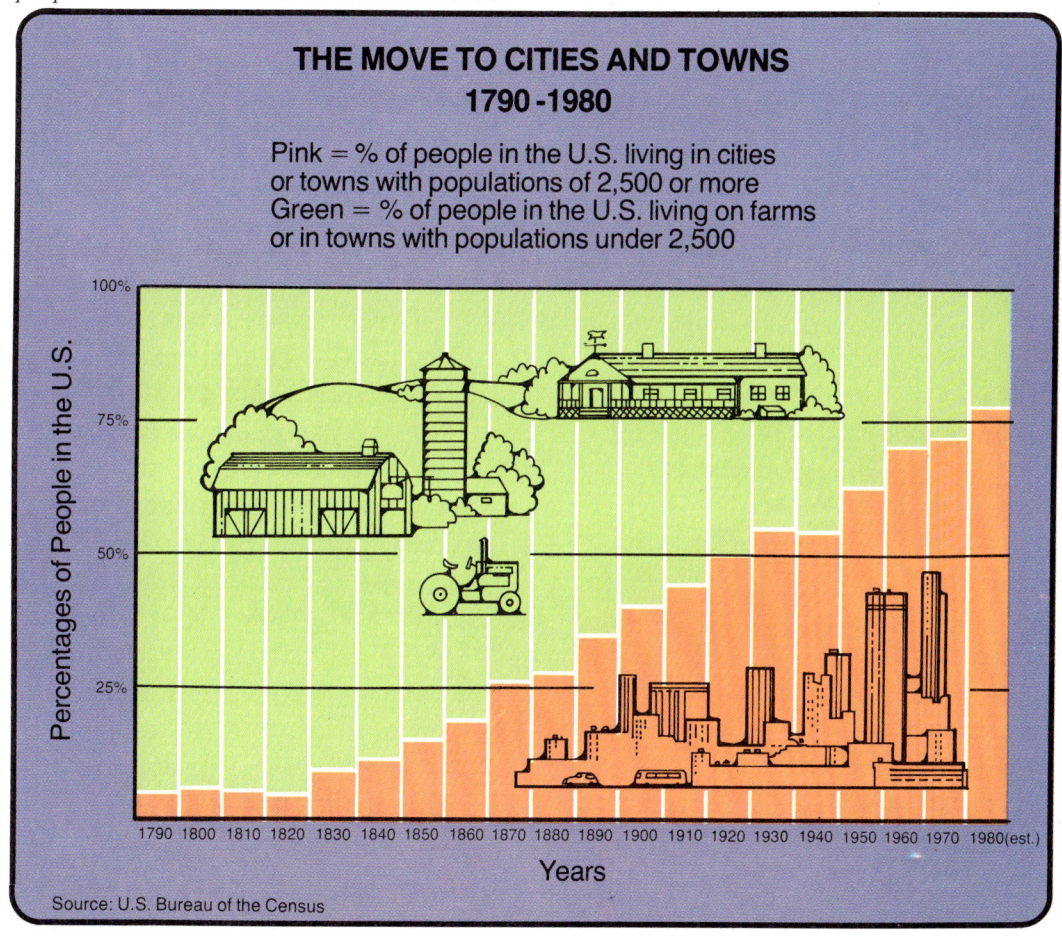

THE MOVE TO CITIES AND TOWNS 1790-1980

Pink = % of people in the U.S. living in cities or towns with populations of 2,500 or more
Green = % of people in the U.S. living on farms or in towns with populations under 2,500

Source: U.S. Bureau of the Census

was generally filled by a mayor, who was chosen by popular election. For many years, particularly in the smaller cities, the council held the chief powers of government.

The rapid growth of American cities in the late 19th century placed great strains on this kind of government organization. Expanding businesses had many needs they thought the city government should deal with. They wanted favorable locations for their plants and tax advantages. The immigrants and the native-born Americans who were moving to the cities wanted housing, education, and even simple friendship and recognition from the city governments. Weak mayors, with little power, found it difficult to meet these demands. Furthermore, the members of the city councils often had conflicting interests. They often found it hard to settle their own differences and make the decisions that were needed.

A natural result of this situation was the rise of the political machine and its boss. The political bosses in the growing cities often were not even elected officials. They were, however, skilled in dealing with office holders and voters. They used their skills to build political machines—powerful political organizations. Power to run the machines came from the ability of the bosses to deliver votes in elections. In return for their votes, immigrants and other newcomers were provided with many government services and other acts of kindness. In return for money, business leaders were given many kinds of favorable treatment.

Today, this system of bosses and machines is generally seen as a crude and dishonest way of running a city government. And, indeed, it often was. One example was the shameful Tweed Ring that gained control of the New York City government in the early 1870s. "Boss" William Tweed and his machine cheated the city of almost $100,000,000 over a two-year period. Some of the money came from graft paid by contractors to members of the Ring. An investigation uncovered a number of dishonest dealings including the payment of almost $3,000,000 to a plasterer for nine months work. In the end, Tweed was tried and sent to prison.

For all the corruption, however, there is another way of looking at boss-rule in the cities of the late 19th century. At the time, bosses were able to provide the services that the weak and inefficient local governments were not able or not willing to provide. It should be added that machine activities were in keeping with the values of the late 19th century. During that period of our history the pursuit of wealth and the doctrine of the survival of the fittest held full sway.

In the early years of the 20th century a number of Americans spoke out against the evils of the city machines. A nationwide reform movement began in an effort to find improved ways to govern cities. From the movement emerged forms of municipal government that we continue to use today.

MAYOR-COUNCIL GOVERNMENTS

One outgrowth of the reform movement was an improvement in the traditional mayor-council form of government. In many cases, the office of mayor was made stronger. In mayor-council cities the mayor is the executive head of government. Today, mayors generally make policy suggestions to city councils and hold veto power over ordinances (local laws) that the councils seek to pass. Mayors often have the power to appoint and remove heads of executive departments. In many cities, however, a number of these department heads are elected.

The tendency today is for mayors to have greater power in the larger cities and less in smaller cities. In our smaller cities, in fact, a mayor may still have very little real power.

Along with certain legal powers, a mayor may have a great deal of informal authority that comes as a result of personal qualities. Through press conferences, and on radio and TV, a mayor can help mold public opinion. As the ceremonial head of a city, a mayor represents the city at public functions, greets important visitors, and makes a number of public statements. All of these things keep the mayor in the public eye. As the executive leader of a city, the mayor also has many contacts with officials in the state and national governments. As a consequence of these many activities some of our mayors have become national figures. They may become deeply involved in national matters far beyond the bounds of their own cities.

In a mayor-council form of government, laws and regulations are enacted by a council. The council—the legislative branch of city government—is generally a one-chamber body of fewer than a dozen members. Council members may be chosen by the city voters at large (by all the voters in the city). Or each member may be chosen separately by the voters in each political ward of the city. In some cities the councils hold daily sessions. In others they meet from time to time, perhaps a few times each month. Council meetings are often open to the public.

The powers of the council, like those of the mayor, vary from city to city. Where the mayor's legal power is weak, the council holds the balance of power. Again, this tends to be the case in smaller cities. In cities with strong mayors, one often finds a struggle for power between the executive and legislative branches. The struggles are much like those between the branches of the state and national governments.

City councils tend to hold the balance of power in smaller cities and lose power as cities grow larger. What are some possible explanations for this tendency?

LOCAL GOVERNMENT: THE AMERICAN WAY

FORMS OF CITY GOVERNMENT

MAYOR–COUNCIL FORM

Voters elect → Mayor → Mayor runs city departments—fire, police, health, welfare, etc.

Voters elect → Council → Council passes city laws.

COUNCIL–MANAGER FORM

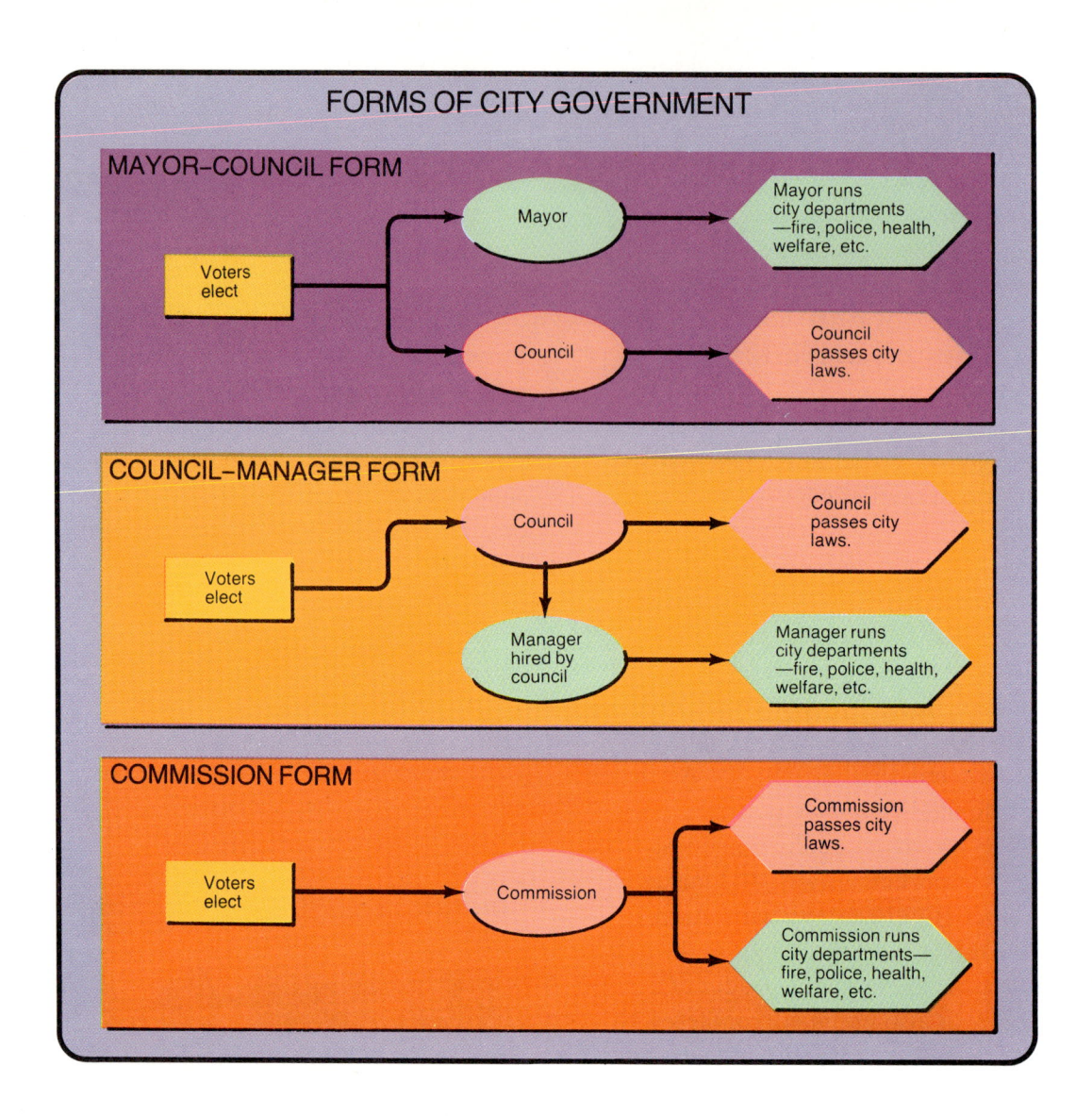

Voters elect → Council → Council passes city laws.

Council → Manager hired by council → Manager runs city departments—fire, police, health, welfare, etc.

COMMISSION FORM

Voters elect → Commission → Commission passes city laws.

Commission → Commission runs city departments—fire, police, health, welfare, etc.

COUNCIL-MANAGER GOVERNMENT

Because of the growing complexities of city government, many cities have adopted a council-manager form of government. It differs from the mayor council form mainly in the creation of the office of city manager. Chosen by the city council, the city manager is generally a professional administrator, who is highly skilled in the management of city affairs.

The council-manager form of government was first adopted in 1908, in the city of Staunton, Virginia. Today the plan is used by two out of every five American cities with populations over 5,000. It tends to be most popular in medium-sized cities. Even so, it is found in a number of larger cities. Miami, Fort Worth, Dallas, Kansas City, San Diego, and Cincinnati all have council-manager forms of government. After Cincinnati adopted the new plan, a local news reporter praised the reformed government:

> "Before 1925, Cincinnati was generally known as one of the worst governed cities in America. Its bad reputation was fully earned under a series of corrupt bosses. . . . In 1924–1925 a group of courageous citizens cleaned house, drew a new charter on the best modern lines, and won a sweeping endorsement from the people.
>
> "The new charter provided for a council of nine members chosen at large . . . and a manager with broad powers over virtually all administrative functions excepting parks, recreation, and one or two lesser matters left to quasi-independent voters. Schools, of course, are separate.
>
> "Councilmen are chosen by ballot without party designations. The names are listed in alphabetical order, and the voter marks his choice in Arabic numerals, 1, 2, 3, 4, and as many more as he likes. The result is a council absolutely representative of the electorate—as good or as bad as it deserves. . . .
>
> "Cincinnati has made tremendous progress and claims with some justice, the distinction of being the best governed of larger American cities. . . ."

This news report was written about 15 years after the Cincinnati experiment began. The report's description of the way in which a council-manager government functions is still basically true today. In most cases, the city manager is given the power to hire and fire department heads. The manager generally has overall direction of such programs as housing, welfare, police protection, and traffic.

It is well to keep in mind, however, that all real power rests with the elected city council. The manager is the agent of the council. The manager is called upon to give advice, but the council makes final decisions about matters of policy.

The manager in the council-manager form of government does not necessarily replace the mayor. Such a government may have both a manager and a mayor. However, the mayor's job is generally ceremonial. In some cases, the council has one of its own members act as ceremonial head of the city.

The council-manager form of government has the virtue of placing the daily operation of city affairs in the hands of a skilled professional. From time to time, however, weaknesses have been found in this form of government. Because managers do not have to campaign to get elected, some lose touch with the wishes of the people. In addition, some city governments have suffered because their councils have not been willing to give the managers enough freedom to run the cities.

COMMISSION GOVERNMENT

Another effort to improve the government of cities—government by commission—began under unusual circumstances. In 1900 a hurricane hit the city of Galveston, Texas. So great was the damage that the existing city government was suspended. A five-member commission was formed to oversee the city's reconstruction. The commission idea proved successful. In 1901 Galveston changed its charter to make an elected commission its form of government. The commission idea caught on quickly. By 1917 some 500 American cities had adopted it.

In recent years the commission form of government has become less popular. It can now be found mainly in

Why do you suppose the people of Galveston chose a commission form of city government to deal with the 1900 disaster?

medium-sized cities. About 10 percent of these American cities have a commission government.

Essentially, commission government is rule by a small group of elected officials—most often five, but sometimes three or seven. The commission acts as both the executive branch and the legislative branch of government. It passes laws, levies taxes, approves city budgets, and oversees the activities of city departments. In some cities the commissioners are heads of city departments. In other cities, they appoint department heads.

Getting the Facts

1. What were some of the problems of big city government in the 19th century?

2. Describe each of the three major forms of city government in the United States today.

Forming an Opinion

■ Which of the three forms of city government do you think would function best in a city of over 100,000 people? Which would be best in a smaller city? Why?

Speaking Out

Theodore J. Lowi

A student of American government, Lowi believes that city government bureaucracies have become the new political machines. He feels that in many cities, elected officials have too little control over the people working for city departments, agencies, and commissions.

"The New Machines are machines because they are relatively irresponsible structures of power. That is, each agency shapes important public policies, yet the leadership of each is relatively self-perpetuating and not readily subject to the controls of any higher authority.

"The New Machines are machines in that the power of each, while resting ultimately upon services rendered to the community, depends upon its cohesiveness as a small minority in the midst of the vast dispersion of the multitude.

"The modern city is now well run but ungoverned because it now comprises islands of functional power before which the modern mayor stands impoverished. No mayor of a modern city has predictable means of determining whether the bosses of the New Machines—the bureau chiefs and the career commissioners—will be loyal to anything but their agency, its work, and related professional norms. These modern machines, more monolithic by far than their ancient brethren, are entrenched by law and are supported by tradition, the slavish loyalty of the newspapers, the educated masses, the dedicated civic groups, and, most of all, by the organized clientele groups enjoying access under existing arrangements."

1. In our large cities, thousands of people work for the city government—in the police, fire, health, housing, welfare, and finance departments, among others. Few of them must stand for election. What are some arguments in favor of giving mayors and other elected officials more control over the staffs of the city departments? What are some arguments against increasing the power of the elected officials?

2. Americans often complain about "bureaucracies." Against what aspects of the bureaucracies do you think the complaints are generally directed? What changes in the management of city bureaucracies do you think would cause people to view them more favorably?

Inquiry

How Are the Cities in Your Area Governed?

Because the United States has become so urbanized, you are likely to be living in or near at least one city. If you are, do the cities in your area have mayor-council, council-manager, or commission forms of government? Whatever the forms, the governments of the cities in your area are probably run in certain special ways that are peculiar to your locality.

In this inquiry exercise, you are asked to study at least one of the city governments in your area. The study suggested here has two purposes. In seeking answers to questions about city government you will need information about (1) the structure and functions of government and (2) the way forces outside the government can, and often do, influence the way the government is run.

In your search for answers, the first kind of information is rather easy to come by. It should not be difficult to obtain certain basic facts about government organization:

- What is the length of term for the mayor, manager, or commission members?
- What is the length of term for council members?
- Are council members elected at large (by all the people in the city) or by wards?
- How often does the council meet?
- What kinds of departments and special boards does the government have?
- Are department heads and board members appointed or elected?

This kind of information, while appropriate to the question at hand, is purely factual. Questions of power and influence are much more difficult to answer. For these, we must often rely on opinion rather than fact. Consequently, as you seek answers to the following questions you are likely to get very different answers from different people and sources.

- If you are studying a mayor-council government, does the office of the mayor seem to be "weak" or "strong"? What legal powers does the mayor have? In using the powers of the office, does the current mayor seem to be strengthening or weakening the position of mayor in any way?
- If you are studying a council-manager government, how long has the manager served? How well qualified does the manager seem to be for the job? Does the manager seem to have too much or too little power?
- If the government you are studying has a council, do the members of the council play a major role in the daily affairs of the city?
- If you are studying a commission form of government, which commissioners seem to have the most power? Why?
- In recent city elections, have there been any signs that voting is being controlled by a political machine? If so, which city officials seem to be most closely associated with the machine?
- What evidence is there of a "spoils system" in the city? That is, to what extent do people get jobs in city government because of their political or personal connections rather than because of their ability?

Inquiry

Questions about who really runs a city can lead one outside the legal framework of city government. In many cases, political power can be found outside city hall. Power may be held by business and labor organizations, by service clubs and by other special interest groups such as those formed by teachers and landlords.

What happens when groups outside the city government decide to use their political power to influence the affairs of the city? In some cases, the city government grants the reasonable or minor demands of the groups. In other cases, the government doesn't need to take any action because the power of one interest group is balanced by the power of another.

Sometimes, however, the actions of interest groups can lead to major problems. An example of such problems can be found in a crisis that developed in New York City in the winter of 1968. It came as a result of a strike by city sanitation workers. So powerful were the striking workers that neither the mayor, John Lindsay, nor the governor of the state, Nelson Rockefeller, was able to come to an agreement with the workers without making important concessions. Week after week the people of the city watched the piles of garbage lining their streets grow larger. Finally, it was decided that the city must meet the major demands of the striking workers.

One observer, political philosopher Walter Lippmann, believed the New

What is this cartoonist's view of the 1968 strike of sanitation workers in New York City? Do you agree or disagree? Why?

LOCAL GOVERNMENT: THE AMERICAN WAY

Inquiry

York crisis had broad implications for all large cities. He viewed the problem as one that cities could not solve, but only manage.

"Living in a big city like New York fits G. K. Chesterton's description of modern civilization. We are, he said, like men at the bottom of the ocean. They get their air and everything else they need through tubes that can easily become tangled and fouled up.

"Robinson Crusoe, the self-sufficient man, could not have lived in New York City. These last few weeks the garbage piled up in the streets, and if the snowstorm that was threatened had come, the traffic would have been impossible. In recent months we have nearly had a standstill of transportation, both horizontal and vertical. The schools have been closed by a teachers' strike, and there have been threats by the police and the firemen.

"New York is a dramatic and conspicuous example of the vulnerability of urban living. Certain services are indispensable to city dwellers. In the past they have been more or less taken for granted. But in our time such services as collecting garbage and operating subways and buses are performed by men who have learned to organize. These men read that this is an affluent society. They hear about the goods and services of affluent people. They realize that by striking they can come nearer to a glittering, affluent good life. They know they have power, and they have not yet tested the limits of that power.

". . . The fact of the matter is that a great modern city has no means of enforcing a law against powerful unions. There is no way of evading the fact that in a city as big as New York only the garbage men can collect the garbage. This is their power. The individual citizen does not have his own incinerator. The police and firemen cannot collect garbage. The courts cannot put in jail or levy fines on thousands of garbage men. . . .

"Modern living is dangerous. We are confronted with a fateful question—can we remain a free society and still provide the great urban masses with the vital services they must have?

"We must remind ourselves that it is not written in any book or enshrined in any law that American democracy will master the problem of modern living. The American way of life was formed in a simple environment when the mass of the people had not yet become dependent, as they are today, upon the restraint and the goodwill and cooperation of the people of their communities."

Analyzing Questions of Political Power

With the Lippmann selection in mind, think of the cities in your area. Consider the following questions.

Can you find any examples of political control by groups outside the city government? What problems, if any, have been created by the use of the power that these groups hold?

Do the people of any residential areas in the city seem to have more political power than other people in other areas? If so, what seem to be the sources of the power held by these people?

"The American way of life," according to Lippmann, "was formed in a simple environment when the mass of the people had not yet become dependent, as they are today, upon the restraint and the goodwill and cooperation of the people of their communities." Are there examples in the cities in your area of the unwillingness of people to cooperate? What are possible steps that could be taken by city governments, voters, or private groups to promote the best interests of all people in the cities?

262 LIFE IN AMERICAN COMMUNITIES

The Government of the Great Metropolitan Areas

Spotted across the American landscape are many large clusters of people. Each cluster forms one of our country's great metropolitan areas. We know each area best by the name of the major city in the area. When we think of metropolitan areas, we generally think of big cities—Seattle, Denver, Houston, Chicago, Atlanta, Boston. However, almost all of the metropolitan areas have, not one, but a number of different units of government. These units have often been formed with little concern for any overall plan. They have simply been set up as needed in response to the steady movement of Americans from country to city and from city to suburbs. Organizing these many government units so that they can work together smoothly is one of the major concerns of every metropolitan area.

PIECEMEAL GOVERNMENT

The New York metropolitan area offers a good example of the piecemeal kind of government often found in metropolitan areas. New York City has its own city government. The New York metropolitan area, however, is spread over parts of three states—New York, New Jersey, and Connecticut. Within this area there are more than 20 separate and independent counties. Each county has its own government. Then, there are the many suburbs. A number of suburban communities have their own city governments. Other suburban communities have become incorporated villages.

To the north of New York City lies Westchester County. To the west lies New Jersey. These areas, along with parts of Connecticut and Long Island in the east and more of New Jersey in the south, are all a part of the New York metropolitan area.

LOCAL GOVERNMENT: THE AMERICAN WAY **263**

Finally, the metropolitan area contains a large number of special districts, each providing a single service—public school districts, water districts, and the like. In all, the New York metropolitan area has about 1,400 units of local government.

As new communities develop around large cities they tend to incorporate as separate cities. This is generally easy to do, for state laws of incorporation have come out of a rural age when most people lived in widely spaced villages and small towns. Once a suburban neighborhood receives its own city charter, it usually remains a separate city. Although the central city may grow larger and begin to surround the suburban city, state laws usually make it hard for one city to take over another. As the metropolitan area expands, a patchwork of separate and independent cities and villages is formed.

In many ways, the people of the suburbs benefit from this kind of patchwork government. They are able to run their own local governments. They can set up their own residential and business zones. They can run their own schools. They can provide most of the government services that they believe are needed. But when problems arise that affect all of the people of the area, the many different suburban governments generally find it quite hard to work together to find answers.

COMMON CONCERNS

The problem with having suburban governments in the outer city is that they are not really little towns and neighborhoods in the open country. The fact is that in the metropolitan areas people's lives are highly interrelated. What happens in one city or village can easily affect people in the surrounding communities. Polluted air and water do not recognize city limits. Crime, fire, and disease can all spread quickly from town to town.

One of the best examples of the common concerns of the suburbs involves the matter of transportation. Many people in the residential suburbs want modern expressways to carry them quickly and easily into the central city. Clearly, these highways cannot be built and maintained by the small cities through which they pass. When new highways are built, generally by the state or national governments, there is a strong tendency for the metropolitan area to grow in their direction. A new expressway may be built across open country. But its very existence serves as a magnet to draw businesses, new construction, and people away from older areas. Thus building an expressway calls for overall and long range planning. It calls for decisions about the way the land in the metropolitan area is to be used. Such planning cannot be done by small, separate cities and villages.

EXPERIMENTS WITH METROPOLITAN GOVERNMENT

The problems of governing metropolitan areas are well known and widely recognized. Yet for many reasons, people are reluctant to make overall changes. For one thing, our heritage of rural government causes many Americans to value small, local units. In the suburbs there is often the fear that taxes might rise after a merger with the central city. There are also personal and political concerns. The suburbs tend to be heavily middle or upper class. Many suburban people are fearful of the central city with its poor neighborhoods. At the same time, groups in the city may be reluctant to give up their control of city politics.

In the face of these many concerns it is not surprising that little progress has been made toward effective government of metropolitan areas. However, in four southern cities—Miami, Atlanta, Nashville, and Jacksonville—major efforts have been made.

Some years ago Miami and other cities in Dade County formed a metropolitan alliance. The desire for a single government was brought to a head by a pollution problem.

Government cooperation in Atlanta has centered around the problem of law enforcement. The metropolitan area now has a single law-enforcement agency. This has made it possible for police officers to adopt a number of anti-crime measures. They are now able to deal with lawlessness in a much more effective manner. Beyond this group effort, however, the metropolitan area remains fragmented.

One of the most ambitious experiments in metropolitan government is that found in the city of Nashville, Tennessee. In 1963 the Metropolitan Government of Nashville and Davidson County was set up. The government is mayor-council. There is one school system and a single law-enforcement agency. Other services of local government—fire protection, water and sewage services, public works, aviation—are also handled by the Metropolitan Government. Within the metropolitan area are about a half a dozen small incorporated cities. But even these "satellite cities" use certain metropolitan services, such as schools. A recently developed metropolitan government in the Jacksonville, Florida area is somewhat like the one in Nashville.

Pollution is especially undesirable in an area that receives much of its income from tourists. What action did the people in Miami take to solve their pollution problems?

Getting the Facts

1. What is a metropolitan area? How are most metropolitan areas governed?

2. Why are Americans in a number of cities experimenting with new forms of metropolitan government?

Examining the Issues

■ Many of the experiments with metropolitan government have focused on a single major problem such as pollution, law enforcement, or schools. Which of the services provided by local governments do you think should be provided by a huge central government? Which do you think should be provided by small local governments?

Review of Basic Ideas

1. Many of the forms of local government found in the United States today are an inheritance from an earlier, more rural period. The democratic ideas about self-government that developed in colonial villages and towns are still very influential. Today, county governments are found in nearly every state. In certain parts of the country, there are town governments, civil townships, and incorporated villages. Throughout the country, there are special districts, each set up to perform a single government service.

2. In the early years of our country, most city governments were run by elected councils. The executive role of mayor grew slowly. The weakness of many 19th century city governments led to the rise of political bosses and machines. In the early 20th century, a reform movement sought to improve city governments. In many cases, the mayors were given increased power. The mayor-council form of government remains the most common form of city government today. A number of cities have adopted a council-manager form of government in the belief that a professionally trained manager could best deal with the many problems of modern cities. Other cities have adopted a commission form of government.

3. The great metropolitan areas of our country are generally made up of a number of independent local governments. The piecemeal nature of local government in these areas cannot disguise the fact that the people of every metropolitan area have many common concerns. To deal with these common concerns, experiments are being made in many areas to find better ways of governing metropolitan areas.

Questions to Think About

1. Why do you think early Americans developed so many different forms of local government?

2. To what extent are counties, New England towns, and civil townships appropriate forms of government for modern urban areas? In what kinds of areas would each of these three forms of government be most appropriate?

3. In a mayor-council form of government, where do you think the majority of the power should rest, with the mayor or with the council? Why?

4. One argument in favor of the council-manager form of government is that modern cities, like modern businesses, are better run by professional administrators. Do you agree or disagree with this statement? Why?

5. What are the advantages and disadvantages of the commission form of local government?

6. In what ways does a modern suburban village resemble an early colonial village? In what ways do the two villages differ?

7. For the large metropolitan areas of our country would you favor overall metropolitan governments, metropolitan alliances to deal with specific area problems, or a continuation of the many local governments now found in the areas? Explain your answer.

Words and Relationships

Define each of the terms in the first column. Then show how each term is related to the item listed opposite it by using both items in a sentence or short paragraph.

1. county — rural conditions
2. congressional township — sections of land
3. incorporated village — state charter
4. special district — government services
5. municipality — self-government
6. political machines — growth of cities
7. ordinance — city council
8. commission government — executive branch
9. metropolitan area — common urban concerns
10. satellite cities — piecemeal government

Building a Future

In this chapter you have studied the many different forms of local government in America. You have also been asked to explore certain features of government in your area. Looking to the future, think of ways that your local government might be changed so that it could better meet the challenges of the coming years.

Think first of the special features of your local area. Every area has its own characteristics. These are related to such factors as historical traditions, geographic features, population characteristics, and political power structures. Taking these things into account, how can government in your local area be improved?

If you live in a metropolitan area, think about these possibilities:

- substituting a single metropolitan government for the many existing city and village governments;
- combining important urban services, such as schools, police, water, and sewage under a single government.

If you live in a smaller urban area with a single city government, consider these possibilities:

- changing the form of government, or strengthening certain features of the present government;
- improving the way in which certain services, such as traffic control are performed.

If you live in a rural area, think about these possibilities:

- reorganizing your village, county, town, or township to make it more efficient;
- combining a number of the local governments in your area.

12 Local Issues: Housing and Education

In the summer of 1969 Americans and, indeed, people around the world, thrilled to the deeds of two American astronauts. For the first time, people walked on the surface of the moon. It was truly a magnificent achievement.

But even as awestruck Americans turned their eyes to the heavens in response to the dramatic act, many of them were also calling attention to pressing problems on the earth.

One problem was housing. Noting the need of millions of families, George Romney, Secretary of the Department of Housing and Urban Development, declared that America must now seek a new goal. With the moon landing achieved, he said, the country's next major goal should be "a decent home for every American." His was not a new idea. The words, in fact, were the same as those written into congressional housing legislation in 1937. But while the moon program was able to reach its goal in the 1960s, the housing program, in Secretary Romney's words, was "losing ground."

Another problem of major concern in 1969 was the country's system of public education. Declaring schools "the business of everyone—everyone who is concerned about the future," the Com-

268 LIFE IN AMERICAN COMMUNITIES

mittee for Economic Development warned:

> "Unless schooling keeps pace with the large demand that will be made on it in the years ahead, the American people will not achieve their personal, community, and national goals."

American desires for adequate homes and good schools are very old goals. From the time of the earliest settlements, comfortable dwellings and some means of educating the young were high on the list of priorities. They remain high today. Yet, they seem to be goals that are more difficult to achieve than the single goal of placing astronauts on the moon.

Issues Affecting the American Family

The family is a social institution as old as civilization. It is not, however, the same kind of institution in all societies. Families function in accordance with the values of their own cultures. And, of course, these values not only differ from place to place, but may change from time to time. In the United States, for example, people have always valued housing and education. But ideas about the nature of good housing and education have changed. Changes in these and other values and in society itself have helped bring about changes in the nature of the American family.

LIFE IN THE TRADITIONAL AMERICAN FAMILY

During the early years of our country, most Americans lived on farms. There were some large estates with hired workers and some plantations and farms with slaves. But most families did their own work without outside help. Each family was, in many ways, a little community. All family members were expected to do their share of the work. In most cases, families were large. The average family had from six to eight children. This was fortunate, for many hands were needed to run the farms.

Female and male roles were, for the most part, clearly defined. In most cases, women and girls ran the household. They prepared the meals, canned fruits and vegetables, baked bread, sewed the family's clothing, and cared for the house and the young children. Men and boys generally built the house, grew the crops, cared for the farm animals, and made the furniture and farm tools.

Young children were expected to work as soon as they were old enough to do simple tasks. A boy would carry in firewood soon after he had learned to walk. By the age of 10 he would be plowing a field for the spring planting. Girls helped their mothers by gathering vegetables from the garden, caring for the younger children, and doing other household tasks. During harvest time, the entire family might be found working together in the fields.

The social roles in most families were clearly understood and accepted. The father was the "head of the house." Legally, everything a family owned belonged to the husband. He could do whatever he wished with the family property. Marriage was regarded by most people as a life partnership. Divorce was rare. In this partnership, the husband had certain rights as family head and basic responsibilities for the

What roles would each of the members of this 19th century family probably have played in building a new life on the Nebraska frontier?

family's well-being. He was expected to be the provider of house and food. He decided how to use any money the family might have. As head of the family, a father usually considered himself responsible for all persons under his roof. Generally a wife felt obliged to abide by her husband's decisions and strict obedience was expected from the children. The father saw to it that the boys learned to read, write, and do simple arithmetic. The education of the girls was often not seen as important. In many families, whatever education the girls received, they picked up from their brothers or from their mother.

THE CHANGING FAMILY IN MODERN AMERICA

Many aspects of life in traditional families are likely to seem strange to people living in modern American families. A great number of changes have taken place in family roles and activities. To better understand the differences between traditional and modern families, let us look briefly at the major changes in society that have so altered the nature of family life.

Major changes came with the Industrial Revolution. The effects of this revolution could be seen in England during the last half of the 1700s. By substituting the use of power-driven machines for hand labor, production was revolutionized. It was a revolution that brought not only a new age of machines, but an age of machines housed in factories, located in cities. Soon families were making fewer things by hand. More and more work was done by machine. People were paid wages for this work. With the money they earned they bought what they needed.

Family life was greatly affected by two important products of the Industrial Revolution: industrialization and urbanization. Through the process of industrialization, machines were placed in factories to form large industries. The existence of jobs in the industries led to urbanization. That is, people who needed jobs came to the cities where so many of the large factories were located.

At first the Industrial Revolution developed slowly in the young United States. By the 1820s, however, a number of factory towns had been set up. By the 1850s industrialization was taking firm hold. Rural families by the thousands were drawn from the farms to the cities. Immigrant families from countries such as Ireland and Germany saw in the busy machines and billowing smokestacks the hope of a new life in a new land.

At the same time, industrialization was also affecting the families that remained on the farms and the immigrants who settled on the land. Railroads brought goods from city factories. Machines were designed to do the work of animals and farm hands. The new machines greatly altered the ways of those who lived in rural America.

Yet farm families continued to live, for the most part, in scattered rural homesteads. Greater changes were seen in the housing patterns of city people. Dwellings in the growing cities of the new industrial America were built side-by-side in row houses or stacked atop one another in tenements.

Activities within the dwellings were also greatly changed. Most fathers and many mothers began to work away from their homes in factories and offices. Food, no longer produced at home, was bought in packages and cans. Clothing was made in factories and called, by the rural-minded, "store clothes."

In the course of these changes the father's authority as head of the family was weakened. Children received less supervision from parents who found it necessary to be away from home for long hours during the working day. As a result, many children developed a new kind of independence. Nor were there as many children born. Some people may have decided to have fewer children because they were no longer living on farms where so many workers were needed. By 1900 the average American family had only about three children. Today the average is about two per family.

The partnership between wives and husbands grew more equal. In the cities, women had a greater opportunity to find jobs outside the home. Attitudes about

What are some of the many ways industrialization has affected life on modern American farms?

What roles do you think the members of an average American family will be playing by the year 2000?

education for women changed. More and more young women attended high school and college. Married women gained the legal right to own property. And in 1920 women gained the right to vote.

Getting the Facts

1. Name at least three ways in which the average American family has changed since the colonial period.

2. What general changes in American society helped bring about changes in the American family?

Forming an Opinion

■ If you plan to have a family, in what ways would you want your family to resemble the average family of the 18th or 19th century? In what ways would you want your family to be different from the traditional pattern? Why?

Good Housing for All: A National Goal

People were drawn to cities because they seemed to offer hope and opportunities. Good housing was part of the dream, but it was a dream for the future. Like the pioneer family willing to live in a crude sod house on the Nebraska frontier, many city people hoped for a comfortable dwelling tomorrow, not today.

For millions of Americans, both rural and urban, that day is now here. They live in comfortable houses. Their homes are filled with the miracles of modern technology. This is not true for all Americans, however. For many the promise of a decent home is still beyond reach.

CHANGING HOUSING PATTERNS

The pattern of city growth was strongly influenced by the railroads. Businesses and factories were set up in the downtown areas near the railroad stations. Houses for workers were built close to the businesses and factories because most workers had to walk to work. Land, however, was scarce. So, it was common to build houses in long rows with no space between them. Space was also saved by building tenements of many stories. Some of the wealthier people lived in town houses. People with a great deal of money could afford houses outside the city near station stops on the railroad lines.

Smaller towns in America were also influenced by the railroads. Trains became rural America's link with the outside world. The towns with railroad

272 LIFE IN AMERICAN COMMUNITIES

stations often became important service centers for the countryside around them.

The arrival of the streetcar brought new housing possibilities for city families. Streetcar fares were reasonably low. As streetcar lines fanned out from the center of the city, new housing often followed. Even families with moderate incomes were able to buy homes with large yards and more privacy. Small neighborhood marketing centers were built to serve people moving to the outskirts of the cities. These new neighborhoods along the streetcar lines became, in some ways, like small towns. The shops and schools that were built in these areas brought people into close and frequent contact.

The coming of the automobile made it possible for homes and neighborhoods to spread in all directions. Houses and roads filled in the empty spaces that streetcar tracks had not reached. Individual houses with grassy lawns became a part of the American way of life. Suburban neighborhoods grew up around large cities. People in smaller towns also found it possible to move away from the downtown area. New businesses were started along the modern highways serving both urban and rural Americans.

Even with the departure of many city families, the houses in the central business districts remained. As they were abandoned by some, others arrived to take up the overcrowded quarters. In the process, buildings were allowed to become shabby and run-down. Many owners hoped to sell the valuable land to new businesses looking for sites in the central city. Often, however, the promise of new business never arrived. So the slums remained. Today they provide housing for many who can afford nothing better. It should be noted, however, that not all central districts have suffered this fate. There are still a number of highly desirable neighborhoods found in the centers of San Francisco, Boston, Philadelphia, and many other American cities.

The fate suffered by many city centers has also befallen the houses built along the streetcar tracks. Although they once seemed far away from the city center, they now seem very close. Many are no longer in desirable neighborhoods. They are often too large for today's

The height of city buildings was limited until safe elevators were developed in the second half of the 19th century. However, builders did everything they could to crowd as many people as possible into the central parts of the cities.

families. Many are not designed to be divided into apartments. So they stand old and almost forgotten. Still, they are used by people too poor to move to the suburbs and by older people who want to be near the center of things. Fortunately, some people have taken pride in these old neighborhoods and have maintained them as desirable places to live. All too often, however, the houses along the early streetcar lines have been allowed to decay in the same way that the inner city slums have.

What solutions would you favor for solving the problem of city slums? Why?

PUBLIC SUPPORT FOR HOUSING GOALS

Through most of our history, housing has been thought of as a private, rather than a public, matter. It was not until the depression years of the 1930s that Americans became interested in using the forces of government to help provide good housing for all families. At that time perhaps one third of the American people were living in dwellings that could be regarded as below minimum standards for decent housing.

To help with the problem, Congress passed the Housing Act of 1937. The purpose of this act was to give aid to communities and states so that they could build "decent, safe, and sanitary dwellings for families of low incomes."

The program had hardly gotten under way when World War II began. War workers were needed in factories, shipyards, and military camps. Temporary houses for these workers had to be built in a hurry. All other housing plans were sidetracked.

When the war was over the federal government again moved into the housing field. In 1947 the Housing and Home Finance Agency was set up. Two years later the Housing Act of 1949 was passed. Its goal was 135,000 new low-cost public housing units a year for the next six years. It set in motion the program that came to be known as "urban renewal."

The purpose of urban renewal has been to rebuild parts of our cities. The program is based on the belief that slum neighborhoods and blighted business areas are problems that must be handled mainly by government rather than by private people and groups. To deal with the problems, city governments have entered into agreements with the national government to acquire land. The national government, in turn, has sold the land to people whom it believes will develop "decent, safe, and sanitary housing" and new business centers. In the process the national government has agreed to pay most of any financial losses that may arise for the cities.

The urban renewal program may appear sound in theory. But it has, at best, produced mixed results. Clearly, it has not provided adequate housing for all Americans. It has definitely failed to provide enough housing for the very poor in the inner cities.

Partly because of these criticisms of government housing programs, Congress and the President, in 1965, combined all government housing agencies and programs and set up a new cabinet level agency—the Department of Housing and Urban Development (HUD). It became the task of the new department to try to bring together all the urban activities of the federal government. One of the first HUD projects was known as the Model Cities program.

The Model Cities program called for the federal government to give financial aid to a number of American cities. Each city was to come up with new ways to handle some of the problems of their own urban areas. Unfortunately, the goals of the program have not always been clear. City officials have often seemed unable to decide what direction the Model Cities plan should take. Should its basic purpose be to help the poor by improving slum areas? Or, should it be used to revive business in city centers? There are a number of other questions that have not been clearly answered. Are the problems of the cities caused mainly by poor housing? Or, are they the product of other factors such as low-income levels and overcrowding.

In some American cities, governments and private citizens are working together in urban "homesteading" projects. People who are willing to spend time fixing up a run-down house may have the house for little or no money.

Such unanswered questions have caused many HUD plans, including the Model Cities program, to be severely criticized. Opponents claim that many projects such as high-rise apartments and new office buildings have actually added to the problems they were meant to solve. Those who favor the HUD programs point to such things as city beautification projects. Many parks, malls, and recreation areas have been financed by HUD. They also call attention to new sewer and water facilities and other health projects.

While HUD, as a department of the federal government, draws up broad plans for urban development, private groups are also at work. Investors are putting money into the renovation of buildings in older areas. In many places, middle and upper class families are moving back into the cities. Often they move so that they will be able to enjoy more of the many cultural advantages our cities have to offer.

Getting the Facts

1. How were American housing patterns affected by the railroad? the streetcar? the automobile?

2. What are some of the causes of slums in many modern American cities?

3. In what ways have private citizens and the federal government tried to solve the problem of urban slums?

Examining the Issues

■ Although the federal government has also set up programs to help rural and suburban home owners, much of the government's attention has been directed toward urban housing problems. To what extent do you think this emphasis is justified? What are some of the arguments that can be offered to support or oppose the emphasis on city housing?

The American Spirit in Education

The United States is the oldest democracy in the world. It also has the world's oldest public school system. Throughout the history of our country we have asked this system to perform very special and very heavy tasks.

The first and greatest task of our schools has been to produce an educated electorate. Without educated voters, self-government could not work.

A second task has been to create a united country. With people and states scattered over a broad area, many believed that unity could not be created without an educational system that fostered the spirit of nationalism.

A third task has been to carry out a process we call Americanization. Schools became places where people, especially immigrants, could learn about the American way of life. Never in the history of the world has such a process occurred on such a large scale in so short a period of time.

A fourth task of our schools has been to support and perpetuate American ideals of equality and justice. In America there have always been forces seeking economic privileges and social distinctions. These forces have been countered by the ideals taught in the schoolrooms of America.

ORIGINS OF THE PUBLIC SCHOOL IDEA

Education was important to many of the Europeans who first settled on the Atlantic Coast of North America. In the beginning, most people favored education in the service of religion. The English settlers at Jamestown established Henrico College in 1619. The chief purpose of the school was to convert the Indians to Christianity. The Dutch, who founded the colony of New Netherlands (later New York), were required by their charter to set up schools. Quakers required all parents in the colony of Pennsylvania to teach their children reading and writing.

An important step toward the public school idea was taken in the Puritan colony of Massachusetts. To follow their

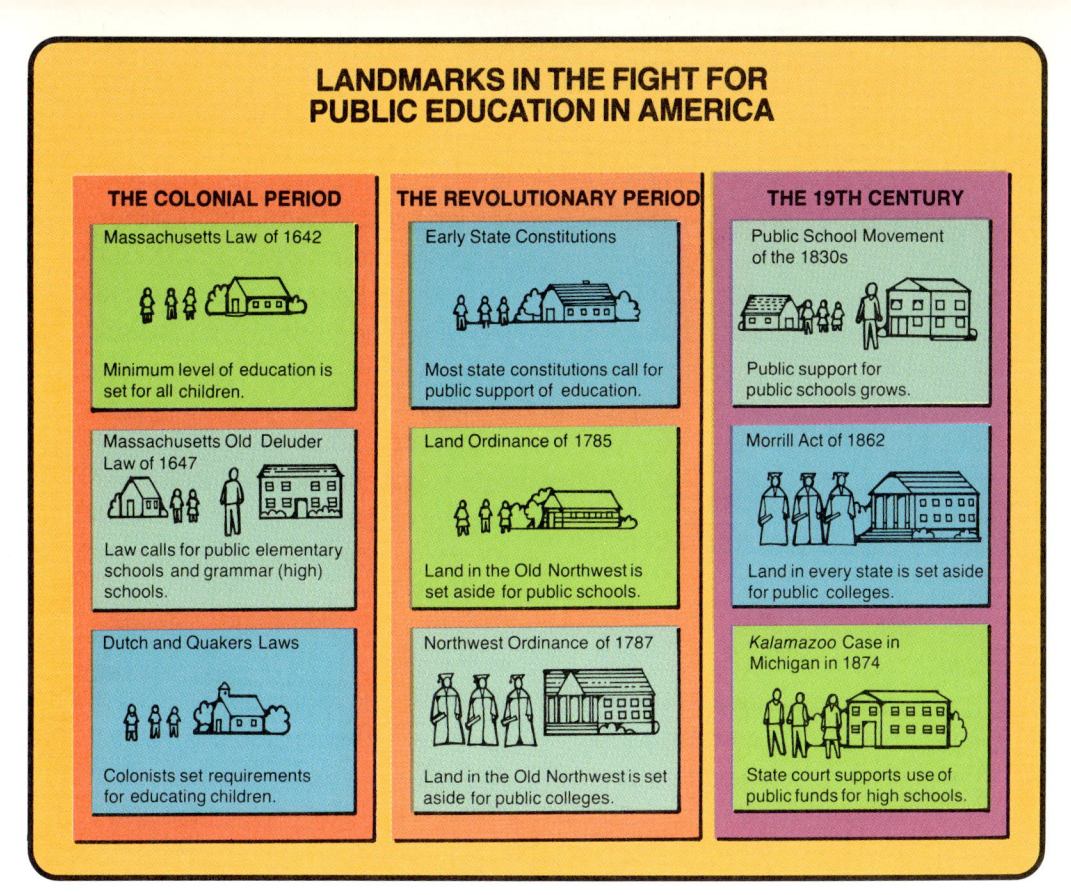

LANDMARKS IN THE FIGHT FOR PUBLIC EDUCATION IN AMERICA

THE COLONIAL PERIOD

Massachusetts Law of 1642
Minimum level of education is set for all children.

Massachusetts Old Deluder Law of 1647
Law calls for public elementary schools and grammar (high) schools.

Dutch and Quakers Laws
Colonists set requirements for educating children.

THE REVOLUTIONARY PERIOD

Early State Constitutions
Most state constitutions call for public support of education.

Land Ordinance of 1785
Land in the Old Northwest is set aside for public schools.

Northwest Ordinance of 1787
Land in the Old Northwest is set aside for public colleges.

THE 19TH CENTURY

Public School Movement of the 1830s
Public support for public schools grows.

Morrill Act of 1862
Land in every state is set aside for public colleges.

***Kalamazoo* Case in Michigan in 1874**
State court supports use of public funds for high schools.

---

religious beliefs, the Puritans needed both educated ministers and literate citizens. They thought that all people of their religion should be able to read the Bible. Thus, the Puritans turned naturally to education. In 1635, only a few years after their first settlement, they established a public high school.

In the next few years public schools were opened in a number of towns and villages. In 1642 Massachusetts passed a law that set a minimum level of education for all children. The law was not always followed, but it established principles that led to a law of greater importance in 1647. The law passed in that year was designed to defeat "that old deluder, Satan."

Frankly religious in its aim, the law of 1647 has often been called the Old Deluder Law. It required that every village with 50 families or more provide a school and a teacher to teach reading and writing. Towns with 100 families or more were required to set up grammar schools. In these schools, boys were to be taught Latin and Greek. The purpose of the grammar schools was to prepare boys for entrance into Harvard College. By passing this law, the Puritans had created a comprehensive public school system, from the elementary grades through college.

Whatever the merits of Puritan education, it was a system set up mainly for males. In some places girls attended the elementary schools. In other places, schooling for children meant schooling only for boys. Beyond the elementary grades, in the grammar schools and college, only boys could enroll. However, many girls were taught by members of their families, ministers, or other interested adults.

LOCAL ISSUES: HOUSING AND EDUCATION

The influence of these Massachusetts laws was felt through much of New England and, indeed, throughout the English colonies. Education in Massachusetts and in many other colonies was strongly motivated by religious needs. Gradually, however, people began to see that schools could also serve the political goals of the American colonies.

EDUCATION AND DEMOCRATIC IDEALS

After the overthrow of British rule, Americans began to develop not only a new form of government but also a new American culture. The American people were of many different religious backgrounds. Schools had been set up to teach the beliefs of these religions. It was also hoped that the schools would produce people who were honorable and virtuous. There was a need for people who could act as leaders in both the government and the churches. The results justified the hopes of the people. After the Revolution, American leaders followed the values stressed in so many of the colonial schools in creating a new form of government based on democratic principles.

Even as the Revolution was being fought, Americans began to write state constitutions. Most of these constitutions called for public support of schools. In this way, the new states formed the basis for a state, rather than a national, system of education.

There was, however, a strong national interest in education. Two important laws affecting education—the Land Ordinance of 1785 and the Northwest Ordinance of 1787—were passed by the Articles of Confederation government. The first law stated that parts of the land in the Northwest Territory must be sold to raise money for the establishment of schools. In the second law we find these words: "Religion, morality, and knowledge being necessary to good government and the happiness of mankind, schools and the means of education shall be forever encouraged." The Northwest Ordinance also set aside land for colleges to serve the people of the territory.

The idea that public schools and colleges should be the responsibility of the state governments was strengthened by the fact that the national Constitution of 1787 made no mention of education. National leaders such as Thomas Jefferson and George Washington, however, lent their support to education. They saw schools as a means for achieving democratic goals. "If a nation expects to be ignorant and free in a state of civilization," said Jefferson, "it expects what never was and never will be." As he was leaving the presidency, George Washington, in his Farewell Address, spoke in favor of public schools: "Promote, then, as an object of primary importance, institutions for the general diffusion of knowledge. In proportion as the structure of a government gives force to public opinion, it is essential that public opinion should be enlightened."

AN EDUCATIONAL AWAKENING

The movement toward public schools developed slowly at first in most of the young states. During the 1830s, however, there was an educational awakening. The desire for public schools spread throughout the country.

The photographs on this page show American schools in the early and late 19th century. What were the goals of the 19th century public schools? To what extend are these still the goals of our public schools?

In the years before the 1830s, there were few public schools. Those that had been set up were generally poor. In some states and communities efforts had been made to increase support for public schools. But the funds that were collected were generally too small to produce good schools. Many Americans still believed that education was a private matter, despite the words of their state constitutions.

In the 1830s a number of people began to speak out in favor of public education. They believed that schools must be free, open to all, and supported by taxes. These beliefs are the basis of the system of public education that we have today. The movement for publicly supported schools was nationwide. Important leaders could be found in all parts of the country.

EXTENDING PUBLIC EDUCATION UPWARD AND DOWNWARD

The great educational drive from the 1830s to the 1850s was to provide public elementary schools for all American children. By the 1860s, elementary schools could be found almost everywhere. There was also growing support for public high schools.

The high school movement grew stronger in 1874 following an action taken by the Michigan Supreme Court. In the *Kalamazoo* case, the court upheld the right of the state of Michigan to use public funds to support high schools. This court action, along with the growing need for a well-educated citizenry, led to the founding of many new public high schools toward the end of the 19th century. By 1900 there were about 6,000 high schools in the United States.

Paralleling the growing number of schools was the growth and improvement of school administration. More and more school systems hired superintendents and other professionals to run their schools.

The idea of providing public education at the college and university level also received growing support. There were about 250 colleges in the country in 1860. Only 17 were publicly supported. An important step toward support of higher education was taken in 1862 when Congress passed the Morrill Act. By the terms of the act, public lands in every state were set aside for the support of colleges of agriculture and mechanical arts. Today 68 of our American colleges and universities—many of them among the nation's best known—are a result of the 1862 law.

The colleges set up by the Morrill Act offered practical training in such fields as engineering and agriculture.

In recent years, many states have set up community colleges or junior colleges. Most offer two-year programs with emphasis on technical as well as academic subjects.

Thus the act provided the kind of education needed in a country that was becoming more and more industrial. The Act also stated that all male high school graduates who applied to public colleges must be admitted. This meant that at least half of the young people in America were given a chance to obtain a college education with the public paying some of the costs.

The idea of public education was extended downward as well as upward. The kindergarten idea first took hold in the 1850s. In 1873, St. Louis became the first city to make kindergartens a part of its public school system.

AMERICANS IN SCHOOL TODAY

One measure of the success of American efforts to provide education for all can be found in enrollment figures for 1970. In that year there were over 200,000,000 people in America. About 60,000,000 of them were enrolled in schools. About 46,000,000 of the people enrolled in schools were students in public schools. Another 5,000,000 were students in schools supported by the Catholic Church. About 700,000 were attending other private, or independent, schools. About 8,300,000 were enrolled in American colleges and universities.

These figures do not show the millions of older Americans enrolled in adult education programs. Truly, the goal of universal education is being achieved in the United States.

INDEPENDENT SCHOOLS

As can be seen in the 1970 enrollment figures, most young people in America attend public schools. There are, however, large numbers in independent

What kind of elementary school did you attend—public, independent, or parochial? What things did you especially like or dislike about your school?

schools. Many independent schools have no church connection. Non-public schools that are supported by religious bodies are often called parochial schools. About 90 percent of the non-public schools in America are parochial schools supported by the Catholic Church. The right to attend either a public or a non-public school has been upheld by the United States Supreme Court. This right is based on the 1st Amendment principle of freedom of religion.

Independent schools are as old as America. In the first colonies there were "dame schools" taught by women in their homes. Some of the independent schools still in existence today began in the colonial years. The Collegiate School in New York City, for example, opened in 1638. During the 19th century, a number of private academies were set up to prepare young men for college. By the middle of the century there were about 6,000 of these academies. Later, with the increased support for public high schools, many of these academies were closed. Independent schools continue, however, to play an important role in American education.

Parochial education supported by the Catholic Church also began with the earliest colonial settlements. There is a record of a Catholic school in St. Augustine, Florida in 1606. But it was in the 19th century that Catholic schools began to flourish. By 1840, there were about 200 Catholic schools in the United States.

With the heavy immigration of Catholics to the United States in the 19th and early 20th centuries, the number of Catholic schools continued to grow. Despite the growing numbers, many Catholic children have always attended public schools. Today it is estimated that only about half of the Catholic children in the United States are enrolled in Catholic elementary schools. Only about one third of the Catholic teenagers attend Catholic secondary schools.

PROBLEMS FACING AMERICAN SCHOOLS

Americans have always expected great things of their schools. In 1970, Dr. George Gallup made a survey of American attitudes toward public schools. After the study had been made, he observed, "People continue to have a high regard for the schools of their community and they believe firmly that education is the royal road to success in America."

Americans seem to have kept their faith in education. Yet many people today are concerned about certain problems facing American schools. Typical are the words of author and former teacher Charles Silberman. In his best-selling book *Crisis in the Classroom,* Silberman wrote, "It is not possible to spend any prolonged period visiting public schools without being appalled by the mutilation everywhere—the mutilation of spontaneity, of joy of learning, of pleasure in creating, of sense of self."

One of the major problems facing the public schools has, for years, been a lack of funds. Money has been needed to pay more adequate salaries to teachers. It has also been needed to build and equip new schools.

Another major problem has been caused by the segregated housing patterns found in many American cities. In a number of places across America segregated neighborhoods still separate different ethnic groups. Since most students attend neighborhood schools, the segregation patterns are often carried into schools and classrooms.

Independent schools are facing many of the same problems. There is the ever-present need for more money. Like the public schools, many private schools have remained racially segregated. Many are segregated by chance or because of their locations. A 1976 decision of the United States Supreme Court made it illegal for independent schools to refuse any applicants for racial reasons.

Because most Americans still have faith in our schools, we continue to look for ways to improve the schools. The schools continue to receive aid from the national government. Teachers remain ready to try new ideas designed to improve teaching and learning. There is concern for those who are educationally disadvantaged. Attention is paid to the needs of students who are especially gifted. Now that we have created a system of universal education, more time can be spent trying to find ways to improve that system.

Getting the Facts

1. What special tasks have Americans expected public schools to perform?

2. In what ways did the following government actions further the idea of public education in America: the Old Deluder Law of 1647; the Morrill Act of 1862; the *Kalamazoo* decision of 1874?

3. What are some of the problems facing public schools today?

Examining the Issues

■ All American states except Mississippi have laws requiring young people to attend school or receive some form of formal education. Why do you suppose most states have passed such laws? Most of the laws were passed in the 19th century. Do you think they are still necessary today? Why, or why not?

Speaking Out

Susan Jacoby

Jacoby is a free-lance writer and student of American immigration. Here she argues that American public schools have not done as much for American immigrants as most Americans think they have.

"The new immigrants are the latest inheritors of one of the most persistent myths of American life: that the public school has served as the chief instrument of assimilation and upward mobility for newcomers to this country. Like all myths that help define a community, the school myth is a compound of fantasy and reality. Experiences like those of Domenica Banca, who will be the first member of her family to attend college, have confirmed the positive side of the myth for generations of Americans. However, the sense of frustration and failure expressed by Johnny Lo has been an equally important part of the immigrant experience with American education during the past 100 years.

"The school myth was most frequently invoked during the Sixties by critics of urban education who asked, "Why can't the schools do for the blacks what they did for the immigrants?" In large measure, the answer to the question is that the schools never accomplished as much for immigrants as Americans thought they did. . . . For most immigrants, entry into American society was facilitated not by books, but by unskilled labor. The school myth has always been an integral part of the larger myth of the American melting pot, and, like the melting-pot thesis itself, is now being subjected to a long-overdue re-evaluation."

---

1. According to Jacoby, public schools have not helped most American immigrants to achieve "upward mobility," or higher living standards. For what reasons may free education alone not have been enough to help many bright young immigrant children to obtain higher living standards?

2. Jacoby favors dual-language programs that allow students to learn school subjects in their native languages. Do you favor or oppose such programs? Explain.

3. What other programs might American public schools offer to assure an equal opportunity for all Americans?

Inquiry

Are Public Schools the Proper Agencies for Achieving Racial Integration?

Of all the problems facing our public schools, none have been more difficult to deal with than those caused by racial segregation. Should the schools be used to achieve racial integration? If so, in what way? Americans have found it very difficult to agree about the answers to these questions. Discussion has generally centered on the education of white and black Americans, but students from other ethnic minorities are also involved.

Before the Civil War, free blacks who lived in the North generally had some access to formal education. Once the war was over, public attention was directed to the education of the newly freed slaves. In most of the southern states, schools were set up on a racially segregated basis. There were some schools for white children and others for black children. Outside the South, the pattern differed from state to state. A school segregation law was upheld by the Indiana state courts in the 1860s. About the same time, however, a similar law was turned down by the courts in Illinois. During the 1880s some states—among them New York, Pennsylvania, and Ohio—passed laws against school segregation. Again, by contrast, California passed laws in the 1880s and 1890s calling for separate schools for Chinese, Mongolian, and American Indian students.

In 1896, the national government acted in favor of racial segregation. In the case of *Plessy v. Ferguson,* the United States Supreme Court ruled that Louisiana had the right to force blacks and whites to travel in separate railroad cars, provided the facilities were equal. In the years following the court ruling, segregation increased. In many places, especially in the South, hotels, restaurants, theaters, and other public facilities were segregated. In the public schools the lines of segregation became tightly drawn, not only in the South but also in the border states and in parts of the North.

The first break in the wall of school segregation came in 1936. In that year, the Supreme Court ordered that a young black student be admitted to the University of Maryland Law School. In 1954, the Supreme Court reversed its 1896 decision. The Court decided that it could no longer give any support to the idea of school segregation. The 1954 case was *Brown v. Board of Education of Topeka.*

More and more Americans support the goal of integration. However, many question the methods. What methods would you favor? Why?

The 1954 Court ruling included the following statements:

"Today, education is perhaps the most important function of state and local governments. Compulsory school attendance laws and the great expenditures for education both demonstrate our recognition of the importance of education to our democratic society. It is required in the performance of our most basic public responsibilities, even service in the armed forces. It is the very foundation of good citizenship. Today it is a principal instrument in awakening the child to cultural values, in preparing him for later professional training, and in helping him to adjust normally to his environment. In these days, it is doubtful that any child may reasonably be expected to succeed in life if he is denied the opportunity of an education. Such an opportunity, where the state has undertaken to provide it, is a right which must be made available to all on equal terms.

"We come then to the question presented: Does segregation of children in public schools solely on the basis of race, even though the physical facilities and other 'tangible' factors may be equal, deprive the children of the minority group of equal educational opportunities? We believe that it does. . . .

"The effect of this separation on their educational opportunities was well stated by the finding in the Kansas case. . . .

" 'Segregation of white and colored children in public schools has a detrimental effect upon the colored children. The impact is greater when it has the sanction of the law; for the policy of separating the races is usually interpreted as denoting the inferiority of the Negro group. A sense of inferiority affects the motivation of a child to learn. Segregation with the sanction of law, therefore, has a tendency to retard the educational and mental development of Negro children and to deprive them of some of the benefits they would receive in a racially integrated school system. . . .'

"We conclude that in a field of public education the doctrine of 'separate but equal' has no place. Separate educational facilities are inherently unequal. Therefore, we hold that the plaintiffs and others similarly situated for whom the actions have been brought are, by reason of the segregation complained of, deprived of the equal protection of the laws guaranteed by the Fourteenth Amendment. . . ."

In the *Brown* decision it was stated that school desegregation should proceed "with all deliberate speed." It was hoped that within a few years all public schools would become integrated, allowing people of all races and ethnic backgrounds to attend school together. Schools in some border states were desegregated quickly. Relatively quiet changes also took place in some parts of the upper South. And, of course, many members of racial minorities who happened to live in integrated neighborhoods in the North had been attending integrated schools for years.

The most widely publicized opposition to integration occurred in the city of Little Rock, Arkansas. When schools opened in September, 1957, there was strong opposition to a federal court order calling for immediate school desegregation. President Eisenhower was forced to send troops to Little Rock to assure that the court order would be obeyed.

In the months and years that followed, it became increasingly clear that states and communities would have to follow the Supreme Court's ruling. There was no longer any legal basis for segregation. However, there remained

Inquiry

'The Roaring Seventies'

What is this cartoonist saying about the progress made in school integration between the 1954 Brown *decision and the early 1970s?*

the problem of *de facto* school segregation. The term *"de facto"* is used to describe school segregation caused by segregated housing.

In some places, an attempt was made to end *de facto* segregation by following an "open enrollment" policy. Under this policy, young people could choose to attend any school in the community. Students, however, had to provide their own transportation. While there were some efforts to use this kind of arrangement, it soon became clear that it did not offer an overall solution. To prevent overcrowding, limits had to be placed on the number of students in each school. Many students could not afford to travel daily to schools outside their own neighborhoods.

In other areas, efforts to achieve racial integration involved sending students by school bus to schools outside their neighborhoods. Early plans called for sending limited numbers of children from inner city ghettos to schools in the suburbs. While some students were bused from the inner city to schools in the outer city, there was little movement of outer city students to inner city schools. Most blacks, Puerto Ricans, and other inner city children remained isolated in their ghetto classrooms.

In 1971, the Supreme Court dealt directly with the problems caused by segregated housing. The Court's new ruling came as a result of a case concerning the public schools in Charlotte-Mecklenburg County, North Carolina. In the years following the *Brown* decision federal courts had taken many steps to end the nation's dual school system. But in a number of places *de facto* segregation remained. In the *Charlotte* decision, the Supreme Court refused to set "rigid guidelines" but stated firmly that the Court's objective was "to dismantle the dual school system."

"The central issue in this case is that of student assignment, and there are essentially four problem areas:

"1. *Racial balances or racial quotas.* The constant theme and thrust of every holding from Brown I to date is that State-enforced separation of races in public schools is discrimination that violates the Equal Protection Clause [of the 14th Amendment]. The remedy commanded was to dismantle dual school systems. . . .

"Our objective in dealing with the issues presented by these cases is to see that school authorities exclude no pupil of a racial minority from any school, directly or indirectly, on account of race; it does not and cannot embrace all the

286   LIFE IN AMERICAN COMMUNITIES

problems of racial prejudice, even when those problems contribute to disproportionate racial concentrations in some schools. . . .

"2. *One-race schools.* The record in this case reveals the familiar phenomenon that in metropolitan areas minority groups are often found concentrated in one part of the city. In some circumstances certain schools may remain all or largely of one race until new schools can be provided or neighborhood patterns change. Schools all or predominantly of one race in a district of mixed population will require close scrutiny to determine that school assignments are not part of State-enforced segregation.

"In light of the above, it should be clear that the existence of some small number of one-race or virtually one-race schools within a district is not in and of itself the mark of a system which still practices segregation by law. The district judge or school authorities should make every effort to achieve the greatest possible degree of actual desegregation and will thus necessarily be concerned with the elimination of one-race schools. . . .

"3. *Remedial altering of attendance zones.* The maps submitted in these cases graphically demonstrate that one of the principal tools employed by school planners and by courts to break up the dual school system has been a frank—and sometimes drastic—gerrymandering of school districts and attendance zones.

"An additional step was pairing, 'clustering' or grouping of schools with attendance assignments made deliberately to accomplish the transfer of Negro students out of formerly segregated Negro schools and transfer of white students to formerly all-Negro schools. More often than not, these zones are neither compact nor contiguous; indeed they may be on opposite ends of the city. As an interim corrective measure, this cannot be said to be beyond the broad remedial powers of a court.

"Absent a constitutional violation, there would be no basis for judicially ordering assignment of students on a racial basis. All things being equal, with no history of discrimination, it might well be desirable to assign pupils to schools nearest their homes. But all things are not equal in a system that has been deliberately constructed and maintained to enforce racial segregation. . . .

"The objective is to dismantle the dual school system.

"4. *Transportation of students.* The scope of permissible transportation of students as an implement of a remedial decree has never been defined by this Court, and by the very nature of the problem it cannot be defined with precision.

"No rigid guidelines as to student transportation can be given for application to the infinite variety of problems presented in thousands of situations.

"Bus transportation has been an integral part of the public educational system for years, and was perhaps the single most important factor in the transition from the one-room schoolhouse to the consolidated school. Eighteen million of the nation's public school children, approximately 39 per cent, were transported to their schools by bus in 1969–70 in all parts of the country. . . .

"An objection to transportation of students may have validity when the time or distance of travel is so great as to risk either the health of the children or significantly impinge on the educational process. District courts must weigh the soundness of any transportation plan in light of what is said in subdivisions (1), (2) and (3) above. . . ."

In the wake of the *Charlotte* ruling, federal district courts ordered the adoption of busing plans in a number of cities. The controversy brought on by these orders was in many ways similar to that which arose in the 1950s following the *Brown* decision. Even the President,

Inquiry

What is this cartoonist's view of the school busing issue? Do you agree or disagree with this view? Why?

Richard Nixon, entered into the controversy. Opposed to the idea of busing children to achieve a racial balance in schools, he ordered government officials to work with school districts "to hold busing to the minimum required by law."

Early in 1972, the controversy over school busing reached a boiling point. Demands for a constitutional amendment to end busing were voiced in many circles. In Congress, a number of anti-busing bills were introduced. Most of them sought to block current busing plans. A compromise bill was passed by the Congress in March. It prohibited any forms of busing that would risk the health of students involved or would send them to "inferior" schools. The bill temporarily stilled demands for stronger anti-busing measures.

The courts themselves could not always agree about the steps that should be taken to achieve school integration. Although a number of district courts issued busing orders, others did not. In 1972, two district judges in Atlanta, Georgia ruled against massive busing in that city. They stated that a major busing effort would be "neither reasonable, feasible nor workable." They warned that further busing would speed the flight of whites from the city and bring about an all black school system. In 1975 a federal court in Detroit decided not to order busing for similar reasons.

These court decisions received some support from an unlikely source—sociologist James Coleman. A report written by Coleman and others in 1966 had often been cited to justify busing as a means of school desegregation. Writing in 1975, he expressed the opinion that the methods being used to bring about school integration were, in fact, producing greater segregation. Like the

288 LIFE IN AMERICAN COMMUNITIES

district court judges in Atlanta and Detroit, he believed that the new methods were in many cases causing whites to flee from the cities to the suburbs. "If integration is going to come to exist in this country," he wrote, "we have to devise ways where after two or three years of integration we won't end up with resegregation."

A number of other sociologists disagreed with Coleman. They argued that his latest study had failed to examine other possible reasons for the large-scale movement of whites from the cities to the suburbs.

Efforts to integrate schools continue today. Many changes are being made in response to court orders. Others are the result of voluntary community action. Court-ordered desegregation through school busing brought violent reactions in Boston, Massachusetts and Louisville, Kentucky in the fall of 1975. At the same time, court-ordered busing was accepted without violence in Omaha, Nebraska and Stockton, California. Voluntary desegregation plans have been successful in Dayton, Ohio and Racine, Wisconsin.

Analyzing the Brown Decision

In the *Brown* decision, the Supreme Court stated that education is "perhaps the most important function of state and local governments." In what ways does the nature of our public school system influence most or all other aspects of American life?

Do you agree or disagree with the Court's statement that "separate educational facilities are inherently unequal"? Explain.

Analyzing the Charlotte Decision

Why did the Court refuse to set "rigid guidelines" for busing? Do you think the Court's decision would have been more or less valuable if strict guidelines had been set? Why?

In the *Charlotte* decision, the Court upheld the use of busing in Charlotte-Mecklenburg County. Having read the more general statements of the decision, why do you think the Court ordered busing in this special case? Under what conditions did the Court state that busing would not be desirable? Under what conditions, if any, would you favor the use of busing? Why?

School Desegregation: Where Do You Stand?

Do you think public schools should be used as a means of achieving integration? Why, or why not? *De facto* segregation of schools would end if all neighborhoods were integrated. What steps, if any, do you think should be taken to encourage integrated neighborhoods?

In both the *Brown* and *Charlotte* cases, the Supreme Court's decisions were unanimous. Even so, the decisions were made by nine people. Many Americans have disagreed with one or both of the decisions. In some communities a majority of the citizens have opposed the decisions. Do you think nine judges should be able to establish educational policy for all school districts? Explain.

Think of the schools in your community. Which are regarded as the best schools? Why? Where are the good schools located? Where do you find the poor schools? Why are they considered poor schools? Would you favor or oppose a local policy that would assign large numbers of students to schools outside their own neighborhoods? Why?

Inquiry

Review of Basic Ideas

1. In the colonial period and in the 19th century, most American families lived on farms. Families were usually large. On farms, they produced most of what they needed. The roles of parents and children were clearly understood. Wives and children generally accepted the need to obey the "head of house." Young boys were likely to receive more education than young girls. In the 19th century, industrialization and the growth of cities led to many changes in the nature of American families. The size of the average family became much smaller. More parents found jobs away from the home. Children grew more independent. Women gained a number of rights and the idea of formal education for women gradually became accepted.

2. Homes in the first industrial cities were usually clustered near the factories and businesses in the downtown area. The coming of the streetcar made it possible for working people to leave the central area and move to houses built along the streetcars lines. With the arrival of the automobile, housing spread in all directions. Over the years, housing in the central areas of many cities decayed. In the 1930s, Congress passed the first of many acts calling for government-supported housing projects. Today private groups and governments at all levels are working to provide better housing for all Americans.

3. The United States has the world's oldest public school system. Americans have always had great faith in education. Our schools have been expected to provide educated voters, help unify and "Americanize" the people of a huge nation, and preserve our democratic ideals. Although there have always been a number of independent schools in America, support for a publicly-supported system of schools grew throughout the 19th century. Today many people are seeking ways to improve our schools. A major controversy has arisen over the question of whether or not our schools should be used to help further racial integration.

Questions to Think About

1. Do you think you would have enjoyed being a member of a farm family in colonial America? Why, or why not?

2. Why could many of the traditional family relationships not be maintained in the industrial cities?

3. In what ways did new developments in transportation change housing patterns in America? What examples of these changes can you find in your own community?

4. Would you support increased government efforts to solve housing problems? Why, or why not? What do you think should be the major goals of government urban renewal and Model Cities programs?

5. What goals do you think American public schools should try to achieve?

6. Why did so many religious leaders favor the establishment of schools in the colonial period? How did the increase in the number of high schools and colleges in the 19th century serve the needs of growing industries and businesses?

Words and Relationships

Define each of the terms in the first column. Then show how each term is related to the item listed opposite it by using both items in a sentence or short paragraph.

1.	urbanization	American families
2.	family roles	colonial farms
3.	suburbs	transportation
4.	urban renewal programs	slums
5.	Northwest Ordinance	colleges
6.	Morrill Act	practical training
7.	parochial schools	religion
8.	racial integration	equality of education
9.	*de facto* segregation	neighborhood schools
10.	busing	desegregation

Building a Future

In recent years there has been much discussion about the way schools may change in the future. Plans have been drawn up for new and different school buildings with elaborate learning centers. On the other hand there are proposals that call for the development of new electronic devices to make it possible for students to acquire much of their education at home. In either case, it is likely that teaching will be viewed more as assistance with learning and less as the giving of information. A number of new courses have been suggested. Many are designed to offer more thorough preparation for the world of work and a world of increasing leisure.

Since you have been in school for some years, you are likely to have many ideas about what school should and should not be. What changes would you like to see in the schools of the future? What changes would you make in school buildings? How would you organize the school day? How long do you think the school year should be? Would you favor developments that would allow students to acquire much of their education at home? What kinds of courses should be taught? What other kinds of educational experiences should be made available? Should there be one kind of school for all students? Or, should students be offered a choice of many different kinds of education?

Citizenship Laboratory

13 The Urban Environment: Transportation, Pollution, and Crime

Through most of American history, the majority of the American people lived on farms. But wherever they settled Americans also built cities. In the colonial years, seaports such as Baltimore were built along the Atlantic Coast. As settlers moved inland, cities rose in the farmlands, the mountains, and the deserts. Indianapolis, Kansas City, Denver, Phoenix—the cities marked the stages of the westward movement. The cities were seen as places of opportunity. In the cities, new ideas and new values flourished.

The new ideas and values that developed in the cities have been the subject of one writer after another. "I loved Chicago," wrote American novelist Theodore Dreiser, speaking of the city as it was in the early years of the 20th century. "It was so strong, so rough, so shabby, and yet so vital and determined. It seemed . . . like a young giant afraid of nothing. . . ."

Indeed, there is nothing more characteristic of our American cities than that they are "forever strange and new." Huge skyscrapers of glass and steel seem to sprout overnight. Grassy, wooded areas on the outskirts of the cities are suddenly changed into busy shopping malls.

With all the changes, much of what is new to the cities is not only strange, but unwelcome. Streets are clogged with crawling automobiles, trucks, and buses. Exhaust fumes burn the eyes. Noises fray the nerves. Fear lurks in dark corners. These are some of the things that make our cities act at times as if they were afraid of their own destinies. Our American cities are still strong. In some ways they are rough and shabby. But they remain vital. The question is how well will our cities be able to deal with those aspects of the urban environment that threaten their existence.

Transporting Urban People

If you live in any of a number of American cities, this report of one winter evening in Washington, D.C. may seem familiar.

"In Washington, the snow came just about the time that that city of transients was dispersing for the long Christmas holiday week-end. Inexorably, the snowball rolled its vicious cycle: local streets iced over, which stalled private cars, which blocked the inter-city buses, which left travelers stranded down the line, which placed added demands on the airports, which had to close runways because of snowdrifts, which delayed passengers already holding tickets, which caused a scramble for cabs, which were stuck on the icy streets."

Even if the weather's fine, people themselves have ways of making trouble. A strike of subway workers in New York City a few years ago offers a good example. When underground transportation stopped, the city had to rely on surface vehicles alone. Automobiles, buses, bicycles, even horses and roller skates, were used. Because the streets were choked with traffic, the very life of the city was in danger. Many people could not get to their jobs. It was difficult to take sick people to hospitals. Food and other goods could not be moved readily.

What happened in New York shows how vital all forms of transportation are to a city's life. For urban Americans, a snow storm or strike further aggravates what one writer has called the "agony of getting anywhere." Automobiles fill the streets and expressways. To end the congestion, new expressways are built. As soon as an expressway is opened, it, too, is filled. Jets carry us from city to city in minutes. Once we have landed, the snail-like movement of traffic makes the trip to home or hotel seem like hours. These problems are found not just in a few large cities. Today they can be found throughout America.

CITY STREETS

In this age of the automobile, the layout of city streets is a matter of great importance. Many problems arise from the fact that most streets were laid out when automobiles were far less numerous than they are today. For that matter, in many of our older cities there are streets that were laid out long before there were even dreams of automobiles.

Sam Walter Foss, in his poem "The Calf Path," tells an interesting tale of how many of our streets may have come about.

> One day, through the primeval wood,
> A calf walked home, as good calves should;
> But made a trail all bent askew,
> A crooked trail as all calves do.
>
> Since then two hundred years have fled,
> And, I infer, the calf is dead.
> But still he left behind his trail,
> And thereby hangs my moral tale. . . .
>
> The forest path became a lane,
> That bent, and turned, and turned again;
> The crooked lane became a road,
> Where many a poor horse with his load
> Toiled on beneath the burning sun,
> And traveled some three miles in one.
> And thus a century and a half
> They trod the footsteps of that calf.
>
> The years passed on in swiftness fleet,
> The road became a village street;
> And this, before men were aware,
> A city's crowded thoroughfare;
> And soon the central street was this
> Of a renowned metropolis;
> And men two centuries and a half
> Trod in the footsteps of that calf.

The inspiration for this poem may have come from many places. There are streets in downtown Boston that are said to follow paths made in early times by cows being driven back and forth between pasture and milking shed. In the lower part of Manhattan there are streets that can be traced back to the old Dutch days of early New York. Even in younger cities such as Minneapolis, there are streets with rural origins. There are probably streets in your own community that were laid out long before any thought could be given to the needs of today's traffic.

As communities developed, it became much more typical to lay out streets according to some overall plan. The plans have tended to follow three general patterns: (1) the checkerboard, or gridiron, pattern; (2) the radial pattern; and (3) the super block pattern.

The checkboard pattern is found most often in the center of large cities. Land is divided into square or rectangular blocks, with straight streets and right-

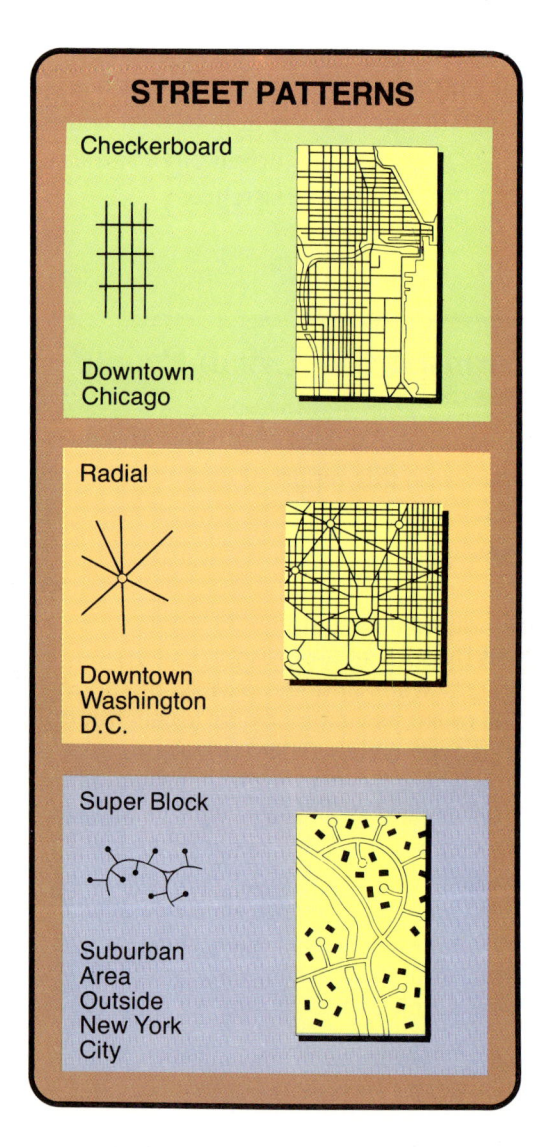

STREET PATTERNS

Checkerboard

Downtown Chicago

Radial

Downtown Washington D.C.

Super Block

Suburban Area Outside New York City

294   LIFE IN AMERICAN COMMUNITIES

Why is the super block pattern of streets generally found in the suburbs rather than in cities or other areas? For what other areas might it be appropriate or desirable?

angled corners. This plan makes it easy for people to find their way about. It also makes traffic control relatively easy. It is not a pattern, however, that lends itself well to rolling or hilly land. Many people find straight lines and square corners monotonous.

A few large cities have streets laid out in a radial pattern. In these cities there are a number of centers from which streets fan out like the spokes of a wheel. Well known examples of this layout can be found in Paris and in Washington, D.C. The pattern, with grand boulevards extending in all directions from major points in the cities, can be very impressive.

The super block pattern is most often found in the suburbs. Streets are laid out according to the topography of the land. Hills, valleys, streams, and lakes are all taken into account. Streets may wind in various directions. Some of them may lead to dead ends. Many people find this kind of arrangement very attractive. Houses and apartment buildings can be built in unusual locations on irregularly shaped lots since there is no need to follow the square layout found in the checkerboard pattern. The super block pattern may also be preferred because its use tends to discourage through traffic. Those who wish to travel quickly generally find it easier to by-pass a super block community.

EXPRESSWAYS IN AN AUTOMOBILE AGE

Expressways are the children of the automobile age. More than anything else, they symbolize the modern shift from travel by foot to travel on wheels.

The photograph below shows only a small part of the expressway system that leads people into, out of, and around the city of Chicago.

THE URBAN ENVIRONMENT: TRANSPORTATION, POLLUTION, AND CRIME

Ignoring traditional patterns of street layout, expressways extend concrete tentacles to and around cities. Some move in reasonably direct lines into the centers of our cities. They pour in thousands of workers each morning and return them to their bedrooms in the suburbs in the evening. Other expressways are laid out in giant circles around cities. These highways allow traffic to by-pass the busy downtown areas. Many of the expressways are part of our federal Interstate Highway System. Work on this system began in the 1950s. It will eventually cost more than $50,000,000,000 and include more than 64,000 kilometers of highway.

AUTOMOBILES IN THE CITIES

The sprawl of the cities, the many new streets, the modern expressways—these are the products of one basic influence, the automobile. For work and for play, the car is ever present in the life of the American. As one automobile manufacturer recently remarked, "America's love affair with the automobile has matured into a marriage."

Just how secure the marriage is can be seen from a few facts. The graph on this page shows the great increase in the number of passenger cars in the United States in the years since 1920. Today there is approximately one car for every two Americans. It has been estimated that if all the cars, buses, and trucks in the United States were stretched out bumper-to-bumper, they would extend the distance from the earth to the moon.

These figures alone are enough to explain the constant stream of cars that passes before our eyes. To handle this

Reading the Graph: *Approximately 60,000,000 automobiles were registered in the United States in 1960. How many were registered in 1940? in 1975?*

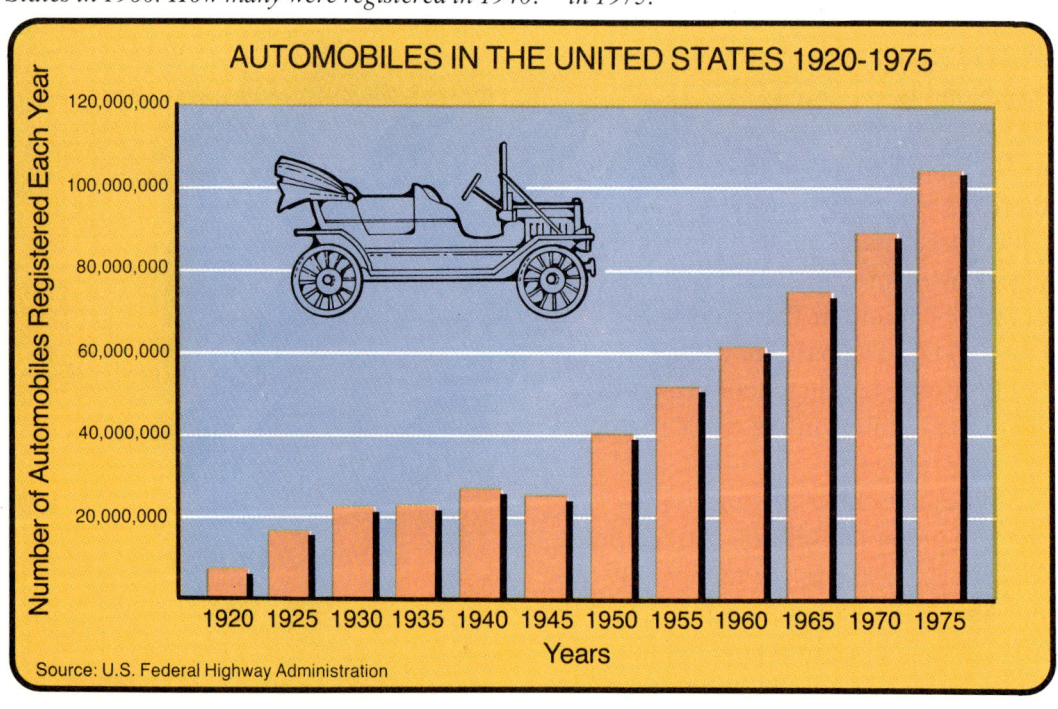

AUTOMOBILES IN THE UNITED STATES 1920-1975

Source: U.S. Federal Highway Administration

LIFE IN AMERICAN COMMUNITIES

stream of cars there are some 6,000,000 kilometers of streets and highways in our country. The problem is that only about 12 percent of these streets and highways are in urban centers. Yet it is in the urban centers that most automobiles are found. It is little wonder that the traffic jam has become a way of life in our cities. The problem is particularly acute in the downtown areas of our largest cities.

To deal with the increasing amount of automobile traffic, a number of short-term solutions have been tried. On many downtown streets parking has been banned. In heavily traveled parts of some cities, most streets carry one-way traffic. In some places large parking lots have been set up at the edge of the downtown business centers. More and more, however, the problem comes to the question of whether our cities will be reshaped to fit the needs of the automobile or whether the use of the automobile in the cities will be greatly limited.

The second choice does not appeal to most urban Americans. People like the automobile's comfort and privacy. They like its flexibility as a means of transportation. Surprisingly, studies show that the automobile is sometimes a cheaper means of transportation than such public carriers as buses and trains.

Even with these advantages, the automobile hardly seems the answer to all of the important problems of urban transportation. Already in many of our large cities, most of the people who work in the business districts have long since turned to public transportation. One observer has noted that if all the people who work in New York City were to travel to work by automobile, "all Manhattan below 50th Street would have to be converted to multiple deck parking garages."

Trying to get out of a city by car at the end of a workday can be an ordeal. Which do you think are stronger, the advantages or the disadvantages of commuting by automobile?

Getting the Facts

1. Name the three general patterns of street layout found in American communities. What are the advantages of each pattern?

2. What are some of the solutions that have been proposed, or are now being used, to solve traffic problems in our cities?

Examining the Issues

■ What are some of the many ways in which automobiles have changed American life styles? Which of the changes do you think have been good? Which do you think have been bad? Explain.

THE URBAN ENVIRONMENT: TRANSPORTATION, POLLUTION, AND CRIME

Inquiry

Will Urban Mass Transit Meet the Cities' Needs?

Shall we Americans continue to build new streets and expressways? Are we ready to turn over our cities more and more to the automobile? Or, are we willing to seek other ways to get to and from the centers of our cities? The alternative to the automobile is urban mass transit—buses, subways, and commuter trains. Here is the way one observer viewed the issue in 1967.

"When former Soviet Premier Nikita Khrushchev visited the U.S. in 1959, he watched amazed as hundreds of cars jammed across San Francisco's Golden Gate Bridge on their way to work. 'Why,' he exclaimed, 'there is only *one man* in most of those cars!'

"The absurd inefficiency of a 4,000-pound [about 1,800-kilogram], 350-horsepower vehicle with a mere 200-pound [about 90-kilogram] payload apparently struck Khrushchev as the height of capitalistic decadence. Yet his observation pointed up the prime barrier facing developers of U.S. urban mass transit: the average American's love for his car. He will endure stifling exhaust fumes, dense traffic jams and exorbitant parking fees for the privilege of traveling door to door in private. Eight out of every 10 U.S. commuters use their cars. Mass transit is considered chiefly the unhappy recourse of the less advantaged. As a result, the once extensive network of rail and bus commuter services—luxurious and relatively swift in their salad days—is now in a state of advanced decay. The wondrous old East Coast trolley—stretching unbroken from New York to Portland, Maine—is long gone. Many newer cities, such as Houston, have almost no mass transit, and it is virtually impossible to get to work without a car.

"Yet the auto's pressure on cities is reaching dangerous proportions. For those who were in Boston on Dec. 30, 1963, what happened seemed but a preview of horrors to come. That afternoon all city traffic ground to a complete halt in a giant traffic jam. It took police until 9 at night to untangle things.

"A return to mass transit is an obvious solution: One track of transit can carry as many people as 20 lanes of highway and eliminate the need for downtown parking. Yet since 1956 the federal government has spent 100 *times* more money on highways than on mass transit. . . .

"Meanwhile, huge chunks of revenue-producing downtown land are being eaten up: between 1962 and 1972, an amount of U.S. land equaling the combined areas of Washington, Boston, San Francisco and Buffalo will be covered with concrete. Over 50% of the total area of sprawling Los Angeles already is either streets, highways or parking lots. 'Soon there will be no point in going anywhere,' shrugs one transit expert, 'because everywhere will be covered with concrete for getting there.' "

New highways are still being built. But some cities have moved aggressively into the field of public transportation. A good example is the Bay Area Rapid Transit built in San Francisco in the early 1970s. A 120-kilometer electric track system links San Francisco with Oakland, Berkeley, and other parts of the metropolitan area. Computer operated trains run at speeds up to 128 kilometers an hour on tracks above and below ground. A shorter, but no less dramatic example is the rail system that opened in Cleveland in 1968. It runs from the downtown area to the airport. Another system opened in the 1960s is the fast rail service called the "Skokie Swift." It links the downtown and suburban areas of Chicago. Still another new

Inquiry

Most of America's extensive mass transit systems are found in cities in the North and East. What are some possible explanations for the fact that there are so few systems in southern and western cities such as Houston and Los Angeles?

system is being built in Washington, D.C. The first section was opened to the public in 1976.

To build these new transit systems cities need huge amounts of money. Where should it come from? Many believe that the federal government should bear a major share of the high costs. Here are the views of one expert, George M. Smerk.

"With but few exceptions, local areas have been unable to meet the transport problem as it exists today, much less gird themselves for the onslaught to come. So great is the magnitude of the problem already, and so impotent are governmentally fragmentized metropolitan areas, that the conclusion appears inescapable, that federal action is needed to help metropolitan areas mount the attack. . . ."

The first major federal effort to aid urban mass transit came in 1970, when Congress passed the Urban Mass Transportation Assistance Act. The law set aside about $3,000,000,000 for public transportation. The sum was to be spent over a five-year period. Much of the money has been used to make improvements in urban commuter service. A number of bus and rail lines have been improved. Some of the money has been used to build new transit systems.

How Would You Travel?

If you could ride a clean, modern train or bus to work each day at half the cost of driving an automobile, what would be your choice? Why?

If the downtown area of a city became so clogged with traffic that nothing could move at any reasonable speed, which of these solutions would you favor: (1) allowing trucks to load and unload only at night and in the early morning; (2) eliminating all taxis; (3) keeping passenger cars out of the downtown area?

Should each city pay for its own transportation system? Or, should the federal government use the tax money collected from all the American people to help pay for the systems?

Would you favor or oppose a law that prohibited commuters from traveling one person to a car?

Polluted Cities

Automobiles move endlessly along city streets. Factories pour out more and more goods. Thousands of people live together in small areas. All contribute to pollution, something with which people in modern America are very familiar.

Pollution means the loss of purity and cleanliness through contamination. We contaminate our air with gases and dirty our water with sewage. We pile up garbage and other wastes. With our many machines we build up noise to damaging levels. Though we desire beauty, we carelessly create ugliness.

POLLUTED SKIES

In the early fall of 1948 the nation was shocked by news from the small industrial city of Donora, Pennsylvania. A warm blanket of air had settled over the city. Waste gases and soot from the factories were trapped close to the ground. Clouds of industrial wastes poured into the air and darkness spread over the city in the middle of the day. When the air finally cleared, 20 people had died and about 5,000 had become ill.

Americans had long been used to dirty air in and near industrial towns and cities. But the Donora episode was the first recorded air pollution disaster in the United States. As a result, people became much more aware of the dangers that lurked in the very air they breathed. The dangers were again underscored in 1952, when a killing fog in London left more than 4,000 people dead in a single week.

As scientists study the effects of air pollution, we become more aware of its dangers to health. It has been found that in heavily populated areas people are far more likely to have colds, pneumonia, asthma, bronchitis, and emphysema. Many believe that a link may exist between air pollution and lung cancer.

Air pollution also affects the environment. It leaves layers of grime on buildings, roads, and metals. It can damage the finish on cars. The United States Public Health Service has estimated that destruction from air pollution costs Americans $12,000,000,000 a year. And this does not include the billions of dollars paid to treat illnesses that may be caused by air pollution.

A major producer of air pollution today is the automobile. Cars, buses, and trucks are said to produce some 60

Many radio stations now include statements about the quality of the air in their weather reports. Because of pollution, the air we once took for granted has become a matter of daily concern.

LIFE IN AMERICAN COMMUNITIES

"AIR!"

What is this cartoonist saying about the state of our urban environment?

percent of the pollutants in our skies. One authority even estimates that in urban centers cars may contribute as much as 85 percent.

To deal with pollution caused by cars, Congress has placed certain limits on the amount of pollution new cars can produce. In addition, automobile manufacturers are trying to find ways of making pollution-free engines. Oil companies are trying to find new gasoline additives that will sharply lower the output of carbon monoxide.

In 1967 Congress passed the Air Quality Act. By its terms, the federal government is able to help state and local governments fight air pollution. Additional federal action came in 1971 when the President set up a three-member board to recommend new environmental control programs.

Many American cities are also taking steps to clean the filth from their air. There are laws that limit the amount of smoke and soot that factories and homes may produce. Health departments may also act to control smoke. Industries are cooperating by spending millions of dollars to clean the air.

More and more people are beginning to understand that the narrow band of air that envelops the earth is precious. If we destroy it we will not be able to survive.

POLLUTED WATER

Not many years ago Americans became aware of the fact that a wasteland was developing in a most unlikely place. The place was a great inland sea—Lake Erie. Formed some 12,000 years ago by an advancing sheet of ice, Lake Erie became a treasure house of biological life. Up to 1925 people were catching one of the lake's fish, the cisco, at the rate of 12,000,000 kilograms a year. Suddenly, in 1926, the cisco catch dropped to about 3,000,000 kilograms. By 1965 the catch had dropped to only 480 kilograms. This was but one example of the toll pollution was taking on life in the lake.

Much of the pollution was traced to large industrial cities along and near Lake Erie's southern and western shores. Buffalo dumped waste from flour mills and from chemical, cement, and steel plants. Cleveland's industries dumped chemicals, acids, oils, and other waste products. Toledo added waste from its glass industries and other large plants. Detroit dumped waste from its automobile factories and petroleum refineries. Added to all this was the treated and untreated human sewage from every city and town around the lake. Finally, fertilizers and insecticides washed in from the surrounding farmlands.

Aware that Lake Erie could soon become a completely dead body of water, efforts were made to save this important resource. Many of these efforts have been successful. Through pollution control measures, Lake Erie is slowly being returned to a more natural state. Efforts are also being made to control the pollution of the other Great Lakes.

The water needs of 20th century Americans border on the fantastic. Clean water is needed, of course, for drinking. Families need great amounts of water for washing machines, air conditioning, and plumbing. But these needs hardly compare with those of industry. Up to 250,000 liters of water may be needed to produce one metric ton of steel.

Our oceans, rivers, and lakes serve as water resources. Because the oceans border many states and the rivers often cross state lines, the federal government has taken a hand in the problem. Water pollution is handled at the national level by the Federal Water Quality Administration. Its job is to keep a watchful eye on any changes that may threaten our water resources.

TRASH AND GARBAGE

To the liquid and solid wastes that pollute our waters can be added the mountains of solid wastes that threaten to smother us on land. The figures are too large for us to imagine. In 1970, we Americans threw away 6,300,000 automobiles and 100,000,000 tires. In the same year, we threw away 48,000,000,000 cans and 28,000,000,000 bottles. These items, together with other kinds of solid waste, amounted to a total of 3,500,000,000 metric tons for the year. It was an average of more than 2 kilograms a person each day. Estimates are that by 1980 the average will rise to almost 4 kilograms a person each day.

Numbers like these become more meaningful when we think of unsightly automobile graveyards, smelly trash heaps, and uncollected garbage. Piles of trash and garbage are a health hazard. Disease is spread by flies and other insects attracted to garbage that is left out in the open. Garbage is also a breeding ground for rats. It is estimated that as many as 14,000 people are bitten by rats each year in the United States.

Scientists and engineers are trying to find better methods of getting rid of the huge amounts of trash Americans throw away each year. What methods do you think could be used to solve a different aspect of the problem—to cut down the amount of trash that is thrown away?

Most cities use one of two methods to dispose of solid wastes. They either dump it in open areas or burn it in incinerators. Where dumps are left open, they are not only ugly and smelly, but also breeding places for rats, flies, and other insects. When rainwater runs through these dumps it pollutes streams and underground water. To overcome these problems some cities have resorted to the use of landfill. Layers of earth are used to cover the dumped wastes. The landfill areas may then be made into parks and recreational areas. But here, too, there is a problem. City after city is running out of landfill sites. Burning wastes in giant incinerators also presents a problem. The incinerators themselves produce smoky wastes that pollute the air around them.

Neither burning nor dumping seems to offer an answer. In 1969 a federal survey reported that "94 percent of all land disposal operations and 75 percent of municipal incinerators are unsatisfactory from the standpoint of public health, efficiency of operation, or protection of natural resources." The survey went so far as to term the situation "a national disgrace."

The picture is not entirely bleak, however. Scientists and engineers are busily at work finding new ways to treat solid wastes. One answer may be greater use of recycling. The general idea is to change solid wastes into useful materials. Through recycling, auto bodies can be melted down to produce more steel. Used glass can be melted and reshaped into bottles. Paper can be reprocessed and used again. Scientists also find that some solid wastes can be used as fuel to produce steam and electricity. Doubtless, many other ideas will be explored.

NOISE POLLUTION

Our modern cities are technological wonderlands. Filled with machines of every kind, the cities throb to the roar of traffic, the blare of horns, the whine of sirens, and the steady beat of jackhammers. The sounds of the machine age also pierce the silence of our homes. We learn to live with the sounds of washing machines, air conditioners, stereos, radio, and TV. All these things are elements that make up the sounds that envelop our lives.

We use the word "noise" to describe sounds that are unwanted. Noise, then, may be thought of as the pollution of silence.

We are all aware that what is one person's noise may be another person's music. This is certainly the case with the thunderous sounds that pour from the amplifiers of a rock band. Sounds have different meanings for different people. When a very quiet vacuum cleaner was developed, many people would not buy it. Because it made so little noise they believed the cleaner would not do a good job.

Whatever one's feelings about different sounds, it is clear that noise can be a menace to health. A report from the American Health Foundation states that noise "effects virtually every bodily function." The report goes on to point out that noise "probably has much to do with emotion ailments, and persistent exposure to high noise levels can cause permanent deafness." There is also evidence that persistent noise can reduce a person's efficiency. In a study done by an eastern university it was found that the output of workers in offices and factories improved when noise levels were lowered.

Perhaps even more important than a temporary reduction in efficiency is the possibility of permanent loss of hearing from high levels of sound. Some researchers have found evidence that permanent damage to hearing may be caused by listening continuously to such loud sounds as those produced by amplified rock music.

We measure sound with a unit called a decibel. One decibel is the lowest sound that can be heard by the best human ear. The chart on the next page shows that even a whisper measures about 20 decibels. Generally speaking, we are comfortable with sounds up to about 60 decibels. At a level of about 100, most people become uncomfortable. A level of 150 can be quite painful. You may have had this kind of painful experience listening to the whine of a jet engine. It has been estimated that in our American cities the noise level has been rising about one decibel each year since the mid-1940s.

Governments at all levels and a number of interested citizen groups are taking steps to end the growing pollution of our environment by noise. The federal government is presently spending millions of dollars on noise control. Most of the money is going into efforts to control the noise levels of jet airplanes. Some, however, is begin directed into research that seeks ways of reducing noise in industry. Laws dealing with noise are being passed by some state and

COMMON NOISE LEVELS

Jet plane taking off	~150 dB
Pneumatic riveter or air raid siren	~130 dB
Amplified rock music	~120 dB
Motorcycle or subway train	~100 dB
Busy city street	~70 dB
Normal conversation	~60 dB
Quiet city street	~50 dB
Quiet area in the suburbs	~40 dB
Whisper	~20 dB
Leaves rustling in the wind	~10 dB

Decibels scale: 0–200

- 0 dB: FIRST LEVEL HEARD BY HUMAN EAR
- 80 dB: DANGER LEVEL
- 120 dB: BEGINNING OF PAIN
- 180 dB: DEADLY LEVEL

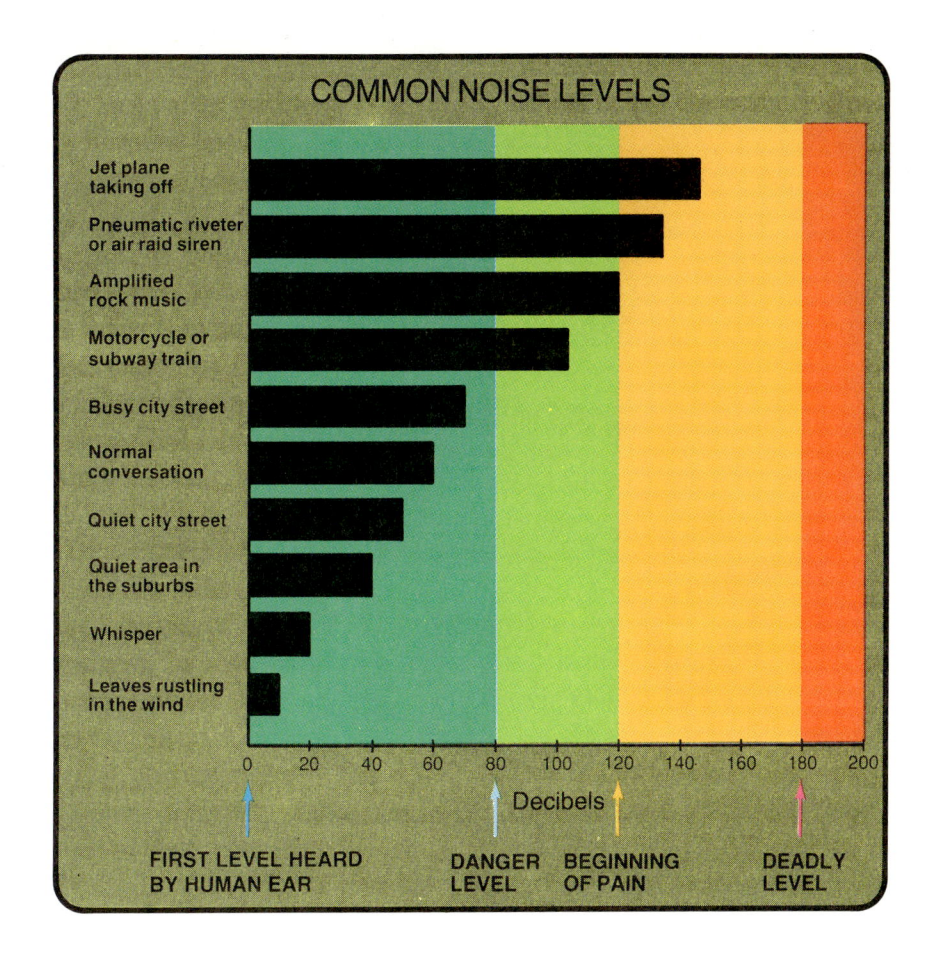

local governments. These may be no more than laws that restrict honking of automobile horns. A few cities have set up new building codes that require soundproofing of apartments and office buildings. Businesses are searching for ways to produce quieter machines. Quieter mufflers are being made for buses and trucks.

Two of the citizen groups working for a quieter society are the National Council on Noise Abatement in Washington, D.C. and a group in Chicago called Citizens Against Noise. Much of the work of these and other groups is directed toward making the public aware of the dangers of noise pollution.

Typical is this message in a newspaper ad paid for by a New York group, Citizens for a Quieter City: "Noise pollution won't kill you. It can only drive you nuts or make you deaf."

VISUAL POLLUTION

Pollution is not just poisonous air, dirty water, disease-carrying garbage, and nerve-wracking noise. Pollution also includes ugly scenes that disturb our sense of beauty. Each picture on the next page shows a scene that many find ugly. You may have seen some of these forms of visual pollution in your own community. You have probably looked at such scenes all of your life.

THE URBAN ENVIRONMENT: TRANSPORTATION, POLLUTION, AND CRIME

How would you define visual pollution? What steps, if any, do you think should be taken to end various forms of visual pollution?

There are automobile graveyards. These dumping grounds for wrecked and worn out cars litter the landscape around cities and towns across America. There are billboards that scream their messages to people traveling on our highways. They mark with ugliness what were once quiet meadows and fields. There are giant shovels digging coal in strip mines. Here, before the shovels arrived, there were tree-covered slopes that charmed the eye and controlled the water. The list could go on and on.

What makes the problem of visual pollution so difficult to solve is that it is often related to things we need and want. We want automobiles. Advertising is an important part of business. Coal is needed to supply energy. A number of efforts are being made to deal with the problems caused by these needs. In many places, automobile graveyards are being fenced off from the public view. Some attempts are being made to limit outdoor advertising. Today most strip miners must agree to restore the land after the coal is taken.

Getting the Facts

1. What are the major causes of air and water pollution in the United States? What is being done to deal with these problems?

2. Why are many of the present methods for getting rid of trash not likely to be good long-term solutions? What other long-term solutions are now being suggested?

Examining the Issues

■ What are some of the reasons why almost every form of pollution has increased over the last century? Do you think scientists will be able to solve most of our pollution problems? Or do you think we will eventually be forced to give up many of our modern conveniences?

What Can Individuals Do to Fight Pollution?

None of us can escape the pollution of our environment. It is all around us. While large scale pollution of air and water must be dealt with by industries, laws, and government regulations, remedies for much of the pollution around us are much closer at hand. We, as individuals can do our part to bring about a more wholesome environment. Consider these examples of things young Americans have done to fight pollution.

- Groups of students gathered in downtown Columbus, Ohio on a busy shopping day with large bags to pick up litter.
- Young people in Pawtucket, Rhode Island dredged up a truck load of bottles, cans, old tires, and other debris from a river that runs beside a historic mill.
- Scouts in Los Angeles cleaned up a large park so they could use it as a gathering place and camping ground.
- Junior high students in Pittsburgh formed a Clean Air for Youth group to write and distribute pamphlets about pollution.
- A youth group in Chester, Connecticut set up a Council for Community Action to work on local environmental problems.

There are probably a number of things that could be done to fight pollution in your own neighborhood or community. Here are a few possibilities:

- Look around your school grounds. Is there anything there that could be improved or made more attractive?
- Do people burn leaves or trash in your neighborhood? If so, do any of the other people in the neighborhood find this bothersome? Is there a city ordinance against it?
- Are there streets or alleys in your neighborhood that are strewn with trash? Is there a park nearby that is often littered with paper? What efforts are made by your local government to clean up the streets and parks? In what ways might individuals be able to help end this kind of pollution?
- Are there polluted streams in your neighborhood? If so, what is the major cause of pollution? How serious is the problem? What could be done to make people more aware of the situation?

Is it likely that individual action would be able to solve this pollution problem? Why, or why not?

THE URBAN ENVIRONMENT: TRANSPORTATION, POLLUTION, AND CRIME

Speaking Out

John C. Esposito

As a member of a consumers' rights group led by lawyer Ralph Nader, John C. Esposito conducted a study of air pollution. Here Esposito states his belief that the problem of pollution is really the old problem of power.

"In a disturbingly real sense, air pollution is a new way of looking at an old American problem; concentrated and irresponsible corporate power. 'Clean Air Buffs' who fail to recognize this fact of economic and political life had best begin organizing nature walks or collecting butterflies. . . . The Task Force has illustrated how the public's hope for clean air has been frustrated by corporate deceit and collusion, by the exercise of undue influence with government officials, by secrecy and the suppression of technology, by the use of dilatory legal maneuvers, by special government concessions, by high-powered lobbying in Congress and administrative agencies and—in ultimate contempt for the people—by turning a deaf ear to pleas for responsible corporate citizenship.

"If we are to restore the balance of our ecological system, we must bring balance to our political system. Those who offer 'solutions' must answer a single question: 'Will your proposal assist in redressing the enormous disparity in power between the people and the corporate polluters?' Unless the answer to this question is affirmative, the 'solution' is no solution; it is merely another palliative.

"The main reason why citizens have no impact on the corporations which they support and which affect their lives and health is that the large corporate polluter refuses to be held accountable to the public. Highly concentrated corporations in tightly knit industries, with but a handful of rivals, are insulated from the public—because their wealth buys legal and scientific apologists, because they are generally bigger and more powerful than government agencies making halfhearted attempts at confrontation, and because they can direct consumer choices away from environmental issues."

1. According to Esposito, why are some businesses able to continue polluting the air?

2. What does Esposito see as the only real way of solving the problem of air pollution?

3. Steps have been taken by the government and by many industries to end air pollution. But problems remain. Would you favor any of these solutions: more government regulations; a breakup of large corporations; a major campaign by interested consumer groups? What are your reasons for supporting or opposing these solutions?

Safety on City Streets

To the problems of traffic and pollution in our cities can be added the danger from crime. If the cities are made for people, then people should be able to walk the streets in safety. They should be able to feel safe in their own homes.

All too often this is not the case. In 1970, a report issued by the FBI stated that people living in large American cities had one chance in 19 of becoming the victim of some kind of serious crime. Serious crime as defined by the FBI included such acts as murder, aggravated assault (an attack meant to kill or injure), rape, robbery, burglary, arson, and car theft. The odds were better for people living in the suburbs and rural areas. People in the suburbs had one chance in 47 of becoming a victim of serious crime. People in rural areas had one chance in 108. On a nationwide basis. Americans had one chance in 36 of becoming a victim of some kind of serious crime.

There were other things equally distressing in the FBI's report. Figures showed that during the 10 years from 1960 to 1970 crime in the United States had almost tripled. There were 2,014,000 serious crimes reported in 1960 and 5,568,200 in 1970. The biggest increases were in arson, robbery, and auto thefts. The general rise in serious crime continued into the 1970s.

VIOLENCE IN THE UNITED STATES

The marked increase in violence during the 1960s caused great concern at all levels of government. It led, in 1968, to the appointment of The National Commission on the Causes and Prevention of Violence. The Commission made its report at the end of 1969. "The decade of the 1960s," the report noted, "was considerably more violent than the sev-

These photographs show two ways Americans have found to protect themselves from violent crime. What other methods would you favor? What are some possible long-range solutions to the problem?

eral decades preceding it and ranks among the most violent in our history." Comparing our country with other countries, the report stated, "The United States is the clear leader among modern, stable democratic nations in its rates of homicide, assault, rape and robbery, and it is at least among the highest in incidents of group violence and assassination." The commission believed that this high level of violence led easily to other major problems. "It is disfiguring our society—making fortresses of portions of our cities and dividing our people into armed camps." As the report further stated, "No society can remain free, much less deal effectively with its fundamental problems, if its people live in fear of their fellow citizens; it is ancient wisdom that a house divided against itself cannot stand."

CRIME IN THE CITIES

When we think of crime we tend to think of violence. Yet violent crimes such as murder, assault, and robbery make up only a small part of all criminal acts that take place in our country. Violence is involved in no more than 10 percent of all reported crimes. Nonviolent crimes include such things as failing to follow traffic laws, carrying a gun without a license, and counterfeiting. Americans are much more likely to be victims of crimes that are nonviolent. A person is five times more likely to die in an automobile accident than to be the victim of homicide.

There has, however, been an increase in crimes of violence in recent years. Such crimes are committed by people of all ethnic groups. They are committed in all parts of the country, in large cities, small towns, and rural areas. Even so the Commission on Violence had these findings to report.

- Violent crime in America is "primarily a phenomenon of large cities," that is, cities with more than 500,000 people.
- In the cities, violent crime is "overwhelmingly" committed by males. The homicide rate is five times higher among males than females. The number of robberies is 20 times higher among males.
- A large number of the violent crimes in the cities are committed by young people between the ages of 15 and 24.
- Violent crimes in the cities are committed "primarily by poor and uneducated persons who have few employment skills."
- A disproportionately large amount of violent crime takes place in city slums.
- Except for robbery, violent crimes tend to be acts of passion among people who know each other well.
- People with previous criminal records commit most of the serious crimes in the cities.

Which of these findings do you find particularly surprising? Can you think of reasons why violent crimes take place more often in large cities? Why do you think violent crimes are more often committed by males? Reports from the 1970s show that the percentage of violent crimes committed by females is rising. What factors might explain this increase? Why do you think so many crimes are committed by young people, poor people, and people with little education? What measures might be taken to keep so many people with criminal records from continuing their lives of crime?

This cartoonist has identified a "crime rise" as one of many urban problems. In what ways do many of the other urban problems noted contribute to the high level of crime in our cities?

Getting the Facts

1. How has the rate of violent crime in America changed over the last few decades?

2. How does the United States compare with other large nations in rate of violent crime?

3. What are some of the generalizations about violent crime in the United States made by the National Commission on the Causes and Prevention of Violence?

Forming an Opinion

■ In 1976, the Democrats' party platform called for a ban on "Saturday-night specials." They were referring to a type of small handgun that is often used to commit violent crimes. Would you favor or oppose this kind of restriction? Do you think it would help reduce the number of violent crimes committed in the United States? What other restrictions on weapons, if any, would you like to see enacted? Why?

THE URBAN ENVIRONMENT: TRANSPORTATION, POLLUTION, AND CRIME

Citizenship Laboratory

Review of Basic Ideas

1. Clogged streets choked with traffic present a major problem in many American cities. Some of the problems are caused by lack of planning in the original layout of the city streets. Even when street layouts are planned, generally following the checkerboard, radial, or super block pattern, there may be problems. A major issue in many urban areas today is whether to build more expressways or place greater emphasis on the development of mass transit systems.

2. The people of American cities and towns suffer from many different forms of pollution. Air pollution may be the cause of a number of different illnesses. Many of our lakes and rivers are polluted. Cities are finding it more and more difficult to dispose of the huge amounts of trash and garbage. The high levels of noise created by modern machines may reduce human efficiency and lead to deafness. Unlike other forms of pollution, visual pollution does not present a health hazard, but it does destroy much of the enjoyment people may derive from their environment. Governments at all levels, industries, citizen groups, and individuals are seeking ways to control pollution.

3. Over the past 20 years, the number of crimes committed in the United States has risen greatly. Violent crimes, however, make up only a small part of the crimes that have been committed. Government statistics show that violent crimes are most often committed in large cities, by young males, and by people who are poor and uneducated.

Questions to Think About

1. Would you favor a policy that attempted to solve traffic problems by making certain city streets open only to particular kinds of vehicles? If so, which kinds of vehicles? Why?

2. What pattern or patterns of street layout do you find in your own community? What pattern do you think would best meet the needs of the people in your community?

3. What are some of the advantages and disadvantages of mass transit?

4. If it were necessary to close down all the chemical plants along the shores of Lake Erie in order to purify the water, would you favor such action? Why, or why not?

5. Which of the noises in your community do you think are most objectionable? What, if anything, should be done to lower the level of these noises?

6. What examples would you use to describe visual pollution?

7. What steps do you think should be taken to reduce the number of violent crimes committed in the United States each year?

Words and Relationships

Define each of the terms in the first column. Then show how each term is related to the item listed opposite it by using both items in a sentence or short paragraph.

1. checkerboard street pattern — traffic control
2. super block street pattern — suburbs
3. expressways — Interstate Highway System
4. mass transit — traffic jams
5. pollution — environment
6. Air Quality Act — coordinating government actions
7. solid waste — landfill areas
8. recycling — bottles and cans
9. decibel — pollution of silence
10. violent crimes — poverty

Building a Future

In cities and towns across America people have set up programs to improve the appearance of their communities. The "City Beautiful" campaigns take a variety of forms. Some forms of small-scale activity are described on page 307 of your textbook. Your textbook also lists suggestions of things that might be done in your own neighborhood.

Beyond these immediate kinds of action, think of the long-range needs of your community. What can be done to bring about relatively permanent improvements in your environment? Are there factories that pollute the air and poison the water? If so, what are the factories and the local government doing about the situation? What could be done to make the public more aware of the problem? How extensive is the problem of visual pollution? Photographs of especially ugly scenes might be used to bring some of the problems to public attention. Is visual pollution, in part, caused by inadequate means for waste disposal? How useful would it be to increase the size of the budget of the local sanitation department? Or, perhaps, the community might consider a voluntary or paid youth corps to repair some of the damages caused by pollution? What actions do you think should be taken to bring about permanent solutions?

Citizenship Laboratory

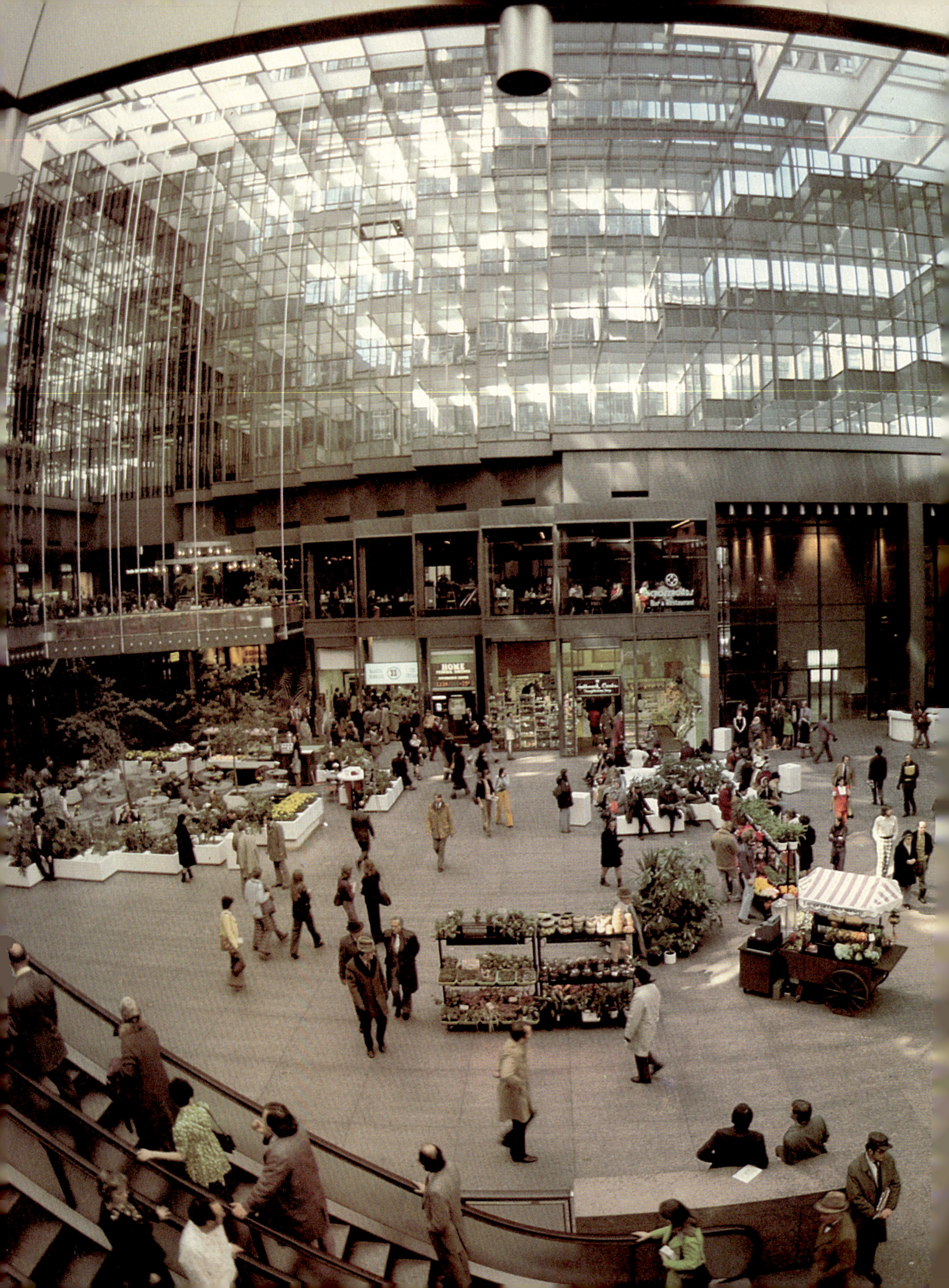
HOME

Unit Five

Economic Life in Modern America

14 Conserving Resources for All Americans

More than a century and a half ago the American writer James Fenimore Cooper wrote a novel called *The Prairie*. In it, he had a trapper say, "The air, the water, and the ground are free gifts to men and no one has the power to portion them out in parcels."

Years later some of the same deep concern about the country's natural resources was much in the mind of President Theodore Roosevelt. It led him to call a national conference on conservation in 1908. Addressing the opening session, the President stated his conviction that "the prosperity of our people depends directly on the energy and intelligence with which our natural resources are used." Such resources, he added, "are the final basis of national power and perpetuity." He warned the conference that "these resources are in the course of rapid exhaustion."

It is easy for Americans today to take such warnings too lightly. In our desire for an ever higher standard of living, we have built a technological society unequaled in human history. To feed this huge technology, we are led to wasteful use of the very resources that have made us so rich. These actions have often polluted our environment

316 ECONOMIC LIFE IN MODERN AMERICA

and made life less liveable, even with all our wealth.

We are now faced with stern realities. The question to some is whether we will be willing to make the decisions that are needed if we are to survive. To even the most hopeful, the question today is whether we can conserve our resources and improve our environment while continuing to make the kind of technological progress that has always been so highly valued in America.

America, Land of Plenty

The people who settled that part of the Western Hemisphere that became the United States found in their new land a great wealth of natural resources. Much of the soil was deep and fertile. It was ready to grow crops in abundance. Hidden within the earth was a wealth of mineral resources. Coal, iron ore, copper, lead, petroleum, gold, and clay and stone for building could all be found in America.

Heavy forests covered more than half of North America. Trees grew so closely together that sunlight could barely filter through. Where there were no forests, broad grasslands provided grazing for cattle and sheep.

Across this rich land ranged wildlife in abundance—buffalo, deer, geese, and countless other animals. Inland streams and waters along the coast were filled with fish.

Over much of this huge land the rain fell heavily enough to supply water for farming. The climate was temperate. This, combined with water and good soil, made for abundant crops. Water from rain and melting snow ran down the slopes to form rivers. Many of these rivers could be used as highways for transportation.

Settlers came to this land of plenty in search of a chance to make a better life. It is this story of a sturdy people, using abundant resources in a land of freedom, that is America's history. A fortunate blending of many forces—natural wealth, political liberty, human ingenuity, and a measure of social equality—helped produce a country of greatness and strength.

AN ERA OF WASTEFULNESS

For the American pioneers, the land was something to be conquered. They saw a wilderness to be overcome, rather than a wealth of resources to be used with care. The wealth, in fact, staggered the imagination. To the early settlers it seemed without end.

Along the Atlantic Coast one of the first tasks was to clear the forest. The wood could be used for shelter and fuel. In the open land among the stumps, food could be grown.

Across the country from the Atlantic to the Pacific, the settler marched with axe in hand. In the forested areas, the settler's advance could be measured by the fresh clearings that were made. For a time, lumbering was America's largest industry. The waste that went with it was enormous. Only the best trees were cut. Often fire was set to the rest of the forest. This killed young seedlings that might have grown into new forests. The cleared lands were plowed for crops. Without the protection of trees and grass, the loose topsoil was washed away by rain. Deep, clear streams and rivers became shallow and muddy.

On the Great Plains west of the Mississippi, the forests thinned out into a sea of rich grasslands. On these lands lived many different groups of Native Americans. The land supported millions of buffalo. When the settlers came, the Native Americans were pushed aside. The buffalo were slaughtered.

Leading the movement into the Great Plains were cattle raisers, driving their herds onto the supposedly inexhaustible range. So great was this boom in livestock in the years following the Civil War that the grasslands of the western states were soon crowded with cattle and sheep. Where sheep grazed, the grass was often cropped so low that it died. Where cattle grazed all year in the same area, the grass was seldom given a chance to renew itself.

With the cattle raisers came also the Plains farmers. The farmers plowed up the fertile land and planted wheat. Not having lumber from trees, many built their houses of sod cut from the topsoil. Exposed to the wind and rain, the soil of the plains quickly lost much of its fertility. Large amounts of soil were blown away. Dust storms became a part of life on the Great Plains.

Wasteful also was the search for mineral wealth. Gold and silver drew a rush of miners to California, Colorado, and other parts of the Great West. Oil brought drillers to Pennsylvania, and

With the help of the United States Army, cattle raisers took much of the American West away from the Native Americans. Their hold on the land, however, was only temporary. The invention of barbed wire in the 1870s made it possible for farmers to fence off the open range.

later to Texas and Oklahoma. Coal brought miners to the valleys of the Appalachians. Iron ore attracted workers to Minnesota.

In the exploitation of our rich mineral resources, the land was attacked with vigor and abandon. Rivers became filled with muck. Topsoil was washed away by hydraulic mining. The richest veins of coal were mined. The rest of the coal was left in the earth. Wasteful practices were also followed in drilling for oil and natural gas.

But, for all the waste, the practices were not considered bad at the time. The Industrial Revolution was in progress. Here were the resources to feed such a revolution. It was a way for the United States to become a rich and powerful country in a hurry. Loggers, farmers, cattle raisers, and miners were helping to build a new industrial civilization. They provided food for the growing cities and minerals for the factories. Many people were able to make great fortunes by gaining control over different resources. It was not a time when most Americans were inclined to take a long look into the distant future. It was easy to believe that America would always be a land overflowing with abundant resources.

CONSERVATION PIONEERS

In the face of this conquest of the American land, a few voices were raised to remind the country of its conservation needs. One of the most important of the early conservationists was a New Englander, George Perkins Marsh. At a time when exploitation was the watchword, Marsh argued that the country's natural resources should be used in a scientific

Much of the early interest in conservation was directed toward saving the unspoiled beauty of the West.

way. It should be the job of government, he believed, to protect our resources for the good of all. In his book *Man and Nature,* published in 1864, he stated, "Man is everywhere a disturbing agent, wherever he plants his foot, the harmonies of nature are turned to discord." Warned Marsh, "The earth is fast becoming an unfit home for its noblest inhabitants."

Among early 20th century conservationists was a crusading Pennsylvanian, Gifford Pinchot. Appointed Chief Forester of the United States in 1898, Pinchot worked to change this obscure government job into an important one. He found ways to accomplish this after Theodore Roosevelt became President in 1901. Though a New Yorker, Roosevelt had had experiences as a rancher and hunter in South Dakota. These experiences increased his interest in the natural environment. He was impressed with Pinchot's idea that the cutting of timber should be regulated so that forests could be used, but also preserved. In his first State of the Union message, Roosevelt called forest and water problems "perhaps the most vital internal question to the United States." Pinchot attacked the forest problem by building up an organization of forest rangers. In 1905, he persuaded the President and Congress to support a law that set up our present system of National Forests.

Pinchot also saw a need for a conservation program to protect our other natural resources. To build public interest, he urged President Roosevelt to call a conservation conference in 1908. This meeting marked the beginning of the modern conservation movement.

GOVERNMENT AND CONSERVATION

The Roosevelt conference brought conservation squarely into the field of government both at the national and state levels. Its first outgrowth was a survey of the country's natural resources. This survey strongly emphasized the need for conservation. As a result, committees were formed in 41 states.

Slow to act at first, government agencies stepped up their activities during the 1930s. Interest was sparked in the spring of 1934 when frightful dust storms began to blow out of western Kansas, Oklahoma, and Texas. Picking up the dry soil of the plains, the westerly winds carried black clouds of dust for hundreds of kilometers. As far east as Boston, people could see dust blown in from the farmlands of the Middle West.

The hardship and misery of the people in this western Dust Bowl so impressed Congress that it passed the Soil Conservation Act of 1935. The act declared soil erosion "a menace to the national welfare." It gave the government both money and power to carry on soil conservation programs.

Like his distant cousin Theodore, President Franklin D. Roosevelt carried his own interest in conservation into his government program. The New Deal program of the 1930s included, for example, the Civilian Conservation Corps. Through this agency, many jobless people were put to work. They built facilities in national parks and planted millions of trees. They built dams and worked on soil erosion problems. Another example was the Tennessee Valley Authority. This project had as one of its major goals the conservation of natural resources in an entire river valley. Other New Deal conservation laws gave protection to grazing land and set up wildlife refuges. Long-range plans for the better use of resources were made.

World War II placed greater demands on the natural resources of our country than had ever been made before. At war's end, President Truman stated in a message to Congress, "During the war we have expended our resources . . . we have torn from the earth copper, petroleum, iron ore, tungsten and every other mineral required to fight a war, without regard to our future supplies." Great demands were also made on the country's resources by wars in Korea and Southeast Asia. Equally demanding have been the requirements of our expanding economy.

The mounting demands on our resources have made recent Presidents even more aware of the problem. Typical was a statement by President John F. Kennedy in a message to Congress in 1962: "We must reaffirm our dedication to the sound practices of conservation which can be defined as the wise use of our natural environment." He added that "in the work of conservation, time should be made our friend, not our adversary."

Getting the Facts

1. What are some of the many natural resources 18th and 19th century settlers found in the United States?

2. In what ways were many of our natural resources wasted in the 18th and 19th centuries? Why were wasteful practices often followed?

3. When did the national government begin to take interest in conservation? What event in the 1930s led to greater government involvement in the field of conservation?

Examining the Issues

■ In what ways do you think the history of the United States would have been different if we had not had an abundance of good soil? How would our history have differed if we had not had so many mineral resources?

Preserving Nature's Balance

President Kennedy's association of the terms "conservation" and "environment" suggests a relationship that has received a great deal of public attention in recent years. Pollution of the environment—air, water, soil—has in a number of ways brought the problems of conservation more directly to the attention of Americans. It has also increased popular interest in the science of ecology. Many are seeking a better understanding of the delicate balance by which nature preserves itself.

ECOLOGY: THE STUDY OF NATURE'S LIFE CYCLE

Ecology is the study of the relationship between living things and their natural environments. Those scientists who seek to understand how nature preserves this delicate balance are called ecologists. Ecologists are interested in the ways that various forms of life depend on one another. In addition, they seek to identify the factors that fit various forms of life into an organic whole.

Undisturbed by people, nature's balance can be described as beginning with the sun. The sun is the source of life energy. From the sun's energy and the nonliving materials in the air and soil, plants create food. Animals, in turn, receive energy by eating plants. Animals also receive energy by eating other animals that have eaten plants. When plants and animals die, their remains are broken down into basic materials called nutrients. This is done by decomposers such as bacteria and fungi. The nutrients are then used again by new plant life.

Outside interference at any stage can upset this delicate life cycle. The cycle, with which we must deal daily, is the way that life on earth has come about. It is the way that life on earth continues. The earth is the only home we have. For this reason, preservation of nature's life cycle is truly a matter of life and death.

THE WORK OF ECOLOGISTS

The ecologist knows that we must maintain a balance in the systems of our environment. Each of the four major systems—air (atmosphere), water (hydrosphere), land (lithosphere), and living organisms (biosphere)—must

What are the advantages and disadvantages of spraying crops? Which do you think are stronger? Why?

remain in balance. Interference with any of these four can affect the other three. If the interference is major the effect can be disastrous. As an example, consider the use of pesticides. A chemical pesticide is used to kill certain unwanted insects. When these insects are killed, other pests may appear in huge numbers because their natural enemies—the unwanted insects—have been destroyed. Again, when unwanted insects are destroyed, certain useful ones may also be killed. It is a chance people always take when they interfere with nature's balance.

In a modern technological society such as ours, there is no way for people to avoid disturbing nature's balance. It is here that the work of the ecologist becomes most important. The ecologist can help answer questions about how much disturbance the system can stand.

Getting the Facts

1. What is meant by the term "nature's life cycle"?

2. What are the four major systems of our natural environment?

Examining the Issues

■ In what ways do human actions interfere with the natural balance of each of the systems in our natural environment? Which of the actions you have described are avoidable? Which are avoidable but desirable? To what extent do you agree that people in modern technological societies cannot avoid disturbing nature's balance?

ECONOMIC LIFE IN MODERN AMERICA

Inquiry

How Many More People Can the Earth Support?

More than 3,500,000,000 people now live on our planet earth. Clearly, the presence of so many people is bound to affect our planet's life—the balance of nature. It is only in recent years, however, that we have become acutely aware of the relationship between the number of people and nature's balance. Our awareness has come because of two important developments. There have been great advances in technology. At the same time, there have been great increases in human population.

Technology is one of the factors that has made this rise in population possible. As recently as 1850 the earth's population stood at only 1,000,000,000. It had taken all of human history to reach this figure. Just 70 years later the earth's population had more than tripled. Population experts now expect a population of 6,000,000,000 or more by the year 2000.

Here in the United States the rise in population has been even more dramatic. This has been brought about by a

Reading the Graph: *In 1880 the population of the United States was about 50,000,000. What was the population in 1920? Which of the 10-year censuses first reported a population over 200,000,000?*

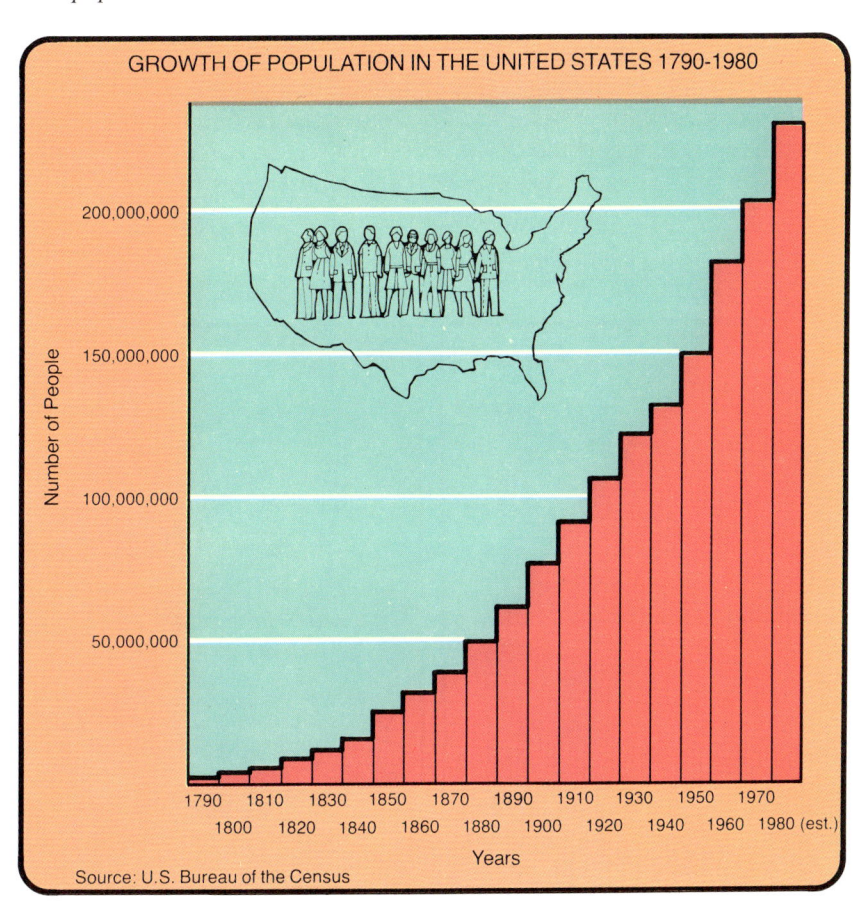

GROWTH OF POPULATION IN THE UNITED STATES 1790-1980

Source: U.S. Bureau of the Census

CONSERVING RESOURCES FOR ALL AMERICANS

Inquiry

combination of natural increase and immigration. The 1850 population of about 23,000,000 has increased approximately 10 times. There are now well over 200,000,000 people in the United States. Projections are that, by the year 2000, the United States will have a population of 250,000,000.

How should we view these huge increases in population? How many people can the earth support? One scientist, Dr. Paul Ehrlich, sees the earth's population "on a collision course with the laws of nature."

"Human values and institutions have set mankind on a collision course with the laws of nature. Human beings cling jealously to their prerogative [right] to reproduce as they please—and they please to make each new generation larger than the last—yet endless multiplication on a finite [limited] planet is impossible. Most humans aspire to greater material prosperity, but the number of people that can be supported on Earth if everyone is rich is even smaller than if everyone is poor. We are told that only economic growth can ease the pain of poverty . . . but we know that the quantity of physical goods, like the human population, cannot grow forever. It is not yet clear precisely when and in what form the collision between the growth ethic and natural limits will occur, but there can be no doubt as to the outcome. Human values and institutions will bend or be crushed by biological and physical realities. . . .

"The present situation, then is somewhat like driving an automobile with failing brakes down a treacherous road at an accelerating speed. So far we have managed to stay on the road, but the task becomes more and more difficult because our brakes become less effective as our speed increases. . . . Mankind's ignorance of the exact carrying capacity of social institutions and the physical environment makes the whole enterprise akin to driving our defective, accelerating automobile down that treacherous road in a heavy fog. In this situation, certain politicians, economists, and technologists who offer us glib reas-

What is this cartoonist saying about population growth? To what extent do you agree or disagree?

surances that no crisis is evident are like blind backseat drivers who urge us to keep our foot on the gas."

An American sociologist, Dr. Valerie Oppenheimer, views the population problem somewhat differently. The problem, he believes, involves the way in which people live their lives as well as the number of people there are. We Americans are a good example of what he means. Our country makes up only about 5 percent of the world's population. It is estimated, however, that each year the people of the United States use 40 percent of the resources consumed by the people of the world. Here is how Dr. Oppenheimer views the general problem.

"As a whole, today's industrialized nations have the capacity to feed populations several times their present size. Indeed, the problem in many of these countries is food surpluses rather than food shortages. Nevertheless, many biological scientists fear that our future survival is increasingly open to question. What worries them is whether the consumption patterns of modern industrialized societies do not pose an unprecedented threat to the natural environment and, thus, to the basic life processes on which we all depend. This threat is increasingly aggravated by large and growing populations.

"... the ... debate ... [is] whether we should blame our environmental problems more on population growth than on our style of life. An either/or debate of this type is probably not the most fruitful approach; nevertheless, good arguments can be made that our life style is the worst culprit in the situation. Thus, it is quite appropriately pointed out that changes in our way of life have far outstripped our population growth in producing pollution and causing other environmental problems. For example, while the United States population has increased by about 50 percent over the past 30 years, the rise in the number of people visiting our national parks—usually by means of the pollution-producing automobiles—has been more than 400 percent.

"Or take electric power. Between 1950 and 1969, when our population grew by about 33 percent, the use of electric power rose by almost 400 percent. The generation of electric power involves, in many cases, the burning of fossil fuels [coal, oil, etc.], and thus contributes significantly to air pollution. . . .

"There is little doubt that changes in how we live, not just increases in the number living, are a major factor in the destruction of our environment. It would be foolhardy, therefore, to suggest that the problem simply be approached . . . by trying to reduce population growth. . . .

"In general, while population growth is not the major culprit in the creation of many of the threats to our environment, it nevertheless does play a part. . . . In the search for technological solutions to the problems of air and water pollution, for example, if the population is growing, the solutions must come faster to offset this population growth. In addition, the larger the population, the more effective the solutions must be. . . ."

Comparing Two Points of View

Think about the population increases in recent times. Who do you think sees the problem more clearly, Dr. Erhlich or Dr. Oppenheimer? Why?

If overcrowding becomes a severe problem what new areas might be opened for human settlement?

What kinds of changes in the life styles of Americans might have to take place if our population increases by, say, one third or one half? Do you think it will be possible to solve our environmental problems if the population rises greatly?

Conserving the Land

The way in which people use the land they live on is an important factor in the relationship between people and the natural environment. In America, land usage presents certain problems. It also presents certain reasons for viewing the future optimistically. One American ecologist stresses the problems, using language that many would probably consider extreme.

"I define as most seriously overpopulated that nation whose people by virtue of their numbers and activities are most rapidly decreasing the ability of the land to support human life. With our large population, our affluence and our technological monstrosities, the United States wins first place by a substantial margin."

In referring to the land, the ecologist is likely to have had more in mind than just soil. Even so, our country has lost a great amount of tillable soil. The United States Department of Agriculture reported that during the 20 years between 1944 and 1964, 53,000,000 acres (about 21,400,000 hectares) of American crop land were shifted to other uses. During the same period only about 10,800,000 hectares were salvaged and returned to the growing of crops. Stated in different terms, the total amount of crop land decreased 7 percent between 1944 and 1964. And this, of course, was in the face of a rapidly growing population that needed more food.

A more optimistic view is that, in terms of soil and climate, the United States is blessed with the greatest food producing capacity of any country in the world. Only about 6 percent of our arable land is now being used for farming. Equally encouraging, is the fact that the soil of almost half of the farmland in the United States can be used year after year with only normal care. It is little wonder that, with a surplus of crop land and an abundance of good soil, our farmlands are the envy of much of the rest of the world.

There is another factor—the American farmer. The typical American farmer, with modern machines and scientific know-how, grows enough food to feed more than 40 other people. A sharp contrast can be seen in many parts of Asia where the average farmer grows barely enough to feed one person. Even in the Soviet Union, with its good farmlands and modern methods, the average farmer grows only enough to feed six other people.

SOIL CONSERVATION

For all our abundance of rich soil, long-range views stress that this valuable gift of nature must not be neglected. As our population grows, thousands of hectares of farmland are transformed each year into suburbs, airports, and highways. And it is estimated that each year more than 1,000,000 hectares of land are allowed to decline in quality.

A major reason for the decline in the quality of soil is loss of soil through erosion. Erosion is a process of gnawing away or eating away. It is usually done by water, wind, or great changes in temperature. For the erosion process to take place, soil must be left exposed and unprotected. This may happen when trees and bushes are cleared from slopes and hillsides. Erosion may also be caused by certain plowing practices, and by allowing livestock to graze too closely.

To stop erosion, various methods of soil conservation have been developed. On land that erodes easily, grass or fast growing trees may be planted. To keep valuable topsoil from being washed or blown away, farmers may sow cover crops such as clover and alfalfa. Rows of trees may be planted to shelter the land from the wind. Where the land slopes, farmers generally plow and plant in curved lines running across the slopes. This is known as "contour" farming. It is an effective practice, because the plowed ridges hold back the water. This allows farmers to avoid the kind of carved out gullies and rocky hillsides so evident in places where careful soil management plans have not been followed.

In addition to the contour farming method, conservation-minded farmers often use the "strip" farming method. This involves planting a strip of crops, a strip of grass, another strip of crops, and so on, along the contour slope of the land.

On steep slopes farmers may build terraces to hold the soil. Terracing has long been used in many different parts of the world. It is found particularly in rice growing areas where water must be retained for long periods of time.

LAND RECLAMATION

Good soil conservation calls for not only the protection of existing soil, but also the reclaiming of land not presently suitable for farming. This may be done by repairing damaged lands. On slopes carved with gullies, small dams may be built or bushes may be planted. The gullies may be filled with brush. On overly grazed lands, livestock may be removed so that the grass can grow again.

Reclamation may also take place on lands not previously thought of as useful for farming. This has been done in dry areas of the American West. To make these dry lands suitable for farming, water has been provided through irrigation.

Land reclamation was first carried on by private people and groups, or by state governments. As early as 1902, however, Congress set up the Bureau of Reclamation. Through the work of this bureau, giant dams have been built in many parts of the West. Behind these dams are huge reservoirs of water.

What two farming methods are being combined in this photograph?

People have been irrigating land for thousands of years. The photograph above shows the results that can be achieved. Note the difference between the productive land at the left and the dry, sunbaked land at the right.

Pumped into irrigation ditches, the water makes it possible for almost useless dry lands to "blossom as the rose." The Bureau has built over 150 major dams and irrigation projects in 17 western states. The Bureau, in fact, has been so active that a report made in 1971 by a private group claimed that the Bureau had done too much. The report stated that the agency had "outlived its usefulness" and should halt its "senseless damming of the West."

Reclamation projects have been set up in other parts of our country to drain swamps and marshes. Although much less extensive than the irrigation and dam projects, these drainage projects have also opened up a number of new farming areas.

Getting the Facts

1. What factors have made it possible for the average American farmer to grow enough food to feed 40 other people?

2. What are some of the methods now being used to conserve soil in the United States? What methods are being used to reclaim land?

Forming an Opinion

■ The ecologist quoted at the beginning of this section takes a dim view of the way land is being used in America today. What facts can be used to support or oppose the ecologist's statement?

Using Mineral Resources Wisely

There is an important difference between soil and minerals. Soil can be used over and over and even rebuilt. Mineral resources are not renewable. When they are gone, they are gone forever. By mineral resources we mean (1) fuels, such as coal, petroleum, and natural gas, (2) metals, such as iron, lead, copper, aluminum, gold, and silver, and (3) other materials, such as clay, building stone, asphalt, and asbestos.

To run an industrial society such as ours, vast amounts of fuel are needed. Early locomotives and other steam engines first used wood and later coal as a source of energy. Discoveries of petroleum made possible the development of gasoline and diesel engines. Natural gas came into use for heating and lighting.

Of these three fuels—coal, petroleum, and natural gas—coal exists in greatest supply. Viewed globally, it is estimated that at the present rate of use we have enough coal to last 1,000 years. This is not the case with petroleum and natural gas. Some estimates run to no more than 30 years for petroleum and 15 years for natural gas. Another mineral that has come into use in recent years as a source of energy is uranium. Uranium reserves are also expected to last no more than 30 years at the present rate of use.

Iron is a basic element in any industrial country. For years high grade iron ore for American industry was found mainly in the rich Mesabi Range in northeastern Minnesota. Here, in the world's largest open-pit iron mine, the vast ore reserves once seemed without end. This is no longer the case. A search by steel companies for high-grade iron now goes on throughout the Western Hemisphere. There remain, however, considerable amounts of low-grade iron ore in the United States.

Similar estimates could be given for other important mineral resources. Briefly stated, American industry has been the largest user of mineral resources the world has ever seen. At the present time, industry in the United States is using almost one third of all minerals being taken out of the earth. And almost all of these metals are in alarmingly short supply.

What can be done to improve the current situation? One answer is a greater use of recycling. Through recycling, huge amounts of iron, glass, and other materials can be ground up, melted down, and used again and again.

Another answer is to use more efficient methods of extraction. In the past, low-grade iron ore has been passed by. Narrow veins of coal have been left unmined. Pockets of natural gas have been allowed to escape into the air. It is now becoming obvious that these profitable but wasteful methods of extraction can no longer be used. We must also continue to look for mineral resources yet unknown. These explorations are now being made both on land and on the ocean floors.

Our dwindling supplies of mineral resources raise a number of other questions. Should we continue to expand the production of our factories? As you search for an answer, remember that not to expand may mean fewer jobs. And, it could possibly lead to lower standards of living. Should we look for ways to build automobiles, refrigerators, and other metal products so that they will last longer? Here, again, a yes answer might lead to fewer jobs and lower living standards. Clearly, such questions remind us that mineral resources are one of our most important conservation problems.

Getting the Facts

1. Which of our mineral resources may be used up within the next 30 years if the present rate of use continues?

2. What are some of the possible solutions to the problem of dwindling mineral resources?

Examining the Issues

■ Which of the products in your home and school are made from minerals? What renewable resources might be used to make the same products?

Conserving and Rebuilding Our Forests

As with minerals, Americans have found themselves blessed with an abundance of forests. Despite years of careless use, the resources of our forests are still abundant. The heaviest concentration of forest lands in the United States today is in the Pacific Northwest. Even so, forests are widely distributed across the country.

At the beginning of the 1970s, the total timber supply in the United States was estimated to be 17,500,000,000 cubic meters. But even such a huge figure can only be a partial source of comfort. Demands on our forests are growing. One estimate is that the demand for lumber in the United States will double in 30 years. This places a great strain on our forest reserves. The pressure can only be met by the wisest possible management—by private companies and by our state and national governments.

FOREST CONSERVATION: PRIVATE AND PUBLIC

The continued existence of our rich forest resources is the result of work by both private groups and government agencies. In recent decades, private lumbering companies have shown great interest in forest conservation. There has been much cooperation between the lumbering companies and state and federal forestry services. Many companies have cutting practices that are as strict as those of the government agencies. Often the companies replant the areas where they have cut timber. Government forestry work is carried on by the United States Forestry Service. Most states also have forestry services.

A number of things are being done, or at least being thought about, to conserve the resources of our forests. Better use is being made of residues from lumbering—slabs, edgings, sawdust. These residues, which were once wasted, make up almost a third of the volume of the lumber. Another answer is found in the use of recycling. Paper and wood

Why is there more concern about our stocks of mineral resources than about our supply of timber?

products can be recycled into useful materials with substantial savings. Lumber is also being conserved through the use of substitutes such as bricks and plastic.

WILDERNESS PRESERVATION

More than just sources of lumber, our forests are useful for recreational purposes. For a nation that is becoming more and more a land of cities, our great expanses of forests are of incomparable value. It was with this in mind that Congress, in 1964, passed the Wilderness Act. In the words of the act, "A wilderness, in contrast with those areas where man and his own works dominate the landscape, is hereby recognized as an area where the earth and its community of life are untrammeled by man, where man himself is a visitor who does not remain."

In carrying out the act, Congress set aside some 60 areas of land owned by the federal government. By the act, these lands were to remain wild and unspoiled. Lands in all parts of the country were included. Forest lands, desert lands, and lake country areas in Minnesota were all set aside.

Getting the Facts

■ In what ways are private companies and government agencies working to conserve American forests?

Examining the Issues

■ One expert estimates that our use of lumber will double in the next 30 years. What factors should be taken into consideration in making this kind of estimate? What changes might make any such estimate prove untrue?

Preserving the Natural Beauty of the Land

Of all our efforts to preserve and protect the natural beauty of our land, none have been more important than those that led to the creation of a national park system. Today there are almost 300 park areas included in the system. Together they cover an area of land larger than the state of Pennsylvania. We now have 38 national parks, 16 historic parks, and a number of historic sites and recreational areas. The parks and other lands within the system are run by the United States National Park Service, a bureau of the Department of the Interior.

The oldest and largest of the national parks is Yellowstone. It covers an area of more than 800,000 hectares in the states of Wyoming, Montana, and Idaho. It was created by an act of Congress in 1872. One hundred years later, in 1972, representatives from almost 100 nations gathered at Yellowstone for a World Conference on National Parks. One purpose of the conference was to celebrate the centennial of a national park movement that had become worldwide.

Here, in the United States, the wonders of Yellowstone are matched by other national parks. Next in size to Yellowstone is the majestic Mt. McKinley National Park in Alaska. Spread over thousands of hectares of land in southern Florida is the haunting Everglades National Park. For breathtaking grandeur few places in the world can match Arizona's Grand Canyon National Park. Of all the national parks, Americans seem to be most fond of the Great Smokey Mountains National Park in the eastern part of Tennessee and the western part of North Carolina. More people visit it each year than any other national park.

The national parks, historic sites, seashores, and lakeshores provide recreation for millions of Americans. The National Park Service also maintains a great deal of its land in its natural state. This land is kept chiefly for its beauty and for scientific study. In these natural areas every effort is made to preserve the balance of nature. Here plant and animal life is left as undisturbed as possible. All the national parks, except Mesa Verde in Colorado with its Indian cliff dwellings, are regarded as natural areas, open to people only when they come as temporary visitors. In these parks, an attempt is being made to preserve the beauty of the land for future generations.

Getting the Facts

1. What are some of the purposes served by our system of national parks?

2. In what part of the United States are most of the national parks found?

Forming an Opinion

■ In recent years many of our national parks have been flooded with tourists. Some officials worry that the natural environment of the parks will be destroyed by this kind of overcrowding. What restrictions, if any, do you think should be placed on tourism in the parks?

Protecting Our Nation's Wildlife

The lands of North America were once a wonderland of wildlife. It was not uncommon for Indians and early settlers to see hundreds of thousands of pigeons flying so closely together that they darkened the sky. The clear, sweet waters of the rivers and lakes teemed with fish. The lonely hunter might come upon a herd of thousands of buffalo ranging the western plains.

ALTERATIONS IN HABITAT

For these animals and others, North America offered a friendly habitat. By habitat, we mean the natural dwelling place or environment of a plant or animal. Much of the story of America is an account of the ways that people have made changes in this natural habitat. In the course of these changes, the nation's wildlife has been a major victim.

The habitat of many kinds of animals was greatly damaged, or even destroyed, by the very presence of settlers. To make way for farms and cities, land had to be cleared. This meant cutting down forests that protected wildlife. It involved plowing up grasslands that had given animals food. The opening of mines and the building of factories brought pollution to many streams, rivers, and lakes. Fish and wild fowl were poisoned by the waters. The rapidly growing populations increased the need for animal products—meat for food and hides for clothing. These human needs and activities, so often destructive of the natural habitat, have proceeded apace down to our own day.

WILDLIFE IN MODERN ENVIRONMENTS

As we take a thoughtful look at the conditions of wildlife in today's environment, certain significant items come to our attention. For one thing, it is not easy for those of us living in cities and large towns to appreciate the relationship between animal life and the balance in nature. Only in abstract terms can most of us understand that the death of birds who live on insects gives these insects a greater opportunity to destroy the crops we plant for food.

An equally significant point is that people and wildlife share the environment. When this environment is polluted, both are affected. Most kinds of wildlife, however, are more sensitive to a polluted environment than people are. For this reason, wildlife is in a position to provide us with early warning signals of the dangers ahead. We have watched harmful pesticides kill certain species of birds. We find signs of mercury in fish. These are but two examples of warnings that we have received in recent years.

Finally, there is something to be said for the joy that wildlife may bring to our lives. The grace of the deer, the song of the mockingbird, the industry of the squirrel—all of these things may add to the pleasure we derive from our environment. Many people believe that all animals have rights. So long as animals do not harm the environment, the belief is that they too have the right to live.

HELP FOR THE NATION'S WILDLIFE

A major concern of those working to preserve wildlife is loss of habitat. Each year new houses, factories, highways, and airports use up about 600,000 hectares of wildlife habitat.

Both national and state governments have taken steps to offset these losses. They have set up bird sanctuaries, game preserves, and other kinds of living space for wild animals. Today there are more than 12,000,000 hectares of land in the National Wildlife Refuge System. At the national level of government, the Fish and Wildlife Service conducts studies. It also provides money for wildlife conservation. At the state level, fish and game agencies regulate fishing and hunting.

Should government preservation efforts be directed toward saving all forms of wildlife? Or do you think some forms of wildlife more worth preserving than others?

There are also a number of private groups at work in the interest of American wildlife. The National Association of Audubon Societies has a special interest in bird life. Fish conservation is the major interest of the Isaak Walton League.

Getting the Facts

1. In what ways can wildlife serve human purposes?

2. What actions are being taken to conserve American wildlife?

Forming an Opinion

■ As you have seen, our national government has set aside a great deal of land for different conservation purposes. Would it make sense to combine all the public lands run by agencies of the federal government in one agency? Why, or why not?

Conserving Water Resources

It is not difficult to understand the importance of water as a resource. All you need to do is to get thirsty. In addition, think about the following facts.

- Almost 4,000 liters of water are needed to produce one liter of milk.
- Almost 200 liters of water are consumed by a single corn plant in the course of a growing season.
- About 400,000 liters of water are needed to make one automobile.
- A paper mill may use 200,000,000 liters of water each day.

All these bits of information point toward the fact that Americans use an average of 6,000 liters of water per person each day. We use it in factories and on farms. We use it to produce electricity. Plants and animals also need large amounts of water. Water is, in short, a kind of life blood of our country and our world. The question is, what are we doing to conserve this life blood?

Almost every stream, river, and lake in the United States is polluted to some degree. Even such huge bodies of water as the Great Lakes and the Great Salt Lake are victims of pollution. It is a problem that has become extremely serious in recent years.

In the years before World War II pollution problems were much less severe. Chemicals and wastes from cities and factories could be handled with some effectiveness in water treatment plants. Excessive pollution was largely confined within certain small areas.

After World War II the rate of city and suburban growth greatly quickened. Expanding industries dumped huge amounts of chemicals into nearby streams and lakes. Growing cities added to the problem by dumping greater amounts of human wastes into local waters.

A major problem today arises from the fact that so many chemicals are poured into our fresh water supplies. Take, for example, the general shift from soap to detergents. Ordinary soap is made of vegetable and animal fats. It can be broken down into natural products by bacteria in the water. Chemical detergents, on the other hand, cannot be so easily decomposed. They may reappear in our drinking water or as foam on the surface of our streams and rivers. Another problem is caused by great amounts of sewage. There are also a number of other dangerous pollutants. Factories may pour heated water into nearby rivers. This thermal pollution can have a damaging effect on both plant and animal life. Another pollutant is the silt that washes from slopes and hillsides. Finally, people today tend to leave calling cards in the form of cans, bottles, tires, and the like, along the shore and on the bottom of lakes and rivers.

Factories are, by all odds, the most important sources of water pollution. City wastes, in the form of sewage and other pollutants, are less than half as damaging as industrial wastes. Farming causes pollution. But it also is less responsible than either factories or cities. Even so, the fertilizers and chemicals used on most farms and the erosion of the soil makes farming a major contributor. Regardless of who is to blame, the fact remains that clean water is everybody's business. It is a problem that we can neither escape nor push aside.

Getting the Facts

■ What general changes in the years since World War II have greatly increased the amount of pollution in American rivers and lakes?

Forming an Opinion

■ It has often been noted that air and water pollution cross state borders. Which of the following do you think best able to deal with the problems caused by these two forms of pollution: (a) private citizens; (b) state governments; (c) regional cooperative groups formed by state governments; (d) the national government? Explain.

Speaking Out

Gus Tyler

Tyler is a labor union leader. He believes that the American culture encourages wasteful use of our natural resources. He finds both businesses and individual people at fault.

"Present waste in America is obscene. While much of it is corporately generated, much of it is personally preferred. Agribusiness may discard thousands of carloads of valuable waste in the form of pods, shells, husks; but individuals leave equally numerous carloads behind on their restaurant plates, in their wastebaskets, in their garbage cans. Soft drink companies may prefer to sell their ades in nonreturnable containers; but consumers also prefer not to bother with the returns. Waste is part of the culture.

"The forms of waste are manifold. Planned obsolescence is a sophisticated form. A car, dishwasher, a vacuum cleaner, an electric light bulb is devilishly designed to break down at a given point, to insure the need for repair (with valuable parts) or total replacement. . . .

"Packaging is another form of waste. Items worth two cents sell for 10 times that amount because of the packaging. . . .

"Much advertising is pure waste. In any one year, a busy executive will toss a piece of a forest into his wastebasket—in the form of unread mail. . . .

"To protect society against this kind of inevitable exhaustion of materials calls for measures to forbid waste of valuable resources—whether soil, trees, air, water, metals, or space. The nation must rethink the Gross National Product to inquire not only as to how big it is but also as to how useful it is in serving man's present and rapidly approaching future needs. It becomes imperative to examine the qualitative as well as the quantitative meaning of the national output."

1. Tyler gives a number of ways in which Americans waste natural resources. What other examples can you think of?

2. What examples can you find of ways in which individuals and businesses act to preserve our natural resources?

3. Tyler believes that we must give thought to our future needs. What actions, if any, do you think should be taken by individuals, businesses, or government?

How Serious Are Our Environmental Problems?

In January of 1969, a great oil well blowout took place off the shore of Santa Barbara, California. With distress and often anger, Americans viewed the results on TV. Millions watched as efforts were made to keep the slimy oil slicks from marring the beautiful beaches and killing the wildlife along the coast. A year later, in recognition of the disaster, a national conference was held in Santa Barbara. Conservationists, political leaders, and ordinary citizens attended. They adopted the following Declaration of Environmental Rights.

"All men have the right to an environment capable of sustaining life and promoting happiness. If the accumulated actions of the past become destructive of this right, men now living have the further right to repudiate the past for the benefit of the future. And it is manifest that centuries of careless neglect of the environment have brought mankind to a final crossroads. The quality of our lives is eroded and our very existence threatened by our abuse of the natural world. . . .

"Recognizing that the ultimate remedy for these fundamental problems is found in man's mind, not his machines, we call on societies and their governments to recognize and implement the following principles:

- We need an ecological consciousness that recognizes man as member, not master, of the community of living things sharing his environment.
- We must extend ethics beyond social relations to govern man's contact with all life forms and with the environment itself.
- We need a renewed idea of community which will shape urban environments that serve the full range of human needs.
- We must find the courage to take upon ourselves as individuals responsibility for the welfare of the whole environment, treating our own back yards as if they were the world and the world as if it were our back yard.
- We must develop the vision to see that in regard to the natural world private and corporate ownership should be so limited as to preserve the interest of society and the integrity of the environment.
- We need greater awareness of our enormous powers, the fragility of the earth, and the consequent responsibility of men and governments for its preservation.
- We must redefine 'progress' toward an emphasis on long-term quality rather than immediate quantity.

"We, therefore, resolve to act. We propose a revolution in conduct toward an environment which is rising in revolt against us. Granted that ideas and institutions long established are not easily changed; yet today is the first day of the rest of our life on this planet. We will begin anew."

Many other Americans were caught up in the same concern. President Nixon issued a statement from the White House a few days after the Santa Barbara conference. "The task of cleaning up our environment," he stated, "calls for a total mobilization by all of us. It involves government at every level; it requires the help of every citizen."

The urgency of the Nixon message was underscored by biologist Dr. Barry Commoner. In an article that appeared at about the same time as the presidential statement, Dr. Commoner warned, "We have time—perhaps a generation—in which to save the environment from the final effects of the violence we have already done it, and to save ourselves from our suicidal folly. . . ."

Inquiry

Inquiry

IF THE ECOLOGY ISSUES DIE, SO DO YOU

'Daddy, what does ecology mean?'

What statements are the two cartoonists and the poster designer making about modern environmental problems? To what extent has each exaggerated to make the point? With which statement do you agree most strongly?

ENVIRONMENTAL CONTROL STUDY CENTER

Such expressions of urgency and concern are directly related to the more general questions of ecology. As important as these questions seem, not everyone believes that the problems call for immediate answers. A leading sociologist, Amitai Etzioni, has called the ecology movement "a fad." Writing in the magazine *Science,* he placed environmental needs far from the top of his list of national priorities.

"This new commitment has many features of a fad: a rapid swell of enthusiasm . . . fanned by mass media. . . . And the commitment is rather shallow. Few citizens seem aware of the costs they will have to bear as taxpayers, consumers, and automobile and home owners. . . .

"The complicated problems that pollution control poses can be handled only in part through a crash program. Public and legislative commitment ought to be built up for a long pull. But even if one day water and air again are as pure as they were before man polluted them, many other environmental problems—from ugly cities to overcrowding—will still be with us.

"Now we should continue to give top priority to 'unfashionable' *human* problems. Fighting hunger, malnutrition, and rats should be given priority over saving wildlife, and improving our schools over constructing waste disposal systems. If we must turn to 'Environment,' first attention should be given to the 57,000 Americans who will *lose their lives* on the roads in 1970."

Also taking issue with the ordering of national priorities is a professor of law, Kenneth S. Tollett. Writing in a publication of the Center for the Study of Democratic Institutions, Professor Tollett noted certain kinds of problems that he believes must be placed higher on a list of national priorities than environment.

"Although I regard the environment problem as serious . . . I do not place it high among my priorities. This because I believe if the pace of excitement about the environment and the quality of life continues unabated, there will be a cop-out on the other priorities. A few redwood trees, condors, whooping cranes, buffaloes, and other picturesque fauna and flora may be preserved for the aesthetic satisfaction of cultural snobs and elitest intellectuals; a few signboards may be removed from highways, and industrial development here and there may be thwarted (to the detriment of the workingman and for the benefit of the leisure class's conspicuous concern for scenic beauty, unoiled surfing waters, and clean and silent air for their luxurious estates, homes and patios); but at the same time hardly anything will be done to clean up the slums, improve medical services for the lower and lower-middle classes, continue expansion of higher educational opportunity, deal with mass transportation problems of our urban centers, and maintain the struggle for economic, racial, and human justice.

"In short, I am of the opinion that the environment movement is a fad which permits . . . affluent white Americans to escape from dealing with the issues involving human survival. . . ."

Deciding Your Priorities

What right do you think people have to a more liveable environment?

Is it fair to call the ecology movement "a fad"? Why, or why not?

What kinds of national priorities do Etzioni and Tollett place above the conservation of the environment?

Where would you place environmental problems in a list of priorities? Why?

Citizenship Laboratory

Review of Basic Ideas

1. Early settlers in America found a land of plenty. The abundance of good soil, mineral wealth, forests, and wildlife helped to breed an attitude of wastefulness. To build personal fortunes and a rich industrial country, Americans exploited our country's natural resources, often with little concern for the future. Conservation of natural resources is largely a 20th century concern. Today almost all Americans are aware, to some degree, of the need to preserve and protect our country's resources.

2. Recent years have brought a growing interest in the science of ecology. Ecology is the study of the relationships between living things and their natural environments. Ecologists stress the need to maintain a balance in the systems of our environment—air, water, land, and living organisms.

3. America is blessed with an abundance of good soil. Using scientific methods, the average American farmer grows enough food to feed about 40 people. In the past, good soil has been damaged by careless farming practices. Today private and public efforts have successfully put an end to erosion of the soil in many areas. Irrigation and drainage projects have made more land available for farming.

4. Mineral resources, unlike soil, are not renewable. Our supply of many minerals is quickly running out. Today minerals are being conserved through recycling and the use of more efficient methods of extracting minerals from the earth.

5. The resources of American forests are renewable. Private and public efforts are being made to replant forests. Recycling and the use of substitute products are also helping to meet the growing demand for forest products.

6. Today the natural beauty of our land is preserved in hundreds of parklands run by the National Park Service.

7. Much of our country's history is an account of ways that the natural habitat has been altered. This has produced a serious loss of wilderness areas and wildlife. The National Wildlife Refuge System has set aside a great amount of land for wildlife conservation.

8. The pollution of water in the United States has increased greatly in the years since World War II with the growth of cities and industries. People are today seeking solutions to preserve this important natural resource.

Questions to Think About

1. What ideas or activities of the conservation pioneers do you think are still useful to the conservation movement today?

2. How are the terms "conservation," "environment," and "ecology" related?

3. What facts can be used to argue that soil conservation practices in the United States have been very successful?

4. The United States has a very short supply of many minerals. Do you think this will make it necessary for the United States to lower its industrial output in the near future? What other solutions might be found?

5. To what extent do you think it necessary for state and national governments to take part in forest conservation?

6. Should preservation of wildlife be a major conservation goal? Why, or why not?

7. Why is water pollution one of the nation's more serious ecological problems? What steps do you think should be taken to control water pollution?

Words and Relationships

Define each of the terms in the first column. Then show how each term is related to the item listed opposite it by using both items in a sentence or short paragraph.

1.	economic growth	natural resources
2.	conservation	future needs
3.	ecology	nature's life cycle
4.	atmosphere	air pollution
5.	hydrosphere	chemicals and detergents
6.	lithosphere	soil erosion
7.	biosphere	wildlife
8.	reclamation	irrigation
9.	recycling	mineral and forest resources
10.	habitat	wildlife preservation

Building a Future

We've all heard the old saying: "Don't cry over spilt milk." We should keep these words in mind when we deal with conservation, or environmental, problems. We must see the problems for what they are today and do what we can about them. Conservation, thus, is both for now and for the future. And it is, as we say, "action oriented."

One of the best ways to learn more about conservation problems is to identify certain ones that are close at hand. If you live in a city some of the most evident problems will likely be caused by air and water pollution. If you live in a suburb or a rural area you may be more conscious of changes in the natural habitat, soil erosion, and the like.

Working individually, or in small groups, identify and explore in depth a number of local conservation problems. On the basis of your studies, prepare written or oral reports for class presentation. Once the reports have been made, consider actions that you and your classmates might take to help solve any of the reported problems. In the process, give priority to those problems with which your group would appear to have the most likely prospect for success.

When you have found a problem that can be attacked, you may wish to bring it to the attention of the people directly affected. Posters, letters, or personal appeals might be used. If the problem does not improve, you may wish to bring it to the attention of local or federal officials.

Citizenship Laboratory

15 Developing National Systems of Transportation and Communication

The United States is, by any measure, a large country. Its boundaries encompass a considerable part of the globe. Look at a map of the United States. What is the approximate distance from Boston to Los Angeles? How far is it from Miami to Seattle? Using a globe, find the approximate distance from Washington, D.C. to Honolulu, Hawaii. Traveling at about 80 kilometers per hour (or about 50 miles per hour), approximately how long would it take you to drive from Portland, Maine to Portland, Oregon?

Ours is a well settled land. Almost anywhere we travel in the United States we find modern cities and cultivated farmlands. This spread of the American population is largely the result of the wealth of natural resources found in all parts of the country.

To settle the land and make use of our many resources, good systems of transportation were needed. Without ships and steamboats, roads and railroads, automobiles and airplanes, the United States could never have become as large and as rich as it is today.

Developments in transportation brought improved means of commu-

ECONOMIC LIFE IN MODERN AMERICA

nication. People did not have to remain isolated in tight little communities. Travel became easier and cheaper for all Americans. The telegraph, telephone, and finally radio and TV brought the outside world closer to every citizen.

Nor did American business need to remain small and localized. With improved methods of transportation and communication, business was able to expand. In doing so, it became more able to provide for the ever-growing needs, not only of Americans, but of people around the world.

A National System of Highways

When we examine the use of highways by motor vehicles in the United States, figures boggle the mind. During one recent year (1975), there were more than 100,000,000 passenger cars registered in the United States. In addition there were some 25,000,000 trucks and buses. During that year, motor vehicles in the United States traveled more than 2,000,000,000,000—2 trillion—kilometers. With about one car for every two Americans, highway travel is easily the most common means of transportation in our country. And, as far as commercial transportation is concerned, more people ride buses than trains or planes.

EARLY ROADS

The sea and the coastal rivers were the first means of travel for early settlers. As people pushed inland, however, the need for roads grew. As early as 1632, we find the colonial legislature in Virginia passing a law stating that "highways shall be laid out in such convenient places as are requisite...." Similar laws calling for roads were passed in other colonies.

Before the end of the 1660s, stagecoaches had been brought from Europe. Running between colonial cities and towns, they carried both people and mail. Stagecoaches were joined in the 1730s by Conestoga wagons. Conestogas—named for the region of Pennsylvania where they were first built—were large, broad-wheeled covered wagons. Used to carry freight, they were pulled by six or more horses. A Conestoga wagon could carry a load of up to four and a half metric tons.

As Americans pushed westward, roads and trails were laid out. Many of these became famous in our country's history. Daniel Boone laid out the Wilderness Road. It linked the Atlantic Coast with settlements in the Ohio Valley. One of the most heavily traveled of the early highways was the National Road. Opened in 1811, it finally extended all the way from Cumberland, Maryland to Vandalia, Illinois.

Linking settlements and trading posts in the Southwest with the eastern states was the Santa Fe Trail. Along this trail, in the 1820s, could be seen Conestoga wagons and people on horseback. They were moving between Independence, Missouri and Santa Fe in what later became the state of New Mexico.

From Independence, in the early 1840s, traders and settlers also followed the Oregon Trail into the Pacific Northwest. With the discovery of gold in California, late in the 1840s, thousands of gold seekers followed this same Oregon Trail as far as Idaho. Then they turned south along the California, or Overland, Trail.

ROADS ACROSS AMERICA

From trails such as these, a road system was developed throughout the United States during the 19th century. At best, however, these roads were crude. Most could be used only by horses, wagons, and buggies. Often they were usable only in good weather. As late as 1904 a study of the roads in the United States showed that while there were more than 3,000,000 kilometers of roads in the nation, only about 30 kilometers of these roads were modern, hard-surfaced highways.

But even as the study was being made, a new vehicle was beginning to appear. The automobile was to revolutionize the American landscape and the American way of life. As these "horseless carriages" chugged along, stirring up clouds of dust, scattering gravel, plowing through mud, and frightening cows and sheep, it became obvious to almost everyone that the roads would have to change.

To meet the needs of the automobile age, a new road system was devel-

Although a great number of good, hard-surfaced roads had been built by the late 1930s, many Americans still had to rely on horse power to solve their automobile problems.

oped. The federal and state governments worked together to build a network of national highways. (You can recognize these highways today by their markers shaped like shields. They give the name of the state, the number of the route, and the letters "U.S.") In addition to helping build these national highways, each state developed its own road system. (The markers for state roads vary in shape from state to state.) Also built were thousands of kilometers of local "feeder" roads. Feeder roads bring people and goods from outlying areas to the main highways.

Construction of the national highway system did not get underway until the middle of the 1920s. So pressing was the need for modern roads, however, that by the middle of the 1930s the system was almost completed.

THE INTERSTATE HIGHWAY SYSTEM

In the years following World War II, the growth of American industry and population made it quite clear that the existing highways could not meet the country's needs. Accordingly, during the 1950s, plans were laid for a national Interstate Highway System. Ultimately it will be a system of almost 70,000 kilometers. Designed to be the country's key highway network, it serves both civilian and defense needs. Funds for the program come from federal excise taxes, such as gasoline taxes, that are levied on highway users. In financing this giant undertaking, the federal government has agreed to pay for 90 percent of the construction. The states must pay the remaining 10 percent of the construction costs.

By 1975 some 60,000 kilometers, or about 85 percent, of the Interstate Highway System had been opened. On almost all of the remaining 15 percent, work was underway. Though designed to carry about a fifth of all the country's highway traffic, the completed interstate system will make up only about 1 percent of all highways in the United States.

Even with its great cost and relatively short length, the interstate system is proving to be a great bargain for the American people. The broad, multi-laned highways have added greatly to the comfort and safety of highway travel. One reason for their greater safety is their limited access feature. This means that vehicles can enter and leave interstate highways only at certain widely spaced places. There are no crossroads and driveways to slow the flow of traffic. No cars or pedestrians can cross directly in front of oncoming traffic.

Getting the Facts

1. What evidence is there that highway travel is the most common means of travel in the United States?

2. What new method of transportation led to the building of good, hard-surfaced roads throughout America?

3. When and why was the Interstate Highway System begun? How has it been financed?

Examining the Issues

■ What groups in America benefit most from a good system of highways? What groups, if any, do not benefit? In what ways do you and your classmates benefit from good highway systems?

Speaking Out

David Hapgood

David Hapgood is a political commentator and a contributing editor to the *Washington Monthly*. Here he compares the federal highway program with the Great Wall of China, built centuries ago. He believes that the highway lobby has far too much power.

". . . The lobby whizzes along on a superhighway it has paved for itself through the jungles of politics at the local, state, and national levels. There are almost no toll gates on that superhighway, and few red lights. The growing number of citizens who want to see more such controls installed have little reason to be hopeful. Despite occasional victories like that of lower Manhattan, most battles against city highways have been lost, mainly because it is the lobby, not the people, that has government support.

"And no wonder. Money is the lifeblood of politics, and the richest blood that flows in the veins of state and local political organizations is derived from highways and their economic side effects. Nothing generates more financial return, legal or otherwise, to those in office than highway construction money, and it is unlikely that any official who wants to stay in Washington will put too many obstacles in the path of that money to the states. . . .

"The financing of the Highway Program was a classic raid on the Treasury. In the annals of lobbying, the highwaymen who executed this coup deserve to be listed alongside those Chinese contractors who convinced the Ch'in emperors to build the Great Wall of China. There are certain similarities between the two operations.

"The Great Wall was supposed to keep out Mongol invaders. The highway lobby's trump card was the claim that what it got Congress to call the 'National System of Interstate and Defense Highways' would serve to move military units in case of war—making opposition to it seem somehow unpatriotic. . . . The Great Wall did not keep the Mongols out, but the Chinese kept on building it over the centuries. Similarly the interstate highways would be of no use in a 24-hour nuclear war . . ."

1. To what extent do you think it fair to compare our interstate highway program with the Great Wall of China?

2. What are the advantages and disadvantages of giving the federal government major control over the development of a huge new highway program?

3. Think about new highways that have been built by the national or state government in your area. Do they seem to meet the needs of the people in your area? What steps might citizens take to assure that the highways built meet local needs?

Railroads in the Nation's Economic Life

That the United States moved into the 20th century without building a national system of hard-surfaced highways was largely due to the earlier development of a railroad network. With railroads running to all parts of the country, there was little concern for anything but local roads.

The importance of the railroads can be illustrated by an event that took place on November 18, 1883. By an agreement among the railroad companies, the United States was divided into four standard time zones—Eastern, Central, Mountain, and Pacific. The system, still being used today, provides time zones that are one hour apart. When it is 11 o'clock in Philadelphia (Eastern Standard Time), it is 10 o'clock in St. Louis (Central Standard Time), nine o'clock in Denver (Mountain Standard Time), and eight o'clock in San Diego (Pacific Standard Time). This has been done to match the movement of the sun from east to west. The 1883 action simply reflected the fact that all parts of the United States had become linked by speedier means of transportation—the railroad.

Before the arrangement of time zones, "local time" was used by cities and even small communities. As long as waterways and poor roads kept travel moving slowly, these many local times offered no great problems. However, with the coming of the railroads and the increased speed of railroad service, however, the use of local time caused no end of confusion.

DEVELOPMENT OF A RAILROAD SYSTEM

Among the first Americans to recognize the need for railroads were business leaders in Baltimore, Maryland. Their trade with the West was being threatened by canals running through New York and Pennsylvania. They decided to compete by building a railroad from Baltimore to the Ohio River. In 1830, about 21 kilometers of the Baltimore and Ohio track were completed. This was the first American railroad of any great length.

So quickly did the railroad idea catch on that by 1835 more than 1,500 kilometers of track were in use. By 1860 there were almost 50,000 kilometers of track.

An important stage in American railroad transportation was reached on May 10, 1869. On that day the Central Pacific Railroad, pushing eastward from California, and the Union Pacific Railroad building westward from Omaha, Nebraska, met at Promontory Point, Utah. This marked the completion of the first chain of railroads to link the country from the Atlantic to the Pacific.

Other transcontinental railroads soon followed. Three were built in the next 16 years. In addition, a vast web of rails was spreading into all parts of the country. By 1916, America's railroads had expanded to their greatest length—over 400,000 kilometers of tracks. Today there are only about 320,000 kilometers of railroad tracks in the United States.

TRANSPORTING PEOPLE

During the century of railway growth after 1830, a great deal of public enthusiasm centered on the railroads. The

In the mid-19th century, a great deal of state and local political activity centered on the planning of new railroad routes. Why do you suppose the politicians in the cities and towns of the Middle West were so interested in the routes chosen for the new railroads?

train was the thing. For hundreds of otherwise isolated towns and villages, the railroad was the only link with the outside world. To a great degree, life in these towns and villages was regulated by the coming and going of the daily passenger train.

The earliest railroad passenger cars were just stagecoaches mounted on wheels. On winter days the only heat was provided by a small stove in each coach. In the warm summer weather people who opened the windows had to bear the discomfort of cinders, smoke, and even hot coals streaming out of the train's engine.

By the 1860s there were many improvements. Some passenger trains had cars for dining and sleeping. Electric lights and steam heat were being used by the 1880s. Other early improvements included air brakes, automatic couplers to connect passenger cars and engine, stronger bridges, and better signal systems.

In the 20th century, steam engines were replaced by diesels. Air conditioning became the rule. In 1934 another innovation—the streamliner—was first put into service. The streamliner got its name from its design. Its smoothly curved lines were meant to cut down wind resistance.

Even with the many improvements in passenger service, in the 20th century other means of transportation replaced the railroad as "the ruler of American transportation." With modern highways, the automobile and bus provided a greater measure of convenience and flexibility. This was particularly true for trips over short distances. The fixed railroad time schedules were much less convenient than private automobiles and local buses. In the skies, airline service offered its own kind of competition. The speed of air travel made it particularly desirable for long-distance trips.

With so many people choosing other forms of transportation, the income of railroads fell. Most lines began to lose millions of dollars a year on their passenger business. This led to the deterioration of equipment and service. By 1970 there were fewer than 400 passenger trains in the United States. Less than 2 percent of all travel between cities was by train.

Today an effort is being made to retrieve some of the passenger travel between cities. High-speed train service is now offered along the heavily traveled route from New York City to Washington, D.C. With electric cars on special rails, the new trains can make the 364-kilometer trip in about three hours. It is hoped that the time might even be shortened to two hours.

A much more extensive program was set up by the Rail Passenger Service Act of 1970. The aim of this act has been to revive railroad passenger service by cutting down the number of trains and improving service. The new service is called Amtrak—a contraction of "American" and "track." It went into operation on May 1, 1971. At first, the new Amtrak system involved only 184 passenger trains. By the mid-1970s there were 225 Amtrak trains. These trains were serving about 425 American cities and towns over a rail network of about 40,000

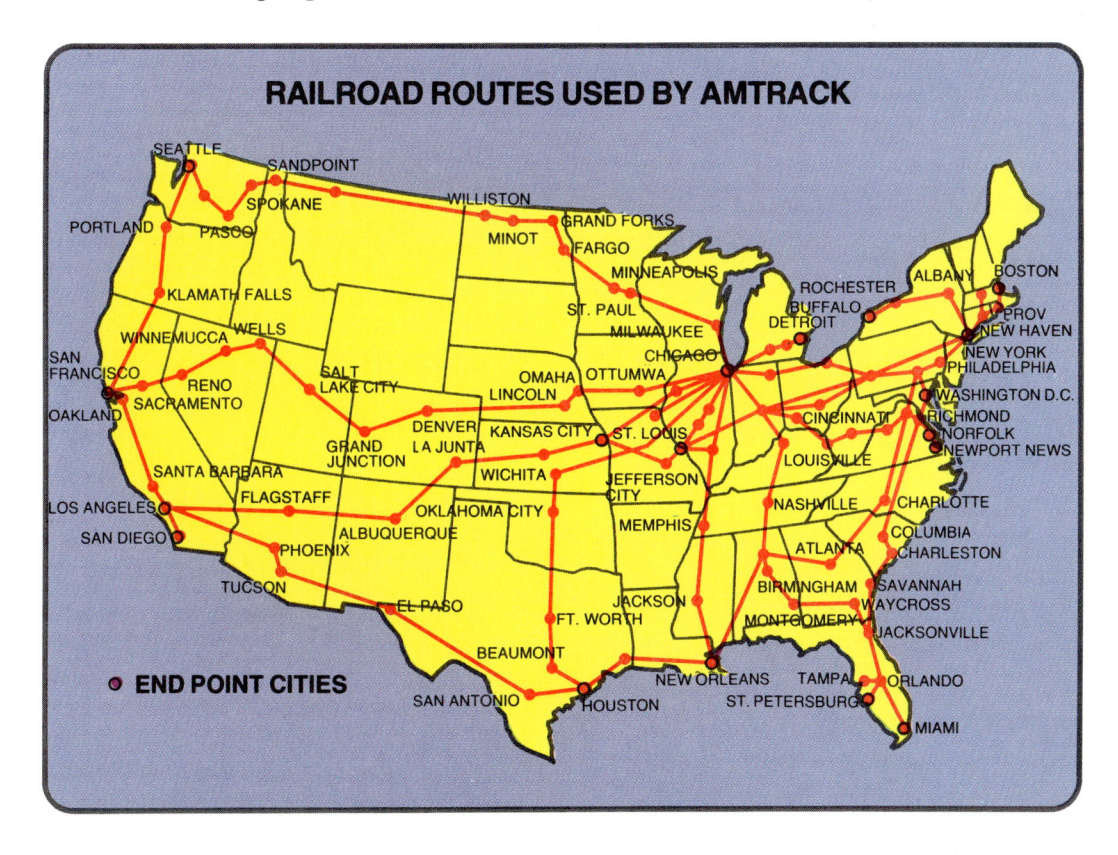

RAILROAD ROUTES USED BY AMTRACK

● END POINT CITIES

DEVELOPING NATIONAL SYSTEMS OF TRANSPORTATION AND COMMUNICATION

kilometers. In taking over most of America's railroad passenger service, this new government corporation hopes to attract many Americans back to train travel. During the first years of Amtrak service, however, the results were mixed. Service on some lines was very popular. In other places there was much less support.

MOVEMENT OF FREIGHT BY RAIL

Passenger service continues to be a matter of some importance. But the most important contribution of the railroad is to our country's economic life. Even with competition from trucks, pipelines, and, to a much lesser extent, cargo airplanes, trains remain our major carriers of freight. Some ground was lost to other kinds of carriers in the 1950s. But trains held their ground in the 1960s. And by the early 1970s they were carrying more than 40 percent of all freight.

To a great extent we Americans live out of freight cars. Fresh fruit and vegetables, meats, and dairy products are brought to us in refrigerator cars. Tank cars carry milk, chemicals, and oil. Stock cars carry cattle. Flat cars carry lumber and machines. Hopper cars carry minerals. Finally, box cars carry all kinds of manufactured goods.

The railroads, to remain competitive, have developed some new ways of moving cargo. One method is often called "piggybacking." Following this method, loaded truck trailers are carried on railroad flat cars. This saves money and reduces the amount of highway traffic. Another new technique is called "containerization." Using this method, a huge metal container is loaded at a warehouse, hauled to a railroad, and loaded onto a flat car. This makes load-

"Piggybacking" has created a new form of transport—half truck, half train. What are some of the many benefits of using this method to carry freight?

ing, unloading, and reloading simpler. The coming years are likely to see other improvements in freight service as the railroads continue to make their contribution to the American economy.

Getting the Facts

1. Give the approximate dates for the following: (a) railroads were first built in the United States; (b) the first transcontinental railroad was completed; (c) the nation's railroad system reached its greatest length.

2. What improvements have recently been made in railroad passenger service? What new methods have made railroad freight service more efficient?

Examining the Issues

■ There is likely to be some form of rail service in or near your community. What passenger services are offered? Has passenger service improved or declined over the last decade? What are possible explanations for any changes in service?

The Modern Age of Air Transport

Movement by air is a 20th century development. Modern aviation is often dated from December 17, 1903. On that day the American Orville Wright, with the help of his brother Wilbur, flew a crate-like airplane 260 meters along the sand dunes at Kitty Hawk, North Carolina. From that date, progress was rapid. Eight years later, in 1911, a plane was flown across the United States. It was not a simple matter, though. The flight took 49 days, only 103 hours of which were spent in the air. Later, in 1919, a seaplane of the United States Navy flew from Newfoundland to England. This was the first successful flight across the Atlantic Ocean. Certainly the most dramatic of all the early flights across the Atlantic, however, took place in 1927. In that year, Charles Lindbergh made the first nonstop solo flight from New York to Paris.

These are but a few of the many achievements that brought the people of the world into the air age. Today the developments of that age make it possible for people to go anywhere on the globe in a matter of hours. As a consequence, old ideas about time and distance have been revolutionized. To a great degree, the airplane has made neighbors of all people everywhere.

PASSENGER TRAVEL BY AIR

The development of airplanes was stimulated by their military use in World War I. During the 1920s, there were repeated efforts to set up regular airline passenger service. Success, however, was very limited.

Progress remained slow during the 1930s. As recently as 1940, regular airlines in the United States carried fewer than 3,000,000 passengers a year.

The photographs below show the interiors of passenger airplanes in the early years of air travel and today. Would you have been one of the adventurous few who traveled by plane in the years before World War II?

DEVELOPING NATIONAL SYSTEMS OF TRANSPORTATION AND COMMUNICATION

It was during the next 30 years that truly remarkable growth in air travel took place. In 1970, airlines in the United States carried over 150,000,000 passengers.

To meet the demands of an ever-growing amount of air travel, larger airplanes were built. By 1970, some new airplanes could carry more than 400 passengers. Supersonic transports, able to fly at twice the speed of sound, were also being built.

The larger airplanes and the growing amounts of traffic placed great burdens on airport facilities. Airports often found it hard to handle the huge planes and the large numbers of passengers they carried. There was also the problem of moving large numbers of people between airports and downtown areas. To meet the mounting demands, airport facilities were expanded. Plans for new and larger airports are now on the drawing boards in cities across the United States.

MOVING GOODS BY AIR

The nature of air travel in the United States can be judged from two figures. During one recent year the airlines accounted for nearly 60 percent of the distance traveled by people in planes, trains, and buses. (The planes were carrying only about one out of every six passengers. The large percentage came from the fact that air passengers generally traveled much longer distances.) By contrast, air freight made up less than 1 percent of American cargo business. Because of limits on the size and weight of their cargo, airplanes cannot cheaply carry many kinds of goods generally carried by trucks and trains.

The small percentage of business in air freight, however, should not lead us to overlook its importance. In many cases, speed of transport is of great value to business. The competition of air freight is being increasingly felt by other carriers. With new super jets and ever-larger airplanes, the amount of business in air cargo seems certain to rise.

Getting the Facts

1. What methods are now being used to improve passenger travel by air?

2. What are the major differences in the amount and forms of freight carried by air and rail?

Forming an Opinion

■ What do you consider the major advantages and disadvantages of traveling by air? For what reasons may people choose trains, buses, or cars instead of planes? Under what conditions would you prefer to travel by air?　by train?　by bus?　by car?

Waterways as Avenues of Trade

In contrast to glamorous new airplanes, historic railroads, and modern highways, the slow quiet traffic along American waterways can easily escape public attention. However, the movement of freight by water is an important part of our country's transportation system. The amount of freight carried on our inland waterways—about 500,000,000,000 metric ton-kilometers a year—runs to such a huge figure that we find it hard to comprehend.

Waterways have one big advantage. They can move goods more cheaply than other forms of transportation can. This is particularly true when moving such heavy, large, and non-perishable products as iron ore, coal, and building materials.

TRANSPORTATION BY RIVER, LAKE, AND CANAL

In earlier times, rivers and lakes were often the most convenient means by which people and goods could move. They became even more useful after 1807. In that year, Robert Fulton demonstrated the first practical use of the steamboat. In the wake of Fulton's trip up the Hudson River aboard his *Clermont*, the United States embarked upon a steamboat era. The steamboat played an important part in the nation's life during the first half of the 19th century.

So important was water transportation during these years that canals were dug to supplement rivers and lakes. Between the years 1825 and 1850 about 6,500 kilometers of canals were opened in various parts of the country.

During the last half of the 19th century, the growth of the railroads diminished the importance of water transportation. Beginning early in the 20th century, however, American waterways gradually gained back much of their earlier significance.

The largest amount of freight carried by water in the United States today is on the Mississippi River and the Great Lakes systems. The Mississippi River system includes a number of large

Many historians believe that the Erie Canal, which connected the Great Lakes and the Hudson River, gave New York City the head start it needed to become our country's largest city.

DEVELOPING NATIONAL SYSTEMS OF TRANSPORTATION AND COMMUNICATION

These tow boats on the Ohio River show another form of "piggybacking." Here the transportation method is half railroad, half boat. What are the advantages of this combination?

rivers that flow into it, such as the Ohio and Missouri rivers. Draining much of the central United States, it has almost 15,000 kilometers of navigable waters. Along these waters move more than a third of all the country's water freight. A comparable amount is carried on the Great Lakes system.

The value of the Great Lakes system was increased by the opening of the St. Lawrence Seaway in 1959. The seaway provides a deep channel from the Great Lakes to the Atlantic Ocean. It makes it possible for ships to penetrate deeply into the American Middle West. By means of the seaway, ships can now travel 3,770 kilometers from the Atlantic Ocean to Duluth, Minnesota at the western end of Lake Superior.

INTRACOASTAL WATERWAYS

There are many rivers in the eastern part of the United States flowing into the Atlantic Ocean. Other American rivers flow south into the Gulf of Mexico. Still others flow into the Pacific Ocean in the West. Rivers and canals along these coasts combine in such a way as to make continuous navigable channels for barges and light vessels.

The intracoastal waterway system along the Atlantic extends for some 2,400 kilometers. Along the Gulf Coast, the system extends about 1,600 kilometers. Although important, the traffic on both of these waterways is less than half the amount found on either the Mississippi or the Great Lakes systems. One reason is that much of the freight that might be carried on intracoastal rivers and canals is, in many cases, moved more cheaply on ocean-going cargo ships.

The intracoastal waterways along the Pacific are used even less than those along the Atlantic and Gulf coasts. But even the Pacific Coast system should not be underrated. The waterways along the Pacific carry a great amount of heavy freight each year.

MERCHANT MARINE

Another important part of our country's transportation system is a fleet of ships known as the Merchant Marine. Ships in this fleet carry people and goods on ocean highways throughout the world.

The American Merchant Marine is made up of three kinds of vessels: passenger-cargo ships, freighters, and tankers. In all three categories the United States is among the world's leading shippers.

At one time, at the end of World War II, the United States owned more than 60 percent of all merchant ships in the world. Since that time, however, transportation of both people and goods has become much more widely distributed among the countries of the world.

America's loss of the leading role in world shipping, however, should not be interpreted as a lack of interest on the part of the United States. In 1970, an act of Congress set up a new program designed to build 300 merchant ships in the next 10 years.

Getting the Facts

1. What two inland waterways carry the majority of American water freight?

2. What services are provided by the Merchant Marine?

Examining the Issues

■ What method or methods would you choose to ship the following items: (a) a metric ton of coal; (b) 100 crates of tomatoes; (c) 2,000 transistor radios; (d) a painting by Leonardo da Vinci? What factors would you have to consider before making each choice?

In 1975 the United States had the seventh largest merchant fleet in the world. Liberia had the largest, followed by Japan, Britain, Norway, Greece, and the Soviet Union. Should efforts be made to regain our post World War II lead? Why, or why not?

DEVELOPING NATIONAL SYSTEMS OF TRANSPORTATION AND COMMUNICATION

Inquiry

Travel Data

Trends in passenger travel between cities in the United States are shown in the three line graphs on the next page. The graphs present information about travel by air, railroad, and intercity bus. The first graph shows the number of passengers carried by air, rail, and bus between 1960 and 1974. The second graph shows the number of kilometers covered by the three means of transportation during these same years. The third graph shows the number of passenger-kilometers traveled. (The passenger-kilometer figures are arrived at by noting how far each passenger traveled and then adding all the distances. Three passengers traveling 10 kilometers each would be 30 passenger-kilometers. One passenger traveling 23 kilometers and another passenger traveling seven kilometers would also be 30 passenger-kilometers.)

Amtrak rail service began in 1971. According to the graphs on the opposite page, what changes occurred in passenger travel by rail between 1971 and 1974? What factors, other than the new service, may have affected trends in rail travel in those years?

These three graphs can be used to answer a number of different kinds of questions. In this exercise, questions will be asked not only to increase your knowledge of intercity passenger travel but also to increase your understanding of the kinds of questions that can be applied to graphs such as these. Six different kinds of questions are asked. Try to answer each question. Then, using that question as a guide, think of other questions of the same nature that can be asked about the data in the graphs.

1. Fact Question. (This kind of question asks for no more than a simple factual answer.) Approximately how many passenger-kilometers did people in the United States travel by intercity bus in 1972?

2. Translation Question. (This kind of question asks that facts be presented in a different form.) Describe in your own words what happened to rail passenger service between 1960 and 1974.

3. Comparison Question. (This kind of question asks for a comparison of different facts.) Compare the trends in rail and bus passenger service between 1964 and 1974.

4. Application Question. (This kind of question asks for certain information to be put to some specific use.) Considering the growth of the nation's population between 1960 and 1974, what do you think the relatively small change in the number of passengers carried by rail and bus and the large increase in the number of passengers carried by air indicates about the ideas and habits of Americans?

5. Synthesis Question. (This kind of question asks that something be created from facts in hand.) From data in the graphs, prepare a brief account of the topic "Trends in U.S. Air Travel Between 1964 and 1974."

6. Evaluation Question. (This kind of question asks you to make a value judgment.) Since the number of passengers carried by rail between 1960 and 1974 decreased, even as the country's population was on the rise, is there any reason to try to save railroad passenger service?

Inquiry

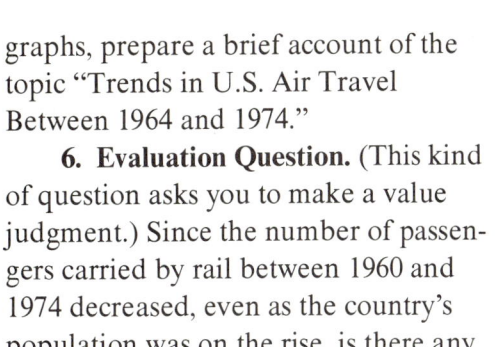

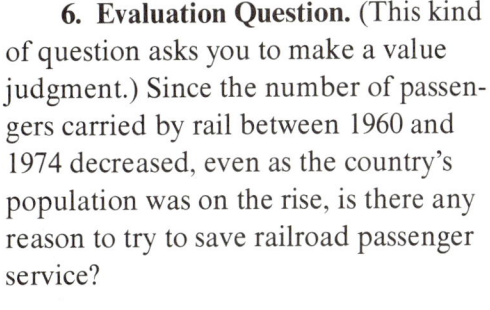

TRAVEL TRENDS

Air, Rail, and Bus Travel in the United States 1960-1974

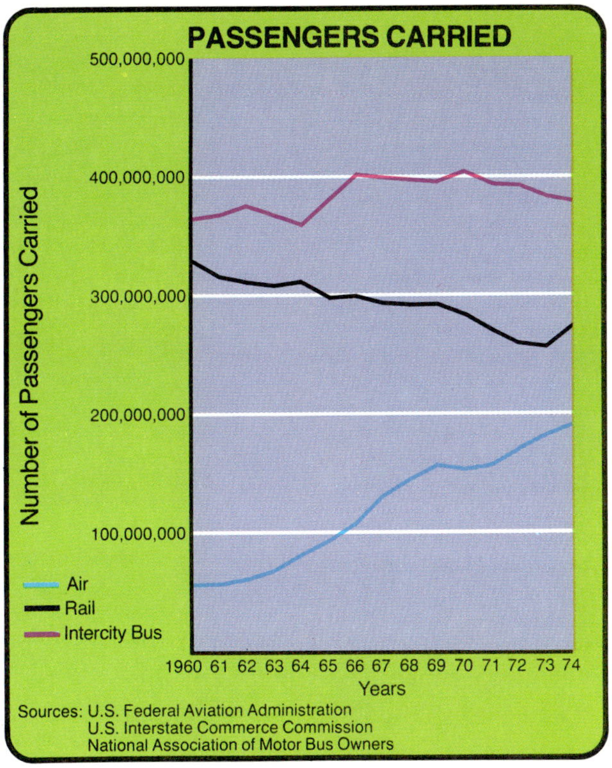

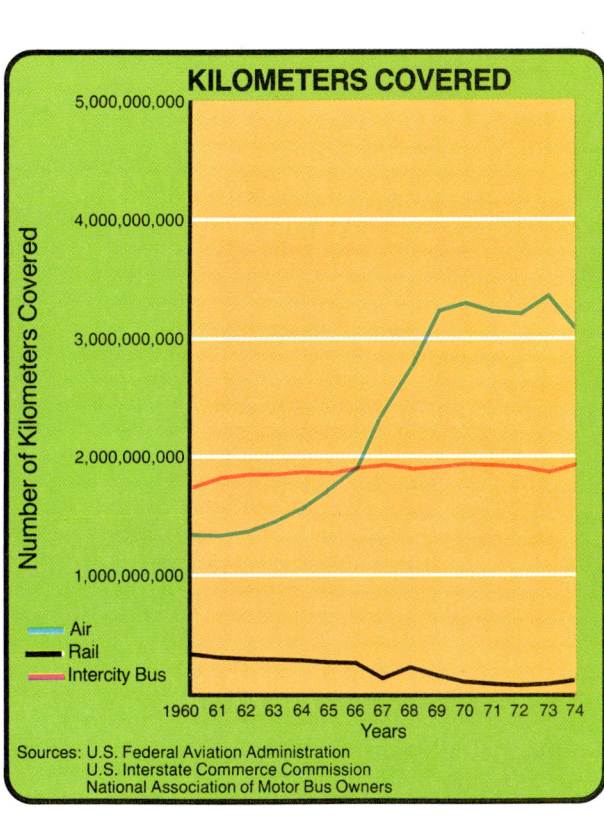

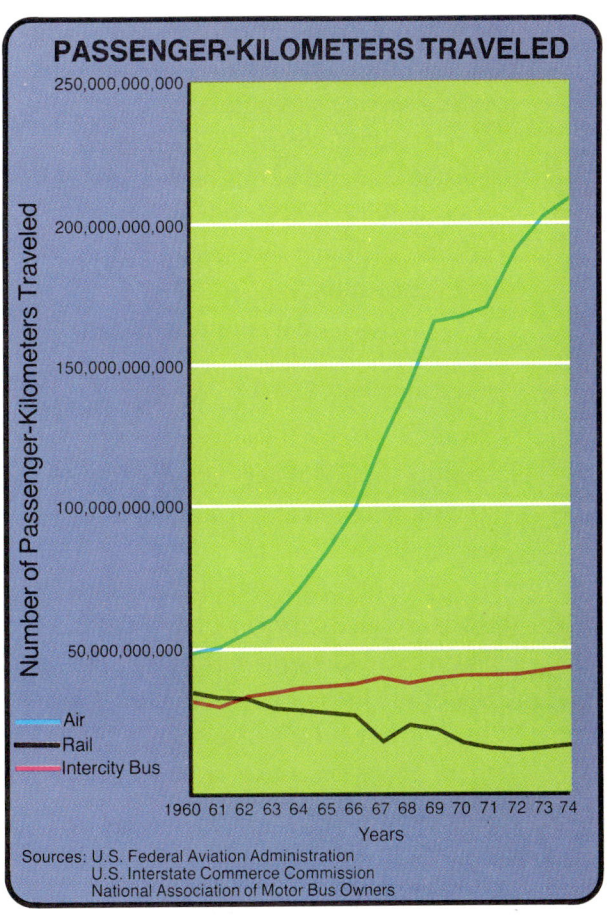

PASSENGERS CARRIED

Y-axis: Number of Passengers Carried (0 to 500,000,000)
X-axis: Years 1960–74

Legend: Air, Rail, Intercity Bus

Sources: U.S. Federal Aviation Administration; U.S. Interstate Commerce Commission; National Association of Motor Bus Owners

KILOMETERS COVERED

Y-axis: Number of Kilometers Covered (0 to 5,000,000,000)
X-axis: Years 1960–74

Legend: Air, Rail, Intercity Bus

Sources: U.S. Federal Aviation Administration; U.S. Interstate Commerce Commission; National Association of Motor Bus Owners

PASSENGER-KILOMETERS TRAVELED

Y-axis: Number of Passenger-Kilometers Traveled (0 to 250,000,000,000)
X-axis: Years 1960–74

Legend: Air, Rail, Intercity Bus

Sources: U.S. Federal Aviation Administration; U.S. Interstate Commerce Commission; National Association of Motor Bus Owners

DEVELOPING NATIONAL SYSTEMS OF TRANSPORTATION AND COMMUNICATION

Systems of Communication

Private automobiles, modern highways, and systems of public transportation are more than just ways of carrying people and goods. They are ways in which people are brought into touch with one another—into communication. There is much more to communication, however, than just face-to-face contacts. Today, in America, we have a number of communications systems. We reach one another by mail, telegraph, telephone, radio, and TV.

POSTAL SERVICE

Letters and other printed matter were delivered by foot or by messengers on horseback even during the earliest years of American settlement. In 1774, a postal service was authorized by the Continental Congress. The first Postmaster General of this new postal service was Benjamin Franklin. Through his efforts post offices were set up throughout the country.

Improvements in postal service came with new developments in transportation. The building of railroads brought faster mail service. In the 20th century, mail delivery was made faster and more efficient through the use of airplanes and new highways.

Early recognition of the value of postal service came in 1829 when the Postmaster General was made a member of the President's Cabinet. Later, in 1872, the Post Office became a department of the executive branch of the federal government.

Recently a major change has been made in our country's mail service. By

Why would mail service be improved if all Americans used zip codes?

an act of Congress in 1970, the Post Office Department was replaced by the United States Postal Service. The Postal Service began operation on July 1, 1971. The chief officer is still called the Postmaster General but is no longer a member of the President's Cabinet. An 11-member Board of Governors now appoints the Postmaster General. The money for running the Postal Service comes from postal fees and from Congress.

Though Congress provides some of the money to run the Postal Service, it has no power to intervene directly. Specifically forbidden under the terms of the new act are political tests or qualifications for post office employees. Such a rule is in sharp contrast to the traditional way of running the Post Office Department. In years past, employees often received their jobs for political reasons.

Even with all the efforts Congress has made to improve mail service, difficulties remain. All too often, the words written on the portico of the main post office building in New York City—"Neither snow nor rain nor heat nor gloom of night stays these couriers from the swift completion of their appointed rounds"—seem in doubt. The real difficulty, however, stems not from the couriers themselves. Nor is it with the people who handle the mail within the post offices. It comes from out-of-date equipment and machines that are expected to handle ever-growing amounts of mail. (Almost 100,000,000,000 pieces of mail pass through the postal system each year. This is as much mail as is sent in all the rest of the world.) Thus, more is needed than just a newly organized service. There is a need for a truly modern service.

RAPID COMMUNICATION BY TELEGRAPH AND TELEPHONE

Possibilities for forms of communication that would be faster than mail service began to be explored in the late 18th and early 19th centuries. Using discoveries about electricity and magnetism, an American artist and inventor, Samuel F. B. Morse, experimented with the idea of a telegraph. His invention made it possible to send coded messages quickly over great distances.

The first telegraph set was completed in 1835. Eight years later, Congress became interested in the idea and provided money for a telegraph line between Washington, D.C. and Baltimore, Maryland. Soon lines were built in other parts of the eastern United

For a short time the Pony Express carried U.S. mail from Missouri to California. The service ended in 1861 when the transcontinental telegraph was completed, giving Easterners and Westerners a faster means of communication.

States. By 1861 a telegraph line ran across the country, from the Atlantic to the Pacific. Five years later, in 1866, a cable was laid under the Atlantic Ocean. It brought telegraph service between the United States and Europe.

Early telegraph messages were sent by small instruments that clicked out dots and dashes in what was called "Morse Code." Modern telegraph messages are much more accurate. They are sent by electronic devices that photograph typed or handwritten messages and send them exactly as typed or written.

The telephone arrived later than the telegraph. The first patent was granted in 1876 to Alexander Graham Bell, a Scottish immigrant who had recently come to the United States. Two years later the first telephone switchboard was opened in Hartford, Connecticut. Shortly after that, telephone service was set up in a number of other American cities. The first long-distance service was opened in 1892 between New York and Chicago. However, coast-to-coast service was not available until 1915.

One of the major improvements in telephone communication was the development of wireless transmission. The idea was first developed by the Italian inventor Marconi late in the 19th century. It made it possible to communicate by telephone without setting up connecting strands of wire. Wireless transmission allows us to make calls from moving trains, automobiles, and ships at sea.

The telephone has become an important part of our personal and business lives. Telephone service has expanded rapidly. It is difficult to realize that in 1900 there were fewer than 1,500,000 telephones in the United States. Today there are that many telephones in a city the size of Detroit or Philadelphia.

COMMUNICATION AND ENTERTAINMENT BY RADIO AND TV

Like the telephone, radio and TV are commonplace features of our life today. More than just a means of communication, however, radio and TV offer hours of entertainment to Americans. Both are much more recent innovations than the telegraph and telephone. And yet they have become important parts of our daily lives. It is now hard to imagine what life must have been like before their arrival.

The first scheduled radio broadcast in the United States took place in 1920. The following year the first radio station—KDKA in Pittsburgh—began operation. Once begun, the idea caught on like wildfire. Radio stations were set up across the country. The 1920s became a kind of radio decade.

Radio continued to grow by leaps and bounds during the 1930s and 1940s. But there were predictions that, with the coming of TV, it would lose much of its popularity. Such has not been the case. Radio has continued to prosper as a means of communication. Major growth is seen today in the number of small stations serving limited geographical areas. To some degree they have replaced the powerful clear channel stations covering entire regions of the country. The smaller stations offer local, as well as national, news. Most of these stations also provide a great deal of musical entertainment.

What are some of the many reasons why the introduction of TV did not end the popularity of radio?

The first regular TV broadcast in the United States came in 1939. But growth was halted by World War II. In the years following the war, this miracle of communication began its meteoric growth. Today more than 95 percent of all American homes have at least one TV set. A recent study reported that in America preschool children spend, on an average, about two thirds of their waking hours in front of a TV set. The study also noted that the average child spends more hours watching TV than the average student spends in the classroom during four years of college.

TV has brought great changes in the leisure-time habits of Americans. It is estimated that, on an average, American adults spend at least 10 years of their lives watching TV. Offering more than just entertainment, however, TV provides access to important events. Through the use of satellites, we have instant visual contact with a large part of the globe. TV also offers many services to industry and business. In a number of ways it is bringing the people of the world into direct visual contact.

Getting the Facts

1. What organization takes care of our country's mail? How is it governed? How is it financed?

2. Give the approximate dates for the following: (a) the first transcontinental telegraph line; (b) the first coast-to-coast telephone service; (c) the first radio station; (d) the first regular TV broadcast.

3. What are some of the many services provided by TV and radio?

Examining the Issues

■ How would your life be altered if all telephone service were eliminated? In what ways would your life change if there were no more radio or TV broadcasts?

What is this cartoonist saying about the influence of TV? Do you agree or disagree?

'He said his first word . . . KILL!'

361

Citizenship Laboratory

Review of Basic Ideas

1. The United States is one of the largest countries in the world. A well settled country, its growth has been made possible by the creation of extensive systems of transportation. Among the most important of these are our modern systems of highways—state, national, and interstate. Trails and roads were important to early settlers. It was the arrival of the automobile, however, that led to the modern highways we have today.

2. The railroads have played an important role in the development of the United States and of the American economy. Although the railroads are no longer as important a means of travel as they once were, much of America's freight is still carried by rail. Efforts are now being made to encourage passenger travel by train.

3. Modern aviation has revolutionized our ideas about time and distance. One of the most important effects of air travel has been to bring all people closer together.

4. Waterways have always been a major means of moving heavy, bulky freight. The busiest waterways in the United States today are the Mississippi River system and the Great Lakes system.

5. The earliest means of communicating over great distances in the United States was by mail. For years, the Post Office Department was run directly by the federal government. Today it has been replaced by the United States Postal Service, run by an 11-member Board of Directors. The major reason for the change was to increase the efficiency of mail service. In the 19th and 20th centuries, scientific discoveries brought forms of communication that were much more rapid than mail. Instant communication is now a global reality. By telegraph, telephone, radio, and TV, the people of the United States and of the world are brought closer together.

Questions to Think About

1. In what ways has geography influenced the development of transportation systems in the United States?

2. What do you think is the single most important form of transportation in the United States today? Explain your answer.

3. What are the greatest benefits of the new Interstate Highway System? What, if any, are the disadvantages of the system?

4. Do you think passenger service by rail will increase or decrease in the future? Why?

5. What are the present limitations to carrying freight by air? For what products would air freight be most useful?

6. What are some of the advantages and disadvantages of transportation by water? For what products would water transportation be most useful?

7. In what ways does the United States Postal Service differ from the earlier Post Office Department?

8. What do you think are the most important services offered by radio and TV? What, if any, changes would you like to see in radio and TV broadcasting policies?

Citizenship Laboratory

Words and Relationships

Define each of the terms in the first column. Then show how each term is related to the item listed opposite it by using both items in a sentence or short paragraph.

1. Interstate Highway System — limited access
2. feeder roads — economic needs
3. standard time zones — rapid travel
4. passenger trains — automobiles
5. containerization — loading time
6. super jets — cargo space
7. intracoastal — waterways
8. Merchant Marine — world trade
9. United States Postal Service — new methods
10. satellites — TV

Building a Future

How adequate is the transportation system in your community? Although the answer may be complicated, the question is worth exploration. A large part of the future of any modern community depends on the means it develops to transport people and goods.

Here are some aspects of local transportation that might be studied.

- What is the layout of roads? Are there plans for new roads? Are there any plans for limiting traffic in any areas?
- What kind of services do buses and trains offer? Are there any plans for improving local mass transport?
- How adequate and how costly is local taxi service?
- Do railroads provide adequate freight service to and from your community?
- If your community has an airport, how adequate is the transportation between the airport and the downtown area? What plans are being made to expand airline service?
- What role, if any, does water transport play in your community's economy?

Bring to class any data that you can find on local transportation issues. Analyze the data in terms of present and future needs. What actions could people in the area take to improve community transportation?

16 The American Economy

We behave in political ways when we take part in the workings of government. We behave in social ways in our families and when we associate with others in groups. We behave in economic ways when we act to fulfill our material wants. Material wants include such things as food, clothing, and housing. They also include services—everything from the services of the filling station operator to the services of the Joint Chiefs of Staff who direct our country's defense.

The economic behavior of Americans has produced our strong American economy. Today our economic system provides for the material wants of people to a degree unmatched in history.

American economic ways have had a long history. They can be traced from the time of the earliest settlements. For much of our history, the production, distribution, and consumption of goods and services was carried on in a rural society. Our early economy was based heavily on agriculture. Today, by contrast, our American economic system is largely industrial. Our society is largely urban. And today, more than ever before, our economic system reaches out to all parts of the globe.

The Development of American Business

We use the word "business" to describe activities by which people produce goods and services and then sell them or buy them. Different kinds of societies carry on business activities in different ways. Here in the United States we have developed a business economy based on the idea of capitalism. Capitalism is an economic system in which private owners and free workers come together to produce goods and services.

BUSINESS ENTERPRISE IN EARLY AMERICA

Early American settlements such as those at Jamestown and Massachusetts Bay were started by English companies. In one sense, then, the settlements were business ventures. From them, the owners of the English companies hoped to make profits.

The New World contained many resources that were wanted in Europe. American lumber, furs, hides, fish, and tobacco all had large markets in Europe. These resources could be traded in Europe for finished products—clothing, metal goods, and so on.

American overseas trade grew quickly. It soon came to involve trade with western and southern Europe, the West Indies, and parts of Asia and Africa. The expansion of overseas trade was, in part, the result of the growth of business within the American colonies themselves. It is true that most of the colonists were small farmers. They produced little more than what was needed for their own families. There were, however, some people who saw farming as a business. They grew crops such as tobacco, rice, and indigo and sold their crops in world markets. At the same time small businesses were being started in the growing towns and cities. Merchants opened stores to serve the needs of townspeople and neighboring farmers. Blacksmiths, furniture makers, millers, and shoemakers found a growing need for their services.

The business economy that developed in America was built along capitalistic lines. It was based on the assumption that both owners and workers were free. A major exception was found on many plantations in the South. There the work was often done by slaves.

A number of laws passed by the English government in the 18th century interfered with the freedom of the colonists to do business. These laws produced much of the agitation that helped bring on the American Revolution.

FROM LOCAL TO NATIONAL BUSINESS

Through the colonial years and during the early years of the new nation, transportation was so poor that most businesses remained small and local. Only on the ocean highways could business be carried on extensively. With the coming of the steamboat, the digging of canals, and the building of railroads, businesses were able to expand within the nation. Farmers in the South and West were able to ship their crops to the East. In return, they received manufactured goods from eastern factories. Minerals, such as coal, oil, and iron ore, were brought together so that giant industries could develop. In these ways, American business, during the last half of the 19th century, became less local and more national in scope.

With the expansion of business came the distribution of finished products on a nationwide basis. The results can be seen today. No matter where we live in the United States, we own the same brands of TV sets. We eat food bearing the same trade names. We find the same labels on our clothing.

BUSINESS ON A GLOBAL BASIS

More than simply national in scope, American business today reaches out to all parts of the world. This is, of course, not a completely new situation. As we have noted, overseas trade was carried on even in colonial times. Modern means of transportation and communication, however, make today's international trade and business broader and more complex.

To manufacture many of today's products, raw materials must be brought together from all parts of the globe. The manufacture of an American automobile offers a useful illustration. To make an automobile some 300 products are brought together from more than 50 countries. The steel body takes manganese from India, nickel from Canada, and chromite from South Africa. The battery and radiator take lead and zinc from Mexico. Tin from Bolivia is

In the 18th and 19th centuries, American ships traded in ports around the world, but the voyages were time-consuming. A mid-19th century trip from Boston to San Francisco took over three months by ship.

Many trade names are known throughout the world. What other American, British, and Japanese trade names have achieved worldwide recognition?

needed for bearings. Copper from Chile is needed for electrical wires. Asbestos for brake linings and aluminum for engine pistons come from Canada. Rubber for tires comes from Malaysia. Finally wool from Australia and burlap from Pakistan are needed for the upholstery. These are but a few examples.

American businesses also build factories in other countries. They do this to be closer to raw materials and markets or because labor costs are generally cheaper in other countries. But even if goods are produced in the United States, they have a way of ending up in all parts of the world. By the same token, the products of foreign businesses have a way of ending up in American markets. The world of business is becoming more and more internationalized. American business invests in natural resources, builds factories, and sells products in every part of the world. Businesses in a number of other countries do the same.

Different countries conduct business in different ways. In the United States businesses operate in a climate of freedom. In many countries, by contrast, businesses operate as an arm of the state. All business decisions are made by the government. One of the responsibilities of American business, and of business in other capitalistic countries, is to show that capitalism works better than other systems.

Getting the Facts

1. What are some of the factors that help explain why 19th century American business activities became less local and more national in scope?

2. In what ways are many modern American businesses dependent upon international trade and business?

Forming an Opinion

■ Today many Americans are looking for ways to become less dependent upon oil produced in the countries of the Middle East. Why do you suppose this seems desirable to so many? What are other possible disadvantages of heavy reliance on international trade? What, on the other hand, are the advantages of conducting business on a global basis?

The American Economic System

All economic systems, including our own, must deal with questions of scarcity. Scarcity is an economic term used to describe the fact that the things we want do not come free or in unlimited amounts. Today, in most parts of the country, even water is sold in limited amounts. A basic lesson of economics, to quote one school of economists, is that we "cannot have our cake and eat it, too. The central problem is *economizing*—making the best use of the scarce productive resources available to us to satisfy our many wants. . . . Resources to satisfy our wants are limited in amount and, therefore, are not free for the asking."

Scarcity is a part of our lives today. It has always existed. And, there is every reason to believe that there will be a scarcity of goods and services in the future. Generally speaking, we tend to want more goods and services than our economy can produce. For this reason, we must try to develop those productive facilities that will most nearly meet our wants and needs.

THE NATURE OF AMERICAN CAPITALISM

A capitalistic system has certain basic features.

- Businesses are owned and operated by private individuals.
- Businesses are run to make profits.
- Credit is used to expand businesses or replace equipment.
- Labor is performed by people who work for wages and salaries.

Strongly influencing each of these features of capitalism in the United States are the ideals of American liberty. Free owners and a free labor force work together in what is often called a system of free enterprise.

Any realistic view of capitalism in the United States must take into account the role of government. It is a role that has grown greatly in recent times. Today few businesses are completely free in their operations. To some degree their activities are regulated by the government. Moreover, many of the goods and services we enjoy today are provided directly by the government.

America has a mixed economic system. It is a system in which Americans as owners of private businesses and Americans working through government seek to satisfy the economic desires of the nation.

THE FORCE OF COMPETITION

In the United States, businesses are free to compete with one another in their efforts to supply our wants and needs. The force of competition leads businesses to find ways of operating more efficiently and effectively. It can also be a means of keeping the price of products from rising too high. So important is competition to the American economic system that the government often acts to promote it.

KINDS OF ECONOMIC ACTIVITIES

Four general kinds of economic activities must be carried out to satisfy our modern needs. These activities are (1) basic production, (2) manufacturing, (3) distribution, and (4) service.

Basic production involves supplying raw materials. Among the most important of these are minerals, lumber, and food. They may be used as they are. Or they may be used to make manufactured goods.

Manufacturing involves changing basic materials into finished products. It is carried on in factories and plants, large and small. Millions of workers are needed to carry out this activity.

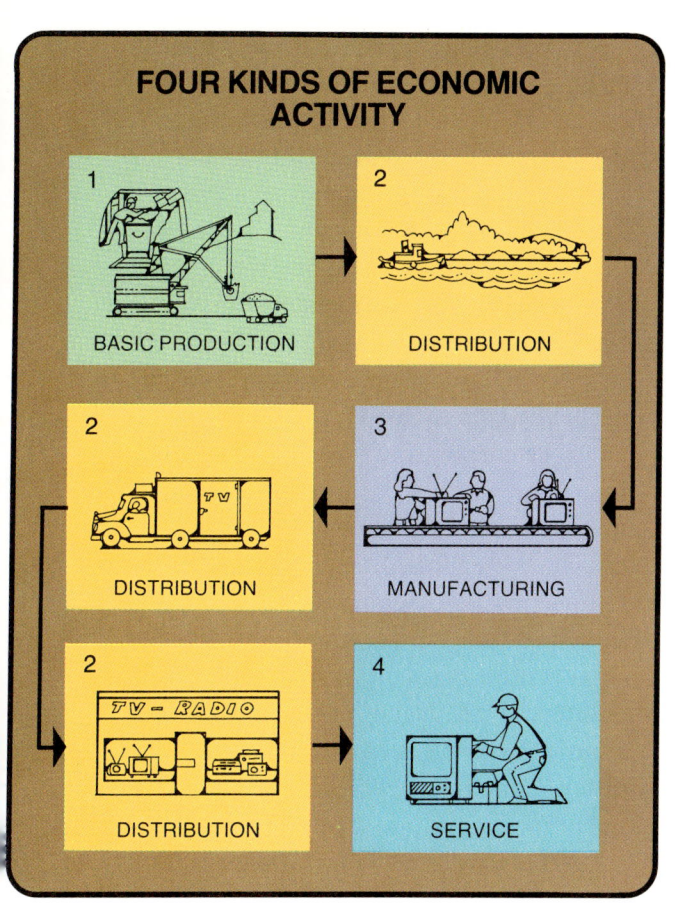

FOUR KINDS OF ECONOMIC ACTIVITY

1. BASIC PRODUCTION
2. DISTRIBUTION
2. DISTRIBUTION
3. MANUFACTURING
2. DISTRIBUTION
4. SERVICE

FACTORS IN THE ECONOMIC PROCESS

To produce the things we want four factors must be combined. These are (1) natural resources, (2) labor, (3) capital goods, and (4) management.

Natural resources are the raw materials of the economic process. They are the coal and iron needed to make steel. They include the fertile soil needed to grow food. They are any of a number of natural products of the land and sea.

Labor is the work that people bring to the process. It can involve anything from the work of highly skilled technicians to the tasks carried out by laborers who have no special skills.

Capital goods are the machines, tools, buildings, and the like, used in production. These goods are a form of

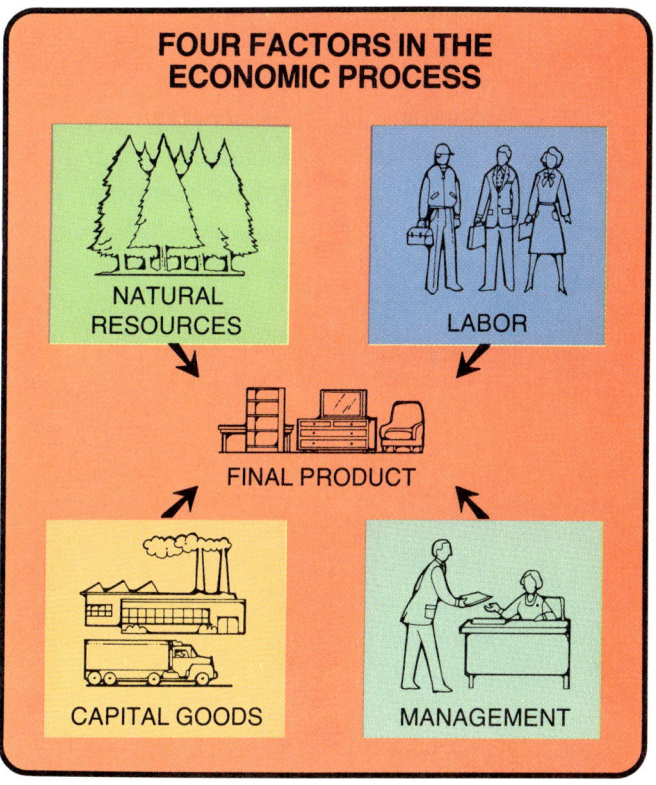

Distribution is the means by which products are made available to consumers. First, some means of distribution is needed to bring raw materials to factories. Then manufactured goods must be carried to warehouses and other storage places. From storage places, distribution agencies move goods to retail stores so that they can be distributed to consumers.

Service activities in America are carried out by many different kinds of specialists. There is need for people who can make mechanical repairs and perform personal services. There is also a need for people who can offer professional services such as those performed by teachers, doctors, and lawyers.

FOUR FACTORS IN THE ECONOMIC PROCESS

NATURAL RESOURCES
LABOR
FINAL PRODUCT
CAPITAL GOODS
MANAGEMENT

THE AMERICAN ECONOMY

accumulated wealth. It is this wealth that a business uses to make more wealth. Capital goods are used to make more of the things that people want.

Management provides a means of organizing the economic process. For production to be carried on efficiently, natural resources, labor, and capital goods must be combined so that they work well together. This calls for managerial skills. Important in even the smallest business, managerial skill becomes even more important as a business grows in size and complexity.

FORMS OF BUSINESS ORGANIZATION

Since our economy is based on the idea of capitalism, we find natural resources, labor, capital goods, and management working together in privately owned businesses. Most of these businesses follow one of four general forms of business organization. These are (1) single proprietorship, (2) partnership, (3) corporation, and (4) cooperative.

A single proprietorship is a single owner business. In these businesses, the owners make all decisions and act as managers. They finance the businesses with their own money and with whatever they are able to borrow. They receive all profits from the businesses. They are also responsible for all of the debts of the businesses. A single proprietorship has the advantage of being easy to set up and run. Its growth, however, is generally very limited. This is mainly because of the difficulty that one owner alone has in acquiring the money needed to greatly expand a business.

The partnership is a form of business with two or more partners. Each partner owns a share of the business, not always in equal parts. All of the partners must agree on the policies that their business will follow. Profits from the business are divided according to an agreement made by the partners when they joined forces. With some exceptions, each partner is responsible for all of the debts of the partnership. It is a form of business organization often used by people in such professions as law, medicine, and architecture.

The corporation is by far the most important form of business organization in America today. Almost all of our country's great manufacturers, transportation companies, communications facilities, and banks are corporations. As legal institutions, corporations receive charters or certificates of incorporation from state governments. The charters describe the nature of the business that the corporations may carry on.

The people who own a corporation are called stockholders. In exchange for money invested in the business, they receive shares of stock. Some owners buy common stock. Such stockholders have the right to vote in the affairs of the corporation. The income from common stock varies. Profits, in the form of dividends, depend upon how well the company is doing. Owners seeking a safer investment are likely to buy preferred stock. This kind of stock pays a fixed dividend each year. However, the preferred stockholder does not have the right to vote in corporation affairs.

Corporations often borrow money by selling bonds. Bondholders are paid interest. They also receive the full value of the bond when it is due. Bondholders, thus, are creditors—people to whom money is owed—rather than owners of a corporation.

Today many American corporations have thousands, or even hundreds of thousands, of stockholders. Since stock can generally be sold without difficulty, a corporation can continue to exist even when some of the owners die. When a corporation has debts to pay, each stockholder has only limited liability for the debts. This means that when debts arise, each stockholder is responsible for only a part of the debt. The size depends on the amount of stock the stockholder has.

The cooperative is a form of business in which a group of producers or consumers work together to benefit all members. Consumer cooperatives are generally set up to buy goods at cheaper prices in large amounts. They may also offer services to their members. Services may include such things as insurance, credit, or health care. Producers' cooperatives are groups of businesses that come together to market their products more efficiently. Members of cooperatives receive a fixed rate of interest on the stock they own.

FARMING AS A BUSINESS

One kind of business in which cooperatives are often useful is farming. Farming is a vital part of the American economy. Our daily need for food emphasizes its importance.

The use of modern technology varies from farm to farm but the general trend is toward large farms run by machines. What are the advantages and disadvantages of this long-range trend for society in general?

THE AMERICAN ECONOMY   **371**

The development of American agriculture is one of the great success stories of our technological age. It is the story of fewer and fewer highly efficient people using modern machinery to produce more and more goods. Through our history, the percentage of Americans living on farms has steadily declined. At the same time our population has steadily grown. This has been possible because those who remained on the farms continued to find better ways to feed a growing population.

As recently as 1950 one out of eight Americans lived on a farm. In 1970, only about one American in 20 lived on a farm. During this same 20-year period the average size of farms in America almost doubled.

These figures, however, do not tell the complete story of the great changes that have taken place in American farming. They do not show how much of our agricultural production is being carried on by a very small number of farmers. In 1969, for example, more than one third of all net farm income went to the owners of 211,000 farms. The remaining income, less than two thirds, went to the owners of about 2,800,000 farms.

Interestingly enough, the majority of the most highly productive American farms are run as family businesses. Such farms have always been the backbone of American agriculture.

In addition to the highly productive family farms there are a few large "factory" farms or "agribusinesses." Often set up as corporations, factory farms are run with the precision of an assembly line. Skillful managers are hired to direct the businesses. Typical of these factory farms are those involved in growing vegetables. These businesses may even include canning factories. With modern equipment, workers may harvest a crop of tomatoes or peas and immediately send the vegetables to other workers who will can them or freeze them.

Of course there are still a number of small farms in the United States that produce only small amounts of agricultural goods. These farms bring their owners little money. Often people living on these farms work at other jobs. The existence of these small farms, hardly businesses at all, inflates the number of farms in the United States. They serve to emphasize the fact that most of our country's agricultural needs are supplied by a small number of highly productive farm businesses.

Getting the Facts

1. Name at least three basic features of capitalism.

2. Manufacturing is one of four general kinds of economic activities carried out in America. What are the other three?

3. What are capital goods?

4. Name at least three of the four different forms of business organization found in the United States today.

5. What are some of the important changes that have taken place in American agriculture over the last 50 years?

Thinking About the Future

■ Which of the four general kinds of economic activities do you plan to become involved in after you finish school? If you plan to enter the private sector of the economy, what form of business organization would you prefer? Why?

Speaking Out

Alice Shabecoff

Shabecoff is the former director of the National Consumer League in Washington, D.C. Here she expresses her concern about the growing power of agribusiness in the United States. She believes that the uniform heavily fertilized products of agribusiness are less appetizing and less healthful than the products grown on smaller farms.

"In the produce bins of neighborhood supermarkets glisten mounds of waxy cucumbers, green tomatoes, plastic bags of radishes, ultra-orange oranges, perfectly formed apples and pears. These are the fruits and vegetables of the nation's food system. The United States Department of Agriculture [USDA] . . . and its agribusiness clients extol America's food system as the world's finest, most efficient, most productive.

"It must be conceded that the supermarket produce section is neat and tidy. . . . The food business has bred for symmetry, sprayed away blemishes, wrapped up shelf life and assured itself high profits. . . .

"The elaborate and not very appetizing or healthful processes that breed, fertilize, spray and extend the shelf life of produce for mass industrial profit are a consequence of the American way of life. The food system is this way because we live in big cities, surrounded by suburban sprawl instead of farmsteads, because our real estate prices and taxes have driven farmers out of business, because the corporate structure as it has evolved —with its tax breaks, its friends in government, its interlocking directorates with banks—eats up the small farmer, replacing agriculture with agribusiness. . . .

"For decades the thrust of USDA research and policy programs has been to aid agribusiness, while thousands of family farms which could raise healthier, fresher produce folded every year. Furthermore, all the agricultural committees in Congress have been almost exclusively filled with agribusiness voices.

"We are also part of the problem. Because somehow we buy strawberries in winter even though they taste like mashed paper, and thus reward and perpetuate the system."

---

1. What reasons does Shabecoff give for the growth of agribusiness? Do you think it would be possible to stop the growing power of agribusiness in the United States? Would it be desirable? Explain.

2. Would you be willing to have fresh fruits and vegetables only during harvest season—with canned products at other times of year? Why, or why not?

3. What role do you think the national government should play in American agriculture?

Government in the American Economy

As noted earlier, the United States has a "mixed economy." Ours is an economy in which both private people and government play important roles. People have always disagreed about just how important the role of government should be. However, people do agree that the role of government is more important now than in years past. Moreover, it is a role played not only by the national government but also by government at the state and local levels.

GOVERNMENT REGULATION OF BUSINESS

One important role that government plays in the American economy is that of regulator of business. The government fills this role in order to protect the interests of all Americans. As long ago as 1906, for example, Congress passed the Federal Food and Drugs Act. This law prohibited the use of harmful chemicals or drugs in medicine and food. A few years later, in 1914, Congress set up the Federal Trade Commission. Among the duties of this commission is the duty of prohibiting false advertising by businesses. In the years since 1914, Congress has set up agencies to regulate the sale of stocks and bonds, airline traffic, atomic energy, and a number of other economic activities.

The state and local governments also engage in business regulation. Banks are inspected by state banking commissions. Restaurants are inspected by local health officers. There are local building codes that set standards for

Some critics of the national Food and Drug Administration argue that it does not test new drugs thoroughly enough. Others argue that the agency delays American use of new medicines. To what extent do you think it necessary to have a government agency to test new medicines and food additives?

homes and other buildings. Various kinds of child labor laws exist in different states. They regulate age of employment, kinds of work, hours of work, and so on.

GOVERNMENT IN BUSINESS

More than just a regulator of business, government in the United States is itself in business. Government is an employer of workers. It is also a producer of goods and services.

The national government produces electricity. It does this at government-built projects such as the Tennessee

Valley Authority and the Hoover Dam on the Colorado River. The national government is also in the banking business. One example is the Small Business Administration which loans money to small businesses. Another is the Export-Import Bank which lends money to foreign countries. The government is in the insurance business. It offers an insurance service through the Federal Deposit Insurance Corporation. The FDIC insures bank accounts if banks fail. The national government also runs a park system and a number of veterans' hospitals.

At the state and local levels, governments run public schools, public colleges, and public universities. State and local parks are also run by these governments. Cities run bus lines and hospitals. Many other examples could be given.

GOVERNMENT AID TO BUSINESS

Still another part of the role of government in our American economy is found in aid government gives to business. It does this in at least two important ways. One is through taxes and government spending. Another is through regulation of our supply of money.

Government receives money from us in the form of taxes. It takes some of this money and pays it to Americans for work they are doing now or work they have done in the past. Payments are made to growers of certain farm products. Money spent for weapons goes, in part, to pay defense workers. Pensions are paid to veterans. Older people receive social security checks.

Government regulates our supply of money through the Federal Reserve System. This system was set up in 1914. You will find it described more fully on pages 378 and 379. The job of the Federal Reserve System is to try to control our country's money supply and, in this way, help business grow or keep business stable.

Getting the Facts

1. What are some of the ways that American businesses are regulated by the national government? by the state governments? by local governments?

2. Name at least four government services that resemble private businesses?

Examining the Issues

■ Between 1930 and 1933 thousands of American banks were forced to close. Millions of Americans lost their savings. As a result the national government set up the FDIC to protect the savings of depositors. Few Americans today would wish to see the end of this government service. Which of the other economic services offered by our governments do you consider equally essential? Why?

Money and Credit in the American Economy

American business activities are carried on with money. Businesses also make use of credit. Without money and credit businesses would have to return to the ancient practice of barter.

Barter allows people to trade one kind of goods for another. Using barter, people may trade their goods or services for goods or other services. Barter was often used in early America because money was scarce. Barter is still used occasionally today. But it would be impossible to carry on complex business operations by barter. For today's business activities we need money.

THE NATURE OF MONEY

Money, in one sense, means metal coins, paper bills, and bank checks. In more general terms, it can mean anything that is widely used and accepted as payment for goods, services, and debts.

People, at different times and in different places, have used all sorts of things for money. Beads, shells, furs, stones, salt, gunpowder, and metals have all been used as money. Many of these things could be used not only as money but also for their own sake. Salt could be used for food. Furs could be used for clothing. This is not the case with our money system. The various kinds of paper we use as money—checks, stocks, bonds, and the like—are worth almost nothing as paper.

Our money system has been developed to suit the needs of our daily economic activities. Our money is easy to

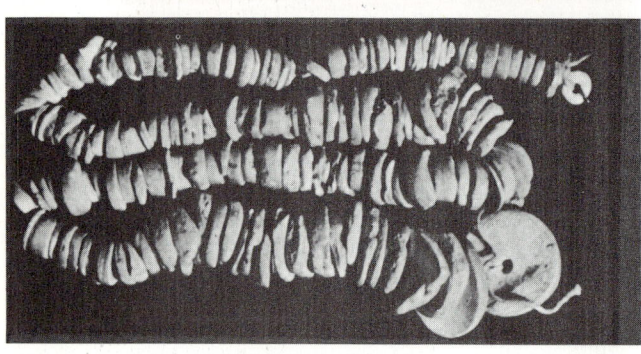

What are the advantages and disadvantages of using each of the four forms of money shown here?

carry. If paper bills wear out, they are easy to replace. The metal coins and paper bills are hard to imitate or counterfeit. And our government takes precautions to prevent counterfeiting. Our money system makes it easy to divide large sums into smaller parts. A $20 bill can be divided into tens, fives, and ones. Quarters can be divided into nickels and dimes. Most important of all, our American money system gives us a quick means of judging cost. In a general way, we know what a dollar is worth and what it will buy.

THE USES OF MONEY

Money, as a part of our economic system, has a number of uses. It isn't enough just to say that money is something we use to buy things. We use money in a number of ways. Among the most important of these uses are (1) as a measure of value, (2) as a medium of exchange, (3) as a means of storing up wealth, and (4) as a measure of amount owed.

Money often serves as a measure of value. We are forever concerned with the price of things. We want to know how much things cost in money. We say a ticket to a concert is $5. A pair of shoes is $30. We don't say that a pair of shoes costs six concert tickets.

This suggests a second use of money. Money can serve as a medium of exchange. You pay a merchant $30 for a pair of shoes. The merchant, in turn, may use some of this money for groceries. You needed shoes. The merchant needed groceries. But it wasn't necessary for the two of you to have what the other needed in order to complete your business transaction. Instead, it was money, serving as a medium of exchange, that made the transaction possible.

This same illustration can be used to explain another use of money. Suppose you wanted a new pair of shoes but did not have enough money to pay for them. You might decide that you did not need new shoes immediately. If so, you might begin to put some of your extra dollars aside so that you could buy the shoes later. Money, in this case, serves as a means of storing up wealth. It is common for both people and businesses to save money for future use. It can be a wise habit, particularly if the money is put to work as it is being saved. While we are storing up wealth, we can put our money to work by investing it or placing it in a bank. Banks make use of our savings by investing them in business or lending them to others.

Finally, a very important use of money is as a measure of amount owed. Here again, think about your need for a pair of shoes. The merchant may agree to let you pay part of the price now and the remainder later. Or you may ask the merchant to charge the entire amount with the understanding that you will pay it all at a later date.

A CREDIT ECONOMY

We often use money as a measure of amount owed in our credit economy. Credit is an important part of our economic life, both for us as individuals and for businesses.

One of the most valued possessions of most Americans is a credit card. Credit cards are used in countless ways, for every manner of business. Certain kinds of cards are useful not just within a community but across the country and around the world. For these reasons, travelers often carry credit cards instead of currency and checks.

Most American businesses are carried on through credit. A corporation may sell bonds that will be repaid with interest at a specific future date. A family may buy a home by obtaining credit in the form of a mortgage. The mortgage will then be paid off monthly over a number of years.

The use of credit is based largely on the creditor's—the lender's—faith in the debtor's ability and willingness to repay the loan and interest charges.

Like individuals and businesses, our governments also depend greatly on credit. Much of the governments' credit is raised through the sale of government bonds. A local board of education may sell bonds to raise money to build a new school. A state government may sell bonds to build new highways. The national government, particularly in times of war, may sell billions of dollars worth of bonds. Government bonds may be bought by private people. Most bonds, however, are bought by financial institutions such as banks and insurance companies.

BANKS AS BUSINESS ENTERPRISES

Banks are an essential part of our American economy. As businesses, banks are set up to provide a place where money can be deposited and exchanged with ease. They are also places where people and businesses can obtain credit.

Banks may be characterized in two different ways. First they may be characterized by the source of their charters.

There are "national banks," which are chartered and supervised by the national government. And there are "state banks," which are chartered and supervised by state governments. Banks may also be characterized by the kind of business they carry on. Most of our banks, whether national or state, fall into one of three categories: (1) commercial banks, (2) savings and loan associations, and (3) trust companies.

Commercial banks are general purpose banks. They are the kind of banks that most of us are likely to know best. Here we can deposit money and write checks on our accounts. Here we can also open savings accounts and receive interest. The activity that keeps the commercial banks in business, however, is making loans. It is the interest from its loans that gives the banks their profits.

Savings and loan associations generally perform fewer banking functions than commercial banks. They are what their name indicates. People can open savings accounts in these banks. People and businesses can also take out loans at these banks.

Trust companies are more specialized banks. They are set up to care for the money and other property of people who desire this kind of service. Most trust companies also offer checking and savings accounts, and make loans. Since most commercial banks have trust departments that perform the same jobs as the trust companies, these two kinds of banks are in many ways similar.

THE FEDERAL RESERVE SYSTEM

Banking activities in the United States are influenced, in important ways, by an agency of the federal government. This

How would you go about choosing a bank from which to obtain a loan?

agency, the Federal Reserve System, was established by an act of Congress in 1913. Its stated purpose is "to maintain sound banking conditions and an adequate supply of credit at reasonable cost for use in commerce, industry, and agriculture." All national banks in the United States are required to be members of the system. Some state banks are also members, although they are not required to join.

The United States is divided into 12 Federal Reserve Districts. There is a Federal Reserve Bank in each district. The district bank is run as a business corporation. All of its stock is owned by banks in the district. The Federal Reserve Banks have no financial dealings with private people or with businesses. They serve merely to provide money and credit to the member banks in the district. These 12 Federal Reserve Banks are, in other words, bankers' banks.

General supervision of the 12 Federal Reserve Banks is in the hands of a Board of Governors. A body of seven members, the board has offices in Washington, D.C. By lending money to member banks at stated rates of interest, the Federal Reserve System is able to exercise some control over the American money system. It also exercises some control by buying and selling bonds on the open market.

The Federal Reserve System is also in charge of issuing paper money. These "Federal Reserve Notes" make up most of the paper money that circulates in the United States. The money is issued by order of the Board of Governors. It is backed by the resources of the Federal Reserve Banks.

Getting the Facts

1. What are some of the different items used as money in our society?

2. Name at least three general ways in which money can be used.

3. In what ways do businesses and governments use credit?

4. Describe the three different kinds of banks found in the United States.

5. What are some of the duties and powers of the Federal Reserve System?

Examining the Issues

■ For many years, Americans have been living through a period of inflation. Wages and prices have risen from year to year. What groups in society are likely to be hurt most by inflation? From time to time the national government has set up wage and price control boards in an attempt to limit inflation. Are you in favor of this kind of control? Why, or why not?

THE AMERICAN ECONOMY

Poverty and Public Welfare in America

One of the goals of our American economy is to produce better lives for all Americans. To do this, the economy must serve alike the rich and the poor, the young and the old. In many ways, the goal is difficult to achieve. Some Americans find it hard to get even the basic necessities of life. Older people may have too little money to live decently. To help people in need is a responsibility accepted by our government. There is always disagreement about the kind and amount of help the government should provide. There is, however, broad acceptance of the need to help. Most of us agree that people or families who do not have the food, clothing, and shelter necessary to live must be helped by government. This belief in helping those who are poverty stricken is shared by people throughout the world.

Government aid to the poor is one aspect of something we generally call public welfare. Here in the United States public welfare includes a number of different government activities. It includes government support of public schools. It includes all of our social security programs and aid to such groups as war veterans, farmers, and workers. The aim of public welfare, in short, is to help people avoid the hazards of daily living. The most important welfare agency in our national government is the Department of Health, Education, and Welfare. The head of HEW is a member of the President's Cabinet. There are also welfare agencies in each of the state governments. At the local level, welfare is an important responsibility of city and county governments.

A HERITAGE OF PUBLIC WELFARE

Our ideas about government responsibility for the care of the needy can be traced to the English poor laws of the late 16th century. Laws similar to the English poor laws could be found in most towns in colonial America. They still form the basis for the approach to relief found in our states and local communities today. According to the laws in England and the American colonies each family was to take care of its own members. When needy people could not get help from their own families, they were expected to turn to friends or private charities. When all else failed, the local government was expected to give aid.

Major responsibility for public welfare remained in the hands of local governments until after the middle of the 19th century. In the 1870s many states began to care for poor people, orphans, and the mentally incompetent. Efforts to get the national government involved in public welfare during these years were strongly opposed. It was not until the Great Depression of the 1930s that the national government became deeply involved in public welfare.

THE NATIONAL GOVERNMENT BECOMES INVOLVED

The United States entered the dark days of the Great Depression in 1929. With so many people out of work, local governments found it impossible to handle the problem. At first, the state governments tried to help. But, by 1933, many

In the early days of the Great Depression, a number of private charities set up bread lines in an attempt to meet the needs of the millions of Americans out of work.

states had also run out of ways to care for the unemployed. It remained for the national government to come to the aid of millions of Americans who were unable to support themselves.

In 1935 the national government began the largest welfare program in our country's history. At that time, Congress gave the President permission to spend about $5,000,000 for emergency relief to needy Americans. That same year, Congress passed the Social Security Act. This law became a permanent part of our country's welfare program. It provided social insurance and financial aid for many people who had never before been helped by government or by private welfare programs. Among those helped were retired people, the unemployed, and mothers with dependent children.

Despite the public welfare efforts that began in the 1930s, large numbers of Americans still live in poverty. In the mid-1960s there were some 30,000,000 Americans living in poverty. To deal with this problem the national government launched what was called a "war on poverty." One result was the Economic Opportunity Act of 1964. The act set up an Office of Economic Opportunity as a part of the national government. The OEO was given the job of running a number of poverty programs. One was the Job Corps. It was set up to provide training and work experience for unemployed young people and job training for older people who were unemployed. The Community Action Program was also set up under the OEO. It was given the job of helping to stimulate local projects. The OEO was also given the power to make loans to poor farmers and farm workers.

The growing importance of the national government in matters of public welfare has been supported by the United States Supreme Court. In 1969, the Court held unconstitutional a Connecticut law that required people who wanted public assistance to live in Connecticut one year before receiving state aid. The practical result of this ruling was to lessen state power over public welfare while increasing the role of the national government.

THE AMERICAN ECONOMY

Great poverty can still be found in the United States, in rural and urban areas, in all parts of the country. What are some of the many different causes of poverty in America?

PUBLIC WELFARE IN A FEDERAL SYSTEM

Today the national government has taken over a great deal of responsibility for public welfare. However, state and local governments still run many parts of the system. This sharing of duties is a basic part of our federal system of government.

One program controlled completely by the national government is a result of the Social Security Act of 1935. The Old Age, Survivors, Disability and Health Insurance program now gives aid to over 30,000,000 Americans each year. Another program run by the government in Washington provides benefits for war veterans. Over 5,000,000 veterans were aided by this government program in 1976.

The national government has general responsibility for another important program—the Supplemental Security Income program. However, the national government runs this program in cooperation with the states. Two groups benefit from the program. One group is made up of people who do not receive social security. The other is made up of people who receive social security but not enough to buy the bare necessities. Almost 4,500,000 people received aid under this program in 1976.

A program called Aid to Families with Dependent Children is run by both the national and state governments. The national government provides most of the money. But the program is run by the state and local governments. There are wide differences in the amounts of

382 ECONOMIC LIFE IN MODERN AMERICA

money various states contribute to the AFDC program. The result is that benefits vary widely from state to state. More than 11,000,000 people received AFDC benefits in 1976. The average monthly payments ranged from $383.70 per family in the state paying the highest benefits to $48.96 in the state paying the lowest.

State and local governments are completely in control of services offered by General Assistance programs. These programs have been set up to offer additional aid that may be needed. They helped about 1,000,000 people in 1976. The average monthly payments ranged from a high of $144.00 to a low of $12.00.

These are but a few examples of the many welfare services found in the United States today. As noted earlier, public welfare includes different forms of insurance, health care, education, and care for the poverty stricken. It is a very necessary part of life in a modern industrialized country such as ours.

Getting the Facts

1. How was public welfare handled in 18th and 19th century America?

2. When and why did the national government first become deeply involved in public welfare?

3. Describe at least two of the welfare programs run mainly by the national government.

Forming an Opinion

■ In what ways can well run programs of public welfare be of value to society as a whole? Which of the programs you have just read about do you think offer the greatest benefits to the entire society? Which, if any, do you think offer little of value to most Americans? Explain.

What is this cartoonist saying about American attitudes toward welfare? How valid do you think the statement is?

"I ALWAYS HATED THOSE... ON WELFARE... NOW I AM ONE!"

Inquiry

What Are the Goals of the American Economy?

We Americans have organized an unparalleled business economy. We know, however, that because of scarcity, business cannot fill all our desires. We have to make choices. To make choices we must first determine our goals. We need to decide in what directions we think our economy should move.

Through the years the American economy has been guided by certain goals. The following list includes a number of goals that have long had strong public support.

- Economic growth—continued increase in the production of goods and services. These increases are expected to bring continued improvements in our living standards.
- Economic stability—no great rises in prices and no great declines in business production. Stability is sought because wild fluctuations bring hardships to many people.
- Economic security—measures that will allow people and businesses to face an uncertain future with confidence.
- Wise use of resources—efficient ways of using our natural resources, our factories and machines, and the skills of American workers.
- Economic freedom—a system in which business is free to operate, workers are free to choose their own jobs, and consumers are free to spend their incomes as they please.
- Economic justice—control of economic activity in the interest of the general welfare. This may involve regulation of businesses by government. It may also involve government action to improve economic conditions for all Americans.

While seeking these economic goals, American businesses have shown a growing concern for our country's social problems. A recent report of the Committee for Economic Development describes the ways in which the economic views of American businesses have changed over the years.

"Business functions by public consent, and its basic purpose is to serve constructively the needs of society—to the satisfaction of society.

"Historically, business has discharged this obligation mainly by supplying the needs and wants of people for goods and services, by providing jobs and purchasing power, and by producing most of the wealth of the nation. This has been what American society required of business, and business on the whole has done its job remarkably well. . . .

"In generating . . . economic growth, American business has provided increasing employment, rising wages and salaries, employee benefit plans, and expanding career opportunities for a labor force . . .

"Most important, the rising standard of living of the average American family has enabled more and more citizens to develop their lives as they wish with less and less constraint imposed on them by economic need. Thus, most Americans have been able to afford better health, food, clothing, shelter, and education than the citizens of any other nation have ever achieved on such a large scale. . . .

"Notwithstanding these accomplishments, the expectations of American society have now begun to rise at a faster pace than the nation's economic and social performance. Concentrated attention is being focused on the ill-being sectors of the population and on ways to bring them up to the general well-being

Although many 19th century factory owners concentrated mainly on making profits, a few showed great concern for the welfare of their workers. A number of the early New England cotton mills were designed to provide bright, cheerful places for the young spinners.

of most of the citizenry. Fundamental changes are also taking place in attitudes, with greater emphasis being put on human values—on individual worth and the qualitative aspects of life and community affairs.

"Society has also become acutely conscious of environmental problems such as air and water pollution produced by rapid economic development and population pressures. And the public has become increasingly concerned about the malfunctioning of important community services such as those provided by the post office, mass transportation, and some utility systems; about inadequacies in education and health care; and about mounting social problems such as poverty, crime and drugs.

"There is now a pervasive feeling in the country that the social order somehow has gotten out of balance, and that greater affluence amid a deteriorating environment and community life does not make much sense.

"The discontinuity between what we have accomplished as producers and consumers and what we want in the way of a good society has engendered strong social pressures to close up the gap—to improve the way the over-all American system is working so that a better quality of life can be achieved for the entire citizenry within a well-functioning community. The goals include:

- elimination of poverty and provision of good health care.
- equal opportunity for each person to realize his or her full potential regardless of race, sex, or creed.
- education and training for a fully productive and rewarding participation in modern society.

Inquiry

- ample jobs and career opportunities in all parts of society.
- livable communities with decent housing, safe streets, a clean and pleasant environment, efficient transportation, good cultural and educational opportunities, and a prevailing mood of civility among people."

In many ways, businesses are now trying to balance economic and social goals. Such a balance, however, is not always easy to achieve. In the following statement, David Eastburn, President of the Federal Reserve Bank of Philadelphia, offers his views on why it is so hard to reach our economic and social goals at the same time. Dividing people into two kinds, Eastburn sees what he calls "Economic Man" as a superb producer and "Social Man" as a person concerned more with happiness than with growth.

"There are two kinds of people in the world today; those who are primarily concerned with making a living and those who are primarily concerned with living with their fellows. The first might be called Economic Man; the second, Social Man.

"One of our main problems these days is that Social Man and Economic Man see the same things differently.

How do you think Eastburn's "Economic Man" would describe this economic activity? What problems might Eastburn's "Social Man" associate with the same activity?

"Social Man urged his Congressman to oppose the supersonic transport because it would make too much noise and might induce skin cancer; Economic Man, if he opposed the SST at all, did so because it would not get off the ground financially.

"Social Man sees the moon shots as an extravagant use of resources at a time when much of the world is starving; Economic Man sees them as spinning off many scientific by-products that someday can improve everyone's standard of living.

"Social Man faithfully lugs his used 'coke' bottles to the neighborhood collection center every Saturday morning for recycling; Economic Man is inclined to feel that if empty bottles were worth anything, somebody would pay for them.

"My point is not that Social Man is soft-hearted and headed, or that Economic Man is a Scrooge but that both have much to learn from each other....

"Economic Man has developed a most sophisticated recipe for growth, and for the past century or so has been proudly serving up his product for us all to consume. The recipe relies heavily on the ingredients of science and technology.

"Scientists must be free to indulge their limitless curiosity about how nature works. Technologists must be free to apply the fruits of science to the satisfaction of human wants. People must want things and be willing to work to get them. Producers must be free to turn out these things with an ever-increasing input of human effort—that is, with ever-increasing productivity.

"Economic Man must say that he attaches no moral connotations to the result. It is neither 'good' nor 'bad'; is simply what people want, and if people want to risk cancer by smoking cigarettes, that is their decision; the system is neutral.

"Actually, Economic Man is seldom content with that position. He really believes that the freedom which the system requires is 'good' and that the system has tremendously improved the physical well-being of mankind, and *that* is 'good.'...

"But Social Man is not so coy about attaching values to economic growth, and, in his eyes, they are not all 'good' ones.

"For most of the past century, he has been striving to round off the rough corners of economic growth. His gadfly efforts have contributed child-labor laws, pure food and drugs, the progressive income tax, Social Security, and countless other reforms.

"Still he is not content. Indeed, he feels he is losing ground....

"When Economic Man first applied technology to the satisfaction of human wants, he was rebelling against the blind laws of nature. Social Man wants to take the process one step further: He is rebelling against the blind forces of growth."

Determining Your Goals

You have just examined a list of traditional American economic goals. You have also read two statements by representatives of the business community. With these in mind, think about the following questions.

Which of the traditional economic goals seem to be contrary to the social goals identified by the Committee for Economic Development? To what extent does it seem likely that we will be able to meet both the economic and the social goals?

According to Eastburn's definition, would you regard yourself as an "economic" person or a "social" person? Explain.

In preparing your own list of economic goals, which items would you place near the top? Why?

Citizenship Laboratory

Review of Basic Ideas

1. Over the past two centuries, American business activities have grown from small local units to huge corporations engaged in business and trade around the world.

2. Our economic system is based on the idea of capitalism. In a capitalistic system, businesses are privately owned, they are run for profits, they depend upon the use of credit, and they are staffed by people who work for wages. The four general kinds of economic activities carried on in America are basic production, manufacturing, distribution, and service. The four factors that must be successfully combined in the American economy are natural resources, labor, capital goods, and management. Most American businesses are set up in one of four ways: single proprietorships, partnerships, corporations, or cooperatives. Modern American farming is a good example of the way technology can be used to increase production.

3. America has a "mixed economy." Both private people and government play important roles in the economy. Governments at all levels work to regulate business activities in the interest of all Americans. Governments also engage in some forms of business activities and offer a number of services to private businesses.

4. Money and credit are an essential part of our economy. Money is used as a measure of value, a medium of exchange, a means of storing up wealth, and a measure of amount owed. Commercial banks, savings and loan associations, and trust companies all offer financial services to people and businesses. The Federal Reserve System, an agency of the national government, regulates banking activities and helps control the nation's money supply.

5. Beginning with the Social Security Act of 1935, public welfare has become increasingly a concern of the national government. Today governments at all levels run a number of programs set up to improve the economic condition of all Americans.

Questions to Think About

1. In what ways have developments in modern industry increased the interdependence of the countries of the world?

2. What are some of the benefits of competition in business activities? What, if any, are the disadvantages?

3. What kinds of businesses might be usefully organized as single proprietorships? What kinds of businesses might best be run as partnerships? Explain.

4. Who are the owners of corporations? Why do corporations sell bonds?

5. In America, capitalism operates as an important part of a "mixed economy." Would you favor more or less government involvement in the economy? Explain.

6. What are some examples of the wide use of credit in our economy? What are some of the advantages and disadvantages of this wide use of credit?

7. Which of the public welfare programs do you think could be best run by

state and local governments? Which do you think could be best run by the national government?

Words and Relationships

Define each of the terms in the first column. Then show how each term is related to the item listed opposite it by using both items in a sentence or short paragraph.

1.	capitalism	freedom
2.	scarcity	goods and services
3.	capital goods	wealth
4.	corporation	stockholders
5.	"agribusiness"	modern technology
6.	"mixed economy"	government regulation
7.	credit economy	government bonds
8.	Federal Reserve System	money supply
9.	commercial banks	loans
10.	public welfare	aid to education

Building a Future

The capitalistic system in America is part of a "mixed economy." We have an economic system in which individuals and government share responsibilities. Our economy seeks to combine private businesses and government action in the interest of the common good.

For a better understanding of the idea of a mixed economy, interview some of the people who run businesses in your community. Ask questions such as these: In what ways does government regulate your business? Are there government businesses competing with your business? How is your business served by government?

A similar kind of study can be carried on with government agencies that have some kind of responsibility for business regulation. Ask government officials about the reasons for the regulation they provide. There may be government agencies in your community that are actively engaged in business activities of their own. What kinds of businesses are these? What purposes do they serve?

After you have made a report of your findings, lead a class discussion of the American economy. To what extent does our economy appear to be private in nature? How strong is government regulation? Is the direction today more toward private or public control of the economy? Which should it be? In other words, would the American economy be better off if it were more nearly private in nature or if it had more public intervention?

Citizenship Laboratory

THE AMERICAN ECONOMY

17 Americans as Workers and Consumers

The 25 years that followed World War II brought a number of important changes in America. For one thing, the nation's population grew some 46 percent. This was rapid growth indeed. The effect of the growth in the United States, however, was not the same as it had been in many other countries. The general tendency had been for rapid gains in population to outdistance increases in production. In many countries growth in population had brought a lowering of the standard of living. Not so in America. Between 1946 and 1970 the output of goods and services rose 138 percent. This was three times as much as the rise in population.

The period was also marked by a large increase in the number of people holding jobs—from just over 55,000,000 to almost 80,000,000. Along with this increase came a shift in the sharing of income. In 1946, Americans who worked for wages and salaries received about 65 percent of the country's income. Twenty-five years later, the share going to this group was more than 75 percent.

It was evident from the shifts in income that more money was being placed in the pockets of a greater number of people. For example, the buying power of a factory worker rose 39 percent. Even more dramatic, the average family income, before taxes, grew by 77 percent.

Increases in the buying power of the average person stimulated the American economy. This was revealed in a number of different ways. Home ownership jumped from 20,000,000 families to about 40,000,000 families. At the close of World War II, fewer than 50 percent of the families in America owned an automobile. Twenty-five years later about 80 percent owned at least one car. Many families had two and three cars.

Added to the growth in production and buying power was the fact that Americans were gaining more and more leisure time. Time spent on vacations rose more than 175 percent.

Finally, for all their spending, Americans were also able to increase their savings. The total value of savings in the United States rose 700 percent.

A Machine Civilization

The growth of the American economy and the social advances of the American people in the years since World War II are a tribute to American workers and their machines. Not until the middle of the 19th century did our technology begin to produce great changes in our way of life. In 1850, for example, American workers worked an average of about 70 hours a week. A hundred years later the average work week was about 40 hours. Over this same period, while the number of workers grew about 900 percent, the country's output of goods and services grew more than 3,000 percent.

This rise in productivity came from a number of factors working together. Production depends a great deal on the amount and quality of the machines that are used. At also depends on the skill and effort of the workers. And, it needs good managers who can keep the process running smoothly.

MACHINES AND POWER

Through most of human history, the energy needed to do work has been supplied not by machines, but by the muscles of people and animals. It has been estimated that, in 1850, almost 95 percent of all work was done with "muscle power." About 80 percent of the work was done by animals. About 15 percent was done by people. "Machine power" was used for only about 5 percent of the work.

The new age of technology replaced muscle power with machines. These machines were powered by mineral fuels—coal, oil, and natural gas. So fast were the advances that, by 1900, machines were doing 38 percent of our work.

The use of machine power grew even faster as the 20th century progressed. Electric power brought an age of electricity. Automobiles took the place of horses and carriages. Atomic energy was harnessed, not only for use in war, but also for peacetime work. Automation and computers replaced many workers, while speeding up the rate of production.

So great was the change that by 1950 only about 6 percent of the energy used in the United States could be called muscle power. The major decrease was in animal power. It fell to less than 2

Computers have created jobs for some workers—programmers, analysts, technicians. At the same time, of course, computers have replaced even more workers. What kinds of human jobs are often done by computer today?

percent. The day of the horse pulling the wagon, or the mule behind the plow, was quickly becoming a thing of the past. People were still using muscle power, but at a much smaller rate.

HUMAN RESOURCES IN PRODUCTION

For all the advances in machine power, people are still an essential part of production in America. The productivity of our country, or of any country for that matter, is still closely related to the quality of its human resources.

A measure of the quality of a country's human resources can be found in the education and skills of the working population. It has been pointed out that one of the main reasons why the economies of Germany and Japan recovered so quickly after World War II was because of the education and skills of the workers in the two countries. A contrast can be seen in countries with less educated and less skilled workers. In these countries, economic development has generally been much slower.

The American labor force can be seen as a highly educated and skilled body of human resources. Such resources, unlike most natural resources, are wasted if they are not used. An unemployed worker means less production. When the number of unemployed reaches into the millions, the losses in goods and services affect us all. Equally important, human resources in America cost money whether or not people are at work. People must somehow be supported. Through public welfare, unemployment insurance, social security, and the like, all Americans are given food to eat, clothes to wear, and shelter over their heads. For these reasons, it makes sense to use our human resources as wisely as we are now seeking to use our natural resources.

Getting the Facts

1. What was the average American work week in 1850? in 1950?

2. About what percentage of work was done by machine in 1850? in 1950?

3. What are some of the factors that help account for the great rise in production of goods and services in the United States over the last century?

Examining the Issues

■ What kinds of machines do you use everyday? What other products that you use were made by machines? In what ways would your life be different without these machines?

Organized Workers in a Capitalistic Society

One means of caring for the interests of a large part of a country's human resources has been found in the organization of labor unions. Unions have been formed by workers in many different fields. Union members may be highly skilled airline pilots. Or they may be people who perform relatively simple tasks on assembly lines.

MASS PRODUCTION CHANGES THE ROLE OF THE WORKER

A good example of mass production is found in the automobile assembly plant. As the body of an automobile moves slowly along the assembly line the principle known as "division of labor" can be clearly seen. According to this principle, tasks are divided among a group of workers. Each worker is a specialist at a certain job. Each job is important, no matter how small or simple it may seem. Take out any step in the process and the automobile would not be complete.

Helping the workers on the assembly line is a great deal of laborsaving machinery. The worker who places the engine block on the moving automobile does not have to strain to lift this heavy item. Each engine body is carried to its proper place on the assembly line by an overhead truck and pulley. This makes it possible for a new car to roll off the assembly line every few minutes.

Compare the job of the automobile worker with that of the carriage maker of an earlier day. The carriage maker was engaged in handicraft work. With some simple tools and a few helpers, the carriage maker built each carriage by hand. Clearly, the number of carriages that could be made in this way was limited. Worker productivity was low. Imagine how few and how costly automobiles would be if such methods were used to build them.

There are a number of other important differences between carriage making and working on an automobile assembly line. The carriage makers either owned their own businesses or worked closely with the owners. Workers on the assembly line, by contrast, generally have little contact with the factory owners. Moreover, their jobs call for only one kind of skill rather than the many skills of the carriage maker. The job of the worker on the assembly line is likely to be one that another worker can learn in a short time. And finally, in an automobile factory, the worker is only one of thousands of workers in a business that has thousands of owners.

What are the greatest benefits of assembly line production? What do you consider the greatest disadvantages?

As we sum up the changes brought by mass production we can see certain reasons for the growth of labor unions. The hundreds of workers brought together in large factories had little personal contact with the owners. Because each worker contributed only a small part of the finished product, workers tended to lose both pride and control over their work. In addition, working conditions and wages in many of the early factories left much to be desired. The hours often ran from sun up to sun down. Few if any precautions were taken to protect workers from injury. Finally, workers could be fired for any reason. It is easy to understand why the workers in these factories might wish for change. Following the principle that "in union there is strength," many workers were attracted by the early labor unions.

EARLY LABOR UNIONS

There were a few small local labor organizations as early as the 1790s. More nearly like today's unions, however, were organizations of workers formed in the textile factories of New England and New York during the 1820s. By the 1860s enough progress had been made to bring about the formation of national unions. The best known was a union formed in 1869. It was called the "Noble Order of the Knights of Labor."

The Knights of Labor had few restrictions on membership. Its rolls were open to all kinds of workers in all kinds of industries. In fewer than 20 years, the Knights grew to a membership of more than 700,000. Its success in membership, however, was also a weakness. The Knights brought a large body of skilled and unskilled workers from many different trades into one loose union. It was thus necessary to deal with the owners of many different companies. During the 1890s the union lost many members along with much of its power.

As the Knights of Labor declined, another national body, the American Federation of Labor, was on the rise. Set up in 1886, the AFL began as a collection of 26 unions. In the federation, each of the member unions ran its own affairs. The parent body was able to strengthen the hand of its member unions in their dealings with management.

The AFL unions were mainly of the craft type. A craft union is one in which the members all work at the same trade—carpenters, bricklayers, and so on. Through the wise leadership of its founder and long-time president, Samuel Gompers, the AFL grew. Many other unions were added to its ranks.

CONFLICT BETWEEN OWNERS AND WORKERS

The AFL and other labor groups were not accepted quietly by the management of American business. Most owners and managers believed that, while American workers were free to sell their services or not as they chose, they should do so as individuals. Unions were regarded as dangerous threats to private property.

Businesses found a number of ways to oppose the unions. Owners sent each other lists of the names of union members. A worker whose name appeared on such a list generally found it very hard to find a job. In the course of being hired, a worker was often required to sign a special contract agreeing not to join a union. When workers tried to form unions, owners sometimes used "lockouts." They closed their factories and everyone was thrown out of work. When workers went on strike, owners often tried to keep their plants open by hiring what was called "scab" labor. "Scab" is a term for a non-union worker who is used as a strikebreaker.

One of the most powerful weapons of management during the early years of labor organization was the injunction. An injunction is a court order forbidding a person or a group of people to do something. Injunctions might forbid union organization. They were often used to forbid strikes. Given the economic beliefs of the time, injunctions were easy to get.

Unions soon found that their most effective means of protest was the strike. This simple act of quitting work is still one of the best means organized workers have found for expressing their freedom as workers.

When using the strike to press their demands, unions are likely to picket the factory or store against which the strike is being waged. Union members or representatives are stationed near the business carrying signs. Their purpose is to discourage others from entering the plant or from doing business while the strike is taking place.

Another weapon long used by unions is the boycott. This is a refusal to buy the products of a business. Union members generally try to persuade others to join them in their boycott.

As unions grew in strength, there was the tendency to insist upon union shops. In a union shop, every worker has to be a union member, or agree to become one, in order to be hired.

Another practice that became popular as unions grew stronger is called "featherbedding." Under a featherbed rule, a union can require an owner to hire and pay workers for certain jobs, whether the jobs are needed or not. This kind of rule can also be used to place a limit on the amount of work done in a day or to specify the kinds of tools a worker must use on a job.

MODERN UNION GROWTH

With weapons such as the injunction and the strike in the hands of owners and workers, the late 1870s, the 1880s, and the early 1890s brought bitter strikes and violence to American factories.

Strikes in the 19th century were often very violent. What are some of the factors that help explain why modern strikes are generally peaceful?

AMERICANS AS WORKERS AND CONSUMERS

Only rarely did the government become involved. The public feeling was that these were private matters, to be handled by owners and workers.

In the early years of the 20th century, there was a change in public attitude. Government began to take more of a hand in the settlement of labor disputes. The public grew more favorably disposed toward the unions. As a consequence, union membership began to grow. In time, laws were passed against a number of the weapons owners had used to stop the unions—the lists of union members, the contracted agreements not to join unions, and the injunctions against strikes.

The total membership in American unions, however, remained relatively small until the middle of the 1930s. One reason was that workers in large industries, such as steel, seemed to find it difficult to form strong unions.

A major change came in 1935, when Congress passed the Wagner Act. This law guaranteed that unions would be given the right to engage in collective bargaining. Owners were required to meet with union representatives and try to reach agreements about such things as wages and working conditions. The Wagner Act thus made it easier to form large and powerful industrial unions. An industrial union is one whose membership is made up of all the people working in a given industry.

To further the growth of industrial unions, a new labor group was formed in the mid-1930s. In 1938 the group officially became the Congress of Industrial Organizations. The CIO included not only many new industrial unions but also some older unions that had split off from the AFL. Later, in 1955, the two large national labor groups merged to form a single group called the American Federation of Labor–Congress of Industrial Organizations.

Since its merger, the AFL–CIO has been the major representative of American workers. In 1970 its ranks included 76 unions with memberships of 25,000 or more. A number of smaller unions were also members of the AFL–CIO.

There are, however, a number of large and powerful unions that do not belong to the AFL–CIO. Among these are the International Brotherhood of Teamsters, the United Automobile Workers, and the United Mine Workers.

Over the last few decades the labor movement has been very successful. Today about one fourth of all American workers belong to unions.

Getting the Facts

1. How is the principle of "division of labor" used in modern industry? In what ways has it affected workers?

2. What methods did factory owners use to try to stop union growth?

3. Name at least three methods used by unions to oppose management decisions.

4. What guarantee did the Wagner Act of 1935 offer union workers?

Forming an Opinion

■ The AFL–CIO is an organization of craft unions and industrial unions. What is the basic difference between the two kinds of unions? Which kind of union, if any, do you think you would prefer if you were (a) an electrician, (b) an assembly-line worker, (c) a clerk in an insurance company? Explain why in each case.

Changing Work in a Changing Society

A major change in American economic life took place in 1956. During that year, for the first time in the history of any country the number of white-collar workers in America grew larger than the number of blue-collar workers. White-collar workers are people who do professional, technical, clerical, or sales work. Blue-collar workers are people who provide labor in industries. Their work may involve manufacturing, mining, construction, or any of a number of other industrial jobs.

The change noted in 1956 was by no means a sudden occurrence. Rather, it was a long-term development brought about by changes in technology. Improvements in technology brought rising standards of living. They also hastened the process of urbanization. More people moved to cities. They had more money to spend. The result was a growth in spending on services. It is a trend that continues today.

For an illustration of these changes, look at the graph on this page. To make the picture more complete, the graph shows not only white- and blue-collar workers but also gray-collar workers and people working on farms. The term "gray-collar" is used for people who perform certain special services. These services include such things as repairing TVs or cars and installing plumbing or electricity. Note the steady fall in the percentage of farmers and farm workers. Note also the steady rise in the percentage of white-collar workers. By contrast, the percentages of blue-collar and gray-collar workers remained fairly constant

Reading the Graph: *In 1920 about 30% of all American workers worked on farms. About 25% of all workers had white-collar jobs. About what percentage of American workers worked on farms in 1975? About what percentage of American workers had white-collar jobs in 1975?*

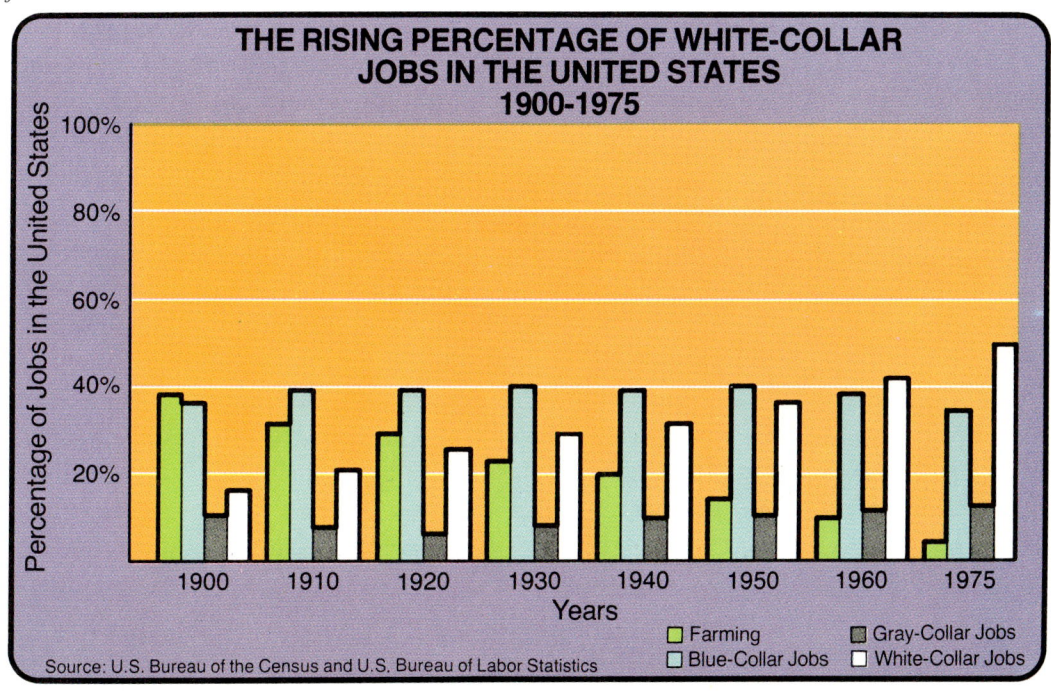

THE RISING PERCENTAGE OF WHITE-COLLAR JOBS IN THE UNITED STATES 1900-1975

Source: U.S. Bureau of the Census and U.S. Bureau of Labor Statistics

Legend: Farming, Blue-Collar Jobs, Gray-Collar Jobs, White-Collar Jobs

25 TOP GROWTH AREAS IN THE UNITED STATES JOB MARKET 1975-1985
(Average Yearly Job Openings Predicted by the U.S. Department of Labor)

OVER 100,000 JOBS A YEAR
- Stenographers and Secretaries
- Retail Salesworkers
- Elementary and High School Teachers
- Mechanics and Repairmen
- Bookkeepers

50,000 TO 100,000 JOBS A YEAR
- Registered Nurses
- Licensed Practical Nurses
- Bank Tellers and Clerks
- Truck Drivers
- Computer Operators
- Cooks and Chefs
- Cosmetologists
- Household Workers

20,000 TO 50,000 JOBS A YEAR
- Accountants
- Carpenters
- Wholesale Salesworkers
- Real Estate Salesworkers and Brokers
- Construction Laborers
- College Teachers
- Personnel Workers

15,000 TO 20,000 JOBS A YEAR
- Doctors
- Drafters
- Social Workers
- Lawyers
- Printers

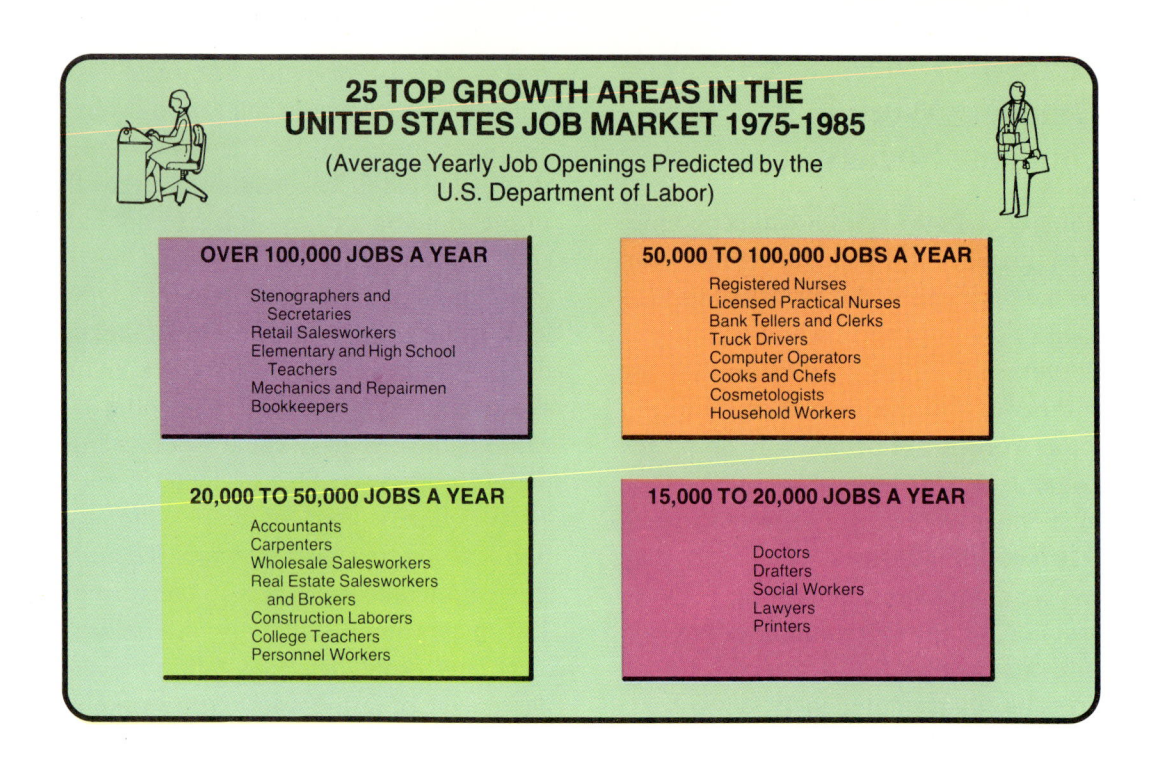

over the years. When we combine the white-collar and gray-collar workers and compare them with the combined blue-collar and farm workers, we get a general picture of a changing American work force. It is, in brief, a shift from the production of goods—raising crops, digging minerals, running assembly lines—to the production of services—giving medical care, providing education, repairing TVs, cleaning clothes.

GROWTH OF SERVICE JOBS

At the beginning of the 20th century seven of every 10 American workers were engaged in the production of goods. Only three workers in 10 were providing services. Those who study labor trends project that at some point in the 1980s the job situation will be just the reverse. Seven of every 10 workers will be providing services. Three in 10 will be producing goods.

We can expect different kinds of service jobs to grow at different rates. For some kinds of services, there may even be declines. In recent years, for example, we have seen a sharp decline in the number of railroad workers. By contrast, the number of workers in other kinds of transportation—trucks, buses, and airlines—has grown larger. Even so, transportation in general is not expected to offer as many job opportunities as certain other fields in the years ahead. It is also likely that the growth of jobs will be slow in fields where workers can be replaced by automation. This includes jobs in banking, retail sales, insurance, and public utilities.

A long-term growth in job opportunities seems very likely in one service area—in government. It is expected that some of this growth will be in the federal government. But the main increases are expected in state and local government jobs. State and local governments are faced with growing demands for more streets and highways. People want more health services and better police and fire protection. These are the kinds of services that require many workers. The one thing that may slow the growth in government job opportunities is lack of money. Recent years have brought major cutbacks in the number of public employees in New York City. However, the demands for state and city services are likely to continue.

There are also a number of likely growth areas in private business. There are mounting demands for health services and medical care. There are also demands for more recreational facilities, private educational opportunities, and a number of repair services.

MORE WOMEN JOIN THE LABOR FORCE

The growth in the number of service jobs has been partly responsible for another major change in American labor patterns. Recent years have seen a steady rise in the number of women working for salaries and wages.

One reason for this change is related to advances in technology. These advances led to a growth in the number of white-collar jobs. These are the kinds of jobs that have traditionally offered the greatest opportunities to women workers. At the beginning of the 1970s, for example, about half of the country's interior decorators were women. Almost two thirds of all medical and health technicians were women. Advances in technology also brought new labor-saving machines to American homes, greatly reducing the amount of time needed for household chores. Because these chores had generally, by tradition, been assigned to women, the technical advances made it possible for more women to seek jobs outside the home.

Of greater long-range importance is the fact that American views about the roles of women and men are changing. Women and men now feel more free to accept or reject traditional roles. Given this freedom, women are moving into all areas of the working world.

CHANGING EDUCATIONAL REQUIREMENTS

The shift to white-collar jobs and jobs in service fields has brought a demand for higher levels of education and skill. The greatest growth in the number of jobs is in professional and technical fields. Workers in these fields need a great deal of education and rather highly developed skills. In blue-collar fields, jobs calling for special skills have grown most quickly.

The graph on the next page shows how educational levels have changed. Note the sharp decreases in the percentages of people who finished only elementary school. Note also the growing percentages who finished high school and entered college. The 1985 percentages are projections by the United States Bureau of Labor Statistics. They serve to emphasize a trend.

The trend shows a general public awareness of the fact that jobs now call for more schooling. There is a growing acceptance of the belief that, as jobs become more technologically advanced, success in the job market calls for more education. Education is becoming more important even in semi-skilled and

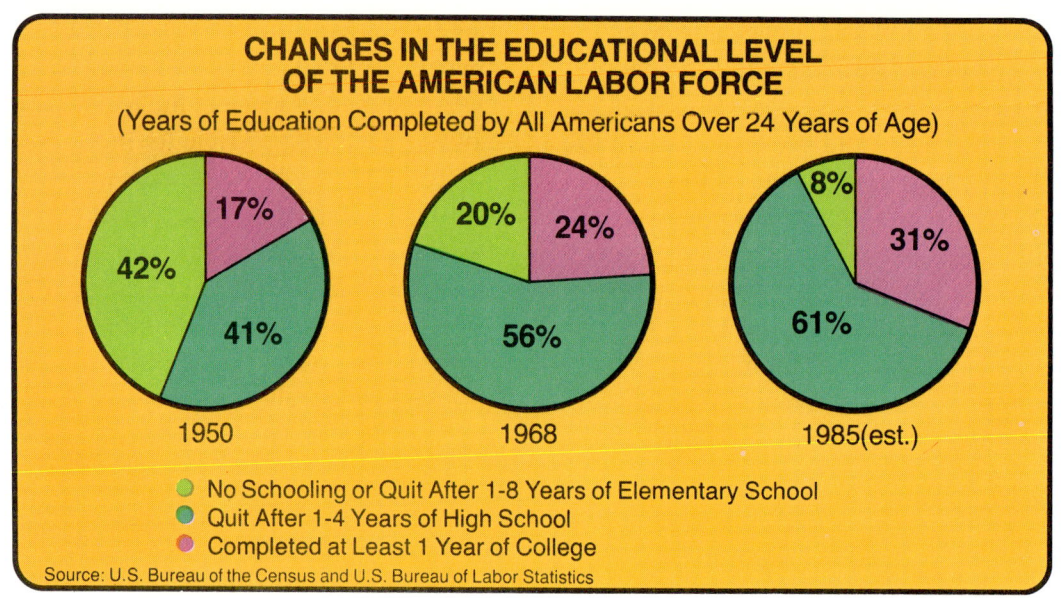

CHANGES IN THE EDUCATIONAL LEVEL OF THE AMERICAN LABOR FORCE

(Years of Education Completed by All Americans Over 24 Years of Age)

1950: 42%, 17%, 41%
1968: 20%, 24%, 56%
1985 (est.): 8%, 31%, 61%

- No Schooling or Quit After 1-8 Years of Elementary School
- Quit After 1-4 Years of High School
- Completed at Least 1 Year of College

Source: U.S. Bureau of the Census and U.S. Bureau of Labor Statistics

Reading Circle Graphs: *In 1950 only about 58% of all Americans over 24 years of age had finished more than 8 years of school. How many Americans over 24 had finished more than 8 years in 1968?*

unskilled jobs. The basic skills of reading, writing, and arithmetic are now essential because of the growing amounts of paper work. A number of traditional ideas about higher education are also changing. A college education was once a reasonably good guarantee of a good job. Today, however, many jobs call for technical skills that may not be offered in many colleges. Technical programs, not college, may be the best choice for many young people.

Even when jobs call for no special education employers often tend to choose the best educated people. The poorly educated worker, thus, is the one who is most likely to end up in an unemployment line.

A good basic education allows a worker to get a foothold in the job market. On the job, a worker is often able to learn new skills. With technological advances, there are changes in the kinds of work jobs require. Businesses often choose to give new training to workers rather than hire new workers.

Getting the Facts

1. What kinds of jobs are described by the terms "white collar," "blue collar," and "gray collar"?

2. What are some of the reasons why there has been a great rise in the number of service jobs over the last century?

3. What factors help explain the major rise in the number of women working for salaries and wages in the United States?

Thinking About the Future

■ What changes do you expect to see in the American working force within your own lifetime? Consider such things as kinds of jobs, length of the average work week, job opportunities for women and members of ethnic minorities, and average age of retirement. What changes would you like to see?

Choosing a Career

In a very practical way, you are part of America and its many resources. How to use yourself wisely as a resource is something you must think about. There are, of course, the things you can do as a responsible citizen. There are also your plans for a career. No doubt, you have already done some thinking about the kind of job you want. Most of us, however, do not make final career decisions quickly. Our career plans are likely to form slowly. And, before you become settled into the world of work, your thoughts about a job will probably change a number of times. The following exercise offers one way of thinking about the world of work—and your own future.

In looking to the future, there are things you need to know about yourself. For one thing, you should think about the relationship between your physical abilities and your career plans. Our concern here, however, is with your other assets. These include your intelligence, your interests, and your aptitudes.

INTELLIGENCE

Intelligence is mental ability—a person's capacity to learn. There are different kinds of mental ability. You may have more of one kind of intelligence, or mental ability. The classmate next to you may have more of another kind. There are, in other words, not only kinds, but also degrees, of intelligence.

Many different tests of mental abilities—intelligence tests—have been developed by psychologists. By taking one of these tests you can get some idea of your own intelligence. Your test results can be compared with the results of thousands of others who have taken the same test.

Just knowing your IQ, however, does not tell you all you need to know about your mental abilities. A number of factors go together to make up intelligence. The following list includes many of these factors.

1. Reasoning. The ability to reason is an important part of intelligence. It is the ability to think straight and make use of logic in solving problems. It is the ability to identify the many sides of an issue and weigh the value of different points of view. It is the ability to use available facts to make wise decisions about future actions. The ability to reason can be useful in almost any kind of work.

2. Verbal Meaning. Words are the symbols with which we reason. Verbal meaning refers to the meanings of ideas expressed in words. Knowing the correct meaning of words helps us when we reason about things. This is why, throughout school, so much attention is paid to vocabulary. The ability to understand the meaning of words, like the ability to reason, is necessary in almost all kinds of work.

3. Verbal Fluency. To understand the meaning of words is one thing. To be able to use them well when you write or speak is another thing. A good command of language is very helpful when you are writing papers, taking part in discussions, or making reports. Verbal fluency can be of great value to sales people, lawyers, teachers, writers—to anyone who has to get ideas across to others.

inquiry

4. Numerical Understanding. This is your ability to work and reason with numbers. It involves your ability to do simple arithmetic. It also involves your understanding of what numbers mean and your ability to solve complex mathematical problems. An understanding of numbers is important in many kinds of work, from running a cash register to solving problems in a physics lab.

5. Spacial Thinking. This is the ability to visualize objects of two or three dimensions in your mind. If you have a high level of spacial ability, you probably are good at putting together jigsaw puzzles. You are also likely to be the kind of person who can look at a blueprint and see in your mind the building or machine that can be made from it. Needless to say, this ability is of great value if you plan to become an architect, engineer, or carpenter.

6. Memory. Memory is the ability to store away things in your mind for future use. It is easy to understand why this is an important part of mental ability. Too often, however, memory is thought of as the only factor in intelligence. This simply is not the case. Memory alone is not enough. There are, for example, extreme cases of people who are virtually walking encyclopedias, who do well at quiz games, but who never seem able to make practical use of their great store of information. Memory is something you can improve with practice. Your ability to remember is likely to be especially good when you are thinking about things in which you have interest.

INTERESTS

Your interests are very much a part of you. This is not to say that you are born with particular interests. However, your

What kinds of interests might lead people to choose jobs such as these?

ECONOMIC LIFE IN MODERN AMERICA

interests are likely to be closely related to your life experiences. Usually you are interested in something because you have enjoyed your experiences with it. New experiences build new interests. For this reason we are often unsure about our interest in something until we have tried it.

Chances are that you have a wide variety of interests, some of them much stronger than others. Still, you may find it hard to identify all of your interests. To help identify interests you may not have considered, answer the following questions.

- What are your favorite subjects in school?
- In what kinds of activities do you show some skill?
- What are some things that people say you are good at?
- Suppose you had completed your general studies in school and now could study anything you wanted to. What would you choose?
- What kinds of jobs or careers would you like to know more about?

APTITUDES

An aptitude is a natural or potential ability to do something. You may be born with certain aptitudes or you may develop them as you grow up. Aptitudes differ from interests. You may have an interest in something but not be able to develop the ability to do it well. You may, for example, have a great interest in music but not be able to sing well.

There are different kinds of aptitudes. Some of the more common ones are described in the following paragraphs. As you read about them, think of your own abilities. In each case, ask yourself whether you rate your own ability as high, average, or low.

1. Academic Ability. Academic ability involves most of the skills you have developed in school. It includes being able to read with understanding, grasp ideas you hear, and solve problems in science and mathematics. Some level of academic ability is necessary for success in college. Academic ability is also needed in all professions and in many kinds of technical work. At the same time it is well to remember that a person can be very successful in some kinds of work with a small amount of academic ability. In many service fields and in some technical work, other kinds of aptitudes are much more important than academic ability.

2. Mechanical and Manipulative Ability. Mechanical aptitude involves the ability to understand how objects are put together. Manipulative ability is skill at using one's hands. Think about the work of automobile mechanics. They must be able to locate trouble spots in engines. After finding out what is wrong, they must use manipulative ability to make the repairs. Their work thus involves not only the ability to locate the difficulty, but also the ability to correct it. This kind of aptitude is needed in many jobs. Architects, dentists, engineers, and watchmakers all need these skills.

3. Clerical Ability. People with a high level of clerical ability are able to use numbers and words with great accuracy. This ability is desirable in many kinds of jobs. In today's work world there are a number of jobs that can be called "clerical." The work demands

Inquiry

patience in dealing with details. Clerical ability may be combined with manipulative ability in secretarial work and computer programming. There are also many other jobs, such as teaching, in which clerical ability can be of great use.

4. Musical Ability. People with musical ability are able to distinguish variations in pitch (musical tones). Such people are also highly sensitive to rhythm (movement and grouping of tones). Of course, if these people wish to play musical instruments, they will also need a great deal of manipulative ability.

5. Artistic Ability. People with artistic aptitudes have a feeling for color and line. They may also be able to draw or sketch well. Then again, artistic ability may involve the ability to use one's mind and hands in other creative ways—with clay, metal, wood, and the like.

6. Social Ability. Social ability—the ability to work well with other people—is an aptitude much needed in today's world. It is hard to think of many kinds of work in which social ability is not of some help. This kind of aptitude is especially useful in social service jobs and in jobs where persuasion is called for. People doing social service jobs—working in schools, hospitals, and welfare agencies—must be able to help and counsel others. To do their jobs well, these people must be able to gain other people's confidence. People doing persuasive work—such as sales work and political work—must be able to persuade others to follow their leadership, to accept their ideas, or to buy their products. In all of these jobs, the ability to relate to others and win their confidence is essential.

What kinds of abilities would you expect most sound engineers to have? What abilities do pediatricians need? What kinds of abilities are generally needed for the careers you have considered for yourself?

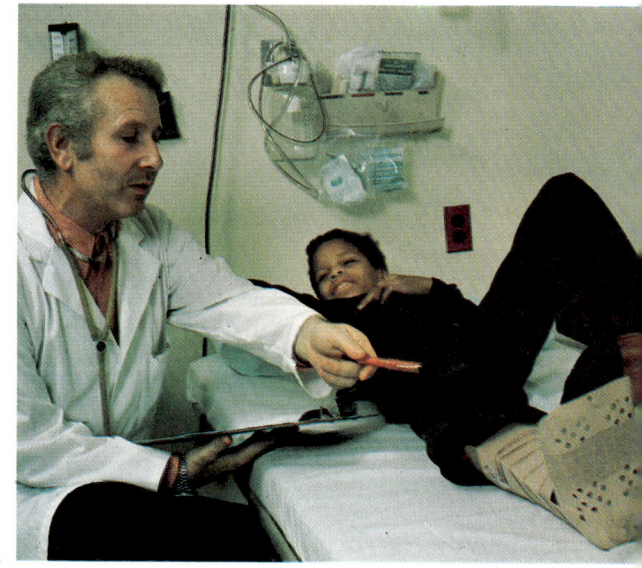

ECONOMIC LIFE IN MODERN AMERICA

The Consumer in the American Economy

Our American economic system depends on a lot of people doing many different kinds of work. Almost every job helps in some way to provide the goods and services that we all need. Each job is of special interest and concern to the person who does it. People who work for wages or salaries are interested in receiving enough income to support themselves and their families comfortably. Managers and owners of businesses are interested in making profits. People who run households are interested in keeping things running smoothly within a personal or family budget.

The fact that people have different kinds of interests can lead to conflicting desires. Consumers may object to the high cost of food and place the blame on farmers. Farmers may object to the price of farm machines. They may feel that the owners and workers in the factories that make the machines are getting too much money. The factory owners may claim that workers' wages are so high that it is hard to make a decent profit. Workers may argue that higher wages increase their buying power and stimulate the economy.

In only one kind of economic activity do all of us meet on common ground. We are all consumers. We all spend money on goods and services. In order to keep our economy in balance, all of us need enough money to buy the goods and services that our economy provides.

A shortage of money in the pockets of one group of consumers can create problems for other groups. Think about the automobile industry. If a few large groups of consumers became unable to buy cars, many assembly lines would close down. With fewer cars being made, steel mills and rubber factories would have to slow their production. Thousands of factory workers would lose their jobs.

THE CONSUMER AS ECONOMIC DECISION MAKER

The choices we make as consumers help determine what will be produced in America. Each day millions of Americans make economic decisions. First, we decide whether to spend our money or save it. If we decide to spend it, we must decide what kinds of goods and services we are going to buy. Such choices are made freely. They are a kind of economic vote. Millions of these votes are

Teenage consumers definitely have an influence on the producers of popular music. What are some of the other products that seem to be heavily influenced by the desires of young consumers?

AMERICANS AS WORKERS AND CONSUMERS

cast every day. From the votes, producers can get a good idea of what consumers want.

Examples of consumer influence can be found in all parts of the economy. In recent years, Americans have shown great interest in small cars made in Europe and Japan. Noting this interest, American automobile producers decided that they must make more small cars of their own.

This shift to small cars to meet consumer demands suggests that in the long run consumers generally get what they want. Taken together, our individual choices as consumers have a very powerful effect on producers. Economists call these combined consumer choices "demand." In a free economy, producers tend to be very aware of "demand." When demand changes, changes in production are likely to follow.

INFLUENCES ON CONSUMER SPENDING

The choices that consumers make are influenced by many different factors. The most important of these is, of course, the amount of buying power in the hands of consumers. Put more simply, our consumer choices are greatly influenced by the amount of money we have to spend. We get this buying power by earning it or by borrowing it through the use of credit. We can also get it by drawing on our savings.

The way in which income is distributed among different groups also has an influence on consumer spending. People with low incomes tend to spend all or most of their money for basics—food, clothing, housing, and the like. People with higher incomes tend to save a larger share of their money. They also tend to spend a large part of their incomes on "luxuries." When most of a country's income goes to a few very wealthy people, the general result is a low level of consumer spending. Everyone buys basics. Few people can afford anything else. When income is distributed more equally, as it is in our country, the amount of consumer spending rises. More people can buy more things.

Another major influence on consumer spending involves the willingness of people to spend money. In recent years growing numbers of Americans have been able to spend or save as they wish. Whether they will spend or save is hard to predict. At times consumers by the millions seem to be in a buying mood. At other times the mood shifts toward savings. People decide that they can make do, for the time being, with what they have. These changing moods can be brought about by any of a number of factors. Perhaps most important is the way people feel about the future. If people are optimistic about the future they tend to buy. If they are pessimistic, they tend to save.

Fashions and fads may also have a powerful influence on consumers. Many people are influenced by the desire to imitate their neighbors. Finally, not to be overlooked, is the powerful influence advertising has on American consumers.

ADVERTISING AND THE CONSUMER

Wherever American consumers turn, there is some form of advertising urging them to buy something. Producers advertise to create demand. It is their

Things Are Not Quite What They Seem

What point is this cartoonist making about some advertisements?

way of communicating with consumers. It is also a means by which producers compete with one another.

From a consumer's point of view, advertising serves a number of purposes. For one thing, advertisements give us information about things we want. We can use ads to compare products. Ads can also introduce us to new goods and services. And, in many cases, ads lead us to desire goods and services that we had never before thought necessary.

The creation of consumer interest and desire calls for great skill on the part of advertisers. To be intelligent consumers, we must study the ways in which advertisers use their skill. We must also remember that the purpose of most ads is not to deceive us, but rather to persuade us. (You will find a discussion of persuasion techniques in Chapter 8.) In some cases, however, the line between deception and persuasion can become blurred. Some ads are very misleading. This is one of the reasons why we have Better Business Bureaus in cities and towns throughout the United States and a Federal Trade Commission in Washington, D.C.

BEING A WISE CONSUMER

There is no magic formula that will tell us how to make wise decisions as consumers. As consumers, our goal is to use our buying power in ways that will give the greatest satisfaction. The following guidelines may help you reach this goal.

- Keep informed about the kinds of goods and services that are available to meet your needs. The more you know about what is available, the more chance you will have to make good choices.
- Decide which choices will give you the greatest satisfaction. As you learn

more about all the different things that are available, the problem of choosing between them is likely to become more difficult. You will need to keep asking yourself: What will give me the most pleasure in the long run?

- Learn more about how to choose the best quality of goods and services at the best price. Look around. Do comparison shopping in search of better values. At the same time, insist on your right as a consumer to know what you are buying. This is as important in seeking services as it is in buying goods.
- Use the help of informed advisers. In every community there are people and groups who can give sound advice about certain kinds of goods and services. Consumer service organizations can be found in most cities. There are also government agencies that set standards of quality for certain goods and services.
- Make intelligent use of advertising. Advertising is an important part of modern business. If used wisely, it can be a helpful source of information. The trick is to avoid being mislead or confused by overly aggressive sales appeals.
- Learn to identify people who might try to take advantage of you. The "confidence story" is as old as history. The "pitch" may be a "free" offer that has strings attached or a "bargain" price that really is no bargain at all.
- Improve your ability to manage money. Money can serve you in many ways. It can be used to buy things that will satisfy your needs. It can be very helpful in emergencies. It can give you security in your later years. If it is to do all these things, however, you must know how to manage it properly. You must keep in mind that choosing to spend money for one thing means not being able to spend it for something else that you may want later.
- Use credit wisely. Low monthly payments often tempt people to buy things they don't really need. Later they may be unable to buy things they do need because they are still making monthly payments for the less important things. If you do make use of credit, remember that the rate of interest being charged may be much larger than it appears to be. Find out what the true rate is. It might be cheaper to obtain credit in the form of a loan from a bank.
- Get the best possible use out of the things you buy. Intelligent consumers know that wise use means careful use. It also means proper upkeep and repair. This applies to everything from a house or car to small personal items.

Getting the Facts

1. What general effect does "demand" have in a free economy?

2. Name at least four important influences on consumer spending.

Examining the Issues

■ Think of the many different ads you see everyday. Have you ever been misled by ads? If so, how? A number of government rulings have attempted to put an end to ads that may be misleading. For example, TV commercials for children's toys can no longer show background props that are not included in the toy package. What other, similar rulings would you favor?

Speaking Out

Bess Myerson

As Commissioner of the Department of Consumer Affairs in New York City, Myerson has fought a number of successful battles in the interests of consumers. However, she believes that in many cases consumers must blame their own bad judgments. This is especially true, she finds, in the use of credit cards.

"No consumer abuse could last longer than it takes you to read this article if consumers did not support its continued existence with their own lack of buying discipline. . . .

"One of the most prevalent self-abuses is the undisciplined use of credit buying. The credit card is perhaps the greatest marketing concept of this century—and, used wisely, can be a blessing to consumers in every income group. Used unwisely, it can be a passport to personal-bankruptcy court. It is no accident that in the past twenty-five years the rise in the distribution of credit cards—now past the two-hundred-million mark—has been accompanied by a disproportionate rise in the number of personal bankruptcies filed each year. Those "convenient" payments do have a way of piling up, and the interest on those payments can eat into a modest budget like an army of happy termites in an old wooden house. . . .

"It is good business for a company to put the credit card within your reach (although we have curbed some of the most enthusiastic abuses of their effort: the unsolicited cards, the undisclosed interest rates and hidden costs, the reduction of the consumer's liability for lost or stolen cards, et cetera), but it may be bad business for you to reach for your credit cards at the slightest whim. That 'pay later' especially for something you didn't really need or want in the first place—has a numbing way of hitting you in the budget when you least expect it, and the effect can be financially fatal. . . .

". . . Consumers will never have a life-style of their own choosing until they liberate their budgets from the psychological assaults that may 'sell' them more than serve them. Purchasing power and willpower are inseparable."

---

1. To what extent do you agree with Myerson's argument that consumers often have only themselves to blame for financial difficulties?

2. Myerson points out that along with the increase in the number of credit cards issued there has been an increase in personal bankruptcies. She believes these two events are directly related. In view of this, would you favor any kind of cutback on the number of credit cards issued? If so, what kind of cutback? If not, why not?

AMERICANS AS WORKERS AND CONSUMERS

Review of Basic Ideas

1. Throughout history a very large part of the energy used in production has been supplied, not by machines, but by humans and animals. Only in the 20th century did machines begin to supply the majority of the power needed to produce our goods.

2. Mass production operates according to the principle of division of labor. The use of mass production has contributed greatly to the growth of labor unions. There were a few small American labor unions in the early years of our country. Large national unions did not emerge, however, until late in the 19th century. The greatest growth in union membership took place in the 1930s. Today, there is one large national union, the AFL–CIO, and a number of large independent unions.

3. Today in the United States there are more white-collar jobs than blue-collar jobs. In part, this is the result of the growing importance of services in our economy. There has also been an increase in the number of women working for salaries and wages and a rise in education requirements for many jobs, both blue-collar and white-collar.

4. We are all consumers, whatever our other economic roles may be. As consumers, we make decisions that help determine the things that will be produced. The basic goal of all consumers should be to use their buying power in ways that will bring the greatest satisfaction.

Questions to Think About

1. In what ways have workers gained by advances in technology? In what ways have workers lost by these advances?

2. Do you think large labor unions would have been formed if mass production had never been introduced? Why, or why not?

3. What weapons have owners used in an effort to prevent union organization? What weapons have workers used to strengthen the power of their unions? Which of these methods do you think are fair? Which do you think unfair? Explain.

4. What are some of the long-range consequences of the trend toward a larger proportion of service jobs in our economy?

5. What are some examples of the way that shifts in consumer demand can bring great changes in the American economy?

6. What are some examples of the ways in which consumer interests and desires are stimulated by fads and advertising?

7. What are some of the advantages and disadvantages involved in the use of credit?

Citizenship Laboratory

Words and Relationships

Define each of the terms in the first column. Then show how each term is related to the item listed opposite it by using both items in a sentence or short paragraph.

1.	division of labor	mass production
2.	lockout	job security
3.	injunction	legal action
4.	picket	strikes
5.	boycott	the general public
6.	union shop	union membership
7.	collective bargaining	union strength
8.	service jobs	government work
9.	consumers	advertisements
10.	demand	changes in production

Building a Future

Helping consumers is one of the many jobs of the federal government. Help comes from a number of agencies in the executive branch. It can also come from laws passed by Congress.

These are some of the ways in which consumer interests are handled by the executive branch:

- The Special Assistant to the President for Consumer Affairs reports directly to the President on a wide variety of matters.
- The Food and Drug Administration keeps an eye on the advertising claims of non-prescription drugs. It also sets rules for packaging food and takes care of many other kinds of consumer concerns.
- The Federal Trade Commission enforces many different kinds of price regulations.

From time to time, Congress passes laws to help consumers. The executive agencies are required to enforce these acts of Congress.

Check current newspapers and news magazines for information about recent consumer activities of the federal government. Which of these activities seem most helpful? What other government actions, if any, do you think should be taken to protect the interests of American consumers?

AMERICANS AS WORKERS AND CONSUMERS

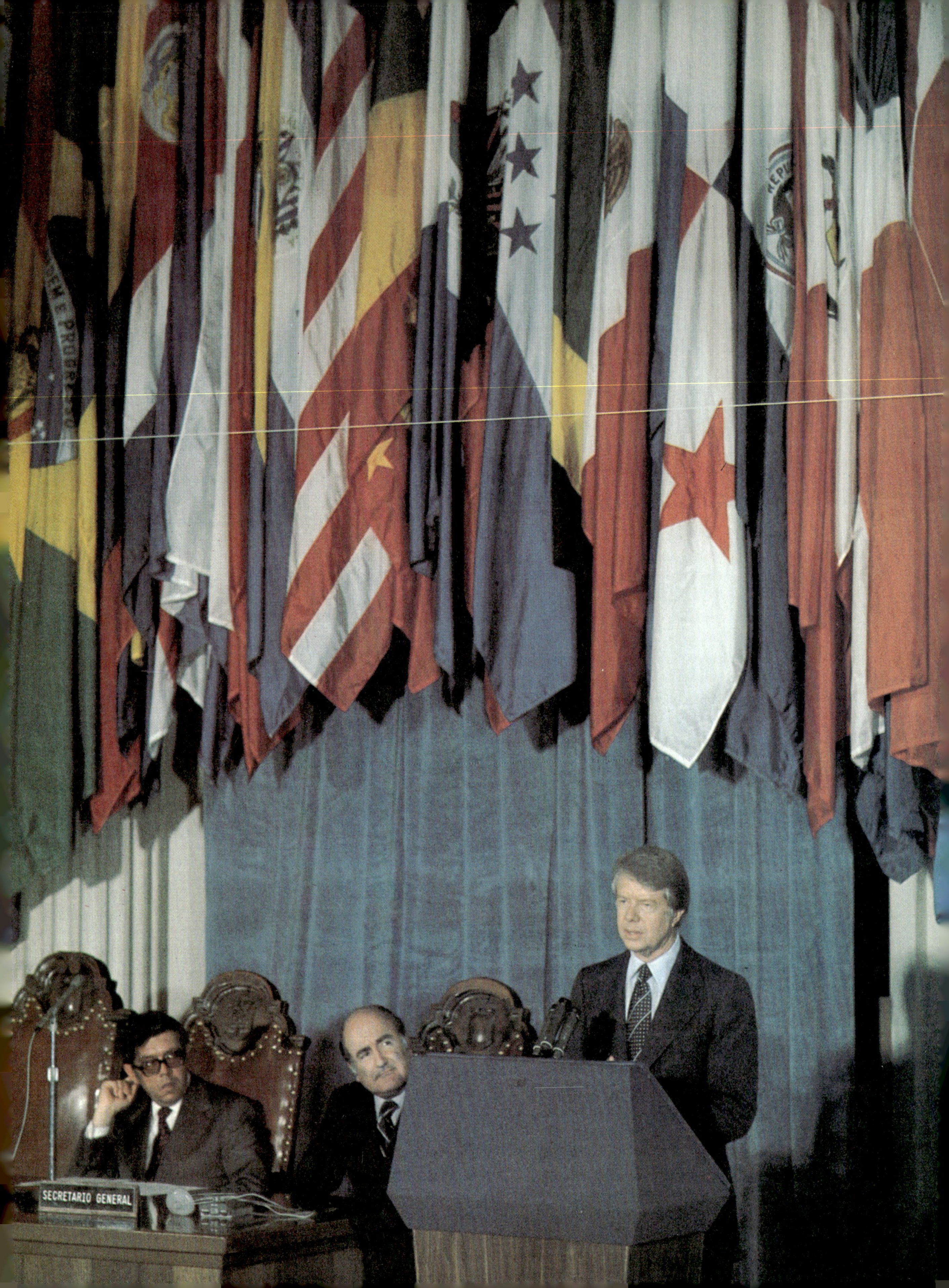
SECRETARIO GENERAL

Unit SIX

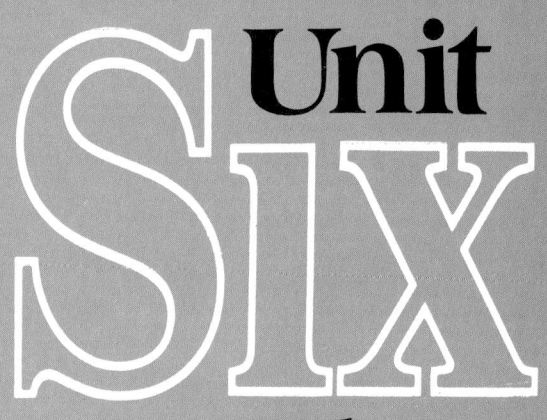

The United States in Today's World

18 The United States as a World Power

As Americans, we are the people of a nation-state—the United States of America. However, we are also the inhabitants of a globe, along with the people of all other nation-states. The world is divided into many separate and independent countries. Some of them have great power. Others have much less power. Some are, in economic terms, well developed. Most, however, have not yet reached the stage of economic development found in the United States.

The presence of a large number of independent countries is one of the important facts of world affairs in the second half of the 20th century. A second important fact is the existence of a number of major centers of power in different parts of the world.

As the world moved into the second half of the 20th century, the two great world powers were the United States and the Soviet Union. With the passage of time, however, other centers of power have emerged. Once powerful countries in western Europe—West Germany, Great Britain, France, and others—have combined to form a powerful economic front. In Asia, a war-torn and defeated Japan has become an industrial giant. Communist China is gaining in political power and searching for ways to further its own economic development. Meanwhile, less powerful countries such as the oil-rich countries of the Middle East are moving ahead with their own development plans.

In today's world, a new reality has emerged. The actions of any country can be a threat to world peace and security. Powerful and weak nations alike can draw people into war. To understand this reality, Americans need only think of the experience of the United States during the 1960s and early 1970s in the small countries of Southeast Asia.

United States' Rise to International Leadership

The United States emerged as one of the world's great powers during World War I. During the war, we sent our allies war materials and other goods. In 1918, we sent American soldiers. Through these activities, the United States demonstrated its great capacity to produce food and factory goods.

In the years before World War I, Americans had devoted most of their energies to activities at home. Americans often had contacts with people and countries beyond our borders. Generally, however, the contacts were neither of great significance nor of long-range importance.

INTERNATIONAL RELATIONS BEFORE 1914

In the years between the American Revolution and World War I, the United States had tried to remove itself from world politics. In its dealings with other countries, our government worked toward two basic goals. One goal was to avoid involvement in European conflicts, turning instead toward the development and expansion of the United States. The second goal was to establish a special role for the United States in the Western Hemisphere—in Central America and South America as well as in North America.

For more than a century these two goals remained the guiding principles of American foreign policy. To achieve them, leaders of the young United States tried to remove the British, French, and Spanish troops that remained in certain neighboring areas after the American Revolution. This was done through treaties, the purchase of Louisiana from the French in 1803, a war with Great Britain in 1812, and the acquisition of Spanish-Florida in 1819.

Along with these activities came the growth of a spirit known as "manifest destiny." Manifest destiny was the dream of an American empire—a land that would reach from the Atlantic to the Pacific. This dream led Americans into Texas, Oregon, and California. It was a part of American activities in the Caribbean Sea, Hawaii, the Philippines, and other Pacific islands.

American expansion was mainly the work of private people and groups. However, with so much of the people's energy centered on westward expansion in North America and the Pacific Ocean, it was natural for the government's foreign policy to be concerned with matters in the same areas. And, from time to time, the government joined private groups in their desire for expansion.

In the 1840s the United States fought a war with Mexico. As a result, the lands between the Louisiana Territory and the Pacific Ocean were added to the United States. In 1867, the government bought Alaska from Russia. The government also took part in activities in the Caribbean Sea and the Pacific Ocean.

Fortunately for the United States, the years between 1815 and 1870 were a time of relative quiet in Europe. After 1870, the powers of Europe began to undertake major new expansion efforts. By then, the United States had become a relatively strong country in its own right.

The years of quiet in Europe made it possible for the United States to achieve a good measure of its second goal, namely, to play a special role in the Western Hemisphere. The first step toward this goal was taken in 1823 by President James Monroe when he issued the Monroe Doctrine. In it, the President stated that the United States would not allow further European colonization of the Western Hemisphere. He also stated that the United States would oppose any attempt on the part of European powers to intervene in the affairs of the countries of the Western Hemisphere.

European powers, at the time, chose not to challenge the Monroe Doctrine. Great Britain's navy controlled the oceans. But, fortunately for the United States, the British chose to follow a policy that, in many ways, supported the Monroe Doctrine. Meanwhile, the United States grew in strength. By the end of the 19th century, the United States found itself able to back the doctrine with its own power.

With posters such as this one, the United States' armed services stressed the glamorous aspects of taking part in World War I, our first war on European soil.

MOVEMENT INTO WORLD POWER STATUS

A more vigorous role in foreign affairs became possible as America's industrial strength grew. Even so, a continuing effort was made to remain uninvolved in the affairs of the great powers. When World War I began in 1914, President Wilson tried to keep the United States out of the war. Within three years, however, American soldiers were fighting in Europe.

When the war was over, President Wilson led the efforts to set up an international peace-keeping organization—the League of Nations. In his own country, however, the long-held desire to remain separated from Europe helped block American membership. At the same time, the United States emerged from the war the most powerful country in the world. In financial terms, America had become the world's creditor. Many countries owed us money. In production, America was soon outstripping all other countries.

Despite this new status, many Americans remained suspicious of commitments outside the Western Hemisphere. Though now among the world's great powers, the United States was reluctant to give up its traditional role of isolation.

THE UNITED STATES AND THE COLD WAR

In 1941, the United States was drawn into World War II by Japan's attack on Pearl Harbor. At the end of the war, America stood preeminent among the great powers. Ours was the only major country not damaged by fighting and bombing. We alone had the ultimate weapon—the atomic bomb. These circumstances made one thing certain: in the future America would have to play an important part in world politics. No longer were the traditional desires to remain uninvolved possible.

Many American leaders hoped that the new United Nations would help bring an era of peace and stability. Their hopes were soon dampened, however, by the expansionist tendencies of the Soviet Union. To counter Soviet moves, American planners developed a doctrine known as "containment." The goal of this new policy was to contain the expansionist tendencies of the Soviet Union. In trying to reach the goal, the United States became involved in

What statement is this cartoonist making about the American policy of containment?

"RATIONALIZE IT! IF WE DON'T FIGHT THEM HERE WE'LL BE FIGHTING THEM IN DOWNTOWN MOSCOW— WE HAVE TO CONTAIN CHINESE COMMUNISM IN ASIA..."

rebuilding the economies of Europe. We helped set up a number of regional alliances. The most important of these was the North Atlantic Treaty Organization—better known as NATO. And finally in 1950, we became involved in a war in Korea.

Out of international developments of the late 1940s and early 1950s, came two great superpowers: the United States and the Soviet Union. The democratic United States and the Communist Soviet Union were, by nature, competing political systems. Both countries had an abundance of economic resources, great military power, and a stockpile of nuclear weapons.

The rivalry of these two powers, and the countries associated with them, led to what has been called the Cold War. Basically a war without battles, it was characterized by economic and political, as well as military, competition. The United States took steps to help its allies improve their economies. The Soviet Union sought the same goals for its satellites. Both tried to gain support for their own political systems from uncommitted countries. Meanwhile, the two powers glared at each other from behind huge arsenals of nuclear weapons.

FRIENDLIER RELATIONS WITH COMMUNIST COUNTRIES

Some change in the Cold War alignments came in the 1960s. Most important perhaps was the break between the Soviet Union and Communist China. At the same time, the United States tried to establish friendlier relationships with the Soviet Union. In the process, the focal point of the American containment policy changed from Europe to Southeast Asia. This led to our involvement in the long, bitter, and costly war in Vietnam. Toward the end of this war, we again turned to a policy of guarded but friendlier relationships with Communist powers. In this case, we sought better relationships with Communist China.

In the 20th century, America has taken part in two world wars and two prolonged Asian conflicts. These facts clearly show the profound change that has taken place in our foreign policy. In today's world, the United States has found it necessary to take a major role in the activities of other lands and peoples.

Getting the Facts

1. What were the two basic goals of American foreign policy in the years before 1914? To what extent were these goals achieved?

2. What factors led the United States to play a greater role in world affairs in the 20th century?

3. What was the United States' policy toward the Soviet Union in the late 1940s and 1950s? How has our foreign policy toward Communist countries changed in recent years?

Forming an Opinion

■ In what ways might the United States benefit from the establishment of good relations with the Soviet Union and Communist China? What problems, if any, do you think could arise as a result of American efforts to establish good relations with the two major Communist powers? What kind of policy do you think the United States should follow in dealing with these countries? Should the policy be the same for both countries? Why, or why not?

Inquiry

Foreign Policy Developments

The last few pages have summarized briefly the rise of the United States to world leadership. Like most summaries, however, what you have just read deals mainly with general trends and major developments. It does not include details about all the important events that have taken place. A knowledge of such events can give a fuller sense of reality to the general story. Obtaining this knowledge is something you can do on your own. It is the kind of exercise you will find particularly enjoyable if you have an interest in history.

To help you, certain important events and developments are listed at the right. Learn something about the meaning of each. As you read about them, other important events may come to your attention. You may wish to include these events in your study. As you study each item, decide how it is related to the summary you have just read in your textbook.

How does this Latin American cartoonist interpret the Monroe Doctrine? Is it a valid criticism of American foreign policy? Why, or why not?

Your school library will have a number of reference books that can be used in your study. Two of the most readily available are standard American history textbooks and encyclopedias.

- Jay's Treaty, 1794, and Pinckney's Treaty, 1795
- Louisiana Purchase, 1803
- Acquisition of Florida, 1819
- The Monroe Doctrine, 1823
- Mexican Cession, 1848
- War with Spain, 1898
- "Open Door" policy, 1899 and 1900
- Interventions in the Caribbean and in Central America, 1901–1934
- The Treaty of Versailles, 1919–1920
- President Franklin D. Roosevelt's Good Neighbor Policy, 1933
- Isolationist activities in the 1930s
- The Truman Doctrine, 1947
- North Atlantic Treaty Organization, 1949
- Southeast Asia Treaty Organization, 1954
- Cuban Missile Crisis, 1962

Interpreting History

In what ways would the United States be different today if there had been no war with Mexico?

In what ways has the policy of the United States in the Caribbean and Central America changed in the years of the 20th century? What are some of the possible reasons for these changes?

The "Open Door" policy dealt with China. The Truman Doctrine dealt with Greece and Turkey. What is the relationship of the United States with these three countries today? In what ways might these earlier policies have had an effect on present relationships?

THE UNITED STATES AS A WORLD POWER

Other Modern Centers of Power

In the years after World War II, the United States and the Soviet Union emerged as the world's two great superpowers. Their positions, however, did not remain unchallenged. Other countries rose from the war's destruction to find their own places in the sun. A number of less powerful countries made plans for greater economic progress. Each was seeking ways to gain a more important position in the family of nations.

GROWTH OF A POWERFUL SOVIET UNION

The huge country of Russia was an important power during the 19th century. The Russians, however, were defeated by the British and the French in the Crimean War in 1856. In 1905, they were again defeated in war, this time by Japan.

During World War I, the disorganized government of the Russian Tsar was overthrown. After three years of civil war and foreign invasion, Russian Communists gained complete control.

Under Communist leaders, the Soviet Union gradually became a major industrial power. Despite the protest of many land owners, thousands of farms were collectivized. That is, the farms were combined and placed under government control. The government also took control of all factories and businesses. Freedom of speech, press, assembly, and religion were suppressed. The Communist Party was the only political group allowed.

Under Communist control, the Soviet Union moved ahead. Much of the progress was the result of the country's great natural resources and the love of the Russian people for their homeland.

During World War II, the major part of Germany's military power was turned against the Soviet Union. In the end, Russia's armies defeated Hitler's main forces, while American, British, and French allies defeated German forces in western Europe.

Following World War II, the Soviet Union sought to expand its power and influence. It helped set up a number of new governments in eastern Europe. Most became, for one reason or another, very supportive of Soviet aims. Soviet leaders worked also to develop their own economy. Gradually, the people of the Soviet Union were given greater, but still limited, freedom of movement and expression. There was major progress in Soviet science. In 1957 the Soviets

For many years Soviet economic planners stressed military weapons and heavy industry. Today planners are showing increased interest in consumer goods.

launched the first space satellite ever produced by human hands. In 1961 they sent the first human into orbit around the earth. Other major scientific achievements followed in the later years of the 1960s and in the 1970s. These included new weapons and greater naval power.

While many of the Communist countries grew economically and militarily, the solid political front of Communist power weakened. This was seen in the greater, but limited, independence of Russian satellite nations in eastern Europe.

TOWARD A UNITED EUROPE

For the past several centuries—at least 500 years—most of the great centers of world power could be found in western Europe. These powers were shaken greatly by the two world wars. In recent years, however, the energetic, well-educated people of these countries, with their democratic governments and modern economies, have once again moved into positions of power.

Much of the progress in Europe has been brought about by cooperative agreements among groups of countries. In 1949, 10 European countries set up the Council of Europe. The aim of the council was to bring about more political and economic unity in Europe. It did not, however, meet with lasting success. Later, in 1952, six countries formed the European Coal and Steel Community. Its goal was to set up a common market for coal and steel produced in the six nations. The six members, in other words, would act as one unit in so far as these two products were concerned.

This arrangement proved so successful that, in 1957, the same six countries created the European Economic Community. The goal was to set up a common market for all the products of the member states. Better known as the Common Market, the European Economic Community proved very effective. During the 1960s, production in the Common Market countries doubled. This was a much greater rate of growth than was found in the United States during the same years.

Working together, the nations of western Europe have a great deal of economic power. Do you think it likely that these nations will ever form a political union to strengthen their economic union? Why, or why not?

Other Europeans were very impressed by the success of the Common Market. Early in 1972, Britain, Ireland, Denmark, and Norway signed treaties that made them members of the market.

Today's Common Market has great political, as well as economic, importance. It now includes a number of major nations in western Europe—Britain, France, West Germany, and Italy—as well as a number of smaller states.

THE UNITED STATES AS A WORLD POWER   **421**

Together these countries form the world's most powerful trading bloc.

THE EMERGENCE OF INDUSTRIAL JAPAN

The post-war industrial and economic advance of western Europe was more than matched by Japan. Thoroughly defeated in World War II, the Japanese people rose from the ashes of atomic destruction to make their islands one of the great powers in the world.

Europeans first arrived in Japan 50 years after Columbus sailed to America. For about a century the Japanese welcomed the European traders and missionaries who came to their shores. In the early 1600s, fearing that European armies might try to take over their islands, the Japanese expelled all foreign people.

Finally, in the 1850s, diplomatic relations were established between Japan and the United States. Trade was begun, not only with the United States, but with a number of European countries. The Japanese soon were competing both economically and militarily with the countries of Europe.

Japan's growing military power led to victory in two wars—one with China in the late 19th century and one with Russia in the early years of the 20th century. In World War I, Japan fought with the Allies against Germany. In the 1930s, however, Japanese military leaders gained control of the government. They led their country into war with China in 1931. In the following years, Japan took over much of East Asia.

A Japanese attack on Pearl Harbor, in 1941, brought war with the United States. Defeat led to an American occupation of Japan that lasted until 1951. During the occupation the Japanese were able to get back on their feet economically. A new government was set up along democratic lines.

Industrial towns look much the same around the world. This factory is located in Kawasaki, a suburb of Tokyo.

The Japanese economy, slow to advance at first, grew quickly in the 1950s and 1960s. By the beginning of the 1970s, Japan had become the third largest industrial power in the world. Japanese automobiles, electronics, and textiles became common in stores around the world.

CHINA IN TODAY'S WORLD

China is in many ways a giant among nations. One out of every four people in the world is Chinese. The greater part live on the huge land area that covers much of eastern Asia.

China has one of the longest recorded histories of any country. One of the most important dates in China's long history is a recent one—1949. In that year Chinese Communists, under Mao Tse-tung, drove the Nationalist government of Chiang Kai-shek from

422 THE UNITED STATES IN TODAY'S WORLD

the mainland of Asia. The Nationalists fled to the island of Taiwan. There they set up a rival government. With economic and military support from the United States, the Nationalists on Taiwan made great economic advances.

The Communist government on the Asian mainland also became intent on economic growth. Large farms owned by wealthy landlords were divided among the poorer people. Later, these same lands were turned into government-run farms or communes.

With so many mouths to feed, and too few farm machines, Chinese agricultural problems are much as they have been through the centuries. The need for modern machines has caused China to turn toward industry. China is still far behind other major powers in the production of trucks, tractors, and other kinds of machines. But China has already become one of the world's larger producers of iron and steel.

Until 1971 the government of Communist China was denied admission to the United Nations. The Nationalist government on Taiwan was the Chinese member of that body. The Nationalist government also had a seat on the Security Council. When Communist China was finally voted into the United Nations, Nationalist China was expelled. By thus joining the family of nations and gaining a seat on the Security Council, Communist China moved forward as an important center of power in the world. The United States had, in years past, worked to keep Communist China out of the United Nations. Relations between the two countries improved, however, in 1972, as a result of President Nixon's visit to China.

Chinese farmers use a variety of methods, ancient and modern. In a country seeking a rapid increase in food production, what are the advantages and disadvantages of government control over farming?

DEVELOPING CENTERS OF POWER

In a rapidly changing world it is hard to predict what the power relationships among different countries will be in the years ahead. When we think about the future, we must take a number of countries into account.

In the Western Hemisphere we must consider our Canadian neighbors in the north and our Latin American neighbors in the south. Canada is, by any measure, a modern country. This close neighbor is our most important trading partner. Canadians also have close economic ties with western Europe and Japan. Latin America has the fastest growing population in the world. Some of the world's most modern cities can also be found here. With many rich resources, industry is booming. In most of the Latin American countries, it is

THE UNITED STATES AS A WORLD POWER

African nations such as Kenya are now making decisions that will greatly affect their future position in the world economy. A basic question for most developing nations is whether to continue stressing exports of valuable natural resources and farm products or to move more heavily into industrial goods.

possible to find both modern urban ways of living and ancient peasant ways.

India is another land of great contrasts. After gaining independence in 1947, India worked to bring about improvements in its economy. But economic improvement has been hindered by the rapid growth of population. Gains in production always seem to be offset by population increases.

Africa is also beginning to make its weight felt in international politics. During the late 1950s and early 1960s, new African countries were set up with breathtaking speed. Most of the new African countries found themselves with weak economies. Many were also plagued with problems caused by ethnic and regional rivalries.

In the early 1970s, the oil-rich countries of the Middle East came rapidly to the fore as an important power bloc. In this part of the world countries such as Iran and Egypt are using their wealth for modernization. Signs of economic growth can be seen in many cities of the Middle East. The growing power of these countries has been felt in the United Nations.

Another Middle Eastern country now making great economic progress is Israel. The desert lands of Israel have been made to flower. Challenged by unfriendly neighbors, this small country has built up a powerful military force.

Getting the Facts

1. Name five major centers of economic and political power.

2. What is the basic purpose of the Common Market?

3. What are some of the problems many of the developing nations must overcome in building their own strong economies?

Examining the Issues

■ In the mid-19th century, French writer Alexis de Tocqueville stated his belief that the United States and Russia would someday be the most powerful nations in the world. At the time Great Britain and France were much more powerful than either the United States or Russia. What factors do you suppose led de Tocqueville to this belief? How can these factors be applied to thoughts about power in the 21st century?

424 THE UNITED STATES IN TODAY'S WORLD

The United States' Position in the World Economy

The United States, as a center of power, is in the mainstream of the world's economic and political life. We are tied in many ways to the affairs of other lands.

AN INDUSTRIAL LEADER

One reason for America's position in today's world may be seen in the bar graph at the right. The graph shows the gross national products of the three leading industrial nations for the years 1960 and 1970. The gross national product, or GNP, is the money value of all goods and services produced by a country during a given year. As you can see, the GNP of the United States was much greater than that of its two closest rivals in 1970. Even so, it should be noted that between 1960 and 1970 both Japan and the Soviet Union had a greater percentage of increase than the United States.

At the close of World War II, the American GNP was far ahead of the GNP of any other country. We in the United States were fortunate because our factories, transportation systems, and communications facilities had not been damaged by the war. The Soviet Union, though victorious, had suffered millions of casualties and its land had been overrun by the Germans. Japan lay in ruins. The same was true of much of western Europe.

With American aid, the countries of western Europe were able to rebuild their factories and their transportation and communication systems. In the Soviet Union, recovery took place without American help. Under American occupation, Japan recovered slowly at first but with greater speed after 1952.

What does the future hold for the United States as an industrial power? There seems every reason to believe that the United States will continue to be the world's industrial leader for the foreseeable future. It seems equally likely that our position in international trade will continue to be strong. There is, however, reason to believe that, in the future, our economy will not be so far ahead of its rivals as it is at present.

Reading the Graph: In 1960 the Soviet Union's GNP was about $230,000,000,000. About how large was Japan's GNP in 1970?

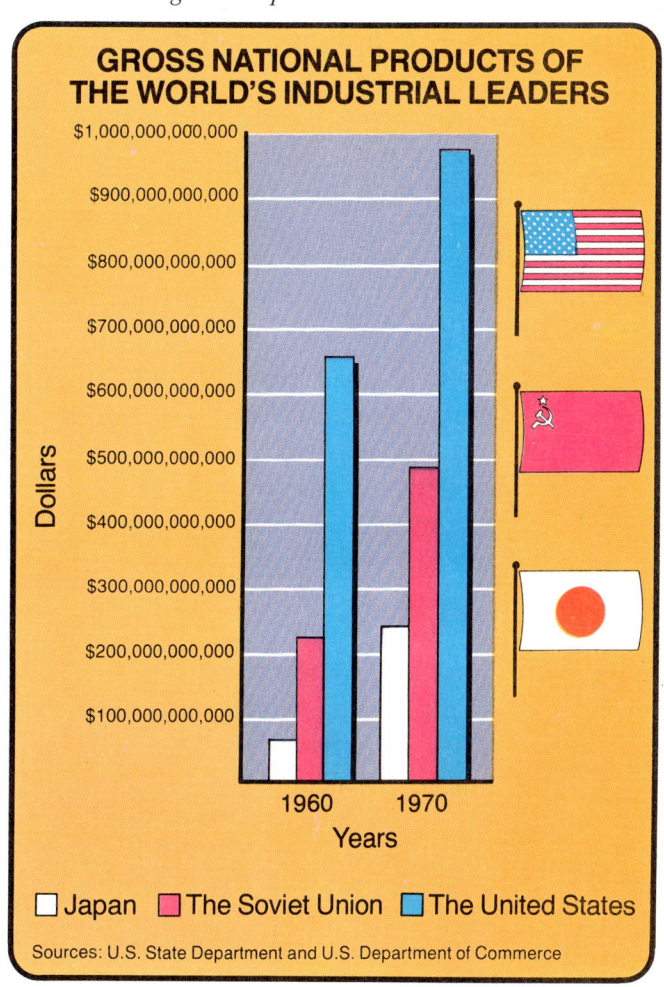

GROSS NATIONAL PRODUCTS OF THE WORLD'S INDUSTRIAL LEADERS

Sources: U.S. State Department and U.S. Department of Commerce

U.S. FOREIGN AID

An important part of American involvement in the world's economic and political affairs in recent times has been America's program of foreign aid. Between 1946 and 1970, the United States gave almost $150,000,000,000 in loans and gifts to more than 100 different countries.

The American aid program began in 1946 with a large loan to Great Britain. The loan was meant to help stimulate the economy of this war-weary ally. The following year, under the Truman Doctrine, the United States sent millions of dollars in economic and military aid to Greece and Turkey. Both countries were threatened by Communist takeovers. Then, in the late 1940s, came the Marshall Plan. Its purpose was to help a number of European countries rebuild economies that had been destroyed by the war.

The emphasis of the foreign aid program changed gradually during the 1950s. The new goal was to provide economic and military aid to countries in Latin America, Asia, and Africa. Through the 1960s the United States spent about $5,000,000,000 a year on military and economic aid. Some of the money was given as gifts. Some was given in the form of low-interest loans.

Foreign aid was often of benefit to American business as well as to the countries being helped. Much of the money given had to be spent to buy American goods. With foreign aid countries bought American machines, motor vehicles, and fertilizers. American farmers were also helped. Billions of dollars worth of surplus crops were sent abroad under a food-for-peace program.

In Latin America, foreign aid was part of a program called Alliance for Progress. In many countries funds were used to support the United States Peace Corps. The Peace Corps was set up in the early 1960s to offer expert advice to countries seeking economic advance. Volunteers in such fields as teaching, farming, and industry were sent to countries around the world.

Whatever the benefits of foreign aid, strong reactions were heard against it in Congress early in the 1970s. Many felt that the United States ought to reduce its commitments around the world. There was the added feeling that more American tax dollars should be spent on problems at home. There was also resentment over our aid to governments run by military rulers.

The growing opposition marked a major turn in American foreign policy. The change did not mean that America was ready to abandon its aid to other countries, but that new approaches were needed.

Getting the Facts

1. How does the United States' GNP compare with the GNPs of other major nations?

2. What were the basic goals of American foreign aid programs in the late 1940s? What have the goals been in the years since 1950?

Examining the Issues

■ What do you consider the greatest achievements of our program of foreign aid in the years since 1945? What problems have been associated with some of the programs? How do you think these problems should be dealt with?

Speaking Out

Hans Morgenthau

A well-known student of international affairs, Morgenthau believes that the United States has lost the faith of many democratic groups in other countries because we have given so much aid to undemocratic leaders.

"In its search for, and support of, allies, the United States has had to weigh its military needs against the political liabilities it might incur by associating itself with a government unpopular at home and abroad. Political preferences must obviously yield to military necessity, and in such a situation the United States has had to act on the principle that Winston Churchill stated in 1941 after the German attack on the Soviet Union when he said that if 'Hitler invaded Hell I would make at least a favorable reference to the Devil in the House of Commons.' Yet there is a difference between dealing with the 'Devil' at arm's length out of necessity and embracing him as a friend, 'our boy,' the champion of freedom, the embodiment of all the virtues. Instead of dealing with the 'Devil' as one businessman with another, in a matter-of-fact way, we have fraternized with him and convinced ourselves that the 'Devil,' since he is on our side, must really be an angel.

"Our attitudes throughout the world have been consistently oblivious of this subtle but crucial distinction. We have proved ourselves incapable of having certain dealings, required by our interests, with foreign governments without identifying ourselves with them politically Since it so happens that most of these governments are unpopular with their own peoples, we have paid for military benefits, such as they are, with a drastic decline in our prestige and influence among those peoples. In many of these nations, America is looked upon, with differing degrees of intensity, not as the last best hope of freedom but as the ally and main support of unpopular regimes."

1. What are some examples of aid given by the United States to undemocratic leaders in the years since World War II?

2. Under what circumstances, if any, do you think the United States should give aid to undemocratic governments?

Inquiry

What Should America's International Trade Policy Be?

Through most of our history, American business and trade have been concentrated mainly within our nation's borders. This has been possible for at least two reasons. We have been blessed with an abundance of natural resources. And our growing population has provided a constantly expanding market for American goods and services. With major exceptions, such as our shipments of crops to Europe and European loans to American businesses in the 19th century, foreign business and trade have made up only a small part of the American economy.

Today this situation is changing. Important American businesses may be found in other countries. Some are located in countries that are just beginning to develop their own modern economies. Many more are found in economically advanced countries where American businesses locate so as to be closer to markets.

There is also a change in the nature of our trade with other countries. Some of our natural resources are running out. American industries now need to import many key raw materials from other lands. To pay for these materials we need to export products of our factories. In doing this, we have to achieve a "favorable balance of trade." When a country exports (sells) more than it imports (buys), it is said to have a favorable balance of trade. More money is received than is spent.

The growth of American foreign trade in the years between 1954 and 1974 can be seen in the graph below.

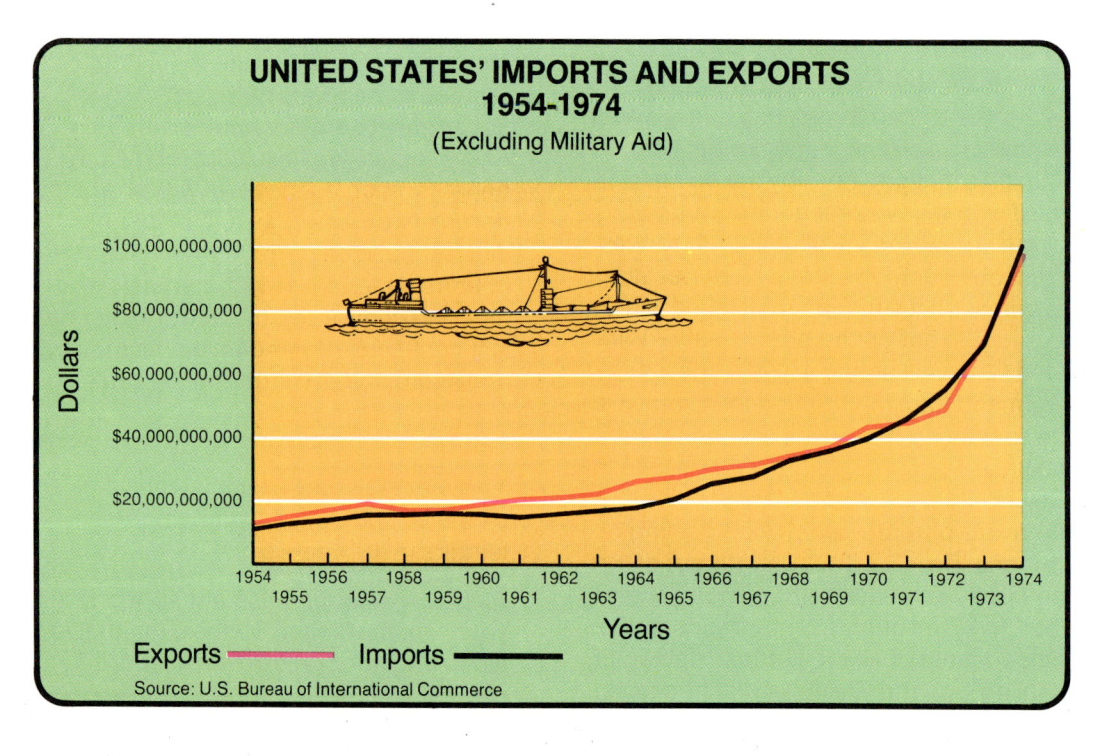

UNITED STATES' IMPORTS AND EXPORTS 1954-1974
(Excluding Military Aid)

Source: U.S. Bureau of International Commerce

THE UNITED STATES IN TODAY'S WORLD

Inquiry

The graph shows the increase in American imports and exports of goods and services as measured in billions of dollars.

Use the following questions to interpret the graph.

1. How much did our exports increase between 1954 and 1974? How much did imports increase during these years?

2. During what period of years did the United States have the most favorable balance of trade?

3. In what years were exports and imports almost the same?

Americans have tended to view the growth of our foreign trade with mixed emotions. In the past, Americans have had certain suspicions of overseas markets and foreign trade. Many worried that foreign goods would sell better than American goods in American markets. There was also the fear, in the early years of our country, that the existence of foreign goods in America would greatly slow the development of American industry. Long ago, in 1824, this kind of concern was expressed by Senator Henry Clay of Kentucky in a speech in the United States Senate. The following words are part of that address:

"The greatest want of civilized society is a market for the sale and exchange of the surplus produce of the labor of its members. This market may exist at home or abroad, or both, but it must exist somewhere if society prospers; and wherever it does exist, it should be competent to the absorption of the entire surplus of production.

"It is most desirable that there should be both a home and a foreign market. But, with respect to their relative superiority, I cannot entertain a doubt. The home market is first in order, and paramount in importance. . . .

"The creation of a home market is not only necessary to procure for our agriculture a just reward for its labors, but it is indispensable to obtain a supply for our necessary wants. If we cannot sell, we cannot buy. . . .

"The superiority of the home market results . . . from its steadiness and comparative certainty at all times . . . from its greater security; and . . . from an ultimate and not distant [increase] of consumption (and consequently of comfort) from increased quantity and reduced prices. . . .

"The measure of the wealth of a nation is indicated by the measure of its protection of its industry; and . . . the measure of the poverty of a nation is marked by that of the degree in which it neglects and abandons the care of its own industry, leaving it exposed to the action of foreign powers. . . ."

Senator Clay's speech was given mainly to convince other members of Congress to set up a protective tariff. A tariff is a tax on goods imported from other countries. A protective tariff is a tax set high enough to keep outside goods from competing successfully with home industries. Protective tariffs have been used through much of our country's history. To many, they seemed especially necessary in the 19th century to protect new American industries. During the 1930s and the years following World War II, the United States, in cooperation with certain other countries, worked for a general reduction of tariffs. In time, however, the competition of industry in other countries began to disturb many Americans. From this came demands for new trade policies that would again protect American industry. The magazine *Newsweek* described the

inquiry

changing views in its issue of March 23, 1970:

"World War II grew in part out of the ruinous international trade war of the Great Depression—and when the bombs had stopped falling, the nations of the free world swore that they would never again permit such provocation. They established a comprehensive framework for reducing trade barriers under a General Agreement on Tariffs and Trade (GATT). With little interruption, the participating nations have seen their prosperity increase ever since in step with ever-expanding, ever-freer world trade.

"Yet, after almost a month of mounting friction, the world's major trading blocs were hurling charge and countercharge of protectionism and bad faith at each other, with veiled threats of retaliation and strong indications that a major trade war was on the verge of breaking out....

"In the world of international trade relations, it is often all but impossible to tell precisely who is right. But the cause of the current battle is fairly clear: It stems from mounting American frustration at seeing the historic U.S. postwar trade surplus . . . shrink to very nearly nothing. At the same time, the U.S. share in total world exports is gradually declining.... But an equally important factor is the basic improvement in the ability of Europe and Japan to produce manufactured goods—particularly technologically sophisticated products in which the U.S. was once supreme...."

Among those most worried about foreign competition were American industrial workers. Their concerns were summarized by I. W. Abel, president of the United Steel Workers, in an address to a national conference of union leaders in March, 1970:

"It is true that as long as there have been nations, there have been problems about what crosses border lines. And nations have had to learn how to get along with each other. In the past, most workers have felt no special concern about foreign trade. But suddenly we have discovered that we have a problem, and for the first time workers are questioning and protesting foreign imports.

"As the name of this conference signifies, all of us are here because of what we call 'The Developing Crisis in International Trade.' We are here because our members have been and are being hurt by imports and they want something done about it....

"Some will make the charge that we are putting on the cloak of protectionism. Those who do so fail to recognize that old concepts and labels of 'free trade' and 'protectionism' have become obsolete . . . we still believe in a healthy expansion of trade with other nations. But our support for the balanced expansion of trade . . . does not mean that such expansion of trade should undercut unfairly the wages and working standards of Americans.... Perhaps the new concept, or more desirable objective in international trade, should be . . . 'fair trade....'

"We believe in competition, but we don't want competition in the U. S.—for our own workers and employers—based on inequity to foreign workers. While we recognize that there can be no international minimum wage, we can demand the elimination of foreign sweatshops. We can insist upon minimum international labor standards—perhaps a United Nations for labor standards...."

Statements such as the one you have just read are of great concern to people who believe in the benefits of free trade. Many worry that feelings such as those expressed by union leader Abel might lead to a fresh round of protectionism in the United States. One group that has long argued for free and

Inquiry

At present the United States is heavily dependent on other countries for coffee and oil. What other products come primarily from other countries? What substitute sources or products could be found if these foreign products were no longer available?

unrestricted foreign trade is the American Importers Association. The following are views of this group as stated in one of their booklets:

"Imports are essential to the economic health and security of America and to the maintenance of a high standard of living for her people. Imports provide materials vital to our defense and industry by making available those materials that are either unavailable or in short supply domestically. These imports are essential, and we could not maintain our

THE UNITED STATES AS A WORLD POWER **431**

Inquiry

present standard of living, to say nothing of growth with the future, if these imports were eliminated. . . . And it must be remembered that if we expect to sell our products abroad, we must buy from abroad. For it is with foreign exchange gained from their exports that other countries buy what we have to sell.

"And last, but certainly not least, the American consumer benefits in many ways from imports. He is given a much wider choice of essential and luxury goods; the prices of the things he buys are kept in line by competition from imports; the industries that supply him are kept technologically progressive by the need to compete here and abroad with the most advanced industries in the world; and his welfare in general gets a helping hand in the battle against inflation . . .

"One of the long-standing challenges to imports raised by protectionists is the allegation that disparate labor costs between U. S. and foreign producers give imports an unfair price advantage in U. S. markets. This challenge is unfounded. Actually, wages are only one part of the cost of production, and, in fact, increased productivity and efficiency in a developed country more than compensate for lower wage costs involved in producing the same or a competitive item in a less-developed country. Other production costs also must be considered, such as fringe benefits, raw material costs, and the cost of borrowing money. Among other industrialized countries these costs frequently outstrip those in the U. S. . . .

"Protectionists, however, would have the American people and the Congress believe that most industrial problems result from the 'flood' of imports. The glaring truth is that only a portion of our imports are 100 percent competitive with American products, and these came in under duty or quotas.

"A great amount of what we import, as has been shown, is not available in the United States, is in short supply here, or is not directly competitive with American products.

"Trade stimulates the growth of our whole domestic economy, and it builds bridges of understanding and cooperation with the rest of the world. The benefits speak for themselves."

In all the discussions of foreign trade, one factor is often overlooked. This is the growing number of giant companies that now have branches in many different countries. Some of these companies are American. Others are foreign. A number are so large that they are able to rival governments in their wealth and power. The following is a description of these giant businesses. It appeared in the magazine *U.S. News and World Report*.

"A powerful new force is emerging in the world, sweeping across national borders and challenging politicians for world leadership.

"It's something called 'multinational companies.'

"These are firms that are rapidly branching out all over the globe, doing billions of dollars' worth of business annually.

"Their economic power is becoming so great that some experts predict in the next decade or two these firms will have a global influence as great as all but the largest nations.

"Multinational firms run manufacturing plants around the world from major industrial centers to remote areas of under-developed countries, supplying jobs for hundreds of thousands.

"Huge financial transactions involving currencies of many nations make these outfits a major factor in international banking and finance.

"Well-staffed sales organizations backed by elaborate merchandising and advertising promotions make the multi-

What advantages do international business activities offer to American society in general? What disadvantages may be involved?

national concern a formidable competitor anywhere in the world it chooses to go.

"More and more of the executives needed to run these far-flung business empires are being recruited locally, tightening the bonds between branch managers and the home office. Many of the giant complexes are American, but a growing number are European or Japanese.

"Out of the top 200 U. S. companies, 80 do 25 percent or more of their business abroad. Of the 200 largest firms outside the U. S., 80 also do a quarter or more of their business in foreign markets. . . .

"Many smaller firms both in America and abroad today are moving heavily into international business, not only as exporters, but as owners of manufacturing and sales subsidiaries in worldwide markets."

In support of multinational companies, one American economist has taken issue with what he describes as the traditional economic view of the world. This view, he says, is of a world "divided into a number of individual nation-states, among which products move freely but the factors of production (land, capital, management) move only with difficulty, if at all." He believes that this view must change. In today's world, he writes, "the production of goods to satisfy consumers' wants and investors' hopes is no longer strictly a national matter. . . . The time of international production is upon us."

A well-known American historian is bothered by this prospect. "If the present tendencies continue," he writes, "the third industrial power in the world, after America and Russia, could be, not Europe, but American industry in Europe."

Analyzing America's Foreign Trade and Investment

The differing views given in the last few pages raise a number of questions.

In what ways are the views expressed by Senator Henry Clay a century and a half ago similar to those expressed by I. W. Abel in 1970?

Why is it desirable for a country to try to export more than it imports?

Do you think governments should limit the amount of money businesses can invest in foreign countries? Explain.

THE UNITED STATES AS A WORLD POWER 433

Citizenship Laboratory

Review of Basic Ideas

1. The United States emerged as a great power during World War I. This new status led to a change in the goals of American foreign policy. In the years before the war, we had tried to avoid involvement in European conflicts, while showing a special interest in the affairs of the Western Hemisphere. After World War I, the United States found it increasingly necessary to play a larger role in world affairs. World War II left the United States and the Soviet Union as the world's two great superpowers. Economic and political rivalry between the two powers led to what has been called the Cold War.

2. Three other important centers of world power have emerged in the years since World War II. Many countries in western Europe have banded together to form the economically powerful Common Market. In the Far East, Japan and Communist China have become major powers.

3. In terms of gross national product, the United States is the world leader. Both the second and third place nations, the Soviet Union and Japan, are far behind the United States in the production of goods and services. The United States also has a strong position in world trade. In order to help other countries develop their economies and to achieve a number of our own political goals, the United States has given billions of dollars worth of foreign aid to countries around the world in the years since World War II. Aid has been both military and economic.

Questions to Think About

1. What were the foreign policy goals of the United States in the years before World War I? What factors made it possible for the United States to reach many of these goals?

2. How has the Cold War rivalry of the United States and the Soviet Union changed in recent years?

3. In what other parts of the world might an economic arrangement similar to the European Common Market be useful?

4. What are some of the strengths and weaknesses of the economy of Communist China?

5. In today's world, the United States, the Soviet Union, Europe, Japan, and Communist China are major centers of power. Within the next century, what other centers of world power do you think will develop? Why do you think they will develop in these areas?

6. What do you think the goals of America's foreign aid program should be? To what countries should aid be given? What forms of aid should be given? Explain your answers.

Words and Relationships

Define each of the terms in the first column. Then show how each term is related to the item listed opposite it by using both items in a sentence or short paragraph.

1.	manifest destiny	expansion
2.	Monroe Doctrine	Western Hemisphere
3.	containment	communism
4.	superpower	nuclear weapons
5.	Cold War	economic and political rivalry
6.	Common Market	economic power
7.	Marshall Plan	foreign aid
8.	Peace Corps	economic development
9.	protective tariff	American industry
10.	multinational companies	global business

Building a Future

Gross national product figures for the United States, the Soviet Union, and Japan in 1960 and 1970 are shown in the graph on page 425. Projecting these figures, a group of economic analysts estimate that in 1980 the gross national products of the three countries will be $1,450 billion for the United States, $900 billion for the Soviet Union, and $570 billion for Japan. If the estimates are correct, the United States will still be ahead, but the rate of economic growth will be slower than in either of the other two countries. In view of this possibility, do you think American business and government should try to speed up our country's rate of economic growth? Why, or why not?

Using the figures on page 425 and the estimates given above, make an estimate of what you think the gross national products of the three countries will be in 1990. (In doing your calculations, keep in mind the percentages of growth between 1960 and 1980.) What other factors should be considered in making these estimates?

In 1970 the combined gross national product of the European Common Market countries was about the same as that of the Soviet Union. What is your prediction about the economic growth of the Common Market group? Do you think the growth will be slower or faster than that of the Soviet Union? Explain.

THE UNITED STATES AS A WORLD POWER

19 Democracy and Other Political Systems

There are over 150 countries in the world today. Each has a political system that is the product of the country's history and its belief about how people can best be served.

Here in the United States we have a political system we call a democracy. Our democratic government follows a written constitution. Technically our government is a republic because the American people rule through their elected representatives. A number of other countries also regard their governments as democracies. Each of these governments has unique characteristics. But in each country the people govern themselves.

Democracy has strong competition from other forms of government. Three fourths, or more, of the world's people live under political systems that are not democratic. Many countries, despite their use of such democratic-sounding words as "republic" and "freedom" have governments controlled by a few leaders rather than by the will of the citizens.

This is an important fact. As never before in history, countries are tied together by instant communications, speeding airplanes, and trade that leaps national boundaries. All countries are

THE UNITED STATES IN TODAY'S WORLD

thus increasingly being brought into close contact. Every government keeps a close watch on the activities of every other government. Each is watching for changes that may affect its own political system.

The interdependence of countries is something with which we will always have to live. As American citizens, we often find it difficult to understand the actions of political systems different from our own. Even governments with political systems most similar to our own sometimes follow policies that we Americans think unwise.

Political Systems and Ideas About Government

Governments are the products of ideas. They are based on beliefs about how people can best be organized to live in groups.

Here in our own country people brought many ideas about government from other lands. In the New World they put these ideas into practice. Once independence was achieved, the ideas were written into the state and national constitutions and laws under which we operate today.

Other countries have had their own historical experiences. But whatever their history or their form of government, all have one thing in common. All countries have some system of rules or laws. The rules may come from a dictator or from a representative assembly. But, for any society to operate, there must be laws. Without them a country cannot function in a peaceful manner.

VALUES AND POLITICAL SYSTEMS

As we examine political systems around the world, it is important to begin with people's values. Values are those ideas that people cherish. They are beliefs about standards of conduct and things that go together to make a good life. They are the moral and ethical codes by which people live.

When we think about different forms of government, there is a basic thought to keep in mind. The kind of government that exists and that will develop in any country depends in part upon the values held by its citizens. The people of a country, in other words, will have their own ideas about what they believe to be a desirable political system.

To understand how this principle works, it is necessary to have some knowledge of the values of different groups of people. Otherwise, it is difficult to understand why much of the world can be happy living under a form of government that is different from our own. How, we may ask, can a Chinese citizen be content to live under Communist rule? How is this kind of rule a reflection of Chinese values? Here we must remember that our values are greatly influenced by the society in which we live. We generally acquire most of our values in our families and other social institutions. All of these institutions can be influenced by government.

In countries where there is little freedom, the young can be taught the values the leaders desire. Thus, through schools, youth organizations, and the like, a dictatorial regime can direct the

In what ways do you think your high school years would be different if you were living in Communist China? In what ways do you think they would be the same?

thoughts of the rising generations. At the same time, the government can take steps to control the thoughts and actions of older citizens.

The transmission of values to coming generations is also the task of free societies such as our own. The difference is that in a democracy the young are given a much greater chance to develop their own values.

Regardless of how much control is exercised over the learning of values, the values of the people in most countries are constantly in a state of change. Thus, when we examine the government of any country, we need to ask a number of different questions about the values of the people. How have these values developed out of the past? What are they today? What directions may they take in the future?

CONFLICTING IDEOLOGIES

Values give rise to ideologies. An ideology may be defined as a group of beliefs that affect the way of life of the people of a country as well as the way a country is governed. Thus, we in the United States have an American way of life that is clearly related to our democratic way of governing ourselves. We have developed our own ways of doing things by putting our American values into action. And we have, in like manner, continued to support a government based on democratic ideas.

Three major political ideologies can be found in the world today: (1) democracy, (2) totalitarianism, and (3) authoritarianism. The government of every country is an adaptation of one of these ideologies. Each ideology involves more than just a system of government.

Each is a way of thinking about human relations, political and otherwise.

Democracy as an ideology has as its major goal the building of a society in which each person has the freedom and opportunity to develop. The rules or laws of such a society are meant to provide each person with opportunities for self-development. In a democratic government the people are the rulers. The government is the servant. The purpose of government is to serve the people.

In contrast, the goal of totalitarianism as a way of life and a form of government is total government control of the people. A totalitarian government seeks to control all the thoughts and activities of the people. The government rules. The people are considered the servants of the government.

Though in many ways the opposite of democratic governments, totalitarian governments often use democratic terms and techniques. There is, for example, much use of the word "freedom." The difference is that under totalitarian rule, people soon learn that they become "free" only when they conform to the will or purposes of the government. That is, of course, not freedom at all. Totalitarian governments also make use of the term "political party." But since only one political party is allowed to function, this is a misuse of the term. The very idea of a political party assumes the existence of many parties competing in free elections.

Another important difference between democracy and totalitarianism involves the use of laws. In a democratic country people may do anything that is not specifically forbidden by law. Furthermore, people may not be punished for any act that is not specifically forbidden at the time the act is committed. In a totalitarian country people may do only what is allowed by the government. Moreover, people may later be punished for acts that at the time are not defined as illegal. This means that people must not only know what the government wants at present but also guess what the government may want in the future.

The way in which laws apply to the actions of public officials also differs in democratic and totalitarian countries. A public official in a democratic country is supposed to do only what the law authorizes. In a totalitarian country a public official may often do almost anything that is not specifically forbidden by the law or government leaders.

There is a tendency for people to use the term authoritarianism to mean the same thing as totalitarianism. This is a mistake. Though both are terms for anti-democratic governments, there are important differences between the two systems. The major goal of an authoritarian government is to control the political activities of the people. In business affairs, family life, religious practices, and so on, the citizen is left relatively free. The main concern of an authoritarian government is that the people do not interfere with the way in which the leaders run the government.

It is perhaps not surprising to learn that most governments throughout history have been authoritarian. This includes most of the governments that function in our world today. In these countries, people have some degree of freedom. They can move freely and express themselves in all but political matters. For these reasons, many people find authoritarianism an attractive system. It allows certain kinds of freedom while not requiring the citizens to exercise political responsibility. The idea is to let someone else do the governing.

The people who wrote our Constitution were well aware of the appeal of authoritarianism. Consequently, in writing the Constitution, they included a separation of powers, checks and balances, and statements of human rights. These things, they hoped, would help prevent the growth of authoritarianism. The democratic government we have today is a tribute to their wisdom.

POLITICAL SYSTEMS IN THE MODERN WORLD

In our world today, there are many examples of each of the three types of government we have just discussed.

A basic feature of today's democratic countries is the presence of two or more political parties. These parties take

In January of 1977 Freedom House, a nonpartisan organization, described the political systems of the world in the manner shown below. With which descriptions do you agree? With which do you disagree? Which have changed greatly since early 1977?

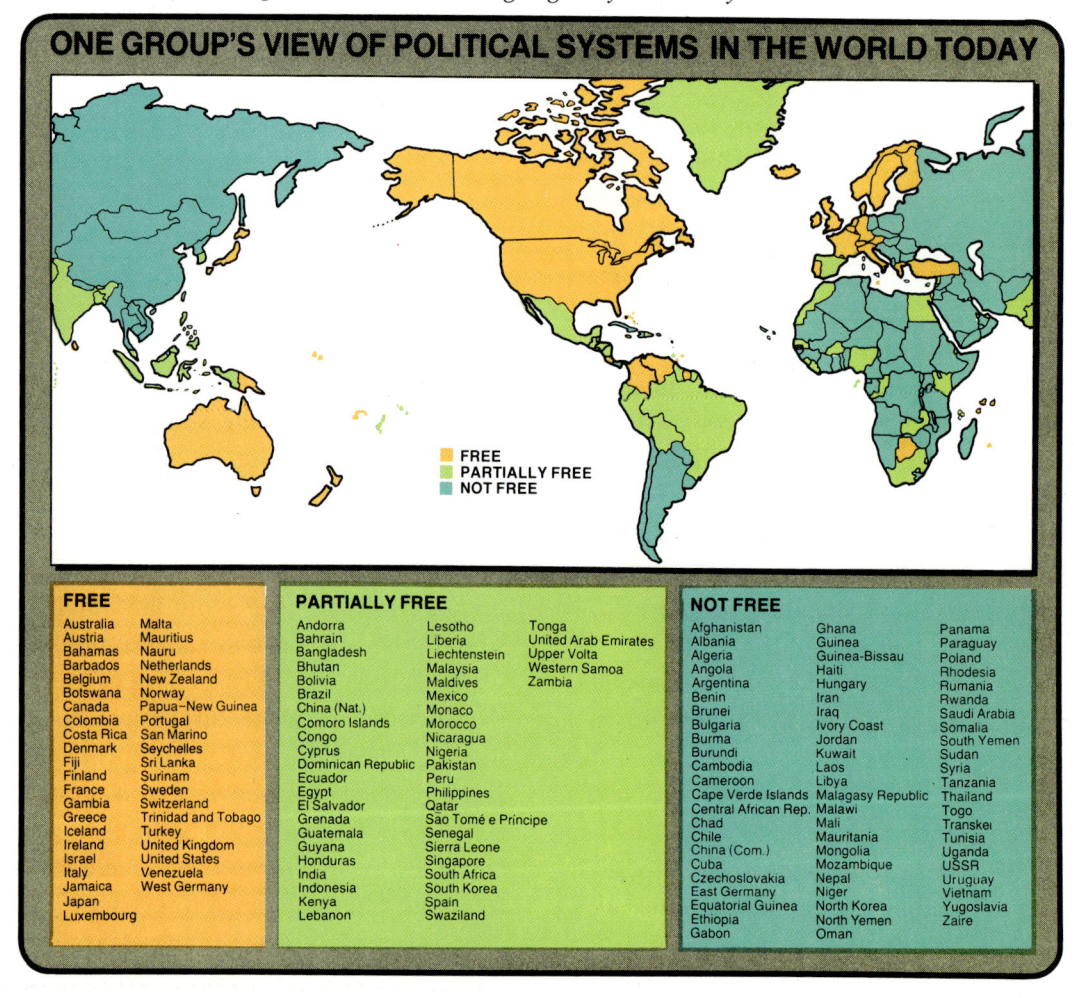

ONE GROUP'S VIEW OF POLITICAL SYSTEMS IN THE WORLD TODAY

FREE
- Australia
- Austria
- Bahamas
- Barbados
- Belgium
- Botswana
- Canada
- Colombia
- Costa Rica
- Denmark
- Fiji
- Finland
- France
- Gambia
- Greece
- Iceland
- Ireland
- Israel
- Italy
- Jamaica
- Japan
- Luxembourg
- Malta
- Mauritius
- Nauru
- Netherlands
- New Zealand
- Norway
- Papua–New Guinea
- Portugal
- San Marino
- Seychelles
- Sri Lanka
- Surinam
- Sweden
- Switzerland
- Trinidad and Tobago
- Turkey
- United Kingdom
- United States
- Venezuela
- West Germany

PARTIALLY FREE
- Andorra
- Bahrain
- Bangladesh
- Bhutan
- Bolivia
- Brazil
- China (Nat.)
- Comoro Islands
- Congo
- Cyprus
- Dominican Republic
- Ecuador
- Egypt
- El Salvador
- Grenada
- Guatemala
- Guyana
- Honduras
- India
- Indonesia
- Kenya
- Lebanon
- Lesotho
- Liberia
- Liechtenstein
- Malaysia
- Maldives
- Mexico
- Monaco
- Morocco
- Nicaragua
- Nigeria
- Pakistan
- Peru
- Philippines
- Qatar
- São Tomé e Príncipe
- Senegal
- Sierra Leone
- Singapore
- South Africa
- South Korea
- Spain
- Swaziland
- Tonga
- United Arab Emirates
- Upper Volta
- Western Samoa
- Zambia

NOT FREE
- Afghanistan
- Albania
- Algeria
- Angola
- Argentina
- Benin
- Brunei
- Bulgaria
- Burma
- Burundi
- Cambodia
- Cameroon
- Cape Verde Islands
- Central African Rep.
- Chad
- Chile
- China (Com.)
- Cuba
- Czechoslovakia
- East Germany
- Equatorial Guinea
- Ethiopia
- Gabon
- Ghana
- Guinea
- Guinea-Bissau
- Haiti
- Hungary
- Iran
- Iraq
- Ivory Coast
- Jordan
- Kuwait
- Laos
- Libya
- Malagasy Republic
- Malawi
- Mali
- Mauritania
- Mongolia
- Mozambique
- Nepal
- Niger
- North Korea
- North Yemen
- Oman
- Panama
- Paraguay
- Poland
- Rhodesia
- Rumania
- Rwanda
- Saudi Arabia
- Somalia
- South Yemen
- Sudan
- Syria
- Tanzania
- Thailand
- Togo
- Transkei
- Tunisia
- Uganda
- USSR
- Uruguay
- Vietnam
- Yugoslavia
- Zaire

THE UNITED STATES IN TODAY'S WORLD

part in free elections. It is through these elections that the people's representatives are chosen.

In authoritarian countries, one person or a small group controls the government. This is done with the support of the military, business leaders, or some combination of powerful groups within the country. The most extreme form of authoritarian government is the absolute monarchy. One person rules with unquestioned authority. Under the monarch is a hierarchy of other privileged people, who form a governing elite. In today's world, there are few absolute monarchs. Modern authoritarian governments are most likely to be military governments, or juntas. Authoritarian leaders, whether military or civilian, generally seek the support of a combination of powerful groups within the country. Support may come from the army, unions, or businesses.

Totalitarian governments differ from authoritarian governments in the degree of control the rulers have over other groups in the country. In totalitarian countries, the government seeks to control all groups. The government does not depend on other powerful groups for support. Instead it uses all groups for its own purposes. The major totalitarian governments of the 20th century have been Fascist governments in Germany and Italy and Communist governments in Russia and China.

Most of today's authoritarian and totalitarian countries have a single political party. Members of this party have a monopoly on governmental offices. Party membership may also be needed for advancement in non-political fields. Elections are generally held. But they are largely meaningless. In a few cases, parties and elections are not used even for the sake of appearances.

The form of government in a country may or may not indicate the kind of political system that the country really has. Great Britain is a monarchy. However, the British have a democratic political system. On the other hand, Iran has a shah, or king, who heads an authoritarian system. The Soviet Union, which is ruled by a Communist party, has a totalitarian system. Yugoslavia is also ruled by a Communist party. But, under the leadership of Marshall Tito, an authoritarian government has emerged. In our own democracy, we have two major political parties. But parts of the country have at times been run by one party.

These illustrations emphasize the point that the government of a country may be a combination of elements from different political systems. The question of whether a government is democratic, totalitarian, or authoritarian may be a matter of degree.

Getting the Facts

1. What are the three major political ideologies found in today's world?

2. How do the three political ideologies differ?

Forming an Opinion

■ Under which of the three different political systems found in today's world would you prefer to live? Why? What do you consider the greatest advantages and disadvantages of living under the other two forms of government?

Democratic Political Systems

Democratic political systems may differ in form. Today's democratic governments, however, all have one thing in common. They all have competing political parties. These parties are able to act as they choose without interference from the government. In free and fair elections, the parties offer candidates for political office. When the votes have been counted, the unsuccessful parties accept the choice of the voters. This is an essential part of democracy.

Here in the United States we hold elections to choose the members of our legislative bodies—Congress, state legislatures, and city councils. We also vote for the heads of our many executive branches—President, governors, and mayors. We do not vote for federal judges. Often, however, judges in the state courts are required to stand for election. This kind of democratic political system seems to meet the needs of the people of our large and diverse country. In other democratic countries, somewhat different forms of government may seem more appropriate.

WESTERN EUROPEAN DEMOCRACIES

Western Europe is the source of much of the world's democratic heritage. In most of the countries, democracy remains the preferred political system. Generally, the European democracies have parliamentary forms of government. This form takes its name from the British Parliament, a long-lived legislative assembly. The legislative body chooses from its membership a prime minister or chief executive who serves as the executive head of the government. Usually, the person chosen is the leader of the political party with the largest number of seats in the legislature.

In a parliamentary government the people vote only for members of the legislative branch. They do not vote directly for the chief executive. The prime minister or chief executive is directly responsible only to the legislature and must be acceptable to the majority in that body. If the legislature casts a vote of "no confidence," the chief executive is supposed to step down to allow the selection of another leader who will carry out the wishes of the majority in the legislature. In many cases, a vote of "no confidence" leads to a call for a general election. The members of the newly elected legislature may then choose a new executive or reelect the executive who has stepped down.

Some democracies in western Europe are organized in other ways. France, for example, has what might be called a presidential form of government. Under the French constitution the people elect a president as well as a legislature. The president is given a great deal of power and may even dissolve the legislature by calling for a new election.

But regardless of the form the government takes, political power in most of the countries of western Europe rests with the people.

WESTERN HEMISPHERE DEMOCRACIES

The democratic heritage of western Europe has been carried to other parts of the Western Hemisphere as well as to our own country. Canada, for example, has a well-defined democracy. Like much of Europe, Canada has a parliamentary form of government. The Parliament chooses a prime minister from among the members of its "lower house" or House of Commons. A large country, Canada is divided into provinces similar to our states. As in our own federal system, power is divided between the national government and the governments of the provinces.

Mexico has no actively competing political parties. It does, however, have many elements of a democratic system. In South America, one of the best illustrations of a strong democracy has long been found in Uruguay. In 1976, however, there was a military take-over of the government of Uruguay. The future of democracy in Uruguay is now in doubt. Steps toward the development of strong democracies have also been made by other South American countries from time to time.

OTHER DEMOCRACIES

The British Empire, during the 18th and 19th centuries, covered a large part of the world. The empire builders carried with them British ideas about democratic government. As a consequence, a number of independent countries, once part of the British Empire, now have democratic governments. This British influence can be found today in the governments of such countries as Australia, New Zealand, and Singapore.

Japan has developed in recent years its own form of democracy. The same is true of the young country of Israel on the shores of the eastern Mediterranean.

A few other democratic countries could be mentioned, but the total num-

The distinction we make between the executive and lawmaking branches of government is not made in the British Parliament or in the other parliamentary governments in Europe. What are the advantages of their system? of ours?

ber is not large. Most of the people of the world do not live in democracies. Because we Americans are so accustomed to a democratic form of government, we are apt to believe that self-government is the direction in which all people will move. The fact is that people in many other countries are busily engaged in organizing governments that are not at all like our own.

Getting the Facts

1. In what general ways are all democratic forms of government alike? In what ways may their governments differ?

2. Name at least five democratic political systems found in the world today.

Examining the Issues

■ Think of your study of world history. What factors do you think have had the greatest influence in leading certain countries to develop democratic forms of government?

Inquiry

Democratic Traditions

Democracy, as a form of government and a way of life, has been evolving for more than 2,500 years. It is a system of human relations that offers a great deal of individual freedom. But it calls for human responsibility as well. Based on the belief that people are able to govern themselves, democracy is a form of government derived from the consent of the governed.

There are countless landmarks in the long history of the democratic tradition. The following list contains only a few of the major landmarks. The purpose of this inquiry is to determine how each of these landmarks may, or may not, have helped further the democratic idea in the world. In other words, you will need to decide which are truly a part of the democratic tradition and which merely make use of democratic words.

You will find information about these items in textbooks of world history, encyclopedias, and books that deal directly with the subjects on the list.

- Judeo-Christian moral and ethical teachings
- Athenian society in ancient Greece
- Roman law
- Magna Charta, 1215
- English Bill of Rights, 1689
- American Declaration of Independence, 1776
- French Declaration of the Rights of Man, 1789
- Abraham Lincoln's Emancipation Proclamation, 1863
- Woodrow Wilson's 14 Points, 1918
- Fundamental Rights and Duties of Citizens, Soviet Union Constitution of 1936
- Rights and Duties of Citizens, Chinese Constitution of 1937
- Franklin D. Roosevelt's Four Freedoms, 1941
- Charter of the United Nations, 1945

What is this cartoonist saying about American democracy? What changes have been made in recent years to help correct the problems noted? What changes do you think are still needed?

HEAR YE! HEAR YE!

Historical Interpretation

Which of the items seem to have had the greatest influence on the development of modern ideas about democracy? Explain why in each case.

Which of the items might be regarded as of little influence, or as even opposed to our ideas about democracy? Why might people or groups opposed to democracy use so many democratic terms?

In your study, what other situations or events did you encounter that may also have contributed a great deal to our ideas about democracy?

Authoritarian Political Systems

In many countries of the world the government is under the rule of a single leader or a small elite. These authoritarian governments may be military dictatorships supported by the country's army. Or, they may be governments supported by one or more civilian groups. Generally these groups are made up of business leaders, land owners, or members of labor unions.

Not uncommonly, authoritarian leaders call their governments democratic. The members of the legislative bodies and the heads of state may be chosen in elections. The difference between this and democracy, however, is that the spirit of these governments is one of semi-permanent leadership by a single person or a small group. The lawmakers and heads of state all follow a single ideology, and the elections are not free.

Authoritarian governments give their citizens no real political freedom. The ruling groups maintain firm control of the reins of government. In most cases, however, the people of the country have considerable freedom in social and economic matters. This is one of the important differences between authoritarian and totalitarian governments.

AUTHORITARIAN GOVERNMENTS IN EUROPE

Under the rule of General Franco, Spain had a long-lived authoritarian government. Franco's government was installed during the course of the Spanish Civil War (1936-39). Guided by a Fascist political philosophy in some ways similar to that of Nazi Germany, the Spanish government worked to strengthen the country's economy. There was some improvement in the standard of living of the people. But political and civil rights were greatly limited. The death of Franco in 1975 offered hopes of greater freedom. In the neighboring country of Portugal, authoritarian governments have been in power since 1933.

A military government was set up in Greece in 1967 after the military leaders staged a coup, claiming that the country was threatened by communism. Greece's king went into exile, leaving the military in total control. The military government was replaced by a civilian government in 1974.

Yugoslavia, which has had a Communist government since 1945, has moved in the direction of less authoritarian control from the central government and greater regional political power. It is a country with two political parties, both of which are Communist dominated. The people of Yugoslavia, however, enjoy considerable freedom of movement and expression.

AUTHORITARIAN GOVERNMENTS IN THE WESTERN HEMISPHERE

Latin America has proven one of the most fertile fields for the growth of authoritarian governments. Most of the Latin American countries won their independence in the early 19th century. Leaders in many of the countries drafted constitutions with the idea of setting up democratic governments. However, the

In many South American countries control of the armed forces guarantees control of the government.

absence of democratic traditions and the presence of unstable conditions worked against true democracy. It soon became apparent that the easiest way to gain political power was through the use of military power. As a consequence, the history of much of Latin America has been that of successful and unsuccessful military revolts.

Stable civilian governments have been set up in some Latin American countries, among them Mexico and Costa Rica. In country after country, however, the threat of revolt remains. As recently as 1970, at least a dozen countries in Latin America had governments that could be characterized as authoritarian military regimes.

AUTHORITARIAN GOVERNMENTS IN AFRICA

Many of the new countries in Africa have followed the Latin American pattern. The majority of the governments of Africa are authoritarian. Some are powerful monarchies, such as the government of the Kingdom of Morocco. Others have one-party governments. Most authoritarian governments in Africa hold elections, but have only one political party.

In many African countries, civilian one-party governments have been replaced by military governments. When the new countries were first formed, the leaders were generally part of a small elite that had led the independence movements. In many cases, the governments they set up were inefficient or corrupt, and the military stepped in to set up a more stable government. In some cases, in Libya and the Zaire Republic, for example, these military governments have been fairly successful. They have provided stable and efficient governments. In most cases, however, military elites have merely replaced civilian elites.

AUTHORITARIAN GOVERNMENTS IN OTHER AREAS

Authoritarian governments can also be found in many other parts of the world. In the Middle East, military regimes have held power in countries such as Iraq and Syria. In southern Asia, authoritarian governments have flourished in a number of countries—Pakistan, Indonesia, and many of the small countries of Indochina. In Indonesia, for example, the end of Dutch rule was followed by a parliamentary form of government. A constitution was proclaimed in 1950, and many people had hopes that a democracy would be established. The government, however, soon came under the strong authoritarian rule of one leader.

THE FUTURE OF AUTHORITARIAN RULE

Whether the many authoritarian governments in today's world will move toward democracy or totalitarianism, or in some other direction, is a question yet to be answered. It is undoubtedly true that people without a tradition of self-government have great difficulty establishing truly democratic governments. On the other hand, it is very likely that there are at least a few people in every country who value the ideas of personal freedom and self-government.

Getting the Facts

1. Which freedoms do people living under authoritarian governments generally have? Which freedoms are the people in these countries generally denied?

2. Name at least five authoritarian political systems that can be found in the world today.

Examining the Issues

■ What are some of the factors that might help explain why there are so many more authoritarian governments than either democratic or totalitarian governments? What changes in authoritarian countries or in the world in general might lead the people in authoritarian countries to set up democracies?

DEMOCRACY AND OTHER POLITICAL SYSTEMS

Totalitarian Political Systems

Totalitarian governments rose to importance during the 20th century. Indeed, some political scientists have claimed that such governments could not have been formed in the years before the 20th century. They argue that governments must have modern mass communication, powerful weapons, and other kinds of advanced technology before they can try to control all aspects of their people's lives. Only in the 20th century has this technology been available. And the technology has been of great use in totalitarianism countries, notably in Fascist Italy and Germany, and in Communist Russia and China.

FASCIST ITALY AND GERMANY

In the years after World War I, Fascist governments came to power in Italy under Benito Mussolini and in Germany under Adolf Hitler. These governments arose in the wake of the social and economic upheavals brought on by the war. Initially they were supported by business, military, and middle class groups. These groups feared socialist or Communist take-overs. They had also suffered from the depressed economic conditions in their countries.

The Fascist leaders promised to restore the national glory of their countries. They also promised to rid their countries of "evil foreign influences." According to the leaders, these were liberals, socialists, Communists, and Jews.

What characteristics of totalitarian governments are shown in this photograph of Hitler and Mussolini?

Finally, the leaders promised to replace the competitive aspects of life with a society in which all people would work together for the good of the country.

In Italy, a police state was set up to protect the rich from the poor. In Germany, the groups that had helped Hitler gain power were turned into tools for implementing Hitler's own racial and political goals. German industry was placed under direct government control through a Four-Year Economic Plan. Churches were regulated. The secret police, the Gestapo, was everywhere rooting out "subversive thought." All independent organizations were either adapted to meet party needs or crushed. These experiments in Fascist totalitarianism were cut short when Italy and Germany lost World War II.

THE RISE OF THE COMMUNIST FORM OF TOTALITARIANISM

Today about one third of the people in the world live under some form of Communist government. The first modern Communist government was set up in Russia after the Russian Revolution in 1917. Subsequent events have caused this revolution to be regarded as one of the truly important episodes in history.

The ideas that gave rise to modern communism came from the writings of German philosopher Karl Marx. In 1847, as a struggling young writer, he published, along with his friend Frederick Engels, a pamphlet called *The Communist Manifesto*. Later, he wrote a much longer work entitled *Capital*.

In his writings, Marx examined human society in terms of its economic structure. His own western society, he believed, was engaged in a "class

Marx expected revolution to come first in the highly industrialized countries of western Europe—not in Russia.

struggle." The struggle was between the capitalist owners and those who worked for them. Marx thought that under a capitalist system the working class would naturally be used for the advantage of the owners. The only way the workers could end this situation, he thought, was by violent revolution against the capitalist class. After this working class revolution, all economic facilities—factories, railroads, power plants, and so on—would be taken over by the people.

The program Marx set forth appealed to many. However, it soon proved to have important weaknesses. Marx predicted that the workers in the capitalist countries of Europe would grow progressively poorer. This poverty would help bring about the revolution. These workers have, instead, become much better off. Marx also thought that the governments of capitalist countries

DEMOCRACY AND OTHER POLITICAL SYSTEMS

would come under the sole control of the capitalist class. On the contrary, governments in capitalist countries continue to be strongly influenced by many different groups. Among these are the military, labor unions, and ethnic, racial, and religious groups. Nevertheless, for all his miscalculations about the future of Europe, Marx's ideas have had a great influence on political systems and political thinking around the world. In part, this is due to the fact that people in many of the poorer countries feel that change is not coming fast enough.

COMMUNISM IN THE SOVIET UNION

The founder of the Communist system in the Soviet Union was a Russian named Nikolai Lenin. Lenin became converted to Marxist communism as a young man. As a speaker and writer, he carried his ideas beyond his land into western Europe during the early years of the 20th century. Typical of his message were these lines: " 'Freedom' is a grand word, but under the banner of freedom for industry the most predatory wars were waged, under the banner of freedom of labor, the working people were robbed."

Lenin was out of the country when revolution flared up in Russia in 1917. Returning quickly, he took command of the small but well-organized Bolshevik Communist Party. Though representing only a small part of the Russian people at the time, the Bolsheviks were able to gain control of the disorganized government of Russia. From that time forward no free elections have been held.

The first head of the new Soviet government was Lenin. When Lenin died, his place was taken by Joseph Stalin. Stalin ruled as an iron-fisted dictator for a quarter of a century, from 1928 to 1953. In 1936 a new constitution was written. This constitution, under which the Soviet Union still operates, calls for a two-house legislative body called the Supreme Soviet. The Supreme Soviet elects a Presidium. The head of this body is the chief of state, or President, of the Soviet Union. There is also a Council of Ministers, the head of which is the prime minister.

Soviet leaders have often said that their 1936 constitution is democratic. They call attention to the election of members of the Supreme Soviet. They also point to the fact that the constitution contains a list of the "Fundamental Rights and Duties of Citizens." But the fact remains that the government of the Soviet Union is run entirely by the Communist Party and its leaders.

The Russian Communist Party has several million members. In theory, all these many members help direct party affairs. In actuality, the party is directed from the top down. At the top is the Politburo, a body of only a dozen party members. Below the Politburo there is a Central Committee of about 100 members. Below this committee is the All-Union Party Congress, a group of about 1,500 elected representatives.

The leaders of the Soviet government are also the leaders of the Communist Party. These leaders run not only the country's political life but also its economic life. All important industry is government owned. The same is true of businesses. There are also government owned farms, or collectives. Some private ownership of property is allowed.

In a number of cases, people own houses, small plots of land, or small businesses.

The government also has considerable control over the ideas and actions of the people. The Soviet leaders use their power to build and maintain the people's commitment to the principles of communism as set forth by Marx and Lenin.

COMMUNISM IN CHINA

China is the world's most heavily populated country. Like the Soviet Union, it has adopted a political system based on Communist ideas. For 2,000 years the authoritarian governments of the Chinese Empire were able to control much of eastern Asia. Then, during the 19th century, the empire began to break down. In 1911, the newly formed Chinese Republic took steps to unify the country. Its success, however, was limited and its power was challenged in the 1920s by the rising Chinese Communist Party.

The Chinese Communists did not gain great power until after World War II. In the years immediately following 1945 the ruling Nationalist government of Chiang Kai-shek failed to bring security and economic improvement to the Chinese people. This gave the Communists, under the leadership of Mao Tse-tung, a chance to challenge the war-weakened Nationalists. Finally, in 1949, the Communists drove the Nationalist government from the Asian mainland to the nearby island of Taiwan.

The government set up by the Communists was called the People's Republic of China. It remains the ruling government of China today. Ruled by the Communist Party and its leaders, the government allows no form of political opposition.

What is this cartoonist saying about the Communist parties in different European and Asian countries?

Since taking over, the Chinese Communists have worked to bring about economic and social reforms. In many cases, this has been very difficult. Social, educational, and political changes have often appeared to bring more chaos than reform. Economic improvements have often been hindered by a lack of natural resources, too few highly skilled workers, and a large and growing population. Even so, by the early 1970s, China had become a nuclear power and was making a great deal of social and economic progress.

Disagreements over the goals of communism were among the major reasons for growing hostility between China and the Soviet Union. Beginning in the 1960s, the Chinese, feeling that they were the true leaders of Communist revolution in the world, began to speak out against the policies of Soviet leaders. At the same time, they denounced the democratic government of the United States.

In the early 1970s Chinese attitudes began to soften somewhat. In the United States, there was also a softening of attitudes toward Communist China. In 1971, Communist China became a member of the United Nations. The Chinese leaders showed a general desire for open discussions with the United States and others it had regarded as its enemies.

OTHER COMMUNIST GOVERNMENTS

While communism has been most successful in the large countries of Russia and China, it has also won victories in other lands. Since the end of World War II, Communist governments have held power in the Russian satellite countries of eastern Europe—East Germany, Poland, Czechoslovakia, Hungary, Rumania, and Bulgaria. Two other European nations, Albania and Yugoslavia, also have Communist governments. Both, however, have been able to avoid being dominated by the Soviet Union. Albania's closest ties have been with Communist China. Yugoslavia has remained independent in its actions. Indeed, Yugoslavia has received military and economic aid from the United States and has traded freely with the democratic countries of western Europe.

In Northeast Asia, a Communist government has held power in North Korea since the end of the Korean War in the early 1950s. In Southeast Asia, Vietnam has become unified under a Communist government. Communists also run the government of Cambodia.

In the new countries of Africa, both Russia and China have worked to encourage the formation of Communist governments. While some of the new governments have shown Communist sympathies from time to time, Communist ideas have not gained a firm hold in any of the African governments.

The Communist powers have also worked to encourage communism in Latin America. Cuba now has a Communist government. In recent years, there have been military governments with Communist sympathies in Bolivia and Peru. In 1970, the people of Chile elected a president who expounded Communist ideas. Four years later he was overthrown by a military coup.

Getting the Facts

1. What two major forms of totalitarian government have developed in the 20th century?

2. What are some of the predictions made by Karl Marx about the future of the capitalist system?

3. Name at least five totalitarian political systems in today's world.

Thinking About the Future

■ The fate of 20th century totalitarian leaders in Germany and Italy shows that a totalitarian government can in certain cases be overthrown. Do you think any of today's totalitarian governments will change to authoritarian or democratic governments within the next 50 years? Why, or why not? Do you think other nations will set up totalitarian governments some time within the next half century? If so, which ones? Why?

William Shirer and Barbara Tuchman

In a 1975 letter to President Gerald Ford, two historians, William Shirer and Barbara Tuchman, expressed their views about the future of Spain. Note that they believe that Franco's government was totalitarian, not authoritarian. As has been noted, opinions will differ about the nature of the political systems of specific countries. However, there is no question about the fact that Franco's government was not a democracy. What about the future?

"The passing of Generalisimo Franco urgently calls for a fundamental review of United States policy looking to a restoration of democracy in Spain, with political and personal freedoms for its people. Such a review is made imperative by the potential and even imminent jeopardy to vital American interests in Spain and in Europe, including the Atlantic Alliance—should the Spanish people be pushed to violence rather than longer endure life under a totalitarian regime.

"In the event of such an eruption there can be little doubt that other outside nations, the USSR included, will not maintain the stance of neutral observers. A free and democratic Spain, on the other hand, in a free alliance with the democratic world, would be a stable ally in Europe . . .

"In a world torn by so much strife, everyone would wish for a peaceful transition in Spain. The question is: a transition to what, and by whom? A continued totalitarian state, with some mitigation of terror and strictures under a Franco hand-picked successor? A monarchy? What kind: constitutional or absolute? A republic, with republican forms of government, following a free election? . . .

"As the leader of the free world, the United States has a significant obligation to discharge: to help assure freedom in Spain without threat of the kind of violence which could lead to a new civil war. . . . The Spanish people seek no arms or armies from the United States. They seek instead a tangible expression of our country's own faith in democracy as the instrument of progress, to be demonstrated by United States support of freedom for the Spanish people to build their own institutions of democracy, to achieve their own progress."

---

1. What reasons do the two authors give for wanting to see a democracy established in Spain?

2. What steps do they think should be taken by the United States? What steps, if any, do you think should be taken? Explain.

3. Given your own knowledge of political systems and world politics, what do you think will be the future government of Spain? Why?

DEMOCRACY AND OTHER POLITICAL SYSTEMS

Citizenship Laboratory

Review of Basic Ideas

1. The three major political ideologies in the world today are democracy, totalitarianism, and authoritarianism. These ideologies have given rise to different kinds of political systems. The basic difference between totalitarianism and authoritarianism is that the first seeks total control of the lives of citizens. Authoritarianism seeks only political control. Most of the governments in today's world follow one of these three ideologies. Democratic governments allow self-government through free and competing political parties. Authoritarian governments have a single leader or small group of leaders who rule with the support of one or more of the powerful groups within the country. Totalitarian governments are run by a single party that seeks to control all groups in the country.

2. Most democratic governments are found in Europe and North America. However, democracies also exist in other parts of the world, in such countries as Israel, Japan, and Australia.

3. Most of the governments in today's world can be characterized as authoritarian. This form of government is very common in Latin America and Africa.

4. In the years after World War I, both Italy and Germany set up totalitarian governments inspired by Fascist ideologies. The two largest and most important totalitarian governments today are found in the Soviet Union and in Communist China. A number of other countries in eastern Europe and in Asia are also run by Communist parties.

Questions to Think About

1. What tests would you use to distinguish between democratic, authoritarian, and totalitarian political systems?

2. Why is the existence of a king or queen, a president, or a legislature not a good guide to the nature of the political system in a country?

3. In what ways is the democratic government in the United States similar to most democratic governments in Europe? In what ways is our democracy different from most of the European democracies?

4. Most of the people of the world do not live in democratic countries. How would you explain this fact?

5. What are some of the historical reasons why democratic governments have been popular in North America? What are some of the historical reasons why authoritarian governments have been popular in South America?

6. In what ways were the Fascist governments of Italy and Germany similar to the present Communist governments in the Soviet Union and China? In what ways were the Fascist governments different from the present Communist governments?

7. In what areas of the world has communism been most successful? What are some possible reasons for its success in these areas?

Words and Relationships

Define each of the terms in the first column. Then show how each term is related to the item listed opposite it by using both items in a sentence or short paragraph.

1. ideology — values
2. democratic — political parties
3. totalitarian — economic control
4. authoritarian — political responsibility
5. parliamentary — representative government
6. prime minister — legislative branch
7. elite — political control
8. military regime — stable government
9. fascism — national glory
10. communism — class struggle

Building a Future

What will be the future of democracy, as a form of government and as a way of life? How can we help further its growth around the world?

Many American leaders have stressed the importance of education in a democracy. They have maintained that educated voters are an essential part of a democracy. In recent years, some political scientists have insisted that true democracy is possible only in countries that are economically advanced. But neither schools nor modern economies can by themselves assure the existence of democracy. In the 1930s, the people of Germany were well educated. The country was economically advanced. And yet Germany turned to a totalitarian government.

In this connection, it is interesting to note that today only one German country, East Germany, is totalitarian. The other German country, West Germany, is democratic. Think also of the political changes that have taken place in Italy and Japan in the years since World War II. Both of these countries are now democracies. Germany, Italy, and Japan were all defeated by the United States in World War II. Are the changes that have taken place in these countries, to any degree, the result of American influence?

To further the democratic idea, is it better to try to influence a country directly by using American power? Or should we try to influence others by making democracy work here in the United States? Would a combination of methods work best?

Citizenship Laboratory

DEMOCRACY AND OTHER POLITICAL SYSTEMS

20 The Search for a Peaceful World

John Donne, a 17th century poet, once wrote lines about the way each of us is tied to everyone else in the world.

> No man is an island, alone by himself.
> Every man is a piece of the continent.
> If so much as a clod is washed away by the sea,
> Europe is just that much smaller.
> And any man's death makes me smaller,
> Because I am involved in mankind.

What the poet wrote of people is also true of countries.

The meaning of this interrelationship of people and countries was greatly altered in August of 1945. With awful suddenness, atomic bombs were dropped from the sky on the Japanese cities of Hiroshima and Nagasaki. The blasts instantly snuffed out the lives of more than 150,000 people, old and young. The smoke from the ashes signaled a turning point in history. A new kind of world was born. It was a world that people were able to destroy.

Faced with this new reality, the people of the world saw that they must seek more peaceful means of settling their differences. The search has not been easy. We still have far to go in discarding the ways of war. Yet the goal of peace continues to be stated by leader after leader in countries around the world.

American Foreign Policy in the Making

The foreign policies of the United States are the courses of action by which our government seeks to maintain peaceful relations with other countries. This goal is sought in order to protect our national security.

The Constitution gives the President the power needed to set up our foreign policies. The Constitution also gives Congress important powers in our dealings with other countries. Because we are a democracy, however, neither the President nor Congress may act without at least taking into account the opinion of the people. This is one reason why there is so much public discussion of foreign affairs in the United States. It is why American Presidents often hold press conferences or go before the people on radio and TV to explain certain changes in foreign policy. It is why the Foreign Relations Committee of the Senate and the International Relations Committee of the House often hold public hearings. It is why both Democrats and Republicans have long foreign policy statements in their party platforms.

AMERICAN FOREIGN POLICIES: PAST AND PRESENT

From the first years of our country's history, American foreign policies have been influenced by six basic principles.

- We have wanted to maintain our independence as a nation.
- We have wanted to protect our freedom as a people.
- We have, in most cases, tried to find ways to settle our differences with other countries in a peaceful way.
- We have agreed that any peaceful settlement of differences must be based on justice.
- We have wanted to protect our own political and economic interests at home and abroad.
- We have tried to cooperate with other countries in an effort to maintain peace in the world.

From these principles, certain foreign policies have emerged. Two of the most important of these policies have been associated with particular Presidents. President Washington, in his Farewell Address, encouraged the country to follow what might be called a policy of isolationism. His hope was that such a policy would keep the United States from becoming entangled in European conflicts. In 1823, President Monroe issued the Monroe Doctrine. It was designed to prevent foreign powers from interfering with the affairs of countries in the Western Hemisphere.

The nuclear age has produced certain changes in American policy. It has brought a greater need for international cooperation. To help fill this need, the United States meets with other countries in the United Nations. We are also involved in regional groups such as the North Atlantic Treaty Organization—NATO.

The foreign aid program, described on page 426, represents another change in American policy in the years since World War II. The program has been closely related to another postwar policy, the policy of containment. Begun in the late 1940s under President Truman, this policy has, in one form or another, been maintained in an effort to prevent the spread of Communist power.

Another change in policy has also been closely associated with the issues of the Cold War. We now follow a policy of military preparedness. Before World War II, the American people had always been strongly opposed to large armies and navies in times of peace. Since the end of World War II, however, the American government has supported a huge military establishment.

THE PRESIDENT AS POLICY MAKER

The President plays a very important part in the making of American foreign policy. Article II of the Constitution gives the President major powers in foreign affairs.

Even more important than the powers given in the Constitution, however, is the position of the President as our national leader. The President represents American interests in dealings with the leaders of other countries. The President also represents us in world councils. In the final analysis, only the President can speak for the country as a whole.

THE POWER OF CONGRESS IN FOREIGN RELATIONS

The Constitution requires that the President share some responsibilities in foreign affairs with Congress. The President may negotiate treaties with other governments. But such agreements do not become effective until approved by the Senate. The Senate must also approve ambassadors and other high-ranking officers appointed by the President to work in foreign affairs.

The Constitution also gives certain powers to Congress as a whole. Foreign trade is regulated, or controlled, by Con-

---

PRESIDENTIAL POWERS IN FOREIGN AFFAIRS: Given in Article II of the Constitution

To Command the Army and the Navy: Article II, Section 2, Paragraph 1

The President shall be commander in chief of the army and navy of the United States, and of the militia of the several States, when called into the actual service of the United States . . .

To Make Treaties and Appoint Diplomats with the Approval of the Senate: Article II, Section 2, Paragraph 2

He shall have power, by and with the advice and consent of the Senate, to make treaties, provided two thirds of the senators present concur; and he shall nominate, and by and with the advice and consent of the Senate, shall appoint ambassadors, other public ministers and consuls . . .

To Make Temporary Appointments When the Senate Is Not in Session: Article II, Section 2, Paragraph 3

The President shall have power to fill up all vacancies that may happen during the recess of the Senate, by granting commissions which shall expire at the end of their next session.

To Receive Ambassadors: Article II, Section 3

. . . he shall receive ambassadors and other public ministers . . .

gress. Only Congress may declare war. This, however, has become a very thorny issue in the years since World War II. The President can use the country's armed forces in such a way as to make war almost inevitable. (See pages 105–108.) The most important congressional power in foreign relations may be the power to raise money and appropriate it for certain purposes. Without these appropriations, Presidents would not be able to carry out their own policies.

Getting the Facts

1. Name at least three general principles that have influenced American foreign policy over the last two centuries.

2. What powers in the field of foreign affairs does the Constitution give to the President? to Congress?

Examining the Issues

■ Although many American Presidents have sought to maintain peaceful relations with other countries there have been exceptions. What are some of the exceptions? Under what conditions do you think a policy of peaceful relations should be abandoned?

CONGRESSIONAL POWERS IN FOREIGN AFFAIRS: Given in Articles I and II of the Constitution

Senate Must Approve Treaties and the Appointment of Diplomats: Article II, Section 2, Paragraph 2

He [the President] shall have power, by and with the advice and consent of the Senate, to make treaties, provided two thirds of the senators present concur; and he shall nominate, and by and with the advice and consent of the Senate, shall appoint ambassadors, other public ministers and consuls . . .

Congress Provides Money for the Common Defense: Article I, Section 8, Paragraph 1

The Congress shall have power to lay and collect taxes, duties, imposts and excises, to pay the debts and provide for the common defense and general welfare of the United States . . .

Congress Regulates Trade with Foreign Countries: Article I, Section 8, Paragraph 3

[Congress shall have power] To regulate commerce with foreign nations . . .

Congress Has the Power to Declare War: Article I, Section 8, Paragraph 11

[Congress shall have power] To declare war, grant letters of marque and reprisal, and make rules concerning captures on land and water;

Congress Provides Money to Support an Army: Article I, Section 8, Paragraph 12

[Congress shall have power] To raise and support armies, but no appropriation of money to that use shall be for a longer term than two years;

Congress Provides Money to Support a Navy: Article I, Section 8, Paragraph 13

[Congress shall have power] To provide and maintain a navy;

Congress Regulates the Armed Forces: Article I, Section 8, Paragraph 14

[Congress shall have power] To make rules for the government and regulation of the land and naval forces;

THE SEARCH FOR A PEACEFUL WORLD

Providing for National Security

A central part of the foreign policy of any country, including the United States, must be the security of its people. Never has it been so important as in our world today. Countries now have supersonic aircraft and long-range missiles. There is the ever-present threat of nuclear war. In the face of these new realities, the United States maintains a huge defense establishment. We have also entered into mutual security arrangements with other countries. At the same time, we are seeking international agreements for the control of arms. This is being done in an effort to decrease the chance of war.

At one time torpedoes carried by submarines could only be used to attack ships at sea. Today the ballistic missiles carried by nuclear-powered submarines can reach targets more than 6,000 kilometers inland.

THE DEPARTMENT OF DEFENSE

The symbol of our defense establishment is the Pentagon. This huge five-sided office building is located just across the Potomac River from Washington, D.C. Lodged in this building is the Department of Defense.

The Department of Defense is the agency of the federal government that is most responsible for our country's security. Its head, the Secretary of Defense, is a member of the President's Cabinet. The Secretary must, by law, be a civilian rather than a member of the military. Directly under the Secretary are three other civilians. These are the Secretaries of the Army, Navy, and Air Force. Each represents one of the three branches of our armed forces.

Military advice within the Department of Defense comes from the Joint Chiefs of Staff. This group is made up of the country's four top military officers. They are the Chief of Staff for the Army, the Chief of Staff for the Air Force, the Chief of Naval Operations, and the Chairman of the Joint Chiefs of Staff.

The Department of Defense, thus, is a combination of military advice and civilian control. This civilian power over the military is very much a part of the American tradition. It is a means by which decisions about how to use our armed might come ultimately from the people through their elected representatives. As such, it contrasts greatly with the military control found in many countries. In many places, military decisions are made by military officers who control the government. The degree of civilian control found in our country, however, has been questioned by some observers. Among these is former general and President Dwight D. Eisenhower, who warned of a rising "military-industrial complex."

MUTUAL SECURITY ARRANGEMENTS

Our country spends many billions of dollars each year to maintain a huge military establishment. Still, there is the belief that another kind of security arrangement is also needed. This extra security is found in our mutual defense treaties. Through these treaties the security of the United States is tied to the security of many other countries around the world.

It was not until the 1940s that the American people became convinced of the need for such treaties. Traditionally, our country had followed the advice of two early Presidents, Washington and Jefferson. Both had warned that our country should avoid alliances with foreign countries.

The change in direction began shortly after World War II. In 1947 the United States signed the first of a series of mutual defense treaties at a conference in Rio de Janiero, Brazil. Under the terms of this Rio Treaty, the United States and 20 Latin American countries agreed that an armed attack against any country in the Western Hemisphere would be treated as an attack against all American countries.

A similar treaty was signed with a group of countries in western Europe in 1949. Stirred by Soviet supported Communist take-overs of governments in eastern Europe, countries in western Europe and North America formed the North Atlantic Treaty Organization, or NATO. The original NATO members were the United States, Canada, Great Britain, France, Belgium, The Netherlands, Luxembourg, Norway, Denmark, Iceland, Italy, and Portugal. Greece and Turkey were added in 1952, and West Germany in 1955. Under the terms of the treaty, an armed attack against any of the countries in NATO is considered an attack against all. Should an attack take place, each country is obligated to help the country attacked, by the use of armed force if necessary.

A less permanent arrangement, the Southeast Asia Treaty Organization (SEATO), was entered into in 1954. This treaty brought the United States, France, and Great Britain into a defense agreement with the Philippines, Australia, New Zealand, Thailand, and Pakistan. Under its terms, each member agreed that any armed aggression in Southeast Asia would endanger its own peace and safety. SEATO ceased to function effectively after 1975, in the wake of the United States withdrawal from Vietnam.

The United States has a number of other security arrangements in eastern and southern Asia. Our country is obligated in a significant way for the security of Japan, South Korea, and the Republic of China on Taiwan. We also have certain obligations to Australia, New Zealand, and the Philippines.

In addition to these many security arrangements, our government gives military and economic aid to a number of countries in exchange for our use of military bases in the countries.

Finally, it should be noted again that the American foreign aid program gives economic and military aid to a number of countries. In many ways, this

"Shouldn't The Bodyguard Stay More In The Background?"

What is this cartoonist saying about the goals of American foreign aid programs? What do you think the major goals of these program should be?

program can also be thought of as a kind of security arrangement for the United States.

THE CONTROL OF ARMS

While maintaining a strong military and supporting a number of security arrangements with other countries, the United States is also working to bring about the control of arms. We are making efforts to reach agreements with other countries to limit the development of atomic weapons. Efforts are also being made to reduce the size of standing armies and to limit the number of military ships and planes. In 1961, a federal agency was set up to deal with matters of arms control. The stated goal of the United States Arms Control and Disarmament Agency is "to reduce the likelihood of war and to limit its effect if it occurs."

Those who work on arms control in our government, and in other countries as well, are well aware that throughout history most attempts at arms control have failed. They are also, however, aware of something else. Throughout history people have believed that the greater a country's armed strength, the greater its security. This old belief has been changed in important ways by the technological advances that have brought our nuclear age. As far as today's nuclear weapons are concerned, "superiority" is a difficult thing to measure. Indeed, it is a matter of little practical significance. A major nuclear attack by one country against another will be followed by retaliation and mutual destruction.

Our government showed some recognition of this new world situation as early as 1946. At that time, the United States had a monopoly of nuclear weapons. Nevertheless, the United States proposed to the other countries in the United Nations that all dangerous nuclear materials be placed in the hands of an international authority. This authority would own or control the dangerous nuclear materials of all countries. The proposal was not accepted, however, because of objections made by the Soviet Union.

In 1953 President Eisenhower submitted an "Atoms for Peace" proposal to the United Nations. Under the terms of this proposal an international agency would be set up to promote the non-military use of atomic power. The President followed this, in 1955, with his "Open Skies" plan. This plan called for aerial inspection of the United States and the Soviet Union. It also proposed that the two countries exchange military plans. The Soviet Union, however, objected to both of the proposals made by President Eisenhower.

Finally, in 1963, some progress toward arms control was made. In that year, the United States and the Soviet Union signed the Limited Test Ban Treaty. Both countries agreed to end all but underground nuclear tests.

Another step was taken toward stopping the nuclear arms race in 1968 and 1969. During those two years, the United States, the Soviet Union, and more than 40 other countries signed the Non-Proliferation Treaty. The treaty had a number of provisions and safeguards. President Lyndon Johnson called it the "most important international agreement since the beginning of the nuclear age."

Of potentially even greater significance are the Strategic Arms Limitations Talks (SALT). These talks between the United States and the Soviet Union began late in 1969. In a letter to the head of the American delegation, read at the opening session, President Nixon stated, "You are embarking upon one of the most momentous negotiations ever entrusted to an American delegation." At the end of the first round of talks, Soviet leader Brezhnev promised that "the Soviet Union . . . will do its utmost to make these talks useful."

Whether these two powerful countries will be able to agree upon firm measures to limit arms remains a question of great importance. Clearly, such agreements will never be easy to reach. Few matters, however, could be of greater consequence to the future of the world.

Getting the Facts

1. How are the duties of the Department of Defense divided between civilian and military officers? Which of the two groups makes final decisions?

2. With which countries or groups of countries does the United States now have mutual security arrangements?

3. What is the basic purpose of the SALT negotiations?

Examining the Issues

■ Through most of our history, the United States has had a military draft only in times of war. In 1948 a peacetime draft was set up. In 1973 the draft program ended and the armed forces were once again staffed only by volunteers. For what reasons might a country wish to draft military personnel during times of peace? Would you favor or oppose a new peacetime draft? Why?

What statement is this cartoonist making about arms control efforts of the 1970s? Do you think the statement is valid? Why, or why not?

"THERE'S NOTHING LIKE A LITTLE TALK!"

THE SEARCH FOR A PEACEFUL WORLD

Speaking Out

Sidney Lens

Lens is a well-known writer on American politics, industry, and labor. He maintains that our country is controlled by a military-industrial complex. It is his belief that this complex must be torn down if the United States is to survive.

"The complex is not a popular force with disinterested goals. It is, instead, a conglomerate of elites—a military elite, an industrial elite, a banking elite, a labor elite, an academic elite—which seeks its own aggrandizement through global expansion. It has sponsored for that purpose what Hanson Baldwin calls 'a surge of nationalism,' the concept that 'America ought to rule the world.' Harry Truman defined it more specifically as assuring the dominance of free enterprise economies over regimented ones. In economic terms that means enlarging American trade and investment, as well as finding new sources of raw materials. In political terms it means aiding those regimes favorable to America's economic goals. In military terms it means nuclear deterrence (or damage-limitation) to checkmate the only power capable of stymieing those ambitions, the Soviet Union. It translates itself inevitably into military bases around the world, military pacts, contingency agreements, and actual intervention where necessary and feasible, to help friendly regimes that are tottering or friendly forces that aspire to power against neutralists and Communists. The power elite that is now called the military-industrial complex has, in other words, fashioned a blueprint for 'Pax Americana' that would do for the twentieth century what 'Pax Britannica' did for the nineteenth. . . .

"We live, however, at the crossroads of three great revolutions—technological, military, and social. Our very genius can be our undoing unless we abolish war and oppression; but it can lead us, on the other hand, to new vistas to hope, affluence, and security if we apply that technology to life-oriented projects.

"Sanity is the application of intelligence to the need for survival. The first step in that direction, it seems to me, is the dismantling of the military-industrial complex."

1. What does Lens see as the goals of the groups that he identifies as making up the American military-industrial complex?

2. What goals does Lens think the United States should seek instead?

3. "Pax Americana" is Lens's term for peace enforced by the power of the United States. To what lengths do you think the United States should go to enforce peace in the world?

What Role Should the United States Play in World Politics?

During the 1960s, while our government was working to achieve some kind of international control of arms, American military forces were drawn deeper and deeper into a long and costly struggle in Vietnam. At no other time in our history, except during our Civil War, did a conflict create so much bitterness within the country. Among other things, the war raised a fundamental question about American foreign policy. Should our policy have as its major goal our own national interest? Or should the basic goal of our foreign policy be America's responsibility to the world? There is also the question of whether these two goals are really different? Or do both belong under a broad definition of "national interest"?

One of many people who decided to take a fresh look at American responsibility in the world was *New York Times* correspondent C. L. Sulzberger. Writing in the early 1970s, Sulzberger first reviews two paragraphs he wrote in 1950. The rest of his remarks are directed toward America's more recent experience in Vietnam.

" 'The Japanese had been brought up on the theory that they were invincible. They had never been defeated in war. Now all their history books and school books must be rewritten in order to adjust history to facts. Are we Americans suffering from the same psychological superiority complex that affected Japan in 1941?

" 'We have managed to defeat the British in two minor campaigns when they were also fighting the French. We have defeated the Mexicans and Spaniards who were already coming apart at the seams. We have defeated the Germans and the Japanese when we had great allies who gave us time to get ready. How are we going to do alone?'

"I wrote this in Tokyo, May 23, 1950, and later published it textually in my book, 'A Long Row of Candles.' The first part of the answer came rapidly—in 33 days—when North Korea invaded South Korea. Although aided by U. N. token forces, the United States was largely alone in repelling this invasion.

"Our history books depict that war as a victory because, by the time the smoke cleared, the North Koreans were approximately back where they had started from, even if undefeated. But then, as Voltaire wrote, history is nothing but a pack of tricks we play on the dead. There were plenty of dead.

"When Vietnam came around, the United States was really on its own. South Korea, Thailand, Australia and New Zealand helped; but the Americans, with the shaky South Vietnamese, bore the real burden.

"And this time we can't pretend to have won. . . .

"We lost the war in the Mississippi valley, not the Mekong valley. Successive American governments were never able to muster the necessary mass support at home. . . .

"The American people increasingly showed more sympathy and admiration for their enemies than for their allies. . . .

"Like Japan, we will discover the price of defeat. But this is defeat without destruction, brought about, not by a distant little Asiatic Sparta, but by an intimately proximate superpower—our faltering selves."

Regardless of our experience in Vietnam, a number of Americans believe that we must maintain our position as world leader. They believe that such a role is in our country's national

THE SEARCH FOR A PEACEFUL WORLD

Inquiry

interest. This view was clearly expressed by Harlan Cleveland, writing in 1969 as the United States Ambassador to NATO.

"The old cliches about commitment were certainly too global, too focused on what America might do, too American in their conviction that if worst came to worst, we could solve any given problem.

"But the problems are still right there in front of us, and we are committed to tackling them because we have the capacity to act. Science and technology keep producing more power to be internationally contained, more pollution to be internationally controlled. . . . We are all staring, fascinated but paralyzed, at global gaps in wealth and weaponry that seem unbridgeably wide. The tensions and technologies of the 1970's will make imperative new international restraints on national action and new dimensions in international cooperation. At this extraordinary moment of history, we just happen to be the world's strongest economy, its most durable power, and its most creative fount of scientific discovery and technological triumph.

In what ways can a program such as the Peace Corps serve the interests of people in the United States while helping the people in developing countries?

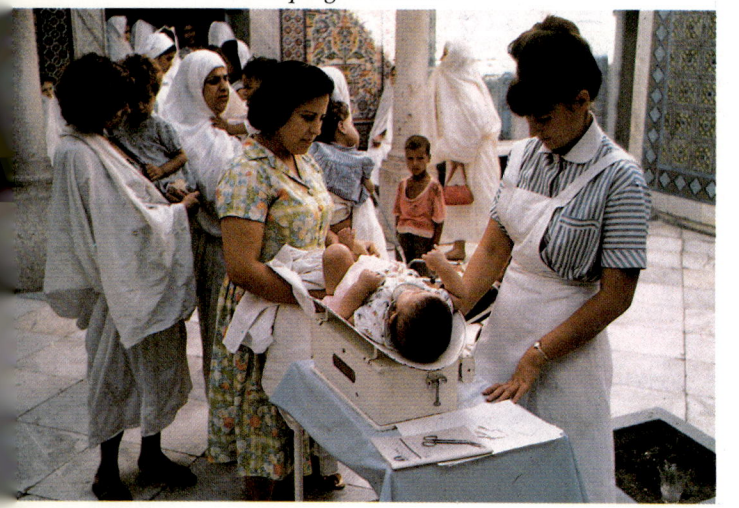

"Withdrawal and anticommitment cannot be our 'thing.' Our problem is not to decide whether we will be involved, but how. Our capacity to act comes in a package with the obligation to choose a course of action. . . .

"We help arm other countries if we perceive a U. S. national interest in their defense—that is, if we judge that not arming them might, in a pinch, require us to undertake their whole defense with our own arms. We join in international development schemes partly because our growing antipoverty commitment at home enlarges our antipoverty commitment abroad, whether we like it or not. But we also help in international development because most Americans vaguely fear the social and political and military consequences—that is, the greater costs—of trying to live in our wealthy manor in the midst of a global slum. We join international organizations . . . and attend international conferences (more than 600 of them each year—15 or 20 in any given week) because there are so many fields in which we can better serve our own interests by pooling them with those of others."

Making Decisions

Americans will have to make a number of decisions about foreign policy in the years ahead. Questions such as the following are sure to be involved.

Should we agree with Sulzberger and regard our country as the big loser in Vietnam?

Is it right, in setting our foreign policy goals, always to place our own national interests first? Why, or why not?

To what lengths do you think the United States should go to meet its obligations to its friends and allies around the globe?

In what ways are the interests of the United States linked to the interests of the other countries of the world?

466 THE UNITED STATES IN TODAY'S WORLD

Searching for a Peaceful World Through the United Nations

In one organization the self-interests of almost all the world's people are represented. This organization is called the United Nations. Not a world government, it is instead a council of independent countries. From its headquarters in New York City, the United Nations seeks to provide means by which countries can gain better understanding of one another and find ways of cooperating in the interests of peace. Its success depends upon the willingness of its members to work together.

FORERUNNERS OF THE UNITED NATIONS

The countries of the world had tried other kinds of international cooperation before the United Nations was formed. Beginning in the mid-19th century there were a number of cooperative agreements. These involved such matters as ocean shipping, telegraph and mail regulations, and controls over drugs.

The first major efforts to deal with the problems of modern warfare were made at meetings held in The Netherlands in 1899 and again in 1907. Our country was a participant in both. The most important result of the meetings was the formation of a world court, the Hague Tribunal, to handle disputes among countries. The meetings, however, had little success in controlling arms.

Before the United Nations, the most important world peace organization was the League of Nations. Formed after World War I, its chief architect was an American, President Woodrow Wilson. The League included almost all of the world's major powers. But despite President Wilson's urgings, the United States did not become a member. The treaty that would have brought our country into the League failed to win the approval of the United States Senate. The League struggled through the 1920s and 1930s. With the outbreak of World War II, however, it ceased to be an effective organization.

During World War II, there were many international conferences and agreements. These were the immediate forerunners of the United Nations. In August, 1941, even before America entered the war, President Roosevelt and British Prime Minister Churchill signed the Atlantic Charter. It stated that "the nations of the world must come to the abandonment of the use of force" and create "a wider and permanent system of general security." A few months later, on January 1, 1942, the two countries, along with 24 other countries, signed the Declaration of the United Nations. This declaration was an agreement to follow the principles stated in the Atlantic Charter. Other conferences and agreements among the major powers in 1943, 1944, and 1945 called for a new world peace organization.

Finally, in April of 1945, more than 1,500 representatives from 46 countries met in San Francisco, California. During two months of meetings, this group framed the Charter—the constitution—of the United Nations.

In contrast to its earlier unwillingness to vote for American membership

Although the United States refused to join the League of Nations in the 1920s, it became a charter member of the UN in the 1940s. Which do you think are stronger, the advantages or the disadvantages of belonging to a permanent world council?

in the League of Nations, the United States Senate overwhelmingly ratified the United Nations Charter. Our country was, in fact, the first to ratify the Charter. The weakness of the League of Nations without the United States and the bitter experiences of World War II were convincing.

GOALS OF THE UNITED NATIONS

Like the Constitution of the United States, the Charter of the United Nations begins with a Preamble. The Preamble lists the four basic goals of the United Nations:

- "To save succeeding generations from the scourge of war, which twice in our lifetime has brought untold sorrow to mankind . . .
- "To reaffirm faith in fundamental human rights, in the dignity and worth of the human person, in the equal rights of men and women and of nations large and small . . .
- "To establish conditions under which justice and respect for obligations arising from treaties and other sources of international law can be maintained . . .
- "To promote social progress and better standards of life . . ."

These four goals are a large order. There can be little disagreement, however, that they are worthy ideals.

STRUCTURE OF THE UNITED NATIONS

The Charter of the United Nations provides a framework for what has become a very elaborate organization. As you can see in the chart on page 469, there are a number of special agencies and commissions. Here we will discuss only the six "principal organs" of the United Nations. These are the General Assembly, the Security Council, the International Court of Justice, the Trusteeship Council, the Economic and Social Council, and the Secretariat.

Representatives from each member country meet in the General Assembly. Each country may send as many as five representatives, but is allowed only one vote. This body supervises all activities of the United Nations. It discusses any questions that come within the scope of the Charter. It elects representatives to the main bodies of the organization, makes recommendations to member countries, and has responsibility for financial matters.

The Security Council has 15 members. Five of the great powers—the United States, Great Britain, the Soviet

468 THE UNITED STATES IN TODAY'S WORLD

Union, France, and China—hold permanent seats on the council. The remaining 10 are non-permanent members. They are selected by the General Assembly for two-year terms. The council investigates disputes between countries. If necessary the council may take action against aggressors in order to preserve peace. All actions, however, except matters of procedure, must be agreed upon by all permanent members. Any one of the five can veto council actions.

The International Court of Justice is a body of 15 members chosen for nine-year terms. They are selected by the General Assembly and the Security Council. The court decides legal disputes between countries. Among the many matters that have been decided by the court are questions about borders and fishing rights. By making such decisions, the Court helps to formulate a body of international law.

The Trusteeship Council supervises the administration of trust territories. Originally, its supervision covered a number of territories that at one time belonged to countries defeated in World War I or World War II. Today, however, very few trust territories remain.

The Economic and Social Council is a body of 27 members elected for three-year terms by the General Assembly. As its title indicates, the council is concerned with economic and social progress in all parts of the world. In carrying out this concern it coordinates the work of a large number of specialized agencies and commissions. Among the better known agencies are the United Nations Children's Fund (UNICEF), the World Health Organization (WHO), the

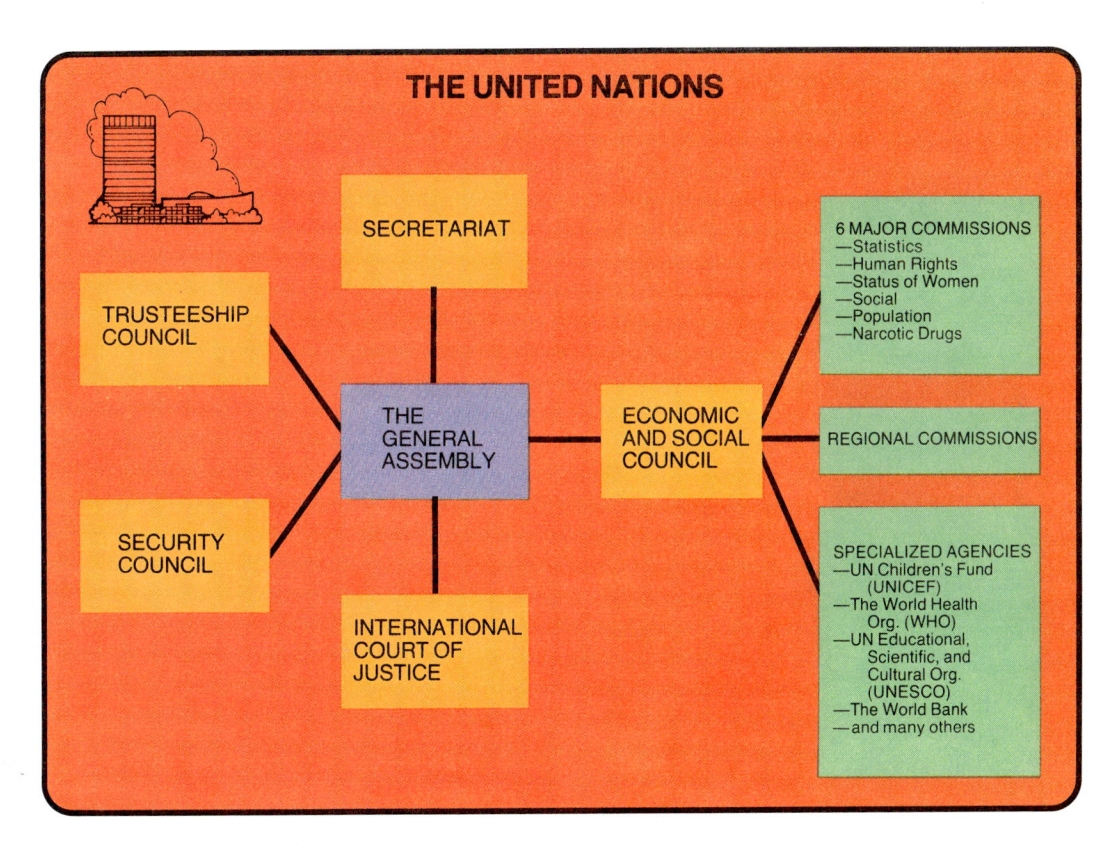

THE UNITED NATIONS

- SECRETARIAT
- TRUSTEESHIP COUNCIL
- SECURITY COUNCIL
- THE GENERAL ASSEMBLY
- INTERNATIONAL COURT OF JUSTICE
- ECONOMIC AND SOCIAL COUNCIL
  - 6 MAJOR COMMISSIONS
    —Statistics
    —Human Rights
    —Status of Women
    —Social
    —Population
    —Narcotic Drugs
  - REGIONAL COMMISSIONS
  - SPECIALIZED AGENCIES
    —UN Children's Fund (UNICEF)
    —The World Health Org. (WHO)
    —UN Educational, Scientific, and Cultural Org. (UNESCO)
    —The World Bank
    —and many others

THE SEARCH FOR A PEACEFUL WORLD

United Nations Educational, Scientific, and Cultural Organization (UNESCO), and the International Bank for Reconstruction and Development (the World Bank). There are a number of other agencies of equal or greater importance.

The photographs below show two of the many different services offered by the Economic and Social Council of the UN. Working with the Indian government, UNICEF has set up a program to improve elementary education in India's schools. UNESCO has helped fund a program that sends pony-cart libraries into remote areas of Thailand.

The Secretariat is the staff organization of the United Nations. It is made up of administrators, secretaries, and clerks who handle the routine day-by-day office work. Its head is the Secretary-General. This official is chosen for a five-year term by the General Assembly. The Secretary-General is the executive head of the United Nations. More than any other official, the Secretary-General sets the tone and direction for the organization.

THE UNITED NATIONS AFTER A QUARTER CENTURY

In the fall of 1970 the United Nations reached the age of 25. Its silver anniversary theme, "Progress and Peace," pointed to the long-held goals of the organization.

To many, the birthday celebration offered a chance to take stock of the organization's achievements and failures. Does it have a future? Will the United Nations be able to meet the needs of the world in the closing decades of the 20th century? These were the kind of questions asked again and again during the anniversary year.

A major success could be seen in the membership figures. The United Nations had grown from 51 member countries in 1945 to 126 in 1970. Equally important, only one country—Indonesia—had ever withdrawn, and it rejoined the very next year. All other countries had somehow been able to overlook their differences enough to try to work together. (The 26th year of the United Nations—1971—brought the expulsion of a member country. When Communist China entered the United Nations, Nationalist China was expelled.) With

470   THE UNITED STATES IN TODAY'S WORLD

so many countries trying to work together, there had been a number of peacemaking achievements—in the Middle East, Kashmir, the Congo, and Cyprus.

In spite of these achievements, the United Nations was criticized by many. A number of people felt that it had not been successful enough in its peace-keeping role. A special commission set up by the United States government directly criticized the failure of the United Nations to fill this basic role.

"Two major shortcomings of the Organization seem to have eroded much of its public support in the United States: first, the failure of its members to make it the paramount means for maintaining international peace and security as was intended in the Charter and second, its misuse as both an unwieldy and ineffective debating society and a propaganda platform."

The commission's conclusion was not unlike that of U Thant, Secretary-General of the United Nations from 1961 to 1971. He stated, "I can report very little progress in the world at large toward the goals of the United Nations Charter . . . Furthermore, I have a strong feeling that time is running out."

However, neither the Secretary-General nor the United States' commission was ready to give up on the United Nations. The commission noted that the United Nations had had a number of successes, not only in peacemaking but also in the work of its specialized agencies. The problems, the commission believed, were the result of outdated procedures. Some new means were needed to strengthen its peace-keeping machinery and to improve its methods of settling disputes.

THE FUTURE OF THE UNITED NATIONS

By the late 1970s, the United Nations had grown to an organization of over 140 members. True, many of these countries are very small. And, the presence of so many small countries brings problems, since each member country, regardless of size, has one vote in the General Assembly. Most countries, however, appear willing to try to get along within the United Nations. There is a continued determination to press for the organization's two main goals: peace and human dignity. Most members recognize the value of working together to deal with the economic and social problems faced by people around the globe. The members realize that the United Nations has helped stop small wars that could have become big ones. Ultimately, they understand that, while the United Nations is not a world government, its peace efforts can help prevent a third world war.

Getting the Facts

1. Name at least three efforts made to achieve international cooperation before the formation of the United Nations in 1945.

2. What are the six "principal organs" of the UN? What powers and duties does each of the six bodies have?

Forming an Opinion

■ The UN is a council of independent countries, not a world government. Do you think there will ever be a world government? Why, or why not? What form of world government would you find most acceptable? What form would you find least acceptable? Explain.

Citizenship Laboratory

Review of Basic Ideas

1. American foreign policy has been influenced by a desire to maintain our country's independence, to protect the freedom of the American people, to settle differences with other countries in a peaceful and just way, to safeguard our political and economic interests at home and abroad, and to cooperate with other countries in efforts to keep peace. The Constitution gives the President the power to make foreign policies. Congress has also been given policy-making powers. In recent years, the President and Congress have clashed over the use of war powers. In the formation of foreign policy, both the President and Congress must take into account the opinion of the American people.

2. The traditional means of achieving foreign policy goals have been affected by the existence of nuclear weapons. This new situation has stimulated the search for new means of dealing with the conflicting interests of different countries without resorting to war. The national security of the United States is protected by a huge military establishment under the Department of Defense. We have mutual security arrangements with a number of countries. We have also made great efforts to reach international agreements for the control of arms.

3. The United Nations is a council of independent countries. It is not a world government. Its stated goals are peace and human justice throughout the world.

Questions to Think About

1. To what extent do the American people influence the making of foreign policy? Given the complex nature of foreign relations, do you think the average American should have any say in foreign policy decisions? Explain.

2. Do you think it is desirable for the United States to have a large army, navy, and air force in peacetime? Why, or why not?

3. What are the advantages of mutual security arrangements such as NATO? What are possible disadvantages of such arrangements?

4. Do you think the great powers will ever be able to arrive at effective arms control agreements? Why, or why not?

5. How would you define "national interest"?

6. What do you see as the strengths and weaknesses of the United Nations? To what extent do you think the United Nations will be able to reach its stated goals?

7. What role do you think the United States should play in the United Nations? How do you think the United States should act when the United Nations decides on policies we oppose?

THE UNITED STATES IN TODAY'S WORLD

Citizenship Laboratory

Words and Relationships

Define each of the terms in the first column. Then show how each term is related to the item listed opposite it by using both items in a sentence or short paragraph.

1.	nuclear age	atomic bomb
2.	isolationism	European conflicts
3.	civilian control	American tradition
4.	mutual security	NATO
5.	Atoms for Peace	nuclear power
6.	Strategic Arms Limitations Talks	arms control
7.	national interest	world responsibility
8.	The Hague Tribunal	international disputes
9.	The League of Nations	United States Senate
10.	Security Council	veto

Building a Future

What will be the future of the United Nations? How do you assess its chances to live and grow? In thinking of these questions, consider some of the criticisms often made about the organization.

- The United Nations is little more than an international debating society.
- The United Nations has no standing army to use to enforce peace.
- Because each country has one vote in the General Assembly, a two-thirds majority can be mustered by a group of members who have less than 10 percent of the world's population.
- This same group, with its two-thirds majority of votes in the General Assembly, provides less than 5 percent of the United Nations budget.
- In one recent but not unusual year, about 60 percent of the members failed to pay their dues.

Which of these, do you think are important criticisms? Are there any that would seem to be insignificant?

The United Nations does provide a meeting place for almost every country in the world. It is possible that the organization will achieve great things in the future. How can it be made to work more effectively for its goals of peace and human dignity? Do you think it is trying to do too much or too little? Do you think the United Nations would be more effective if votes in the General Assembly were based on population? Or, do you think the large nations already have too much power in the organization, especially in the Security Council?

THE SEARCH FOR A PEACEFUL WORLD

Glossary

absentee ballot. A ballot marked by a voter and mailed to the election board before election day.

agribusiness. A large-scale farming operation run as a business, often combining farming and food processing—freezing, canning, and so on. (Also called a factory farm.)

alien. A foreign-born person who is not a citizen.

ambassador. A diplomat of the highest rank who serves as a country's official representative in a foreign country.

amendment. An addition or other change made to improve the original.

appeal. To request that a court case be retried by a higher court in hopes that the decision of a lower court will be overruled.

appellate court. A court that retries cases brought from lower courts.

appellate jurisdiction. The power of a court to retry certain kinds of cases.

apportionment. The division of a state into districts from which elected representatives are to be chosen for the state legislature or for the national House of Representatives.

arable land. Land that is useful for farming.

arms control. Efforts to place international limits on weapons and the size of armies, navies, and air forces.

Articles of Confederation. The document that formed the basis for the government of the United States in the years before the Constitution was accepted. The Articles gave the states much more power than they later had under the Constitution.

assessment. An estimation of the value of property for tax purposes.

Attorney General. The head of the Department of Justice and a member of the President's Cabinet.

authoritarian government. A form of government in which the rules are made by one or a few people and the citizens are allowed some freedom in non-political matters.

bail. An amount of money left by an accused person with a court as a guarantee that the person will return for trial.

ballot. A form used by voters to mark the names of the candidates for whom they wish to vote.

bandwagon device. A propaganda technique used to persuade people to "join the crowd" or "pick a winner."

barter. An economic practice in which people trade one kind of product or service for another.

basic production. An economic term for the work done to supply raw materials such as minerals, lumber, and food.

bicameral. A lawmaking body made up of two houses.

bill. A legislative proposal that has not yet been passed into law.

bill of attainder. A law that punishes a person or group of people without a trial by jury.

Bill of Rights. The first 10 amendments to the Constitution.

bipartisan. Made up of representatives from two political parties.

board of elections. A body, usually made up of representatives of our two major political parties, that runs both primary and general elections.

bond. A certificate sold by governments and corporations to raise money. Those who buy the bonds receive interest payments as well as the full purchase price at the end of a certain period of time.

boss. (See political boss.)

boycott. A refusal to buy the products of a business.

breach of the peace. A legal term for a public disturbance or disorderly conduct by a person or group.

budget. An estimate of income to be received and money to be spent.

bureaucracy. A large group of unelected government officials who conduct the daily affairs of government.

busing. Transporting students to public schools outside their own neighborhoods to achieve a racial balance in public schools.

Cabinet. The official body of advisers to the President, each of whom is head of a major department in the national government.

candidate. A person running for political office.

capital goods. A form of accumulated wealth, including such things as machines, tools, and buildings, that businesses use to create more wealth.

capitalism. An economic system in which businesses are owned and run by private people whose goal is to make profits.

card stacking. A propaganda technique that presents true statements in a misleading way, often by giving much greater coverage to statements that are favorable to the people using the technique.

caucus. A meeting of a group of politicians, all in the same party. Today caucuses are held by both parties in both houses of Congress to choose party leaders and party whips. Members of Congress also met in caucuses to choose presidential candidates until the 1830s when national presidential nominating conventions were first held.

census. A count of population. In the United States a census is taken every 10 years.

charter. A legal statement giving some organization the right to operate in certain ways. State governments grant charters to corporations and to municipalities (cities). State and national governments grant charters to banks.

checkerboard pattern. A street plan with square or rectangular blocks, straight streets, and right-angled corners.

checks and balances. A group of constitutional and traditional rules that help balance power between the three branches of the national government to prevent any one of the branches from becoming all-powerful. A similar system is found in many state governments.

Chief Justice. The head of the United States Supreme Court. All nine justices on the Supreme Court have an equal vote in Court decisions but the Chief Justice does have a few special duties. These include administering the presidential oath of office and presiding over the Senate trial of an impeached President.

citizenship. Membership in a state or nation either by birth or by naturalization.

city council. The elected lawmaking body of a city government.

city manager. A professional administrator hired by a city council to serve as the executive head of the city government.

civic responsibility. A citizen's duty to learn about the way government is run and to act on this information for the public good.

civics. The study of government, politics, and the rights and duties of citizenship.

civil case. A court case involving a dispute between people over private rights such as the right to own property or the rights listed in contracts.

civilian. A person who is not a member of the armed forces.

civil liberty. The protection of citizens from unreasonable government interference.

civil rights. (See civil liberty.)

civil servant. A non-elected government official, generally hired after receiving a high or passing grade on a civil service examination.

civil township. (See township.)

closed primary. A primary election in which each ballot lists the names of the candidates of only one party.

Cold War. A term for the economic and political rivalry of Communist and non-Communist countries in the years after World War II.

collective bargaining. A process by which representatives of labor unions meet with owners or management in an attempt to work out disagreements.

Commander in Chief. The military title given to the President along with the power to command the armed forces and commission military officers.

commercial bank. A general purpose bank that offers checking and savings accounts as well as loans to individuals and businesses.

commission government. A form of city government in which a small group of elected officials serve both executive and legislative functions.

committee system. The organization of members of Congress into small specialized groups so that each group, or committee, can deal with specialized bills.

common law. A body of law based on past decisions by judges rather than on laws passed by lawmaking bodies.

common stock. A form of investment in a corporation that gives a person the right to vote on corporate matters and pays dividends that rise and fall with the profits made by the corporation.

communism. A form of totalitarian government found in the Soviet Union, the People's Republic of China, and certain other countries.

community. A body of people with certain common interests living in the same place under the same rules or laws.

conference committee. A special congressional committee made up of members from both houses, generally set up to change a bill to make it acceptable to the majority in both houses. (Also called a joint conference committee.)

congressional government. A government in which the legislative branch is more powerful than the other branches of government.

congressional township. A section of land surveyed by the national government in the late 18th century.

conservation. The wise management and use of natural resources.

constituents. The voters in the district, state, or other area represented by an elected official.

constitution. A written document that sets up the framework of government and expresses the political principles of a state or nation.

consul. A government official assigned to a foreign city to look after the interests of Americans and American business.

consumer. A person who obtains and makes use of goods and services.

consumer demand. An economic term for the effect on producers made by the combined choices of thousands of consumers.

containerization. Packaging freight in huge containers so that it can be moved more efficiently.

GLOSSARY 475

containment. A foreign policy of the United States in the years following World War II, directed toward stopping further expansion of the Soviet Union.

cooperative. A form of business organization in which a group of producers or consumers work together to benefit all members.

corporate income tax. A tax on business profits.

corporation. A form of business organization owned by stockholders. In order to operate, corporations must be granted state charters.

council. (See city council.)

council-manager government. A form of city government in which an elected council hires a professional manager to run the city departments.

county. A form of local government set up to collect taxes, enforce laws, supervise elections, and provide other local services.

county seat. The town or city where the official business of a county government is handled.

Court of Claims. A federal court set up to hear cases involving suits against the national government.

Courts of Appeal. Eleven federal courts set up to retry cases originally tried by the federal District Courts.

courts of inferior jurisdiction. State courts set up to hear cases involving nonviolent matters such as disputes over small amounts of money, landlord-tenant disagreements, and family quarrels. (Also called "lower courts" and "people's courts.")

craft union. A labor group made up of people all working at the same trade—a group of carpenters or electricians, for example.

credit. A system that allows people, businesses, and governments to pay later for goods, money, or services they receive.

criminal case. A court case that involves a major offense against an individual or society such as murder or robbery.

culture. A society's way of life.

customs. Practices or ways held by a group of people, generally passed down from one generation to another.

Customs Court. A federal court that hears cases involving tariff laws.

customs duties. Taxes charged on products that travellers bring with them into a country.

decibel. A unit used to measure sound.

deed. A legal document that records the ownership or transfer of property.

de facto **segregation.** The existence of public schools attended mainly by students of one racial group as a result of racially segregated—separated—neighborhoods.

demand. (See consumer demand.)

democracy. A society that is ruled by the people.

democratic government. A form of government in which the citizens make the rules, either directly or through representatives they have chosen.

desegregation. Putting an end to separation of racial groups in schools, theaters, and other public places. (Also called integration or racial integration.)

diplomat. An official representative of a country who has been appointed to deal with other countries.

direct primary. (See primary election.)

discrimination. Actions taken against certain people or groups because of prejudice.

distribution. An economic term for the means by which raw materials are made available to manufacturers and finished products are made available to consumers.

district attorney. A lawyer who represents the government in court cases.

District Courts. Federal courts set up throughout the United States to try federal cases. These courts have original jurisdiction—the right to try cases first—over most cases involving federal laws.

dividend. The money paid to the stockholders of a corporation.

division of labor. The way in which jobs are divided among a group of workers in mass production so that each worker can add one small part to the finished product.

double jeopardy. Trying a person twice for the same crime.

dual citizenship. Holding citizenship in two different countries at the same time.

due process of law. Following legal procedures so that people will be protected from unreasonable government actions.

ecology. The science that seeks a better understanding of the relationships between living things and their natural environments.

economic self-sufficiency. The ability to provide for one's own physical needs without outside help.

economy. A term for all the many different activities that provide goods and services in each nation.

elastic clause. A term used to describe Article I, Section 8, Paragraph 18 of the Constitution, the clause that gives Congress the power to make all laws that are "necessary and proper" to carry out the other powers given Congress in the Constitution.

election process. The system that allows citizens to choose their own government officials. Primary elections allow people to nominate candidates for public office. General elections allow people to choose among the candidates nominated in the primaries and elect those they choose to public office.

Electoral College. A group of people who gather at the end of a presidential election to cast the official votes for the President and Vice President.

electorate. Citizens who have the right to vote.

elite. A small group of people who have great political or social power.

emancipation. The act of setting people free.

equity. A set of rules that makes it possible for judges to ignore the strict meaning of the law in order to achieve justice.

erosion. A loss of soil generally caused by wind or water.

estate tax. A tax on money or property left by someone who dies.

ethnic group. A group of people with the same racial or national background and a number of common customs.

excise tax. A sales tax placed on "luxury" goods such as jewelry, cosmetics, and gasoline.

executive branch. The branch of government responsible for carrying out laws passed by the legislative branch.

executive departments. The major departments in the executive branch of the national government run by the members of the President's Cabinet.

export. A product sold to another country.

***ex post facto* law.** A law that punishes a person for an action that was not illegal at the time the action took place.

extraconstitutional. Not mentioned in the Constitution but established by practice or tradition.

factions. Groups with different interests within one political party or other larger group.

factory farm. (See agribusiness.)

fascism. A form of totalitarian government found in Italy and Germany in the years before and during World War II.

featherbedding. A term used to describe a union requirement that owners hire and pay workers for certain jobs whether the jobs are needed or not.

federal courts. The national system of courts in the United States.

federal government. The national government of the United States.

federalism. A system of many governments under one central government with power divided and shared by all.

Federal Reserve System. An agency of the national government set up to regulate the American money system and issue paper money—"Federal Reserve Notes."

feeder road. A road built to connect an outlying area with a major highway.

felony. A serious crime such as murder, rape, or robbery.

feudalism. An economic and social system run by queens or kings and various ranks of nobles, each rank of nobles owing allegiance to the next higher rank.

fine. Money that must be paid as punishment for some offense.

fiscal year. A full year, generally beginning and ending in midsummer rather than in January and December, used in dealing with financial matters.

foreign aid. A government program that gives economic and military assistance to other countries.

foreign policy. The course of action taken by a government in dealing with other countries.

franchise. The right to vote.

franking privilege. The right of congressional representatives to mail personal letters, printed speeches, and other printed materials without paying postage.

free enterprise. A system in which businesses are free to operate as they choose, subject to certain regulations set up to protect the public interest.

free trade. Trade between countries that agree not to set up high tariffs or other high taxes on goods entering their countries.

general election. An election in which voters choose people to fill public offices.

general warrant. (See warrant.)

gerrymandering. Forming election districts in ways that will give one political party control of as many districts as possible.

gift tax. A tax paid by the giver of a gift of money or property that is over a certain specified value.

glittering generalities. A propaganda technique that uses broad and meaningless statements with which almost anyone would agree to influence public opinion.

government. An organization set up to make rules for a large group of people and to provide some kind of authority to enforce the rules.

government corporation. An independent executive agency of the national government set up to carry out certain business-related functions of government.

governor. The executive head of a state government.

grand jury. A body of citizens appointed to hear charges against a person suspected of a crime and decide whether the person should be brought to trial.

gross national product (GNP). The total value of all goods and services produced in a country each year.

habeas corpus. (See writ of *habeas corpus*.)

habitat. The natural dwelling place or environment of a plant or animal.

hearing. A meeting of a congressional committee to consider a bill, sometimes open to the public and in those cases called an open hearing.

ideology. A group of political beliefs that together present a unified view of the way government and society should be run.

immigration. The process by which people leave their own country to settle in another country.

impeachment. An official decision by the House of Representatives that a government official should stand trial for some wrongdoing. Trials following impeachments are held in the Senate.

implied powers. A term for the unspecified powers given Congress in the "elastic clause" of the Constitution to make it possible for Congress to carry out the powers that are specifically mentioned in the Constitution.

import. A product bought from another country.

inalienable rights. Natural rights that cannot be given up or taken away. (Also called unalienable rights.)

income tax. A tax on the earnings of a person (personal income tax) or a business (corporate income tax).

incorporated village. A small community chartered by a state government to carry out the duties of local government.

indentured servant. A person who signs a contract saying he or she will work for another person for a period of time in exchange for some form of aid or service.

independent agency. An executive commission or board set up by Congress to apply the knowledge of experts to certain government problems.

indictment. A formal accusation of guilt made by a grand jury. An indictment must be made before a person can be tried for a crime.

industrialization. The process by which a country or region begins setting up factories and an efficient transportation system to carry manufactured goods.

industrial union. A labor group made up of all the people working in an industry—all steel workers or all automobile workers, for example.

inflation. An economic term for a rise in prices and a drop in the buying power of a dollar.

injunction. A court order forbidding a person or a group of people to do something.

institution. (See social institution.)

integration. Putting an end to the separation of racial groups in schools, theaters, and other public places.

interest. Income received in addition to full repayment of a loan, a bond, or other money that has been borrowed.

interest group. A group of people with common desires and concerns.

Interstate Highway System. The nationwide network of superhighways begun in the 1950s and financed mainly by the national government.

intracoastal waterway. A system of rivers and canals located close to a seacoast.

investigatory function. The congressional right to set up committees to study various social or political issues in an attempt to locate the source of a problem.

isolationism. A belief that the United States should avoid becoming involved in European political affairs.

Joint Chiefs of Staff. A group of military advisers who work with the civilian head of the Department of Defense.

joint committee. A congressional committee made up of members of both houses of Congress set up to deal with matters of interest to both houses.

joint conference committee. A special kind of congressional joint committee set up to revise a bill so that it will be acceptable to the majority of the members of both houses of Congress.

judicial branch. The branch of government that is responsible for interpreting, or giving meaning to, laws.

judicial review. The power of the United States Supreme Court to declare laws unconstitutional.

junket. A pleasure trip taken by a government official at public expense.

junta. A small group, generally made up of military officers, in control of an authoritarian government.

jurisdiction. A court's right to hear certain kinds of cases. Original jurisdiction over a case gives a court the right to hear the case first. Appellate jurisdiction over a case gives a court the right to retry the case.

justice of the peace. The judge presiding over a lower state court located in a small town or rural area.

labor. The work that is done to produce goods and services.

landfill area. An area that was first used as a dumping place for trash and garbage and then covered with earth so that it could be used for other purposes.

land reclamation. Making land useful for farming by repairing damaged land or by building dams, draining marshes, or otherwise changing the natural environment.

laws. Rules of conduct enforced by government.

legislative branch. The lawmaking branch of government.

legislative oversight. The power of the legislative branch to watch over the running of executive agencies and the spending of government money.

libel. False or unproved statements in writing that injure the reputation of a person.

license. An official permit obtained from government for a sum of money that gives a person the right to drive a car, truck, or other vehicle, run a business, or take part in some sport such as hunting or fishing.

limited access feature. The widely spaced entrances and exits found on many new highways including the interstate highways.

literacy law. A law stating that a person must be able to read and write in order to be granted some right such as the right to immigrate to a country.

lobbying. The work that interest groups do to influence lawmakers and other government officials to act in their favor.

local government. Any of a number of governments—city, county, township, town, village, and so on—set up at a level lower than state government.

lockout. A term used to describe the act of a business owner who closes a factory and throws everyone out of work in order to stop the formation of a union or any other labor activity the owner opposes.

long ballot. An election ballot that contains lists of candidates for many different offices.

lower house. A term for the larger house in a two-house lawmaking body. Members of the lower house generally represent smaller areas than the members of the upper house and often have shorter terms. The House of Representatives is the lower house of Congress.

machine. (See political machine.)

majority leader. The leader of the political party that holds the larger number of seats in the Senate or the House of Representatives.

majority party. The political party that holds the larger number of seats in the Senate or the House of Representatives.

management. The people who oversee the activities in a business, factory, or other economic organization to make sure that things go smoothly.

manager. (See city manager.)

manifest destiny. The popular 19th century belief that the people of the United States should control all of the land between the Atlantic and Pacific coasts.

manufacturing. Changing raw materials into finished products.

mass production. A manufacturing process set up to make a large number of the same product quickly, often on an assembly line.

mass transit. The movement of large numbers of people by bus, subway, commuter train, or other public carriers.

mayor. The elected executive head of a city government.

mayor-council government. A form of city government with an elected mayor as executive head and an elected council with lawmaking powers.

media. Various forms of communication including radio, TV, newspapers, and books.

Merchant Marine. The publicly and privately owned ships in each nation that carry people and goods on ocean highways.

metropolis. A large city.

metropolitan area. An urban area made up of a large city and a number of smaller communities in the surrounding area.

metropolitan government. One government set up to provide some or all services of local government for all the people in a metropolitan area.

militia. A body of private citizens prepared to unite as a military force in emergencies and other times of need.

minority leader. The leader of the political party that holds the smaller number of seats in the House of Representatives or Senate.

minority party. The political party that holds the smaller number of seats in the Senate or House of Representatives.

minority rights. Guarantees that those groups who do not have large enough numbers or great enough power to control a government will be allowed to enjoy equal rights of citizenship.

misdemeanor. A crime less serious than a felony, including such things as bribery and disturbing the peace.

mixed economy. An economic system in which both private businesses and government play important roles.

multinational companies. Giant economic concerns that carry on business and run factories in many different countries.

municipality. A city that has been given a charter of self-government by the state government.

mutual security arrangement. An agreement between countries that calls for general action if the political freedom of any one of the countries is threatened.

name calling. A propaganda technique that assigns unproven "good" or "bad" labels ("an honest speech" or "a Communist plot") to people, groups, or things that are favored or opposed.

national committee. The political group at the top of the Democratic and Republican party organizations. The basic job of the national committee is to try to elect the party's presidential candidate.

national debt. The money owed by the national government to bondholders and others.

National Guard. A militia (military force) run by a state government and subject to call by either the state government or the national government in emergencies or during natural disasters.

national nominating conventions. Meetings held every four years by the Republican and Democratic parties to write party platforms and choose candidates for President and Vice President. (Also called presidential nominating conventions.)

naturalization. The process by which a foreign-born person gains citizenship.

natural resources. Products of the earth—minerals, water, and plants—that people use to satisfy human needs.

nature's balance. A balance of the four systems of our natural environment: air, water, land, and living organisms.

"new" immigrants. Groups of people, chiefly from southern and eastern Europe, who came to the United States in the late 19th century and after.

noise pollution. The act of contaminating the environment with sounds that are unpleasant and sometimes unhealthy.

nominate. To make an official suggestion that a person be considered as a candidate for public office.

nominating conventions. (See national nominating conventions.)

"old" immigrants. Groups of people, chiefly from the British Isles and northern Europe, who came to the United States in large numbers before the late 19th century.

oligarchy. A form of government run by a few powerful people.

open enrollment. A policy that permits students to choose the public school they wish to attend, subject to limitations on the overall number of students in each school.

open primary. A primary election in which the names of all candidates of all political parties are printed on each ballot.

ordinance. A law passed by a city council.

original jurisdiction. The power of a court to hear certain kinds of cases first.

pardon. The release of a convicted or imprisoned person by a governor or the President.

parliamentary government. A form of government in which the leaders of the lawmaking body also carry out all executive duties.

parochial school. A private school supported by a religious body.

parole. The release, by a governor or the President, of a convicted prisoner who has not yet served a full term.

partnership. A business owned by two or more people who share profits and are all totally responsible for any debts of the business.

party. (See political party.)

party platform. A statement of the goals and beliefs of a political

GLOSSARY **479**

party. The Democratic and Republican parties draw up platforms every four years at their national nominating conventions.

party whip. An assistant to a majority leader or minority leader in the House of Representatives or the Senate.

passport. A government document that allows a person to leave one country and enter another.

patent. A government document that gives a person or group exclusive rights to such things as inventions.

personal income tax. A tax on the earnings of individuals, collected by the national government, by many state governments, and by some local governments. National and most state personal income taxes are based on ability-to-pay, with higher rates charged for higher incomes.

personal liberty. Individual rights involving such things as freedom of speech, freedom of religion, and protection of property.

persuasion. Efforts by people and groups to influence others to buy or do something.

petition. A written request signed by a large number of people and sent to the government or any other authority that is in a position to grant or reject the request.

petit jury. A group of citizens appointed to hear a case tried in court and make some decision about guilt or responsibility.

picket. To position union members carrying signs of protest in front of a business or factory against which a strike is being waged.

pigeonhole. To hold a bill in a congressional committee indefinitely without taking any action on it.

piggybacking. Placing truck trailers filled with freight directly on railroad flat cars so that there is no need to unload and reload the freight at the end of the rail trip.

plain folks appeal. A propaganda technique that emphasizes the "average" person and the traditional American way of life.

platform. (See party platform.)

pocket veto. The presidential power to kill a bill received within 10 days of the end of a congressional session by simply holding the bill.

political boss. The head of a political machine. Bosses often hold no elected office.

political liberty. The right of citizens to take part in the running of their government.

political machine. A political organization in local or state government set up in an attempt to control elections and the actions of politicians.

political party. An organization of private citizens and government office holders whose goal is to gain the election of party candidates and leadership of government.

polling place. A place where voting takes place.

pollution. The loss of purity through contamination.

populism. A political ideology that stresses the interests of the "common" people and the need for government action to aid these interests.

Preamble. A statement of purpose and goals found at the beginning of the United States Constitution.

precinct. A subdivision of a city or other local government set up as a voting or law-enforcement district.

preferred stock. A form of investment in a corporation that gives a person a fixed dividend—the same interest payment each year or term—but does not give a person a vote in corporate matters.

presidential government. A government in which the President and the executive branch are more powerful than any other branch of government.

presidential nominating conventions. (See national nominating conventions.)

presidential preference primary. A special kind of primary election in which the voters of a state express their feelings about presidential candidates. In some states these primaries lead to the selection of convention delegates who are required to follow the wishes of the voters. In other states delegates are allowed to ignore the results of the presidential preference primary.

presidential succession. A term used to describe the way the office of the President will be filled if the President dies or becomes unable to fill the office. The order of succession is Vice President, Speaker of the House, President *pro tempore* of the Senate, followed by the members of the President's Cabinet.

President *pro tempore*. The Senate official chosen to preside over meetings when the Vice President of the United States is unable to preside.

primary election. An election in which voters are given a chance to nominate candidates who will run for political office.

prime minister. The executive head of a parliamentary government.

private sector. Those parts of society that are maintained by the use of private wealth.

progressive tax. A tax based on ability-to-pay, with a higher rate charged for higher incomes or higher priced goods.

propaganda. The use of various methods to persuade people to think and act in certain ways, often through devices that present a one-sided view of the truth.

property tax. A tax on land, buildings, automobiles, and other forms of private property.

protectionism. A government policy that makes use of high tariffs—taxes on goods imported from other countries—to protect the interests of the country's own businesses and industries.

protective tariff. A high tax placed on certain goods imported from other countries in order to discourage imports and aid the country's own manufacturers.

public education. Schools and other educational facilities that are financed and run by government.

public investment. (See public sector.)

public opinion. A collection of individual opinions on questions and issues. The term is also used to describe the majority view on any question or issue.

public sector. Those parts of society that are set up and run by government with tax money.

public welfare. The well-being of the people in a country. The term is also used to describe government programs such as aid to farmers, poverty-stricken people, and the aged, set up to promote the well-being of specific groups of people.

quota system. A policy that places limits on the number of people from different groups who will be allowed to do something such as enter a college or immigrate to a country.

racial integration. (See integration.)
racial segregation. (See segregation.)
radial pattern. A street plan in which streets fan out from a number of central spots.
reapportionment. The redrawing of the state districts from which representatives are chosen, generally to follow changes in population.
recycling. Changing used products into useful materials.
refugee. A person who has fled his or her country because of dangerous conditions such as war, revolution, or government actions against certain groups of people.
register. To sign an official statement in order to receive some privilege, such as the right to vote, for which one is qualified.
regressive tax. A tax that sets one rate for all taxpayers.
regulatory commission. An independent executive agency set up by Congress to watch over certain aspects of the country's economy.
renewable resources. Natural resources such as forests and water that can be reproduced by planting or used endlessly.
representative democracy. A form of government in which the people rule indirectly through their elected representatives. (Also called a republic.)
reprieve. An official delay in carrying out a legal sentence, at the command of a governor or the President.
republic. A form of government in which the people rule indirectly through their elected representatives. (Also called a representative democracy.)
reserved powers. Those powers, not mentioned in the Constitution, that are given in very general terms to the states in the 10th Amendment.
revenue. Money collected by a government.
revenue sharing. A government program in which money collected by the national government is shared with city and state governments.
rural. A term used to describe farmlands and very small towns and villages. The United States Bureau of the Census defines "rural" as communities with fewer than 2,500 people.

sales tax. A tax on goods and services paid by the person who buys them.
satellite city. A small city lying within the metropolitan area surrounding a large city.
satellite nation. A country whose government is heavily influenced by the decisions of another more powerful and generally larger country.
savings and loan association. A banking institution that offers savings accounts, loans, and in some cases checking accounts.
scab. A term used to describe a worker who opposes a labor union's policy by working as a strikebreaker during a strike.
scarcity. An economic term used to describe the fact that the things we want do not come free or in unlimited amounts.
search warrant. (See warrant.)
secret ballot. A ballot marked by a voter in private.
segregation. The separation of different races in schools, theaters, and other public places.
selectmen. The people elected to carry out the daily activities of a New England town government.
self-incrimination. Giving evidence against one's self in court.
self-sufficiency. (See economic self-sufficiency.)
short ballot. An election ballot that contains the names of candidates for only a few offices.
single proprietorship. A form of business owned by one person.
slander. False or unproved statements spoken aloud that injure the reputation of a person.

social institution. A formally or informally organized body that serves some human need and generally has an influence on the values that a person forms. Families, schools, and churches are examples of social institutions.
social security. A welfare program, run by the national government, that provides aid to a number of people including people who are retired, unemployed, or disabled.
society. A large group of people with common interests. The term "society" is also used to describe the largest social body with which a group of people feel a strong relationship—in most cases, the people of one's own country.
Speaker of the House. The presiding officer of the House of Representatives, elected by the members of the House.
special district. A unit of local government set up to carry out one task such as running a school or providing clean water.
split ticket. A ballot on which a voter has selected candidates from two or more parties rather than just one party.
standing committee. A congressional committee in the House of Representatives or the Senate that has been set up on a permanent basis to deal with some special area of interest.
state central committee. The Republican and Democratic party organization in each state set up to coordinate the work of the city and county committees.
State of the Union message. An annual report made by the President to the Congress, including suggestions about laws the President would like to see passed in the coming year.
states' rights. The general powers given to the states in the 10th Amendment. The term is also used to describe groups who favor strengthening the powers of state governments.
statutory law. A law passed by a lawmaking body such as the Congress, a state legislature, or a city council.
steering committee. A committee set up by each political party in each

house of Congress to consider matters of policy and help get bills favored by the party passed into law. The steering committees in the Senate are often called policy committees.

stock. An investment in a corporation that gives a person a share in the ownership of the corporation and pays interest in the form of dividends.

stockholders. The owners of a corporation.

straight ticket. A ballot on which a voter has selected candidates from one party only.

suburbs. Communities located around the central or largest city in a metropolitan area.

suffrage. The right to vote.

super block pattern. A street plan in which streets are laid out according to the natural features of the land, generally with a number of curves and dead ends.

supreme court. The name given the highest court in the federal court system and in most state court systems.

tariff. A tax on goods brought into a country from another country.

taxes. Money collected by government to pay the costs of running the government.

test case. A case appealed to the United States Supreme Court in an attempt to get a ruling that will affect, not only the case being tried, but similar cases and situations throughout the country.

testimonial. A propaganda technique in which a well-known person endorses a product or political candidate, generally with no special qualifications for judging the product or politician.

third party. A term used to describe minor political parties that have been formed from time to time in the United States, generally because of a feeling that the two major parties were ignoring issues or not handling them well.

totalitarian government. A form of government in which the rules are made by one or a few people and an attempt is made to gain total control over the citizens' lives.

town. An urban community smaller than a city. The term is also used in a special sense to describe a form of local government found in New England in which citizens generally have the right to vote directly on town laws in town meetings.

town meeting. A gathering of citizens in a New England town to discuss local problems and vote on ways of handling the problems.

township. A form of local government found in parts of the East and Middle West set up to take care of such matters as schools and local roads. (Also called a civil township.)

transcontinental. Across the continent; in the United States, from the Atlantic Coast to the Pacific Coast.

transfer device. A propaganda technique in which a connection is made between something most people like or dislike and something else about which most people have no strong feeling.

treason. Attempting to overthrow one's government or giving aid to the enemies of one's government.

trial court. One of many courts where trials begin.

trial jury. (See petit jury.)

trust company. A bank that specializes in the long-term management of large sums of money and other forms of property.

two-party system. A political system in which two major political parties share and compete for government power.

unalienable rights. Natural rights that cannot be given up or taken away. (Also called inalienable rights.)

unconstitutional. Opposed to the meaning of the Constitution.

unicameral. A lawmaking body made up of only one house.

unincorporated village. A small community that does not have a charter of local self-government.

union shop. A union requirement that every worker in a factory or business has to be a union member or agree to become one in order to be hired.

upper house. A term for the smaller house in a two-house lawmaking body. Members of the upper house generally represent larger areas than the members of the lower house and often have longer terms. The Senate is the upper house of Congress.

urban. A term used to describe cities and towns. The United States Bureau of the Census defines "urban" as communities with more than 2,500 people.

urbanization. The movement of people away from farms and villages into cities and towns.

urban renewal. The rebuilding of the run-down parts of cities.

values. Those things that people believe are right and good and their ideas about what is desirable.

vandalism. The act of destroying property or damaging the appearance of property.

verdict. The final decision of a petit, or trial, jury.

veto. An executive refusal to sign a legislative bill into law.

ward. A subdivision of a city set up as a voting or administrative district.

warrant. A court order that gives a law-enforcement officer the power to make an arrest or search private property. Warrants given out by American courts almost always list specific people, places, or things and give reasons for the arrest or search. In most cases, general warrants—warrants that do not give specific details—are illegal.

watchers. People placed in polling places by political parties or candidates to make sure the election is being run honestly.

whip. (See party whip.)

White House. The official home of the President and the place where many presidential advisers and staff members work.

writ of *habeas corpus*. A court order requiring that an arrested person be given a hearing before a judge who must decide whether or not the person should be kept in jail before being tried.

THE CONSTITUTION OF THE UNITED STATES

Our Constitution provides the basic framework for the government of the United States. The entire Constitution and the first 26 amendments are printed in black type on the following pages. The words that appear in color—the headings and explanations—have been added to make your study of the Constitution more rewarding.

Preamble

We, the people of the United States, in order to form a more perfect union, establish justice, insure domestic tranquillity, provide for the common defense, promote the general welfare, and secure the blessings of liberty to ourselves and our posterity, do ordain and establish this Constitution for the United States of America.

The Preamble explains the reasons for writing the Constitution and lists the goals the writers wished to achieve.

Article I. The Legislative Department

Section 1. Congress

All legislative powers herein granted shall be vested in a Congress of the United States, which shall consist of a Senate and House of Representatives.

National lawmaking power is given to a Congress of two houses.

Section 2. The House of Representatives

1. Term and Election. The House of Representatives shall be composed of members chosen every second year by the people of the several States, and the electors in each State shall have the qualifications requisite for electors of the most numerous branch of the State legislature.

Members of the House of Representatives are given two-year terms. All people who have the right to vote for members of their state legislature are given the right to vote for members of the House.

2. Qualifications for Members. No person shall be a representative who shall not have attained to the age of twenty-five years, and been seven years a citizen of the United States, and who shall not, when elected, be an inhabitant of that State in which he shall be chosen.

A member of the House of Representatives must be at least 25, have been a citizen for at least seven years, and live in the state that elects him or her.

3. Representation Based on Population. Representatives and direct taxes shall be apportioned among the several States which may be included within this Union, according to their respective numbers, which shall be determined by adding to the whole number of free persons, including those bound to service for a term of years, and excluding Indians not taxed, three fifths of all other persons. The actual enumeration shall be made within three years after the first meeting of the Congress of the United States, and within every subsequent term of ten years, in such manner as they shall by law direct. The number of representatives shall not exceed one for every thirty thousand, but each State shall have at least one representative; and until such enumeration shall be made, the State of New Hampshire shall be entitled to choose three, Massachusetts eight, Rhode Island and Providence Plantations one, Connecticut five, New York six, New Jersey four, Pennsylvania eight, Delaware one, Maryland six, Virginia ten, North Carolina five, South Carolina five, and Georgia three.

The number of representatives from each state in the House of Representatives depends on the population of the state. Each state will have at least one representative and a census will be taken every 10 years to measure population. Two parts of this paragraph no longer apply: (1) direct taxes can now be collected not just by population but also by income following the 16th Amendment; (2) "three fifths of all other persons" refers to slavery and was changed by the 13th and 14th Amendments.

4. Filling Vacancies. When vacancies happen in the representation from any State, the executive authority thereof shall issue writs of election to fill such vacancies.

If a member of the House resigns or dies the governor of the state must call a special election to choose a replacement.

5. Officers and Impeachment. The House of Representatives shall choose their speaker and other officers, and shall have the sole power of impeachment.

The Speaker of the House, to be chosen by the members of the House, is made the presiding officer of the body. The House of Representatives is given the power to impeach—accuse of wrongdoing—any federal official.

Section 3. The Senate

1. Number of Members, Selection, and Term. The Senate of the United States shall be composed of two senators from each State, chosen by the legislature thereof for six years; and each senator shall have one vote.

Each state will have two senators, each with a term of six years. The statement that senators are to be chosen by the state legislatures was changed by the 17th Amendment, which gave the people the right to vote directly for senators.

2. End of Term and Filling Vacancies. **Immediately after they shall be assembled in consequence of the first election, they shall be divided as equally as may be into three classes. The seats of the senators of the first class shall be vacated at the expiration of the second year, of the second class at the expiration of the fourth year, and of the third class at the expiration of the sixth year, so that one third may be chosen every second year; and if vacancies happen by resignation, or otherwise, during the recess of the legislature of any State, the executive thereof may make temporary appointments until the next meeting of the legislature, which shall then fill such vacancies.**

One third of the senators will stand for election every two years. The statement that governors may appoint replacements when senators die or resign was changed by the 17th Amendment, which calls for special elections unless the state legislature gives the governor the power to appoint a replacement.

3. Qualifications for Members. **No person shall be a senator who shall not have attained to the age of thirty years, and been nine years a citizen of the United States, and who shall not, when elected, be an inhabitant of that State for which he shall be chosen.**

A senator must be at least 30, have been a citizen for at least nine years, and live in the state that elects her or him.

4. Presiding Officer. **The Vice President of the United States shall be President of the Senate, but shall have no vote, unless they be equally divided.**

The Vice President of the United States is made the presiding officer of the Senate—the President of the Senate—but is allowed to vote only when an extra vote is needed to break a tie.

5. Other Officers. **The Senate shall choose their other officers, and also a president *pro tempore,* in the absence of the Vice President, or when he shall exercise the office of President of the United States.**

The President *pro tempore*, to be chosen by the senators, will preside in the absence of the Vice President.

6. Trials of Impeachment. **The Senate shall have the sole power to try all impeachments. When sitting for that purpose, they shall be on oath or affirmation. When the President of the United States is tried, the chief justice shall preside: and no person shall be convicted without the concurrence of two thirds of the members present.**

The Senate is given the power to try federal officials who have been impeached by the House of Representatives. A two-thirds vote is needed to convict an official. Normally the presiding officer of the Senate, the Vice President, presides over trials of impeachment. But if the President is being tried the Vice President would have a personal stake in the outcome. Therefore the Chief Justice of the United States Supreme Court presides over a trial of the President.

7. Conviction of Federal Officials. **Judgment in cases of impeachment shall not extend further than to removal from office, and disqualification to hold and enjoy any office of honor, trust or profit under the United States; but the party convicted shall nevertheless be liable and subject to indictment, trial, judgment and punishment, according to law.**

If the Senate convicts an impeached official, the official will be removed from office and never again be allowed to hold a federal office. The official may then be tried in a regular court.

Section 4. Elections and Meetings

1. Regulation of Elections. **The times, places, and manner of holding elections for senators and representatives, shall be prescribed in each State by the legislature thereof; but the Congress may at any time by law make or alter such regulations, except as to the places of choosing senators.**

The state legislatures are given the right to set the time, place, and rules for electing members of Congress. Congress may, however, make changes in these matters.

2. Meeting Times. **The Congress shall assemble at least once in every year, and such meeting shall be on the first Monday in December, unless they shall by law appoint a different day.**

Congress must meet at least once a year. This clause was added to make sure that no President would be able to put an end to regular meetings of Congress. The 20th Amendment changed the opening date from December to January.

Section 5. Rules and Procedures

1. Admission of Members and Quorum. **Each House shall be the judge of the elections, returns and qualifications of its own members, and a majority of each shall constitute a quorum to do business; but a smaller number may adjourn from day to day, and may be authorized to compel the attendance of absent** members, in such manner, and under such penalties as each House may provide.

Each house can refuse to admit a new member by a majority vote. Officially, a quorum—in this case, a majority of the members of a house—is needed to carry on the business of a house. But the need for a quorum can be ignored if none of the members present object. Members can set up penalties to encourage absent members to attend.

2. House Rules. Each House may determine the rules of its proceedings, punish its members for disorderly behavior, and, with the concurrence of two thirds, expel a member.

Each house can make its own rules for carrying on its work and for punishing members who do not follow the rules. A two-thirds vote is needed to expel a member.

3. Journal. Each House shall keep a journal of its proceedings, and from time to time publish the same, excepting such parts as may in their judgment require secrecy; and the yeas and nays of the members of either House on any question shall, at the desire of one fifth of those present, be entered on the journal.

Each house must keep and publish a record of its meetings. Members of a house, however, may vote to keep some parts of their meetings secret.

4. End of Meetings. Neither House, during the session of Congress, shall, without the consent of the other, adjourn for more than three days, nor to any other place than that in which the two Houses shall be sitting.

Both houses must agree on the time for ending a session.

Section 6. Privileges and Limitations

1. Salaries and Freedom from Arrest. The senators and representatives shall receive a compensation for their services, to be ascertained by law, and paid out of the Treasury of the United States. They shall in all cases, except treason, felony and breach of the peace, be privileged from arrest during their attendance at the session of their respective Houses, and in going to and returning from the same; and for any speech or debate in either House, they shall not be questioned in any other place.

Members of Congress are paid by the national government, not by the states. A member cannot be arrested while attending a session of Congress except for the offenses noted in the clause. Members are also allowed to speak freely in debates.

2. Holding Other Offices Forbidden. No senator or representative shall, during the time for which he was elected, be appointed to any civil office under the authority of the United States, which shall have been created, or the emoluments whereof shall have been increased during such time; and no person holding any office under the United States shall be a member of either House during his continuance in office.

While they are members of Congress, senators and representatives cannot be appointed to fill newly created federal jobs or jobs for which there has just been an increase in salary.

Section 7. Making Laws

1. Money Bills. All bills for raising revenue shall originate in the House of Representatives; but the Senate may propose or concur with amendments as on other bills.

All bills for raising money must start in the House of Representatives. The Senate may, however, suggest changes in money bills.

2. How Bills Become Laws. Every bill which shall have passed the House of Representatives and the Senate, shall, before it becomes a law, be presented to the President of the United States; if he approve he shall sign it, but if not he shall return it, with his objections to that House in which it shall have originated, who shall enter the objections at large on their journal, and proceed to reconsider it. If after such reconsideration two thirds of that House shall agree to pass the bill, it shall be sent, together with the objections, to the other House, by which it shall likewise be reconsidered, and if approved by two thirds of that House, it shall become a law. But in all such cases the votes of both Houses shall be determined by yeas and nays, and the names of the persons voting for and against the bill shall be entered on the journal of each House respectively. If any bill shall not be returned by the President within ten days (Sundays excepted) after it shall have been presented to him, the same shall be a law, in like manner as if he had signed it, unless the Congress by their adjournment prevent its return, in which case it shall not be a law.

Both houses of Congress must agree on all parts of a bill before it is passed and sent to the President. A bill becomes a law in any of the following cases: (1) the President signs it; (2) the President vetoes the law in objection and both houses pass it by a two-thirds vote; (3) the President fails to return a bill to the Congress within a 10-day period during a congressional session. A bill does *not* become a law if (1) either house fails to pass a vetoed law by a two-thirds vote, or (2) the President receives the bill within 10 days of the end of a congressional session and holds it without signing it—a pocket veto.

3. The President's Veto Power. Every order, resolution, or vote to which the concurrence of the Senate and House of Representatives may be necessary (except on a question of adjournment) shall be presented to the President of the United States; and before the same shall take effect, shall be approved by him, or being disapproved by him, shall be repassed by two thirds of the Senate and House of Representatives, according to the rules and limitations prescribed in the case of a bill.

All congressional actions except a vote to end a session must be presented to the President for approval or veto. Any veto can be overruled by a two-thirds vote in both houses of Congress.

Section 8. Powers Given to Congress

The first 17 paragraphs of Section 8 list specific powers. These are called the "enumerated powers." The last paragraph of Section 8 gives Congress the "implied powers" that will be needed to carry out the other powers.

1. Collecting Taxes. The Congress shall have power to lay and collect taxes, duties, imposts and excises, to pay the debts and provide for the common defense and general welfare of the United States; but all duties, imposts and excises shall be uniform throughout the United States;

Congress has the power to collect taxes and pay national debts. All special taxes must be the same in all parts of the country.

2. Borrowing Money. To borrow money on the credit of the United States;

Congress may borrow money needed by the federal government.

3. Regulating Trade. To regulate commerce with foreign nations, and among the several States, and with the Indian tribes;

Congress is given the power to set rules for trade with foreign countries and between states—interstate commerce.

4. Passing Naturalization and Bankruptcy Laws. To establish an uniform rule of naturalization, and uniform laws on the subject of bankruptcies throughout the United States;

Congress has the power to decide which people may immigrant to the United States and become citizens. Congress may also pass laws concerning the payment of personal and business debts.

5. Coining Money and Setting Up a System of Weights and Measures. To coin money, regulate the value thereof, and of foreign coin, and fix the standard of weights and measures;

Congress is in charge of the national money system and deciding upon the value of foreign money. Congress also has the power to set up the official system of weights and measurements to be followed throughout the country.

6. Punishing Counterfeiters. To provide for the punishment of counterfeiting the securities and current coin of the United States;

Congress may set up rules for punishing people who make counterfeit—false—money.

7. Setting Up Post Offices. To establish post offices and post roads;

Congress is given the power to set up a national system of post offices and the roads that will be needed to carry the mail quickly.

8. Passing Patent and Copyright Laws. To promote the progress of science and useful arts by securing for limited times to authors and inventors the exclusive right to their respective writings and discoveries;

Congress may pass laws that prevent other people from using the work of inventors and authors without permission.

9. Setting Up a System of Federal Courts. To constitute tribunals inferior to the Supreme Court;

Congress has the power to set up a system of federal, or national, courts to work under the United States Supreme Court.

10. Punishing Piracy. To define and punish piracies and felonies committed on the high seas, and offenses against the law of nations;

Congress may decide how to punish robberies and other crimes that take place at sea.

11. Declaring War. To declare war, grant letters of marque and reprisal, and make rules concerning captures on land and water;

Congress alone has the power to declare war. Letters of marque and reprisal were once used to give private citizens the right to capture enemy ships.

12. Raising an Army. To raise and support armies, but no appropriation of money to that use shall be for a longer term than two years;

Congress may set up and pay the expenses of an army but money for an army must be voted upon at least every two years.

13. Maintaining a Navy. To provide and maintain a navy;

Congress may also use government money to support a navy.

14. Regulating the Armed Forces. To make rules for the government and regulation of the land and naval forces;

Congress may set up rules for running the armed forces, including today the Air Force.

15. Calling Forth the State Militias. To provide for calling forth the militia to execute the laws of the Union, suppress insurrections and repel invasions;

The state military forces—now called the National Guard—may be used by Congress in cases of rebellion or invasion.

16. Regulating the State Militias. To provide for organizing, arming, and disciplining the militia, and for governing such part of them as may be employed in the service of the United States, reserving to the States respectively the appointment of the officers, and the authority of training the militia according to the discipline prescribed by Congress;

Congress may set up rules for running the state military forces. But each state has the right to appoint militia officers and carry out the rules set by Congress.

17. Governing Federal Land. To exercise exclusive legislation in all cases whatsoever, over such district (not exceeding ten miles square) as may, by cession of particular States and the acceptance of Congress, become the seat of the government of the United States, and to exercise like authority over all places purchased by the consent of the legislature of the State in which the same shall be, for the erection of forts, magazines, arsenals, dockyards, and other needful buildings; and

With the permission of the states involved, Congress may take direct control over land needed by the national government. Included here is the land needed to set up a national capital and run the armed forces.

18. Implied Powers. To make all laws which shall be necessary and proper for carrying into execution the foregoing powers, and all other powers vested by this Constitution in the government of the United States, or in any department or officer thereof.

This "elastic clause" permits Congress to pass laws that are "necessary and proper" to carry out the other powers given to Congress in the Constitution.

Section 9. Powers Forbidden to the National Government

1. Ending the Slave Trade. The migration or importation of such persons as any of the States now existing shall think proper to admit, shall not be prohibited by the Congress prior to the year one thousand eight hundred and eight, but a tax or duty may be imposed on such importation, not exceeding ten dollars for each person.

In the years before 1808, Congress was forbidden to pass any law to end the importation of slaves from other countries.

2. Suspending the Writ of Habeas Corpus. The privilege of the writ of *habeas corpus* shall not be suspended, unless when in cases of rebellion or invasion the public safety may require it.

Except in cases of rebellion or invasion, an accused person has the right to make use of a writ of *habeas corpus*—a court order calling for a hearing before a judge who must decide whether or not to keep the person in jail.

3. Passing Bills of Attainder and Ex Post Facto *Laws.* No bill of attainder or *ex post facto* law shall be passed.

Congress cannot pass two kinds of laws: (1) bills of attainder—laws that punish people without giving them trials by jury; and (2) *ex post facto* laws—laws that punish people for actions that took place before the laws were passed.

4. Collecting Unequal Taxes. No capitation, or other direct, tax shall be laid, unless in proportion to the census or enumeration hereinbefore directed to be taken.

Following this clause, Congress must base taxes on population and tax all people equally. The 16th Amendment made it possible for Congress to tax people "unequally" by placing taxes on incomes.

5. Taxing Trade Between States. No tax or duty shall be laid on articles exported from any State.

Congress cannot tax goods sent from one state to another.

6. Giving Unfair Advantage to the Trade of Any State. No preference shall be given by any regulation of commerce or revenue to the ports of one State over those of another: nor shall vessels bound to, or from, one State be obliged to enter, clear, or pay duties in another.

Congress may not pass laws that would favor the ports of any state over those of another.

7. Misusing Government Money. No money shall be drawn from the Treasury, but in consequence of appropriations made by law; and a regular statement and account of the receipts and expenditures of all public money shall be published from time to time.

Congress must approve all uses of government money.

8. Granting Titles of Nobility. No title of nobility shall be granted by the United States: and no person holding any office of profit or trust under them, shall, without the consent of the Congress, accept of any present, emolument, office, or title of any kind whatever, from any king, prince, or foreign State.

No federal official has the power to grant a title of nobility. In addition, no federal official may receive a title or gift from another country without the approval of Congress.

Section 10. Powers Forbidden to the States

1. Powers Completely Forbidden. No State shall enter into any treaty, alliance, or confederation; grant letters of marque and reprisal; coin money; emit bills of credit; make anything but gold and silver coin a tender in payment of debts; pass any bill of attainder, *ex post facto* law, or law impairing the obligation of contracts, or grant any title of nobility.

Only the national government can make treaties with foreign governments and coin money. Note that many of the things that were forbidden to the national government in Section 9 are forbidden to the states in this paragraph of Section 10.

2. Setting Trade Laws Is Limited. No State shall, without the consent of the Congress, lay any imposts or duties on imports or exports, except what may be absolutely necessary for executing its inspection laws: and the net produce of all duties and imposts laid by any State on imports or exports, shall be for the use of the Treasury of the United States; and all such laws shall be subject to the revision and control of the Congress.

Congress has basic control over trade with foreign countries and trade between the states.

3. Military Rights Are Limited. No State shall, without the consent of Congress, lay any duty of tonnage, keep troops, or ships of war in time of peace, enter into any agreement or compact with another State, or with a foreign power, or engage in war, unless actually invaded, or in such imminent danger as will not admit of delay.

Congress has basic control over military actions.

Article II. The Executive Department

Section 1. The President and Vice President

1. Executive Power and Term. The executive power shall be vested in a President of the United States of America. He shall hold his office during the term of four years, and, together with the Vice President, chosen for the same term, be elected as follows:

National executive power is given to the President. (Executive power is the power needed to execute, or carry out, laws and perform the other duties of a government leader.) Both the President and the Vice President are given four-year terms.

2. The Electoral College. Each State shall appoint, in such manner as the legislature thereof may direct, a number of electors, equal to the whole number of senators and representatives to which the State may be entitled in the Congress: but no senator or representative, or person holding an office of trust or profit under the United States, shall be appointed an elector.

The American people do not vote directly for the President. Instead they choose electors who, in turn, choose the President and Vice President. The number of electors in a state is equal to the number of senators and representatives the state has in Congress.

3. The Original Method of Election. The electors shall meet in their respective States, and vote by ballot for two persons, of whom one at least shall not be an inhabitant of the same State with themselves. And they shall make a list of all the persons voted for, and of the number of votes for each; which list they shall sign and certify, and transmit sealed to the seat of the government of the United States, directed to the president of the Senate. The president of the Senate shall, in the presence of the Senate and House of Representatives, open all the certificates, and the votes shall then be counted. The person having the greatest number of votes shall be the President, if such number be a majority of the whole number of electors appointed; and if there be more than one who have such majority, and have an equal number of votes, then the House of Representatives shall immediately choose by ballot one of them for President; and if no person have a majority, then from the five highest on the list the said house shall in like manner choose the President. But in choosing the President, the votes shall be taken by States, the representation from each State having one vote; a quorum for this purpose shall consist of a member or members from two thirds of the States, and a majority of all the States shall be necessary to a choice. In every case, after the choice of the President, the person having the greatest number of votes of the electors shall be the Vice President. But if there should remain two or more who have equal votes, the Senate shall choose from them by ballot the Vice President.

Following the method in this paragraph, the person who receives the majority of the votes in the Electoral College becomes President and the person who receives the next largest number of votes becomes Vice President. In case of a tie or other difficulty the House of Representatives chooses the President and the Senate chooses the Vice President. The 12th Amendment brought a major change in this method: the election of the Vice President is now done on a second ballot.

4. Time of Elections. The Congress may determine the time of choosing the electors, and the day on which they shall give their votes;

which day shall be the same throughout the United States.

Congress has the power to set the time for a nationwide election of presidential electors and the time for the Electoral College's vote.

5. Qualifications of the President. **No person except a natural-born citizen, or a citizen of the United States, at the time of the adoption of this Constitution, shall be eligible to the office of President; neither shall any person be eligible to that office who shall not have attained to the age of thirty-five years, and been fourteen years a resident within the United States.**

The President must be a citizen by birth, be at least 35, and have lived in the United States for at least 14 years.

6. The President's Death or Disability. **In case of the removal of the President from office, or of his death, resignation, or inability to discharge the powers and duties of the said office, the same shall devolve on the Vice President, and the Congress may by law provide for the case of removal, death, resignation, or inability, both of the President and Vice President, declaring what officer shall then act as President, and such officer shall act accordingly, until the disability be removed, or a President shall be elected.**

If the President dies, resigns, or becomes unable to fill the office, the Vice President becomes President. Congress may set up an order of succession to follow the Vice President in case the Vice President also is unable to fill the office. The 25th Amendment adds further details.

7. The President's Salary. **The President shall, at stated times, receive for his services a compensation, which shall neither be increased nor diminished during the period for which he shall have been elected, and he shall not receive within that period any other emolument from the United States, or any of them.**

The President's salary may not be increased or decreased during the President's term in office.

8. Oath of Office. **Before he enter on the execution of his office, he shall take the following oath or affirmation:—"I do solemnly swear (or affirm) that I will faithfully execute the office of President of the United States, and will to the best of my ability, preserve, protect and defend the Constitution of the United States."**

These words are repeated by each incoming President at the inauguration ceremony.

Section 2. Powers Given to the President

1. Military Powers, Executive Departments, Reprieves, and Pardons. **The President shall be commander in chief of the army and navy of the United States, and of the militia of the several States, when called into the actual service of the United States; he may require the opinion, in writing, of the principal officer in each of the executive departments, upon any subject relating to the duties of their respective offices, and he shall have power to grant reprieves and pardons for offenses against the United States, except in cases of impeachment.**

The President is Commander in Chief of the armed forces, following the desire of the constitution makers to keep civilian control over military leaders. The President's Cabinet is not mentioned in the Constitution, but this paragraph does mention that the President may seek the advice of the heads of executive departments. The President may also grant reprieves (postponements of legal sentences) and pardons (the release of people convicted of crimes) except in cases of impeachment.

2. Treaties and Appointments. **He shall have power, by and with the advice and consent of the Senate, to make treaties, provided two thirds of the senators present concur; and he shall nominate, and by and with the advice and consent of the Senate, shall appoint ambassadors, other public ministers and consuls, judges of the Supreme Court, and all other officers of the United States, whose appointments are not herein otherwise provided for, and which shall be established by law: but the Congress may by law vest the appointment of such inferior officers, as they think proper, in the President alone, in the courts of law, or in the heads of departments.**

The President can make treaties but they must be approved by two thirds of the senators. The President can appoint diplomats and judges of the United States Supreme Court with the approval of the majority of the senators. Congress may make decisions about the way officials in lower offices should be chosen.

3. Temporary Appointments. **The President shall have power to fill up all vacancies that may happen during the recess of the Senate, by granting commissions which shall expire at the end of their next session.**

The President may make temporary appointments when the Senate is not in session.

Section 3. Presidential Duties

He shall from time to time give to the Congress information of the state of the Union, and recommend to their consideration such measures as he shall judge necessary and expedient; he may, on extraordinary occasions, convene both Houses, or either of them, and

in case of disagreement between them with respect to the time of adjournment, he may adjourn them to such time as he shall think proper; he shall receive ambassadors and other public ministers; he shall take care that the laws be faithfully executed, and shall commission all the officers of the United States.

The President must make "State of the Union" reports to Congress informing the members of executive matters and making suggestions about laws. In special cases, the President may call Congress into session and adjourn sessions of Congress. The President is also responsible for dealing with foreign ambassadors, carrying out national laws, and commissioning military officers.

Section 4. Reasons for Impeachment

The President, Vice President, and all civil officers of the United States, shall be removed from office on impeachment for, and conviction of, treason, bribery, or other high crimes and misdemeanors.

This section lists the crimes for which a President or any other federal official may be removed from office.

Article III. The Judicial Department

Section 1. The Federal Courts

The judicial power of the United States shall be vested in one Supreme Court, and in such inferior courts as the Congress may from time to time ordain and establish. The judges, both of the Supreme and inferior courts, shall hold their offices during good behavior, and shall, at stated times, receive for their services, a compensation which shall not be diminished during their continuance in office.

National judicial power is given to the United States Supreme Court and any other federal courts that Congress sets up. All federal judges are given lifetime terms.

Section 2. Powers and Duties of the Federal Courts

1. All Federal Courts. The judicial power shall extend to all cases, in law and equity, arising under this Constitution, the laws of the United States, and treaties made, or which shall be made, under their authority;—to all cases affecting ambassadors, other public ministers and consuls;—to all cases of admiralty and maritime jurisdiction;—to controversies to which the United States shall be a party;—to controversies between two or more States;—between a State and citizens of another State;—between citizens of different States,—between citizens of the same State claiming lands under grants of different States, and between a State, or the citizens thereof, and foreign States, citizens or subjects.

This paragraph lists the kinds of cases that can be tried by federal courts. The 11th Amendment made one change: cases "between a State and citizens of another State" are now tried in state courts.

2. The United States Supreme Court. In all cases affecting ambassadors, other public ministers and consuls, and those in which a State shall be party, the Supreme Court shall have original jurisdiction. In all the other cases before mentioned, the Supreme Court shall have appellate jurisdiction, both as to law and fact, with such exceptions, and under such regulations as the Congress shall make.

The Supreme Court is given original jurisdiction—the right to try cases first—over all cases in which diplomats and states are involved. The Court is given appellate jurisdiction—the right to retry cases—over all other federal cases.

3. Trial by Jury. The trial of all crimes, except in cases of impeachment, shall be by jury; and such trial shall be held in the State where the said crimes shall have been committed; but when not committed within any State, the trial shall be at such place or places as the Congress may by law have directed.

All federal criminal cases, except cases of impeachment, must be tried by jury in the state where the crime took place.

Section 3. Treason

1. Definition of Treason. Treason against the United States shall consist only in levying war against them, or in adhering to their enemies, giving them aid and comfort. No person shall be convicted of treason unless on the testimony of two witnesses to the same overt act, or on confession in open court.

Treason is clearly defined. Conviction must be based on the statements of two witnesses or a free confession.

2. Punishment for Treason. The Congress shall have power to declare the punishment of treason, but no attainder of treason shall work corruption of blood, or forfeiture except during the life of the person attainted.

Congress may decide how to punish an act of treason, but only the guilty person may be punished, not the person's family.

Article IV. The Federal System

Section 1. Respect Due to Each State's Laws

Full faith and credit shall be given in each State to the public acts, records, and judicial proceedings of every other State. And the

Congress may by general laws prescribe the manner in which such acts, records, and proceedings shall be proved, and the effect thereof.

All laws, court decisions, and public records of each state must be respected by the other states.

Section 2. Duties of States to Other States

1. Equal Treatment of All Citizens. The citizens of each State shall be entitled to all privileges and immunities of citizens in the several States.

States must treat the citizens of other states in the same way they treat the citizens of their own state.

2. Returning Escaped Criminals. A person charged in any State with treason, felony, or other crime, who shall flee from justice, and be found in another State, shall on demand of the executive authority of the State from which he fled, be delivered up to be removed to the State having jurisdiction of the crime.

If a person who is to be tried for a crime in one state escapes to another state the governor of the second state must see that the person returns to the state in which the crime was committed.

3. Returning Escaped Slaves. No person held to service or labor in one State, under the laws thereof, escaping into another, shall, in consequence of any law or regulation therein, be discharged from such service or labor, but shall be delivered up on claim of the party to whom such service or labor may be due.

The 13th Amendment changed this paragraph by ending slavery.

Section 3. New States and Territories

1. New States. New States may be admitted by the Congress into this Union; but no new State shall be formed or erected within the jurisdiction of any other State; nor any State be formed by the junction of two or more States, or parts of States, without the consent of the legislatures of the States concerned as well as of the Congress.

Congress is given the power to admit new states to the United States. If the land of any other state is used to make a new state, the permission of the state legislature of the older state is also needed.

2. Federal Territory and Property. The Congress shall have power to dispose of and make all needful rules and regulations respecting the territory or other property belonging to the United States; and nothing in this Constitution shall be so construed as to prejudice any claims of the United States, or of any particular State.

Congress is given the power to govern all territory and any other land that belongs to the federal government. (The word "territory" as it is used here means land that has not yet been formed into states.)

Section 4. National Protection of the States

The United States shall guarantee to every State in this Union a republican form of government, and shall protect each of them against invasion; and on application of the legislature, or of the executive (when the legislature cannot be convened) against domestic violence.

The national government is responsible for helping each state to keep its republican, or representative, form of government. National help is required when any state is threatened by invasion or rebellion.

Article V. Amending the Constitution

The Congress, whenever two thirds of both Houses shall deem it necessary, shall propose amendments to this Constitution, or, on the application of the legislatures of two thirds of the several States, shall call a convention for proposing amendments, which, in either case, shall be valid to all intents and purposes, as part of this Constitution, when ratified by the legislatures of three fourths of the several States, or by conventions in three fourths thereof, as the one or the other mode of ratification may be proposed by the Congress; provided that no amendment which may be made prior to the year one thousand eight hundred and eight shall in any manner affect the first and fourth clauses in the ninth section of the first article; and that no State, without its consent, shall be deprived of its equal suffrage in the Senate.

An amendment can be proposed in two ways: (1) by two thirds of the members of both houses of Congress, or (2) by two thirds of the state legislatures. In order for an amendment to become a part of the Constitution, three fourths of the states must approve. States with small populations are protected by the statement that forbids an amendment that would change the equal representation of states in the Senate.

Article VI. Government Under the Constitution

1. Old Debts. All debts contracted and engagements entered into, before the adoption of this Constitution, shall be as valid against the United States under this Constitution, as under the Confederation.

The new government set up by the Constitution must pay the debts of the Articles of Confederation government it is replacing.

2. Federal Laws over State Laws. This Constitution, and the laws of the United States which shall be made in pursuance thereof; and all treaties made, or which shall be made, under the authority of the United States, shall be the supreme law of the land; and the judges in every State shall be bound thereby, anything in the Constitution or laws of any State to the contrary notwithstanding.

State and local governments must obey the Constitution, federal laws, and federal treaties.

3. The Official Oath. The senators and representatives before mentioned, and the members of the several State legislatures, and all executive and judicial officers, both of the United States and of the several States, shall be bound by oath or affirmation to support this Constitution; but no religious test shall ever be required as a qualification to any office or public trust under the United States.

All federal and state officials must take an oath to obey the Constitution. No religious qualifications can be set for any public office in the United States.

Article VII. Ratifying the Constitution

The ratification of the conventions of nine States shall be sufficient for the establishment of this Constitution between the States so ratifying the same.

Done in Convention by the unanimous consent of the States present the seventeenth day of September in the year of our Lord one thousand seven hundred and eighty-seven, and of the independence of the United States of America the twelfth, in witness whereof we have hereunto subscribed our names.

The Constitution was completed in 1787 and signed by 39 delegates from 12 states. It went into effect in 1788 after nine of the 13 states had ratified, or accepted, it.

Amendments to the Constitution

The first 10 amendments, the Bill of Rights, were added in 1791.

Article I. The 1st Amendment

Freedom of Religion, Speech, Press, Assembly, and Petition. Congress shall make no law respecting an establishment of religion, or prohibiting the free exercise thereof; or abridging the freedom of speech, or of the press; or the right of the people peaceably to assemble, and to petition the government for a redress of grievances.

American citizens have the right to choose their own religions, speak and print their views openly, hold public meetings, and send formal requests—petitions—to the government.

Article II. The 2nd Amendment

The Right to Bear Arms. A well regulated militia, being necessary to the security of a free State, the right of the people to keep and bear arms, shall not be infringed.

States may set up militias and citizens may own rifles and guns.

Article III. The 3rd Amendment

The Right Not to Quarter Troops. No soldier shall, in time of peace, be quartered in any house, without the consent of the owner, nor in time of war, but in a manner to be prescribed by law.

In times of peace, citizens cannot be forced to let soldiers live in their homes. Even in times of war, a congressional law must be passed before people can be forced to quarter troops.

Article IV. The 4th Amendment

The Right of Privacy. The right of the people to be secure in their persons, houses, papers, and effects, against unreasonable searches and seizures, shall not be violated, and no warrants shall issue, but upon probable cause, supported by oath or affirmation, and particularly describing the place to be searched, and the persons or things to be seized.

In order to search a person's home, a law-enforcement officer must first get a warrant from a judge. The warrant must describe the place to be searched and give a reason for the search.

Article V. The 5th Amendment

The Right to a Grand Jury Hearing, Protection from Double Jeopardy and Self-Incrimination, and the Right to Due Process of Law. No person shall be held to answer for a capital, or otherwise infamous crime, unless on a presentment or indictment of a grand jury, except in cases arising in the land or naval forces, or in the militia, when in actual service in time of war or public danger; nor shall any person be subject for the same offense to be twice put in jeopardy of life or limb; nor shall be compelled in any criminal case to be a witness against himself, nor be deprived of life, liberty, or property, without due process of law; nor shall private property be taken for public use without just compensation.

With the exceptions noted, people cannot be brought to trial for serious crimes unless a grand jury decides that they should be tried. People who are judged innocent of crimes cannot be tried again for the same crimes, nor can people be forced to testify against themselves in criminal cases. The government must always follow proper legal procedures in dealing with citizens or their property.

Article VI. The 6th Amendment

The Rights of the Accused in Criminal Cases. In all criminal prosecutions, the accused shall enjoy the right to a speedy and public trial, by an impartial jury of the State and district wherein the crime shall have been committed, which district shall have been previously ascertained by law, and to be informed of the nature and cause of the accusation; to be confronted with the witnesses against him; to have compulsory process for obtaining witnesses in his favor, and to have the assistance of counsel for his defense.

People accused of crimes must be given "speedy" trials. They must be told what the charges are and be allowed to call their own witnesses. Finally, they must be given a lawyer if they cannot afford one.

Article VII. The 7th Amendment

The Right to a Trial in Civil Cases. In suits at common law, where the value in controversy shall exceed twenty dollars, the right of trial by jury shall be preserved, and no fact tried by a jury shall be otherwise reexamined in any court of the United States, than according to the rules of the common law.

Following the conditions noted, people have the right to jury trials in non-criminal cases. (Common law is law based on past decisions of judges rather than on laws passed by lawmaking bodies.)

Article VIII. The 8th Amendment

Fair Bail, Fair Fines, and Fair Punishment. Excessive bail shall not be required, nor excessive fines imposed, nor cruel and unusual punishments inflicted.

The courts may not treat accused and convicted people in cruel or unfair ways. (Bail is the money accused people may be allowed to leave with a court as a guarantee that they will return for trial.)

Article IX. The 9th Amendment

Rights Not Listed. The enumeration in the Constitution of certain rights shall not be construed to deny or disparage others retained by the people.

The fact that a right is not specifically listed in the Constitution does not mean that the people do not have that right.

Article X. The 10th Amendment

Powers Reserved for the States and the People. The powers not delegated to the United States by the Constitution, nor prohibited by it to the States, are reserved to the States respectively, or to the people.

All powers that the Constitution does not give directly to the national government or forbid to the states are to be held by the states and the people.

Article XI. The 11th Amendment

Cases Involving Suits Against States. The judicial power of the United States shall not be construed to extend to any suit in law or equity, commenced or prosecuted against one of the United States by citizens of another State, or by citizens or subjects of any foreign State.

Added in 1798, this amendment states that suits against a state government must be tried in a state court in the state involved. This changes a small part of Article III, Section 2, Paragraph 1.

Article XII. The 12th Amendment

Electing the President and Vice President. The electors shall meet in their respective States, and vote by ballot for President and Vice President, one of whom, at least, shall not be an inhabitant of the same State with themselves; they shall name in their ballots the person voted for as President, and in distinct ballots the person voted for as Vice President, and they shall make distinct lists of all persons voted for as President and of all persons voted for as Vice President, and of the number of votes for each, which lists they shall sign and certify, and transmit sealed to the seat of government of the United States, directed to the president of the Senate;—The president of the Senate shall, in the presence of the Senate and House of Representatives, open all the certificates and the votes shall then be counted;—The person having the greatest number of votes for President shall be the President, if such number be a majority of the whole number of electors appointed; and if no person have such majority, then from the persons having the highest numbers not exceeding three on the list of those voted for as President, the House of Representatives shall choose immediately, by ballot, the President. But in choosing the President, the votes shall be taken by States, the representation from each State having one vote; a quorum for this purpose shall consist of a member or members from two thirds of the States, and a majority of all the States shall be necessary to a choice. And if the House of Representatives shall not choose a President whenever the right of choice shall devolve upon them, before the fourth day of March next following, then the Vice President shall act as President, as in the case of the death or other constitutional disability of the President. The person having the greatest number of votes as Vice President shall be the Vice President, if such number be a majority of the whole number of electors appointed, and if no person have a majority, then from the two highest numbers on the list, the Senate shall choose the Vice President; a quorum for the purpose shall consist of two thirds of the whole number of senators, and a majority of the whole number shall be necessary to a choice. But no person constitutionally ineligible to the office of President shall be eligible to that of Vice President of the United States.

Added in 1804, this amendment states that the Electoral College must cast separate votes for President and Vice President, thus changing the method in Article II, Section 1, Paragraph 3. The 12th Amendment also notes that the choice must be made "before the fourth day of March," the day the presidential term was set to begin. The 20th Amendment changed the first day of the presidential term to January 20th.

Article XIII. The 13th Amendment

Section 1. *The End of Slavery.* Neither slavery nor involuntary servitude, except as a punishment for crime whereof the party shall have been duly convicted, shall exist within the United States, or any place subject to their jurisdiction.

Added in 1865, this amendment freed the slaves in all states and territories of the United States.

Section 2. *Enforcement.* Congress shall have power to enforce this article by appropriate legislation.

Congress is given the power to enforce the 13th Amendment. Note that similar enforcement sections are written into many of the later amendments.

Article XIV. The 14th Amendment

Section 1. *Definition of Citizenship and Limits on State Power.* All persons born or naturalized in the United States, and subject to the jurisdiction thereof, are citizens of the United States and of the State wherein they reside. No State shall make or enforce any law which shall abridge the privileges or immunities of citizens of the United States; nor shall any State deprive any person of life, liberty, or property, without due process of law; nor deny to any person within its jurisdiction the equal protection of the laws.

Added in 1868, the 14th Amendment defines American citizenship and says that the state governments may not deny any citizens "equal protection of the laws." In the broadest sense, this section calls upon each state government to give citizens of each state the same rights that citizens of the United States are given in the Bill of Rights.

Section 2. *Representation in Congress.* Representatives shall be apportioned among the several States according to their respective numbers, counting the whole number of persons in each State, excluding Indians not taxed. But when the right to vote at any election for the choice of electors for President and Vice President of the United States, representatives in Congress, the executive and judicial officers of a State, or the members of the legislature thereof, is denied to any of the male inhabitants of such State, being twenty-one years of age, and citizens of the United States, or in any way abridged, except for participation in rebellion, or other crime, the basis of representation therein shall be reduced in the proportion which the number of such male citizens shall bear to the whole number of male citizens twenty-one years of age in such State.

With the end of slavery, it became necessary to change the special way of counting people for taxation and representation given in Article I, Section 2, Paragraph 3. All people must be counted equally. Changes in the number of representatives each state has in the national House of Representatives must follow the new count of population. This section also calls for a reduction in the number of representatives given to any state that denies voting rights to any eligible adult male.

Section 3. *Loss of Political Rights.* No person shall be a senator or representative in Congress, or elector of President and Vice President, or hold any office, civil or military, under the United States, or under any State, who, having previously taken an oath, as a member of Congress, or as an officer of the United States, or as a member of any State legislature, or as an executive or judicial officer of any State, to support the Constitution of the United States, shall have engaged in insurrection or rebellion against the same, or given aid or comfort to the enemies thereof. But Congress may by a vote of two thirds of each House, remove such disability.

No person who has taken an oath to support the Constitution and then taken part in a rebellion against the United States may hold a state or federal office unless Congress, by a two-thirds vote of both houses, passes a law giving the person the right to hold office. This section was added to punish Confederate leaders. Congressional laws later restored the rights of these leaders.

Section 4. *Confederate Debts.* The validity of the public debt of the United States, authorized by law, including debts incurred for payment of pensions and bounties for services in suppressing insurrection or rebellion, shall not be questioned. But neither the United States nor any State shall assume or pay any debt or obligation incurred in aid of insurrection or rebellion against the United States, or any claim for the loss or emancipation of any slave; but all such debts, obligations and claims shall be held illegal and void.

The federal government refuses to pay any of the debts of the Confederate States.

Section 5. *Enforcement.* The Congress shall have power to enforce, by appropriate legislation, the provisions of this article.

Article XV. The 15th Amendment

Section 1. *Voting Rights for Black Americans.* The right of citizens of the United States to vote shall not be denied or abridged by the United States or by any State on account of race, color, or previous condition of servitude.

Added in 1870, this amendment states that no citizen can be denied the right to vote because of race or the fact that the person was once a slave.

Section 2. *Enforcement.* The Congress shall have power to enforce this article by appropriate legislation.

Article XVI. The 16th Amendment

Income Taxes. The Congress shall have power to lay and collect taxes on incomes, from whatever source derived, without apportionment among the several States, and without regard to any census or enumeration.

Added in 1913, the 16th Amendment gives Congress the power to collect taxes based on income.

Article XVII. The 17th Amendment

Section 1. *Direct Election of Senators.* The Senate of the United States shall be composed of two senators from each State, elected by the people thereof, for six years; and each senator shall have one vote. The electors in each State shall have the qualifications requisite for electors of the most numerous branch of the State legislatures.

Added in 1913, this amendment gives the people of each state the right to vote directly for the two senators from their state. The right to choose senators had originally been given to the state legislatures in Article I, Section 3, Paragraph 1.

Section 2. *Filling Vacancies in the Senate.* When vacancies happen in the representation of any State in the Senate, the executive authority of such State shall issue writs of election to fill such vacancies: *Provided,* That the legislature of any State may empower the executive thereof to make temporary appointments until the people fill the vacancies by election as the legislature may direct.

If a senator dies or is unable to complete a term in Congress, the state governor may call a special election or, with the permission of the state legislature, appoint someone to fill the office.

Section 3. *Present Senators Not Affected.* This amendment shall not be so construed as to affect the election or term of any senator chosen before it becomes valid as part of the Constitution.

The amendment will not have any affect on the term of office being completed by any senator already in Congress (in or before 1913).

Article XVIII. The 18th Amendment

Section 1. *Prohibition.* After one year from the ratification of this article the manufacture, sale, or transportation of intoxicating liquors within, the importation thereof into, or the exportation thereof from the United States and all territory subject to the jurisdiction thereof for beverage purposes is hereby prohibited.

Added in 1919, this amendment made it illegal to make, sell, or transport intoxicating liquor. The amendment was cancelled, or repealed, in 1933.

Section 2. *Enforcement.* The Congress and the several States shall have concurrent power to enforce this article by appropriate legislation.

Both Congress and the states are given the power to enforce the amendment.

Section 3. *Time Limit for Ratification.* This article shall be inoperative unless it shall have been ratified as an amendment to the Constitution by the legislatures of the several States, as provided in the Constitution, within seven years from the date of the submission hereof to the States by the Congress.

If three fourths of the states do not approve the amendment within seven years the amendment will not take effect. (The amendment was, however, approved by the states in 1919.) Note that similar time limits are placed on the ratification of many of the later amendments.

Article XIX. The 19th Amendment

Section 1. *Voting Rights for American Women.* The right of citizens of the United States to vote shall not be denied or abridged by the United States or by any State on account of sex.

Added in 1920, this amendment states that no citizen may be denied the right to vote because of sex.

Section 2. *Enforcement.* The Congress shall have power to enforce this article by appropriate legislation.

Article XX. The 20th Amendment

Section 1. *National Terms of Office Begin in January.* The terms of the President and Vice President shall end at noon on the 20th day of January, and the terms of senators and representatives at noon on the 3d day of January, of the years in which such terms would have ended if this article had not been ratified; and the terms of their successors shall then begin.

Added in 1933, this amendment states that the President and Vice President shall take office on January 20th. (The previous date for taking office had been March 4th.) The terms of members of Congress begin on January 3rd.

Section 2. *Congressional Sessions Begin in January.* The Congress shall assemble at least once in every year, and such meeting shall begin at noon on the 3d day of January, unless they shall by law appoint a different day.

The first session of a newly elected Congress will begin on January 3rd. (The previous date for a new session had been in December of the year after the election of new members.) The 20th Amendment is often called the "Lame Duck" Amendment because it put an end to the practice of allowing members of Congress who had been defeated in November elections—"lame ducks"—to continue to pass laws for a full year.

Section 3. *Death of a President Before the Beginning of a Term.* If, at the time fixed for the beginning of the term of the President, the President-elect shall have died, the Vice President-elect shall become President. If a President shall not have been chosen before the time fixed for the beginning of his term, or if the President-elect shall have failed to qualify, then the Vice President-elect shall act as President until a President shall have qualified; and the Congress may by law provide for the case wherein neither a President-elect nor a Vice President-elect shall have qualified, declaring who shall then act as President, or the manner in which one who is to act shall be selected, and such person shall act accordingly until a President or Vice President shall have qualified.

If a President-elect dies before taking office, the Vice President-elect becomes President. Congress has the power to appoint a President if both the President-elect and the Vice President-elect are unable to fill the office.

Section 4. *Death of a President Chosen by the House of Representatives.* The Congress may by law provide for the case of the death of any of the persons from whom the House of Representatives may choose a President whenever the right of choice shall have devolved upon them, and for the case of the death of any of the persons from whom the Senate may choose a Vice President whenever the right of choice shall have devolved upon them.

Whenever the Electoral College fails to reach a majority, the House of Representatives has the right to choose the President. If the person chosen dies before taking office, Congress has the right to appoint a President.

Section 5. *Date the Amendment Takes Effect.* Sections 1 and 2 shall take effect on the 15th day of October following the ratification of this article.

Section 6. *Time Limit for Ratification.* This article shall be inoperative unless it shall have been ratified as an amendment to the Constitution by the legislatures of three fourths of the several States within seven years from the date of its submission.

Article XXI. The 21st Amendment

Section 1. *Repeal of National Prohibition.* The eighteenth article of amendment to the Constitution of the United States is hereby repealed.

Added in 1933, this amendment cancels the 18th Amendment. It is no longer a federal offense to make, sell, or transport intoxicating liquors.

Section 2. *States Can Prohibit Alcohol.* The transportation or importation into any State, Territory, or possession of the United States for delivery or use therein of intoxicating liquors, in violation of the laws thereof, is hereby prohibited.

States, territories, or possessions of the United States may, if they wish, continue the ban on intoxicating liquors within their own borders.

Section 3. *Time Limit for Ratification.* This article shall be inoperative unless it shall have been ratified as an amendment to the Constitution by conventions in the several States, as provided in the Constitution, within seven years from the date of submission hereof to the States by the Congress.

Article XXII. The 22nd Amendment

Section 1. *Limit on Presidential Terms in Office.* No person shall be elected to the office of the President more than twice, and no person who has held the office of President, or acted as President, for more than two years of a term to which some other person was elected President shall be elected to the office of the President more than once. But this Article shall not apply to any person holding the office of President when this Article was proposed by the Congress, and shall not prevent any person who may be holding the office of President, or acting as President, during the term within which this Article becomes operative from holding the office of President or acting as President during the remainder of such term.

Added in 1951, the 22nd Amendment states that no one may be elected to the presidency more than twice. In addition, a Vice President who has served more than two years as President may be elected to the presidency only once.

Section 2. *Time Limit for Ratification.* This article shall be inoperative unless it shall have been ratified as an amendment to the Constitution by the legislatures of three fourths of the several States within seven years from the date of its submission to the States by the Congress.

Article XXIII. The 23rd Amendment

Section 1. *Voting Rights for the People in Washington, D.C.* The District constituting the seat of Government of the United States shall appoint in such manner as the Congress may direct: A number of electors of President and Vice President equal to the whole number of senators and representatives in Congress to which the District would be entitled if it were a State, but in no event more than the least populous State; they shall be in addition to those appointed by the States, but they shall be considered, for the purposes of election of President and Vice President, to be electors appointed by a State; and they shall meet in the District and perform such duties as provided by the twelfth article of amendment.

Added in 1961, this amendment gives the people living in Washington, D.C. the right to vote for presidential electors.

Section 2. *Enforcement.* The Congress shall have power to enforce this article by appropriate legislation.

Article XXIV. The 24th Amendment

Section 1. *Poll Tax Voting Requirements Outlawed.* The right of citizens of the United States to vote in any primary or other election for President or Vice President, for electors for President or Vice President, or for Senator or Representative in Congress shall not be denied or abridged by the United States or any State by reason of failure to pay any poll tax or other tax.

Added in 1964, this amendment says that state governments may not force citizens to pay any special tax in order to vote for federal officials.

Section 2. *Enforcement.* The Congress shall have power to enforce this article by appropriate legislation.

Article XXV. The 25th Amendment

Section 1. *The President's Death or Resignation.* In case of the removal of the President from office or his death or resignation, the Vice President shall become President.

Added in 1967, the 25th Amendment adds new details to the process already set up for filling the office of a President between elections. Section 1 simply states that the Vice President replaces a President who dies or resigns.

Section 2. *Filling the Office of Vice President.* Whenever there is a vacancy in the office of the Vice President, the President shall nominate a Vice President who shall take the office upon confirmation by a majority vote of both Houses of Congress.

If the office of Vice President becomes vacant, the President may, with the approval of Congress, appoint a new Vice President.

Section 3. *A President Unable to Fill the Office.* Whenever the President transmits to the President *pro tempore* of the Senate and the Speaker of the House of Representatives his written declaration that he is unable to discharge the powers and duties of his office, and until he transmits to them a written declaration to the contrary, such powers and duties shall be discharged by the Vice President as Acting President.

If a President informs the officers of Congress that he or she is unable to carry out the duties of the office, the Vice President is given the power to act as President.

Section 4. *A President Who Seems Unable to Fill the Office.* Whenever the Vice President and a majority of either the principal officers of the executive departments or of such other body as Congress may by law provide, transmit to the President *pro tempore* of the Senate and the Speaker of the House of Representatives their written declaration that the President is unable to discharge the powers and duties of his office, the Vice President shall immediately assume the powers and duties of the office as Acting President.

Thereafter, when the President transmits to the President *pro tempore* of the Senate and the Speaker of the House of Representatives his written declaration that no inability exists, he shall resume the powers and duties of his office unless the Vice President and a majority of either the principal officers of the executive department or of such other body as Congress may by law provide, transmit within four days to the President *pro tempore* of the Senate and the Speaker of the House of Representatives their written declaration that the President is unable to discharge the powers and duties of his office. Thereupon Congress shall decide the issue, assembling within 48 hours for that purpose if not in session. If the Congress, within 21 days after receipt of the latter written declaration, or, if Congress is not in session, within 21 days after Congress is required to assemble, determines by two-thirds vote of both Houses that the President is unable to discharge the powers and duties of his office, the Vice President shall continue to discharge the same as Acting President; otherwise, the President shall resume the powers and duties of his office.

If the Vice President and the majority of the members of the Cabinet inform the officers of Congress that the President is unable to carry out the duties of the office, the Vice President is given the power to act as President. If the President objects, Congress has the power to decide, by a two-thirds vote, who shall act as President.

Article XXVI. **The 26th Amendment**

Section 1. *Voting Rights for Young Americans.* The right of citizens of the United States who are eighteen years of age or older to vote shall not be denied or abridged by the United States or by any State on account of age.

Added in 1971, this amendment gives people over 17 years of age the right to vote in all elections.

Section 2. *Enforcement.* The Congress shall have power to enforce this article by appropriate legislation.

Index

Abel, I.W., 430
academies, 281
Adams, John, 202
adjournment of Congress, 99
advertising, 179, 180, 188–191, 406–407, 408
Africa: economic growth, 424; governments in, 447; U.S. aid to, 426
aged, aid to, 375, 381, 382
agricultural colleges, 280
agriculture: as business, 371–373; in China, 423; factory farms, 372, 373; family farms, 372; Great Plains, 318, 320; interest groups, 185–186; land reclamation, 327–328; soil conservation, 320, 326–327; technology and, 372; tillable soil in U.S., 326; in U.S.S.R., 420, 450–451; water pollution caused by, 302, 335
Agriculture, Department of, 113, 326
Aid to Families with Dependent Children program, 382–383
Air Force Academy, 111–112
Air Force Chief of Staff, 111, 460
airplanes: development of, 351–352; freight, 352; noise pollution caused by, 36, 304; passenger travel, 351–352, 356–357
air pollution, 300–301
Air Quality Act of 1967, 301
Alabama, taxes in, 235
Alaska: local government, 248; taxes, 235
Albania, 452
alcohol, prohibition of, 55–56, 206
aliens, 18
Alliance for Progress, 426
alliances, 457, 461
ambassadors, 99, 111
amendment process, 55–56
amendments: *see* constitutional amendments
American Anti-Slavery Society, 184
American Association for the United Nations, 184
American Bar Association, 186
American Civil Liberties Union, 184
American Farm Bureau Federation, 185
American Federation of Labor (AFL), 185, 394, 396
American Federation of Labor–Congress of Industrial Organizations (AFL-CIO), 185, 227, 396
American Importers Association, 431–432
American Independent Party, 207
American Medical Association, 186
American Party, 206
American Retail Federation, 184
Amtrak, 349–350
Anti-Defamation League of B'nai B'rith, 186
Anti-Masonic Party, 206
Anti-Saloon League, 184
appellate courts, 136, 140–141
appellate jurisdiction, 136
apportionment: *see* reapportionment
aptitudes, 403–404
Arizona, taxes in, 235
Arkansas, taxes in, 235
armed forces, 71, 73, 98–99, 104, 105–108, 111–112, 224–226, 460–463, 464, 465–466; *see also* militias; National Guard
Armenia, immigrants from, 10
arms, right to bear, 155–156
arms control, 462–463
Army Chief of Staff, 111, 460
Articles of Confederation, 48, 51, 97, 278
assembly lines, 393
association, freedom of, 154, 159
Athens, self-government in, 45, 57
Atlanta, Georgia, 265, 288
Atlantic Charter, 467
atomic bomb: *see* nuclear weapons
atomic energy, 391, 462
atomic weapons: *see* nuclear weapons
Attorney General, 110, 112, 141
Australia: government, 443; SEATO, 461; Vietnamese War, 465
Austria, immigrants from, 9
authoritarianism, 44, 438–441, 445–447, 453
automation, 391
automobiles: air pollution caused by, 300–301; consumer demand and, 406; development of, 273, 344–345; number in U.S., 296, 343, 391; production of, 366–367, 393; traffic problems caused by, 293–294, 296–299
availability principle, 127

bail, 166
Bailey, Stephen K., 81–82
Baker v. Carr (1962), 93
ballots: absentee, 214; in general elections, 213; long, 214–215; paper, 214; in primary elections, 212; secret, 214; short, 214–215
Baltimore and Ohio Railroad, 347
banks: commercial, 378; Federal Deposit Insurance Corporation, 375; Federal Reserve System, 375,

378–379; national, 378; savings and loan, 378; state, 378; trust companies, 378
barter, 375–376
Belgium, 461
Bell, Alexander Graham, 360
Better Business Bureaus, 407
bicameral legislatures, 68–71, 91–92, 93
Bill of Rights, 48–49, 50, 55, 77, 150, 154–167, 168, 173; *see also* constitutional amendments
bills, congressional, 84, 85
bills of attainder, 75–76, 152
birth, citizenship by, 17–18, 19, 24
Black Panthers, 38
blacks: education, 282, 284–289; population (1790), 6; segregation, 282, 284–289; voting rights, 48, 59, 150, 169, 218; *see also* slavery
board of elections, 213–214
Bolivia, 452
Bolsheviks, 450
bondholders, 370–371
bonds, 230, 370–371, 378
books, opinion formation and, 180–181
Boone, Daniel, 30, 343
boroughs, 248
bosses, political, 254
Boston, Massachusetts, 289, 294, 298
boycotts, 395
Brezhnev, Leonid, 463
Brown v. Board of Education of Topeka (1954), 138–139, 284–285, 286, 289
Bryce, James, 177
budgets: federal, 109, 229–230; state and local, 230–231
Buffalo, New York, 302
Bulgaria, 452
bureaucracy, 209–210, 259
business: agriculture as, 371–373; capitalism and, 368; in China, 423; colonial, 365; communications and, 365–366; competition, 32–33, 368; credit and, 368, 375–379; in Europe, 421–422; foreign trade, 365–367, 423, 426, 428–433; interest groups in, 184; in Japan, 422; multinational, 432–433; national government and, 71, 109, 111–114, 226, 368, 374–375; organization of, 370–371; social responsibilities of, 384–387; state government and, 90, 374–375; technology and, 226, 391–392, 393; transportation and, 365–366; in U.S.S.R., 420, 450–451
busing, 209, 286–289

Cabinet: 99, 110–114; *see also* names of specific departments
California: expansion of U.S., 415; mineral resources, 318, 343; representation in Congress, 69; schools, 284; taxes, 235
California (Overland) Trail, 344
Cambodia, 108
Canada: economy, 423; government, 442–443; immigrants from, 10–11; NATO, 461
canals, 6, 347, 353, 365
capital goods, 369–370
capitalism, 365, 367, 368
careers, 398–399, 401–404
Castro, Fidel, 11
cattle raising, 318
caucus, 82, 206
Cedarhurst, New York, 36
Census, Bureau of the, 113, 247
census figures: and immigration (graph), 8; immigration laws, use of, 15–16; population growth, 323–324; in 1790, 6; from 1790 to 1980 (graph), 323; and urbanization (graph), 253
Central Pacific Railroad, 347
Chamber of Commerce of the United States, 184
Charlotte-Mecklenburg County, North Carolina, 286, 289
charters: bank, 378; business, 90; city, 253; village, 251
Chavez, Cesar, 186
checks and balances, system of, 52–54, 55, 74–77, 100–102, 137–138
Chesterton, G. K., 262
Chiang Kai-shek, 422–423, 451
Chicago, Illinois, 292, 298
Chief Justice of the Supreme Court, 139
Children's Bureau, 113
Chile, 452
China, immigrants from, 10, 14, 16
China, People's Republic of (Communist): agriculture, 423; and Albania, 452; communism in, 422–423, 451–452; economy, 414–415, 423, 451; industry, 423; and the UN, 423, 452, 470–471; and U.S., 418, 423, 452; and U.S.S.R., 418, 451–452
China, Republic of (Nationalist): economy, 423; loss of mainland, 422–423, 451; and the UN, 423, 470–471; and U.S., 461
Chinese Exclusion Act of 1882, 14
Chisholm, Shirley, 172
Churchill, Winston, 467
Cincinnati, Ohio, 7, 256–257

cities: crime rate in, 309–311; growth of, 253, 263–264, 271, 272–274, 292–295; housing, 271, 272–276; pollution, 300–307; problems of, 240, 261–262, 263–264, 273–276, 292–311; transportation systems, 264, 272–273, 293–299
citizenship: by birth, 17–18, 19, 24; definition, 17, 19; by naturalization, 18–19, 24
city government: charters, 253; commission form of, 257–258; council-manager system of, 256–257; development of, 253–254; employees, 259–262; experiments with, 256–258, 264–265; interest groups and, 261–262; mayor-council system, 253–255; political machines, 213, 254
civic responsibility, 19, 176, 177, 179, 183, 192–195
Civil Aeronautics Board, 114
civil cases, 130–131
Civilian Conservation Corps, 320
civil rights: *see* liberty
civil servants, 102
civil townships, 251
Civil War, 59, 89
Clermont, 353
Cleveland, Grover, 15, 204
Cleveland, Harlan, 466
Cleveland, Ohio, 302
closed primaries, 212
Coast Guard, 112, 113
Coast Guard Academy, U.S., 112
Cold War, 417–418, 458
collective bargaining, 396
collective farms, 420, 423, 450
colleges: enrollment in, 280, 399–400; national government support, 280; state government support, 90
Collegiate School, 281
colonies: business, 365; education, 276–278, 281; government in, 46–48, 247–250; immigration to, 6; liberty in, 46–48; trade, 365; voting in, 47–48
Colorado: mineral resources, 318; taxes, 235
Commager, Henry Steele, 107
Commander in Chief, 98–99
Commerce, Department of, 113
commercial banks, 378
commission government, 257–258
Commission of Inter-Governmental Relations, 238–239
Commission on the Status of Women, 171–172

Committee for Economic Development, 268–269, 384–386
committees, congressional, 83–84
Commoner, Barry, 337
common law, 129–130, 166
Common Market, 421–422
communication networks: and business, 366; and opinion formation, 104, 179–182; postal service, 358–359; radio, 104, 181, 197, 360; telegraph, 359–360; telephone, 360; television, 104, 181, 182, 197, 360–361
communism: in Africa, 452; in Asia, 452; in China, 422–423, 437, 441, 451–452; in Europe, 420–421, 445, 452; in Latin America, 452; Marx and, 449–450; in U.S.S.R., 420–421, 441, 450–451
Communist China: *see* China, People's Republic of
Community Action Program, 381
competition, 32–33, 368
computers, 391
Conestoga wagons, 343
Congress: adjournment, 99; and the checks and balances system, 52–54, 74–77, 100–101, 137–138; committee system of, 83–84; and foreign policy, 105–108, 458–459; and the lawmaking process, 84–85; leaders, 81–82; limits on power, 5, 52–54, 74–77, 88, 151–152; organization, 68–71, 80–84; powers, 52–53, 67, 71–74, 84, 100–101, 105–108, 136, 137–138; qualifications for members, 70; representation, 68–70, 78–79; sessions, 80–81; terms of members, 70; *see also* House of Representatives; Senate
congressional districts, 78–79
congressional privileges, 80
congressional townships, 251
Congress of Industrial Organizations (CIO), 185, 396
Connecticut: colonial government, 46–47; in metropolitan area, 263; taxes, 235
conservation: and ecology, 321–322; of forests, 319–320, 330–331; government and, 320–321, 327–328, 330–332, 334; and land reclamation, 327–328; mineral resources, 328–329; pioneers in, 316, 319–320; soil, 320, 326–327; of wilderness areas, 331–334; wildlife, 333–334
Constitution, U.S.: acceptance of, 55, 68–69; amendment of, 50, 55–56;
and the checks and balances system, 52–54, 74–77, 100–101, 137–138; on Congress, 52–54, 67–77, 80–81, 105, 458–459; on the court system, 52, 55, 136–138; and democracy, 48–49, 440; and division of national power, 49, 52–54; elastic clause, 72–73; and federalism, 49, 50–51; interpretation of, 48, 150; and limited government, 49, 54–55; Preamble to, 26, 30; on the President, 52–54, 97–102, 105, 458; rights guaranteed by, 131, 150–173; on slavery, 5, 74–75, 168; on treason, 153; on trial by jury, 75–76, 131, 152, 164–166; on voting rights, 150, 168–170, 218; writing of, 48–56; *see also* Bill of Rights; constitutional amendments; Supreme Court
constitutional amendments: 1st Amendment, 77, 154–155, 159–160, 182, 183, 281; 2nd Amendment, 155–156; 3rd Amendment, 155; 4th Amendment, 156–157; 5th Amendment, 131, 161–164, 169; 6th Amendment, 77, 131, 164–165; 7th Amendment, 131, 165–166; 8th Amendment, 131, 166; 9th Amendment, 167; 10th Amendment, 77, 167; 12th Amendment, 119–120; 13th Amendment, 5, 150, 168; 14th Amendment, 17, 89, 93, 150, 155, 168–169, 285; 15th Amendment, 150, 168, 169, 218; 16th Amendment, 76, 234, 238; 17th Amendment, 67–68; 18th Amendment, 55–56, 206; 19th Amendment, 150, 169, 171, 218; 21st Amendment, 55–56, 206; 22nd Amendment, 101–102; 26th Amendment, 150, 170, 218
Constitutional Convention, 48
constitutions, state, 50, 54, 91, 92, 122, 125, 131, 278
consuls, 111
consumers: advertising and, 406–409; as decision makers, 405–406; guides for, 407–408; influences on, 406; living standard, 390–391
containment policy, 417–418, 457–458
Continental Congress, 358
contour farming, 327
conventions, presidential nominating, 116–118, 206, 208–211, 213
Coolidge, Calvin, 123
Cooper, James Fenimore, 316
cooperatives, 371
corporations, 90, 234, 370–371
Costa Rica, 446
council-manager government, 256–257
Council of Economic Advisers, 109
Council of Europe, 421
Council of Ministers (U.S.S.R.), 450
counsel, right of, 165
county government, 248–249
county seats, 248
courts: appellate, 136, 140–141; federal court system, 136–141; functions of, 128–132; judges, 128–130, 132–135, 138–139, 144, 147; state court system, 141–145; trial by jury, 131–135, 161, 164–166; work load, 143, 145; *see also* names of specific courts
Courts of Appeal, federal, 140
credit, 368, 370–371, 377–378, 408–409
crime: in cities, 309–311; figures, 309; party platforms on, 209
Crimean War, 420
criminal cases, 130–131
Cuba: government in, 452; immigrants from, 11, 16
Cuban missile crisis, 419
culture: definition, 29; and values, 29–33
customs duties, 236–237
Czechoslovakia: government, 452; immigrants from, 9

Dade County, Florida, 265
Dallas, Texas, 256
Davidson County, Tennessee, 265
Declaration of Environmental Rights, 337
Declaration of Independence, 4, 31, 48, 58–59, 171, 224
Declaration of Seneca Falls, 171
declaration of war, 71, 105–108, 459
Defense, Department of, 111–112, 460–461
deficits, 232
Delaware: local government, 248; taxes, 235
democracy: and education, 176, 276, 278, 438; growth of, 45–49, 57–59, 442–444; principles of, 24, 44, 438–441; in U.S., 24, 46–49, 436, 442, 455; in the world, 442–444
Democratic Party: history of, 202–206; Jacksonian, 203; organization, 200–201; platform

(1976), 208–211; presidential nominating conventions, 116–118; regional aspects, 204
Denmark: Common Market, 421; immigrants from, 8; NATO, 461
Dennis, Jack, 13
departments, executive: *see* Cabinet; names of specific departments
depression, 204, 380–381
desegregation of schools: *see* segregation
Detroit, Michigan, 194, 302
discrimination: against Asians, 14, 284; against blacks, 59, 169, 282, 284–289; against immigrants, 7, 14–16; religious, 4, 7, 14; against women, 57–58, 59, 171–172
District Attorney, 141
District Courts, federal, 140–141, 287–288
District of Columbia, 17, 23
districts, congressional, 78–79
dividends, 370
division of labor, 393
Dixiecrat Party, 207
Dominican Republic, 107
Donne, John, 456
Donora, Pennsylvania, 300
double jeopardy, 161–162
Douglas, William O., 158
Dreiser, Theodore, 292
due process of law, 161, 163–164, 169
Dust Bowl, 318, 320

Earhart, Amelia, 30
Eastburn, David, 386–387
East Germany, 452, 455
Easton, David, 13
ecology, 321–322, 337–339
Economic and Social Council of the United Nations, 468–470
Economic Opportunity, Office of, 381
economies, foreign: African, 424, 426; Canadian, 423; Chinese, 422–423, 451; European, 417–418, 421–422, 426, 433, 435; Japanese, 422, 425, 435; Latin American, 423–424, 426; Middle Eastern, 424; Soviet, 420, 425, 435, 450–451
economy, U.S.: agriculture and, 371–373; banks, 378–379; business, 364–371, 384–387; capitalism, 365, 368; consumers, 405–409; goals of, 384–387; government involvement in, 226, 368, 374–375, 378–379, 389; gross national product, 224–225, 425; living standard, 25, 390–391; manufacturing, 368–370, 391–394, 397–398; mixed, 368, 374, 389; money system, 375–379; productivity, 326, 390–393, 397; workers, 390–400, 405
education: and blacks, 282, 284–289; busing, 286–289; colonial, 276–278, 281; democracy and, 176, 276, 278, 438; employment and, 399–400; functions of, 25, 276, 283, 438; and local government, 230–231, 248–251, 280; and national government, 278, 280, 282, 284–289; religion and, 276–278, 280–281; segregation, 282, 284–289; and state government, 90, 230–231, 278, 279, 284; Supreme Court decisions, 281, 282, 284–289; values and, 25, 438; *see also* independent schools; parochial schools; public schools
Efron, Edith, 182
Ehrlich, Paul, 324–325
Eisenhower, Dwight D., 117, 285, 460–461, 462–463
elastic clause, 72–73
elections: conduct of, 213–214; congressional, 67–70; Electoral College, 67–68, 119–121; general, 213; of governors, 122; improvement of, 214–216; of judges, 144; presidential, 67–68, 101–102, 116–121, 199, 201, 202–208, 213; presidential nominating conventions, 116–118, 206, 208–211, 213; primary, 212–213; *see also* ballots; voting
Electoral College, 67–68, 119–121
Elizabeth I, Queen of England, 46
emancipation amendments, 168–169
Emergency Quota Act of 1921, 15
energy: party platforms on, 209; supplies, 328–329
Engels, Frederick, 449
England: *see* Great Britain
environmental protection: *see* conservation
equality, ideal of, 31, 58–59
equal protection of the laws, 169
equal representation, 78–79, 92–93
equal rights: *see* liberty
Equal Rights Amendment, 171–172, 211
equity, 129–130
Erie Canal, 6, 353
Esposito, John C., 308
estate taxes, 236
Etzioni, Amitai, 339
European Coal and Steel Community, 421
European Economic Community: *see* Common Market
excise taxes, 235
executive agencies, 114
executive branch: *see* President
executive departments: *see* Cabinet; names of specific departments
Export-Import Bank, 375
ex post facto laws, 75–76, 152
expression, freedom of, 154, 158, 159–160
expressways, 295–296

factories: *see* industry
families: and industrialization, 270–272; and opinion formation, 178; roles in, 269–272; size of, 269, 271; and socialization process, 25, 178; and state government, 90; and urbanization, 270–272
farming: *see* agriculture
fascism, 441, 445, 448–449
featherbedding, 395
federal budget, 109, 229–230
Federal Bureau of Investigation (FBI), 112, 309
Federal Council of Churches of America, 186
Federal Deposit Insurance Corporation (FDIC), 375
Federal Food and Drugs Act of 1906, 374
federal government: *see* national government
federalism, 49, 50–51, 89, 91, 95, 141, 238–241
Federalist Party, 202–203, 205
Federal Reserve System, 375, 378–379
federal system: *see* federalism
Federal Trade Commission, 114, 374, 407, 411
Federal Water Quality Administration, 302
felony, 130
feudalism, 45
Finland, 8
"fireside chats," 104, 181
Fish and Wildlife Service, 334
Fitzhugh, George, 59
Five Towns, New York, 36
Florida: expansion of U.S., 415; taxes, 235
Food and Drug Administration, 374, 411
foreign aid, U.S., 426, 457
foreign policy, U.S.: Alliance for Progress, 426; arms control, 462–463; Atlantic Charter, 467;

Cold War, 417–418, 458; toward Communist countries, 417–418, 423, 426, 452, 457–458, 461–463, 465; Congress and, 105–108, 458–459; containment, 417–418, 457–458; Defense Department and, 460–461; toward Europe, 415–418, 426, 455, 457, 461; foreign aid program, 426, 457; history of, 415–419, 426, 455, 457–458, 461–463, 465, 467–468; isolationism, 415–417, 457, 461, 466; toward Latin America, 11, 415–416, 419, 426, 457, 461; manifest destiny, 415; Marshall Plan, 426; Monroe Doctrine, 416, 419, 457; mutual security arrangements, 461–462; national security and, 109, 460; NATO, 457, 461; nuclear weapons, 456, 460, 462–463; party platforms on, 209; Peace Corps, 426; President and, 99, 104, 105–108, 109, 111, 457–458; Rio Treaty, 461; SEATO, 461; State Department, 111; Truman Doctrine, 426; UN, 457, 467–468; Vietnamese War, 105–108, 415, 465
Foreign Policy Association, 184
forests: conservation of, 319–320, 330–331; exploitation of, 317
Fort Worth, Texas, 35, 256
Foss, Sam Walter, 293–294
France: Common Market, 414, 421; government, 442; Louisiana Purchase, 415; NATO, 461; political parties, 200; SEATO, 461; UN, 468–469
Franco, Francisco, 445, 453
Frank, Jerome, 133–134
Franklin, Benjamin, 358
freedom of association, 154, 159, 183
freedom of expression, 154, 158, 159, 198
freedom of religion, 4, 30, 47, 154, 281
freedom of speech, 154, 159–160
freedom of the press, 47, 154
free enterprise, 368
Fritchey, Clayton, 120
Fulton, Robert, 353
Fundamental Orders of Connecticut, 46–47

Gadsden Purchase, 11
Gallup Polls, 218, 282
Galveston, Texas, 257
garbage, pollution caused by, 302–304

General Agreement on Tariffs and Trade (GATT), 430
General Assembly of the United Nations, 468–470, 473
general elections: *see* elections
general warrants, 157
Georgia, taxes in, 235
Germany: fascism in, 441, 448–449; immigrants from, 6, 7; *see also* East Germany; West Germany
Gerry, Elbridge, 78
gerrymandering, 78–79
Gettysburg Address, 24
gift taxes, 236
gold rush, 318, 343–344
Goldwater, Barry M., 241
Gompers, Samuel, 394
Goodman, Louis E., 133, 134–135
government: authoritarian, 44, 438–441, 445–447, 453; colonial, 46–48, 247–250; constitutional, 48–56, 436; democratic, 44, 436, 438–444, 455; federal form of, 49–51, 443; limited, 54–55; totalitarian, 44, 199, 438–441, 448–453; *see also* city government; local government; national government; state government; names of specific countries
governor: as administrative head, 124; duties of, 122, 123–124; election of, 122; as legislative leader, 123–124; powers of, 122–124
grand juries, 132, 161
Great Britain: American colonies and, 47, 48, 224, 247, 365; Common Market, 414, 421–422; government, 45–46, 441, 442, 443; Industrial Revolution, 270; law in, 129; NATO, 461; SEATO, 461; UN, 467, 468–469; U.S. aid to, 426
Great Depression, 204, 380–381
Great Lakes, 301–302, 335, 353–354
Great Plains, 318, 320
Great Salt Lake, 335
Greece: ancient, 45, 57, 246; government today, 445; immigrants from, 9; NATO, 461; U.S. aid to, 426
Green, Philip, 118
gross national product (GNP): of Japan, 425, 435; of U.S., 224–225, 425, 435; of U.S.S.R., 425, 435
Gulf of Tonkin, 105–106, 108
gun control laws, 156

habeas corpus, writ of, 74–75, 151–152

Hague Tribunal, 467
Hamilton, Alexander, 202
Hapgood, David, 346
Harvard College, 277
Hawaii: expansion of U.S., 415; statehood, 51; taxes, 235
Health, Education, and Welfare, Department of, 113, 225, 380
health insurance program, 210
health problems caused by pollution, 300–301, 302, 304
Henrico College, 276
Henry VIII, King of England, 46
Hewlett, New York, 36
highways: early American, 343–344; expressways, 295–296; Interstate Highway System, 296, 345, 346; national government and, 51, 298, 345, 346; state government and, 51, 90, 231, 345; *see also* automobiles; transportation
Hiroshima, 456
Hitler, Adolf, 448–449
hospitals, 90
House of Burgesses, 47
House of Representatives (national): committees, 83–84; daily activities, 83–84, 86–87; election process, 67–68; leaders, 81–82; members' privileges, 80; representation in, 67–70, 78–79; special powers, 71, 74, 119–120
housing: Model Cities program, 275; national government and, 268, 274–275; party platforms on, 210; segregation, 282, 286; slums, 272–276; transportation and, 272–274; urban renewal programs, 274–275
Housing Act of 1937, 268, 274
Housing and Home Finance Agency, 274
Housing and Urban Development, Department of, 113, 268, 275
Humphrey, Hubert H., 102, 240–241
Hungary: government, 452; immigrants from, 9
Hutchinson, Anne, 47

Iceland, 461
Idaho, taxes in, 235
ideologies, political, 438–440
Illinois: schools, 284; taxes, 235
Immigration and Nationality Act of 1952, 16
Immigration and Nationality Act of 1965, 16
Immigration and Naturalization Service, 112

INDEX **503**

immigration to the U.S.: from Africa, 2, 3, 5; from Asia, 2, 3, 10, 14, 16, 17; colonial, 6; and discrimination, 7, 14–16; from Europe, 2, 3, 4, 6–10, 14–17; figures on, 3, 6, 8 (graph); laws concerning, 14–17, 18–19, 71, 72; reasons for, 3–11, 16; from the Western Hemisphere, 10–11, 16–17; *see also* names of specific countries
impeachment, 74, 101, 139
implied powers, 72
import taxes: *see* tariffs
income taxes: corporate, 234; personal, 233, 234, 238; 16th Amendment, 76, 234, 238
incorporated villages, 251
incorporation, laws of, 251
indentured servants, 4
independent agencies, 114
independent schools: beginning, 281; enrollment, 280; Supreme Court decision, 282
independent voters, 218
India, 424
Indiana: education, 284; taxes, 235
Indian Affairs, Bureau of, 112
Indians: *see* Native Americans
indictments, 132
Indochina, 447
Indonesia: government of, 447; withdrawal from UN, 470
industrialization, 225–226, 238, 270–272, 280, 319, 365–366, 391–394
Industrial Revolution, 270–272, 319
industry: as cause of pollution, 300–302, 304–305, 335; in China, 423; in Europe, 270, 421; interest groups, 184; in Japan, 414, 422; lumber, 317, 330–331; mass production, 393; productivity, 390–393; technology and, 391–392; in U.S.S.R., 420, 450; *see also* labor unions; workers
inflation, 210
injunctions, 395
Institute for Propaganda Analysis, 188
integration: *see* segregation
intelligence, 401–402
interest groups: defined, 183; forms of, 183–186; and government, 183, 261–262; influence of, 183; power of, 183, 261–262
Interior, Department of the, 112
International Bank for Reconstruction and Development (World Bank), 470

International Brotherhood of Teamsters, 396
International Court of Justice, 468, 469
international relations: *see* foreign policy
Interstate Highway System, 296, 345, 346
Inwood, New York, 36
Iowa, taxes in, 235
Iran, 441
Iraq, 447
Ireland: Common Market, 421; immigrants from, 4, 6–7; potato famine, 4, 6
Isaak Walton League, 334
isolationism, 415–417, 457, 461, 466
Israel: economy, 424; government, 443
Italy: Common Market, 421; fascism, 441, 448–449; immigrants from, 9; NATO, 461

Jackson, Andrew, 203
Jacksonian Democrats, 203
Jacksonville, Florida, 265
Jacoby, Susan, 283
James I, King of England, 58
Jamestown, Virginia, 247, 276, 365
Japan: economy, 422, 425, 433, 435; government, 443, 455; gross national product, 425, 435; immigrants from, 10, 14, 16; industry, 414, 422, 430; trade, 422, 430, 433; and U.S., 422, 425, 455, 461; and U.S.S.R., 420
Jefferson, Thomas, 102, 202, 278
Job Corps, 381
jobs, 397–400
John, King of England, 45
Johnson, Andrew, 101
Johnson, Lyndon B., 16, 105–106, 463
Johnston, Mrs. Jimmie, 217
Joint Chiefs of Staff, 111–112, 460
judges: responsibility, 128, 129–130, 132, 133–135, 139; selection, 144, 147; term of office, 144
judicial branch: *see* courts; Supreme Court
judicial review, principle of, 49, 55, 137
jury, trial by: constitutional right to, 75–76, 131, 152, 164–166; criticism of, 133–134; defense of, 134–135; grand, 132, 161; petit, 132
Justice, Department of, 18, 112, 141
justice of the peace, 142

Kalamazoo case, 279
Kansas: Dust Bowl, 320; taxes, 235
Kansas City, Missouri, 194
KDKA, radio station, 360
Kennedy, John F., 127, 156, 320–321
Kennedy, Robert F., 156
Kentucky, taxes in, 235
Khrushchev, Nikita, 298
Kilpatrick, James J., 232
King, Martin Luther, Jr., 59, 156
Knights of Labor, 394
Know-Nothing Party, 206
Korean War, 107, 418, 465

Labor, Department of, 113
labor unions: boycotts, 395; collective bargaining, 396; craft, 394; early, 394; featherbedding, 395; growth, 394–396; industrial, 396; as interest groups, 185; membership, 185, 396; opposition to, 394–396; organization of, 185, 394–396; pickets, 395; reasons for, 393–394; strikes, 395; union shop, 395; Wagner Act, 396; *see also* names of specific unions
La Follette, Robert M., 207
Lake Erie, 301–302
Land Ordinance of 1785, 250–251, 278
land reclamation, 327–328
Laos, 107–108
Laski, Harold J., 238
Latin America: communism in, 452; economy, 423–424; governments in, 443, 445–446, 452; immigrants from, 11, 16–17; Rio Treaty, 461; U. S. aid to, 426; *see also* names of specific countries
law: civil cases, 130–131; common, 129, 165–166; criminal cases, 130–131; English, 129; equity, 129–130; interpretation of, 128, 129–130; need for, 25–26, 43–44, 129; statutory, 129; *see also* courts; judges; lawmaking powers; Supreme Court
lawmaking powers: local, 249, 253; national, 52–54, 67, 71–77, 84–85, 100, 137; state, 77, 89–93, 122, 123–124
Lawrence, Massachusetts, 192
Lawrence, New York, 36
Lazarus, Emma, 14
League of Nations, 416, 467–468
League of Women Voters, 184
legislative branch: *see* Congress; House of Representatives; Senate

504 INDEX

legislatures, state: powers of, 90–91, 122; representation, 92–93; structure, 91–92
Lenin, Nikolai, 450
Lens, Sidney, 464
Lewis, James Hamilton, 86
liability, limited, 371
libel, 159
liberty: in colonies, 46–48, 161; constitutional guarantees, 150–170; definition, 42–44; and law, 43–44
Liberty Bell, 42
Liberty Bonds, 42
Libya, 447
licenses, 237
Limited Test Ban Treaty, 463
Lincoln, Abraham, 24, 129, 152, 204
Lindsay, John, 261
Lippmann, Walter, 261–262
literacy tests, 14–15
Little Rock, Arkansas, 285
loans, 378
lobbying, 184
local government: budget, 229, 230–231; city, 253–262; county, 248–249; employment opportunities, 398–399; of metropolitan areas, 263–265; New England town, 249–250; origins, 247–251; revenue sharing, 238–241; special districts, 251; taxes, 234–236, 237; township, 250–251; types of, 247–265; village, 251; *see also* city government
Locke, John, 43–44, 58–59
lockouts, 395
London, England, 300
Los Angeles, California, 246, 298
Louisiana: local government, 248; Supreme Court decision, 284; taxes, 235
Louisiana Purchase, 415
Lowi, Theodore J., 259
lumber industry, 317, 330–331
Luxembourg, 461

Madison, James, 183
magazines, opinion formation and, 180, 197
Magna Charta, 45–46, 151
Maine, taxes in, 235
management, 369, 370
Management and Budget, Office of, 109, 229
manifest destiny, 415
manufacturing: *see* industry
Mao Tse-tung, 422, 451

Marconi, Guglielmo, 360
Marsh, George Perkins, 319
Marshall, Thurgood, 147
Marshall Plan, 426
Marx, Karl, 449–450
Maryland, taxes in, 235
Massachusetts: colonial government, 161; courts, 144; schools, 276–278; taxes, 235
Massachusetts Bay, 365
mass media: development of, 360–361; and government, 179, 182; influence on public opinion, 104, 179–181, 197, 361; use by politicians, 104, 181, 255
mass production, 393
mass transit, 298–299
mayor-council government, 253–255
mayors, 253–255, 257
McCarthy Era, 153
McGee, Gale, 106–107
media: *see* mass media
Medicare, 86
melting pot theory, 13
Merchant Marine, 354–355
Mesabi Range, 329
metropolis, 246; *see also* cities; city government
metropolitan areas: *see* cities; city government
Mexico: government in, 443, 446; immigrants from, 11
Meyerson, Bess, 409
Miami, Florida, 256, 265
Michigan: schools, 279; taxes, 235
Middle Ages, 45
military: *see* armed forces
Military Academy, U.S.: *see* West Point
militias, 71, 73, 98, 155
Milwaukee, Wisconsin, 7
mineral resources: conservation of, 328–329; exploitation of, 318–319
Minneapolis, Minnesota, 294
Minnesota: mineral resources, 319, 329; taxes, 235
minority groups, 49, 158; *see also* names of specific groups
misdemeanor, 130
Mississippi, taxes in, 235
Mississippi River, 353, 354
Missouri, taxes in, 235
Model Cities program, 275
monarchies, 58, 199, 441
money: Federal Reserve System, 375, 378–379; management of, 408; nature of, 376–377; uses of, 377
Monroe, James, 416, 457
Monroe Doctrine, 416, 457

Montana, taxes in, 235
Morgenthau, Hans, 427
Morocco, Kingdom of, 447
Morrill Act of 1862, 280
Morse, Samuel F.B., 359–360
Morse Code, 360
movies, influence on public opinion, 181
multinational companies, 432–433
municipal government: *see* city government
Municipal Voters' League of Chicago, 184
Mussolini, Benito, 448
mutual security arrangements, 461–462

Nader, Ralph, 308
Nagasaki, 456
Nashville, Tennessee, 265
National American Woman Suffrage Association, 184
National Association for the Advancement of Colored People, 186
National Association of Audubon Societies, 334
National Association of Manufacturers, 184
National Catholic Welfare Conference, 186
National Civil Service Reform League, 184
National Commission on the Causes and Prevention of Violence, 143, 309–310
National Conference of State Governors, 216
National Council on Noise Abatement, 305
national debt, 230
national defense, 23–24, 109, 209, 460–463
National Education Association, 186
National Farmers' Union, 185–186
National Forests, 320
national government: branches, 52, 67–68, 97, 136; budget, 109, 229–230; and business, 71, 109, 111–114, 226, 368, 374–375; checks and balances, 52–54, 55, 74–77, 79, 100–102, 137–138; conservation activities, 112, 320–321, 327–328, 330–332, 334; and consumers, 411; and education, 113, 276, 278, 280, 282, 284–289; employees, 102, 224–225; employment opportunities, 398; federal court system,

INDEX **505**

136–141; federalism, 49, 50–51, 89, 91, 95, 141, 238–241; growth of, 224–226; housing programs, 113, 268, 274–275; independent agencies, 114; judicial review, 49, 55, 137; and labor, 113, 396; money system, 375, 378–379; national debt, 230; postal service, 358–359; power over states, 89, 91; public welfare programs, 113, 380–383; revenue sharing, 240–241; spending by, 224–225, 229–230, 232; taxes, 233–237, 238; and transportation, 113, 296, 299, 345, 346, 349–350; *see also* Congress; Constitution; foreign policy; President; Supreme Court
National Grange, 185
National Guard, 124, 155
national nominating conventions, 116–118, 206, 208–211, 213
National Parks, 331–332
National Park Service, 331–332
National Road, 343
National Security Council, 109
National Wildlife Refuge System, 334
Native Americans: immigration from Asia, 2–4; Plains, 318; population, 4; voting, 218; white settlers and, 4
naturalization, citizenship by, 18–19, 24
natural resources: conservation of, 319–322, 326–335; exploitation of, 317–319; in U.S., 25, 317–319, 326, 329, 330; use of, 369
nature, balance of: *see* ecology
Naval Academy, U.S., 111
Nebraska: state legislature, 91–92; taxes, 235
Negroes: *see* blacks
Netherlands, 461
Nevada, taxes in, 235
New Deal, 181, 320
New England town, 249–250
New Hampshire, taxes in, 235
New Jersey: in metropolitan area, 263; taxes, 235
New Mexico: expansion of U.S., 343; taxes, 235
New Netherlands, 276
newspapers, influence on public opinion, 179–180, 197
New York: in metropolitan area, 263; schools, 284; taxes, 235
New York City, 78–79, 194, 261–262, 263–264, 293, 294, 297, 298
New York Weekly Journal, 47
New Zealand, 443, 461, 465

Nixon, Richard M., 95, 99, 101, 239–240, 337, 423, 463
Noble Order of the Knights of Labor, 394
noise pollution, 36, 304–305
nominating conventions: *see* presidential nominating conventions
Non-Proliferation Treaty, 463
North Atlantic Treaty Organization (NATO), 457, 461
North Carolina, taxes in, 235
North Dakota, taxes in, 235
North Korea, 452, 465
Northwest Ordinance, 51, 278
Northwest Territory, 51, 250, 278
Norway: economy, 421; immigrants from, 8; NATO, 461
nuclear weapons, 105, 418, 456, 460, 462–463

Office of Economic Opportunity, 381
Office of Management and Budget, 109
Ohio: schools, 284; taxes, 235
oil, 318–319
Oklahoma: Dust Bowl, 320; mineral resources, 318–319; taxes, 235
Old Age, Survivors, Disability and Health Insurance program, 382
Old Deluder Law, 277
open primaries, 212–213
"Open Skies" plan, 462–463
opinions: development of responsible, 177, 179, 192; influences on, 178–191; propaganda and, 188–191; *see also* public opinion
Oppenheimer, Valerie, 325
order: *see* law
ordinances, 249, 255
Oregon: expansion of U.S., 415; taxes, 235

Pakistan, 447, 461
Panama Canal, 114
pardons, 100, 124
parishes, 248
Parliament, British, 442
parliamentary government, 442–443
parochial schools: beginning, 281; enrollment, 280–281; growth, 281
parole boards, 124
parties: *see* political parties
partnerships, 370
passports, 111
Patent Office, U.S., 141
Peace Corps, 426
Pearl Harbor, 417, 422

Pennsylvania: colonial government, 47; mineral resources, 318; schools, 276, 284; taxes, 235
Pentagon, 111, 460
People's Party, 207
People's Republic of China: *see* China, People's Republic of
Pericles, 57
Peru, 452
pesticides, 322, 333
petit juries, 132, 133–135
Philadelphia, Pennsylvania, 48
Philippine Islands, 461
pickets, 395
Pinchot, Gifford, 319–320
platforms, political, 208–211
Plessy v. Ferguson (1896), 284
Poland: government, 452; immigrants from, 9
political bosses, 254
political machines, 213, 254
political parties: functions, 199–200; history of, 198, 202–207; organization of, 200–201; in other countries, 200, 440–441; platforms, 208–211; President as leader of, 103; public opinion and, 177–178; third-party movements, 200, 206–207; two-party system, 200, 202; *see also* names of specific parties
political systems: *see* government
polling places, 213–214
pollution: air, 300–301; garbage, 302–304; noise, 36, 304–305; visual, 305–306; water, 35, 301–302, 335, 337
population, U.S.: growth, 323–325, 390; and immigration (graph), 8; Native American, 4; in 1790, 6; from 1790 to 1980 (graph), 323; urban, 253
population, world, 323
Populist Party, 207
Portugal, 445, 461
Postal Service: *see* United States Postal Service
Postmaster General, 358
Post Office Department, 358
Preamble to the Constitution, 26, 30
President: advisers of, 109; appointment powers, 98–100; availability, 127; Cabinet of, 99, 110–114; as ceremonial head, 103–104; and the checks and balances system, 52–54, 76–77, 100–101; as Commander in Chief, 98–99; election of, 67–68, 116–121, 127, 201, 213; and the federal budget, 109, 229; and foreign policy, 98,

99, 100, 105–108, 109, 111, 458; growth in power, 102–109; independent agencies, 114; influence on public opinion, 104; lawmaking powers, 52–54, 76–77, 98, 99, 100; limits on the power of, 73–74, 100–102; as party leader, 103; power of, 52–54, 76–77, 97–108, 458; State of the Union message, 69, 98; *see also* names of specific Presidents
presidential nominating conventions, 116–118, 206, 208–211, 213
presidential preference primaries, 213
presidential succession, 114
President of the Senate, 81, 82
President *pro tempore*, 81
press, freedom of the, 47, 154, 159
primary elections: *see* elections
prisons, 90
privacy, right of, 156–157
private schools: *see* independent schools
productivity, 390, 391–392
profit, 368
Progressive Party (Bull Moose), 207
Progressive Party (1924), 207
Progressive Party (1948), 207
prohibition, 55–56, 206
Prohibition Party, 206
Promontory Point, Utah, 347
propaganda: forms of, 188–190; misuse of, 188
property taxes, 236, 238
protective tariffs, 429
public housing: *see* housing
public opinion: definition, 177–178; and political parties, 177–178
public schools: administration, 280; attitudes toward, 278–279, 282; busing, 286–289; desegregation, 284–289; elementary schools, 276–277, 279; enrollment figures, 280; functions of, 276; growth, 276–280; higher education, 280; high schools, 279; kindergarten, 280; national government, 278; religion and, 276–278; state government, 90, 230–231, 278; *see also* education
public welfare, 90, 211, 380–383
Puerto Rico: immigrants from, 11; as part of U.S., 11, 17, 24
Puritans, 276–277

Quakers, 276
quartering of soldiers, 155
quotas, immigration, 15–17

racial discrimination, 14, 59, 169, 282, 284–289
radio: development of, 360; influence on public opinion, 104, 181, 197
Rail Passenger Service Act of 1970, 349
railroads: and city growth, 272–273; development, 6, 10, 347–349, 365; freight, 350; passenger service, 347–350; and time zones, 347; transcontinental, 347
reapportionment, 79, 92–93
Reclamation, Bureau of, 327–328
recycling, 303–304, 329, 330–331
Red Scare, 153
Reedy, George, 115
religion: discrimination and, 4, 7, 14; education and, 276–278, 280–281; freedom of, 4, 30, 47, 154, 281; interest groups and, 186
reprieves, 100, 124
republic, 66
Republican Party: formation of, 203–204; history of, 203–206; organization, 200–201; platform (1976), 208–211; presidential nominating conventions, 116–118; regional aspects, 204
reserved powers, 77, 167
resources: *see* natural resources
Reston, James, 106
revenue: *see* taxes
revenue sharing, 91, 240–241
Revolutionary War, 48, 155, 202
Rhode Island: courts, 144; taxes, 235
Rickover, H. G., 88
right of privacy, 156–157
right to bear arms, 155–156
right to counsel, 164–165
Rio Treaty, 461
Ripon, Wisconsin, 204
roads: *see* highways
Rockefeller, Nelson, 123, 261
Rome (ancient), 45, 57–58
Romney, George, 268
Roosevelt, Eleanor, 171–172
Roosevelt, Franklin D., 104, 123, 181, 320, 467
Roosevelt, Theodore, 207, 316, 319–320
Rubin, Jerry, 38
rules: need for, 25–26; school, 27–28
Rumania: government, 452; immigrants from, 9
Russia: *see* Union of Soviet Socialist Republics
Russian Revolution of 1917, 449, 450

St. Augustine, Florida, 281
St. Lawrence Seaway, 114, 354
St. Louis, Missouri, 7, 280
sales taxes, 235
San Diego, California, 256
San Francisco, California, 298, 467
San Mateo, California, 38–39
Santa Barbara, California, 337
Santa Fe, New Mexico, 247
Santa Fe Trail, 343
satellite cities, 265
satellite nations, 421
savings and loan associations, 378
scab, 395
Scammon, Richard M., 219
scarcity, principle of, 367–368, 384
school desegregation, 284–289
schools: *see* education; independent schools; parochial schools; public schools
Scotland, immigrants from, 6
search warrants, 156–157
Seattle, Washington, 36–37, 194
Secretariat of the United Nations, 468, 470
Secretary-General of the United Nations, 470, 471
secret ballots, 214
Secret Service, 111
Security Council of the United Nations, 468–469
segregation: *de facto,* 286; education, 282, 284–289; housing, 282, 286; public facilities, 284
selectmen, 249–250
self-incrimination, protection from, 161, 162–163
Senate (national): committees, 83–84; daily activities, 83–84, 86–87; election process, 67–68; Foreign Relations Committee, 107, 457; leaders of, 81–82; and the League of Nations, 467–468; members' privileges, 80; representation, 68–69, 93; special powers, 73–74
Seneca Falls, New York, 171
Shabecoff, Alice, 373
sheriffs, 249
Shirer, William, 453
Silberman, Charles, 282
Singapore, 443
single proprietorships, 370
slander, 159
slavery: in colonies, 5; and the Constitution, 5, 74–75, 168–169; end of, 59, 168; and 19th century political parties, 203, 204; slave trade, 5, 74–75
slums, 272–276

INDEX **507**

Small Business Administration, 375
Smerk, George M., 299
Smith, Alfred E., 127
socialization: in other countries, 437–438; process of, 25, 178; television and, 181, 361
Social Security Act, 381, 382
social security benefits, 86, 375, 380–382
soil: conservation, 320, 326–327; dust storms, 318, 320; erosion, 326–327; exploitation of, 317–318; reclamation, 327–328; tillable, in U.S., 326
Soil Conservation Act of 1935, 320
Sons of Liberty, 42
South Carolina, taxes in, 235
South Dakota: ranching, 319; taxes, 235
Southeast Asia Treaty Organization (SEATO), 461
South Korea, 461, 465
Soviet Union: *see* Union of Soviet Socialist Republics
space programs, 268–269, 420–421
Spain: colonies in America, 11, 415; government, 445, 453
Speaker of the House, 81–82
special districts, 251
speech, freedom of, 154, 159–160
split ticket, 215
Springfield, Illinois, 37–38
stagecoaches, 343
Stalin, Joseph, 450
State, Department of, 110, 111
state courts, 141–142
state government: budget, 229, 230–231; and business, 90; conservation activities, 320, 330, 334; constitutions, 50, 54, 91, 92, 122, 125, 278; and education, 90, 276–279, 284–289; employment opportunities, 398–399; federalism, 50–51, 89, 91, 95, 238–241; governors, 122–125; legislatures, 89–93; powers, 50–51, 89–91; public welfare programs, 90, 380–383; revenue sharing, 240–241; spending by, 230–231; state court systems, 141–142; taxes, 234–237, 238; and transportation, 51, 90, 230–231, 345; *see also* governor; state legislatures
state legislatures: powers of, 90–91, 122; representation, 92–93; structure, 91–92
State of the Union message, 69, 98
States' Rights Democratic Party (Dixiecrats), 207
Statue of Liberty, 14, 42

statutory laws, 129
Staunton, Virginia, 256
steamboats, 353, 365
stock, 370–371
stockholders, 370–371
straight ticket, 214–215
Strategic Arms Limitations Talks (SALT), 463
streetcars, 273
streets, city, 293–295
strikes, 261–262, 293, 395
strip mining, 306
suburbs: government, 263–265; transportation, 264, 295
Sulzberger, C. L., 465
Supplemental Security Income program, 382
Supreme Court, U.S.: appointment to, 67–68, 100, 137; and the checks and balances system, 52–54, 77, 100, 101, 136–138; on congressional districts, 79; on double jeopardy, 162; on due process of law, 163–164; on education, 281, 282, 284–289; judicial review, 55, 137; lawmaking powers, 54; on public welfare, 381; on reapportionment of state legislatures, 93; on right of counsel, 165; on school desegregation, 282, 284–289; size of, 138; test cases, 137, 138–139; types of cases before, 136, 138; *see also* Supreme Court decisions
Supreme Court decisions: *Baker v. Carr* (1962), 93; *Brown v. Board of Education of Topeka* (1954), 284–285; *Gideon v. Wainwright* (1963), 165; *Plessy v. Ferguson* (1896), 284; *Swan v. Charlotte-Mecklenburg* (1971), 286–287; *Westberry v. Sanders* (1964), 79
Swan v. Charlotte-Mecklenburg (1971), 286–287
Sweden, immigrants from, 8
Syria: government, 447; immigrants from, 10

Taiwan, 423, 461
tariffs, 234, 236, 238, 429
taxes: corporate income, 234; customs duties, 236–237; estate, 236; excise, 235; federalism and, 238–241; gift, 236; growth of, 224–226, 229, 232, 238; income, 233–234, 238; licenses and fees, 237; local government and, 229, 230–231, 234–236, 237, 238–241; national government and, 229–230, 232, 233–237, 238–241; party platforms on, 211; personal income, 233, 234, 238; progressive, 233; property, 236, 238; purpose of, 233–234; regressive, 235; sales, 235; state government and, 229, 230–231, 234–236, 237, 238–241
technology: advances in, 390–393, 398–400; agriculture and, 372; business and, 226; communications and, 225–226, 359–361; industry and, 390–393; population increase and, 323
telegraphs, 359–360
telephones, 360
television: development of, 181, 360–361; influence on public opinion, 181, 182, 197, 361; socialization process and, 181, 361
Tennessee: representation in legislature, 92–93; taxes, 235
Tennessee Valley Authority, 114, 320, 374–375
terracing, 327
territory, U.S.: expansion of, 51, 415–416; Old Northwest, 51, 250, 278; today, 23–24
test cases, 137, 138–139
Texas: county government, 248; Dust Bowl, 320; expansion of U.S., 415; mineral resources, 318–319; taxes, 235
Thailand, 461, 465
Thant, U, 471
third-party movements, 200, 206–207
time zones, 347
Tito, Josip, 441
Tocqueville, Alexis de, 171
Toledo, Ohio, 302
Tollett, Kenneth S., 339
totalitarianism, 44, 199, 438–441, 448–452, 453
town government, 249–250
town meetings, 249–250
townships, 250–251
trade: colonial, 365; expansion, 365–367; foreign, 428–433; tariffs, 233–234, 236, 429
trade unions: *see* labor unions
transportation: airplanes, 351–352; automobiles, 273, 293–297, 298, 300–301, 344–345; business and, 365–366; cities and, 264, 272–274, 293–299; Conestoga wagons, 343; employment opportunities in, 398; expressways, 295–296; highways, 51, 90, 231, 295–296, 298, 343–345, 346; mass transit, 298–299; Merchant Marine, 354–355; and the national government, 51, 71,

296, 298–299, 345, 346, 349–350; party platforms on, 211; pollution caused by, 300–301, 304–305; railroads, 6, 10, 272–273, 347–350, 365; stagecoaches, 343; and state governments, 51, 90, 231, 345; steamboats, 353, 365; streetcars, 273; suburbs and, 264; waterways, 6, 347, 352–355, 365
Transportation, Department of, 113
treason, 153
Treasury, Department of, 110, 111
treaties, 71, 74, 99, 100, 457, 461, 463
trial by jury: constitutional right to, 131, 164–166; criticism of, 133–134; defense of, 134–135; grand, 132, 161; petit, 132
Truman, Harry S, 84, 86, 320, 426, 457–458
Truman Doctrine, 426
trust companies, 378
Trusteeship Council of the United Nations, 468, 469
Tubman, Harriet, 30
Tuchman, Barbara, 60, 453
Turkey: immigrants from, 10; NATO, 461; U.S. aid to, 426
Tweed, "Boss" William, 216, 254
two-party system, 200
Tyler, Gus, 336

unemployment, 211, 381
unicameral legislatures, 91–92
unincorporated villages, 251
Union of Soviet Socialist Republics: agriculture, 420, 450–451; arms control, 462–463; business, 420, 450–451; and China, 418, 451–452; Cold War, 417–418; communism in, 420–421, 441, 450–451; economy, 420, 425, 435, 450–451; government, 420, 450–451; gross national product, 425, 435; industry, 420, 450; space program, 420–421; and the UN, 468–469; and U.S., 417–418, 425, 427, 462–463
Union Pacific Railroad, 347
unions: *see* labor unions
union shops, 395
United Auto Workers, 396
United Mine Workers, 396
United Nations: achievements, 470–471; beginnings of, 467–468; Charter, 467–468; criticism, 471, 473; Economic and Social Council, 468, 469–470; General Assembly, 468; goals, 468; International Court of Justice, 468, 469; membership, 423, 467, 468–469, 470–471; and nuclear power, 462; Secretariat, 468, 470; Secretary-General, 470, 471; Security Council, 468–469; structure, 468–470; Trusteeship Council, 468, 469; U.S. entry, 457, 467–468
United Nations Children's Fund (UNICEF), 469–470
United Nations Educational Scientific and Cultural Organization (UNESCO), 470
United States: *see* economy; foreign policy; national government; population, U.S.; territory
United States Arms Control and Disarmament Agency, 462
United States Bureau of Labor Statistics, 399
United States Court of Customs and Patent Appeals, 140–141
United States Courts of Appeal, 140
United States Customs Court, 140–141
United States District Courts, 140, 141
United States Forestry Service, 330
United States Patent Office, 141
United States Postal Service, 358–359
United States Public Health Service, 300
United States Supreme Court: *see* Supreme Court
universities: enrollment figures, 280; national government support, 280; state government support, 90
University of Maryland Law School, 284
urbanization, 225, 238, 253–254, 270–274, 293–294
Urban Mass Transportation Assistance Act, 299
urban renewal, 274–275
Uruguay, 443
Utah, taxes in, 235

values: basic American, 29–33; definition of, 26, 29
vandalism, 194
Vermont: admitted to Union, 51; taxes, 235
veterans, 375, 380
veto, 54, 76–77, 100, 124
Vice President, 52, 81–82, 97, 114, 119
Vietnamese War, 105–108, 418, 465
Vikings, 8
villages: history, 247; incorporated, 251; unincorporated, 251
Virginia: colonial government in, 47, 343; taxes, 235
Virgin Islands of the United States, 17, 24
voting: blacks and, 48, 169, 218; in colonies, 47–48; 18-year-olds, 170, 218; Native Americans, 48, 218; voter preferences, 218–219; women, 48, 169, 171, 218; *see also* ballots; elections
Voting Rights Act of 1965, 169

Wagner Act, 396
Wallace, George C., 207
Wallace, Henry, 207
War, Secretary of, 110
War on Poverty, 381
warrants, 156–157
Washington, D.C., 72, 293, 298, 299
Washington, George, 99, 103, 110, 202, 278, 457, 461
Washington, taxes in state of, 235
water pollution, 35, 301–302, 335, 337
waterways: canals, 6, 347, 353, 365; freight, 352–355; intracoastal, 354
welfare, 90, 380–383
Wesberry v. Sanders (1964), 79
West Germany: economy, 392, 414, 421; government, 455; NATO, 461
West Point, 111
West Virginia, taxes in, 235
Wheaton, Illinois, 194
Whig Party, 203, 205
White House, 104, 109
Wildavsky, A.B., 117–118
Wilderness Act of 1964, 331
wilderness preservation, 331–334
Wilderness Road, 343
wildlife conservation, 333–334
Williams, Roger, 47
Wilson, Woodrow, 42, 123, 204, 416, 467
Wisconsin, taxes in, 235
women: discrimination against, 48, 57–58, 59, 127, 171–172; employment of, 399; roles of, 269–272, 399; voting, 48, 57, 59, 150, 169, 171, 218, 219
Woodmere, New York, 36
workers: blue-collar, 397–398; education and, 399–400; farm, 186, 397–398; gray-collar, 397–398; mass production, 393–394; productivity, 390–393; service jobs, 398–399; technological advances and, 391–393,

397–400; white-collar, 397–398, 399; women, 399; *see also* labor unions
World Health Organization (WHO), 469
World War I, 415, 416, 420, 422, 467
World War II, 417, 420, 422, 425, 449, 451, 457, 458, 461, 467
Wright, Orville, 351
Wright, Wilbur, 351
Wriston, Walter B., 34
Wyoming, taxes in, 235

youth: civic responsibility and, 192–195; rights of, 159–160, 163–164; voting, 150, 170, 218, 221
Yugoslavia, 441, 445, 452

Zaire Republic, 447
Zenger, John Peter, 47

Every reasonable effort has been made to trace the owners of copyright materials in this book, but in some instances this has proven impossible. The publishers will be glad to receive information leading to more complete acknowledgments in subsequent printings of the book, and in the meantime extend their apologies for any omissions.

ARTICLES AND BOOKS

UNIT ONE **Chapter 1:** p. 13 from *Children in the Political System* by Jack Dennis and David Easton. Copyright © 1969 by McGraw-Hill. Used with permission of McGraw-Hill Book Company. **Chapter 2:** p. 34 from "Liberty, Leadership and License" by Walter B. Wriston, 1976 speech given at the University of Chicago. Used with permission./pp. 35–39 from *Life,* Vol. 69, No. 14, October 2, 1970. Used with permission of Time/Life Syndication Service. **Chapter 3:** pp. 57–58 from *Historical Selections* by Hutton Webster, © 1929 by D. C. Heath./p. 60 from "On Our Birthday—America as Idea" by Barbara Tuchman, *Newsweek,* July 12, 1976. Used with permission of the author.

UNIT TWO **Chapter 4:** pp. 81–82 from *The New Congress* by Stephen K. Bailey. Used with permission of St. Martin's Press, Inc./p. 88 from "The Decline of Congressional Power" by H.G. Rickover, *The New York Times,* April 27, 1972. © 1972 by The New York Times Company. Reprinted with permission. **Chapter 5:** p. 106 from "The Press, the President and Foreign Policy" by James Reston, *Foreign Affairs,* Vol. 44, No. 4, July 1966. Now part of his book *The Artillery of the Press,* published by Harper and Row for the Council on Foreign Relations. Used with permission./p. 115 from *The Twilight of the Presidency* by George Reedy, © 1970 by World Publishing Company. Used with permission./p. 117 from "Our National Nominating Conventions Are a Disgrace" by Dwight D. Eisenhower, *Reader's Digest,* July 1966. Reprinted by permission of Doubleday & Company, Inc./pp. 117–118 from "On the Superiority of National Conventions" by Aaron B. Wildavsky, *The Review of Politics,* Vol. 24, July 1962. Used with permission./p. 118 from "Political Conventions? Yes, But . . ." by Philip Green, *The Christian Science Monitor,* September 13, 1968. Quoted by permission from The Christian Science Monitor. © 1968 The Christian Science Publishing Society. All rights reserved./p. 120 from "Dangers of the Electoral College" by Clayton Fritchey, *Harper's Magazine,* August 1967. Copyright © 1967, by Minneapolis Star and Tribune Co., Inc. Reprinted from the August 1967 issue of *Harper's Magazine* by permission of the author.

UNIT THREE **Chapter 7:** p. 158 from *Points of Rebellion* by William O. Douglas. Copyright © 1969 by William O. Douglas. Reprinted by permission of Random House, Inc./ p. 173 from *Anti-Democratic Attitudes in American Schools* by H.H. Remmer. Copyrighted by Northwestern University Press. **Chapter 8:** p. 182 from "The Free Mind and the Free Market" by Edith Efron, *Vital Speeches of the Day,* Vol. 40, No. 17, June 15, 1974. Used with permission./p. 195 adapted from *Adolescent Development and Adjustment* by Lester D. and Alice Crow. Copyright 1956 by McGraw-Hill. Used with permission of McGraw-Hill Book Company. **Chapter 9:** p. 217 from a letter written by Mrs. Jimmie Johnston to the *Farm Journal,* May 1976. Used with permission of the *Farm Journal.*/p. 218 from *The Gallup Opinion Index,* Report No. 131, 1976. Used with permission of The Gallup Opinion Index, Princeton, New Jersey./p. 219 from "The American Voter: A 1970 Profile" by Richard M. Scammon, *AFL–CIO American Federationist,* August 1970. Used with permission. **Chapter 10:** p. 227 from "Public Investment, America's New Future," *AFL–CIO American Federationist,* March 1971. Used with permission./p. 232 from an article by James J. Kilpatrick, *Nashville Banner,* January 19, 1976. Used with the permission of the author./p. 238 from "The Obsolescence of Federalism" by Harold J.

Laski, *The New Republic,* May 3, 1939. Used with permission./pp. 240–241 from *Airwaves,* Vol. 1, No. 1, April/May 1971, published by Allegheny Airlines. Used with permission.

UNIT FOUR **Chapter 11:** p. 259 from the foreword by Theodore J. Lowi to *Machine Politics* by Harold Gosnell, University of Chicago Press, 1968 (2nd Ed.). Used with permission./p. 262 from "Lindsay and Rockefeller at Odds" by Walter Lippmann, *Newsweek,* February 26, 1968. Copyright Newsweek, Inc., February 26, 1968. **Chapter 12:** p. 269 from *Innovation in Education: New Directions for the American School,* Research and Policy Committee of the Committee for Economic Development, 1968./p. 283 from "I No Understand the Teacher" by Susan Jacoby, *Saturday Review,* April 5, 1975. Used with permission. **Chapter 13:** p. 293 from "The Agony of Getting Anywhere," *Newsweek,* January 9, 1967. Copyright Newsweek, Inc., January 9, 1967./p. 294 from "The Calf Path" in *Whiffs from Wild Meadows* by Sam Walter Foss. Reprinted by permission of Lothrop, Lee & Shepard Co./p. 298 from "Mass Transit versus More Highways" by Chris Welles, *Life,* Vol. 62, May 12, 1967. Used with permission of Time/Life Syndication Service./ p. 299 from *Urban Transportation: The Federal Role* by George M. Smerk, University of Indiana Press, 1965. Used with permission./p. 308 from *Vanishing Air* by John C. Esposito. Copyright © 1970 by The Center for the Study of Responsive Law. All rights reserved. Reprinted by permission of Grossman Publishers.

UNIT FIVE **Chapter 14:** pp. 324–325 from *Human Ecology: Problems and Solutions* by Paul R. Ehrlich, Anne H. Ehrlich, and John P. Holdren. W.H. Freeman and Company. Copyright © 1973. Used with permission./p. 325 reprinted with permission from *Headline Series #206, Population* by Valerie K. Oppenheimer. Copyright June 1971 by the Foreign Policy Association, Inc./p. 336 from "The Re-Creative Society" by Gus Tyler, *AFL–CIO American Federationist,* July 1976.

Used with permission./p. 339 from "The Wrong Top Priority" by Amitai Etzioni, *Science,* Vol. 168, May 22, 1970. Copyright 1970 by the American Association for the Advancement of Science. Used with permission of author./p. 339 from "What Price Ecology?" by Kenneth S. Tollett. Reprinted with permission from the July 1970 issue of *The Center Magazine,* a publication of the Center for the Study of Democratic Institutions in Santa Barbara, California. **Chapter 15:** p. 346 from "The Highwaymen" by David Hapgood, *Inside the System—A Washington Monthly Reader,* edited by Charles Peters and Timothy J. Adams. Used with permission of Praeger Publishers, Inc. **Chapter 16:** p. 373 from "Supermarket Waxworks: The Agribusiness Market Gardens" by Alice Shabecoff, *The Nation,* January 31, 1976. Used with permission./pp. 384–386 from *Social Responsibilities of Business Corporations,* Research and Policy Committee of the Committee for Economic Development, 1971./pp. 386–387 from "Social Man and the New Stationary State" by David P. Eastburn, *Business Review,* May 1971. Used with permission of the Federal Reserve Bank of Philadelphia.

UNIT SIX **Chapter 18:** p. 427 from "The Principles of Propaganda" by Hans Morgenthau, Democratic Advisory Council, Advisory Committee on Foreign Policy, May 31, 1960. Used with permission./p. 430 from "A Growing Battle of Trade Barriers," *Newsweek,* March 13, 1970. Copyright Newsweek, Inc., March 13, 1970./pp. 431–432 from *How Imports Benefit America,* American Importers Association. Used with permission./pp. 432–433 from "On the Way: Companies More Powerful Than Nations," *U.S. News & World Report,* July 19, 1971. Copyrighted by U.S. News & World Report. **Chapter 19:** p. 453 from "Franco's Death: The Challenge" by William L. Shirer and Barbara W. Tuchman, *The Nation,* December 6, 1975. Used with permission. **Chapter 20:** p. 464 reprinted with permission from Sidney Lens, *The Military-Industrial Complex,* Pilgrim Press.

Copyright © 1970 by Sidney Lens./p. 465 from "Sackcloth and Ashes" by C.L. Sulzberger, *The New York Times,* July 9, 1971. © 1971 by The New York Times Company. Reprinted with permission./p. 466 from "The Road Back to Internationalism" by Harlan Cleveland, *The Atlantic,* May 1969.

ILLUSTRATIONS

UNIT ONE: xiv, Wally McNamee from Woodfin Camp & Assoc.; **Chapter 1:** 2, Sybil Shackman from Monkmeyer; 3 (top), Monkmeyer; 3 (bottom), T. Fujihira from Monkmeyer; 5, Ruth Riley; 7, Bettmann Archive; 9, Brown Brothers; 10, Dolores McCutcheon Brown from Monkmeyer; 12 (left), Brown Brothers; 12 (right), Bettmann Archive; 13, Michal Heron from Monkmeyer; 14, Bettmann Archive; 16, from *The Herblock Gallery,* Simon & Schuster, 1968; 18, Sybil Shelton from Monkmeyer; 19, Mimi Forsyth from Monkmeyer; **Chapter 2:** 22, George Zimbel from Monkmeyer; 24, UPI; 25 (left), Edith Reichmann from Monkmeyer; 25 (right), T. Fujihira from Monkmeyer; 27, S. Falk from Monkmeyer; 28, Frink from Monkmeyer; 29 (top), Donald L. Miller from Monkmeyer; 29 (bottom), Mimi Forsyth from Monkmeyer; 32 (left), Bert Whitman, *Phoenix Gazette,* from Rothco; 32 (right), *Saturday Review,* from Rothco; 33, NASA; 34, Medford Taylor from Black Star; 35, Fort Worth Chamber of Commerce; 36, David Hamill; 37 (top), Alan Pitcairn from Grant Heilman; 37 (bottom), The Greater Springfield Chamber of Commerce; 38, Bill Anderson from Monkmeyer; **Chapter 3:** 42, UPI; 43, Leonard Freed from Magnum; 45, Brown Brothers; 46, 47, Bettmann Archive; 51, UPI; 54, Partymiller, *York Daily Record,* Penn., from Rothco; 55, Herblock, *The Washington Post;* 58, Colonial Williamsburg; 60, 61 (top), UPI; 61 (bottom), Bill Anderson from Monkmeyer.

UNIT TWO: 64, Burt Glinn from Magnum; **Chapter 4:** 66 (top), Monkmeyer; 66 (middle), Edith

Reichmann from Monkmeyer; 66 (bottom), 69, UPI; 70 (both), Grant Heilman; 78, Bettmann Archive; 83, 87, Paul Conklin from Monkmeyer; 88, UPI; 90, Donald L. Miller from Monkmeyer; 91, Sam Falk from Monkmeyer; 92, UPI; 93, from *Straight Herblock,* Simon & Schuster, 1964; **Chapter 5:** 96, Dennis Brack from Black Star; 99, Paul Conklin from Monkmeyer; 100, 103, 104, UPI; 107 (left), McDarrah; 107 (right), Monkmeyer; 108, Wide World; 112 (top), UPI; 112 (bottom), T. Fujihira from Monkmeyer; 115, UPI; 117 (both), 118, UPI; 121, from *The Herblock Gallery,* Simon & Schuster, 1968; 122, Grant Heilman; 123, 125, UPI; **Chapter 6:** 128, John Sanford from Monkmeyer; 130, Paul Conklin from Monkmeyer; 132, Mimi Forsyth from Monkmeyer; 134, Strickler from Monkmeyer; 139, UPI; 143, Michal Heron from Monkmeyer; 145 (top), Pierotti, from Ben Roth Agency; 145 (bottom), Hutton, Philadelphia *Inquirer.*

UNIT THREE: 148, Paul Fusco from Magnum; **Chapter 7:** 150, Dennis Brack from Black Star; 151, UPI; 154, Bill Anderson from Monkmeyer; 155, from *Straight Herblock,* Simon & Schuster, 1964; 156 (left), Mimi Forsyth from Monkmeyer; 156 (right), Brown Brothers; 158, UPI; 160, Mimi Forsyth from Monkmeyer; 164, editorial cartoon by Pat Oliphant, copyright *The Denver Post,* reprinted with permission of Los Angeles Times Syndicate; 165, Wallmeyer; 169, Brown Brothers; 170, Paul Fusco from Magnum; 172 (left), Hugh Rogers from Monkmeyer; 172 (right), Alex Webb from Magnum; **Chapter 8:** 176, 178, 180, Mimi Forsyth from Monkmeyer; 182, CBS Photo; 185 (both), Mimi Forsyth from Monkmeyer; 186, Michal Heron from Monkmeyer; 187, Morris of A.P. Newsfeatures; 188, from *Herblock's Here and Now,* Simon & Schuster, 1955; 189, Bettmann Archive; 190, courtesy ILGWU; 191 (left), courtesy Litton Industries; 191 (right), Connecticut Mutual Life; 193 (top left), McDarrah; 193 (top right), Mimi Forsyth from Monkmeyer; 193 (bottom), Sam Falk from Monkmeyer; **Chapter 9:** 198, J.M. Zalcensztajn; 200, Dennis Brack from Black Star; 203, Culver Pictures; 204 (both), UPI; 208, Caraballo from Monkmeyer; 210 (left), Dennis Brack from Black Star; 210 (right), UPI; 212, Bill Anderson from Monkmeyer; 215, Grant Heilman; 216, Culver Pictures; 217, Mimi Forsyth from Monkmeyer; 219 (top), Lardner, *The State,* Columbia, S.C., from Rothco; 219 (bottom), Bert Whitman, *Phoenix Gazette,* from Rothco; **Chapter 10:** 222, Mimi Forsyth from Monkmeyer; 223, UPI; 225, 227 (left), Hugh Rogers from Monkmeyer; 227 (right), UPI; 232, 233, Fred Ward from Black Star; 237, Department of Motor Vehicles, State of New York; 239, Knox, *Nashville Banner;* 240 (left), Bender, *Waterloo Daily Courier,* Iowa, from Rothco; 240 (right), Liederman, *Long Island Press,* from Rothco.

UNIT FOUR: 244, Bill Grimes from Black Star; **Chapter 11:** 246, J.R. Eyerman from Black Star; 248, Brown Brothers; 249, Nathan Benn from Black Star; 250, Grant Heilman; 255, Hugh Rogers from Monkmeyer; 258, Brown Brothers; 259, Lew Merrim from Monkmeyer; 261, editorial cartoon by Pat Oliphant, copyright *The Denver Post,* reprinted with permission of Los Angeles Times Syndicate; 263, Charles Moore from Black Star; 265, Michal Heron from Monkmeyer; **Chapter 12:** 268, Bill Anderson from Monkmeyer; 270, Solomon D. Butcher Collection, Nebraska State Historical Society; 271, Grant Heilman; 272, Mimi Forsyth from Monkmeyer; 273, Brown Brothers; 274, Stanley Rice from Monkmeyer; 275, Monkmeyer; 279 (left), Bettmann Archive; 279 (right), Brown Brothers; 280, Paul Conklin from Monkmeyer; 281, Wide World; 283, Hugh Rogers from Monkmeyer; 284, Mimi Forsyth from Monkmeyer; 286, Darcy; 288, editorial cartoon by Pat Oliphant, copyright *The Denver Post,* reprinted with permission of Los Angeles Times Syndicate; **Chapter 13:** 292, Bettmann Archive; 295 (top), Doug Wilson from Black Star; 295 (bottom), Grant Heilman; 297, FPG; 299 (left), Murray Greenberg from Monkmeyer; 299 (right), Michal Heron from Monkmeyer; 300, Dr. Richard D. Jones; 301, editorial cartoon by Pat Oliphant, copyright *The Denver Post,* reprinted with permission of Los Angeles Times Syndicate; 303, J. Cron from Monkmeyer; 306 (all), 307, Grant Heilman; 308, 309 (top), UPI; 309 (bottom), McDarrah; 311, from *The Herblock Gallery,* Simon & Schuster, 1968.

UNIT FIVE: 314, Tony Howarth from Woodfin Camp & Assoc.; **Chapter 14:** 316, Grant Heilman; 318, Bettmann Archive; 319, American Museum of Natural History; 322, Grant Heilman; 324, Liederman, *Long Island Press,* from Rothco; 327, 328, 330, 334, 336, Grant Heilman; 338 (top), Peter Vadnai; 338 (bottom left and right), Darcy, *Newsday;* **Chapter 15:** 342, Grant Heilman; 344, Bettmann Archive; 346, Mimi Forsyth from Monkmeyer; 348, Bettmann Archive; 350, Union Pacific Railroad; 351 (left), Bettmann Archive; 351 (right), Pan Am; 353, Bettmann Archive; 354, Hugh Rogers from Monkmeyer; 355, courtesy of Seatrain Lines, Inc.; 356, Amtrak; 358, Mimi Forsyth from Monkmeyer; 359, Bettmann Archive; 361 (top), Mimi Forsyth from Monkmeyer; 361 (bottom), Darcy, *Newsday;* **Chapter 16:** 364, Fred Ward from Black Star; 366, Bettmann Archive; 367, James Theologos from Monkmeyer; 371 (left), Monkmeyer; 371 (right), Tom Ebenhoh from Black Star; 373, Mimi Forsyth from Monkmeyer; 374, UPI; 376 (top left), J.M. Zalcensztajn; 376 (top right), E. Sackler for American Museum of Natural History; 376 (bottom left and right), McDarrah; 379, Rogers from Monkmeyer; 381, Gregor from Monkmeyer; 382 (left), Monkmeyer; 382 (right), UPI; 383, Sawyer Press, Los Angeles; 385, Bettmann Archive; 386, Grant Heilman; **Chapter 17:** 390 (top), Grant Heilman; 390 (bottom), Sybil Shackman from Monkmeyer; 392, Merrim from Monkmeyer; 393, Paul Conklin from Monkmeyer; 395, Bettmann Archive; 402 (top), Hugh Rogers from Monkmeyer; 402 (bottom), RCA; 404 (left), Freda Leinwand from Monkmeyer; 404 (right), Rhoda Sidney from Monkmeyer; 405, Zimbel from Monkmeyer; 407, Yardley, *Baltimore Sun;* 409, J.M. Zalcensztajn.

UNIT SIX: 412, Dennis Brack from Black Star; **Chapter 18:** 414, NASA; 416, Division of Military History, Smithsonian Institute; 417, editorial cartoon by Pat Oliphant, copyright *The Denver Post,* reprinted with permission of Los Angeles Times Syndicate; 419, Bettmann Archive; 420, UPI; 421, Edith Reichmann from Monkmeyer; 422, Patrick Morin from Monkmeyer; 423, Monkmeyer; 424, Grant Heilman; 427, T. Fujihira from Monkmeyer; 431 (top), James Theologos from Monkmeyer; 431 (bottom), UPI; 433, T. Fujihira from Monkmeyer; **Chapter 19:** 436, Monkmeyer; 438, Susan W. Dryfoos from Monkmeyer; 440, data from *Freedom at Issue,* January–February 1977, published by Freedom House, used with permission; 443, Bettmann Archive; 444, Herblock; 446, 448, UPI; 449, Brown Brothers; 451, *Het Parool,* Amsterdam, from Rothco; 453, Latham from Monkmeyer; **Chapter 20:** 456, 460, UPI; 462, from *Herblock's Here and Now,* Simon & Schuster, 1955; 463, Calvi–France, from Rothco; 464, Wide World; 466, Conklin from Monkmeyer; 468, UN; 470 (top), C. Srinivasan for UN; 470 (bottom), UN.